Artificial Neural Nerworks

Artificial Neural Nerworks

Editor:

Prof. Dr. Zoran Gacovski, Ph.D.

ArclerPress

www.arclerpress.com

Artificial Neural Nerworks

Editor: Prof. Dr. Zoran Gacovski, Ph.D.

708 3rd Avenue, 6th Floor
New York
NY 10017
United States of America
www.arclerpress.com

ISBN: 978-1-68094-459-4

Library of Congress Control Number: 2016951151

About the Editor

Prof. Dr. Zoran Gacovski, Ph.D.

Dr. Zoran Gacovski has earned his PhD degree at Faculty of Electrical engineering, Skopje. His research interests include Intelligent systems and Software engineering, fuzzy systems, graphical models (Petri, Neural and Bayesian networks), and IT security. He has published over 50 journal and conference papers, and he has been reviewer of renowned Journals. In his career he was awarded by Fulbright postdoctoral fellowship (2002) for research stay at Rutgers University, USA. He has also earned best-paper award at the Baltic Olympiad for Automation control (2002), US NSF grant for conducting a specific research in the field of human-computer interaction at Rutgers University, USA (2003), and DAAD grant for research stay at University of Bremen, Germany (2008). Currently, he is a professor in Computer Engineering at European University, Skopje, Macedonia.

Contents

List of Contributors

Tielin Zhang
Institute of Automation, Chinese Academy of Sciences, Beijing, China
University of Chinese Academy of Sciences, Beijing, China

Yi Zeng
Institute of Automation, Chinese Academy of Sciences, Beijing, China

Bo Xu
Institute of Automation, Chinese Academy of Sciences, Beijing, China

Ning Ning
Data Storage Institute, Agency for Science, Technology and Research, Singapore

Guoqi Li
Department of Precision Instrument, Tsinghua University, Beijing, China
Center for Brain-Inspired Computing Research (CBICR), Tsinghua University, Beijing, China

Wei He
Data Storage Institute, Agency for Science, Technology and Research, Singapore

Kejie Huang
Singapore University of Technology and Design, Dover, Singapore

Li Pan
Data Storage Institute, Agency for Science, Technology and Research, Singapore

Kiruthika Ramanathan
Data Storage Institute, Agency for Science, Technology and Research, Singapore

Rong Zhao
Singapore University of Technology and Design, Dover, Singapore

Luping Shi
Department of Precision Instrument, Tsinghua University, Beijing, China
Center for Brain-Inspired Computing Research (CBICR), Tsinghua University, Beijing, China

Shinichi Tamura
NBL Technovator Co., Ltd., 631 Shindachimakino, Sennan 590-0522, Japan

Yoshi Nishitani
Department of Radiology, Graduate School of Medicine, Osaka University, Suita 565-0871, Japan

Chie Hosokawa
Biomedical Research Institute, AIST, Ikeda, Osaka 563-8577, Japan

Tomomitsu Miyoshi
Department of Integrative Physiology, Graduate School of Medicine, Osaka University, Suita 565-0871, Japan

Hajime Sawai
College of Health and Human Sciences, Osaka Prefecture University, Habikino, Osaka 583-8555, Japan

Wei Li,
College of Automation, Huazhong University of Science and Technology, Wuhan 430074, China
Image Processing and Intelligent Control Key Laboratory of Education Ministry of China, Wuhan 430074, China

Miao Wang
College of Automation, Huazhong University of Science and Technology, Wuhan 430074, China
Image Processing and Intelligent Control Key Laboratory of Education Ministry of China, Wuhan 430074, China

Yapeng Li
College of Automation, Huazhong University of Science and Technology, Wuhan 430074, China
Image Processing and Intelligent Control Key Laboratory of Education Ministry of China, Wuhan 430074, China

Yue Huang
College of Automation, Huazhong University of Science and Technology, Wuhan 430074, China
School of Electrical and Electronic Engineering, East China Jiaotong University, Nanchang 330013, China

Xi Chen
College of Automation, Huazhong University of Science and Technology, Wuhan 430074, China
Image Processing and Intelligent Control Key Laboratory of Education Ministry of China, Wuhan 430074, China

Hani Omar
Institute of Information Management, National Chiao Tung University, Hsinchu 300, Taiwan
Computational Intelligence Technology Center, Industrial Technology Research Institute, Chutung, Hsinchu 310, Taiwan

Van Hai Hoang
The University of Danang, Campus in Kon Tum, No. 129 Phan Dinh Phung Street, Kon Tum 580000, Vietnam

Duen-Ren Liu
Institute of Information Management, National Chiao Tung University, Hsinchu 300, Taiwan

Elizabeth Martinez-Zeron
Facultad de Informática, Universidad Autónoma de Querétaro, Querétaro, México

Marco A. Aceves-Fernandez
Facultad de Informática, Universidad Autónoma de Querétaro, Querétaro, México

Efren Gorrostieta-Hurtado
Facultad de Informática, Universidad Autónoma de Querétaro, Querétaro, México

Artemio Sotomayor-Olmedo
Laboratory of Artificial Intelligence, Faculty of Engineering, Universidad Autónoma de Querétaro, Querétaro, México

Juan Manuel Ramos-Arreguín
Facultad de Informática, Universidad Autónoma de Querétaro, Querétaro, México

Itedal Sabri Hashim Bahia
Ministry of Higher Education and Scientific Research, Baghdad, Iraq

Jie Wang
School of Science, Beijing Jiaotong University, Beijing 100044, China

Jun Wang
School of Science, Beijing Jiaotong University, Beijing 100044, China

Wen Fang
School of Economics and Management, Beijing Jiaotong University, Beijing 100044, China

Hongli Niu
School of Science, Beijing Jiaotong University, Beijing 100044, China

Deepti Moyi Sahoo
Department of Mathematics, National Institute of Technology Rourkela, Rourkela, Odisha 769 008, India

S. Chakraverty
Department of Mathematics, National Institute of Technology Rourkela, Rourkela, Odisha 769 008, India

Fahed Awad

Depatment of Network Engineering & Security, Jordan University of Science & Technology, Irbid, Jordan

Rufaida Shamroukh
Depatment of Computer Engineering, Jordan University of Science & Technology, Irbid, Jordan

Yongtae Do
Electronic Control Major, Division of Electronic & Electrical Engineering, Daegu University, 712-714, South Korea

Xiaoqing Luo
School of IoT Engineering, Jiangnan University, Wuxi, China

Xiaojun Wu
School of IoT Engineering, Jiangnan University, Wuxi, China

Gulshan Kumar
Department of Computer Application, Shahed Bhagat Singh State Technical Campus, Punjab, India

Krishan Kumar
Department of Computer Science & Engineering, Punjab Institute of Technology, Punjab, India

Manar Maraqa
Department of Management Information Systems, Al-Isra' Private University, Amman, Jordan;

Farid Al-Zboun
College of Information Technology, Ajloun National University, Ajloun, Jordan;

Mufleh Dhyabat
College of Information Technology, AL al-Bayt University, Mafraq, Jordan;

Raed Abu Zitar

School of Engineering and Technology, New York Institute of Technology, Amman, Jordan.

Jamal Salahaldeen Majeed Alneamy
Software Engineering Department, Computer and Mathematics Science College, University of Mosul, Mosul, Iraq

Rahma Abdulwahid Hameed Alnaish
Software Engineering Department, Computer and Mathematics Science College, University of Mosul, Mosul, Iraq

Yuhua Chen
Department of Electrical and Computer Engineering, University of Houston, Houston, USA

Subhash Kak
Department of Computer Science, Oklahoma State University, Stillwater, USA

Lei Wang
Department of Electrical and Computer Engineering, University of Houston, Houston, USA

Junjia Yuan,
College of Automation, Harbin Engineering University, Harbin 150001, China

Hao Meng
College of Automation, Harbin Engineering University, Harbin 150001, China

Qidan Zhu
College of Automation, Harbin Engineering University, Harbin 150001, China

Jiajia Zhou
College of Automation, Harbin Engineering University, Harbin 150001, China

Wei-Bo Chen
National Science and Technology Center for Disaster Reduction, New Taipei City 23143, Taiwan

Wen-Cheng Liu
Department of Civil and Disaster Prevention Engineering, National United University, Miaoli 36063, Taiwan
Taiwan Typhoon and Flood Research Institute, National Applied Research Laboratories, Taipei 10093, Taiwan

B. Krishna
Deltaic Regional Center, National Institute of Hydrology Kakinada, Andhra Pradesh, India

Y. R. Satyaji Rao
Deltaic Regional Center, National Institute of Hydrology Kakinada, Andhra Pradesh, India

P. C. Nayak
Deltaic Regional Center, National Institute of Hydrology Kakinada, Andhra Pradesh, India

Jafar Keighobadi
Faculty of Mechanical Engineering, University of Tabriz, Tabriz, Iran.

Khadijeh Alioghli Fazeli
Faculty of Mechanical Engineering, University of Tabriz, Tabriz, Iran.

Mohammad Sadeghi Shahidi
Faculty of Mechanical Engineering, University of Tabriz, Tabriz, Iran.

Preface

Artificial neural networks are graphical structures whose initial purpose was to emulate the human brain. They were introduced in 1943 by McCulloch and Pits and, since then, they have evolved in a very powerful computational tool. In 1958 Rosenblatt introduced the perceptron – a two-layered learning network based on simple math rules. The structure of an artificial neural network consists of an input layer, an output layer and of one or more hidden layers. The nodes in the network represent the neurons, while the links represent synapses. All links are weighted and these weights are adaptable, as they can be adjusted according to a learning algorithm. The usage of artificial neural networks today is inevitable in areas such as machine learning, data mining, pattern recognition, and automation control. Typical applications include: image and voice recognition, fraud detection, biometric user authentication (e.g. fingerprint and eye retina recognition), and complex control algorithms (e.g. aircraft motion control). This edition contains relevant, state-of-the-art research on artificial neural networks, categorized in four sections.

Section 1 focuses on Biological neural networks, describing: spike activity prediction based on multi-neuron spike train data, neuromorphic persistent firing networks, code spectrum and code flow of cultured neural networks, and brain network construction method for exploring age-related functional reorganization.

Section 2 focuses on the application of artificial neural networks in forecasting and prediction, describing: sales forecasting based on ARIMA, airborne pollution forecasting by neuro-fuzzy algorithms, forecasting revenue by using a case study involving a national insurance company from Iraq, financial time series prediction, and health assessment of multi-store shear buildings.

Section 3 focuses on Learning neural networks, describing: human detection by neural network image processing, camera image formation using a feedforward neural network, medical image fusion based on pulse coupled neural networks, artificial neural networks for intrusion detection, recognition of Arabic sign language, heart disease diagnosis utilizing hybrid fuzzy wavelet neural network, and hybrid neural network architecture for online learning.

Section 4 focuses on the application of artificial neural networks in modeling and control applications, describing: course control of under-actuated ship based on nonlinear robust neural network, water quality modeling in reservoirs, time-series modeling of river flow, and modeling and control of an AGV.

Editor
Prof. Dr. Zoran Gacovski, Ph.D.

INTRODUCTION

Artificial Neural Networks are relatively crude electronic models based on the neural structure of the brain. The brain basically learns from experience. It is natural proof that some problems that are beyond the scope of current computers are indeed solvable by small energy efficient packages. This brain modeling also promises a less technical way to develop machine solutions. This new approach to computing also provides a more graceful degradation during system overload than its more traditional counterparts.

These biologically inspired methods of computing are thought to be the next major advancement in the computing industry. Even simple animal brains are capable of functions that are currently impossible for computers. Computers do rote things well, like keeping ledgers or performing complex math. But computers have trouble recognizing even simple patterns much less generalizing those patterns of the past into actions of the future.

Now, advances in biological research promise an initial understanding of the natural thinking mechanism. This research shows that brains store information as patterns. Some of these patterns are very complicated and allow us the ability to recognize individual faces from many different angles. This process of storing information as patterns, utilizing those patterns, and then solving problems encompasses a new field in computing. This field, as mentioned before, does not utilize traditional programming but involves the creation of massively parallel networks and the training of those networks to solve specific problems. This field also utilizes words very different from traditional computing, words like behave, react, self-organize, learn, generalize, and forget.

Analogy to the Brain

The exact workings of the human brain are still a mystery. Yet, some aspects of this amazing processor are known. In particular, the most basic element of the human brain is a specific type of cell which, unlike the rest of the body, doesn't appear to regenerate. Because this type of cell is the only part of the body that isn't slowly replaced, it is assumed that these cells are what provide us with our abilities to remember, think, and apply previous experiences to our every action. These cells, all 100 billion of them, are known as neurons. Each of these neurons can connect with up to 200,000 other neurons, although 1,000 to 10,000 is typical.

The power of the human mind comes from the sheer numbers of these basic components and the multiple connections between them. It also comes from genetic programming and learning.

The individual neurons are complicated. They have a myriad of parts, sub-systems, and control mechanisms. They convey information via a host of electrochemical pathways. There are over one hundred different classes of neurons, depending on the classification method used. Together these neurons and their connections form a process which is not binary, not stable, and not synchronous. In short, it is nothing like the currently available electronic computers, or even artificial neural networks.

These artificial neural networks try to replicate only the most basic elements of this complicated, versatile, and powerful organism. They do it in a primitive way. But for the software engineer who is trying to solve problems, neural computing was never about replicating human brains. It is about machines and a new way to solve problems.

Artificial Neurons and How They Work

The fundamental processing element of a neural network is a neuron. This building block of human awareness encompasses a few general capabilities. Basically, a biological neuron receives inputs from other sources, combines them in some way, performs a generally nonlinear operation on the result, and then outputs the final result. Figure 1 shows the relationship of these four parts.

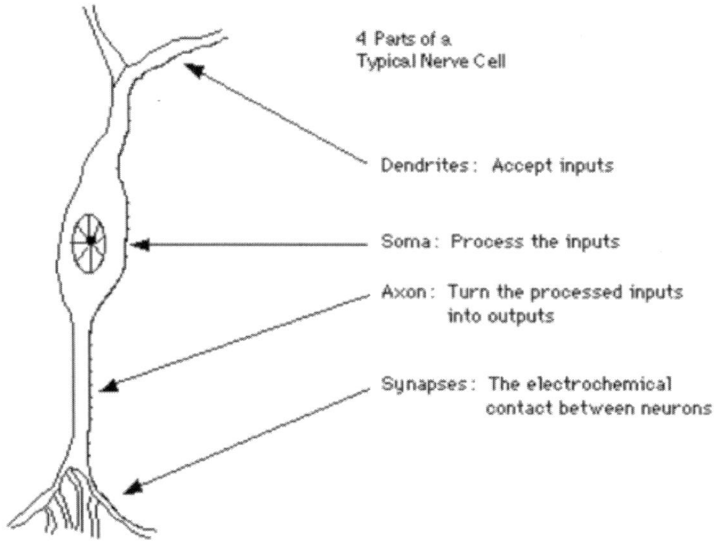

Figure 1: A Simple Neuron.

Within humans there are many variations on this basic type of neuron, further complicating man's attempts at electrically replicating the process of thinking. Yet, all natural neurons have the same four basic components. These components are known by their biological names - dendrites, soma, axon, and synapses. Dendrites are hair-like extensions of the soma which act like input channels. These input channels receive their input through the synapses of other neurons. The soma then processes these incoming signals over time. The soma then turns that processed value into an output which is sent out to other neurons through the axon and the synapses.

Recent experimental data has provided further evidence that biological neurons are structurally more complex than the simplistic explanation above. They are significantly more complex than the existing artificial neurons that are built into today's artificial neural networks. As biology provides a better understanding of neurons, and as technology advances, network designers can continue to improve their systems by building upon man's understanding of the biological brain.

But currently, the goal of artificial neural networks is not the grandiose recreation of the brain. On the contrary, neural network researchers are seeking an understanding of nature's capabilities for which people can engineer solutions to problems that have not been solved by traditional computing.

To do this, the basic unit of neural networks, the artificial neurons, simulates the four basic functions of natural neurons. Figure 2 shows a fundamental representation of an artificial neuron.

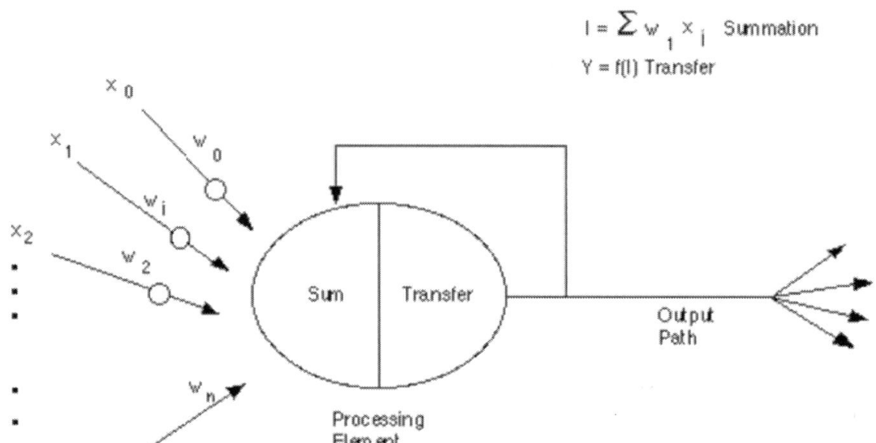

Figure 2: A Basic Artificial Neuron.

In Figure 2, various inputs to the network are represented by the mathematical symbol, x(n). Each of these inputs are multiplied by a connection weight. These weights are represented by w(n). In the simplest case, these products are simply summed, fed through a transfer function to generate a result, and then output. This process lends itself to physical implementation on a large scale in a small package. This electronic implementation is still possible with other network structures which utilize different summing functions as well as different transfer functions.

Some applications require "black and white," or binary, answers. These applications include the recognition of text, the identification of speech, and the image deciphering of scenes. These applications are required to turn real-world inputs into discrete values. These potential values are limited to some known set, like the ASCII characters or the most common 50,000 English words. Because of this limitation of output options, these applications don't always utilize networks composed of neurons that simply sum up, and thereby smooth, inputs. These networks may utilize the binary properties of ORing and ANDing of inputs. These functions, and many others, can be built into the summation and transfer functions of a network.

Other networks work on problems where the resolutions are not just one of several known values. These networks need to be capable of an infinite number of responses. Applications of this type include the "intelligence" behind robotic movements. This "intelligence" processes inputs and then creates outputs which actually cause some device to move. That movement can span an infinite number of very precise motions. These networks do indeed want to smooth their inputs which, due to limitations of sensors, come in non-continuous bursts, say thirty times a second. To do that, they might accept these inputs, sum that data, and then produce an output by, for example, applying a hyperbolic tangent as a transfer functions. In this manner, output values from the network are continuous and satisfy more real world interfaces.

Other applications might simply sum and compare to a threshold, thereby producing one of two possible outputs, a zero or a one. Other functions scale the outputs to match the application, such as the values minus one and one. Some functions even integrate the input data over time, creating time-dependent networks.

Electronic Implementation of Artificial Neurons

In currently available software packages these artificial neurons are called "processing elements" and have many more capabilities than the simple artificial neuron described above. Those capabilities will be discussed later in this report. Figure 3 is a more detailed schematic of this still simplistic artificial neuron.

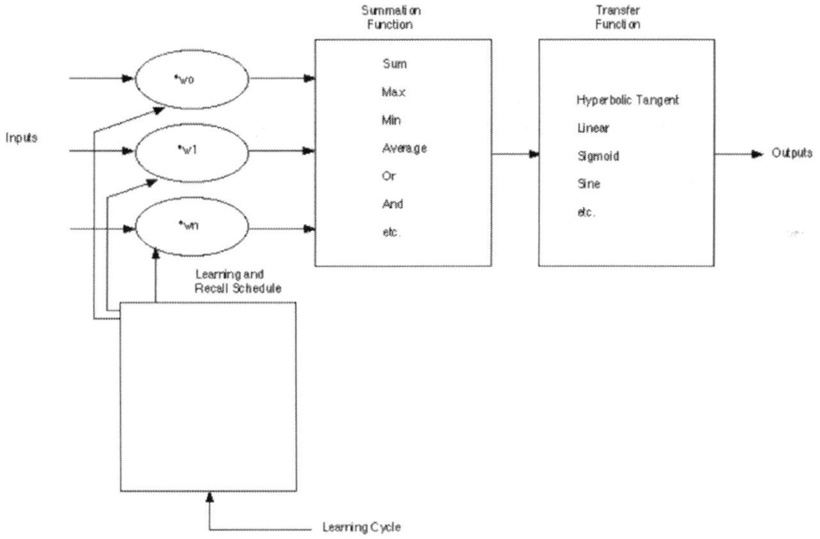

Figure 3: A Model of a "Processing Element".

In Figure 2.2.3, inputs enter into the processing element from the upper left. The first step is for each of these inputs to be multiplied by their respective weighting factor (w(n)). Then these modified inputs are fed into the summing function, which usually just sums these products. Yet, many different types of operations can be selected. These operations could produce a number of different values which are then propagated forward; values such as the average, the largest, the smallest, the ORed values, the ANDed values, etc. Furthermore, most commercial development products allow software engineers to create their own summing functions via routines coded in a higher level language (C is commonly supported). Sometimes the summing function is further complicated by the addition of an activation function which enables the summing function to operate in a time sensitive way.

Either way, the output of the summing function is then sent into a transfer function. This function then turns this number into a real output via some algorithm. It is this algorithm that takes the input and turns it into a zero or a one, a minus one or a one, or some other number. The transfer functions that are commonly supported are sigmoid, sine, hyperbolic tangent, etc. This transfer function also can scale the output or control its value via thresholds. The result of the transfer function is usually the direct output of the processing element. An example of how a transfer function works is shown in Figure 4.

This sigmoid transfer function takes the value from the summation function, called sum in the Figure 4, and turns it into a value between zero and one.

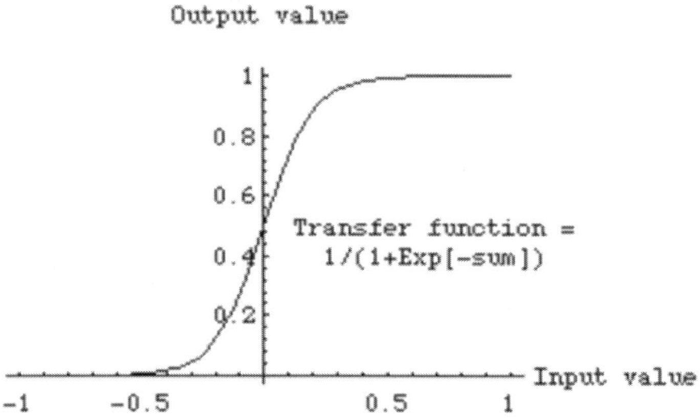

Figure 4: Sigmoid Transfer Function.

Finally, the processing element is ready to output the result of its transfer function. This output is then input into other processing elements, or to an outside connection, as dictated by the structure of the network.

All artificial neural networks are constructed from this basic building block - the processing element or the artificial neuron. It is variety and the fundamental differences in these building blocks which partially cause the implementing of neural networks to be an "art."

Artificial Network Operations

The other part of the "art" of using neural networks revolves around the myriad of ways these individual neurons can be clustered together. This clustering occurs in the human mind in such a way that information can be processed in a dynamic, interactive, and self-organizing way. Biologically, neural networks are constructed in a three-dimensional world from microscopic components. These neurons seem capable of nearly unrestricted interconnections. That is not true of any proposed, or existing, man-made network. Integrated circuits, using current technology, are two-dimensional devices with a limited number of layers for interconnection. This physical reality restrains the types, and scope, of artificial neural networks that can be implemented in silicon.

Currently, neural networks are the simple clustering of the primitive artificial neurons. This clustering occurs by creating layers which are then connected to one another. How these layers connect is the other part of the "art" of engineering networks to resolve real world problems.

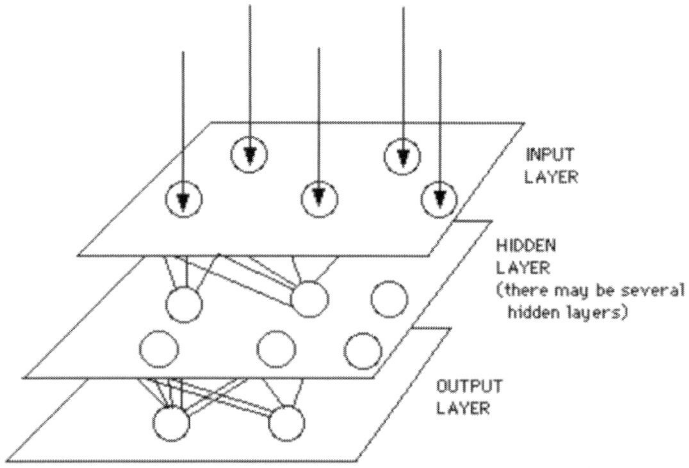

Figure 5: A Simple Neural Network Diagram.

Basically, all artificial neural networks have a similar structure or topology as shown in Figure 5. In that structure some of the neurons interfaces to the real world to receive its inputs. Other neurons provide the real world with the network's outputs. This output might be the particular character that the network thinks that it has scanned or the particular image it thinks is being viewed. All the rest of the neurons are hidden from view.

But a neural network is more than a bunch of neurons. Some early researchers tried to simply connect neurons in a random manner, without much success. Now, it is known that even the brains of snails are structured devices. One of the easiest ways to design a structure is to create layers of elements. It is the grouping of these neurons into layers, the connections between these layers, and the summation and transfer functions that comprises a functioning neural network. The general terms used to describe these characteristics are common to all networks.

Although there are useful networks which contain only one layer, or even one element, most applications require networks that contain at least the three normal types of layers - input, hidden, and output. The layer of input neurons receives the data either from input files or directly from electronic sensors in real-time applications. The output layer sends information directly to the outside world, to a secondary computer process, or to other devices such as a mechanical control system. Between these two layers can be many hidden layers. These internal layers contain many of the neurons in various interconnected structures. The inputs and outputs of each of these hidden neurons simply go to other neurons.

In most networks each neuron in a hidden layer receives the signals from all of the neurons in a layer above it, typically an input layer. After a neuron performs its function it passes its output to all of the neurons in the layer below it, providing a feed forward path to the output.

These lines of communication from one neuron to another are important aspects of neural networks. They are the glue to the system. They are the connections which provide a variable strength to an input. There are two types of these connections. One causes the summing mechanism of the next neuron to add while the other causes it to subtract. In more human terms one excites while the other inhibits.

Some networks want a neuron to inhibit the other neurons in the same layer. This is called lateral inhibition. The most common use of this is in the output layer. For example in text recognition if the probability of a character being a "P" is .85 and the probability of the character being an "F" is .65, the network wants to choose the highest probability and inhibit all the others. It can do that with lateral inhibition. This concept is also called competition.

Another type of connection is feedback. This is where the output of one layer routes back to a previous layer. An example of this is shown in Figure 6.

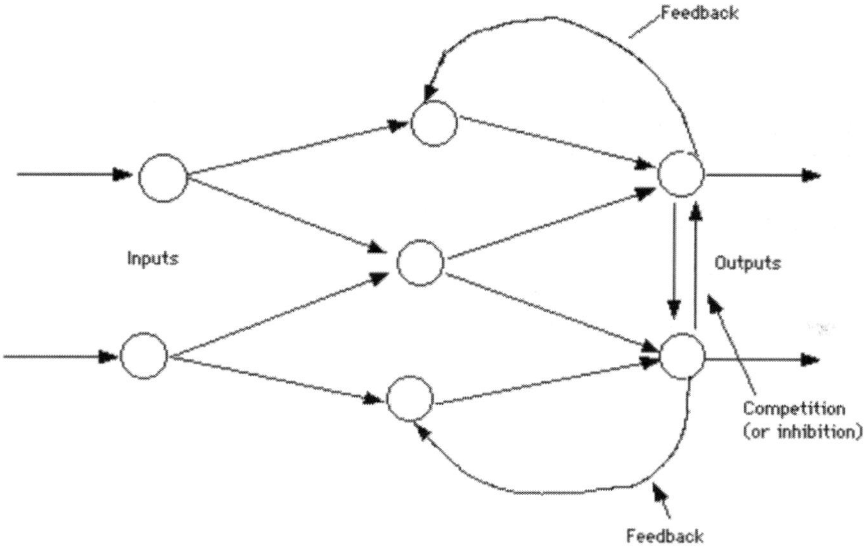

Figure 6: Simple Network with Feedback and Competition.

The way that the neurons are connected to each other has a significant impact on the operation of the network. In the larger, more professional software development packages the user is allowed to add, delete, and control these connections at will. By "tweaking" parameters these connections can be made to either excite or inhibit.

How Do Neural Networks Differ From Conventional Computing?

To better understand artificial neural computing it is important to know first how a conventional 'serial' computer and it is software process information. A serial computer has a central processor that can address an array of memory locations where data and instructions are stored. Computations are made by the processor reading an instruction as well as any data the instruction requires from memory addresses, the instruction is then executed and the results are saved in a specified memory location as required. In a serial system (and a standard parallel one as well) the computational steps are deterministic, sequential and logical, and the state of a given variable can be tracked from one operation to another.

In comparison, ANNs are not sequential or necessarily deterministic. There are no complex central processors, rather there are many simple ones which generally do nothing more than take the weighted sum of their inputs from other processors. ANNs do not execute programed instructions; they respond in parallel (either simulated or actual) to the pattern of inputs presented to it. There are also no separate memory addresses for storing data. Instead, information is contained in the overall activation 'state' of the network. 'Knowledge' is thus represented by the network itself, which is quite literally more than the sum of its individual components.

What Applications Should Neural Networks be used for?

Neural networks are universal approximators, and they work best if the system you are using them to model has a high tolerance to error. One would therefore not be advised to use a neural network to balance one's cheque book! However they work very well for:

- capturing associations or discovering regularities within a set of patterns;
- where the volume, number of variables or diversity of the data is very great;
- the relationships between variables are vaguely understood; or,
- the relationships are difficult to describe adequately with conventional approaches.

What are their Limitations?

There are many advantages and limitations to neural network analysis and to discuss this subject properly we would have to look at each individual type of network, which isn't necessary for this general discussion. In reference to backpropagational networks however, there are some specific issues potential users should be aware of.

Backpropagational neural networks (and many other types of networks) are in a sense the ultimate 'black boxes'. Apart from defining the general architecture of a network and perhaps initially seeding it with a random numbers, the user has no other role than to feed it input and watch it train and await the output. In fact, it has been said that with backpropagational, "you almost don't know what you're doing". Some software freely available software packages (NevProp, bp, Mactivation) do allow the user to sample the networks 'progress' at regular time intervals, but the learning itself progresses on its own. The final product of this activity is a trained network that provides no equations or coefficients defining a relationship (as in regression) beyond it's own internal mathematics. The network 'IS' the final equation of the relationship.

Backpropagational networks also tend to be slower to train than other types of networks and sometimes require thousands of epochs. If run on a truly parallel computer system this issue is not really a problem, but if the BPNN is being simulated on a standard serial machine (i.e. a single SPARC, Mac or PC) training can take some time. This is because the machines CPU must compute the function of each node and connection separately, which can be problematic in very large networks with a large amount of data. However, the speed of most current machines is such that this is typically not much of an issue.

What are their Advantages over Conventional Techniques?

Depending on the nature of the application and the strength of the internal data patterns you can generally expect a network to train quite well. This applies to problems where the relationships may be quite dynamic or non-linear. ANNs provide an analytical alternative to conventional techniques which are often limited by strict assumptions of normality, linearity, variable independence etc. Because an ANN can capture many kinds of relationships it allows the user to quickly and relatively easily model phenomena which otherwise may have been very difficult or imposible to explain otherwise.

SECTION I: BIOLOGICAL NEURAL NETWORKS

CHAPTER 1 BIOLOGICAL NEURAL NETWORK STRUCTURE

Tielin Zhang, Yi Zeng and Bo Xu

Keywords: Neural Network Structure Prediction, Spike Prediction, Time-Order Strategy, Co-Occurrence Strategy, Spreading Activation

INTRODUCTION

The micro-scale brain anatomy and activities of the neurons are essential for understanding how the brain works and the nature of human intelligence. The general motivation of this paper comes from the fact that neuronal structure and activities are closely connected with each other even though it is usually very hard to get both neural anatomical structure and spike activity by electrophysiology or imaging method at the same time. The general idea is that even without nanoscale imaging techniques (which cannot scale well), it is still possible to reconstruct the neural network structure and predict spike activities by analyzing the spike train data.

From the structure perspective, we propose that multi-neuron spike train data can be used as an alternative source to predict the neural network structures, and here we discuss two concrete strategies for neural network structure prediction based on this kind of data. Multi-neuron spike train data is composed of spike trains from multiple neurons recorded in the same time interval. The data typically shows whether a specific neuron generates a spike or not at a specific time. Two strategies are proposed for neural network structure prediction: 1) the time-ordered strategy: synapses exist between neurons that generate spikes at the two neighborhood time points (i.e. the time point N and N-1); 2) the spike co-occurrence strategy: synapses exist between neurons that fire together at the same time slot. This strategy is consistent with the Hebb's law "cells that fire together, wire together".

Citation: Zhang, T. , Zeng, Y. and Xu, B. (2015) Biological Neural Network Structure. International Journal of Intelligence Science, 5, 102-111. doi:10.4236/ijis.2015.52010.

From the function perspective, for each neuron in a neural network, its behavior is not only decided by its own property, but also very relevant to its contexts (e.g. other neurons in the same network). Hence, effective prediction of neural spike activities in a network context requires at least the following three major efforts: 1) response prediction of a single neuron towards a stimulus; 2) obtaining the detailed network structure, with synapse information among neurons; 3) modeling signal transmission based on the neural network. We use the neuron simulator to build detailed single pyramidal cells for the first effort. The network structure is built by the methods introduced above, while the spreading activation method based on the two previous efforts is introduced for the third effort. We use part of the spike train data to build the neural network structure and the model for neural activity prediction and the rest is for validation.

In order to validate the proposed methods and strategies, we use the data based on calcium imaging technology. Among different kinds of calcium imaging method, one of them is named functional Multi-neuron Calcium Imaging (fMCI), namely, multi-neurons loading of calcium fluorophores. The advantages of fMCI include: 1) recording en masse from hundreds of neurons in a wide area; 2) single-cell resolution; 3) identifiable location of neurons; and 4) detection of non-active neurons during the observation period. These advantages enables us acquire necessary spike train data discussed above to support the investigation and validation of proposed problems and methods. The paper is structured as follows: Section 2 briefly introduce related work, Section 3 explain the detailed neural network structure and spikes prediction method as well as their relationships, and Section 4 describes the experiments and results to show the prediction accuracy, finally conclusion is made in Section 5. This paper refines and extends the work introduced in [1] and [2].

RELATED WORK

From the structure perspective, most common approaches for obtaining the micro-level neural network structure is typically based on brain slicing and reconstruction with nanoscale imaging [3] [4]. This method can accurately locate the position of neurons, synapses and even dendritic spines. But at the same time, complex and weak nanoscale images make image repairing, synapse recognition and 3D structure reconstruction cost too much time. Based on current brain slicing and imaging techniques, it is still difficult to get synaptic scale neural network structures for a small group of neurons, let alone bigger network. In addition, tissues after slicing are with no functional reactions any more. This makes advanced research on neuronal functions based on the reconstructed neural network nearly impossible.

From the activity perspective at the nanoscale, electrophysiology techniques and calcium imaging techniques are frequently used. The electrophysiology techniques detect and save the neurons' time dependent soma voltage [5]. This technique is with accurate temporal resolution but poor space resolution. In addition, it can only record few neurons' voltage at one time. While calcium fluorescence imaging techniques detect the changes on neurons' voltage values by monitor cell calcium changes, it can monitor the activity of a hundred to thousand neurons simultaneously both in vitro and in vivo [6]. The maximum number of neurons monitored by calcium fluorescence is around 100,000 cells for zebrafish [7]. Stetter uses transfer entropy method to reconstruct the network which requires no prior statistics and connections assumptions, and the work focuses on excitatory synaptic links, and network clustering topology [8]. Takahashi investigates the calcium imaging experiments including imaging, spikes detection and some network analysis tasks. He and coauthors conclude that the network fits for power-law scaling of synchronization properties and network connection probability varies from different network scales [6].

METHODOLOGY

Although the functional data are collected by functional multi-neuron calcium imaging techniques, the missing of relevant structures from anatomical method still makes analysis about the dynamic causality for the whole network hard. Here we propose architecture to analyze the spike train data to predictively reconstruct the microlevel network structure, and predict neuronal activities based on the reconstructed network.

The methodology introduced here relies on spike train data generated by various kinds of techniques (e.g. fMCI and electrophysiology experiments). In this paper, we use the experimental data from the mouse memory task [6]. Spontaneous spiking activities are still happening in slices of the mouse brain hippocampus CA1 area when it was taken out of the body for not a long time. These spikes show the special task related network function in hippocampus, such as memory retention. The understanding of these kinds of data can greatly speed up the procedure of memory research.

As Figure 1 shows, calcium images and neuron voltages from mouse slices data are collected by fMCI method. Neural voltage signals based on the fMCI technique are with low Signal to Noise Ratio (SNR). Hence, signal processing to filter noise is necessary. Here we use Fast Fourier Transform (FFT) and Inverse Fast Fourier Transform (IFFT) methods to filter the high frequency noises so that spiking signals can be detected precisely. Then two methods to convert neural spike signals to neural structure are introduced, namely, the co-occurrence strategy and the time-ordered strategy. As a step forward, we propose a spike activity prediction method based on the predicted neural network, the spreading activation theory and single pyramidal neuron models.

Voltages Signal Processing

Voltages signals from calcium imaging are so closed combined with noise that high frequency filter must be applied for further spikes detection. The processing procedure mainly includes the following four parts: 1) using FFT to transform time sequence signals to frequency signals; 2) using high frequency filters to eliminate signal noises; 3) using IFFT to transform frequency signals back to time series signals; 4) deciding the voltage threshold to detect spiking signals. As Figure 2 shows, after signal transformation from time series to frequency and back again by FFT and IFFT, high frequency noises are filtered and spike signals are detected.

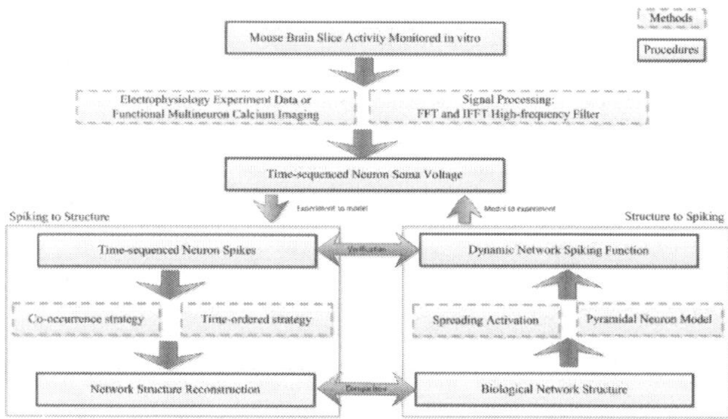

Figure 1: The overall architecture for predicting neural network structure and neuronal activities based on spike train data.

From Spikes to Neuronal Structures

In this paper, two strategies are discussed and used to realize the procedure of converting spike signals to neural network structure:

1) The time-ordered strategy: synapses exist between neurons that generate spikes at the two neighborhood time points (the time point N and N-1);
2) The spike co-occurrence strategy: synapses exist between neurons that fire together at the same time slot. This strategy is consistent with the Hebb's law "cells that fire together, wire together".

Based on the proposed two different strategies, two neurons that may share a connection might be connected from tens to hundreds of times. Each time of connection is with the same unit strength. However, more times of connection between neurons indicate the higher probability for the existence of synapse. As shown in Figure 3, the network is rebuilt by combination of two methods. The upper panel in Figure 3 shows the spikes states of 62 neurons in different time slot. The bottom left panel shows the present spike transfer (in green line). The bottom right panel shows the connection probability of different neurons.

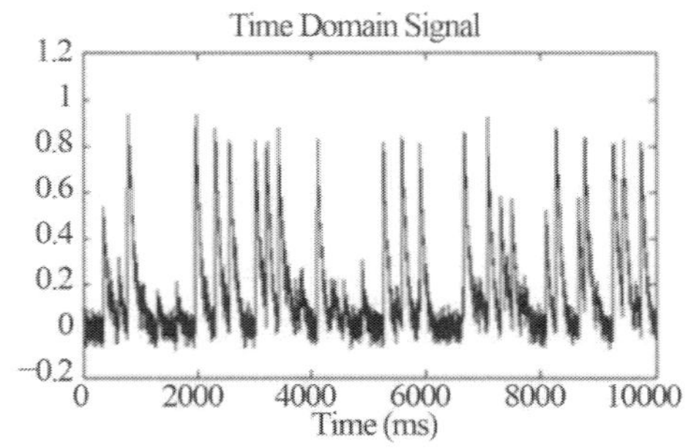

(a)

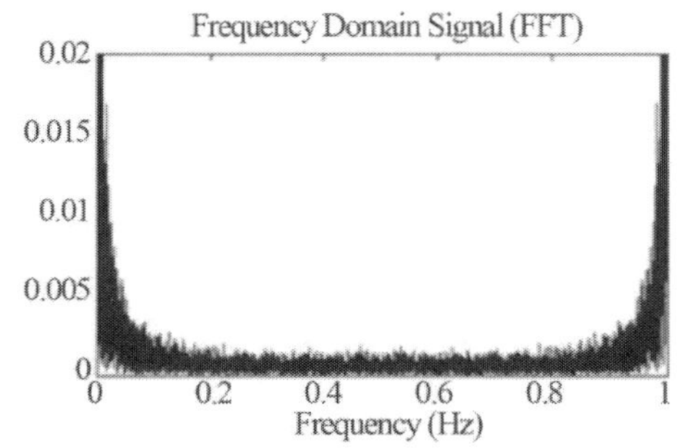

(b)

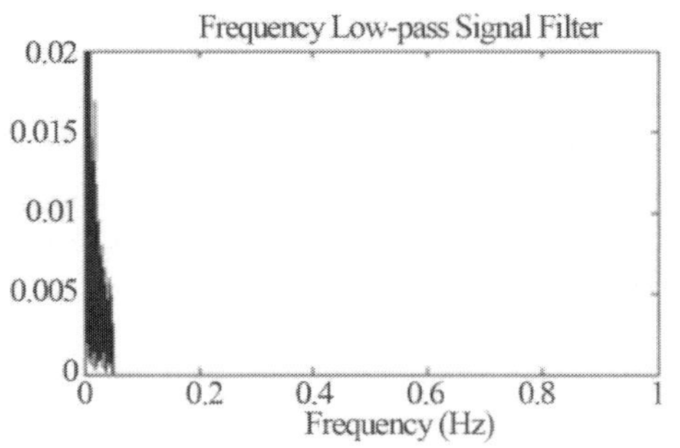

(c)

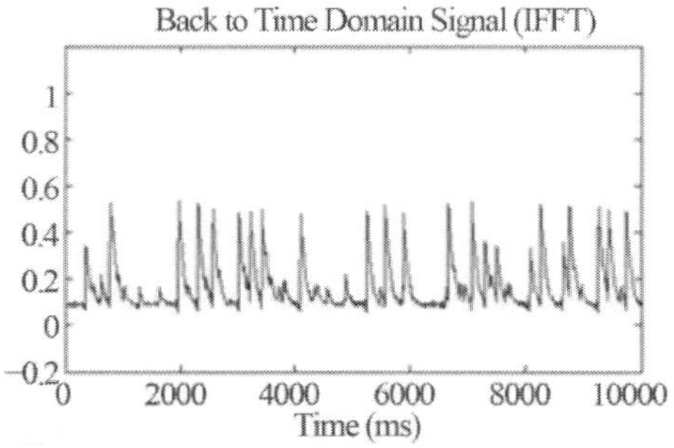

(d)

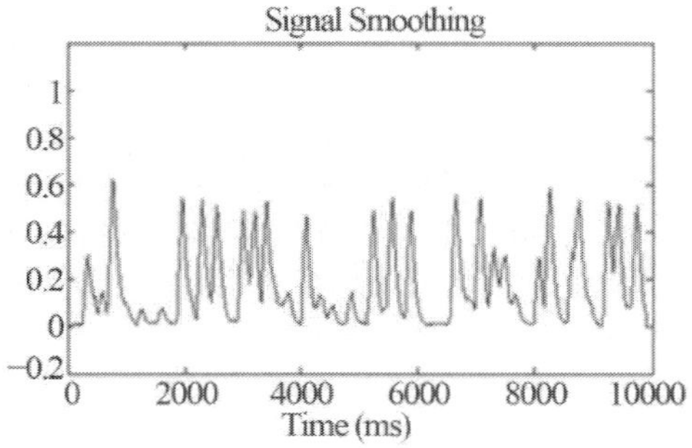

(e)

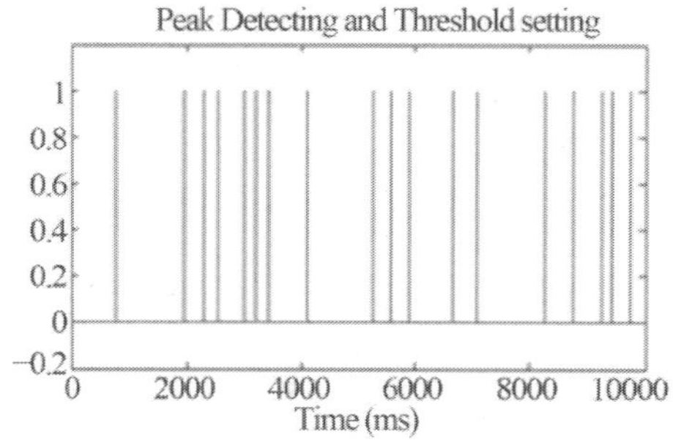

(f)

Figure 2: Neural activity signal processing. a) Original time series signals; b) FFT frequency signals; c) High frequency filter; d) IFF-Ttime series signals; e) Signal smooth process; f) Voltage threshold method of spiking detection.

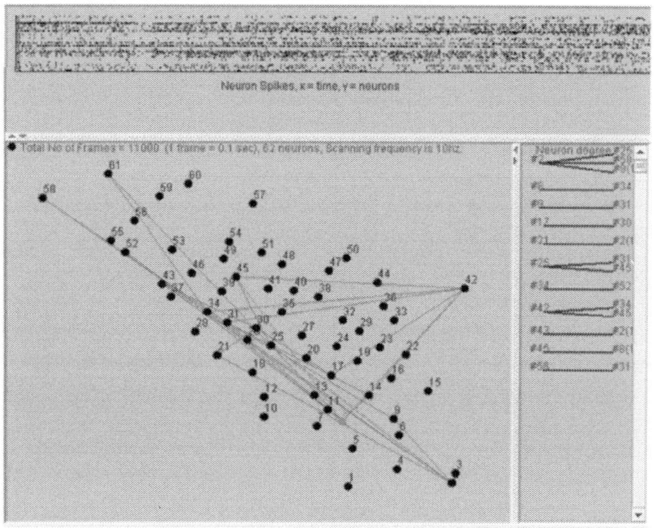

Figure 3: Network structure prediction procedure.

Spike Prediction Based on Spreading Activation

With the reconstructed micro-level neural network based on the methods proposed in Section 3.2, combined with single neuron models, we can predict spike activities for the neurons in observation. Here we first introduce a single neuron model as a foundation. Then we propose a spreading activation based spike prediction method, which utilize the single neuron model and the predicted neural network.

Since pyramidal neuron is widely distributed in mouse hippocampus (more than 90%) [9], here we introduce the single neuron model of a kind of pyramidal neuron in mouse brain hippocampus CA1 area for the simulation of the neuronal activities. Its neural structure obtained from http://neuromorpho.org/ (ID: NMO_08800) is shown in Figure 4(a). Neuron model contains three basic kinds of ion channels, namely potassium channel, sodium channel and calcium channel. Potassium ion channels mainly include four subtypes, namely K^+ -A^+ channel, basic potassium channel, slow Ca^{2+}-dependent potassium channel and calcium-activated potassium channel. The calcium ion channel contains l-calcium channel and basic calcium channel. The sodium ion channel is H-current kind of sodium channel. In addition, detailed ion channel parameters in different model sections such as soma, axon and dendrite are varied from each other. Neuron response with given voltage stimuli is shown in Figure 4(b). Special response from high stimuli voltage can be found in Figure 4(c), which shows the detailed neuron model with more ion channels (not only basic H-H kind of Na^+ , K^+ , Ca^{2+}), not just leaky integrate-and-fire kind of spiking model. It is able to describe the property of neuronal refractory period well in this model. This detailed pyramidal neuron model built in neuron [10] [11] is essential to understanding and simulation of brain network function.

Spreading activation (SA) was proposed in cognitive psychology for understanding human memory. It is also widely used for searching associative network, neural network or semantic network [12]. The SA network is briefly illustrated in Figure 5. In this paper, this method is applied to the micro scale for understanding neural network activities and predicting spikes.

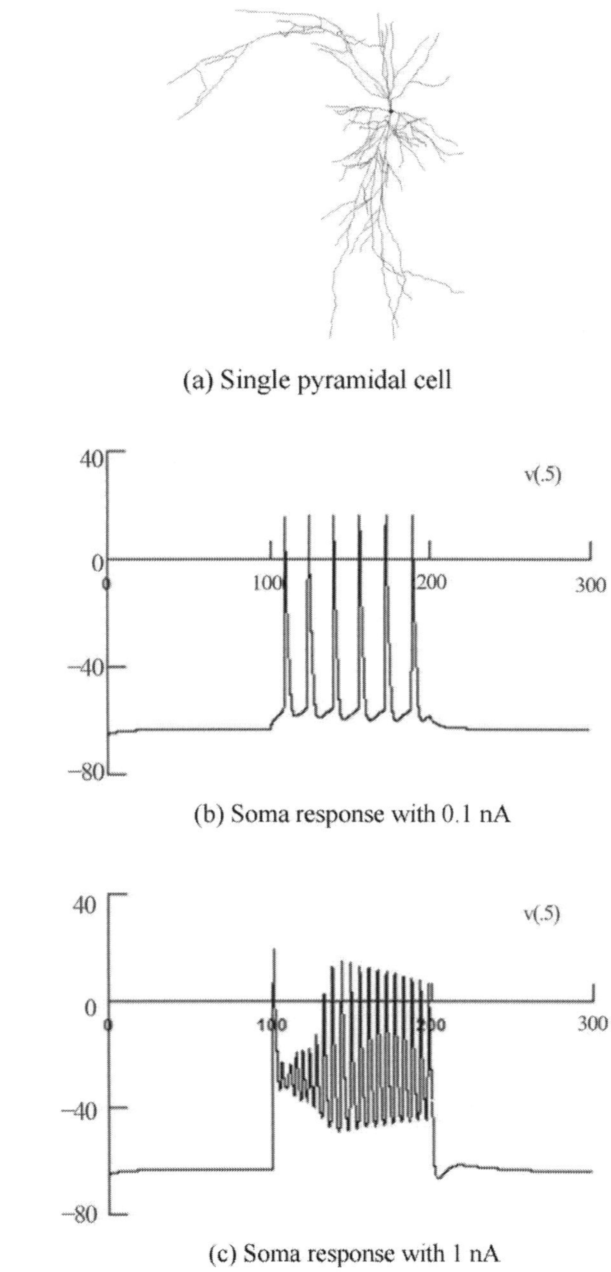

(a) Single pyramidal cell

(b) Soma response with 0.1 nA

(c) Soma response with 1 nA

Figure 4: Single pyramidal cell's reaction with voltage stimulus (0.1 nA to 1 nA). The morphology of the pyramidal cell (a) is from http://neuromorpho.org/ (ID: NMO_08800).

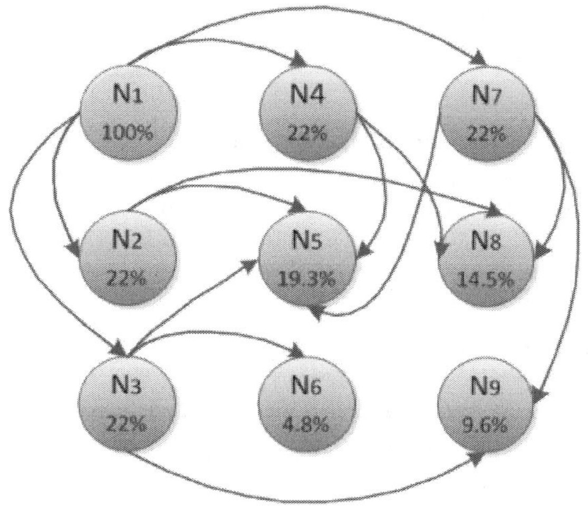

Figure 5: An illustration of the SA network mechanism.

Here we utilize some biology evidence to enhance SA method. The two important variables in SA is the decay factor D and the voltage threshold F. As Figure 6 shows, electrical stimulation action experiment is simulated by Neuron software on real pyramidal cell in mouse hippocampus CA1 area introduced above. Both voltages in soma and dendrites are monitored. As Equation (1) shows, since the voltage decay between two neurons is mainly caused by dendrites instead of axons, we can calculate the average voltage decay range as the universal decay which is fit for the decay factor in SA method. Based on the calculation, the value of D should be 0.22. As Equation (2) shows, voltage threshold F can be the neuron spiking threshold which is set as −56 mv based on [13].

$$D = \frac{\max\left[\frac{\sum_1^{N_{dend}} V_{dend} - V_{th}}{N_{dend}}\right]}{\max\left[V_{soma} - V_{th}\right]} \tag{1}$$

$$F = V_{th} \tag{2}$$

D is the decay factor in SA method which can be biologically described as the voltage decay. N_{dend} is the number of neuronal dendrites. V_{dend} is the voltage of the dendrite section. V_{th} is the resting potential of neuron. F, which represents the spreading threshold factor in SA, is described by pyramidal cell voltage threshold.

The SA method is initiated by activating some neurons as source nodes and then iteratively propagates or spreads that activation to other neurons. During the propagation procedure, the values from original neurons decay according to different weights of neighbor neurons. The activation will terminate when the values go below the threshold for activation [12]. The detailed SA based method for spike prediction is described as follows.

Spreading Activation Based Method for Spike Prediction:

[1] Initialize the main parameters including voltage threshold F (ranging from zero to one) and decay factor D (ranging from zero to one).

[2] Initialize the network and set all neuron activation value *A[i]* to zero. Set some origin nodes in A*[i]* a larger number compared to the voltage threshold F.

[3] For each links [*i, j*], connect the source *[i]* with target *[j]*, adjust $A[i] = A[j] + A[i] * W[i, j] * D$

[4] If a target neuron activation value is larger than threshold F, adjust activation value to F_{max}.

[5] Once a neuron has fired, it may not fire again for preventing repeated firing and loops in a refractory period (experimentally set as 10 iteration times).

[6] Neurons whose activation values exceed the voltage threshold F should be marked for firing on the next spreading activation cycle.

[7] Procedure terminates when no more neurons fire or the number of iterations exceeds the maximum value (experimentally set as 10 iteration times).

EXPERIMENTS AND RESULTS

The Pathway Prediction Results

Data of the rat hippocampus CA1 pyramidal cell layer based on fMCI is used for neural network structure prediction (including 8 datasets, and each of them records spike activities for 62 to 226 neurons. The datasets were imaged with the frequency of 10 Hz [6] [14]) using the upper two proposed strategies.

We validate the accuracy of the neural network structure prediction strategies based on the following steps. The overall prediction accuracy is an average value based on the 8 dataset. For each of the dataset: 1) Equally divide one dataset as 20 sub datasets according to the time intervals (The sub datasets are denoted as S1,...,S20). Select the first 80% of the sub datasets (S1,...,S16) for neural network structure construction, and validate the pathway using the rest of the 20% sub dataset (Here we assume that if the predicted pathway is correct, it should cover the neuronal connections based on the rest of the 20% sub datasets); 2) Select another 80% of the sub datasets for neural network structure construction, and the rest for validation, and repeat this step until all the sub datasets have been selected for validation. 3) The prediction accuracy is the average value of the 20 predictions.

There are several important observations and indications based on the prediction results. 1) Although the two prediction strategies seem entirely different, the neural network structures based on the two different strategies are very relevant (The correlation is significant with the Pearson correlation value 0.958). It indicates that al- though the proposed strategies are different, the results from the two different strategies do not have major conflicts, instead they are very consistent, and support each other. 2) The neural network structure prediction accuracy for the time-ordered strategy is 83.4%, and the accuracy for the spike co-occurrence strategy is 80.5%. When we group the two neural network structures together (denoted as the merged strategy), the prediction accuracy reaches 89.3%. Figure 7 shows the prediction accuracy for each of the dataset using the proposed strategies. This result indicates that better prediction can be made when the predicted pathways from the two strategies are combined together. 3) 27% of the possible connections among neurons are selected for the time-ordered strategy, while 25% of the connections are selected by the spike co-occurrence strategy. If the two results are grouped together, 32% of the possible connections are included. The results seem good, since the coverage is not high (and is consistent with the observation by using electro-microscopy techniques [15] [16]), while the predicted accuracy for possible neural network structure reaches 89%. Comparing with other correlation strategies, merged strategy shows better prediction accuracy results as Figure 8 shows.

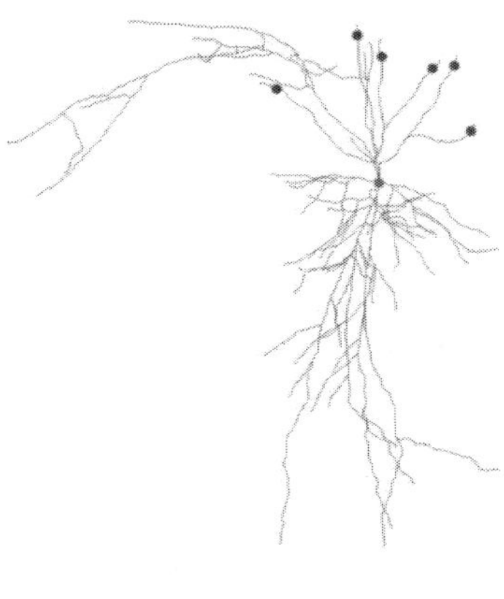

(a)

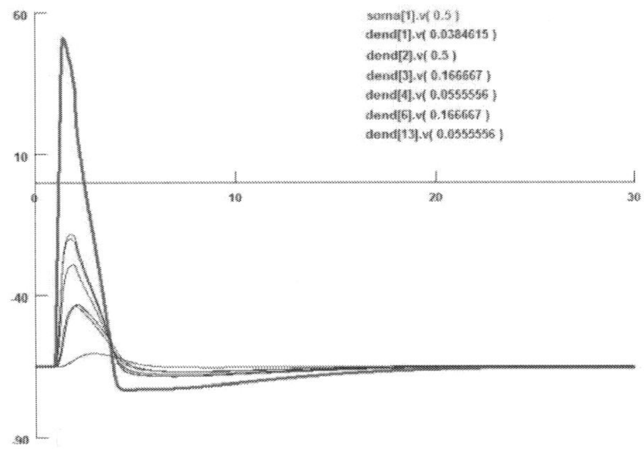

(b)

Figure 6: Pyramidal cell morphology and electrical activity simulation. a) Single pyramidal cell voltage, probe method to ensure the section voltages in soma (red point) and dendrites (blue points); b) Different synapse sections and soma voltage changing by multi stimuli from six neurons. Both soma *[i], v[j]* and dendrite [*i*], *v[j]* sections are built in this model, *i* stands for the section id, *j* denotes the detection probe position. The average decay factor is calculated by means of these six voltages.

The proposed method is validated on the data in which the distance of two neurons is within approximately 400 μm [17]. Whether the proposal is applicable when the distance goes further needs to be validated. In addition, our current result is based on fMCI data from rat brain slices. In our future work, we will investigate the possibility of using the proposed method on fMCI in-vivo imaging data.

Spike Prediction Results

Assume a specific neuron (denoted as n1) is connected with N neurons in the network and its action potential is V, the post synaptic neurons of n1 receive transmitted signals from n1. When one synaptic transmission is done and the signal reaches the post synaptic soma, its contribution to this soma is around 5 mv [18]. The overall contribution to the voltage of the soma (denoted as P) is represented as P = N ×5 mv , which is obtained by summing up all the contribution from each of the post synaptic potential, while P is used as the stimulus to generate next action potentials. Each of the potential P for the N neurons that connects to a specific neuron can be obtained through the upper calculation process. Having the structure of the neural network, we predict the neuron which owns the largest value of P will generate a spike in a refractory period (experimentally set as 10 iteration times).

In order to validate the proposed method, the data from the rat hippocampus CA1 pyramidal cell layer using fMCI is used (including 8 datasets, and each of them records spike activities from 62 to 226 neurons. The datasets were pictured with the frequency of 10 Hz [6] [14]). Since the time slot during two neighborhood pictures is 100 ms, signal transmissions may have looped for several rounds. Hence, iterations of the spreading activation process are needed. The spike prediction accuracy for each of the dataset is shown in Figure 9.

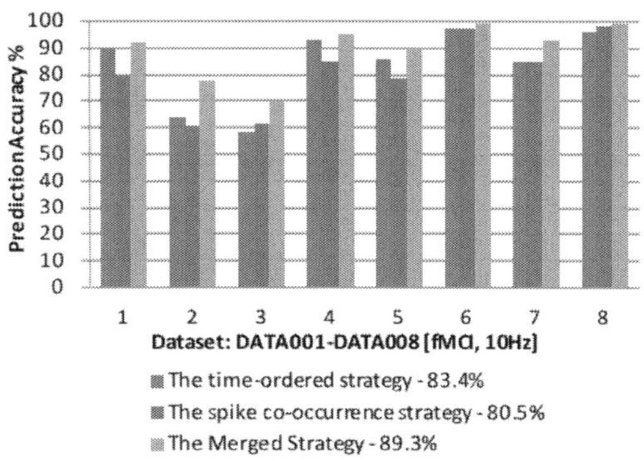

Figure 7: Neural pathway prediction accuracy based on fMCI multi-neuron spike train dataset.

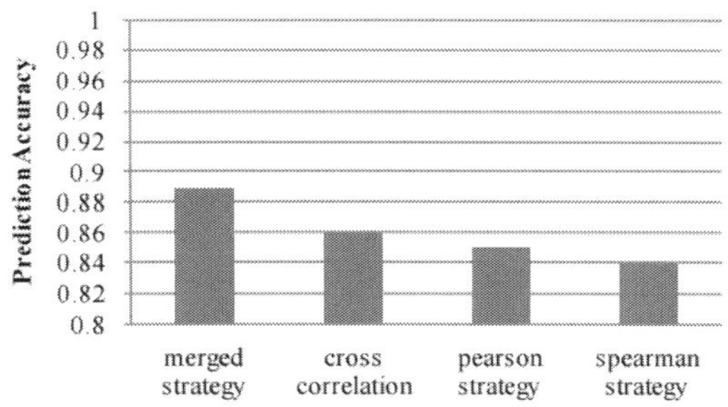

Figure 8: Accuracy made by the merged strategy and other correlation strategies.

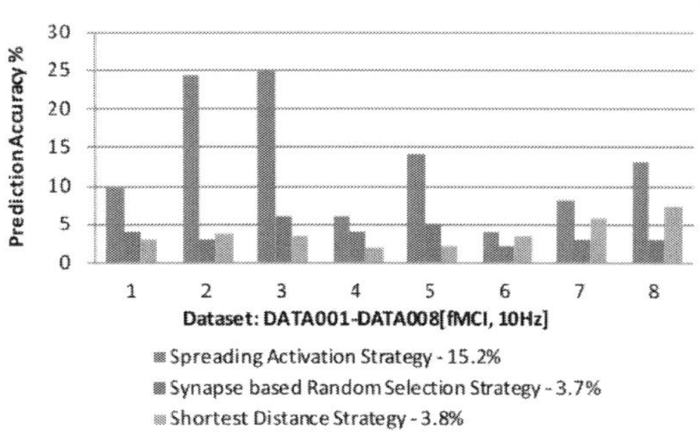

Figure 9: Neural spike prediction accuracy based on different strategies.

As a comparative study, we introduce two alternative strategies, namely the shortest distance strategy (the neuron which owns the shortest distance compared to other post synaptic neurons will be fired), and the synapse based random selection strategy (randomly select a neuron from the set of post synaptic neurons). As shown in Figure 1, the spreading activation based strategy outperforms other two strategies and the average prediction accuracy on 8 datasets is around 15.2%, at least three times better than the other two strategies (the average prediction accuracy for shortest distance strategy is 3.8%, while the synapse based random selection strategy is 3.7%). The validation shows that the proposed spreading activation strategy is potentially effective for predict- ing neural spikes in the neural network.

CONCLUSION

In this paper, two strategies to predict neural network structure ares proposed and high accuracy experiment results are showed in Section 4.1 and proved their efficiency. This effort makes the rebuilt network structure without anatomy slicing possible. Although restricted by the experimental data, the size of the rebuilt network is around hundred neurons, it still shows great potential for handling larger network reconstruction tasks. Further, the spiking prediction method gives us a view point to analyze the special condition in which we can acquire only structure data. As the first try, this paper only compared with some commonly used methods, such as cross correlation, Pearson and Spearman strategies. More methods will be taken into consideration for comparative studies in the future, such as Granger causality method. One further potential efforts for this work is that spiking functional activities from prediction model can further be used to guide biological experiment signal processing, such as which kind of spikes are noises while others are not.

ACKNOWLEDGEMENTS

This paper is supported by the Brain Engineering project funded by Institute of Automation, Chinese Academy of Sciences. The authors would like to thank anonymous reviewers for constructive comments.

REFERENCES

1. Zeng, Y., Zhang, T.L. and Xu, B. (2014) Neural Pathway Prediction Based on Multi-Neuron Spike Train Data. Proceedings of the 23rd Annual Computational Neuroscience Meeting (CNS 2014), Québec City, 26-31 July 2014, 6.
2. Zhang, T.L., Zeng, Y. and Xu, B. (2014) Neural Spike Prediction Based on Spreading Activation. Proceedings of the 23rd Annual Computational Neuroscience Meeting (CNS 2014), Québec City, 26-31 July 2014, 7.
3. Sporns, O., Tononi, G. and Kötter, R. (2005) The Human Connectome: A Structural Description of the Human Brain. PLoS Computational Biology, 1, e42.http://dx.doi.org/10.1371/journal.pcbi.0010042
4. Arenkiell, B.R. and Ehlers, M.D. (2009) Molecular Genetics and Imaging Technologies for Circuit-Based Neuroanatomy. Nature, 461, 900-907.http://dx.doi.org/10.1038/nature08536

5. Mukamel, R. and Fried, I. (2011) Human Intracranial Recordings and Cognitive Neuroscience. Annual Review of Psychology, 63, 511-537.http://dx.doi.org/10.1146/annurev-psych-120709-145401

6. Takahashi, N., Sasaki, T., Usami, A., Matsuki, N. and Ikegaya, Y. (2007) Watching Neuronal Circuit Dynamics through Functional Multineuron Calcium Imaging (fMCI). Neuroscience Research, 58, 219-225. http://dx.doi.org/10.1016/j.neures.2007.03.001

7. Kettunen, P. (2012) Calcium Imaging in the Zebrafish. In: Islam, S., Ed., Calcium Signaling, Springer Netherlands, Heidelberg, 1039-1071.

8. Stetter, O., Battaglia, D., Soriano, J. and Geisel, T. (2012) Model-Free Reconstruction of Excitatory Neuronal Connectivity from Calcium Imaging Signals. PLoS Computational Biology, 8, e1002653. http://dx.doi.org/10.1371/journal.pcbi.1002653

9. Mira, J. and Sánchez-Andrés, J.V. (1999) Foundations and Tools for Neural Modeling. Proceedings of International Work-Conference on Artificial and Natural Neural Networks, Vol. I, Alicante, 2-4 June 1999, 29.

10. Carnevale, N.T. and Hines, M.L. (2006) The Neuron Book. Cambridge University Press, Cambridge, UK. http://dx.doi.org/10.1017/CBO9780511541612

11. Dayan, P. and Abbott, L.F. (2001) Theoretical Neuroscience: Computational and Mathematical Modeling of Neural Systems. MIT Press, Cambridge.

12. Anderson, J.R. (1983) A Spreading Activation Theory of Memory. Journal of Verbal Learning and Verbal Behavior, 22, 261-295. http://dx.doi.org/10.1016/S0022-5371(83)90201-3

13. Yue, C.Y., Remy, S., Su, H.L., Beck, H. and Yaari, Y. (2005) Proximal Persistent Na^{+}Channels Drive Spike Afterdepolarization and Associated Bursting in Adult CA1 Pyramidal Cells. The Journal of Neuroscience, 25, 9704-9720.http://dx.doi.org/10.1523/JNEUROSCI.1621-05.2005

14. Yue, C.Y., Remy, S., Su, H.L., Beck, H. and Yaari, Y. (2011) High-Speed Multi-Neuron Calcium Imaging Using Nipkow-Type Confocal Microscopy. Current Protocols in Neuroscience, 2, Unit 2.14. http://www.hippocampus.jp/data

15. Gómez-Di Cesare, C.M., Smith, K.L., Rice, F.L. and Swann, J.W. (1997) Axonal Remodeling during Postnatal Maturation of CA3 Hippocampal Pyramidal Neurons. Journal of Comparative Neurology, 384, 165-180.

16. Fujisawa, S., Matsuki, N. and Ikegaya, Y. (2006) Single Neurons Can Induce Phase Transitions of Cortical Recurrent Networks with Multiple Internal States. Cerebral Cortex, 16, 639-654. http://dx.doi.org/10.1093/cercor/bhj010

17. Sasaki, T., Matsuki, N. and Ikegaya, Y. (2007) Metastability of Active CA3 Networks. The Journal of Neuroscience, 27, 517-528. http://dx.doi.org/10.1523/JNEUROSCI.4514-06.2007

18. Lodish, H., Berk, A., Zipursky, S.L., Matsudaira, P., Baltimore, D. and Darnell, J. (2000) Molecular Cell Biology. 4th Edition, Freeman and Company, New York.

CHAPTER 2

MODELING NEUROMORPHIC PERSISTENT FIRING NETWORKS

Ning Ning, Guoqi Li, Wei He, Kejie Huang, Li Pan, Kiruthika Ramanathan, Rong Zhao, and Luping Shi

Keywords: Neuron Model, Neuromorphic, Persistent Firing, Slow Integration, Spiking Network, Working Memory

INTRODUCTION

Understanding how human brain represents, stores, and processes information is one of the greatest unsolved mysteries and fundamental challenges of science today. Over the past century, since Lapicque introduced the integrate-and-fire model of the neuron in 1907 [1] , computational neuroscientists have developed several mathe- matical and computational neural models. Generally, one approach in computational neuroscience involves creating biologically realistic models, where information about the biological details of neurons including their electrochemistry, biochemistry, and detailed morphology and connectivity are also included [2] , such as Hodg- kin-Huxley [3] and compartment models [4] . Another approach involves building qualitative models to capture the spiking nature and the essential elements of the behavior with simplified complexity, for example, leaky in- tegrate-and-fire [5] , FitzHugh-Nagumo [6] , Morris-Lecar [7] , Hindmarsh-Rose [8] , Wilson [9] , Resonate-and- Fire [10] and Izhikevich [11] neuron models.

However, as neuroscience continues to advance rapidly, more and more complex neuronal behaviors and brain dynamics are revealed. This has posed challenges for neural modeling as conventional neuron models fail to reflect the newly-discovered complexity of neural systems, such as the persistent firing phenomenon recently observed in rodent hippocampal inhibitory neurons [12] . In the classic viewpoint about the information flow in the nervous system, synaptic inputs are received and integrated in the dendrites only on a timescale of millise- conds to seconds, and when the depolarized somatic membrane potential exceeds the threshold, action potentials are triggered at the axon hillock and propagate along the axon. However, recent discovery reveals that some ac- tion potential began at the distal end of axon instead of at the axon hillock. A much slower form of potential in- tegration is observed which leads to persistent firing in distal axons of rodent hippocampal and neocortical in- terneurons [12] . The slow integration lasts from tens of seconds to minutes in distal axon, so does the persistent firing. During the persistent firing, the somatic depolarization is not observed, implying that axon may perform its own neural computations without any involvement of the soma or dendrites.

In this paper, we propose a new computationally-efficient artificial neuron model that account for all-known neural behaviors. In this model, axon is an independent computational unit complementary to the classic somatic computational unit which evokes action potentials. Compared to the soma which integrates dendritic inputs in a timescale of milliseconds to seconds, the axon integrates the spikes evoked by soma in a timescale of tens of second to minutes, and consequently determines the persistent firing behavior of the axon. Besides the computa- tional model, a neuromorphic model of persistent firing neurons and its analog circuit are also proposed. In ad- dition, a polychronous spiking network [13] with persistent firing inhibitory interneurons is simulated, which may assist the development of spiking network-based memory and bio-inspired computer system.

PERSISTENT FIRING NEURON MODEL

The conventional models such as Izhikevich neuron model [11] are incapable of simulating the important newly- discovered

Citation: Ning, N. , Li, G. , He, W. , Huang, K. , Pan, L. , Ramanathan, K. , Zhao, R. and Shi, L. (2015) Modeling Neuromorphic Persistent Firing Networks. International Journal of Intelligence Science, 5, 89-101. doi:10.4236/ijis.2015.52009.

phenomenon of persistent firing induced by axonal slow integration, as a recent discovery in neuro- physiology reveals that interneurons can slowly integrate spiking, share the output across a coupled network of axons and respond with persistent firing even in the absence of input to the soma or dendrites. To this end, we extend the Izhikevich neuron model by modeling the axonal slow integration, which can be mathematically de- scribed by Equations (1)-(6):

$$v' = 0.04v^2 + 5v + 140 - u + I \quad (1)$$

$$u' = a(bv - u) \quad (2)$$

$$w' = -fw \quad (3)$$

with the auxiliary resettings:

$$\text{if } v \geq 30 \text{ mV, then } v \leftarrow c,\ u \leftarrow u + d,\ w \leftarrow w + e \quad (4)$$

$$\text{if } w \geq w_p, \text{ then } (a,b,c,d,e) \leftarrow (a,b,c,d,e)_p \quad (5)$$

$$\text{if } w \leq w_n, \text{ then } (a,b,c,d,e) \leftarrow (a,b,c,d,e)_n \quad (6)$$

where $' = d/dt$, t is the time, w describes the hyper theoretical potential of the axonal leaky integrator, v and u are the dimensionless variables that describe the membrane potential, the membrane recovery, respec- tively. Parameters $a,\ b,\ c,\ d,\ e$ and f are dimensionless, a describes the timescale of u, b represents the sensitivity of u to the subthreshold fluctuations of v, c is the after-spike reset value of the membrane potential, d describes the after-spike reset of u, e represents the after-somatic-spike axonal accumulation in the passive conduction mode, and f is the value describing the rate of the axonal leak. In Equations (5) and (6), w_p is the high threshold (rising edge) value of w to trigger the persistent firing mode of axon, and w_n is the low threshold (falling edge) value of w for the axon to return to passive conduction mode. $(a,b,c,d,e)_p$ and $(a,b,c,d,e)_n$ describe the parameter sets of $a,\ b,\ c,\ d,\ e$ variables when the axon is in the persistent firing mode and passive conduction mode, respectively.

This model extends the Izhikevich neuron model [11] described by Equations (1)-(2), which well captures the somatic spiking dynamics. By modifying the $a,\ b,\ c,\ d$ variables in Equations (1), (2), and (4), different firing patterns can be generated. One important concept of our model is the axon-dependent switch of the axonal firing patterns through dynamically selecting different variable set of $a,\ b,\ c$ and d.

The axon is modeled as a slow leaky integrator, which is capable to alter the axonal functions between passive conduction and persistent firing modes, depending on the potential of axonal integrator. In the passive conduc- tion mode, the axon acts as a transmission cable in which stable propagation occurs once an action potential is evoked by synaptic inputs. In the persistent firing mode, in which the parameters in the model are chosen to set the dynamical system to be self-oscillatory, axon acts as a bistable oscillator which does not require stimulus from dendrites to sustain the persistent firing of action potentials.

In contrast to the somatic leaky integrator which accounts for the integration of dendritic inputs, the axonal leaky integrator has a larger time constant for its integration and leakage, integrating incoming spikes generated in the axon hillock in the timescale from tens of seconds to minutes, due to its slow rate of leakage f, as de- scribed in Equation (3). When the potential in the axonal leaky integrator exceeds w_p, which denotes the high threshold (rising edge), the persistent firing will be triggered, and the firing pattern is determined by the para- meter set of $(a,b,c,d,e)_p$. If there are no somatic spikes accumulated in the axon, the potential w decreases at the rate of f. When w reaches the low threshold (falling edge), the axon w_n returns to passive conduc- tion mode, and the $a,\ b,\ c,\ d,\ e$ variables in the model are reset to $(a,b,c,d,e)_n$.

We have simulated the persistent firing neuronal behaviors under two stimulation protocols, with the parame- ters summarized in Table 1. The simulation results under step/pause stimulation protocol [12] are shown in Figure 1. We applied 1-second current step of 500 pA during each 10-second sweep to the simulation model. During the sweeps of the step/pause input stimulus, it is observed that the somatically evoked action potentials appear when the synaptic input stimulus is presented and disappear when the stimulus is removed (Figure 1(a)). When w accumulates to a level higher than the high threshold w_p, persistent firing occurs (Figure 1(a)), 12th sweep), after which w decreases monotonically due to axonal leakage and no stimulus (Figure 1(d)). The per- sistent firing ends when w is lower than the low threshold w_n. It should be noted that in this model, the rest- ing potential of persistent firing spikes is about 20 mV below the one of somatically evoked action potentials, which fits well with the data from current-clamp recordings in the persistent firing neurons [12] [14] . We emu- late this phenomenon through switching the parameter c in Equation (4) between c_p and c_n.

The variation of persistent firing frequency was also simulated (Figure 1(b) and Figure 1(c)). As the firing frequency can be tuned by the parameter b in Equation (2), the decrease of persistent firing frequency ob- served in the current-clamp experiment can be emulated in the model through defining the following relation- ship between parameter b and f.

Table 1: Simulation parameters

Step/Pause protocol	*Long Pulse protocol*
$(a,b,c,d,e)_p = (0.1,5,-85,0,0)$	$(a,b,c,d,e)_p = (0.1,0.3,-85,0,0)$
$(a,b,c,d,e)_n = (0.1,0.2,-65,2,0.001)$	$(a,b,c,d,e)_n = (0.1,0.2,-65,2,0.012)$
$f = 5\times10^{-4}$	$f = 8\times10^{-4}$
$w_n = 0.2$, $w_p = 0.84$	$w_n = 0.2$, $w_p = 2.1$
$I = 500$ pA	$I = 15$ pA

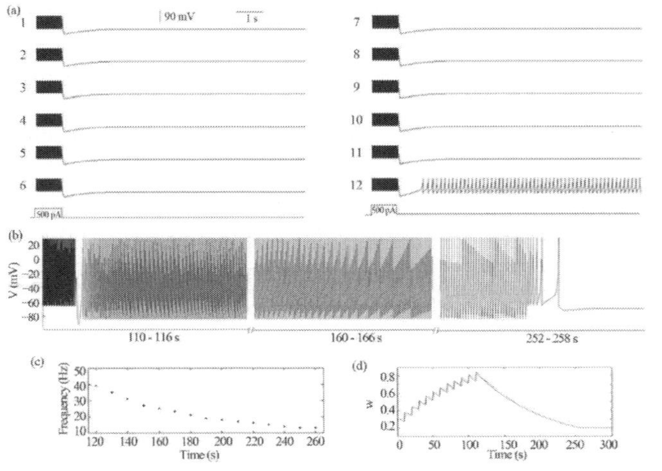

Figure 1: Simulation of persistent firing neuron model. (a) The waveform of membrane potential. The simulation used the same stimulation protocol as the experiment of whole-cell current-clamp recording by Sheffield et al [12] . To evoke persistent firing, 1-s current step of 500 pA was delivered to the neuron during each 10-s sweep (left, sweeps 1 - 6; right, sweeps 7 - 12). In this simulation, persistent firing was evoked after the 12th sweep, and the total number of evoked action potentials before persistent firing was 1278. (b) The waveform of persistent firing, which lasted over 2 minutes. The total number of evoked axonal action potentials was 3073. The simulation reflects the decrease of instantaneous firing frequency, which was shown in the current-clamp experiment. (c) The instantaneous firing frequency of persistent firing action potentials, which decreased from 40 Hz at the onset of persistent firing to 12 Hz at the end of persistent firing as the parameter b decreased in this simulation. (d) The time response of w, which represents the hypertheoretical potential of the axonal leaky integrator.

if persistent firing action potential is generated, then $b \leftarrow b(1-f)$ (7)

The instantaneous firing frequency of axon-evoked action potentials attains its maximum (40 Hz) at the onset of persistent firing, and decreases over time till the end of persistent firing.

We also applied the stimulation with a 40-second long pulse of 15 pA current to the persistent firing neuron model described by Equations (1)-(7) with a different parameter set (Table 1). The simulation results are shown in Figure 2. The repeated somatic current stimuli eventually trigger the persistent firing that outlasts the current stimuli by more than 30 seconds.

By tuning the parameters of e, f, w_p and w_n, we can set different time scales for the axonal slow integra- tion, allowing the model to accommodate different types of neurons with different persistent firing behaviors.

MODEL ANALYSIS

In this section, we present the mathematical analysis on the conditions which guarantee the existence of the persistent firing behavior in the neuron. Let. $X=[uvw]'$ Equations (1)-(3) can be rewritten as:

$$X' = F(X) + HI = X^{\mathrm{T}}AX + BX + C + HI \quad (8)$$

where I is the input current, A, B, C and H are the corresponding matrices determined by

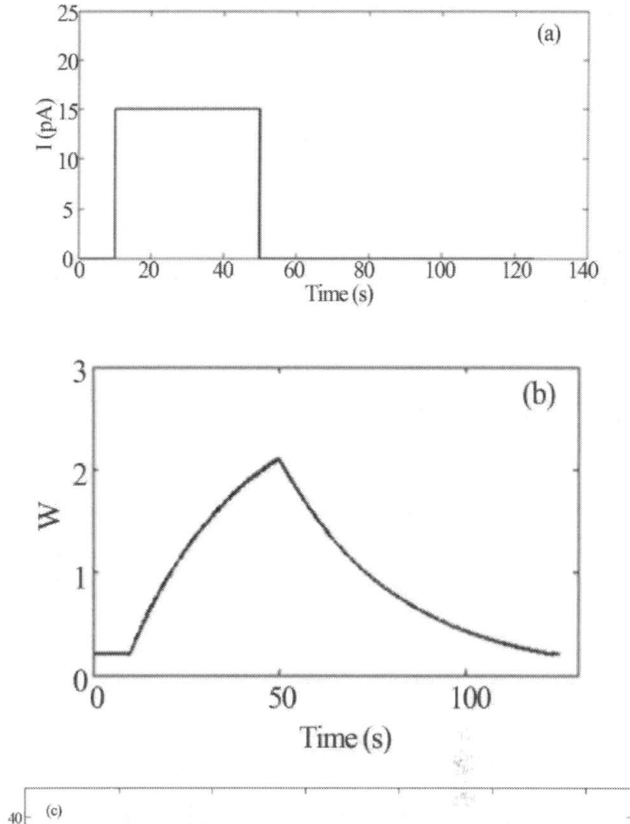

Figure 2: Simulation of persistent firing neuronal behaviors with long pulse stimulation protocol. (a) The input stimulus. A pulse of current with 15 pA amplitude lasts 40 seconds as the synaptic input to the neuron. (b) Time response of W, the variable describing the potential of the axonal leaky integrator. (c) Time response of V, which describes the membrane or axon potential. The first part is the fast spiking waveform of V when the 15pA current step is present, and the second part is the persistent firing waveform of V.

Equations (1)-(3). When the input current I is not present, the equilibrium points of the dynamic system in Equation (8) are the solutions of the Equation $F(X)=0$, the two equilibrium points are obtained $X_1=\left[-12.5\left(5-b+\sqrt{\Delta}\right)-12.5\left(5-b+\sqrt{\Delta}\right)0\right]'$ and. Here, we assume that $\Delta = 2.6 + b^2 - 10b > 0$ and it is noted that X_1 is a stable equilibrium point while X_2 is unstable. Based on the analysis of stability of the equilibrium points and the nonlinear dynamic characteristic of Equation (8), the following conditions can be summarized to guarantee the existence of the persistent firing behavior.

Condition 1. The input current I satisfies that $\forall v \in R$ such that $0.04v^2+(5-b)v+140 \geq 0$, i.e,

$$I \geq \left|\min\left\{0.04v^2+(5-b)v+140\right\}\right|.$$

Condition 2. The condition $w > w_p$ is satisfied no later than the time when I is removed.

Condition 3. When $w > w_p$, the parameter c is denoted as c_p in Equation (5) (during the persistent firing period) is chosen to be the value such that $c > -12.5(5-b-\sqrt{\Delta})$.

Condition 1 means that there is no equilibrium point for the equation $F(X)+HI=0$ which gives $X' AX + BX + C + HI = 0$. Otherwise, X may approach the equilibrium point and not change any more even when I is present. In this case, it is impossible for persistent firing to exist. Condition 2 requires that the neu- ron fires a sufficient number of spikes to ensure that $w > w_p$ before I is removed. Condition 3 implies that, during the persistent firing period, $0.04v^2+(5-b)v+140>0$ should be guaranteed at the interval $-12.5(5-b-\sqrt{\Delta}) \le v \le c_p$.

In the above analysis, we choose b to be such that $\Delta > 0$. Now we analyze the case that $\Delta \le 0$. It can be shown that there is no real equilibrium point or at most a unstable equilibrium point for the equation $F(X)=0$. Then Condition 1 is achieved even if $I=0$. The persistence firing can be always observed no matter whether the Conditions 2 and 3 are satisfied or not. However, in this case, the nonlinear system $X = F(X)+HI$ is un- stable. This is the reason that generally b is suggested to be chosen as a value such that $\Delta > 0$.

The geometrical approach provides a clear and insightful perspective of investigating the characteristics of dynamical system of neuron [15] , and is therefore adopted to analyze the persistent firing model. We choose conveniently to conduct geometrical analysis on the phenomenon of persistent firing due to a long-lasting pulse stimulation (Figure 2 and Figure 3(a)) rather than on that due to a pulse train (Figure 1), since the geometry of the former is less complicated yet retains significant information regarding the time evolution of the dynamical

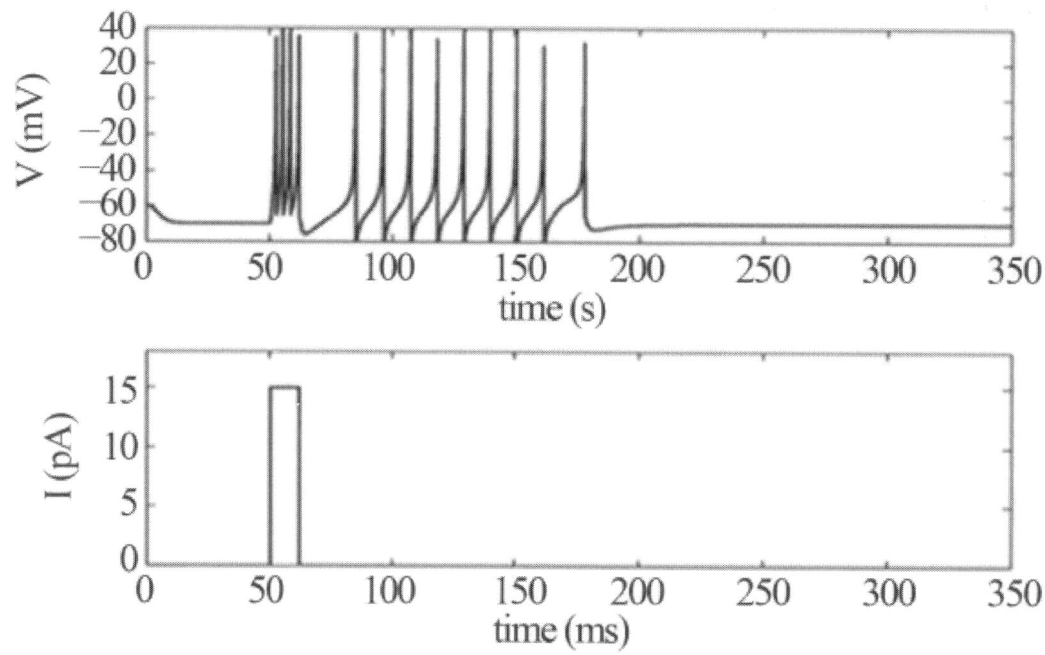

(a)

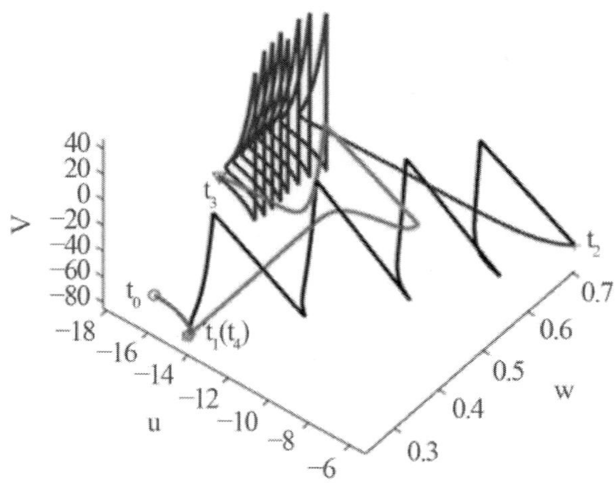

(b)

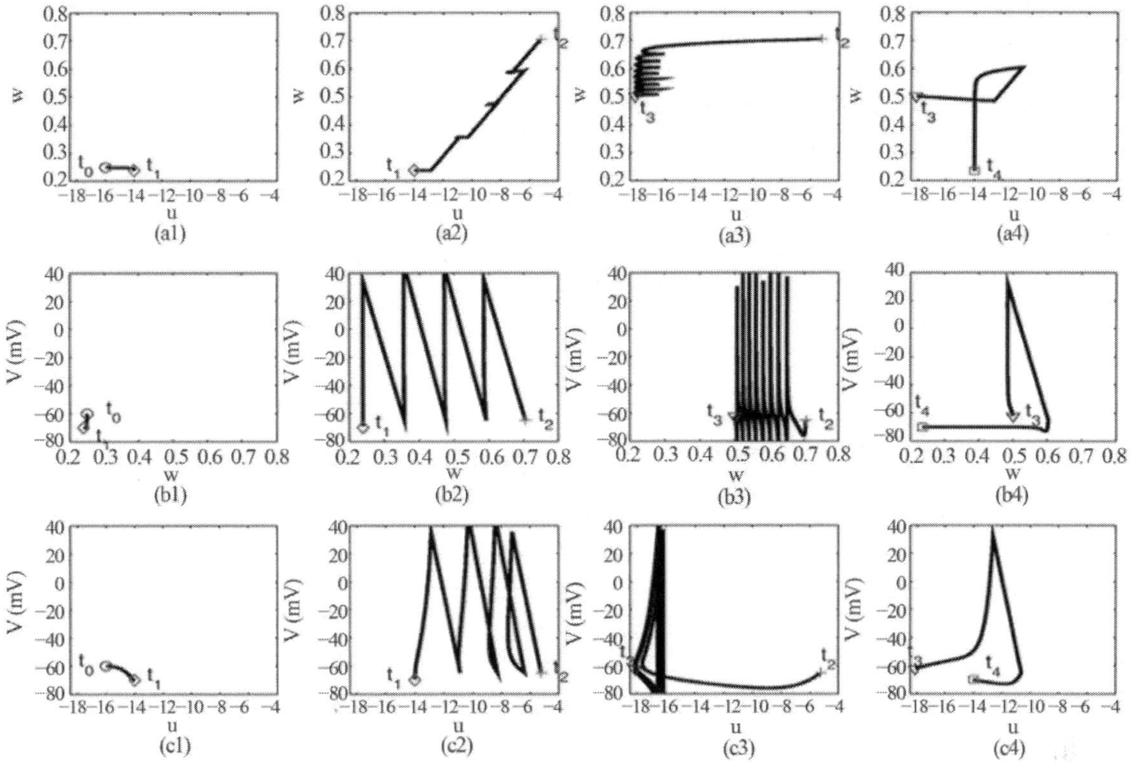

(c)

Figure 3: (a) Persistent firing induced by an input current pulse; (b) Trajectory of state variables u, v, w in three-dimensional phase space; (c) The three rows are projections of the 3-D trajectory. Figure 3(b) of persistent firing on the uw (a1-a4), wv(b1-b4), and uv(c1-c4) phase planes, respectively; the four columns repre- sent the four stages of the whole process of persistent firing: stage 1 (a1, b1, c1), stage 2 (a2, b2, c2), stage 3 (a3, b3, c3), and stage 4 (a4, b4, c4), respectively.

system of neuron, such as the stable equilibrium and the threshold values, as shown in Figure 3(b) where the geometrical trajectory of the state variables u, v, w is plotted in three-dimensional phase space. It is worth mentioning that a new set of values in Table 2 is assigned to the model's parameters to further reduce the com- plexity of the geometry, as shown in Figure 3(a) and Figure 3(b). For the convenience of analysis, the projec- tions of the 3-D trajectory on the uw, wv, and uv phase planes are illustrated in Figure 3(c), where five points in time (t_0, t_1, t_2, t_3, t_4) are labeled on the curves, so as to partition the whole course of persistent firing into four temporal stages:

Stage 1: During the time range of $t_0 \to t_1$, the system begins with its initial state at t_0, converges to a stable equilibrium, stay there until t_1. The stable equilibrium can be calculated to be $[-70,-14,0]'$.

Stage 2: During the time range of $t_1 \to t_2$, the system exhibits action potential evoked by a rectangular cur- rent signal, which also leads to the persistent firing in the next stage.

Stage 3: During the time range of $t_2 \to t_3$, the system exhibits persistent firing, which is triggered at t_2 when w reaches the upper threshold $w_p = 0.7$, and terminates at t_3 when w reaches the lower threshold value $w_n = 0.5$.

Stage 4: During the time range of $t_3 \to t_4$, the system returns to the state of stable equilibrium and rests there.

NEUROMORPHIC MODEL OF THE ARTIFICIAL NEURON

Since the last two decades, there has been a continuing interest in developing the neuromorphic circuits and sys- tems that mimic the operation of biological neurons and brains, which enables considerably faster and more energy-efficient emulations of the neurons and neural systems. Due to the computational simplicity of our model, it is rather straightforward to implement the proposed neuron model in hardware, either in digital circuits or analog circuits. There have been several circuit implementations of Izhikevich neuron model and its variants [16] [17] . Thus in our case it is intuitive to add a leaky integrator emulating the axon, as well as the switching devices for selecting one of two sets of a, b, c, d, e parameters, which may be stored in memory devices, e.g. non- volatile memory.

A conceptual design of the proposed artificial neuron are shown in Figure 4, where the axonal spikes are ori- ginated from the unstable state of the neuron circuit and the artificial neuron is considered as a parameter-de- pendent dynamic system. The parameters of such dynamic system can be stored in non-volatile memory devices. Through modifying the parameter values in the memory, the spiking neuron unit can alter the axonal dynamics between the passive conduction mode and the persistent firing mode.

We have built the neuromorphic model based on the concept design with SPICE and Verilog-A languages, and simulated the model in Synopsys® HSPICE Simulator. The circuit model is shown inFigure 5(a) and Figure 5(b). The soma membrane circuit (Figure 5(a)) essentially implements the Izhikevich neuron model [10] , which includes a SPICE block describing Equations (1)-(2), an adder, a Schmitt trigger and two NMOS transis- tors (M1, M2) as switches. The stimulus I is the only external input to the soma unit, which also requires to fetch a parameter set of a, b, V_p and c from its memory during the operation. The Schmitt trigger imple- mented in Verilog-A, compares the membrane potential v with V_p (peak of the spike, typically 30 mV) and c (rest potential, typically −65 mV), and produces the output C_v, of VDD only when $> V_p$, and GND only when $v < c$. When C_v is high (VDD), which means a spike is generated, the two NMOS switches (M1, M2) are turned on thus the potentials of u and v are reset to u_{new} and c, respectively. When C_v is low (GND), the potentials of u and v remain to be solely determined by Equations (1)-(2) in the SPICE block.

Table 2: Simulation parameters

$(a,b,c,d,e)_p$	=	$(0.1,0.3,-85,0,0)$
$(a,b,c,d,e)_n$	=	$(0.1,0.2,-85,2,0.12)$
f	=	5×10^{-4}
w_n	=	0.5
w_p	=	0.7
I	=	15 pA

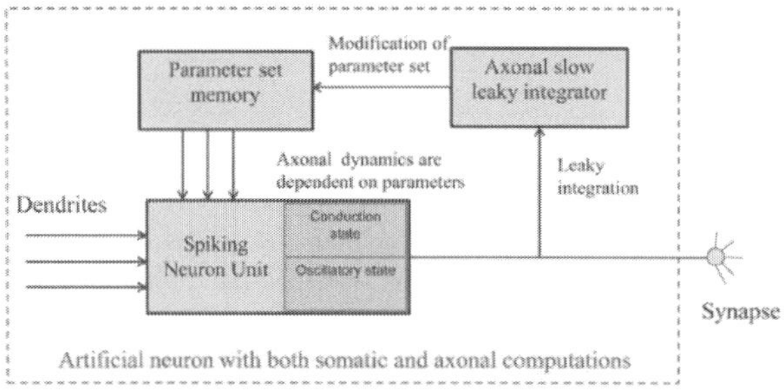

Figure 4. Conceptual design of the proposed artificial neuron.

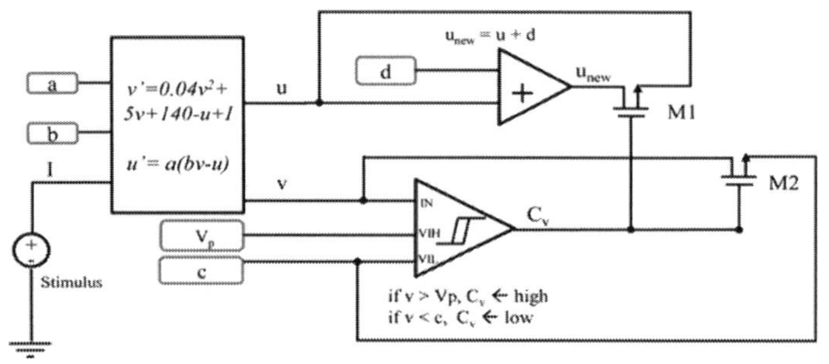

(a)

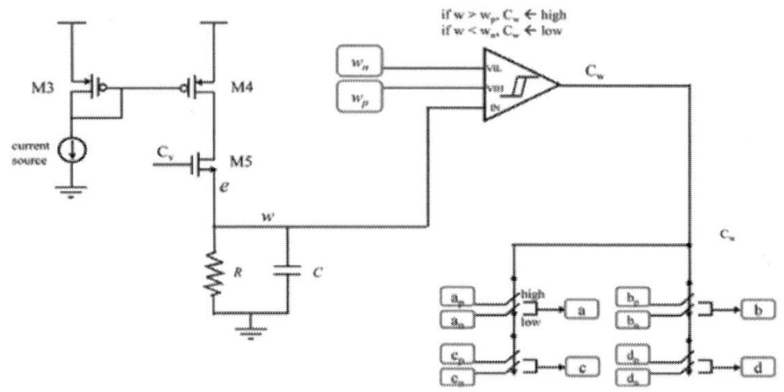

(b)

Figure 5. (a) The soma membrane circuit; (b) The axon circuit.

In the axon circuit (Figure 5(b)), a parallel RC circuit implements the axonal leaky integrator. When the soma membrane is generating a spike, C_v is high (VDD) and NMOS M5 will be turned on and pull the current from the current mirror (M3, M4), and charge the RC leaky integrator, increasing the axon potential w. The potential w is compared with w_n and w_p by a Schmitt trigger, which produces the output C_w of VDD when $w > w_p$ (the persistent firing should start) and GND when $w < w_n$ (the persistent firing should stop). The C_w signal controls five 2-way switches, which subsequently determine the value of x to be x_n or x_p, where $x \in \{a,b,c,d,e\}$, and the neuron spiking dynamics.

Based on the long-pulse stimulation protocol and the circuit parameters given in Table 3, the simulation re- sults of the circuit are shown in Figure 6. It should be noted that the values of the stimulus current I and si- mulation time here are different from those discussed in the previous section, with the purpose of achieving simpler implementation in the circuits. Nevertheless, it can be clearly seen that after we continuously applied the stimulus current for a period of time and stopped the input, the persistent firing of spikes was triggered, lasted for a similar duration, and finally stopped, depending on the level of axonal integrator potential w.

Table 3: Circuit simulation parameters

$(a,b,c,d,e)_p$	=	$(0.1\ \text{V}, 0.3\ \text{V}, -85\ \text{mV}, 0\ \text{V}, 0.1\ \text{mA})$
$(a,b,c,d,e)_n$	=	$(0.1\ \text{V}, 0.2\ \text{V}, -65\ \text{mV}, 2\ \text{mV}, 0.1\ \text{mA})$
f	=	0.2
w_n	=	40 mV
w_p	=	90 mA

PERSISTENT FIRING SPIKING NETWORK

We have used this model to simulate a spiking network of 1000 randomly connected neurons. The network takes into account of axonal conduction delays [18] and spike-timing-dependent plasticity (STDP), which is consi- dered to be "polychromous" [13] . The network consists of 800 excitatory neurons with regular spiking pattern [11] and 200 inhibitory neurons. As around 80% of EGFP-positive interneurons were found to have persistent firing behavior by repeated somatic current injection [12] , we set in the 80% simulation, or 160 of the inhibitory neurons to be capable of persistent firing while the remaining 20% are fast spiking inhibitory neurons.

Each excitatory neuron is connected to 100 random neurons, and each inhibitory neuron, including persistent firing neuron, is randomly connected to 100 excitatory neurons only. Each synaptic connection has a fixed in- teger conduction delay between 1 ms and 20 ms. The conduction delay in the range of 1 - 20 ms is randomly as-signed to all excitatory synapses, while the 1 ms delay are assigned to all inhibitory synapses [13] . The synaptic connections are modified according to the STDP rule [19] . The implementation of the STDP function is based on Equation (9):

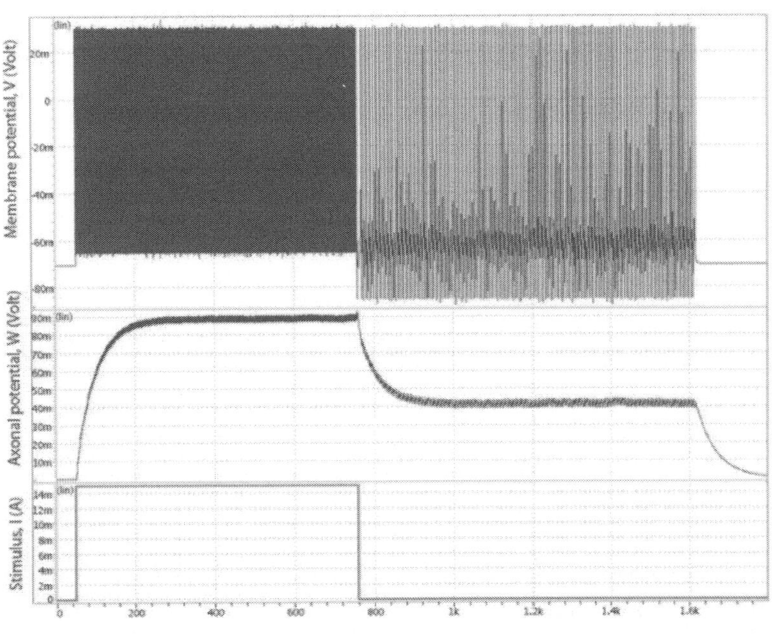

Figure 6: Circuit simulation results of the artificial neuron, showing that after a continuous applied stimulus stops, the slow integration in the axon leads to persistent firing of spikes. Top: the membrane potential V; Middle: the potential of axonal integrator W; Bottom: the stimulus current I.

$$W(\Delta t) = \begin{cases} A^{+}e^{-\Delta t/\tau^{+}}, & \text{for } \Delta t > 0 \\ -A^{-}e^{\Delta t/\tau^{-}} & \text{for } \Delta t < 0 \end{cases} \tag{9}$$

where $\Delta t = t_{post} - t_{pre}$, $W(\Delta t)$ represents the strength of synapse connection, A^{+} and A^{-} depend on the maximum synaptic strength, and τ^{+} and τ^{-} are time constants determining the time window of STDP.

A simplified example of the spiking network structure is illustrated in Figure 7(a). The raster plots of 1-second firing activities in the 1000-neuron spiking network with persistent firing inhibitory interneurons are shown in Figure 7(b). One can see from Figure 7(b) that the network exhibits asynchronous dynamics. Differ- ent rhythmic activities can be identified, ranging from 3 Hz to 8 Hz. Dense vertical columns indicate there are occasional episodes of synchronized firings. As the firing rate of the inhibitory neurons (fast spiking) is higher than that of excitatory neurons (regular spiking), there are generally more firings for inhibitory neurons. The persisting firing of inhibitory interneurons in the network, leads to reciprocal inhibition in a longer timescale and thus shut down the activities for a longer period (Figure 7(b) middle column). The synchronization of persis- tent firing interneurons could contribute to the beta and gamma oscillation, whose frequency ranges are close to the persistent firing frequency [20] .

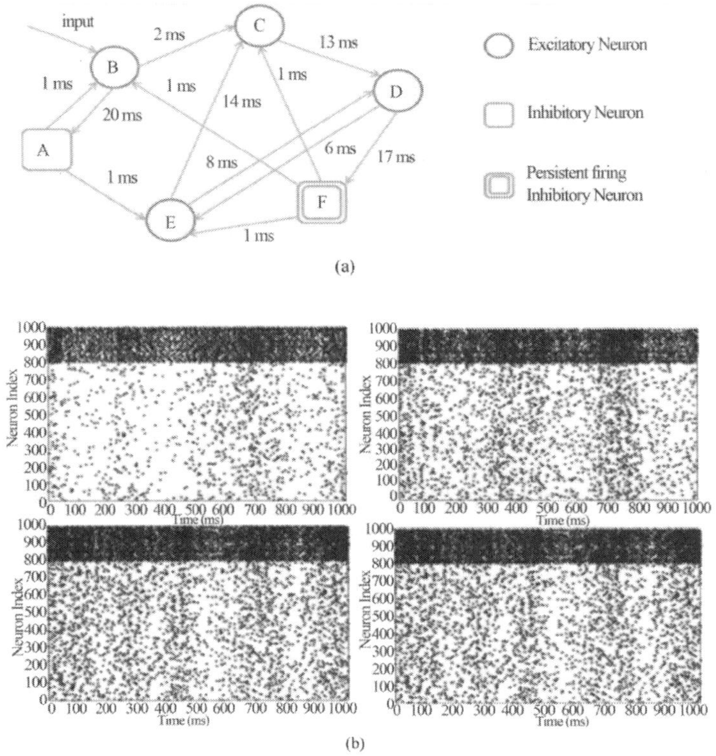

Figure 7: (a) A simplified example of the persistent firing spiking network structure. Among the neurons ranging from A to F in the network, (B, C, D, E) represent the excitatory neurons, and (A, F) represent inhibitory neurons in which F is capable for persistent firing. (b) Raster plots of spike activities in the spiking network of 1000 neurons including persistent firing inhibitory interneurons. Each raster plot shows the 1-second segment of the firing activity. Neurons indexed from 1 to 800 are excitatory neurons, and neurons indexed from 801 to 1000 are inhibitory. Within the 200 inhibitory neurons, there are 160 randomly selected neurons with persistent firing capability. Horizontally continuous dotted lines with neuron index in the range of 801 - 1000 indicate there are persistent firings of action potentials in inhibitory neurons.

DISCUSSION

The possible functions of the persistent firing were suggested to be related to working memory [12] . The ability to maintain the persistent firing of action potentials without on-going stimulation provides a mechanism of stor- ing the information for a short period of time. This mechanism is similar to our working memory [21] -[23] , which actively holds a limited amount of information [24] in the absence of stimuli. Working memory has been extensively explored from perspectives of highly abstract top levels in the domains of psychology, neuroscience and anatomy, but there are much less work from perspectives of bottom level of biological neurons [25] -[30] . It is still unknown how working memory is represented within a population of cortical neurons.

The presented simple model of persistent firing neurons enables further investigation of possible functions of persistent firing, especially the relationship between working memory and persistent firing, and the neural cor- relate of working memory. Recently, we have proposed a model of short term persistent habituation [31] , con- sisting of a persistent firing neuron and a habituating synapse, to explore the presynaptic learning and memory. The interaction of persistent firing axonal and presynaptic processes increases the retention time of the synaptic conductance and therefore the recovery time, and continues the learning of short term habituation for the duration of persistent firing. This leads to a working memory for habituation.

Through incorporating the persistent firing dynamics in spiking networks with axonal delays and STDP learning rules, we can further investigate the interaction of polychronization and persistent neural activities. In the polychronous spiking network, the number of co-existing polychronous groups far exceeds the number of neurons in the network, resulting in an unprecedented memory capacity of the system [13] . Thus it would be in- teresting to investigate how working memory is presented in the polychronous network, and simulate a bio-plausible working memory system with increased memory capacity. To this end, we are working towards the development of artificial cognitive memory with the objective of developing a novel function-driven memory technology in comparison to conventional density-driven storage technology [32] . The models of persistent fir- ing neuron and spiking network presented in this paper can be used in the simulation of cognitive memory ar- chitectures.

Due to the computational simplicity of our model, it is straightforward to implement the model in hardware. We have developed a neuromorphic model of persistent firing neurons [33] , which reproduces the neuronal per- sistent firing behavior by integrating somatic and axonal computational processes of different timescales. Con- sidering there are many existing VLSI implementations of Izhikevich neuron model and its variants [16] [34] - [36] , the proposed neuron model can be conveniently implemented in silicon by incorporating the axonal leaky integrator into the Izhikevich VLSI designs, enabling a considerably faster emulation of the neural systems with persistent neural activity in a highly parallel manner.

CONCLUSION

Ning Ning, Guoqi Li,*, Wei He, Kejie Huang, Li Pan, Kiruthika Ramanathan, Rong Zhao, Luping Shi, Based on the recent discovery in neurophysiology which revealed that interneurons can slowly integrate spiking, share the output across a coupled network of axons and respond with persistent firing even in the absence of input to the soma or dendrites, we proposed a new model of persistent firing neuron to bridge the gap between the conventional models and the newly-discovered phenomenon. In this work, we presented and discussed the mathematical and neuromorphic models of the artificial neuron, as well as a persistent firing polychronous spiking network which exhibits asynchronous dynamics. The artificial neuron we proposed, being computationally efficient yet bio-plausible, would be useful to construct and simulate the large scale models of animal or human cortex, which provides a neuromorphic platform for further investigation of the possible functions of persistent firing and their roles in animal and human brain, especially for exploring the relationship between working memory and persistent firing spiking network-based memory and the bio-inspired computer systems.

REFERENCES

1. Lapicque, L. (1907) Recherches quantitatives sur l'excitation electrique des nerfs traitee comme une polarization. Jour- nal of Physiol Pathol Générale, 9, 620-635.
2. Sandberg, A. and Bostrom, N. (2008) Whole Brain Emulation: A Roadmap. Future of Humanity Institute, Oxford University, Technical Report #2008-3.
3. Hodgkin, A.L. and Huxley, A.F. (1952) A Quantitative Description of Membrane Current and Its Application to Conduction and Excitation in Nerve. The Journal of Physiology, 117, 500-544. http://dx.doi.org/10.1113/jphysiol.1952.sp004764
4. Brette, R., Rudolph, M., Carnevale, T., Hines, M., Beeman, D., Bower, J.M., Diesmann, M., Morrison, A., Goodman, P.H., Harris Jr., F.C, et al. (2007) Simulation of Networks of Spiking Neurons: A Review of Tools and Strategies. Journal of Computational Neuroscience, 23, 349-398. http://dx.doi.org/10.1007/s10827-007-0038-6
5. Mihalas, S. and Niebur, E. (2009) A Generalized Linear Integrate-and-Fire Neural Model Produces Diverse Spiking Behaviors. Neural Computation, 21, 704-718. http://dx.doi.org/10.1162/neco.2008.12-07-680
6. Fitzhugh, R. (1961) Impulses and Physiological States in Theoretical Models of Nerve Membrane. Biophysical Journal, 1, 445-466. http://dx.doi.org/10.1016/S0006-3495(61)86902-6
7. Morris, C. and Lecar, H. (1981) Voltage Oscillations in the Barnacle Giant Muscle Fiber. Biophysical Journal, 35, 193-213. http://dx.doi.org/10.1016/S0006-3495(81)84782-0
8. Rose, R.M. and Hindmarsh, J.L. (1989) The Assembly of Ionic Currents in a Thalamic Neuron I. The Three-Dimen- sional Model. Proceedings of the Royal Society of London. Series B. Biological Sciences, 237, 267-288. http://dx.doi.org/10.1098/rspb.1989.0049
9. Wilson, H.R. (1999) Simplified Dynamics of Human and Mammalian Neocortical Neurons. Journal of Theoretical Biology, 200, 375-388. http://dx.doi.org/10.1006/jtbi.1999.1002
10. Izhikevich, E.M. (2001) Resonate-and-Fire Neurons. Neural Networks, 14, 883-894.http://dx.doi.org/10.1016/S0893-6080(01)00078-8
11. Izhikevich, E.M. (2003) Simple Model of Spiking Neurons. IEEE Transactions on Neural Networks, 14, 1569-1572. http://dx.doi.org/10.1109/TNN.2003.820440
12. Sheffield, M.E.J., Best, T.K., Mensh, B.D., Kath, W.L. and Spruston, N. (2011) Slow Integration Leads to Persistent Action Potential Firing in Distal Axons of Coupled Interneurons. Nature Neuroscience, 14, 200-207. http://dx.doi.org/10.1038/nn.2728
13. Izhikevich, E.M. (2006) Polychronization: Computation with Spikes. Neural Computation, 18, 245-282. http://dx.doi.org/10.1162/089976606775093882
14. Ning, N., Yi, K.J., Huang, K.J. and Shi, L.P. (2011) Axonal Slow Integration Induced Persistent Firing Neuron Model. Lecture Notes in Computer Science, 7062, 469-476.http://dx.doi.org/10.1007/978-3-642-24955-6_56
15. Izhikevich, E.M. (2007) Dynamical Systems in Neuroscience: The Geometry of Excitability and Bursting. The MIT Press, Cambridge.
16. Wijekoon, J.H. and Dudek, P. (2008) Compact Silicon Neuron Circuit with Spiking and Bursting Behaviour. Neural Networks, 21, 524-534.http://dx.doi.org/10.1016/j.neunet.2007.12.037
17. Wijekoon, J.H. and Dudek, P. (2008) Integrated Circuit Implementation of a Cortical Neuron. Proceedings of the

IEEE International Symposium on Circuits and Systems, Seattle, 18-21 May 2008, 1784-1787.

18. Swadlow, H.A. (1985) Physiological Properties of Individual Cerebral Axons Studied in Vivo for as Long as One Year. Journal of Neurophysiology, 54, 1346-1362.
19. Song, S., Miller, K.D. and Abbott, L.F. (2000) Competitive Hebbian Learning through Spike-Timing-Dependent Synaptic Plasticity. Nature Neuroscience, 3, 919-926.http://dx.doi.org/10.1038/78829
20. Bartos, M., Vida, I. and Jonas, P. (2007) Synaptic Mechanisms of Synchronized Gamma Oscillations in Inhibitory Interneuron Networks. Nature Reviews Neuroscience, 8, 45-56.http://dx.doi.org/10.1038/nrn2044
21. Baddeley, A. (1992) Working Memory. Science, 255, 556-559.http://dx.doi.org/10.1126/science.1736359
22. Durstewitz, D., Seamans, J.K. and Sejnowski, T.J. (2000) Neurocomputational Models of Working Memory. Nature Neuroscience, 3, 1184-1191. http://dx.doi.org/10.1038/81460
23. Egorov, A.V., Hamam, B.N., Fransen, E., Hasselmo, M.E. and Alonso, A.A. (2002) Graded Persistent Activity in Entorhinal Cortex Neurons. Nature, 420, 173-178. http://dx.doi.org/10.1038/nature01171
24. Miller, G.A. (1956) The Magical Number Seven, Plus or Minus Two: Some Limits on Our Capacity for Processing Information. Psychological Review, 63, 81-97.http://dx.doi.org/10.1037/h0043158
25. D'Esposito, M., Detre, J.A., Alsop, D.C., Shin, R.K., Atlas, S. and Grossman, M. (1995) The Neural Basis of the Central Executive System of Working Memory. Nature, 378, 279-281. http://dx.doi.org/10.1038/378279a0
26. Goldman-Rakic, P.S. (1995) Cellular Basis of Working Memory. Neuron, 14, 477-485.http://dx.doi.org/10.1016/0896-6273(95)90304-6
27. Miller, E.K., Erickson, C.A. and Desimone, R. (1996) Neural Mechanisms of Visual Working Memory in Prefrontal Cortex of the Macaque. The Journal of Neuroscience, 16, 5154-5167.
28. Amit, D. and Mongillo, G. (2003) Spike-Driven Synaptic Dynamics Generating Working Memory States. Neural Computation, 15, 565-596.http://dx.doi.org/10.1162/089976603321192086
29. O'Reilly, R.C. and Frank, M.J. (2006) Making Working Memory Work: A Computational Model of Learning in the Prefrontal Cortex and Basal Ganglia. Neural Computation, 18, 283-328. http://dx.doi.org/10.1162/089976606775093909
30. Szatmary, B. and Izhikevich, E.M. (2010) Spike-Timing Theory of Working Memory. PLoS Computational Biology, 6, e1000879. http://dx.doi.org/10.1371/journal.pcbi.1000879
31. Ramanathan, K., Ning, N., Dhanasekar, D., Li, G., Shi, L.P. and Vadakkepat, P. (2012) Presynaptic Learning and Me- mory with a Persistent Firing Neuron and a Habituating Synapse: A Model of Short Term Persistent Habituation. International Journal of Neural Systems, 22, Article ID: 1250015. http://dx.doi.org/10.1142/S0129065712500153
32. Shi, L.P., Yi, K.J., Ramanathan, K., Zhao, R., Ning, N., Ding, D. and Chong, T.C. (2011) Artificial Cognitive Memory—Changing from Density Driven to Functionality Driven. Applied Physics A, 102, 865-875. http://dx.doi.org/10.1007/s00339-011-6297-0
33. Ning, N., Huang, K.J. and Shi, L.P. (2012) Artificial Neuron with Somatic and Axonal Computation Units: Mathematical and Neuromorphic Models of Persistent Firing Neurons. Proceedings of the 2012 International Joint Conference on Neural Networks (IJCNN), Brisbane, 10-15 June 2012, 1-7.
34. van Schaik, A., Jin, C., McEwan, A. and Hamilton, T.J. (2010) A Log-Domain Implementation of the Izhikevich Neuron Model. Proceedings of 2010 IEEE International Symposium on Circuits and Systems (ISCAS), Paris, 30 May-2 June 2010, 4253-4256.
35. Li, G.Q., Ning, N., Ramanathan, K., Wei, H., Pan, L. and Shi, L.P. (2013) Behind the Magical Numbers: Hierarchical Chunking and the Human Working Memory Capacity. International Journal of Neural Systems, 23, Article ID: 1350019.http://dx.doi.org/10.1142/S0129065713500196
36. Li, G.Q., Wen, C.Y., Li, Z.G., Zhang, A.M., Yang, F. and Mao, K.Z. (2013) Model-Based Online Learning with Kernels. IEEE Transactions on Neural Networks and Learning Systems, 24, 356-369. http://dx.doi.org/10.1109/TNNLS.2012.2229293

CHAPTER 3

CODE SPECTRUM AND CODE FLOW OF CULTURED NEURAL NETWORKS

Shinichi Tamura, Yoshi Nishitani, Chie Hosokawa, Tomomitsu Miyoshi and Hajime Sawai

INTRODUCTION

Many generator models and analyzing methods of spike trains from neurons including artificial models, such as spike-coding metrics [1], spatiotemporal coding models [2–8], synchronous action models [9–13], and pseudorandom code detection methods [14] have been proposed.

On the other hand, we identified the sequence "1101" within the poststimulus time histogram (PSTH)/instantaneous firing rate (IFR) of a cultured neuronal network in Baljon et al. [15] (Figure 1) as well as our own network [16, 17] (Figure 2). The sequence "1101" is the core portion of the reversal M-sequence "1101000" which is a typical pseudorandom sequence [18–21]. Electric circuits generating pseudorandom sequences are well known. Furthermore, it has been shown that, in a cultured neuronal network on a multielectrode, pseudorandom-like sequences (codes), including "1101", are detected, and they flow with some spatial decay curve [22]. We call the chart of the appearance frequencies of short code (e.g., length <8) versus various codes (in number) "code spectrum." Each cultured neuronal network is characterized by a specific code spectrum curve. That is, the curve shape seems to depend on the characteristics of neurons and the network configuration, including the weight distribution in the network. Therefore, we may consider it as a "signature" of the network. In the present study, we performed a simulation of code spectrum from a multielectrode on a 2D mesh neural network using neurons with fluctuating characteristics of refractory period and output delay time around each given intrinsic characteristic from time to time; that is, parameters of each neuron varied intrinsically and temporarily. Connection weights between neurons are randomly generated on the basis of a given statistical property. In this paper, expression "neuronal network" is mainly used for natural one, and "neural network" is for artificial one.

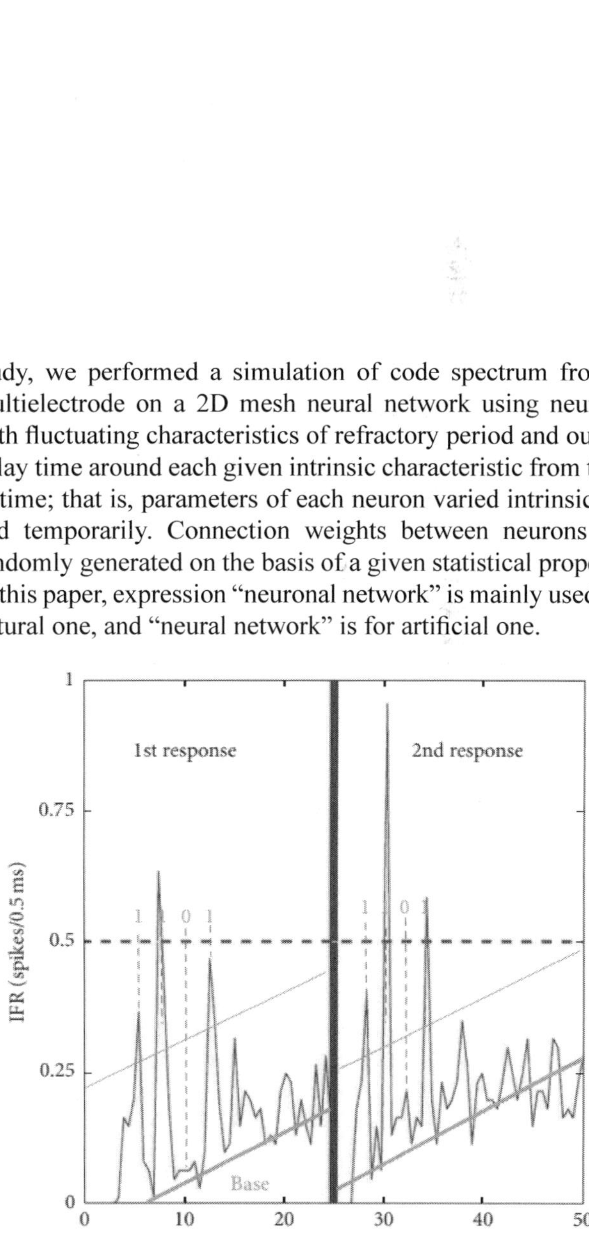

Figure 1: First and second responses "1101" in the instantaneous firing rate (IFR) of cultured neuronal tissue after two electrical stimulations as shown in [15] with additional interpretation (courtesy of Baljon et al.; reproduction permission provided by APS).

Citation: Shinichi Tamura, Yoshi Nishitani, Chie Hosokawa, Tomomitsu Miyoshi, and Hajime Sawai, "Code Spectrum and Code Flow of Cultured Neural Networks," Computational Intelligence and Neuroscience, vol. 2016, Article ID 7186092, 12 pages, 2016. doi:10.1155/2016/7186092.

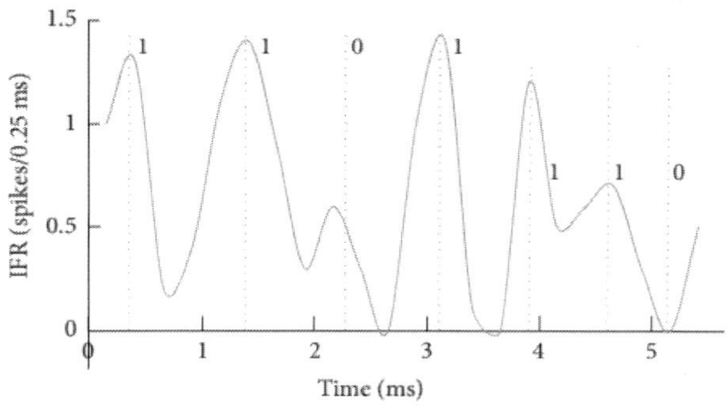

Figure 2: Instantaneous firing rate (poststimulus time histogram) where the sequence "1101" was observed. Since the timing becomes dispersed within trials, the peak positions and shapes gradually changed as time elapsed. Particularly, there was a tendency of risings and peaks to become faster than the regular timing, which is led by the fastest spike among the dispersed spikes as well as the slowest spike to be cancelled by the succeeding fastest negative spike (effectively supposed; pulling down the tail of peak), and lowering the peak height [16, 17].

SIMULATION

Network Configuration

We performed a computer simulation to observe spike propagation on a 2D network with a 33 × 33 2D mesh of neurons. Each neuron has connection weights to and from eight neighboring neurons, as shown in Figure3.

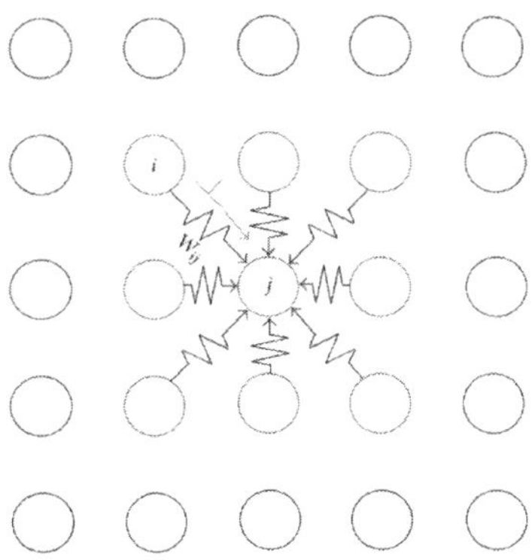

Figure 3: Inputs to neuron j in a 2D mesh neural network. Each neuron j (red) receives input spikes from eight neighboring neurons (blue) such as i through connection weights $w_{ij} \in [-1, 1]$. Neuron j integrates such weighted spikes during its accepting period and outputs a spike after a delay time if the integrated value exceeds zero.

The weight of the network is given as follows:

$$w_{ij} = F\left[(1+c)\,u - c\right], \quad w_{ij} \in [-1, 1], \; w_{ij} \not\equiv w_{ji}, \tag{1}$$

where $i = (i_x, i_y); j = (j_x, j_y); i_x, i_y, j_x, j_y \in \{1, 2, \ldots, 33\}$; $i \neq j; \max\{|i_x - j_x|, |i_y - j_y|\} = 1$; and $F[x]$ is a truncation function such that

$$F[x] = \begin{cases} 1 & 1 \le x \\ x & -1 < x < 1 \\ -1 & x \le -1, \end{cases} \tag{2}$$

c is positive parameter such that $0 < c \le 3$ controls weight balance of positive and negative values and u is a random variable with uniform distribution such that $0 \le u < 1$.

In short, if c increases, the number of negative weights increases. For example, if $c = 1/3$, weight w_{ij} distributes uniformly in $[-1/3, 1]$; that is, the ratio of positive to negative weights is 3 : 1. This ratio is a typical one in real neuronal networks. In 2D mesh artificial neural network model with weights to and from every eight neighboring neurons, however, weight distribution must be different because of different network shape and every eight neighboring weight is generated randomly, which usually does not result in zero. Of course, such models can be designed that first decide whether or not the weight exists and then decide on the weight value if it exists. For simplicity, we have designed that no connections between adjacent neurons (i.e., not connected; weight zero) are effectively realized by suppressions with negative weights. If c=1, w_{ij} distributes in $[-1, 1]$ uniformly; that is, the ratio of positive to negative weights is 1 : 1. If c=3, w_{ij} distributes in $[-1, 1]$ but not uniformly; that is, the ratio of positive to negative weights is 1 : 4. Although the setting of weights was simple, the result was not much different from that obtained using separate settings of the weight values and their positive or negative signs.

Characteristics of Neurons

The neuron model used here is shown in Figure 4, which is a type of integrate-and-fire model without leak [25]. Neuron n accumulates weighted inputs during the accepting period A_{nk}. If the accumulated weighted input becomes positive and the neuron is not in its refractory period, the neuron n outputs a spike after a delay time D_{nk} as the kth firing. Some parameters used in the simulation are given as examples below.

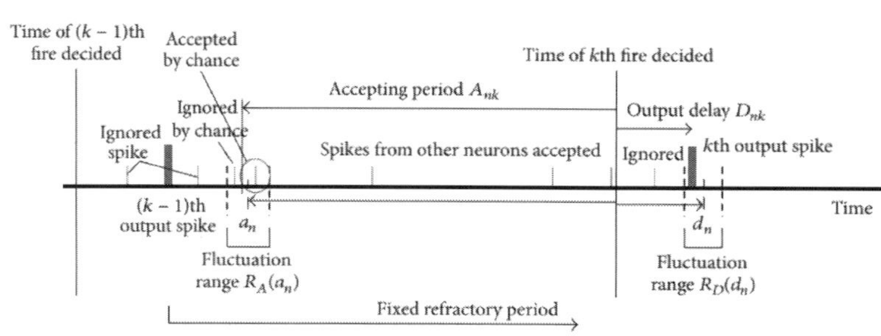

Figure 4: Integrate-and-fire model without leakage but with fluctuation in the parameters of neuron n. Each neuron has an inherent accepting period a_n and output delay time d_n. These parameters vary with time within certain ranges $R(a_n)$ and $R_D(d_n)$, respectively. Neuron n inte-

grates weighted input spikes during the accepting period A_{nk} for the kth firing, and after the refractory period ends, it decides whether the integrated value exceeds zero for firing at every time point. If so, it outputs the kth output spike with delay time D_{nk}. That is, $A_{nk} \in R(a_n)$, and likewise, $D_{nk} \in R_D(d_n)$.

A basic accepting period *an* intrinsic to neuron n is randomly generated in each network within a range $a_n \in \{a_{0-2}, a_{0-1}, a_0, a_{0+1}, a_{0+2}\}$with a probability of 1/5 for each, where a_0 is a fixed common parameter value through the network, and the unit time (bin) is 0.1 ms. The actual instantaneous accepting period *Ank* of neuron n at the kth firing is further randomly given within the fluctuation range $R_A(a_n)$ around a_n; that is, $A_{nk} \in R_A(a_n)$.The instantaneous refractory period is implicitly assumed as slightly smaller than *Ank*. The accepting period can also be called input integration or the accumulating period for firing. Roughly speaking, the accepting and refractory periods can be regarded as the same. The software can stimulate neurons with arbitrary spatiotemporal patterns. Typically, a combination of three neurons is simultaneously stimulated such that the states of the neurons are set to "1" at time 1 (bin no. 1). The reason why we stimulated three neurons simultaneously instead of only one neuron is that, in wet experiments, many neurons around an electrode seem to be simultaneously stimulated by an electrical stimulation; and secondly, parallel stimulation to multiple neurons seems to promote stable propagation of excitation according to computer simulations.

Parameters used in the simulation are as follows.

Basic accepting period a_0 is a preassigned network parameter such as 20, 30, . . . , 100, where unit time (bin width) is 0.1 ms. Instantaneous accepting period $A_{nk} \in R_A(a_n) = \{a_{n-1}, a_n, a_{n+1}\}$ is randomly selected at the kth firing with the probability *pa*, $1-2\times p_a$, and p_a, respectively, and $p_a = 1/12$. This value defines how much the instantaneous accepting period fluctuates from time to time. If we increase *pa* or expand the range $R(a_n)$, the fidelity of communication or information flow decreases. The above value is determined by considering a trade-off between such considerations and attaining 99% communication fidelity

Details will be presented in our coming paper.

Similarly, the output delay is as follows. Basic output delay time *dn* is randomly selected from {2, 3, . . . , 8} with a probability of 1/7 each. Instantaneous output delay time $D_{nk} \in R(d_n) = \{d_{n-1}, d_n, d_{n+1}\}$, and $p_d = 1/12$, similar to $R_A(an)$.

We have utilized an integrate-and-fire model without leaks, but instead we used a model incorporating a fluctuating period of acceptance. Our model is more stringent than the leaky integrate-and-fire model because our model randomly neglects old spikes, while the leaky model neglects them gradually. However, from our simulations, ignoring a portion of the spikes in any type is not fatal and not essential but only influences the quality of communication. This property is a strong point of neural networks that are composed of essentially fluctuating neurons. The fluctuating time parameters are concentrated in the two parameters—the accepting period, preceding the fire deciding time and the output delay time, following this time. These designs were determined by balancing the degree of complication, essential precision of results, and computation time.

Results of a preliminary experiment of stimulating a 9 × 9 mesh neural network are shown in Figure 5, where three neurons were stimulated at time t=0. We can observe "spike waves" propagating from source stimulations, and the waves often behave like Synfire [9, 10]. Further, the code flow may be regarded as a component of such spike waves. It is possible to acquire codes in wet experiments and compare them with the simulation. In the present study, however, as a preliminary step, we focused on simulating not only the entire spike waves but also the flow of codes.

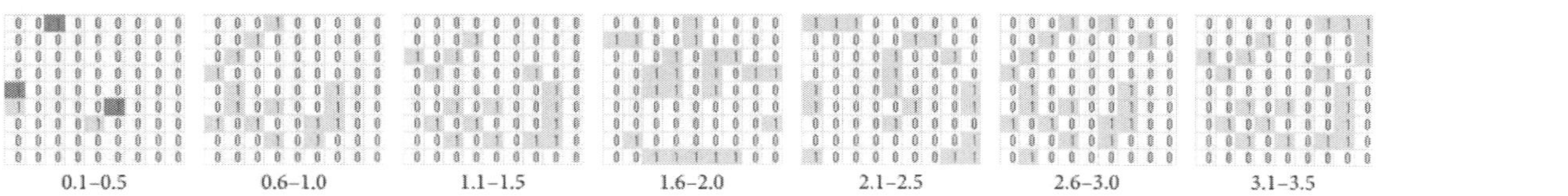

Figure 5: Spike waves generated on a 2D mesh neural network. Green spots indicate stimulation point. "0.1–0.5 ms" means an accumulation result of firing at 0.1 ms, 0.2 ms, . . . , 0.5 ms. This suggests that the codes are a part of these "spike waves."

Arrangement of Multielectrode

Figure 6 shows the arrangement of a multielectrode on a 33 × 33 2D mesh neural network. Each neuron has directional connections with eight neighboring neurons. Each electrode gathers spikes from two to nine surrounding neurons. The major differences from the wet experimental configuration [22] are as follows: (1) there are no neurons and no connections outside the explicit 1089 neurons, (2) neurons are placed on a regular lattice, which is different from an irregularly shaped cultured neuronal network, and (3) distances between electrodes are smaller than those in the cultured neuronal network. It can be said that difference (3) is a smaller scale of (1) and it corresponds to the fact that we regard the spike data from different electrodes as independent events. That is, in (1) and (3), we neglect the behavior of neurons outside the noted neurons.

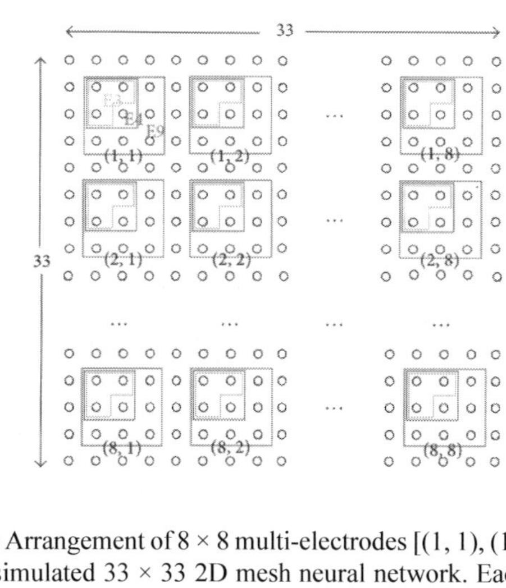

Figure 6: Arrangement of 8 × 8 multi-electrodes [(1, 1), (1, 2), . . . , (8, 8)] on a simulated 33 × 33 2D mesh neural network. Each electrode

acquires spikes of two to nine neurons. For example, "E9" showing 3 × 3 block of neurons (I) indicated with (1, 1) shows that electrode (1, 1) collects spikes from nine neurons. In addition, "E3" and "E4" are likewise; "E2" and "E5"–"E8"are not shown. Spectrum, cross-correlation, or probability distribution data obtained from electrode Em is expressed as "E_m" in the text. Connections between eight neighboring neurons are randomly generated with given stochastic characteristics.

Component Code Spectrum

By changing the basic accepting period a_0 and the positive and negative weight balance parameter c, we can generate spike trains for each type of electrode E_m catching from m ($m = 2, 3, \ldots, 9$) surrounding neurons. We then decode the spike trains to obtain code spectra for each m. We call such a spectrum Em "component spectrum." Figure 7 shows an example of simulated spike trains caught by electrode E_m.

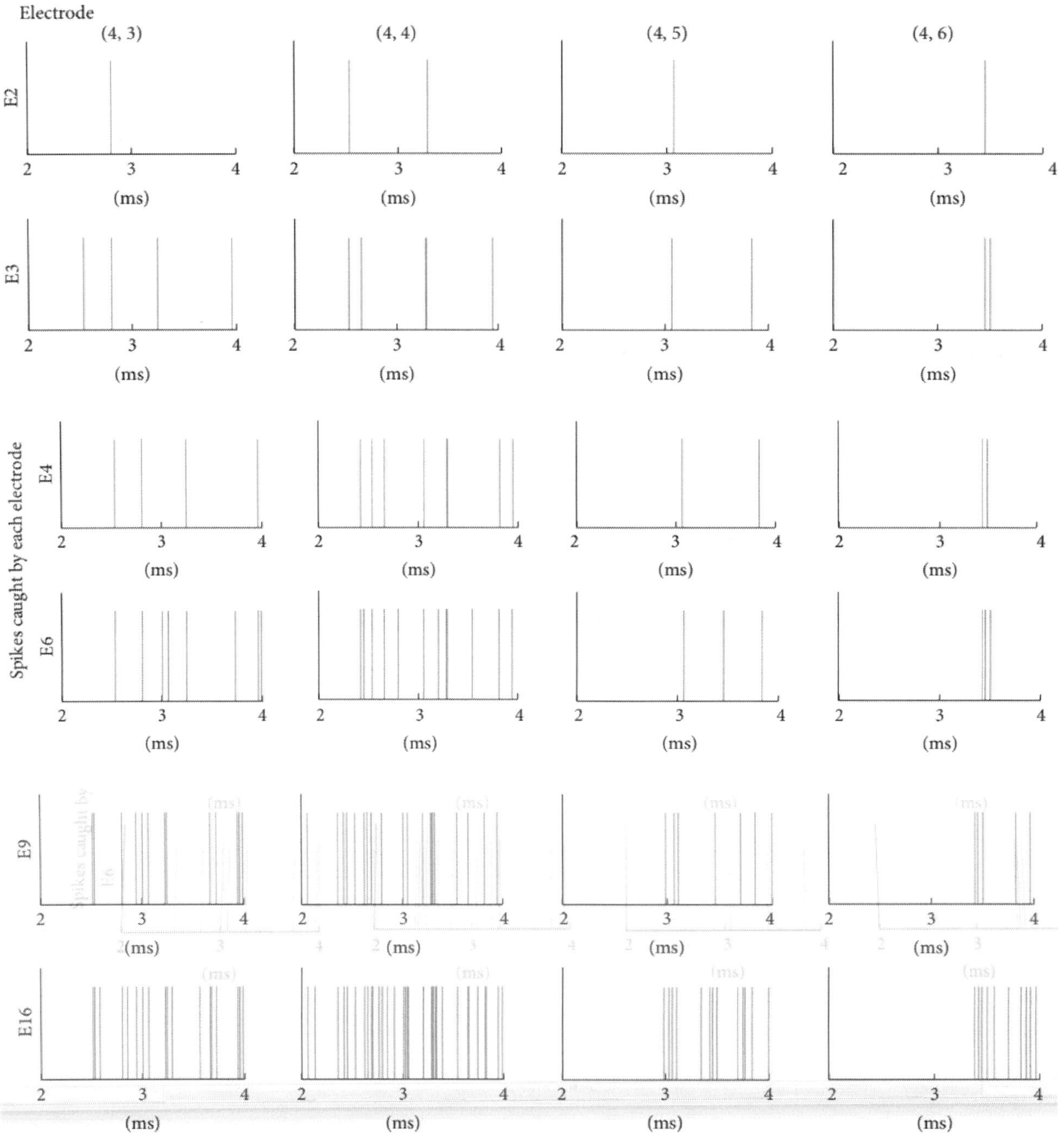

Figure 7: An example of simulated spike trains caught by Em during 2.0–4.0 ms after stimulation with $a0 = 8.0$ ms and $c = 2.5$. Initial stimulations were given to around electrodes (1, 1) at 0.1 ms and (1, 5) at 0.5 ms.

Figure 8 shows examples of component code spectra of simulated spike sequences of some a_0 (median of accepting period A_{nk}) and the connection weight parameter c. Practically, the number of neurons emitting spikes to each electrode changes electrode by electrode according to its statistical distribution. Therefore, the actual observed code spectra will be mixed according to the probability distribution of the number of neurons m around the electrodes.

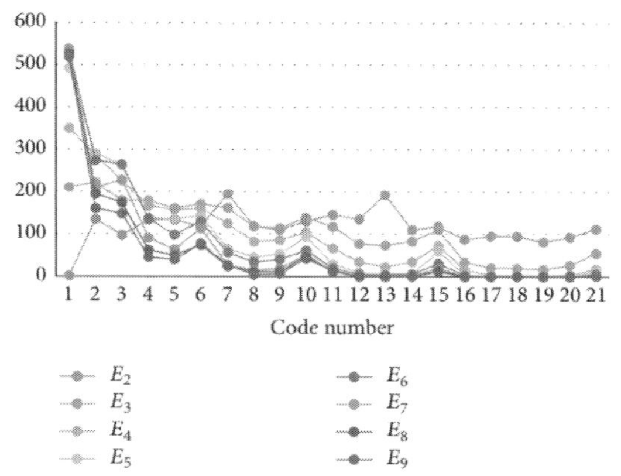

(a) a_0 = 6 ms c = 0.1

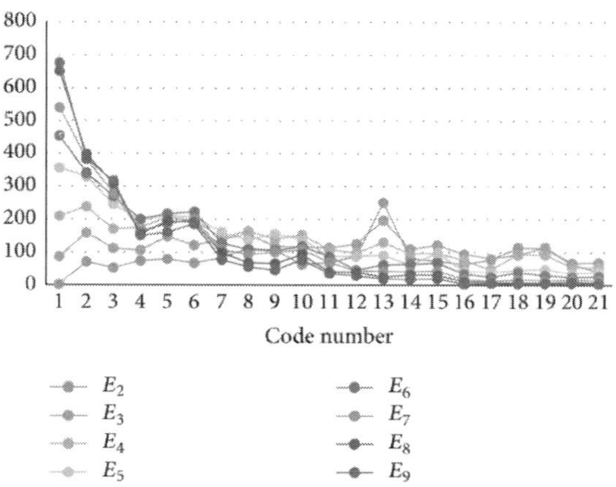

(b) a_0 = 6 ms c = 1.5

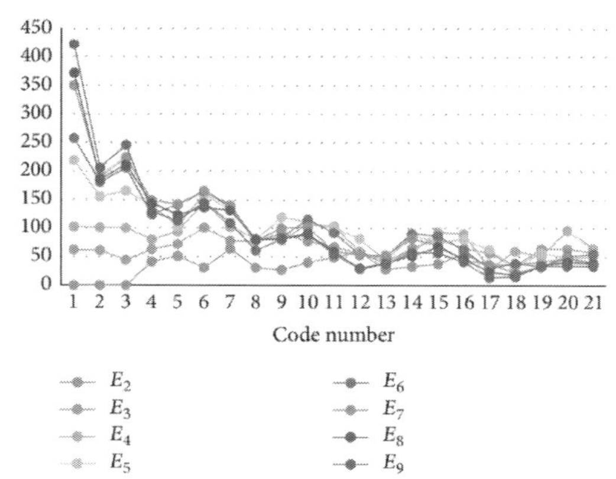

(c) a_0 = 9 ms c = 1

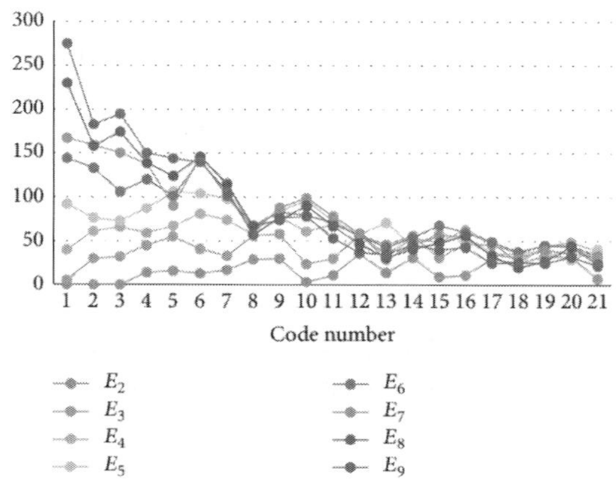

(d) a_0 = 9 ms c = 2

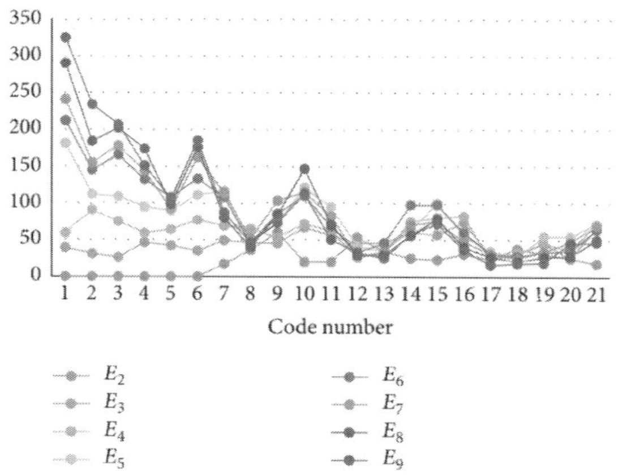

(e) a_0 = 10 ms c = 1

Figure 8: Code spectrum components E_m for several parameters of accepting period a_0 and positive and negative weight balance c. The horizontal line represents code numbers (1, 2, . . . , 21) whose number of "1"s in the code is 3. That is, code 1 = "111," code 2 = "1011," code 3 = "1101," code 4 = "10011," code 5 = "10101," ... code 21 = "11000001" [22]. The vertical line represents the total number of codes detected during the first 200 ms after stimulation (2000 time bins of 0.1 ms/bin) and from 63 electrodes.

Spectrum Fitting with Components

The blue curve in Figure 9(a) shows the results of the average number of codes detected in recorded spike trains of 9 trials for code numbers 1–21 (code spectrum) from 63 electrodes of Sample A during 200 ms after stimulation expressed as 2000 times the bin data. Sample A is the same as that presented in [22].

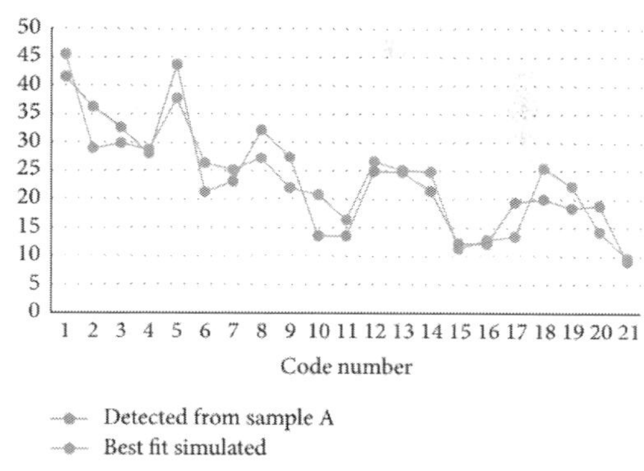

(a) Sample A (9 trials). Estimated a_0 = 8 ms, c = 2.5, and probability distribution of E_m (m = 2, 3, . . . , 9) is (0.3, 0.1, 0, 0, 0, 0.05, 0, 0.55), with a normalized RMS error of 0.179

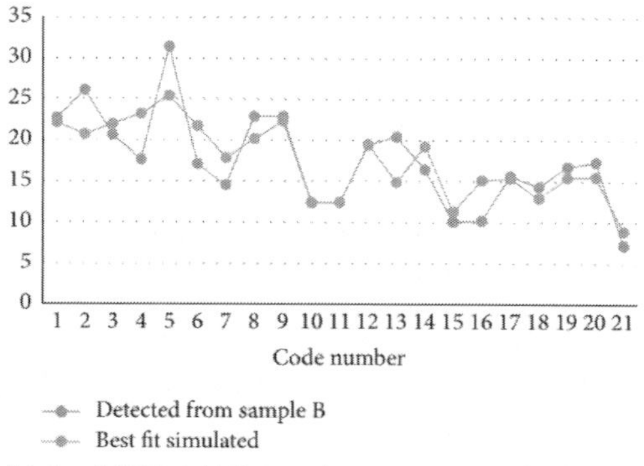

(b) Sample B (23 trials). Estimated a_0 = 9 ms, c = 2, and probability distribution of E_m (m = 2, 3, . . . , 9) is (0.3, 0.1, 0, 0, 0, 0.05, 0, 0.55), with a normalized RMS error of 0.181

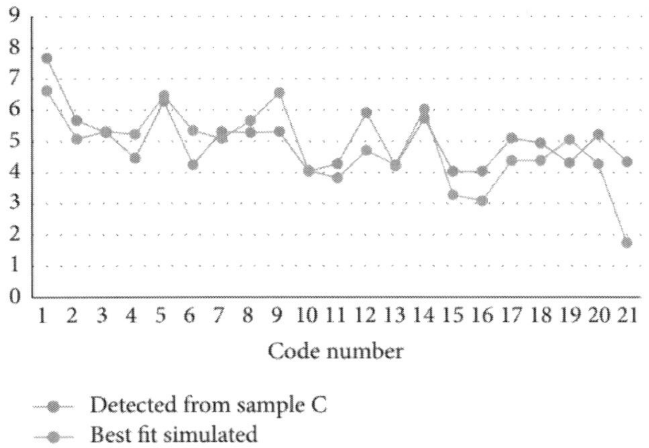

(c) Sample C (26 trials). Estimated $a_0 = 9$ ms, $c = 2.5$, and probability distribution of E_m ($m = 2, 3, \ldots, 9$) is (0.263, 0.158, 0, 0.053, 0.053, 0.053, 0.421, 0), with a normalized RMS error of 0.180

Figure 9: Code spectra. The blue curve shows the average of trials of an experimental number of codes detected from 63 electrodes in spike trains during 200 ms after stimulation expressed with 2000 time bins of 0.1 ms. The bit width of the code is 0.6–2.0 ms (6–20 bins). Codes are detected with 1% time accuracy, although practically several % because of the 0.1 ms bit width. This curve can be considered as the "signature" of spike trains. The orange curve is the best fit to code spectrum using a simulation spectrum.

The orange curve in Figure 9(a) shows the best fit to the number of codes detected in spike trains of 2000 time bins of Sample A using code spectra E_m of artificially generated spike sequences with different accepting periods a_0 and connection weight parameters c and probability distribution of E_m. Although this is an inverse problem and imperfect, the estimation of neuronal parameters a_0, c, and probability distribution of E_m is possible to some extent.

Table 1 shows the normalized squared error of a simulated code spectrum to that of recorded data of Sample A with a changing probability distribution of E_m, that is, a combination of component code spectra for various a_0 and c values.

Some root mean square (RMS) error data are not shown (shown as "—") because the number of codes detected was too small to calculate the component code spectrum as such spikes disappeared within the given time. Tables 2 and 3 show that of Sample B in Figure 9(b) and Sample C in Figure 9(c), respectively.

Table 1: Normalized RMS error for various parameters of neurons used to fit the data in Figure 9(a). Bold and italic values show the first and second best fits, respectively. Typical a_0 and c values were estimated as 8.0 ms and 2.5, respectively.

c	a_0 (ms)					
	5.5	6.0	7.0	8.0	9.0	10.0
0.1	0.464	0.315	0.565	—	—	—
0.3	0.442	0.283	0.581	0.904	—	—
1.0	0.393	0.252	*0.182*	0.212	0.327	0.349
1.5	0.326	0.240	0.208	0.230	0.269	0.286
2.0	0.301	0.246	0.203	0.212	0.186	0.310
2.5	—	0.470	0.580	**0.179**	0.192	—
3.0	—	0.321	—	0.328	0.319	0.674

Table 2: Normalized RMS errors for various parameters of neurons used to fit the data in Figure 9(b)

c	a_0 (ms)					
	5.5	6.0	7.0	8.0	9.0	10.0
0.1	0.502	0.322	0.577	—	—	—
0.3	0.484	0.288	0.577	0.890	—	—
1.0	0.438	0.259	0.197	0.233	0.335	0.340
1.5	0.361	0.243	0.210	0.248	0.271	0.283
2.0	0.320	0.256	0.188	0.241	**0.1809**	0.304
2.5	—	0.477	0.605	0.203	*0.1814*	—
3.0	—	0.325	—	0.317	0.332	0.680

Table 3: Normalized RMS errors for various parameters of neuron used to fit the data in Figure 9(c)

c	a_0 (ms)					
	5.5	6.0	7.0	8.0	9.0	10.0
0.1	0.518	0.290	0.461	—	—	—
0.3	0.509	0.223	0.440	0.777	—	—
1.0	0.515	0.291	0.252	0.204	0.222	0.223
1.5	0.430	0.275	0.253	0.196	0.197	0.187
2.0	0.399	0.257	0.263	0.256	*0.186*	0.215
2.5	—	0.491	0.656	0.213	**0.180**	—
3.0	—	0.324	—	0.354	0.358	0.631

Expansion of E_m

In some cases, the best estimation of the probability distribution of E_m had a large value at E_9, suggesting that there are more than nine neurons around the electrode. Therefore, we increased the number m to $_{16}$. Figure 10 shows the expanded code spectral components up to E_{16}. Although E_2–E_9 have various shapes, E_9–E_{16} have a similar shape. When the best fit process included a large number of parameters, the computation time was long.

Therefore, it may be reasonable to regard E_9 as the representative component of E_9–E_{16} to decrease the computation time.

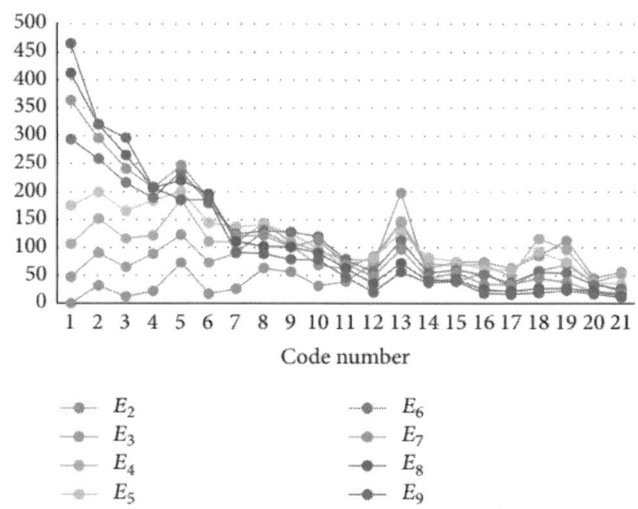

(a) $a_0 = 7$ ms $c = 2$ $E_{2\text{–}9}$

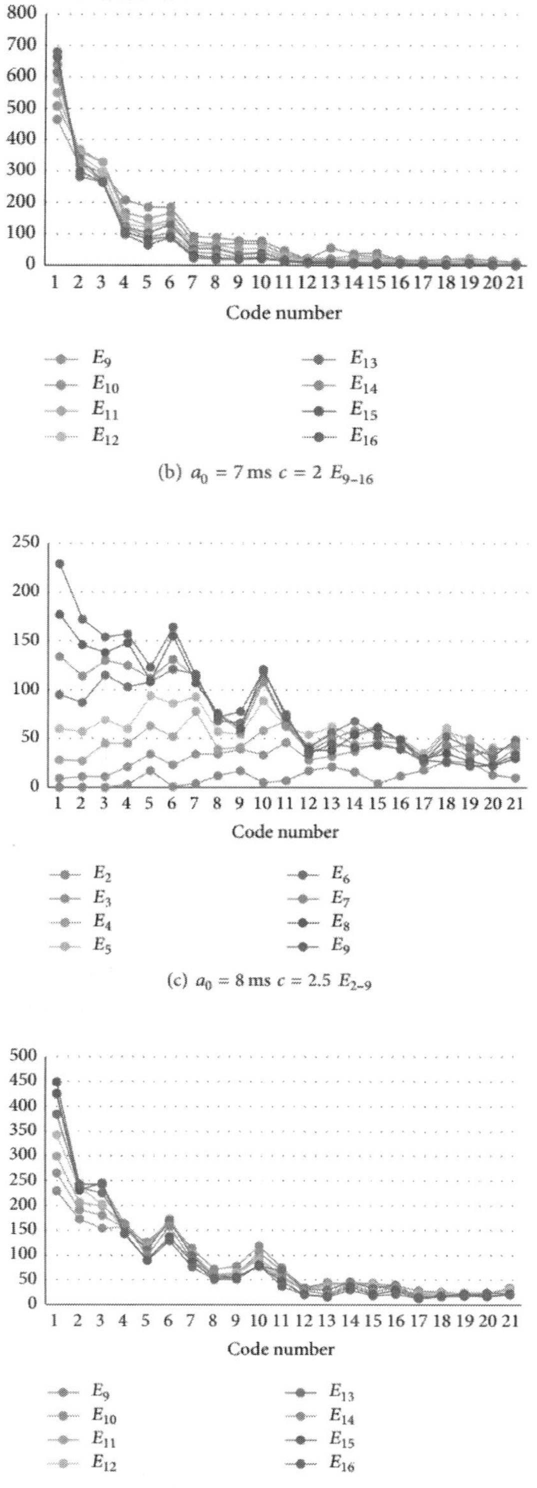

(b) $a_0 = 7$ ms $c = 2$ E_{9-16}

(c) $a_0 = 8$ ms $c = 2.5$ E_{2-9}

(d) $a_0 = 8$ ms $c = 2.5$ E_{9-16}

Figure 10: Expanded spectrum components up to E_{16}. (a) Code spectrum components E_2–E_9 for $a_0 = 7$ ms and c=2. (b) Expansion to E_9–E_{16} of (a). (c) Code spectrum components E_2–E_9 for $a_0 = 8$ ms and c = 2.5. (d) Expansion to E_9–E_{16} of (c).

Maximum Cross-Correlations

Because the simulation size was limited, the separation distances between the electrodes were very small (1–4 times of the neuron pitch). Nevertheless, using the same method as used in [22] for the natural neuronal network, we calculated the maximum crosscorrelation $\Phi(C)$ of a trial among eight and 20 neighbors between a time frame difference of 0.5 (ms) for E_2–E_{16} and 14 major codes C (Figure 11). However, since the electrodes were located relatively closer than in [22], and therefore cooccurrence probability of each code between two electrodes was expected higher, normalization of cross-correlation by code length was not applied. As shown in Figure 11(a), in case of E_4 and E_5, the maximum cross-correlation is rather flat in comparison with that of Sample A of the natural neuronal network of [22]. The characteristics of E_6–E_{11} (Figure 11(b)) decreased according to the code number, which roughly represents the code length. Although not shown in figures, E_{12}–E_{16} showed a more steep decreasing tendency

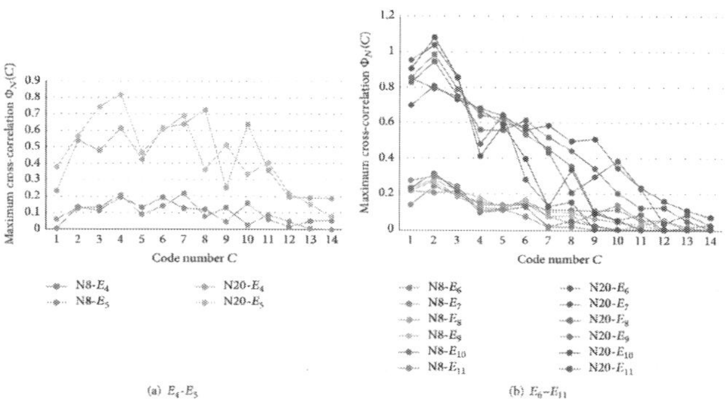

Figure 11: Maximum cross-correlation $\Phi(C)$ of a trial among eight (8N) and 20 (20N) neighbors with a time frame difference of 0.5 ms for 14 major codes C.

DISCUSSION AND CONCLUSIONS

In the present study, we constructed a 2D mesh neural network model and an input/output (I/O) functional model of neurons. A 2D mesh model may differ from a real natural cultured neuronal network, which will have a nonhomogeneous distribution of neurons [26]. The I/O functional model of neurons has certain intrinsic and instantaneous fluctuations of the refractory period and output delay time [11]. There may be some discrepancies compared with real natural cultured neurons; however, we have shown that from the perspective of the code spectrum of spike trains, it is possible to simulate the electrical activity of a neuronal network on a multielectrode plate (MED plate) with a 2D mesh neural network model. Moreover, it was possible to estimate the neuronal network parameters to some extent by recording spike trains with electrode without sorting. For example, though there is no guarantee to be true ones, estimated typical accepting periods were 8-9 ms, and refractory periods were also estimated as almost the same which are within range (5–10 ms) of a text book [27].

The detected codes were composed of spikes from different neurons because we acquired codes with bit widths ranging from 0.6 to 2.0 ms; in cases of 4-bit code, code lengths are mainly less than 6 ms (= 2 ms × 3 [spans of 4-bit code]). These values are generally shorter than the refractory period of neurons, which is estimated to be more than 8 ms in our cases. This suggests that it is unnecessary to add sorting processing to the spikes obtained from each electrode in case of analyzing by code with length less than 8 ms. That is, spikes forming the codes under our conditions originate from different neurons, and it may be possible to analyze circuit states around the electrodes. We need not to deal with E_1 whose spike interval is more than 8 ms. In our case, although we statistically analyzed all the 63 electrodes (except for the stimulating electrode) together, it may be possible to analyze individual electrodes, which may give more precise distribution of E_m; that is, we can determine whether neurons near a certain electrode compose a specific circuit such as a linear feedback shift register (LFSR) [14].

We used simulated code spectrum components to analyze the wet experimental spectrum of a cultured neuronal network. It is true, however, there are problems of (1) besides codes are not always orthogonal, (2) some of the extracted codes may be false such that composed of overlapped spike combination by chance [22]. To reduce such effects, it may be effective to improve the statistical background such as increasing the number of spike trains to suppress the statistical variation of the code spectrum components, because the present data were acquired from only one spike train of one trial each, that is, from the 63 electrodes, which are not necessarily perfectly independent.

A 2D mesh neural network can generate spike waves, as shown in Figure 4. Thus, the code flow observed on a cultured neuronal network can be regarded as a fragment of "spike waves." Code not only works as a marker of the spike waves but also provides information or clues about the circuit's shape. In other words, the code spectrum reflects the circuit shape, including the weight distribution, neuron characteristics, and its role in communication around each electrode. Therefore, it may be considered as a kind of network signature.

Furthermore, spike waves will establish asynchronous multiplex communication links as well as multiplex communication within a synchronous neural network [23, 28] where various pseudorandom-like codes are observed. For communication within this network, each neuron or group of neurons cannot receive entire spike waves, but rather a specific part of the wave, that is, a pseudorandom-like code or a spatiotemporal combination of codes.Then, based on the communication links as presented in Figure 12 [24, 29], information will be processed by an intelligence mechanism in the brain. Under these conditions, information will be radiated as spike waves from source neurons and then widely propagated via the neuronal network.There has been substantial research on behavior of a spike intensity wave as a global macrotask including cardiac electric propagation [30–32]. Although it may be true that most neurons work to relay spikes as a part of spike waves, destination neurons in a communication task are limited in number and must select signals sent to them from among the various spike waves based on spike trains containing codes that are a fragment of each spike wave or a spatiotemporal combination of these codes. This task is local and should not be treated as conventional "intensity" level wave information, but rather as "locally phasic" level wave information incorporated in the spatiotemporal pattern of locally arriving spikes including codes. In artificial brain research, though through concentrated digital synaptic switching, effect of communication is shown [33].The present study serves a base of communication tasks in natural 10 Computational Int intelligence, as illustrated in Figure 13. These studies of spike waves will lead to higher-order reasoning/intelligence in the brain via communication [8, 34].

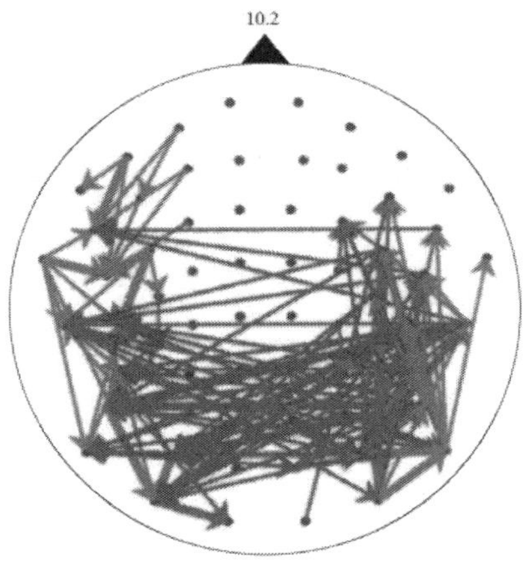

Figure 12: Time-shift diagram of 10.2 Hz MEG, for a number counting task [23, 24]. Red arrow < 5 ms < green < 10 ms < blue. We can see that red arrow with lag time < 5 ms runs within each hemisphere, and blue > 10 ms across the callosum.

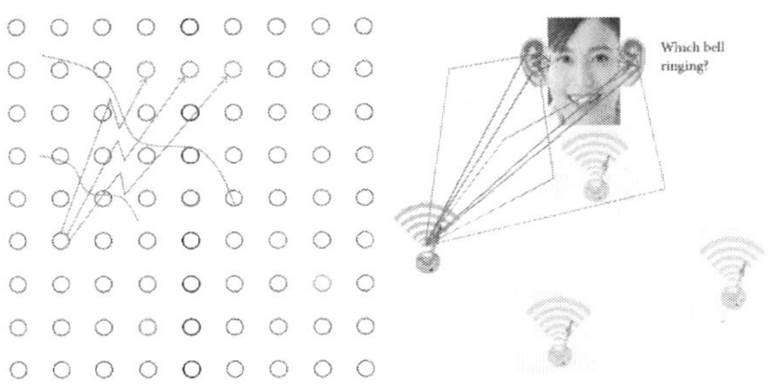

(a) The top three receiving neurons can detect the specific transmitting neuron among the four neurons from the spike wave fragment as a combination of spike codes (the spatiotemporal spike pattern)

(b) The same mechanism allows us to perceive where a bell is ringing in our surrounding atmosphere

Figure 13: Illustration of the communication within the neural network based on spatiotemporal pattern recognition. Each neuron can perform the roles of transmitting, receiving, and simply as a transmission media.

Our results, including those reported in [22], are summarized as follows:

(1) We are investigating an intelligence mechanism with the maintenance of correspondence between wet experiments and simulation.

(2) We identified a pseudorandom sequence (code) "1101" for PSTH in the literature as well as from our experience which should provide clues about neuronal circuits around electrodes.

(3) A code spectrum as an extension of code "1101" was obtained from cultured neuronal networks and simulations. (4) A code spectrum can be considered as a "signature" of its associated network by which some characteristics can be estimated, including the refractory period and weight distribution.

(5) A code can function as a mark on a spike wave. We have shown that to some extent, wave propagation preserves the codes. This finding was documented by movies as well as quantitatively.

Future studies will address the following:

(i) communication based on codes as a part of spike waves,

(ii) organization of communication links to derive intelligence functions.

ACKNOWLEDGMENTS

This study was supported in part by the Grant-in-Aid for Scientific Research of Exploratory Research 21656100, 25630176, and Scientific Research (A) 22246054 of Japan Society for the Promotion of Science.

REFERENCES

1. B. Cessac, H. Paugam-Moisy, and T. Viéville, "Overview of facts and issues about neural coding by spikes," Journal of Physiology Paris, vol. 104, no. 1-2, pp. 5–18, 2010.
2. O. Kliper, D. Horn, B. Quenet, and G. Dror, "Analysis of spatiotemporal patterns in a model of olfaction," Neurocomputing, vol. 58–60, pp. 1027–1032, 2004.
3. K. Fujita, Y. Kashimori, and T. Kambara, "Spatiotemporal burst coding for extracting features of spatiotemporally varying stimuli," Biological Cybernetics, vol. 97, no. 4, pp. 293–305, 2007.
4. I. Tyukin, T. Tyukina, and C. van Leeuwen, "Invariant template matching in systems with spatiotemporal coding: a matter of instability," Neural Networks, vol. 22, no. 4, pp. 425–449, 2009.
5. A. Mohemmed, S. Schliebs, S. Matsuda, and N. Kasabov, "Training spiking neural networks to associate spatio-temporal input-output spike patterns," Neurocomputing, vol. 107, pp. 3–10, 2013.
6. B. A. Olshausen and D. J. Field, "Emergence of simple-cell receptive field properties by learning a sparse code for natural images," Nature, vol. 381, no. 6583, pp. 607–609, 1996.
7. A. J. Bell and T. J. Sejnowski, "The 'independent components' of natural scenes are edge filters," Vision Research, vol. 37, no. 23, pp. 3327–3338, 1997.
8. S. Tamura, Y. Mizuno-Matsumoto, Y.-W. Chen, and K. Nakamura, "Association and abstraction on neural circuit loop and coding," in Proceedings of the 5th International Conference on Intelligent Information Hiding and Multimedia Signal Processing (IIHMSP '09), pp. 414–417, IEEE, Kyoto, Japan, September 2009.
9. M. Abeles, Local Cortical Circuits: An Electrophysiological Study, Springer, Berlin, Germany, 1982.
10. M. Abeles, "Synfire chains," Scholarpedia, vol. 4, no. 7, article 1441, 2009.
11. E. M. Izhikevich, "Polychronization: computation with spikes," Neural Computation, vol. 18, no. 2, pp. 245–282, 2006.
12. M. Perc, "Fluctuating excitability: a mechanism for self-sustained information flow in excitable arrays,"Chaos, Solitons & Fractals, vol. 32, no. 3, pp. 1118–1124, 2007.
13. H. Zhang, Q. Wang, M. Perc, and G. Chen, "Synaptic plasticity induced transition of spike propagation in neuronal networks," Communications in Nonlinear Science and Numerical Simulation, vol. 18, no. 3, pp. 601–615, 2013.
14. Y. Nishitani, C. Hosokawa, Y. Mizuno-Matsumoto, T. Miyoshi, H. Sawai, and S. Tamura, "Detection of M-sequences from spike sequence in neuronal networks," Computational Intelligence and Neuroscience, vol. 2012, Article ID 862579, 9 pages, 2012.
15. P. L. Baljon, M. Chiappalone, and S. Martinoia, "Interaction of electrically evoked responses in networks of dissociated cortical neurons," Physical Review E, vol. 80, no. 3, Article ID 031906, 2009.
16. S. Tamura, Y. Nishitani, C. Hosokawa et al., "Pseudo random sequences from neural circuits," inProceedings of the International Forum on Medical Imaging in Asia (IFMIA '12), P. 1-44, Daejeon, Republic of Korea, November 2012, http://www.nbl-technovator.jp/NBL_Tech/paper/IFMIA48.pdf.
17. T. Shinichi, Y. Nishitani, C. Hosokawa, et al., "M-sequence family from cultured neural circuits," inProceedings of the 3rd International Workshop on Computational Intelligence for Bio-Medical Science and Engineering (CIMSE '12), pp. 466–471, Taipei, Taiwan, October 2012, http://www.nbl-technovator.jp/NBL_Tech/paper/MseqPSTH-Taipei3.pdf.
18. R. C. Dixon, Spread Spectrum Systems, John Wiley & Sons, 1976.
19. D. V. Sarwate and M. B. Pursley, "Crosscorrelation properties of pseudorandom and related sequences,"Proceedings of the IEEE, vol. 68, no. 5, pp. 593–619, 1980.
20. S. W. Golomb and G. Gong, Signal Design for Good Correlation: for Wireless Communication, Ctyptography, and Rader, Cambridge University Press, Cambridge, UK, 2005.
21. Y. M. Elyada and D. Horn, "Can dynamic neural filters produce pseudo-random sequences," inArtificial Neural Networks: Biological Inspiration—ICANN 2005, vol. 3696 of Lecture Notes in Computer Science, pp. 211–216, Springer, Heidelberg, Germany, 2005.
22. S. Tamura, Y. Nishitani, C. Hosokawa et al., "Spike code flow in cultured neuronal networks,"Computational Intelligence and Neuroscience, In press.
23. T. Kamimura, Y. Yagi, S. Tamura, and Y.-W. Chen, "Multiplex communication with synchronous shift and weight learning in 2D mesh neural network," Automation, Control and Intelligent Systems, vol. 3, no. 5, pp. 63–70, 2015.
24. Y. Mizuno-Matsumoto, K. Okazaki, A. Kato et al., "Visualization of epileptogenic phenomena using cross-correlation analysis: localization of epileptic foci and propagation of epileptiform discharges,"IEEE Transactions on Biomedical Engineering, vol. 46, no. 3, pp. 271–279, 1999.
25. W. Gerstner and W. M. Kistler, Spiking Neuron Models. Single Neurons, Populations, Plasticity, Cambridge University Press, 2002.
26. D. J. Watts and S. H. Strogatz, "Collective dynamics of 'small-world' networks," Nature, vol. 393, no. 6684, pp. 440–442, 1998.

27. J. Koester and S. A. Siegelbaum, “Propagated signaling: the action potential,” in Principles of Neural Science, E. Kandel, J. Schwartz, T. Jessell, S. Siegelbaum, and A. J. Hudspeth, Eds., chapter 7, p. 157, McGraw-Hill, New York, NY, USA, 5th edition, 2013.

28. S. Tamura, Y. Nishitani, T. Kamimura et al., “Multiplexed spatiotemporal communication model in artificial neural networks,” Automation, Control and Intelligent Systems, vol. 1, no. 6, pp. 121–130, 2013.

29. Y. Mizuno-Matsumoto, M. Ishijima, K. Shinosaki et al., “Transient global amnesia (TGA) in an MEG study,” Brain Topography, vol. 13, no. 4, pp. 269–274, 2001.

30. M. Perc, “Spatial coherence resonance in excitable media,” Physical Review E, vol. 72, no. 1, pp. 1–6, 2005.

31. K. Takahashi, S. Kim, T. P. Coleman et al., “Large-scale spatiotemporal spike patterning consistent with wave propagation in motor cortex,” Nature Communications, vol. 6, article 7169, 2015.

32. P. Spector, “Principles of cardiac electric propagation and their implications for re-entrant arrhythmias,” Circulation: Arrhythmia and Electrophysiology, vol. 6, no. 3, pp. 655–661, 2013.

33. P. A. Medolla, J. V. Arthur, R. Alvarez-Icaza, et al., “A million spiking-neuron integrated circuit with a scalable communication network and interface,” Science, vol. 345, no. 6197, pp. 668–673, 2014.

34. S. Tamura, Y. Nishitani, C. Hosokawa, Y. Mizuno-Matsumoto, and Y.-W. Chen, “Base of brain intelligence: information flow in cultured neuronal networks and its simulation on 2D mesh network,” in Proceedings of the 11th International Conference on Natural Computation and the 12th International Conference on Fuzzy Systems and Knowledge Discovery (ICNC-FSKD ‘15), IEEE Circuits and Systems Society, Zhangjiajie, China, August 2015, http://www.nbl-technovator.jp/NBL_Tech/paper/1551.pdf.

CHAPTER 4

A NOVEL BRAIN NETWORK CONSTRUCTION METHOD FOR EXPLORING AGE-RELATED FUNCTIONAL REORGANIZATION

Wei Li, Miao Wang, Yapeng Li, Yue Huang, and Xi Chen

INTRODUCTION

Healthy aging, along with many age-related diseases, is generally accompanied by cognitive functional deficits, such as reduced performance in memory and motor execution [1, 2], resulting from abnormalities in brain's structural and functional systems [3, 4]. Previous studies have illustrated that, in terms of structural changes, such functional degradations are related to loss of gray matter and thinning of cerebral cortex [5, 6]. Researchers are also currently attempting to explore aging from the perspective of alterations in functional system [7–9]. Owing to its noninvasive and mature data acquisition and processing, resting-state functional magnetic resonance imaging (fMRI) technology has become an important means to study these functional changes in the brain. fMRI has been providing abundant lines of evidence demonstrating variations in brain function during aging [4].

Since Watts and Strogatz [10] proposed small-world network in 1998 and Barabasi and Albert [11] proposed scale-free network in 1999, complex network theory has become increasingly important in exploring the nature of complex systems. Studies on the complex network of the brain, which is one of the most complex systems, elucidate the brain connectivity on the level of network topological organization, providing new insights into brain complexity [12, 13]. Numerous meaningful results have been obtained from exploring the changes in structural [3, 14] and functional brain networks [2, 15–17] of aging, as well as of age-related diseases, such as Alzheimer's disease (AD), Parkinson's disease, and stroke [18, 19]. Functional connectivity focuses on the relationship among different brain regions [20] and is usually established by the correlation of blood oxygenation level-dependent time courses between nodes [21]. Pearson correlation analysis, being the most frequently used functional brain network construction method, has been widely applied to explore the brain mechanism of aging and age-related diseases [7, 8, 22–24].

Numerous studies have demonstrated that reorganization in brain networks and changes in brain connectivity occur during aging [4, 19]. Alterations in brain network properties, such as efficiency and clustering coefficient, are also observed in aging [15, 16, 25, 26]. However, the consistency of the graph properties of brain networks within a group is sometimes not very satisfactory [27]. Some scientists cannot obtain statistically significant differences in some graph properties between different groups. Some studies even got disparate or contradicting changes in normal aging or age-related diseases [19, 28]. For example, Achard and Bullmore [25] found a higher global efficiency but no significantly different local efficiency was observed in the young group; this result is inconsistent with those obtained by Wu et al., indicating that the young group showed lower global efficiency but higher local efficiency than the elderly group [26]. Moreover, in terms of age-related diseases, such as AD, Stam et al. [29] showed that, compared with the healthy control group, the average path length of AD patients is longer, and the clustering coefficient does not change. However, Supekar et al. [30] showed that, compared with the healthy control group, AD patients demonstrate lower clustering coefficient, whereas the average

Citation: Wei Li, Miao Wang, Yapeng Li, Yue Huang, and Xi Chen, "A Novel Brain Network Construction Method for Exploring Age-Related Functional Reorganization," Computational Intelligence and Neuroscience, vol. 2016, Article ID 2429691, 15 pages, 2016. doi:10.1155/2016/2429691.

shortest path does not significantly change. In addition, Zhao et al. [24] found a significant difference in clustering coefficient between AD patients and healthy controls, whereas Sanz-Arigita et al. [31] could not obtain significant changes. Given that the reproducibility of fMRI datasets cannot be guaranteed [32], the study results bear much uncertainty. Some studies have shown that certain topological properties of functional brain network of the same group at two different time periods collected in the same test set also exhibit differences [33, 34].

The reasons for the abovementioned problems are possibly the individual differences not related to research factors we investigated within the group, as well as the differences in data preprocessing (such as band filtering and noise removal methods) [33, 34]. Moreover, the existing network modeling methods cannot fully extract significant differences between groups. Therefore, finding methods to improve SNR of data collection, to extract meaningful features from the collected datasets, and to explore new brain network construction methods will be of great significance for brain network analysis to strengthen consistency within group and highlight the differences between groups. Scientists have started working on this endeavor. For example, Liang et al. [34] reported that different filter bands affect the consistency of brain network analysis; meanwhile, Braun et al. [33] illustrated that the processing methods of MRI data possibly affect the reliability and robustness of brain network.

This paper proposes a novel brain network construction method, namely, subnetwork voting (SNV) method with sliding window, to explore age-related functional reorganization. This novel brain network modeling approach aims to reduce the impact caused by individual differences within group in brain network analysis and consequently weaken the differences within group and highlight the differences between groups. We hope that this method can help improve the reliability of brain network analysis in exploring aging and related diseases.

MATERIALS AND METHODS

Subjects

A dataset of 28 right-handed healthy adults, including 14 young adults (6 males, 8 females; mean age: 23.71 years old; range: 19–30 years old) and 14 elderly adults (7 males, 7 females; mean age: 67.57 years old; range: 60–79 years old), was collected by the International Consortium for Brain Mapping (ICBM), which is a subdataset in the 1000 Functional Connectomes Project (http://fcon_1000.projects.nitrc.org/).

Data Preprocessing

The first five images in raw data of each subject were discarded by ICBM to ensure magnetization equilibrium. Data preprocessing was performed using SPM8 (http://www.fil.ion.ucl.ac.uk/spm/). We first conducted slice timing; that is, all the datasets were corrected in time domain. Realignment was subsequently employed to remove movement artifact in the fMRI time series. We then normalized the datasets by using a standard template. The processed images were smoothed by using a standard 4*4*4 FWHM kernel, drifted, and filtered to the frequency range of 0.06–0.11 Hz [12, 17].The dataset for each subject was then segmented into 90 brain regions defined by AAL atlas [35].

Classic Construction Method for Functional Brain Network

For the time courses of 90 regions extracted from each subject, Pearson correlation was used to calculate the relationship between every two time courses of brain regions; thus, the correlation matrix of 90 $*$ 90 of each subject can be obtained. Previous studies have indicated that the properties of functional brain network are consistent with the actual brain model when the functional brain network density is 8–16% [7, 8, 17, 36]. Therefore, the functional brain networks of the young and the elderly individuals were established at a network density range of 8–16% to compare the topological properties (global efficiency, mean clustering coefficient, transfer coefficient, small-world value, and number of long edges) of the functional brain networks of young and old individuals in a large range of network densities.

SNV Method to Construct Functional Brain Network

In this study, we proposed the use of SNV method to establish functional brain network. The specific steps are as follows.

We set the density of functional brain networks to ND%; the length of time courses obtained by data preprocessing was L and the width of the sliding window was W ($W<L$).

For the time courses with length L of 90 brain regions extracted from the preprocessing datasets of each subject, we first extracted $L-W+1$ subseries with length W through window sliding (Figure 1(a)).

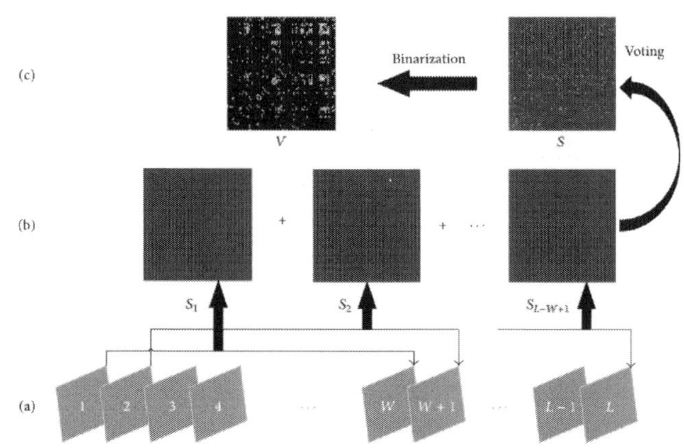

Figure 1: Process in the SNV method. (a) $L-W+1$ subseries with length W were extracted through window sliding; (b) binary subnetwork matrix S_i ($i = 1, 2, \dots, L - W + 1$) with density ND% was obtained by subseries; (c) the subseries were then summed up to obtain the voting matrix S, which was fixed to the binary voting network matrix V with density of ND%.

For all the ith ($i = 1, 2, \dots, L - W + 1$) subseries of the 90 brain regions of each subject (these subseries were extracted from the original time courses with the same starting and ending time points), Pearson correlation method was used to calculate 90 $*$ 90 correlation coefficient matrix C_i ($i = 1, 2, \dots, L - W + 1$), resulting in the construction of a brain subnetwork. According to the descending absolute value, the top ND percent elements of matrix Ci were set to 1, and the remaining elements were set to 0. As a result, an entitled binary subnetwork matrix S_i ($i = 1, 2, \dots, L - W + 1$) with density ND% was obtained (Figures 1(a) and 1(b)).

We summed up all binary matrices S_1, S_2, S_3,...,$_{L-W+1}$ and obtained a voting matrix $S=S_1 + S_2 + S_3 +\cdots+S_{L-W+1}$ (Figure 1(b)). Given that the functional brain network was established with density ND%, the top ND percent elements of matrix S (whose value is between 0 and $L-W+1$) were set to 1, and the remaining elements were set to 0. We obtained the final desired binary voting network matrix V (Figure 1(c)), which describes the brain connectivity.

When more than one element is equal to the last one of the top ND percent element in S (whose value was T), then determining which elements should be set to 1 only depending on the voting matrix is difficult. We then used weight information of subnetwork sequence to make a decision. We calculated the absolute value of all elements in C_i and summed up these values to obtain$C = |C_1|+|C_2|+\cdots+|C_{L-W+1}|$. Among the elements in S whose values are equal to T, we chose the ones demonstrating the largest absolute value with the same position in C; these values represent the largest weight of connectivity and thus were set to 1.

The length of a time course in our study is 128. To obtain the best values of window width in our modeling approach, we constructed the brain networks by using the SNV method with a window width of 10–120 and found that the rational window width is 90–100. Therefore, the experiments in our study were performed based on $W = 90$, 95, and 100. We will give reason for the selection of window width and discuss this issue in Section 4.

Support Vector Machine (SVM) for Classification

This study used the SVM approach to classify the young and the elderly subjects to evaluate the SNV method in functional brain network construction. K-fold cross-validation was applied herein. Specifically, we randomly split the entire population into 14 folds, each consisting of one young and one elderly individual. We used 13 folds as training sample set, leaving one fold as testing sample set. The training and testing processes looped 14 times with a distinct testing fold in each time. The accuracy, sensitivity, and specificity were averaged across the 14 classifications. A linear kernel was applied in SVM, and two sets of classification features were considered in our experiments. The first set consisted of all the five network properties mentioned above. The other set, based on the first set, was optimized with nodal information and removed network properties showing no significant difference between groups (only the small-world value was removed according to this criterion). A two-sample t-test was performed to compare the node degrees of each node between the young and elderly groups in the training sample set, and those showing significant difference (FDR correction at q value of 0.05) were appended to the feature set. The nodes demonstrating significant difference based on SNV method were shown in Table 1 and Figure 2.The features were scaled from 0 to 1 before inputting them into SVM in both cases.

Table 1: Regions showing significant difference in node degree.

Region	Hemisphere	AAL ID	Cluster
Precentral gyrus	Left	1	Parietal-(pre)motor
Superior occipital gyrus	Left	49	Occipital
Thalamus	Left	77	Subcortical
	Right	78	Subcortical
Temporal pole, superior temporal gyrus	Right	84	Medial temporal

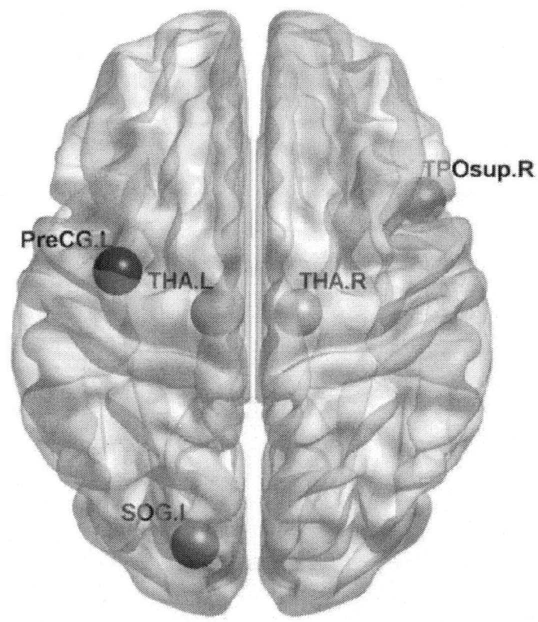

Figure 2: Regions showing significant difference in node degree. Different colors represent different clusters to which the nodes belong. Dark blue: parietal-(pre)motor; light blue: occipital; green: subcortical; brown: medial temporal.

RESULTS

Differences in the Topological Properties between the Young and Elderly Adults

With a network density of 8–16%, the topological properties of functional brain network in young and elderly groups were calculated based on classic method and SNV method (in this study, $W = 90$, 95, and 100), respectively, as shown in Figure 3 (take $W = 90$, e.g.). Compared with the topological properties of functional brain networks of young group, the global efficiency and the number of long edges of elderly group both declined to different extent. In addition, the mean clustering coefficient, transfer coefficient, and small-world property showed different degrees of increase. The difference between the brain functional networks, which are constructed by the SNV method, remained consistent with that by the classic method.

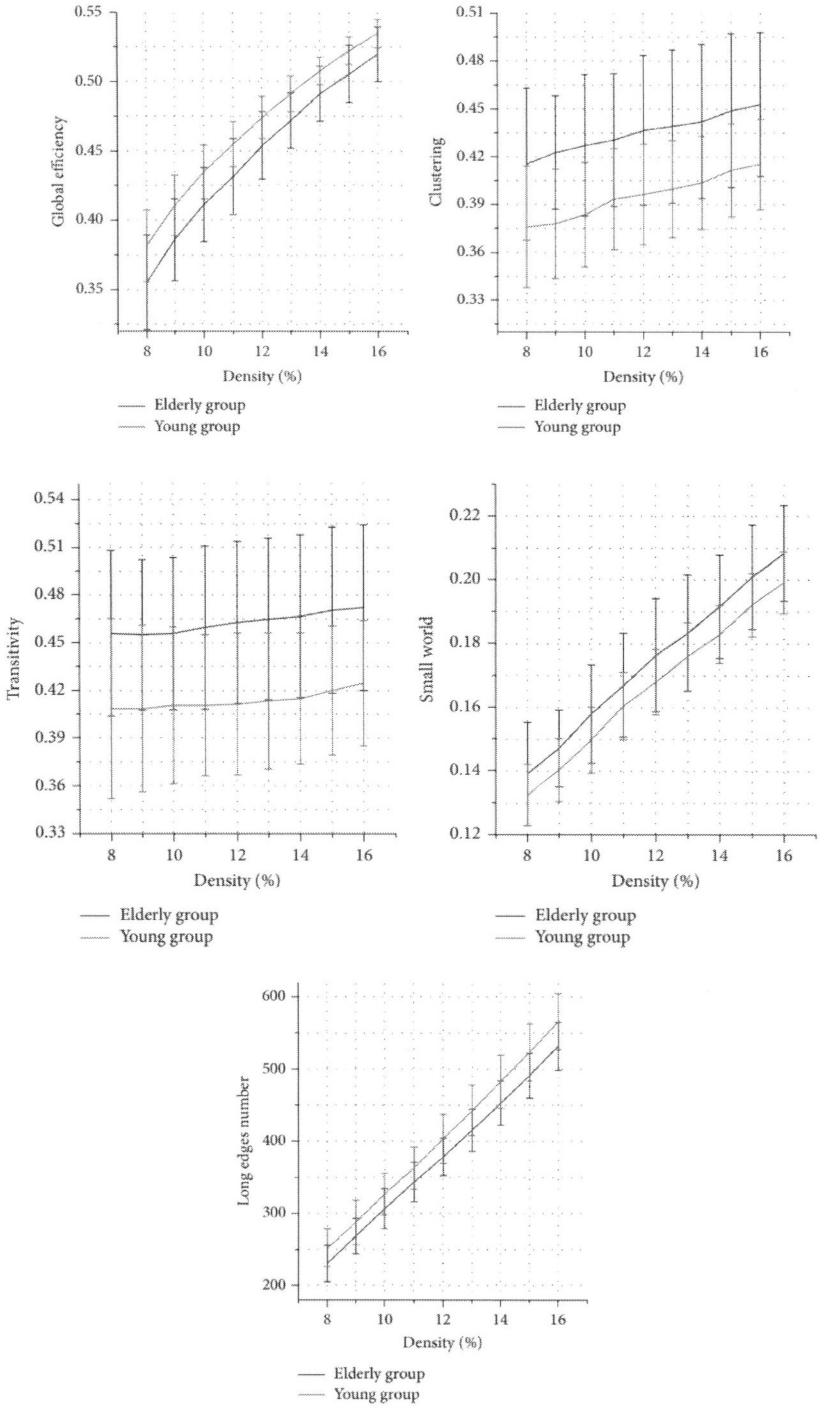

(a) Network properties with SNV method ($W = 90$)

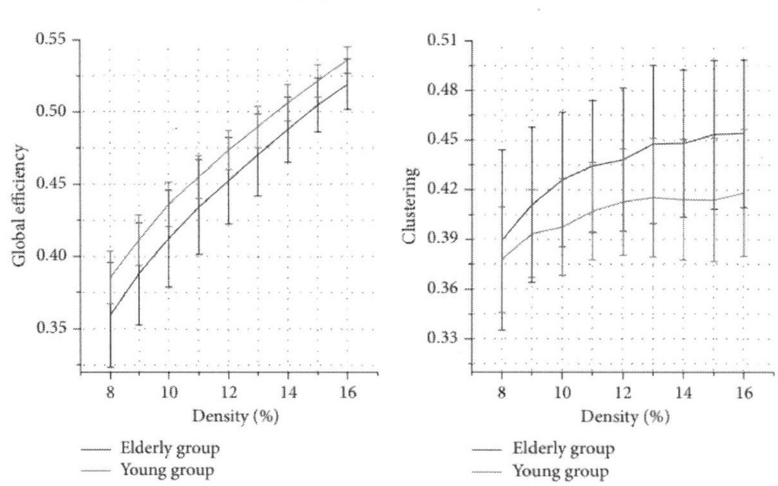

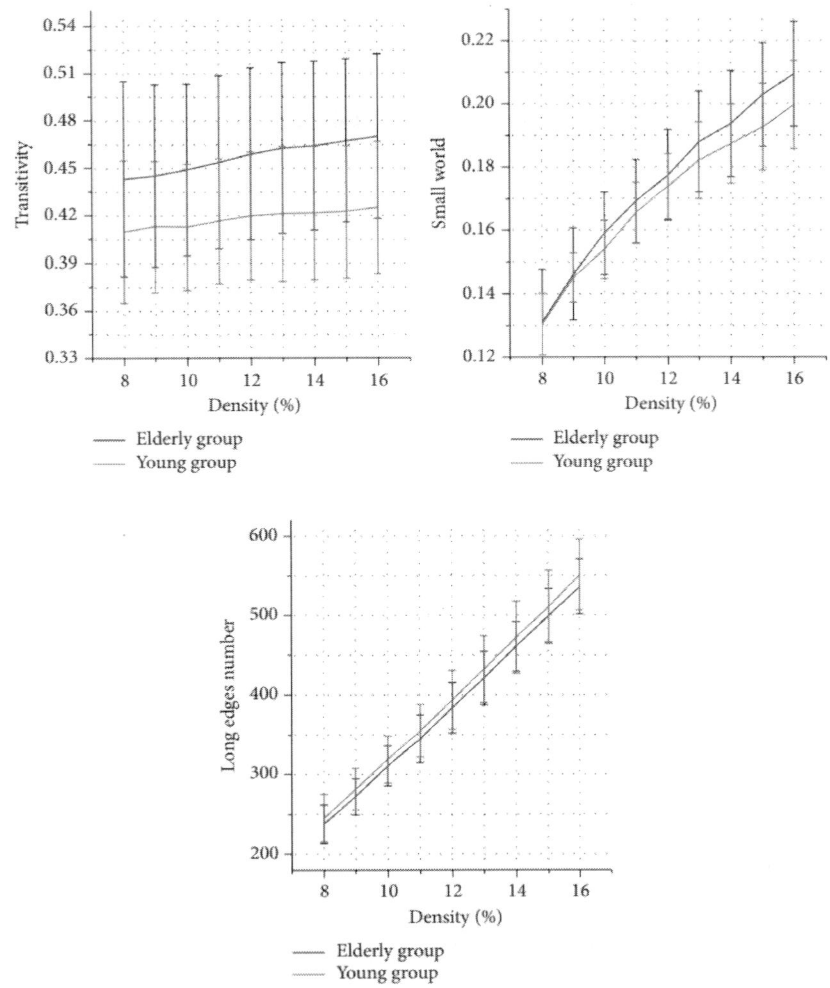

(b) Network properties with classic method

Figure 3: Topological properties of networks constructed by (a) SNV method ($W = 90$) and (b) classic method. The black and red lines represent the elderly and young groups, respectively. The error bars represent standard deviation. The difference between the networks, which were constructed by the SNV method, of the young and elderly groups remained consistent with the classic method.

Statistical Analysis of Topological Properties of Brain Networks

We performed a t-test for the topological properties based on both network construction methods to compare the differences between the young and elderly groups. Figure 4 shows the P values that were uncorrected for multiple comparison, which are convenient for straightforward comparison of magnitudes. Only 60 sets of network property comparisons in the classic method showed significant difference ($P < 0.05$). However, there were 92 sets showing significant difference in the SNV method, more than one and a half times that in classic method. Except for the small-world value and the number of long edges, 98.77% of the P values in SNV method showed significant difference ($P < 0.05$), indicating that the SNV method can identify much more statistically significant differences, which cannot be discovered when using the classic brain network construction method. Compared with the classic method, the P values of various topological properties by the SNV method significantly decreased in all of the three window widths (permutation test, $P < 0.05$ in efficiency, $P < 0.01$ in other properties). In our 135 sets of statistic comparisons, the P values of 124 sets (91.85%) decreased. In addition, 98.89% of the P values decreased at a network density range of 9–14%. When FDR correction was implemented for multiple comparisons at q value of 0.05, only 27 sets of comparisons showed significant difference in the classic method. However, there were 80 sets showing significant difference in the SNV method, nearly three times that in classic method.

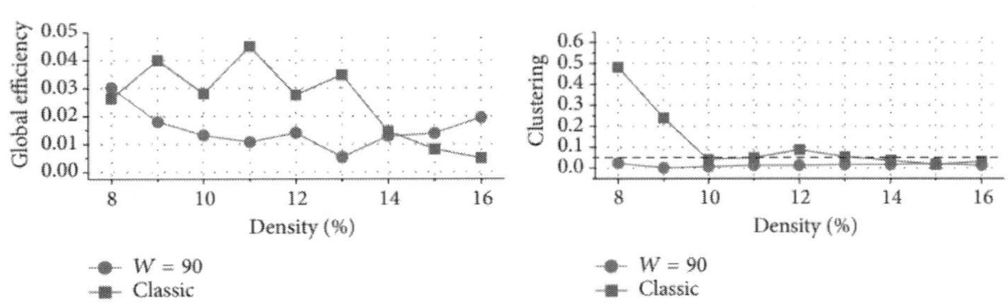

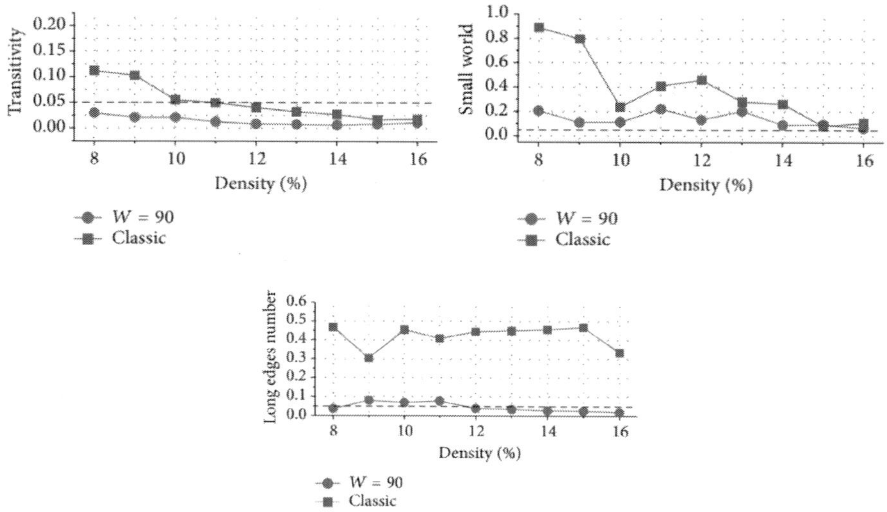
Transitivity
Density (%)
W = 90
Classic
Small world
Density (%)
W = 90
Classic
Long edges number
Density (%)
W = 90
Classic

(a) $W = 90$

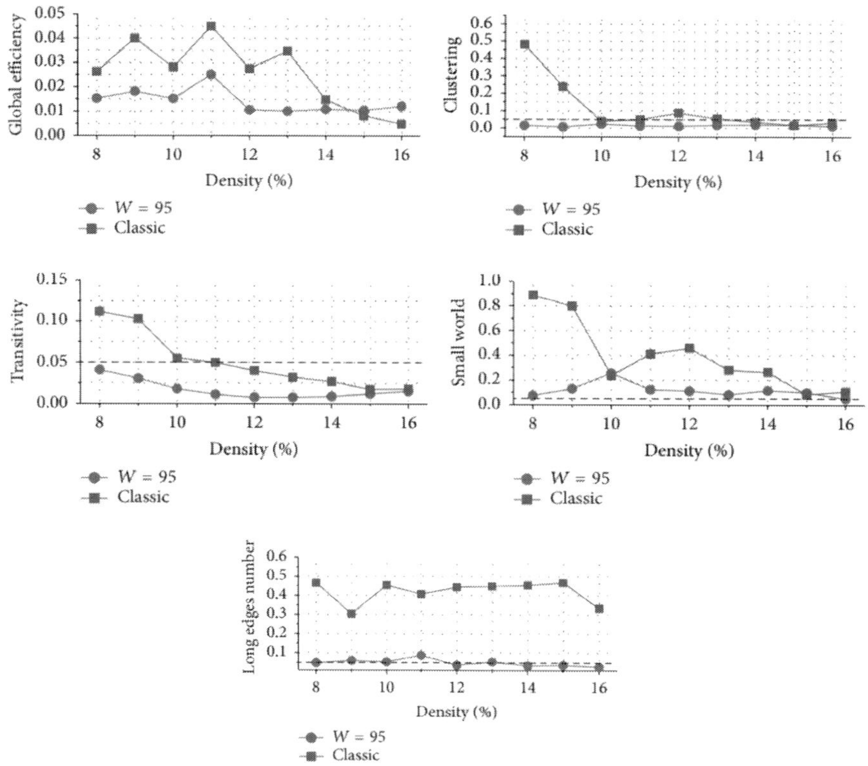
Global efficiency
Density (%)
W = 95
Classic
Clustering
Density (%)
W = 95
Classic
Transitivity
Density (%)
W = 95
Classic
Small world
Density (%)
W = 95
Classic
Long edges number
Density (%)
W = 95
Classic

(b) $W = 95$

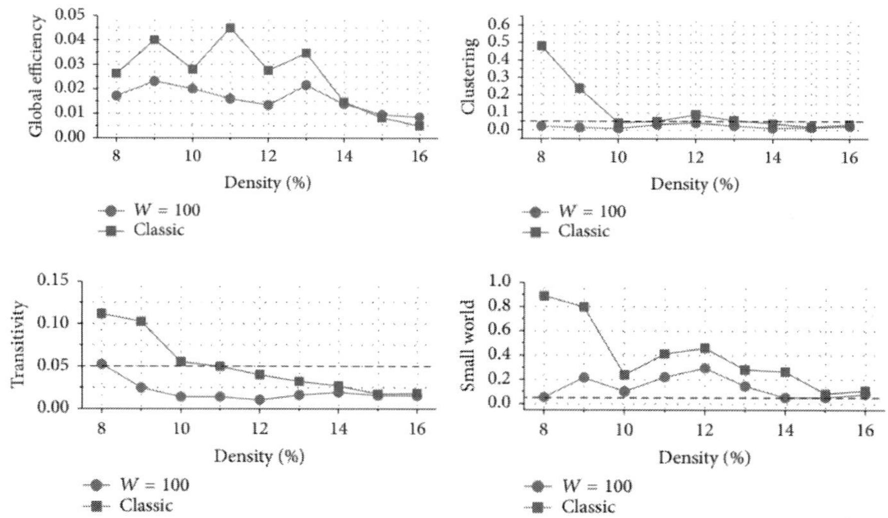
Global efficiency
Density (%)
W = 100
Classic
Clustering
Density (%)
W = 100
Classic
Transitivity
Density (%)
W = 100
Classic
Small world
Density (%)
W = 100
Classic

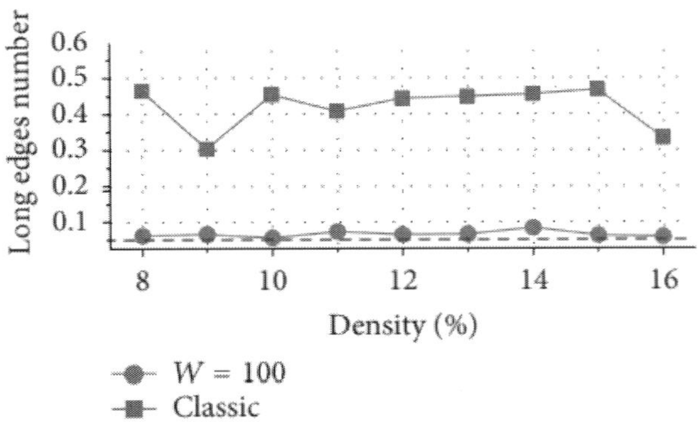

(c) $W = 100$

Figure 4: Statistical analysis of topological properties of the networks produced using the SNV ($W = 90$, 95, and 100) and classic methods. The blue and red lines represent P values obtained through the classic and SNV methods, respectively. Compared with that of the networks constructed by the classic method, P values of topological properties of the networks constructed by the SNV method significantly decreased (permutation test, $P < 0.05$ in efficiency, < 0.01 in other properties).

Classification Results of the Young and Elderly Individuals Using SVM

We used the classic and SNV methods to build a functional brain network for each subject in the young and old groups, and then we attempted to use SVM as a classifier to classify the testing dataset into two groups. To analyze the impact of different window widths on classification, we performed classification experiment at $W = 90$, 95, and 100.

Table 2 and Figure 5(a) show the accuracy rate of classification in the first set of classification features. The overall mean accuracy rate of the classic method was 62.3%. Compared with that classic method, the SNV method used in this study significantly improved the accuracy to 72.8% (permutation test, $P < 0.01$ in all of the three window widths). The highest accuracy was 82.1% (permutation test, $P < 0.01$; and the 95% confidence interval was 69.6–94.7%). Moreover, the sensitivity (Table 3 and Figure 5(b)) improved significantly from 65.9% to 76.7% (permutation test, $P < 0.01$ in all of the three window widths). The specificity (Table 4 and Figure 5(c)) also improved significantly from 58.7% to 68.8% (permutation test, $P < 0.01$ in all of the three window widths).

Table 2: SVM accuracy in the first feature set.

Density	8%	9%	10%	11%	12%	13%	14%	15%	16%
W									
90	0.714	0.679	0.714	0.714	0.643	0.750	0.786	0.821	0.786
95	0.750	0.643	0.679	0.679	0.714	0.679	0.786	0.786	0.786
100	0.714	0.679	0.714	0.750	0.750	0.714	0.679	0.786	0.750
Classic	0.536	0.571	0.714	0.571	0.643	0.607	0.643	0.607	0.714

Accuracy was significantly higher in the SNV method than in the classic method (permutation test, $P < 0.01$ in all of the three window widths).

Table 3: SVM sensitivity in the first feature set.

Density	8%	9%	10%	11%	12%	13%	14%	15%	16%
W									
90	0.786	0.643	0.714	0.786	0.643	0.786	0.857	0.929	0.857
95	0.714	0.643	0.714	0.714	0.786	0.714	0.857	0.857	0.857
100	0.714	0.643	0.714	0.786	0.786	0.786	0.714	0.857	0.857
Classic	0.643	0.643	0.714	0.643	0.714	0.643	0.643	0.571	0.714

Sensitivity was significantly higher in the SNV method than in the classic method (permutation test, $P < 0.01$ in all of the three window widths).

Table 4: SVM specificity in the first feature set.

Density	8%	9%	10%	11%	12%	13%	14%	15%	16%
W									
90	0.643	0.714	0.714	0.643	0.643	0.714	0.714	0.714	0.714
95	0.786	0.643	0.643	0.643	0.643	0.643	0.714	0.714	0.714
100	0.714	0.714	0.714	0.714	0.714	0.643	0.643	0.714	0.643
Classic	0.429	0.500	0.714	0.500	0.571	0.571	0.643	0.643	0.714

Specificity was significantly higher in the SNV method than in the classic method (permutation test, $P < 0.01$ in all of the three window widths).

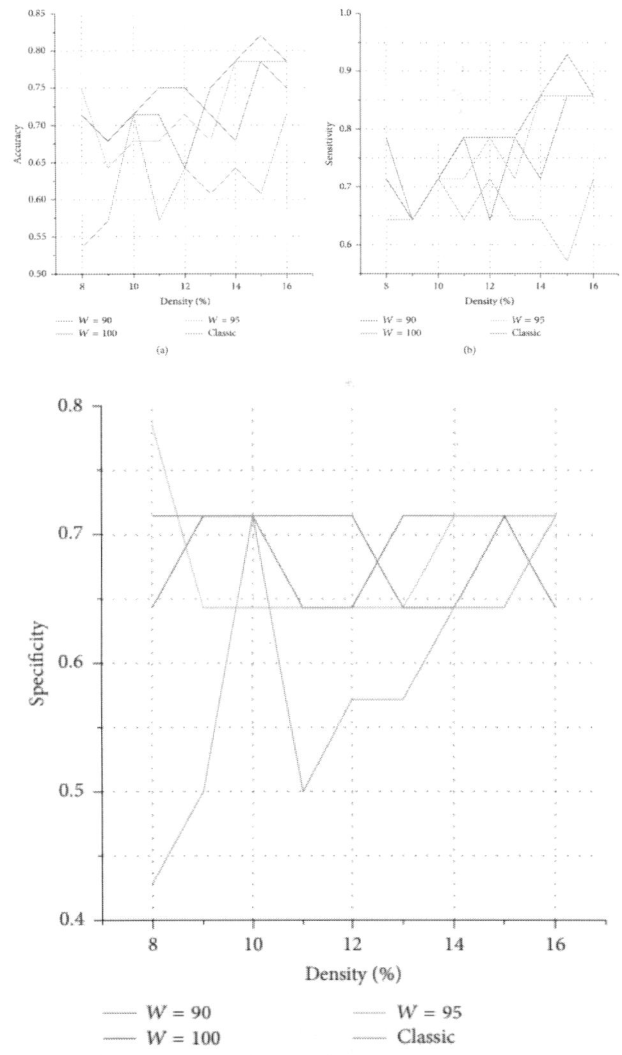

Figure 5: SVM classification results of young and elderly adults in the first feature set. Compared with classic network construction method, (a) accuracy, (b) sensitivity, and (c) specificity of classification based on the SNV method in the first feature set improved significantly.

The other set of classification features was optimized with nodal information, and the differences in node degree were prominent within parietal-(pre)motor, occipital, subcortical, and medial temporal systems (Table 1 and Figure 2) as revealed by the partition method based on a hierarchical clustering analysis as performed by Salvador et al. [37]. With the optimized feature set (Table 5 and Figure 6(a)), the overall mean accuracy rate of classification improved significantly from 67.5% in the classic method to 76.5% in the SNV method (permutation test, $P < 0.001$ at $W = 90, 95$; $P < 0.05$ at $W = 100$). In addition, the highest accuracy reached up to 89.3% (permutation test, $P < 0.01$; and the 95% confidence interval was 78.5–100%) when using the SNV method at $W = 90$ and density = 10%, which is consistent with or better than those obtained by the following similar studies: Vergun et al. [38] classified the young and elderly individuals based on the same dataset downloaded from 1000 Functional Connectomes Project with an accuracy of 84%. Supekar et al. [39] and Dosenbach et al. [40] reached an accuracy of 91% in classifying the children and adults by using the SVM method, respectively. Although these results were not that comparable because of the methodology and differences in raw data, they can still reflect to some extent the superiority of the SNV method. Furthermore, the sensitivity (Table 6 and Figure 6(b)) improved significantly from 66.7% to 81.2% (permutation test, $P < 10e-4$ at $W = 90, 95$; no significant difference was observed at $W = 100$). The specificity (Table 7 and Figure 6(c)) improved significantly from 68.3% to 71.7% (permutation test, $P < 0.01$ at $W = 100$; no significant difference was observed at $W = 90, 95$).

Table 5: SVM accuracy in the optimized feature set.

Density	8%	9%	10%	11%	12%	13%	14%	15%	16%
W									
90	0.786	0.893	0.821	0.821	0.786	0.714	0.786	0.786	0.750
95	0.857	0.821	0.821	0.821	0.750	0.750	0.750	0.679	0.679
100	0.750	0.821	0.857	0.643	0.750	0.714	0.679	0.679	0.679
Classic	0.714	0.643	0.679	0.714	0.714	0.643	0.643	0.643	0.679

Accuracy was significantly higher in the SNV method than in the classic method (permutation test, $P < 0.001$ at $W = 90, 95$; $P < 0.05$ at $W = 100$).

Table 6: SVM sensitivity in the optimized feature set.

Density	8%	9%	10%	11%	12%	13%	14%	15%	16%
W									
90	0.786	0.929	0.929	0.929	0.929	0.786	0.857	0.857	0.857
95	0.929	0.857	0.929	0.929	0.857	0.857	0.857	0.714	0.714
100	0.714	0.857	0.857	0.643	0.786	0.643	0.643	0.643	0.643
Classic	0.714	0.714	0.714	0.714	0.714	0.643	0.571	0.571	0.643

Sensitivity was significantly higher in the SNV method than in the classic method (permutation test, $P < 10e-4$ at $W = 90, 95$; no significant difference was observed at $W = 100$).

Table 7: SVM specificity in the optimized feature set.

Density	8%	9%	10%	11%	12%	13%	14%	15%	16%
W									
90	0.786	0.857	0.714	0.714	0.643	0.643	0.714	0.714	0.643
95	0.786	0.786	0.714	0.714	0.643	0.643	0.643	0.643	0.643
100	0.786	0.786	0.857	0.643	0.714	0.786	0.714	0.714	0.714
Classic	0.714	0.571	0.643	0.714	0.714	0.643	0.714	0.714	0.714

Specificity was significantly higher in the SNV method than in the classic method at one window width (permutation test, $P < 0.01$ at $W = 100$; no significant difference was observed at $W = 90, 95$).

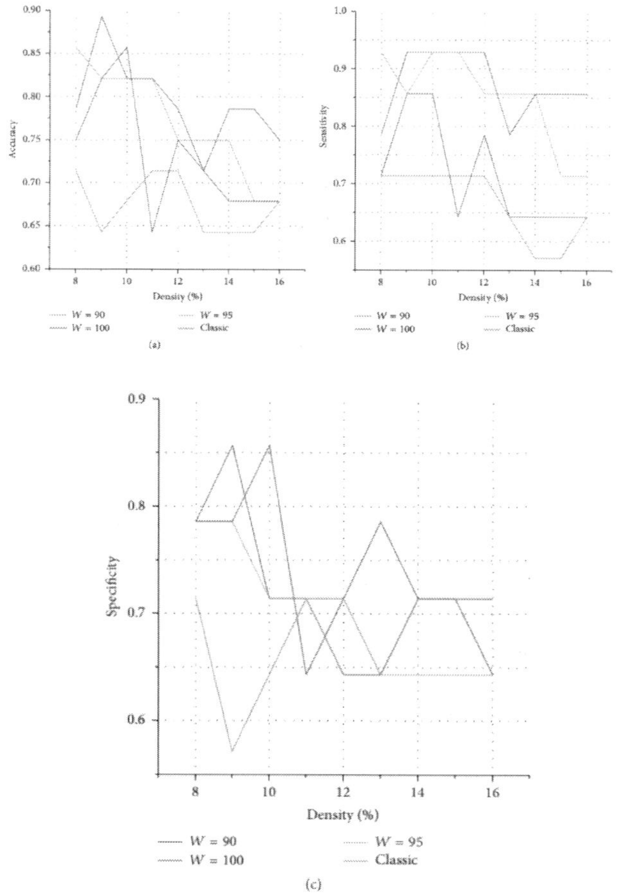

Figure 6: SVM classification results of young and elderly adults in the optimized feature set. Compared with classic network construction method, (a) accuracy, (b) sensitivity, and (c) specificity of classification based on the SNV method in the optimized feature set improved significantly.

DISCUSSION

Differences in Topological Properties of Brain Network between the Young and Elderly Adults

The cognitive and memory functions of the brain generally decline with aging [41]. Different aspects of studies provide different explanations for this phenomenon. In terms of structural changes, previous studies have suggested that reduction in gray matter density and thinning of cortex may cause the decline in brain function during aging [5, 6]. With the recent development in graph theory and complex network, scientists have started to study aging and related diseases from the perspective of functional brain network, and they generally consider the decrease in cognitive and memory as a direct consequence of reduced efficiency and number of long edges in functional brain network during aging [3, 7–9, 15]. This present study observed the same results. From the perspective of physiology, this phenomenon is possibly caused by the changes and reconnection of the brain synapses.

Mean clustering coefficient is the average of clustering coefficient in all nodes in a network and indicates the extent of local cliquishness or local efficiency of information transfer [10, 42]. Numerous studies have demonstrated that brain networks evolved from an integrated system to a distributed one during aging [2, 14,16], which is consistent with the observed increasing clustering coefficient in our study. Although both the old and young groups showed normal small-world architecture in the functional brain networks, increased clustering and decreased efficiency were found in elderly subjects, implying a degeneration process wherein the brain system shifted from a small-world network to a regular one along with normal aging [16, 26].

Transfer coefficient is the ratio of "triangles to triplets" in the network [43], from another aspect to measure the degree of tightness and easy exchange of information between network nodes. This study found that the transfer coefficient in the elderly group also increased to a certain degree. This finding is possibly caused by the increased linkages in the elderly group to maintain information transfer among different brain regions, which can be seen as an adaptive process of the brain during aging.

In this study, we found that the changes in the brain network properties during aging as revealed by the SNV method are consistent with those revealed by the classic method, indicating the validity of the SNV method. In other words, the SNV method did not result in false positive differences. By combining the previous results with ours, we consider that reorganizations occur in the brain network during aging, and differences do exist between the young and elderly groups on the level of functional brain network.

Analysis of P Values

This study calculated the topological properties and then performed statistical tests to compare the young and elderly groups. Similar experiments were performed in many previous studies. Sometimes studies capture statistically significant differences in some properties, whereas only nonsignificant differences were observed at times. For example, Wang et al. [7, 8] found reduction in global efficiency in the elderly group but did not observe significant differences in clustering coefficients. By contrast, significant differences in clustering coefficients were found in some other studies [2, 16]. One possible reason for this issue is that the approach employed in constructing brain networks cannot fully extract the "intrinsic edges" to avoid the useful signal being buried into noises. Our results showed that, under different network densities, the SNV method revealed much more significant differences, which cannot be discovered by the classic method. On this basis, the SNV method can better highlight the differences between the young and elderly groups according to various topological properties.

We also utilized another independent dataset consisting of nine AD patients and nine healthy controls to validate the performance of the SNV method (for more demographics and experiments, see Supplementary Materials available online at http://dx.doi.org/10.1155/2016/2429691). The brain networks were obtained in the same manner. The SNV method similarly revealed much more significant differences, and the *P* values of the network properties obtained using the SNV method significantly decreased compared with the classic method (Supplementary Figure 1).

These experimental results indicated that this novel method offers an apparent advantage in exploring significant alterations in aging or age-related diseases. This method reveals more differences, which the classic method cannot discover in brain network analysis, and thus this novel method is significant in exploring dynamic brain pathology.

SVM Classification

SVM is a machine learning method that can be trained and is widely used in nonlinear function classification. A good classification performance of the same kind of SVM reveals the consistency within group and the differences between groups. Our study used SVM to classify the samples into young group or elderly group. On the basis of both sets of features, the results showed that the accuracy, sensitivity, and specificity of the SNV method improved significantly in different sliding window widths compared with the classic method. That is, our SNV method can better highlight the differences between groups, making classification into two classes easier. Particularly for the optimized feature set, nodal information was combined with global network properties to improve classification accuracy. Given that the small-world value did not reveal significant difference at any density or any window width, which is consistent with the finding that a human brain exhibits small-world architecture in both the young and the elderly individuals [19], we removed this property from the feature set to avoid redundant characteristics. As we can see in Table 1, the nodes demonstrating significant difference were found in parietal-(pre)motor, occipital, subcortical, and medial temporal systems, which is consistent with a study by Chou et al. [44]. Moreover, St Jacques et al. [45] found an age-related difference in brain regions, such as the precentral area, for subsequent memory of negative stimuli, and Cao et al. [15] also found that brain regions showing significant age-related changes in weighted degree centrality were predominantly located in several default-mode regions. These regions exhibiting changes were also found in our results.

The highest accuracy in our study reached up to 89.3%. Compared with homologous researches, our method provided a preferable result based on a relatively small optimized feature set. In previous studies, Vergun et al. [38] reached 84% with 100 connection features, Supekar et al. [39] reached 91% with connectivity patterns between subcortical and primary sensory regions, and Dosenbach et al. [40] reached 91% with 200 functional connections.

This study obtained similar results from the independent dataset, indicating that our modeling method can fully extract effective characteristics from brain networks for classification. Furthermore, being a novel brain network construction method, the SNV method could help explore human normal aging or age-related diseases. Through the SNV method, the optimized mixed feature set can be possibly regarded as a remarkable biomarker, and an effective auxiliary diagnosis indicator based on SVM may be developed for future study or for clinical applications.

Impact of the Sliding Window Width on Brain Network Modeling

This study used the sliding window widths of 90, 95, and 100 to establish the functional brain network of the young and the elderly groups. To analyze the impact of window width on our modeling approach, we constructed the brain networks by using the SNV method at window widths from 10 to 120 and calculated the *P* values of five network properties between groups. For easier visualization, we showed the results based on the middle density (12%) in Figure 7. At window widths below 90, the *P* values were generally increasing with decreasing window width. By contrast, at window width above 100, the overall performance rapidly deteriorated. Hence, the rational window width is 90– 100.

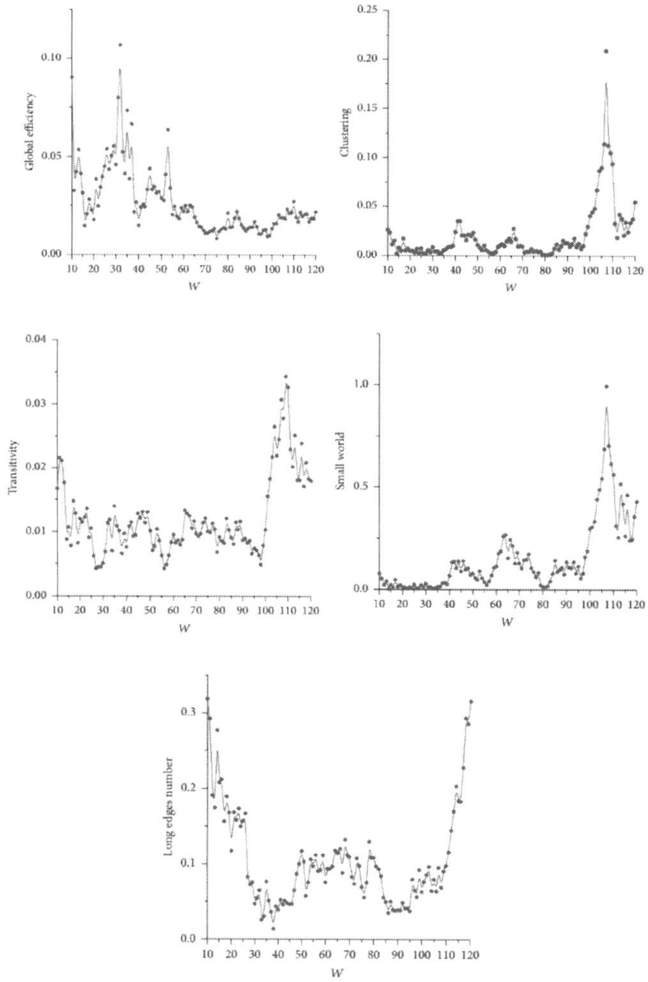

Figure 7: *P* values at window widths of 10–120. Dark gray dots represent *t*-test *P* values. Red solid lines represent B-spline-based nonparametric fits of *P* values. *P* values of all five network properties decreased to a relatively low level at a window width of 90–100.

Given that the TR of scans in our study was 2.0 s, window width of 90 equaled the scan duration of 3 min. In a review, Birn et al. [46] mentioned that many test-retest fMRI studies validated the reliability of functional connectivity using scan duration of 3–11 min and concluded that an increasing scan length can improve reproducibility. Van Dijk et al. [47] studied the intrinsic functional connectivity in human brain, and one of the most important conclusions was that correlation strengths can be stable at an acquisition time of as brief as 5 min. In addition, Gonzalez-Castillo et al. [48] suggested the use of longer scans above approximately 10 min. Although the context and ROIs of the above studies vary, they all suggested a relatively long but flexible scan duration of more than at least 3 min to achieve stable functional connectivity. Therefore, when the sliding window width is considerably narrow, the reliability of subnetworks constructed by Pearson correlation decreases, and thus the confidence of the SNV method declines. On this basis, subnetwork will be reliable when the scan duration of the subseries was longer than 3 min; that is, the window width should be above 90.

Moreover, although relatively stable brain connectivity can be acquired under a long scan duration, the performance of the brain network constructed by the classic method with full-length scans remained unsatisfactory because the effects of noise and individual difference are unavoidable during fMRI acquisition. For example, two uncorrelated time courses can be quite correlated when noise is added to time courses, resulting in a spurious edge in the network. We therefore introduced "voting" when constructing brain network to promote the discriminability of identifying a spurious edge. That is to say, "voting," to a large extent, reduces the false positive rate of identifying an edge. In this way, we can obtain the most intrinsic edges among those "stable edges." The brain network composed of these intrinsic edges can improve the consistency within group and highlight the differences between groups.

Given this, when the sliding window width is considerably wide, the number of subnetworks will be considerably small in our modeling, and the active effect of the final voting process will be reduced. The experimental results demonstrated this inference. Figure 7 suggests that better modeling results will be obtained when the window width is lower than 100, which provides sufficient number of subnetworks for voting. In this case, the number of the subnetworks was maintained above 25. The conclusion was also supported by the supplementary dataset.

Limitations

Some limitations in our SNV method must be clarified. First, our method can only be applied to dataset that contains a sequence of elements, such as BOLD time course from fMRI, and is not appropriate when applied to single-variable dataset, such as cortex thickness from structural MRI, in which case an individual network cannot be constructed by correlation method. We therefore cannot split a raw data sequence into windowed subsequences. Second, our classification feature lacks mechanistic interpretability. Although a simple or low-dimensional feature in our study can greatly save calculating resources and avoid overfitting, it in turn cannot comprehensively represent the whole brain network, indicating that we cannot figure out the connectivity by nodal information in feature vector. Third, the selection of window width in window-sliding method is an open issue in recent years [49, 50]. We usually choose a window width through the rule of thumb to avoid spurious fluctuation in network state [50]. Although our window widths were verified by experimental results, a data-driven method is urgently needed to address this issue, and that will be one of our studies in the future.

ACKNOWLEDGMENT

This work was supported by the National Natural Science Foundation of China (61473131, 60905024, and 70903026).

REFERENCES

1. T. Hedden and J. D. E. Gabrieli, "Insights into the ageing mind: a view from cognitive neuroscience,"Nature Reviews Neuroscience, vol. 5, no. 2, pp. 87–96, 2004.
2. R. Sala-Llonch, C. Junqué, E. M. Arenaza-Urquijo et al., "Changes in whole-brain functional networks and memory performance in aging," Neurobiology of Aging, vol. 35, no. 10, pp. 2193–2202, 2014.
3. Z. J. Chen, Y. He, P. Rosa-Neto, G. Gong, and A. C. Evans, "Age-related alterations in the modular organization of structural cortical network by using cortical thickness from MRI," NeuroImage, vol. 56, no. 1, pp. 235–245, 2011.
4. C. Grady, "The cognitive neuroscience of ageing," Nature Reviews Neuroscience, vol. 13, no. 7, pp. 491–505, 2012.
5. A. M. Fjell, L. T. Westlye, I. Amlien et al., "High consistency of regional cortical thinning in aging across multiple samples," Cerebral Cortex, vol. 19, no. 9, pp. 2001–2012, 2009.
6. E. R. Sowell, B. S. Peterson, P. M. Thompson, S. E. Welcome, A. L. Henkenius, and A. W. Toga, "Mapping cortical change across the human life span," Nature Neuroscience, vol. 6, no. 3, pp. 309–315, 2003.
7. L. Wang, Y. Li, P. Metzak, Y. He, and T. S. Woodward, "Age-related changes in topological patterns of large-scale brain functional networks during memory encoding and recognition," NeuroImage, vol. 50, no. 3, pp. 862–872, 2010.
8. L. Wang, C. Yu, H. Chen et al., "Dynamic functional reorganization of the motor execution network after stroke," Brain, vol. 133, no. 4, pp. 1224–1238, 2010.
9. W. Zhu, W. Wen, Y. He, A. Xia, K. J. Anstey, and P. Sachdev, "Changing topological patterns in normal aging using large-scale structural networks," Neurobiology of Aging, vol. 33, no. 5, pp. 899–913, 2012.·
10. D. J. Watts and S. H. Strogatz, "Collective dynamics of 'small-world' networks," Nature, vol. 393, no. 6684, pp. 440–442, 1998.
11. A.-L. Barabasi and R. Albert, "Emergence of scaling in random networks," Science, vol. 286, no. 5439, pp. 509–512, 1999.
12. E. Bullmore and O. Sporns, "Complex brain networks: graph theoretical analysis of structural and functional systems," Nature Reviews Neuroscience, vol. 10, no. 3, pp. 186–198, 2009. ·
13. Y. He and A. Evans, "Graph theoretical modeling of brain connectivity," Current Opinion in Neurology, vol. 23, no. 4, pp. 341–350, 2010.
14. D. Meunier, E. A. Stamatakis, and L. K. Tyler, "Age-related functional reorganization, structural changes, and preserved cognition," Neurobiology of Aging, vol. 35, no. 1, pp. 42–54, 2014.
15. M. Cao, J.-H. Wang, Z.-J. Dai et al., "Topological organization of the human brain functional connectome across the lifespan," Developmental Cognitive Neuroscience, vol. 7, pp. 76–93, 2014.
16. Z. Liu, L. Ke, H. Liu, W. Huang, and Z. Hu, "Changes in topological organization of functional PET brain network with normal aging," PLoS ONE, vol. 9, no. 2, Article ID e88690, 2014.
17. D. Meunier, S. Achard, A. Morcom, and E. Bullmore, "Age-related changes in modular organization of human brain functional networks," NeuroImage, vol. 44, no. 3, pp. 715–723, 2009. ·
18. G. Rodriguez, D. Arnaldi, and A. Picco, "Brain functional network in Alzheimer's disease: diagnostic markers for diagnosis and monitoring," International Journal of Alzheimer's Disease, vol. 2011, Article ID 481903, 10 pages, 2011.
19. J. Sun, S. Tong, and G.-Y. Yang, "Reorganization of brain networks in aging and age-related diseases,"Aging and Disease, vol. 3, no. 2, pp. 181–193, 2012.
20. K. J. Friston, C. D. Frith, P. F. Liddle, and R. S. J. Frackowiak, "Functional connectivity: the principal-component analysis of large (PET) data sets," Journal of Cerebral Blood Flow and Metabolism, vol. 13, no. 1, pp. 5–14, 1993.
21. H.-J. Park and K. Friston, "Structural and functional

brain networks: from connections to cognition,"Science, vol. 342, no. 6158, Article ID 1238411, 2013.

22. R. L. Buckner, J. Sepulcre, T. Talukdar et al., "Cortical hubs revealed by intrinsic functional connectivity: mapping, assessment of stability, and relation to Alzheimer's disease," Journal of Neuroscience, vol. 29, no. 6, pp. 1860–1873, 2009.

23. K. Onoda and S. Yamaguchi, "Small-worldness and modularity of the resting-state functional brain network decrease with aging," Neuroscience Letters, vol. 556, pp. 104–108, 2013.

24. X. Zhao, Y. Liu, X. Wang et al., "Disrupted small-world brain networks in moderate Alzheimer's disease: a resting-state fMRI study," PLoS ONE, vol. 7, no. 3, Article ID e33540, 2012.

25. S. Achard and E. Bullmore, "Efficiency and cost of economical brain functional networks," PLoS Computational Biology, vol. 3, no. 2, article e17, 2007.

26. K. Wu, Y. Taki, K. Sato et al., "Age-related changes in topological organization of structural brain networks in healthy individuals," Human Brain Mapping, vol. 33, no. 3, pp. 552–568, 2012.

27. X. Guo, Z. Jin, X. Feng, and S. Tong, "Enhanced effective connectivity in mild occipital stroke patients with hemianopia," IEEE Transactions on Neural Systems and Rehabilitation Engineering, vol. 22, no. 6, pp. 1210–1217, 2014.

28. L. K. Ferreira and G. F. Busatto, "Resting-state functional connectivity in normal brain aging,"Neuroscience & Biobehavioral Reviews, vol. 37, no. 3, pp. 384–400, 2013.

29. C. J. Stam, B. F. Jones, G. Nolte, M. Breakspear, and P. Scheltens, "Small-world networks and functional connectivity in Alzheimer's disease," Cerebral Cortex, vol. 17, no. 1, pp. 92–99, 2007. ·

30. K. Supekar, V. Menon, D. Rubin, M. Musen, and M. D. Greicius, "Network analysis of intrinsic functional brain connectivity in Alzheimer's disease," PLoS Computational Biology, vol. 4, no. 6, Article ID e1000100, 2008.

31. E. J. Sanz-Arigita, M. M. Schoonheim, J. S. Damoiseaux et al., "Loss of 'Small-World' networks in Alzheimer's disease: graph analysis of fMRI resting-state functional connectivity," PLoS ONE, vol. 5, no. 11, Article ID e13788, 2010.

32. A. J. Schwarz and J. McGonigle, "Negative edges and soft thresholding in complex network analysis of resting state functional connectivity data," NeuroImage, vol. 55, no. 3, pp. 1132–1146, 2011.

33. U. Braun, M. M. Plichta, C. Esslinger et al., "Test-retest reliability of resting-state connectivity network characteristics using fMRI and graph theoretical measures," NeuroImage, vol. 59, no. 2, pp. 1404–1412, 2012.

34. X. Liang, J. Wang, C. Yan et al., "Effects of different correlation metrics and preprocessing factors on small-world brain functional networks: a resting-state functional MRI study," PLoS ONE, vol. 7, no. 3, Article ID e32766, 2012.

35. N. Tzourio-Mazoyer, B. Landeau, D. Papathanassiou et al., "Automated anatomical labeling of activations in SPM using a macroscopic anatomical parcellation of the MNI MRI single-subject brain," NeuroImage, vol. 15, no. 1, pp. 273–289, 2002.

36. E. Bullmore and O. Sporns, "The economy of brain network organization," Nature Reviews Neuroscience, vol. 13, no. 5, pp. 336–349, 2012.

37. R. Salvador, J. Suckling, M. R. Coleman, J. D. Pickard, D. Menon, and E. Bullmore, "Neurophysiological architecture of functional magnetic resonance images of human brain," Cerebral Cortex, vol. 15, no. 9, pp. 1332–1342, 2005.

38. S. Vergun, A. S. Deshpande, T. B. Meier et al., "Characterizing functional connectivity differences in aging adults using machine learning on resting state fMRI data," Frontiers in Computational Neuroscience, vol. 7, article 38, 2013.

39. K. Supekar, M. Musen, and V. Menon, "Development of large-scale functional brain networks in children," PLoS Biology, vol. 7, no. 7, Article ID e1000157, 2009.

40. N. U. F. Dosenbach, B. Nardos, A. L. Cohen et al., "Prediction of individual brain maturity using fMRI,"Science, vol. 329, no. 5997, pp. 1358–1361, 2010.

41. D. C. Park and P. Reuter-Lorenz, "The adaptive brain: aging and neurocognitive scaffolding," Annual Review of Psychology, vol. 60, pp. 173–196, 2009.

42. V. Latora and M. Marchiori, "Efficient behavior of small-world networks," Physical Review Letters, vol. 87, no. 19, Article ID 198701, 2001.

43. G. Fagiolo, "Clustering in complex directed networks," Physical Review E—Statistical, Nonlinear, and Soft Matter Physics, vol. 76, no. 2, part 2, Article ID 026107, 2007. ·

44. Y.-H. Chou, N.-K. Chen, and D. J. Madden, "Functional brain connectivity and cognition: effects of adult age and task demands," Neurobiology of Aging, vol. 34, no. 8, pp. 1925–1934, 2013. ·

45. P. L. St Jacques, F. Dolcos, and R. Cabeza, "Effects of aging on functional connectivity of the amygdala for subsequent memory of negative pictures: a network analysis of functional magnetic resonance imaging data," Psychological Science, vol. 20, no. 1, pp. 74–84, 2009. ·

46. R. M. Birn, E. K. Molloy, R. Patriat et al., "The effect of scan length on the reliability of resting-state fMRI connectivity estimates," NeuroImage, vol. 83, pp. 550–558, 2013.

47. K. R. A. Van Dijk, T. Hedden, A. Venkataraman, K. C. Evans, S. W. Lazar, and R. L. Buckner, "Intrinsic functional connectivity as a tool for human connectomics: theory, properties, and optimization," Journal of Neurophysiology, vol. 103, no. 1, pp. 297–321, 2010.

48. J. Gonzalez-Castillo, D. A. Handwerker, M. E. Robinson et al., "The spatial structure of resting state

connectivity stability on the scale of minutes," Frontiers in Neuroscience, vol. 8, article 138, 2014.

49. E. A. Allen, E. Damaraju, S. M. Plis, E. B. Erhardt, T. Eichele, and V. D. Calhoun, "Tracking whole-brain connectivity dynamics in the resting state," Cerebral Cortex, vol. 24, no. 3, pp. 663–676, 2014.

50. N. Leonardi and D. Van De Ville, "On spurious and real fluctuations of dynamic functional connectivity during rest," Neuroimage, vol. 104, pp. 430–436, 2015.

SECTION II: FORECASTING AND PREDICTION APPLICATIONS

CHAPTER 5

A HYBRID NEURAL NETWORK MODEL FOR SALES FORECASTING BASED ON ARIMA AND SEARCH POPULARITY OF ARTICLE TITLES

Hani Omar, Van Hai Hoang, and Duen-Ren Liu

INTRODUCTION

Forecasting is an important part of many aspects of our lives, and sales forecasting plays a major role for enterprises in making business plans more accurate and gaining competitive advantage. Enhancing sales and operations planning through forecasting analysis and business intelligence is demanded in any industry and business. Convenience stores allow people to buy things at anytime and anywhere. They have a huge market in Taiwan and many publishing providers (e.g., magazine business) want to cooperate with them. Magazine businesses need plans for enhancing sales, distribution, storage space, and high quality predictions. Accurate sales forecasting can reduce inventory costs and shortages. It would increase profits for the business by reducing wasted resources and allow planning for appropriate future production.

Most studies have depended on historical sales data for forecasting sales, but the sales of magazines are also affected by the contents of the magazines. The contents are represented by the stories (articles) and their titles. Popular content can often boost sales, so it is an important field to consider when forecasting sales. For example, a magazine reporting celebrity gossip, for example, Faye Wong's extramarital affair, will attract readers who like her and want to know about her to buy the magazine. Thus, magazine sales will increase due to the popularity of the magazine contents. Before customers make decisions, they usually search for a product via the Internet in websites and blogs. Thus, search indexes of product data received via the Internet can be useful in deriving the popularity of products for building prediction models. Search terms related to the products can be decided manually. However, the terms manually decided may be limited when approximating consumer preferences. In this paper, information retrieval techniques are adopted to extract words from article titles. The popularity measures of article titles are then analyzed by using the search indexes obtained from Google search engine. The derived popularity denotes consumer interests in the contents of the magazines. The higher values of search indexes from the Google search engine indicate higher popularity and interest in magazine contents.

Several forecasting models, such as regression models [1–3], exponential smoothing and Box-Jenkins models [4–7], neural networks [8–12], or fuzzy system models [13–15], have been developed and implemented in different sectors of business. Many researchers have achieved accurate sales forecasting by using a time series method such as the autoregression (AR), moving average (MA), and autoregressive moving average (ARMA). Previous studies used statistical methods to make the trends stable. These methods found the maximum likelihood fitting to be ARMA [5]. The major limitation is the preassumed linear form of the models of AR, MA, and ARIMA. That is, a linear correlation structure is assumed among the time series values; no nonlinear patterns can be captured by the ARIMA model [16].

Time series are generally recognized as nonlinear and/or nonstationary. Due to these two properties, the system should be sensitive enough to capture the uniqueness of a time series and should replicate this in prediction. Traditional time series methods are confined to the assumption of linearity; however,

Citation: Hani Omar, Van Hai Hoang, and Duen-Ren Liu, "A Hybrid Neural Network Model for Sales Forecasting Based on ARIMA and Search Popularity of Article Titles," Computational Intelligence and Neuroscience, vol. 2016, Article ID 9656453, 9 pages, 2016. doi:10.1155/2016/9656453.

some data are nonlinear. In order to overcome the limitations of the traditional methods, many researchers are using soft computing techniques such as fuzzy logic, neural networks, fuzzy neural networks, and evolutionary algorithms.

Neural networks are reported to be such a method. Artificial neural networks (ANNs) have more noise tolerance than conventional regression-based empirical modeling, having the ability to learn complex systems with incomplete and corrupted data. In addition, they are more flexible, having the capability of learning dynamic systems through a retraining process using new data patterns with proper training data set [17, 18]. Forecasting reliability of the proposed neural networks was expressed in terms of forecasting error performance based on statistical and graphical methods. The most common learning mechanism is the "backpropagation" approach. The Backpropagation Neural Network (BPNN) is a supervised learning network well suited for prediction [19, 20].

In our preliminary work [21], we have proposed a BPNN popularity method, a sales forecasting model based on Backpropagation Neural Network (BPNN) where the inputs are historical sales and the popularity indexes of magazine article titles. In this study, we extend and enhance our preliminary work by proposing a novel hybrid ARIMA-BPNN popularity model for sales forecasting based on the prediction result of time series forecasting and the popularity of article titles. The proposed hybrid model uses the historical sales data, popularity of article titles, and the prediction result of a time series, Autoregressive Integrated Moving Average (ARIMA) forecasting method to learn a BPNN-based forecasting model. More specifically, our proposed BPNN model considers not only historical sales data but also the popularity of article titles. Besides, our proposed hybrid model uses the prediction output of ARIMA as input for the BPNN and uses the BPNN for forecasting future sales. The motivation for the hybrid model comes from the following perspectives. First, it is often difficult in practice to determine whether a time series data under study is generated from a linear or nonlinear underlying process or whether one particular method is more effective than the other in forecasting. Second, real-world time series are rarely purely linear or nonlinear. They often contain both linear and nonlinear patterns. The ARIMA model cannot deal with nonlinear relationships while the neural network model alone is not able to handle both linear and nonlinear patterns effectively. Several empirical studies have also suggested that combining several different models can improve forecasting accuracy [16, 22]. However, existing studies have not considered the effects of content popularity on sales. Our proposed hybrid BPNN model considers the popularity of article titles and prediction output of ARIMA can be a more effective approach for sales forecasting.

Our proposed forecasting model is experimentally evaluated by comparing with conventional sales prediction techniques. The experimental result shows that our proposed forecasting method outperforms conventional techniques which do not consider the popularity of title words. Our proposed hybrid ARIMA-BPNN popularity method also outperforms the BPNN popularity method presented in our preliminary work.

Section 2 provides related work on the methodology of forecasting. Section 3 describes a proposed hybrid methodology for forecasting sales. The experimental results and evaluation of our dataset using our proposed models are in Section 4. Section 5 provides a discussion of the results and analysis of real data supplied from a Taiwanese magazine. The conclusion is in Section 6.

RELATED WORK

There are many forecasting methods, and they are very important for managers and businessmen. Forecasting allows them to anticipate future operating expenses, enables more confident strategic decisions, and increases business efficiency. Additionally, it can be applied to identifying key areas in a business operation that operators can influence proactively. Therefore, developing AI systems for this kind of prediction is not simple [23]. There are two types of forecasting, traditional and nontraditional forecasting methods.

Traditional Forecasting Methods

These techniques are easy to develop and implement. Traditional methods include time series regression, moving average (MA), Autoregressive Integrated Moving Average (ARIMA), and exponential smoothing [24,25]. ARIMA is a popular traditional method used to analyze stationary univariate time series data. The main idea of ARIMA is to build a mathematical model with historical data to represent the regular pattern of a time series. Then, using this model and historical values, forecast the future values of this time series. There are usually three main stages to building an ARIMA model, including model identification, model estimation, and model checking. Model identification is the most crucial stage in building ARIMA models [26]. ARIMA is the method introduced by Box-Jenkins and has been used in various fields [1] and this model is a great predictor in the linear modeling problems but has poor performance for nonlinear problems. The ARIMA model is a generalization of the ARMA model, which integrates an autoregression (AR) and moving average (MA). Regression analysis is a method of investigating the relationships between variables, while moving average is a time series constructed by taking the averages of several sequential values of another time series.

Nontraditional Forecasting Methods

A number of researchers have developed nonlinear forecasting models for predicting stocks or sales [27]. Neural networks (NN) represent the nonlinear forecasting model and can be applied to time series modeling without assuming a priori function forms of models to find the nonlinear relationship between inputs and outputs [28]. Traditional time series methods may not be able to capture nonlinear patterns in data. NN modeling is a promising alternative for overcoming these limitations. Neural processors are designed based on cross correlation between inputs and the weights [29]. For instance, when training a neural network, the expected and real outputs of each sample of training set are compared, and the error information is used to modify the weights and thresholds [30, 31]. In a feed-forward network, there can be several hidden layers, with each layer having one or more nodes. The number of hidden layers and the number of nodes in each hidden layer are usually determined by a trial-and-error procedure [32]. A type of ANN, the multilayer perceptron trained by a backpropagation algorithm, has been utilized in many fields for forecasting. When compared to other traditional methodologies the backpropagation procedure is one of the most appropriate procedures for forecasting, especially for nonlinear data. Backpropagation is updating the weights in each perceptron to justify the real results as matching or approaching the desired result. Figure 1 shows a model of a neural network.

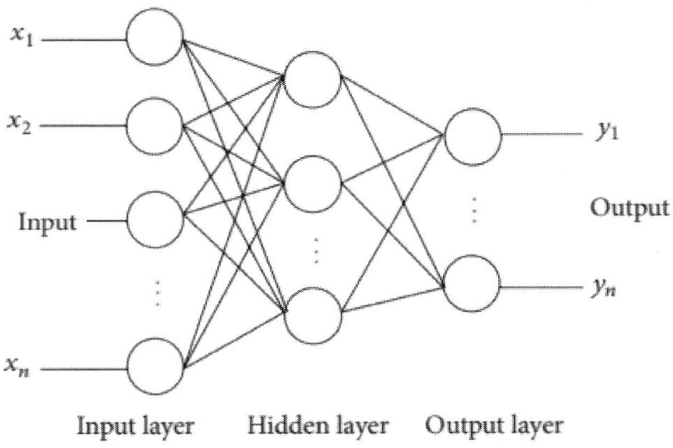

Figure 1: Neural network model.

Each model may have shortages related to the model itself or related to data. Thus, combining different models as hybrid models is used to overcome these shortages or enhance the performance. For example, an ANN predictor may give more accurate load forecasts during the morning hours, while a linear regression predictor may be superior for evening hours. Hence, a method that combines different types of predictors may outperform any single type of predictors [33]. Furthermore, weighted combination methods can increase the prediction accuracy by assigning greater importance to predictors of higher credit [34]. Traditional statistical models such as Autoregressive Integrated Moving Average (ARIMA) are linear prediction models. These models have been constrained to using linear functions in past observations. Several classes of nonlinear models have been proposed to overcome the restrictions of the linear models and account for certain nonlinear situations. ARIMA and ANN models have achieved successes in both linear and nonlinear domains [16]. Areekul et al.'s [35] hybrid model depends on using the ARIMA and ANN jointly. Their model used the ARIMA as a forecasting method for the linear component of the time series data and used ANN to forecast the residual as a nonlinear component. They combined the predicted values from the time data series and its residuals to improve forecasting accuracy.

THE HYBRID METHODOLOGY BASED ON THE POPULARITY OF ARTICLE TITLE WORDS

Popular article titles and headlines attract readers to buy the magazine and play a major role in sales. In this paper, we use the popularity of words in titles and headlines to improve the accuracy of forecasting. Information retrieval techniques are adopted to extract words from article titles. We then analyze the contents (title words) of magazine articles to measure the popularity of magazines based on the search indexes of title words derived from Google search engine. We propose forecasting with the Backpropagation Neural Network with popularity (BPNN-POP). Also, we propose a hybrid (Hybrid-POP) model with popularity combining the BPNN-POP and Autoregressive Integrated Moving Average (ARIMA) using popularity.

Our proposed forecasting models have preprocesses, starting with finding the correlation of sales, extracting the title words (phrases) from our data, finding the popularity of a magazine's content, and normalizing both the popularity and historical sales data. Our model (Hybrid-POP) uses historical sales data as input for an ARIMA. We then use the predicted value from the ARIMA and the historical sales data as input for the BPNN-POP, which uses popularity for forecasting sales. Therefore, a pattern of linear data and nonlinear data time series can be captured (Hybrid-POP). Figure 2 depicts our model (Hybrid-POP) with Autoregressive Integrated Moving Average and Backpropagation Neural Network with popularity.

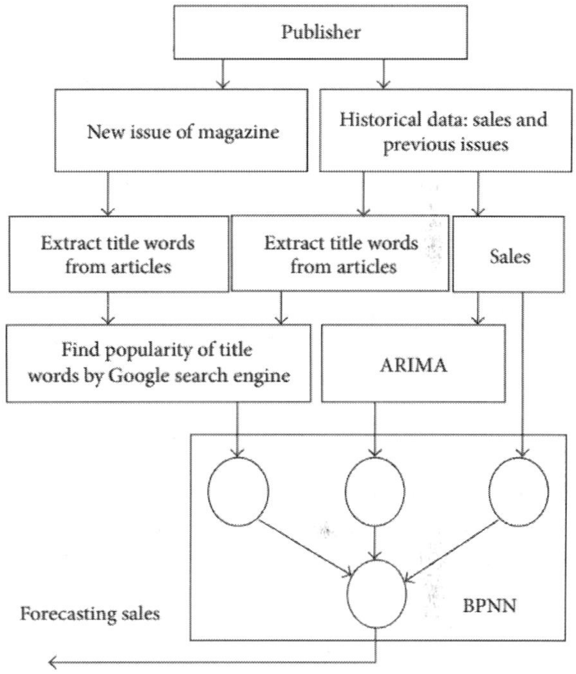

Figure 2: Hybrid ARIMA-BPNN popularity model.

Popularity Analysis of Magazine Content

Sales of publications such as magazines may be influenced by factors including content, social stratification, age, gender, locations of outlets, and historical sales data. In this research, we concern ourselves with historical sales data and the contents of a magazine. Historical sales data is commonly used as input for most forecasting models, but there is a need to normalize sales by dividing the sales over the maximum of all sales of magazine issues. Popular content can usually attract consumer interest and boost magazine sales. Therefore, we extract title words from magazine articles to obtain title word search indexes (volumes) using Google search. There are different ways to judge popularity. Google is the largest web search engine company; its search service is very powerful and useful.

Information retrieval techniques are adopted to extract words from article titles. The popularity of a title word can be derived from the Google engine to determine how many webpage volumes they have related to the title word. The Google engine also can restrict results to a particular time frame, (e.g., from October 1st, 2010, to October 3rd, 2010), and the results can show the number of retrieved webpages related to the title word in a time window. Generally, more retrieved webpages for the title word indicate higher popularity. Figure 3 shows an example of using a Google search engine to find the volume of usage for the word "java". The search engine is used to derive the popularity scores of title words by finding the search indexes, that is, the number of webpages for each title word during a one-month search period before the publication date of each issue. We accumulate the popularity scores of all title words for each issue and use them to represent the popularity index of the issue:

$$P_t = \sum_{j=1}^{N_t} R_{t,j}, \tag{1}$$

where P_t is the popularity index of issue t; N_t is the number of title words in issue t; and $R_{t,j}$ is the outcome of the Google search for title word j in issue t. The popularity indexes are normalized by dividing the maximum value over all issues.

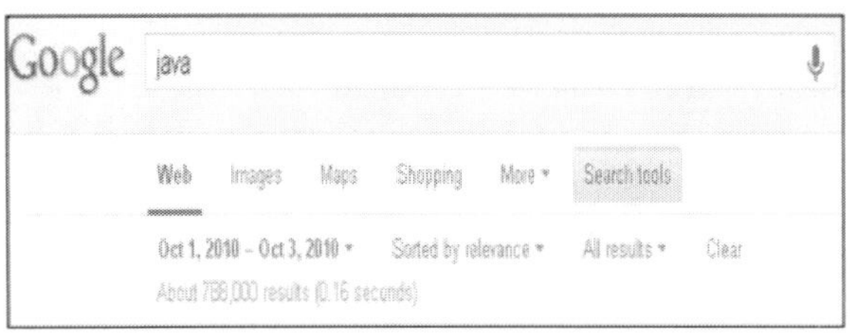

Figure 3: Using Google search.

Autoregressive Integrated Moving Average (ARIMA)

ARIMA has been one of the popular linear models for time series forecasting during the past three decades [16].

In this research, we aimed to use it as part of our adopted hybrid forecasting model and as a benchmark for testing the effectiveness of our proposed model. The ARIMA model is nonseasonal and has parameters. In the ARIMA(p, d, q) model, (p) is the number of autoregressive terms; (d) is the number of nonseasonal differences; and (q) is the number of lagged forecast errors in the prediction equation [36]. ARIMA has the following model:

$$\begin{aligned}&\left(1-\varphi_1 L-\varphi_2 L^2-\cdots-\varphi_p L^p\right)(1-L)^d\, y_t\\&=c+\left(1-\psi_1 L-\psi_2 L^2-\cdots-\psi_q L^q\right)\varepsilon_t,\end{aligned} \tag{2}$$

where φ_i (i = 1, 2, . . . , p) and ψ_j (j = 1, 2, . . . , q) are the model parameters. p is an order of autoregressiveness, and q is an order of moving average part while d represents order differencing. ε_t is white noise and is assumed to be independently and identically distributed with a mean of zero and a constant variance of σ^2. ARIMA was developed as a practical approach [37]. This methodology includes three iterative steps of model identification, parameter estimation, and diagnostic checking.

In the identification step, remaining stationary is necessary for building an ARIMA model. Therefore, data series have statistical characteristics such as a mean and variance that are constant over time. Parameters are estimated linearly when the model is specified, and nonlinear data series are estimated by minimizing the measure of errors. The last step is basically to check if model assumptions about the errors εt are satisfied. If the model is not adequate, a new model should be identified, which is again followed by the steps of parameter estimation and model verification [16].

Backpropagation Neural Network with Popularity

BPNN is a common method of teaching artificial neural networks how to perform a given task. It is a supervised learning method, consisting of a network system containing a large number of simple processing elements which are fully interconnected. In order to make the actual output close to any complex nonlinear mapping, its information processing procedure includes backpropagation, forward propagation, and weight adjustment. BPNNs are a type of feed-forward artificial neural networks. Feed-forward neural networks consist of an input layer, a hidden layer, and an output layer, as depicted in Figure 2. Each layer is formed by a number of nodes, and each node represents a neuron. The data flow in one direction and answers are obtained solely based on the current set of inputs. A BPNN has the same structure as a forward artificial network but is trained with a backpropagation algorithm in which incidences of training samples are entered from the input layer, and the outputs are calculated through the operation of corresponding functions and connection weights between the nodes [38]. The output error is obtained by comparing the calculated values with the target outputs. Sigmoid function is usually used as the activation function in the hidden layer of backpropagation:

$$f(I) = \frac{1}{1-e^{-I}}, \tag{3}$$

where I is the next formula and

$$I = \sum_{j=1}^{n} w_{mn} x_n, \tag{4}$$

where w_{mn} ($i = 0, 1, \ldots, m; j = 1, 2, \ldots, n$) are the connection weights, m is the number of hidden nodes, n is the number of input nodes, and x is the input value. We used a metric to calculate the difference between the real sales and the predicted values. There are many metrics, but one of them is enough to use for adjusting the (interconnections) weights in the neural network model.

In our proposed model of the Backpropagation Neural Network with popularity (BPNN-POP), we used three inputs; two inputs represented the sales of the previous two issues (Issue t_1 and Issue t_2) before the target issue (Issue t_3) and the third input represented the popularity of article titles and headlines for the target issue. Figure 4 demonstrates a BPNNPOP with three inputs, including previous sales of the last two issues. The third input is the normalized popularity (POP t_3) of the target issue.

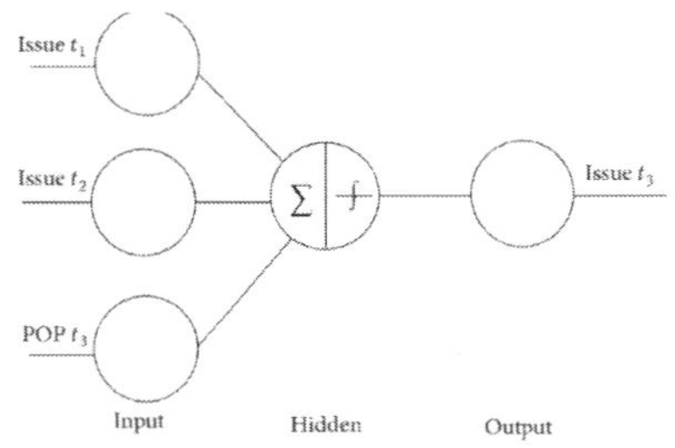

Figure 4: Three inputs for the BPNN-POP.

Hybrid ARIMA-BPNN Popularity Model

Our proposed model adopts the hybrid model (Hybrid-POP) for forecasting sales. In the hybridization, the ARIMA is used to forecast sales of a target issue by using the sales of previous two issues.

Predicted sales from the ARIMA are used as input for the BPNN-POP along with sales from the previous two issues and the popularity of the target issue. The implementation of Hybrid-POP has four inputs, as shown in Figure 5. The first two inputs represent the sales of the previous two issues (Issue t_1 and Issue t_2) before the target issue (Issue t_3) for forecasting. The third input represents the normalized popularity of the target issue. The fourth input represents the forecasting value of the target issue using ARIMA. Using the univariate ARIMA model has constraints. ARIMA is not tolerant of any extreme values in data and should be reestimated after every new data point. BPNNs are more tolerant of extreme values in data as compared to the ARIMA. Another constraint is the nature of data as being either linear or nonlinear. For these reasons, we use the hybrid model (Hybrid-POP) combining the ARIMA and the Backpropagation Neural Network using popularity to predict sales of a target issue. In the first step of our hybrid system, an ARIMA model is used to model the linear part of the time series and to create the ARIMA forecast. In the next step, the outputs of ARIMA are used as inputs for the artificial neural network and trained using known input and output training data to model the nonlinearity part of the time series. This method emphasizes the effects of previous sales and the popularity of article titles in the BPNN's forecasting method as well as the effect of the ARIMA by using the predicted value from it as an input to the neural network. The Hybrid-POP can thus tolerate more extreme values without reestimating the process. Moreover, attractive titles and headlines in magazines have an effect on buyer preferences for these publications. The proposed Hybrid-POP uses the popularity of article titles to enhance the accuracy of forecasting.

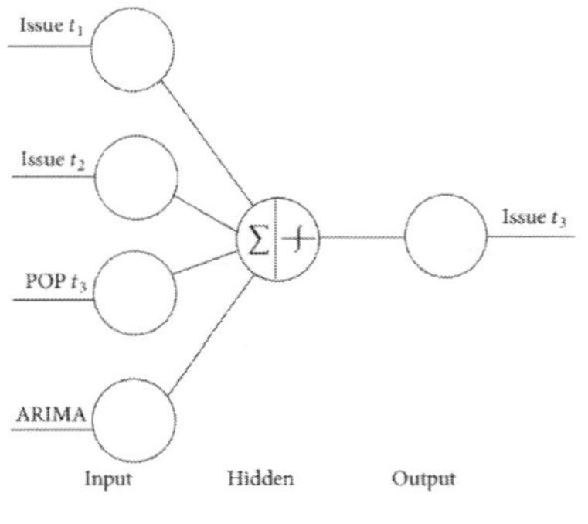

Figure 5: Four inputs for the hybrid ARIMA-BPNN popularity model (Hybrid-POP).

EXPERIMENT AND EVALUATION

In this section, we conduct experiments on our forecasting method and other methods and compare them to find out what we can achieve by using the popularity of magazine contents in our adopted hybrid method for forecasting, as described in Section 3.

Experiment Set-Up

In this section, we describe our sales forecasting model utilizing ARIMA, Backpropagation Neural Networks (BPNNs), and the popularity indexes of magazine article titles. We implemented our hybrid forecasting model using sales data from a Chinese magazine categorized as a weekly magazine. The data set includes article titles from 133 weekly issues sold through stores from June 2009 to December 2011. We chose the 50 stores with the highest correlations of sales and popularity indexes of magazine issues. We used the first 80 weeks of sales for each of the top 50 stores as the training set and the remaining 53 weeks of sales as the testing set.

Extracting the words from the titles and headlines of magazine is part of the preprocessing. We used the Google search engine to derive popularity scores of the extracted words of titles for each issue during a specific time period. We used one month as a period time to determine popularity. Note that the store sales (the numbers of sold items) are normalized to derive the normalized numbers of sold items during the processing of various forecasting methods. We normalized the store sales and popularity scores by dividing the store sales over the maximum of all store sales and the popularity scores over the maximum of all popularity scores, respectively. The following equation shows how to normalize the store sale (the number of sold items) for each issue (weekly issue):

$$\text{Normalize}(\#\ \text{item}_t) = \frac{\#\ \text{item}_t}{\text{Max}(\#\ \text{item})}, \tag{5}$$

where # item$t$ is the number of sold items for issue t and Max(# item) is the maximum number of sold items in stores. The normalization of popularity scores is derived similarly.

Evaluation Metrics

The forecasting quality depends on the residuals of the actual number of sold items for each issue and the predicted number of items for that issue. There are many measurements to evaluate the residuals. We used the Root Mean Square Error (RMSE), which evaluates the average residuals for predicted sales (the numbers of sold items) as defined in the following:

$$\text{RMSE} = \sqrt{\frac{1}{N}\sum_{t=1}^{N}(\text{Sales}_t - \text{prediction}_t)^2}, \tag{6}$$

where N is the number of issues in the testing set, Sales$t$ is the actual number of sold items for issue t, and prediction$t$ is the predicted number of items for issue t by the forecasting method. The magazine issue is published weekly. We also used RMSE in the BPNN in the learning step. The network "learns" by adjusting the interconnections (called weights) between layers in the BPNN. Thus, the RMSE is an appropriate evaluation metric in this work for adjusting the weights in the BPNN and evaluating our hybrid method in comparison to

BPNN and ARIMA. We should note that RMSE could also be calculated based on the normalized values of Sales$t$ and prediction$t$ by using (5).

Methods Compared in the Experiment

In the forecasting field, many methods have been used and there is no definitive claim for the most accurate forecasting method for any data time series. Comparison is a way to see the more accurate forecasting method for our data set. We used the Autoregressive Integrated Moving Average (ARIMA) and the Backpropagation Neural Network (BPNN) without popularity on titles and headlines as benchmarks. Mean Root Square Error (MRSE) was used as a metric to estimate the improvement of the accuracy of our Backpropagation Neural Network with popularity (BPNN-POP) and our hybridization of ARIMA and BPNN-POP (Hybrid-POP) when comparing with other methods. We use multilayer perceptron function from WEKA 3.6.13 to implement BPNN with the following values: the learning rate is 0.1, the momentum is 0.2, decay is False, seed is 0, and training time is 500 epochs. The computational cost of BPNN for each epoch requires $O(N \times w)$ time, where N is the number of training samples and w is the number of weights in the neural network. For 500 epochs, the computational cost of BPNN is approximate to (N^2). The computational cost of ARIMA is linear time (N). The hybrid model (Hybrid-POP) used the historical number of sold items, popularity, and the predicted number of items from the ARIMA forecasting model as inputs. The computational cost of the hybrid model also depends on the BPNN model. Accordingly, the computational cost of the Hybrid-POP is (N^2).

Autoregressive Integrated Moving Average (ARIMA)

We used the number of sold items of the previous two issues to forecast the target issue using the ARIMA model. We assumed five different parameters for the ARIMA to identify the model. We randomly select 10 stores to conduct experiments on identifying the best parameters for the ARIMA model. Figure 6 shows the average RMSE for sample of our data set for each of the following: ARIMA(1, 0, 0), ARIMA(0, 0, 1), ARIMA(1, 0, 1), ARIMA(1, 1, 1), and ARIMA(2, 1, 1). Note that the RMSE of each store is calculated based on the normalized values of the actual numbers of sold items and predicted numbers of items. As seen in Figure 6, ARIMA(2, 1, 1) is more appropriate than the others. Therefore, we used it as one of our methods. We used the output of ARIMA(2, 1, 1) as an input for BPNN in our Hybrid-POP method to capture the linear and nonlinear patterns of our time data series for each issue of the magazine.

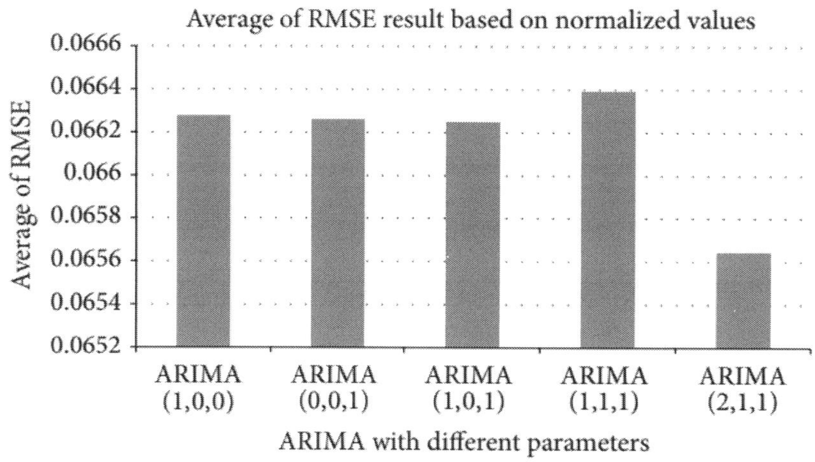

Figure 6: Average of RMSE (by normalized values) for ARIMA(p, i, q) with different values of parameters.

Backpropagation Neural Network without Popularity (BPNN)

The Backpropagation Neural Network was used as the forecasting model for nonlinear data. This is the typical forecasting method, which depends on historical number of sold items data. We used the number of sold items of the previous two issues of our target issue as input for the BPNN. We used the RMSE for measurement and for adjusting the interconnections. In this model, we used one hidden layer. After using the training set in the BPNN, the testing set was used to get the predicted values from two models.

Backpropagation Neural Network with Popularity (BPNN-POP)

In our proposed model of the Backpropagation Neural Network with popularity (BPNN-POP), we used three inputs; two inputs represented the number of sold items of the previous two issues and the third input represented the popularity of titles and headlines for the target issue, as demonstrated in Figure 4. In this model, we used one hidden layer. After using the training set in the BPNN, the testing set was used to get the predicted values from two models.

Hybrid ARIMA with BPNN-POP (Hybrid-POP)

Our proposed model adopted the hybrid model for forecasting sales. In the hybridization, the ARIMA was used to forecast number of items of the target issue by using the number of sold items of the previous two issues. Predicted numbers of items from the ARIMA were used as input for the BPNN-POP along with number of sold items from the previous two issues and the popularity of target issue, as shown in Figure 5. The patterns of the linear and the nonlinear data time series can be captured using this hybrid model.

Experiment Results

In the experiment, we implemented Hybrid-POP and BPNN-POP methods as our proposed models using popularity as the main input. Other methods, such as Autoregressive Integrated Moving Average, ARIMA(2, 1, 1) using historical sales data and BPNN with historical sales data without popularity, were used as benchmarks. Root Mean Square Error was used as an evaluation metric to compare the accuracy of each method. Figure 7 shows the RMSEs of 50 stores (horizontal axis) for different forecasting methods, where the RMSE of each store is calculated based on the actual numbers of sold items and predicted numbers of items. From the figure, the BPNNs were lower than for the ARIMA for most of the stores in our dataset. Some stores had lower RMSEs using the ARIMA. Due to the nature of data and its fluctuations, it is difficult to judge BPNN or ARIMA as fit models for our data. After using the BPNN-POP, the RMSEs became lower than the RMSEs of the BPNN and the ARIMA for the stores in our dataset. The RMSEs for Hybrid-POP were the lowest when compared to other methods. The forecasting accuracy was improved when we used historical number of sold items data, popularity, and the predicted number of items from the ARIMA forecasting model as inputs for our Hybrid-POP.

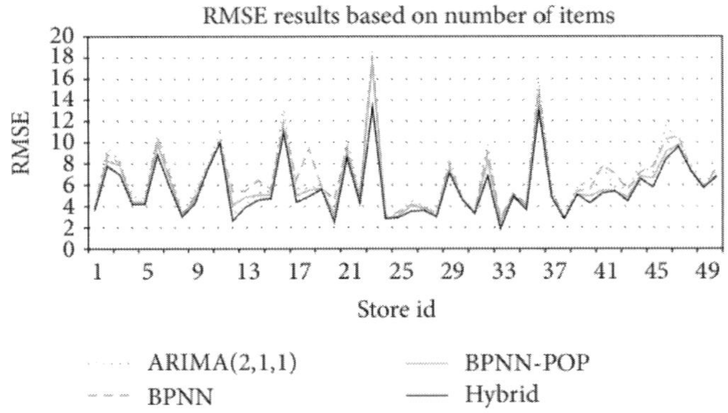

Figure 7: RMSE (by number of items) of 50 stores for ARIMA, BPNN-POP, and Hybrid-POP.

The Effects of Popularity

Figure 7 shows that using the popularity of magazine title words as an input for the BPNN-POP and Hybrid-POP helps to enhance forecasting accuracy by reducing the RMSE and making it lower than the ARIMA and BPNN. On the other hand, when ARIMA is used, the RMSEs for some stores in our dataset were lower than in the BPNN while others were higher, as shown in Figure 7. However, after using popularity as an input for BPNN-POP, the RMSEs became lower for all the stores. This implies that popularity enhances the accuracy of forecasting, and it indicates that attractive titles and headlines in magazines have an effect on buyer preferences for these publications. Therefore, the popularity of title words can be used to choose the most appropriate titles and headlines to increase sales and benefits.

The Effects of Using the Hybrid Approach

When using Root Mean Square Error as an evaluation metric, as we show in Figure 7, neither the BPNN nor ARIMA fits for all stores in our dataset, due to the nature of some of the data and fluctuations in data. Some stores had linear sales and others nonlinear. In predicting sales, the ARIMA is fit for stores which have linear sales, while neural networks are the best fit for nonlinear stores. The Hybrid-POP model combining the ARIMA and BPNN-POP was used to capture linear patterns and nonlinear patterns of sales for each store. The experiment results are shown in Figure 8. The results represent the average of RMSE for 50 stores in the test set, where the RMSE of each store is calculated based on the actual numbers of sold items and predicted numbers of items.

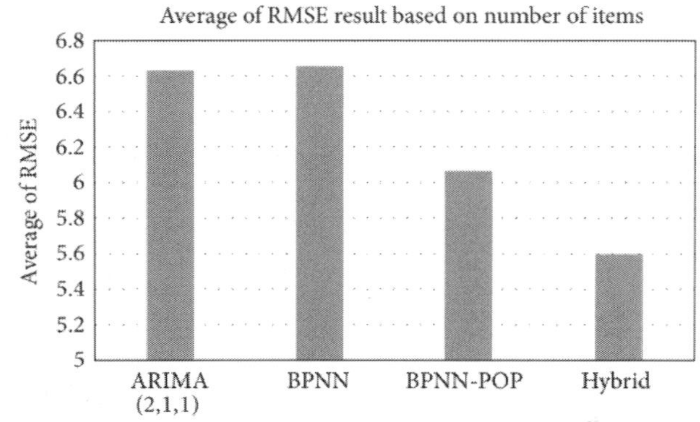

Figure 8: Average of RMSE (by number of items) for ARIMA(2, 1, 1), BPNN, BPNN-POP, and Hybrid-POP.

We note that the RMSE is calculated by considering the residuals of actual number of sold items for each issue and the predicted number of items for that issue, as defined in (6). The maximum number of actual weekly sales (sold items of an issue) of a store is 58. The difference in the average RMSE between BPNN-POP and Hybrid-POP is 0.466 based on the number of sold items. Accordingly, the difference is about 0.8% in percentage, which is important in improving the total sales of stores.

The Hybrid-POP performed better than the other forecasting methods in our experiment. This implies that the Hybrid-POP conducts and captures both linear and nonlinear patterns in our data, and it is more appropriate for our data. The Hybrid-POP model helps to overcome judgment on the behavior of data and uses popularity to improve forecasting.

DISCUSSION

As shown in Figure 8, using popularity of magazine contents makes the BPNN-POP more accurate and overcomes shortcomings of the traditional forecasting methods represented here by ARIMA and the BPNN without popularity. However, there are both linear and nonlinear sales in the stores, so neither model fits our data. The BPNN-POP using popularity enhanced the accuracy and was a better fit for our data than the ARIMA and BPNN.

The ARIMA model was used to capture the linear pattern in our dataset, and Backpropagation Neural Networks were used to capture the nonlinear pattern. For some stores, using the ARIMA model could be better than using the BPNN, or vice versa. We used the Hybrid-POP to improve the forecasting results by combining the ARIMA and BPNN-POP models to deal with the many potential influencing factors, such as sampling model uncertainty and structure changes. Real-world time series are rarely purely linear or nonlinear. Figure 8shows that our Hybrid-POP presents a superior and reliable alternative to conventional methods. When they are combined, our Hybrid-POP model is superior to both the ARIMA and BPNN in all points and is also better than our BPNN-POP.

CONCLUSION

In this paper, a novel hybrid neural network model is proposed for sales forecasting based on the popularity of article titles. In the publishing industry, the popularity of headlines and titles plays a main role in reader decisions to buy or not to buy. Our proposed hybrid BPNN model considers not only historical data but also the popularity of article titles. The information retrieval techniques and Google search engine were used to derive the popularity of article titles. Using content popularity as an input into the Backpropagation Neural Network has added value to the forecasting process and increased accuracy when compared to the conventional forecasting methods. Existing studies have not considered the effects of content popularity on sales. Moreover, our proposed hybrid model uses the prediction output of ARIMA as input for the BPNN and uses the BPNN for forecasting future sales. Combining the ARIMA and BPNN can utilize the advantages of both methods, thus enabling our proposed hybrid model to capture linear and nonlinear patterns in sales data. Our experimental results show that our proposed forecasting method outperforms conventional techniques which do not consider the popularity of title words. These results imply that our proposed hybrid BPNN model considers the popularity of article titles and prediction output of ARIMA can be a more effective approach for sales forecasting.

Magazine sales may be affected by the locations of stores. It is interesting to analyze the sales/locations of stores and the popularity indexes of magazine issues to find which area is positively correlated with content popularity. In our future work, we will classify the stores spatially and integrate our proposed models with the popularity indexes of magazines in particular areas to enhance sales forecasting.

REFERENCES

1. C. S. Bos, P. H. Franses, and M. Ooms, "Inflation, forecast intervals and long memory regression models,"International Journal of Forecasting, vol. 18, no. 2, pp. 243–264, 2002.
2. L. Ji and A. J. Peters, "Forecasting vegetation greenness with satellite and climate data," IEEE Geoscience and Remote Sensing Letters, vol. 1, no. 1, pp. 3–6, 2004.
3. A. D. Papalexopoulos and T. C. Hesterberg, "A regression-based approach to short-term system load forecasting," IEEE Transactions on Power Systems, vol. 5, no. 4, pp. 1535–1547, 1990. ·
4. C. C. Holt, "Author's retrospective on 'Forecasting seasonals and trends by exponentially weighted moving averages'," International Journal of Forecasting, vol. 20, no. 1, pp. 11–13, 2004. ·
5. R.H.Jones,"MaximumlikelihoodfittingofARMAmodels to time series with missing observations,"Technometrics, vol. 22, no. 3, pp. 389–395, 1980.
6. J. H. Park, Y. M. Park, and K. Y. Lee, "Composite modeling for adaptive short-term load forecasting,"IEEE Transactions on Power Systems, vol. 6, no. 2, pp. 450–457, 1991.
7. R. D. Snyder, A. B. Koehler, R. J. Hyndman, and J. K. Ord, "Exponential smoothing models: means and variances for lead-time demand," European Journal of Operational Research, vol. 158, no. 2, pp. 444–455, 2004. ·
8. D. Olson and C. Mossman, "Neural network forecasts of Canadian stock returns using accounting ratios," International Journal of Forecasting, vol. 19, no. 3, pp. 453–465, 2003.
9. S. M. Rabiee and H. Baseri, "Prediction of the setting properties of calcium phosphate bone cement,"Computational Intelligence and Neuroscience, vol. 2012, Article ID 809235, 8 pages, 2012.
10. S. Thomassey and M. Happiette, "A neural clustering and classification system for sales forecasting of new apparel items," Applied Soft Computing, vol. 7, no. 4, pp. 1177–1187, 2007.
11. H. Yoo, "Short term load forecasting using a self-supervised adaptive neural network," IEEE Transactions on Power Systems, vol. 14, no. 2, pp. 779–784, 1999.
12. G. P. Zhang and M. Qi, "Neural network forecasting for seasonal and trend time series," European Journal of Operational Research, vol. 160, no. 2, pp. 501–514, 2005. ·
13. T. Chen and M.-J. J. Wang, "Forecasting methods using fuzzy concepts," Fuzzy Sets and Systems, vol. 105, no. 3, pp. 339–352, 1999.
14. A. Fiordaliso, "A nonlinear forecasts combination method based on Takagi-Sugeno fuzzy systems,"International Journal of Forecasting, vol. 14, no. 3, pp. 367–379, 1998.
15. P. A. Mastorocostas, J. B. Theocharis, and V. S. Petridis, "A constrained orthogonal least-squares method for generating TSK fuzzy models: application to short-term load forecasting," Fuzzy Sets and Systems, vol. 118, no. 2, pp. 215–233, 2001.
16. P. G. Zhang, "Time series forecasting using a hybrid ARIMA and neural network model,"Neurocomputing, vol. 50, pp. 159–175, 2003.
17. S. Amornwattana, D. Enke, and C. H. Dagli, "A hybrid option pricing model using a neural network for estimating volatility," International Journal of General Systems, vol. 36, no. 5, pp. 558–573, 2007.
18. C.-H. Huang, C.-K. Feng, H.-H. Hsu, N. C. Tang, and T. K. Shih, "A collaborative virtual world application to the hyper-interaction platform," Journal of Internet Technology, vol. 8, no. 4, pp. 493–503, 2007.
19. C.-Y. Chen, J. R.-C. Hsu, M.-H. Cheng, and C.-W. Chen, "Experiments on mixing and dissipation in internal solitary waves over two triangular obstacles," Environmental Fluid Mechanics, vol. 8, no. 3, pp. 199–214, 2008.
20. D. E. Rumelhart, G. E. Hinton, and J. R. Williams, "Learning representations by back-propagating errors," Nature, vol. 323, pp. 533–536, 1986.
21. H. A. Omar and D.-R. Liu, "Enhancing sales forecasting by using neuro networks and the popularity of magazine

article titles," in Proceedings of the 6th International Conference on Genetic and Evolutionary Computing (ICGEC '12), pp. 577–580, IEEE, Kitakushu, Japan, August 2012.

22. A. Jain and A. M. Kumar, "Hybrid neural network models for hydrologic time series forecasting," Applied Soft Computing, vol. 7, no. 2, pp. 585–592, 2007.

23. H. Pan, C. Tilakaratne, and J. Yearwood, "Predicting Australian stock market index using neural networks exploiting dynamical swings and intermarket influences," Journal of Research and Practice in Information Technology, vol. 37, no. 1, pp. 43–54, 2005.

24. V. Gosasang, W. Chandraprakaikul, and S. Kiattisin, "A comparison of traditional and neural networks forecasting techniques for container throughput at bangkok port," The Asian Journal of Shipping and Logistics, vol. 27, no. 3, pp. 463–482, 2011.

25. C. Mitrea, C. Lee, and Z. Wu, "A comparison between neural networks and traditional forecasting methods: a case study," International Journal of Engineering Business Management, vol. 1, no. 2, pp. 19–24, 2009.

26. C.-S. Ong, J.-J. Huang, and G.-H. Tzeng, "Model identification of ARIMA family using genetic algorithms," Applied Mathematics and Computation, vol. 164, no. 3, pp. 885–912, 2005.

27. D.-Y. Chiu, T.-S. Chen, and Y.-C. Pan, "Using improved BPN/Cauchy machine and genetic algorithms to build an efficient neural network and to forecast Taiwanese electronic stock indexes," Journal of Financial Studies, vol. 16, no. 4, p. 213, 2008.

28. D.-Y. Chiu and C.-C. Lin, "Exploring internal mechanism of warrant in financial market with a hybrid approach," Expert Systems with Applications, vol. 35, no. 3, pp. 1237–1245, 2008.

29. H. M. El-Bakry and Q. Zhao, "Fast normalized neural processors for pattern detection based on cross correlation implemented in the frequency domain," Journal of Research and Practice in Information Technology, vol. 38, no. 2, pp. 151–170, 2006.

30. B. Yuan and W. Liu, "Measure oriented training: a targeted approach to imbalanced classification problems," Frontiers in Computer Science, vol. 6, no. 5, pp. 489–497, 2012.

31. Z. Bosnić and I. Kononenko, "An overview of advances in reliability estimation of individual predictions in machine learning," Intelligent Data Analysis, vol. 13, no. 2, pp. 385–401, 2009.

32. R. S. Govindaraju, "Artificial neural networks in hydrology. I: preliminary concepts," Journal of Hydrologic Engineering, vol. 5, no. 2, pp. 115–123, 2000.

33. S. Kiartzis, A. Kehagias, A. Bakirtzis, and V. Petridis, "Short term load forecasting using a Bayesian combination method," International Journal of Electrical Power and Energy Systems, vol. 19, no. 3, pp. 171–177, 1997.

34. V. Petridis and A. Kehagias, Predictive Modular Neural Networks: Applications to Time Series, Springer Science & Business Media, 2012.

35. P. Areekul, T. Senjyu, H. Toyama, and A. Yona, "A hybrid ARIMA and neural network model for short-term price forecasting in deregulated market," IEEE Transactions on Power Systems, vol. 25, no. 1, pp. 524–530, 2010.

36. C. W. Granger, "Long memory relationships and the aggregation of dynamic models," Journal of Econometrics, vol. 14, no. 2, pp. 227–238, 1980.

37. B. Gep, G. M. Jenkins, and G. C. Reinsel, Time Series Analysis: Forecasting and Control, Holden-Dag, Oakland, Calif, USA, 1976.

38. X. Zhang, Y. Liu, M. Yang, T. Zhang, A. A. Young, and X. Li, "Comparative study of four time series methods in forecasting typhoid fever incidence in China," PLoS ONE, vol. 8, no. 5, Article ID e63116, 2013.

CHAPTER 6

METHOD TO IMPROVE AIRBORNE POLLUTION FORECASTING BY USING ANT COLONY OPTIMIZATION AND NEURO-FUZZY ALGORITHMS

Elizabeth Martinez-Zeron, Marco A. Aceves-Fernandez, Efren Gorrostieta-Hurtado, Artemio Sotomayor-Olmedo, and Juan Manuel Ramos-Arreguín

Keywords: Neuro-Fuzzy models, Ant Colony Optimization, Airborne Pollution

INTRODUCTION

In recent years, the environment has been affected by the presence of particulate pollutants such as the Ozone (O_3), NO_2 nitrogen oxide, carbon monoxide CO, sulfur dioxide (SO_2) and particulate matter less than 10 microns PM_{10} (≤ 10 microns) and Particles less than 2.5 micrometers $PM_{2.5}$(≤ 2.5 microns) [1] . For this reason, pollution monitoring has been necessary for large cities with high concentration of population and industries.

During several years the air quality in Mexico City for prevention of toxicity levels in health and the environment have been observed and evaluated [1] .

Measures were performed to obtain information efficiency and reliability of the air quality. Some of these contributions consists in predicting pollution levels such as the work of Cortina [2] , who forecast levels of ozone pollution in the city of Guanajuato in Mexico by using neural networks, Aceves [3] takes modeling variables between relative humidity and temperature level of contamination. Sotomayor [4] uses support vector machines and kernel functions particulate ozone (O_3), (PM_{10}) and nitrogen dioxide in Mexico City.

Patterns of pollution levels do not show linear behavior [3] [4] whereby a pattern is generated in clusters can be represented by several linear functions, this for ease of interpretation. In this case study, Fuzzy C means is used to generate clusters which have similar characteristics, subsequently establish the cluster centers as membership functions in a fuzzy system [3] , Also, neuro-fuzzy inference system (ANFIS) with multiple inputs and one output ("Multiple-Inputs-Single-Output" or MISO) is used to approximate nonlinear functions [5] [6] . Subsequently, three models are generated by the above steps after obtaining improved by using the algorithm of ant colony optimization (ACO) prediction. This methodology shows that it is possible to improve existing algorithms to predict the levels of particulate pollutants, in this case study in Mexico City.

Fuzzy inference methods

A Fuzzy Inference System (FIS) is basically a logic that allows intermediate values defined between conventional evaluations as Yes/No, True/False, etc.

A FIS is the main unit of a fuzzy logic system, the part where the decision is made, by constructing appropriate rules based on the theory of fuzzy sets. The rules are constructed linguistically (IF-THEN-) having the general form of "If A Then B" where A and B are (collections of) propositions containing linguistic variables linked by connectors (AND, OR) to make the correct decision-making [7] .

A fuzzy inference system consists of 5 blocks as described in Figure 1.

Citation: Martinez-Zeron, E. , Aceves-Fernandez, M. , Gorrostieta-Hurtado, E. , Sotomayor-Olmedo, A. and Ramos-Arreguín, J. (2014) Method to Improve Airborne Pollution Forecasting by Using Ant Colony Optimization and Neuro-Fuzzy Algorithms. International Journal of Intelligence Science, 4, 81-90. doi: 10.4236/ijis.2014.44010.

Fuzzy inference system operates as follows: The input data are treated by a method of fuzzification then the Fuzzy rules are formed and the already fuzzyfied input data are analyzed. Defuzzification method is used to convert the value obtained after analysis with fuzzy rules to obtain an output value applicable to the real world.

The steps taken by fuzzy reasoning, i.e. inference operations on rules IF - THEN performing the FIS, are:

- Compare the input variables with the membership functions for the linguistic value of each part, this process is called fuzzyfication.
- Combine by an operator ($t-$norm, usually multiplication or minimum) the membership values to obtain the weight of each rule.
- Add the resulting output to produce a crisp, this step is called defuzzification.

A fuzzy rule has a general structure in a fuzzy model as shown on equation (1):

$$\text{If } x \text{ is } A \text{ and } y \text{ is } B \text{ THEN } z = f(x,y) \tag{1}$$

where A, B fuzzy sets in the previous data sets are, $z = f(x,y)$ is a consequent function. Usually $f(x,y)$ is polynomial in the input variables x and y, the output of the system with a fuzzy region specified by the predecessors of the rule.

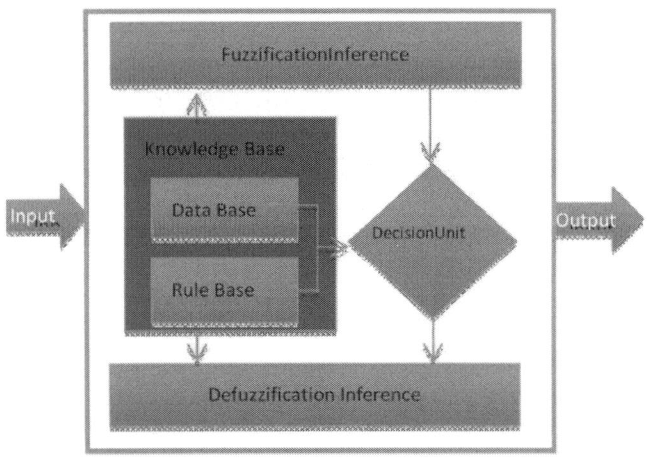

Figure 1: Block Diagram of a Generic Fuzzy inference system.

A typical rule in FIS model has the form as shown in equation (2) [8] :

$$\textbf{IF Input 1} = x \textbf{ AND Input 2} = y, \textbf{THEN Output is } z = ax + by + c \tag{2}$$

The final output of the FIS system is the weighted average of all the outputs of the rules:

$$\text{Final Ouput} = \frac{\sum_{i=1}^{N} w_i z_i}{\sum_{i=1}^{N} w_i} \tag{3}$$

The Takagi-Sugeno model or TSK model proposed in 1985 [8] [9] , is widely used in the theoretical analysis, application control and Fuzzy Modeling.

A Fuzzy system needs a precedent and consequent to express a logical connection between the input and output data used as a basis to produce the desired behavior of the system.

Clustering

Clustering is the grouping of data based on certain criteria that clusters have similar properties and characteristics, clusters are based mainly on the distance interpreted as similarity [10] .

Fuzzy C-means

Fuzzy C-Means (FCM) is a clustering method which allows a data to belong in one or more clusters, this method developed by Dunn [11] and improved by Bezdek [10] , is often used for pattern recognition, it is an iterative optimization algorithm that minimizes the cost function given by:

$$J = \sum_{k=1}^{n} \sum_{i=1}^{c} \mu_{ik}^{m} \left\| x_k - v_i \right\|^2 \tag{4}$$

where n is the number of data, c is the number of clusters, x_k is the kth data point, v_i is the center of the ith cluster, μ_{ik} is the degree of membership of the kth data in the ith cluster, m is any real number greater than 1, (typically $m = 2$) [10] . The degree of membership μ_{ik} is defined by:

$$\mu_{ik} = \frac{1}{\sum_{j=1}^{c} \left(\frac{\left\| x_k - v_i \right\|}{\left\| x_k - v_j \right\|} \right)^{2/(m-1)}} \tag{5}$$

Starting with the desired number of cluster c and an initial randomly chosen center for each cluster v_i, $v_i = 1, 2, 3, L, c$, FCM will converge in a solution to v_i which represents both a local minimum or a point function cost [10] . This clustering method uses fuzzy partition such that each point can belong to several clusters with different membership values between 0 and 1. Fuzzy c-means, has predefined parameters such the weight of the exponent m and the number of clusters.

To measure the effect of clustering algorithm, validity and accuracy are required. Validity: If the algorithm can find all internal type in the data collected. Truth: If the algorithm can set the same kind of data to the same group, different types of data at different clusters. We define the rate of decline of Clustering (C_r) to measure the effect of clustering [7] :

$$C_r = \frac{m_{\text{best}}}{m_{\text{result}}} \times 100 \tag{6}$$

m_{best} is best clustering number and m_{result} is the actual number of cluster after clustering.

$$v_i = \frac{\sum_{x \in X} (\mu_C(x))^m}{\sum_{x \in X}^{n} (\mu_C(x))^m}, \quad 1 \le i \le k \tag{7}$$

After determining the number of clusters, the value of m, and the stopping criterion the FCM algorithm performs two steps, first calculates the membership functions using equation (5), as a second step updates the proto types using equation (7) the two steps are repeated iteratively to achieve the stability criterion, in which the change of the output values by the previous equations is minimal. The Figure 2 shows an example FCM function.

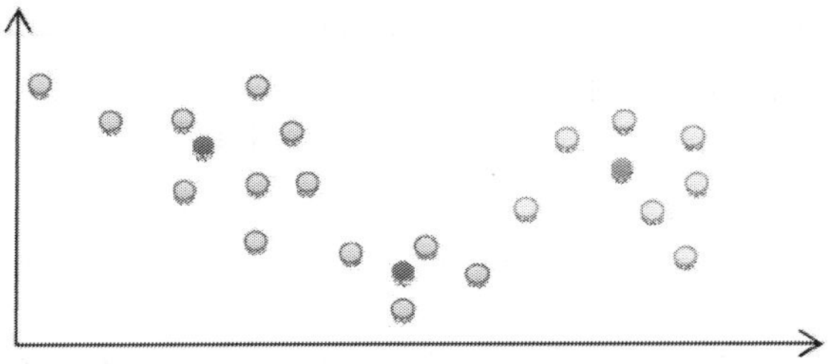

Figure 2: Example of Fuzzy C-Means showing three different clusters with a set of data points each, and their centroids.

The Adaptive Neuro-Fuzzy Inference System (ANFIS)

This method is a type of neural network that is based on a method for the process of fuzzy modeling to learn information about a data set by generating fuzzy rules, this is called neuro-fuzzy, this architecture was proposed by Jang in 1993 [12] . Has a network structure with directional links connecting a number of nodes. Each node has a function with adjustable or fixed parameters.

The classical ANFIS consists of 5 layers with specific tasks as show in Figure 3 [13] .

First Layer (Layer 1). Layer one is performed the input fuzzification. That is, each entry will set a value of belonging that only covers the total of the input variables to be treated [13] . This is expressed in mathematical terms as follows:

$$\mathrm{Out}_{ij}^{(1)} = \mu_j\left(\mathrm{In}_i^{(1)}\right) \tag{8}$$

While:

$\mathrm{Out}_{ij}^{(1)}$ is the layer 1 node's output which corresponds to the j-th linguistic term of the i-th input variable. The membership is:

$$\mu_j = \frac{1}{1+\left|\frac{x_i - c_{ij}}{a_{ij}}\right|^{bo}}, \quad i = 1,\cdots,\mathrm{NumInVars},\ j = 1,\cdots,\mathrm{NumIntTer} \tag{9}$$

While the parameters $\left(a_{ij}, b_{ij}, c_{ij}\right)$ are referred to as premise parameters or non-linear parameters and they adjust the shape and the location of the membership function.

Second Layer (Layer 2 from Figure 3). Executes the fuzzy AND of the antecedent part of the fuzzy rules. This results to each node's output being the product of all of its inputs (every input term node that is connected to that rule node) [14] :

$$\mathrm{Out}_k^{(2)} = w_k = \prod_{i=1}^{N_{\mathrm{Inputs}}} \mathrm{Out}_{ij}^{(1)}, \tag{10}$$

For all the terms nodes j connected to the k-th the rule node, $k = 1,\cdots,\mathrm{NumRules}$

Third layer (Layer 3 from figure 3). Normalizes the membership functions (MFs).

The output of the k-th node is the firing strength of each rule divided by the total sum of the activation values of all the fuzzy rules. This results in the normalization of the activation value for each fuzzy rule. This operation is simply written as:

$$\mathrm{Out}_k^{(3)} = \overline{w_k} = \frac{\mathrm{Out}_k^{(2)}}{\sum_{m=1}^{N_{\mathrm{Rules}}} \mathrm{Out}_m^{(2)}}, \quad k = 1,\cdots,\mathrm{NumRules} \tag{11}$$

Fourth layer (Layer 4 from figure 3) executes the consequent part of the fuzzy rules. Each node k in this layer is accompanied by a set of adjustable parameters $a_{1k},\ a_{2k},\ \cdots,\ a_{N_{\mathrm{Inputs}}k},\ a_{0k}$ and implements the linear function:

$$\mathrm{Out}_k^{(4)} = \overline{w_k} f_k = \overline{w_k}\left(a_{1k}\mathrm{In}_1^{(1)} + a_{2k}\mathrm{In}_2^{(1)} + \cdots + a_{N_{\mathrm{Inputs}}k}\mathrm{In}_{N_{\mathrm{Inputs}}k}^{(1)} + a_{0k}\right), \quad k = 1,\cdots,\mathrm{NumRules} \tag{12}$$

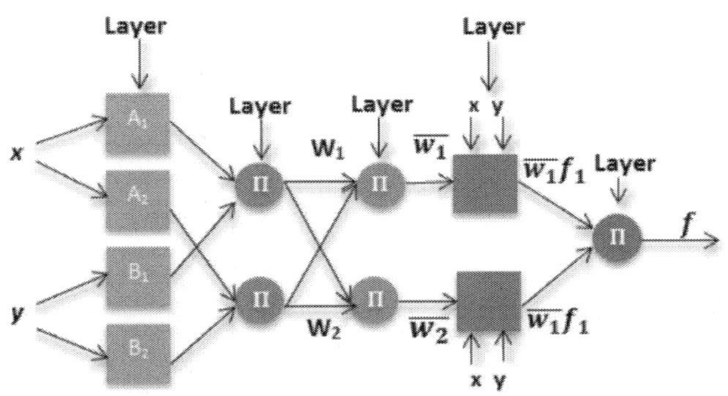

Figure 3: ANFIS architecture.

The weight w_k is the normalized activation value of the k-th rule, calculated by from equation (7). Those parameters are called consequent parameters or linear parameters of the ANFIS system and are adjusted by the RLS algorithm.

Layer 5 computes the output of fuzzy system by summing up the outputs of layer fourth.

$$\mathrm{Out}^{(5)} = \sum_{k=1}^{N_{\mathrm{Rules}}} \mathrm{Out}_k^{(4)} = \sum_{k=1}^{N_{\mathrm{Rules}}} \overline{w_k} f_k = \frac{\sum_{k=1}^{N_{\mathrm{Rules}}} w_k f_k}{\sum_{k=1}^{N_{\mathrm{Rules}}} w_k} \tag{13}$$

Optimization

The optimization algorithm is a numerical method which finds a value $xi \in Rn$, where Rn is an n-dimen- sional search space, which minimizes or maximizes the function optimization $J(x)$; through the systematic selection of values of the variable xi using some restrictions. Here, $J(x)$ is called the objective function. A feasible solution that minimizes or maximizes the objective function is called an optimal solution [15] .

As mentioned in [15] the techniques used for providing solution to complex combinatorial optimization problems have evolved from constructive methods to local search methods and finally to population-based algorithms. These techniques are classified as: Extensive and not exhaustive. These non-analytical computational techniques are based, and the classification is performed based on the solution space.

Exhaustive optimization techniques are those that guarantee always find the optimal (maximum or minimum) walking in the worst case the whole solution space (which can be considerably large) [16] .

Non-exhaustive techniques rely on getting good enough solutions without exceeding the time constraints established or memory. Solutions are based on steps taken to find new solutions that approximate the optimal solution more, increasing quality.

Some of the best known are:

- Genetic Algorithms
- Taboo search
- Ant Colony Optimization
- Greedy Randomized Adaptive Search Procedure (GRASP).
- Scatter Search
- Simulated Annealing

Ants Colony Optimization

The ant colony optimization (ACO) is a bio-inspired technique of classification based on the external behavior of a real ant colony when foraging. This algorithm was created in 1992 by Dorigo [17] .

The ACO algorithm solves complex problems of combinatorial optimization in various fields of engineering, commerce, industry, among others. When a problem does not have a polynomial equation that describes it belongs to the NP-hard problems. The results provided by ACO can be approximated to address the combinatorial optimization problemsas shown in the Figure 4. [18] .

The probability of an ant k to choose the next node, where x is the current state and y is the next state we have:

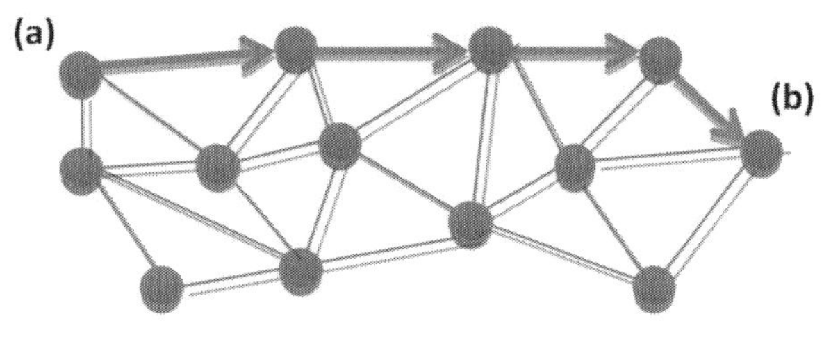

Figure 4: Example of ACO where ants choose the shortest path from node 1 to node 2.

$$p_{xy}^{k}=\frac{(\tau_{xy}^{\alpha})(\eta_{xy}^{\beta})}{\sum(\tau_{xy}^{\alpha})(\eta_{xy}^{\beta})} \qquad (14)$$

where:

η_{xy} is the level of convenience that has a transition state, $\frac{1}{d_{xy}}$ d_{xy} is the distance.

τ_{ij} is the trace levels, or that the amount of pheromone which will be deposited in a state of transition.

β is a parameter that controls the influence of η_{xy}.

α is a parameter that controls the influence of τ_{xy}.

Updated Trail

Pheromone must be updated because this changes which followed the iterations by offering increased likelihood based on the accumulated experience [19] .

In this case the level of pheromone raises based on the best solution path according to equation (14)

$$\tau_{ij}=(1-\rho)\tau_{ij}+\Delta\tau_{ij} \qquad (15)$$

where: $\rho\in(0,1]$ It is the persistence factor trail

$$\Delta\tau_{ij}=\sum_{k=1}^{\text{NrosAnts}}\Delta\tau_{ij} \qquad (16)$$

Accumulating trace is proportional to the quality of solutions.

$$\Delta\tau_{ij}=\begin{cases}\frac{1}{L_k}, & \text{if ant } k \text{ used edge } p_i, p_j;\\ 0, & \text{otherwise.}\end{cases} \qquad (17)$$

L_k Represents the objective value of the solution k (in the denominator for minimization problems).

Every time an ant travels a node applies the rule:

$$t_{ij}\leftarrow(1-\varphi)\times t_{ij}+t_0 \qquad (18)$$

$\varphi\in(0,1]$ Decrement pheromone parameter.

The stop condition

This process is iterative until it stops for compliance with established criteria

METHODOLOGY

In Figure 5, the environmental monitoring map shown in Mexico City, in this study we only evidence in the northwest area of the spring season.

The list of the sites used in this contribution is shown on figure 5, whilst the proposed methodology for this contribution is shown in the figure 6.

The monitoring stations used for this case study were chosen due to data availability and specific industrial or polluted areas.

Since obtaining data from such stations is filtered data, i.e., data values are complete and validated readings are sought.

Figure 5: Monitored areas.

The data are arranged in time series along the day; hence the clustering is performed to generate the characteristics of groups depending on pollution levels. These are grouped according through the fuzzy c means algorithm, which generates fuzzy clusters, based on a center that iteratively changes to accommodate more data groups. This provides greater robustness for modeling. Data modeling is performed using a fuzzy logic system, wherein each generated center is interpreted as fuzzy rules language.

The fuzzy system is improved with training data, which in this case, the training data are data from a previous year validated dataset. The training is through the use of neuro-fuzzy system AN-FIS which generates a more robust data modeling system.

The training is carried out using of neuro-fuzzy system ANFIS which generates a more robust data modeling system.

Three models for the prediction of air quality are generated; these models are subject to the ant colony optimization algorithm to improve the prediction closer to an outcome more accurately. Such three models along with the real measured data and its corresponding prediction are shown onFigure 7.

The mean square error for each model generated with neuro-fuzzy and neuro-fuzzy with ACO to measure the difference between the estimated and the model.

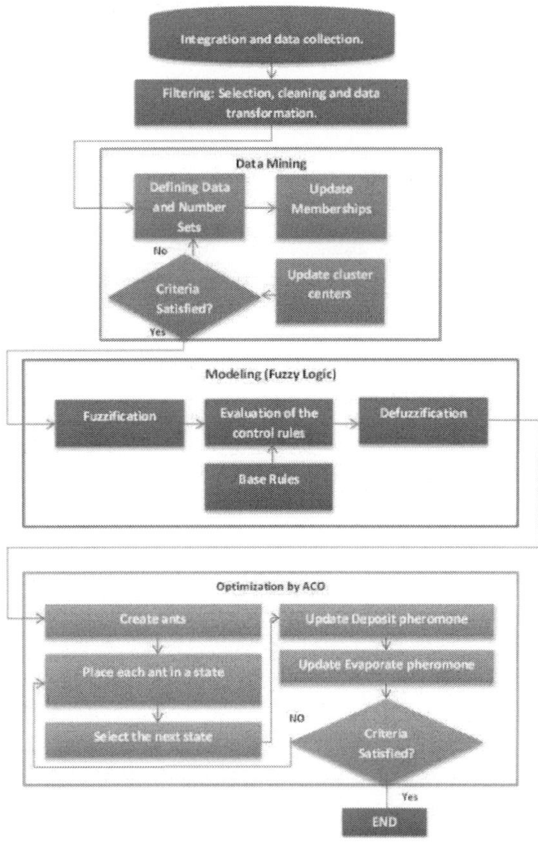

Figure 6: Proposed methodology.

RESULTS AND DISCUSSION

The models are created using Fuzzy Logic where the rules are formed by clustering, the ANFIS to improve each model and make each one more accurate and the ACO algorithm use these three models to improve the forecast having different options base on the three previous models. The models are named Mod 2 Mod 1 and Mod 3, respectively. These models are generated based on the characteristics of the stations, i.e. stations show greater similarity between their measurements generate a model.

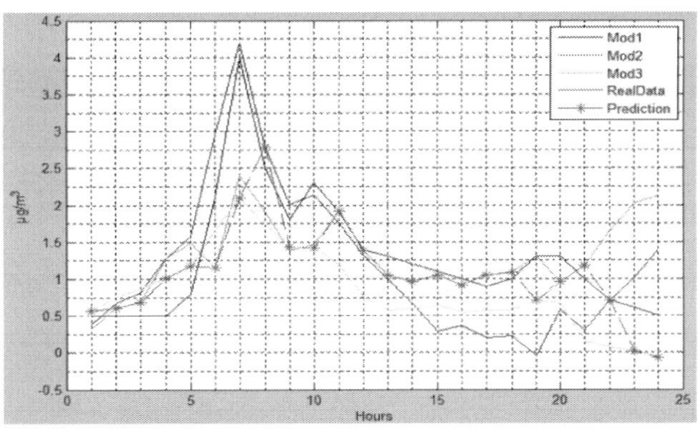

Figure 7: Model selection by ACO.

The results are shown on table 1 and table 2. CO is sensed to the northwest, with three models generated based on the area in 2009, and data validation are the stations belonging to the same area but in 2010. Likewise the table 2 is showing the models of Ozone (O_3). In the following tables the mean square error, it can be seen that is closer to the real value, the prediction of stations Station 1, Station 2, Station 3 and Station 4 based Mod 1, Mod 2 and Mod 3 models. The station in which there was no good approximation was at Station 1.

Table 1: Results of spring in northwestern federal district with CO pollutant.

	Station 1	Station 2	Station 3	Station 4
Mod 1	0.845	0.431	0.678	0.652
Mod 2	1.732	0.591	0.572	0.890
Mod 3	0.97	2.540	1.041	0.860
Mod ACO	0.882	0.373	0.559	0.594

Table 2: Results of spring in northwestern federal district with O_3pollutant.

	Station 1	Station 2	Station 3	Station 4
Mod 1	0.0067	0.0143	0.0116	0.0103
Mod 2	0.0193	0.0124	0.0283	0.0179
Mod 3	0.0078	0.0213	0.0407	0.0718
Mod ACO	0.0074	0.0100	0.0103	0.0117

Figure 7 shows how the algorithm is based on the nearest location from the current node to the next node following the ACO algorithm as shown on equations (14)-(16) and the methodology shown on figure 6. The influence of the pheromone that can choose the model that is closest to the actual data, likewise considering also the shortest distance.

The figure 7 shows the comparison between the models created by the trained logic system with ANFIS and the ACO model. This to appreciate the difference between the accuracy for each model generated with neuro- fuzzy and neuro-fuzzy improved with ACO.

CONCLUSIONS

The algorithms based on swarm intelligence are feasible for solving problems different than the typical machine learning methods. It has shown that a combination of modeling and optimization methods may be used to improve the prediction for this type of non-linear problem. Such combination of methods showed that systems working cooperatively is well complemented and integrated to generate a task system.

For these reasons ACO is an algorithm that provides an improvement in the prediction of contamination if used properly. ACO prediction has a point of view on the combinatorial type issue, and thus, the use of this algorithm improves the contaminants prediction by making the shortest search and the use of pheromone provides a best approximation to real data.

ACKNOWLEDGEMENTS

Elizabeth Martinez-Zeron, Marco A. Aceves-Fernandez, Efren Gorrostieta-Hurtado, Artemio Sotomayor-Olmedo, Juan Manuel Ramos-Arreguín This work was made possible through funding provided by the National Council of Science and Technology CONACYT.

REFERENCES

1. http://www.calidadaire.df.gob.mx/calidadaire/index.php?opcion=4&opcionrecursostecnicos=3
2. Cortina. M. (2012) Aplicación de inteligencia artificial a la predicción de contaminantes atmosféricos. Tesis Doctoral, E.T.S.I. Telecomunicación (UPM).
3. Aceves-Fernández, M.A., Sotomayor-Olmedo, A., Gorrostieta-Hurtado, E., Pedraza-Ortega, J.C., Tovar-Arriaga, S. and Ramos-Arreguin, J.M. (2011) Performance Assessment of Fuzzy Clustering Models Applied to Urban Airborne Pollution. 2011 21st International Conference on Electrical Communications and Computers (CONIELECOMP), San Andres Cholula, 28 February-2 March 2011, 212-216.
4. Sotomayor-Olmedo, A., Aceves-Fernández, M.A., Gorrostieta-Hurtado, E., Pedraza-Ortega, C., Ramos-Arreguín, J.M. and Vargas-Soto, J.E. (2013) Forecast Urban Air Pollution in Mexico City by Using Support Vector Machines: A Kernel Performance Approach. International Journal of Intelligence Science, 3, 126-135. http://dx.doi.org/10.4236/ijis.2013.33014
5. (2005) Adaptive Neuro-Fuzzy Inference Systems (ANFIS). In: Nedjah, N. and de Macedo Mourelle, L., Eds., Fuzzy Systems Engineering: Theory and Practice. Vol. 181, Springer, Rio de Janeiro, 53-83.
6. Adaptive Neuro-Fuzzy Inference Systems (ANFIS) Library for Simulink Ilias S. Konsoulas M.Sc., CEng, MIET.
7. Aceves-Fernandez, M.A., Sotomayor-Olmedo, A., Gorrostieta-Hurtado, E., Pedraza-Ortega, J.C., Ramos-Arreguín, J.M, Canchola-Magdaleno, S. and Vargas-Soto, E. (2011) Advances in Airborne Pollution Forecasting Using Soft Computing Techniques. In: Popovic, D., Ed., Air Quality: Models and Applications, INTECH Publisher, Querétaro, 1-14.http://dx.doi.org/10.5772/16273
8. Sugeno, M. and Kang, G.T. (1988) Structure Identification of Fuzzy Model. Fuzzy Sets and Systems, 28, 15-33. http://dx.doi.org/10.1016/0165-0114(88)90113-3
9. Takagi, T. and Sugeno, M. (1985) Fuzzy Identification of Systems and Its Application to Modeling and Control. IEEE Transactions on Systems, Man and Cybernetics, SMC-15, 116-132.
10. Bezdek, J.C. (1981) Pattern Recognition with Fuzzy Objective Function Algoritms. Plenum Press, New York. http://dx.doi.org/10.1007/978-1-4757-0450-1
11. Dunn, J.C. (1973) A Fuzzy Relative of the ISODATA Process and Its Use in Detecting Compact Well-Separated Clusters. Journal of Cybernetics, 3, 32-57. http://dx.doi.org/10.1080/01969727308546046
12. Jang, J.S.R. (1993) ANFIS: Adaptive-Network-Based Fuzzy Inference System. IEEE Transactions on Systems, Man and Cybernetics, 23, 665-685.
13. Ghanbari, A., Abbasian-Naghneh, S. and Hadavandi, E. (2011) An Intelligent Load Forecasting Expert System by Integration of Ant Colony Optimization, Genetic Algorithms and Fuzzy Logic. 2011 IEEE Symposium on Computational Intelligence and Data Mining (CIDM), Paris, 11-15 April 2011, 246-251.
14. Adaptive Neuro-Fuzzy Inference Systems (ANFIS) Library for Simulink
15. Muñoz, M., López, J. and Caicedos, E. (2008) Inteligencia de enjambres: Sociedades para la solución de problemas (una revisión). Ingeniería e Investigación, 28, 119-130.
16. Carretero, J.C.O., Cánovas, D.G. and Pereira, F.D.Q.

(2008) Técnicas Heurísticas para Problemas de Diseño en Telecomunicaciones.

17. Dorigo, M. (1992) Optimization, Learning and Natural Algorithms. Ph.D. Thesis, Politecnico di Milano, Italian.

18. Calixto, C.A.C. (2005) Implementacion En Hidroinformática De Un Método De Optimización Matemática Basado En La Colonia De Hormigas. Tesis no publicada, Pontificia Universidad Javeriana, Bogota, Colombia.

19. Kole, A., Chakrabarti, P. and Bhattacharyya, S. (2013) An Ant Colony Optimization Algorithm for Uncapacitated Facility Location Problem.

CHAPTER 7

USING ARTIFICIAL NEURAL NETWORK MODELING IN FORECASTING REVENUE

Itedal Sabri Hashim Bahia

Keywords: ANN, Regression Analysis, Forecasting Revenue, National Insurance Company

INTRODUCTION

The insurance is a strategic sector between other economic sectors, it provides an economic protection to the human and material resources and it acts as a shield protects the national economy against financial crises. The insurance plays a key role in the growth and stability of various economic sectors and contributes effectively in achieving the objectives of the economic development plans due to the financial weight that this sector occupying driven by the outstanding role, and that the insurance companies play in compiling the national savings which requires a high financial skills from the insurance companies to ensure its continuation in the market and to achieve a high level of profits through meeting their obligations towards policyholders rights.

There is no doubt that the developments in the insurance sector and the expected changes in the next era enforce to deploy new analysis methods to monitor the financial work of the insurance companies especially the finance and investment. Therefore the financial analysis adopts a great importance in various areas of economic activities and this importance is increasing particularly in the banking sector and insurance entities that came from the nature of the banks and insurance companies works which is related to money collections from the depositors and policyholders.

The importance of financial analysis is not only because it represents a tool to assess performance and management's efficiency, but it also for its necessity in the financial planning processes.

The financial analysis methods aim to identify the extent of the outcome that resulted from applying the legal policies and implementing the decisions in the companies and the ability of these companies to fulfill their obligations towards the policyholders, as well as to assist and enable the financial supervisors to monitor the policies implementation of the insurance companies, they also aim to help the investor in identifying the activity and the finance solvency of these companies.

In order to forecast problems more accurately in management, an Artificial Neural Network (ANN) model has been applied in many varieties of business decision making. For example, ANN is widely used by companies for forecasting bankruptcy, customer churning, stock price forecasting and many other areas. We used generated regression and ANN method to forecast the insurance premiums revenue of the insurance company.

HISTORICAL EXTRACT ABOUT THE COMPANY

The company was established according to act No. 56 of 1950. Upon issuance of the public companies act No. 22 for the year 1997 and in accordance with the requirements of the above act the company became a state company vide the establishment certificate No. 54 on the 24th Dec. 1997 issued by the minister of Trade/companies registrar [1].

Citation: I. Bahia, "Using Artificial Neural Network Modeling in Forecasting Revenue," International Journal of Intelligence Science, Vol. 3 No. 3, 2013, pp. 136-143. doi:10.4236/ijis.2013.33015.

The nature of activity in the company is illustrated in two points:

First: The company transacts all types of general Insurance Marine, fire and Accident, Motor, Agricultural, Engineering Insurance and life assurance and Reinsurance. The company also gives advice in various insurance cases.

Second: The company invests its financial revenues in different faces of investment i.e. real estates investment, deposits and transfers, sharing in other firms capitals [1].

Investment Company

The company has invested its revenues in several fields for continuity and to obtain profits through the following:

1. Awarding loans for people to establish specific projects against annual interest.
2. Deposit cash flow in banks against proper annual interest.
3. The company uses part of its cash flow by sharing in private and mixed sector firms to obtain good returns.
4. The company has invested its property of building and lands by renting them to people to have good invested returns.

Commissions granted by the company to its official and public marketing staff differs according to the types of insurance and marketing channels as shown in the following attached schedule inTable 1 [1].

RELATED WORK

Mehdi Safdari [2] used neural network models and Monte Carlo simulation to estimate and forecast the Iran budget deficit. First stipulated fundamental variables and model, studied stationary of the variables and were unstable some variables. Most variables were stationary including structural breaks and the computed Zivot-Anders and Gregory-Hansen tests. Then there was a little chaotic time series in the review chaos by Lyapunov exponents. More using the neural network model to examine and forecast budget deficit. In the end, forecasted optimal budget deficit with using Monte Carlo simulation in the presence of uncertainty caused by government policies. Expected results of Monte Carlo prediction show what should it be and neural network prediction shows what it is.

Table 1: General Insurance in the company [1].

Type of Ins	Unified Commission for Agents	Unified commission for official salesmen and by contract %
Fire	18%	13%
Theft	20%	15%
Houshold and combined	23%	20%
Hotel	20%	18%
public liability	20%	18%
Cash in safe Or in transit	20%	18%
Plate glass	20%	18%
Fidelity Guarantee	20%	18%
Individual personal Accident	22%	16%
Group personal Accident	10% for the first ID. Millions of premium 5% for the second ID. Millions of premium 1% for above that not exceeding ID. 80000/- And in aggregate not exceeding ID. 230000/- and 50% of commission on renewal	Same
Comprehensive Motor	10%	8%
Livestock	18%	13%
poultry	20%	15%
Crop	10%	10%
Livestock	8%	5%
Crop	10%	10%
Agricultural Vehicles	10%	10%
Engineering	10%	8%

Mohammad Sarchami and Mehdi Eftekhari [3] forecasting per share earnings in investments is very important because it is a significant factor in methods of stock evaluation; and in most of these cases, it is a fundamental factor in investing in the stock market. In order to forecast per share earnings using an "artificial neural network with an error backward propagation algorithm" and an "artificial neural network with a genetic algorithm", 61 firms in 7 financial years, from the beginning of 1381 until the end of 1387, with 9 variables (8 input variables and 1 output variable) were chosen; from which 3843 (61 × 7 × 9) data points were extracted. The hypotheses are based on the idea that: 1) an artificial neural network with an error backward propagation algorithm is able to forecast the earnings of per share; 2) a neural network with a genetic algorithm is able to forecast the earnings per share; and 3) the neural network with the error backward propagation algorithm has less error in forecasting the earnings per share than the neural network with the genetic algorithm. To test the hypotheses, the results confirm all hypotheses.

Greg Tkacz and Sarah Hu [4], financial and monetary variables have long been known to contain useful leading information regarding economic activity. In this paper, the authors wish to determine whether the forecasting performance of such variables can be improved using neural network models. The main findings are that, at the 1-quarter forecasting horizon, neural networks yield no significant forecast improvements. At the 4- quarter horizon, however, the improved forecast accuracy is statistically significant. The root mean squared forecast errors of the best neural network models are about 15 to 19 per cent lower than their linear model counterparts. The improved forecast accuracy may be capturing more fundamental non-linearities between financial variables and real output growth at the longer horizon.

Abbas Vahedi [5] predicted of stock price in Tehran Stock Exchange Using Artificial Neural Network for annual data from 2000 to 2008. In this regard this approach is established with investment income, stock sales income, earnings per share and net assets as independent (Input) variables. Results showed that estimation and predictions of stock price with Artificial Neural Network are possible and have suitable and stronger results. Best architecture is a network with two hidden layer and twelve two neuron in hidden layers with hyperbolic tangent transfer function both in hidden and output layers with Quasi-Newton training algorithm.

Pei-Chann Chang, Chen-Hao Liu, Jun-Lin Lin, Chin-Yuan Fan and Celeste S.P. Ng [6], stock forecasting involves complex interactions between market-influencing factors and unknown random processes. In this study, an integrated system, CBDWNN by combining dynamic time windows, case based reasoning (CBR), and neural network for stock trading prediction is developed and it includes three different stages: 1) screening out potential stocks and the important influential factors; 2) using back propagation network (BPN) to predict the buy/sell points (wave peak and wave trough) of stock price and 3) adopting case based dynamic window (CBDW) to further improve the forecasting results from BPN. The system developed in this research is a first attempt in the literature to predict the sell/buy decision points instead of stock price itself. The empirical results show that the CBDW can assist the BPN to reduce the false alarm of buying or selling decisions. Nine different stocks with different trends, i.e., upward, downward and steady, are studied and one individual stock (AUO) will be studied as case example. The rates of return for upward, steady, and downward trend stocks are higher than 93.57%, 37.75%, and 46.62%, respectively. These results are all very promising and better than using CBR or BPN alone.

Rob Law and Norman Au [7], apart from simple guesswork, time-series and regression techniques have largely dominated forecasting models for international tourism demand. This paper presents a new approach that uses a supervised feed-forward neural network model to forecast Japanese tourist arrivals in Hong Kong. The input layer of the neural network contains six nodes: Service Price, Average Hotel Rate, Foreign Exchange Rate, Population, Marketing Expenses, and Gross Domestic Expenditure. The single node in the output layer of the neural network represents the Japanese demand for travel to Hong Kong. Socially published annual data in the period of 1967 to 1996 were used to build the neural network. Estimated Japanese arrivals were compared with actual published Japanese arrivals. Experimental results showed that using the neural network model to forecast Japanese arrivals outperforms multiple regression, moving average, and exponent smoothing (1999 Elsevier Science Ltd. All rights reserved).

R. G. Hoptroff [8] is intended as a "hands-on" practical discussion of how and why neural networks are used in forecasting and business modeling. The need for forecasting is briefly examined. The theory of the multilayer perceptron neural network is then covered both qualitatively and in mathematical detail, including the methods of back-propagation of error and independent validation. The advantages of the neural net approach to forecasting, namely nonlinear modelling capability, plausible interpolations and extrapolations, robustness to noise, illconditioning and insufficient data, and ease of use, are discussed. Finally, some working notes are offered for the practical implementation of neural nets in forecasting, and four real-life examples are given from the pursuits of econometrics, sales forecasting, market modeling, and risk evaluation.

ANN

ANNs offer a computational approach that is quite different from conventional digital computation. Digital computers operate sequentially and can do arithmetic computation extremely fast. Biological neurons in the human brain are extremely slow devices and are capable of performing a tremendous amount of computation tasks necessary to do every day complex tasks, commonsense reasoning and dealing with fuzzy situations. The underlining reason is that, unlike a conventional computer, the brain contains a huge number of neurons, information processing elements of the biological nervous system, acting in parallel.

ANNs are thus a parallel, distributed information processing structure consisting of processing elements interconnected via unidirectional signal channels called connection weights. Although modeled after biological neurons, ANNs are much simplified and bear only superficial resemblance. Some of the major attributes of ANNs are: 1) they can learn from examples and generalize well on unseen data, and 2) are able to deal with situation where the input data are erroneous, incomplete or fuzzy [9].

Individual Neuron

The individual processing unit in ANNs receives input from other sources or output signals of other units and produces an output as shown in **Figure 1**. The input signals (x_i) are multiplied with weights (W_{ji}) of connection strength between the sending unit "i" and receiving unit "j". The sum of the weighted inputs is passed through an activation function. The output may be used as an input to the neighboring units or units at the next layer. Assuming the input signal by a vector $x(x_1, x_2, \cdots, x_n)$ and the corresponding weights to unit "j" by $W_j(W_{j1}, W_{j2}, \cdots, W_{jn})$, the net input to the unit "j" is given by Equation (1). The weight (W_{j0} = b) is a special weight called bias whose input signal is always +1 [9].

$$Net_j = \sum W_{nj} X_n + W_{j0} = W_{jx} + b \qquad (1)$$

METHODOLOGY

An Artificial Neural Network is making of Artificial

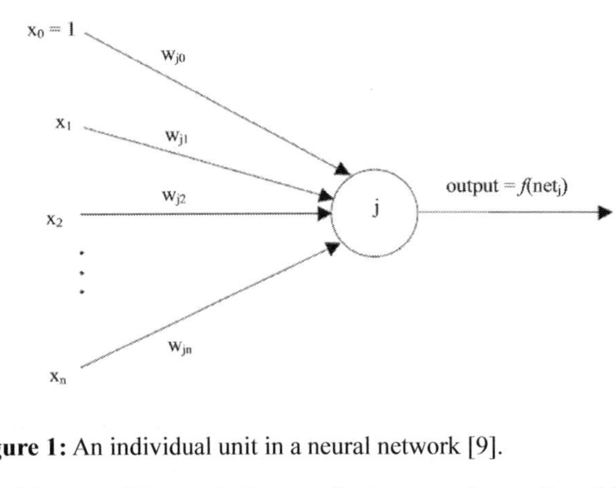

Figure 1: An individual unit in a neural network [9].

Neurons. Neuron is the smallest processing unit and is the base of neural network operation. The greatest advantage of a neural network is its ability to modeling complex nonlinear relationship without a priori assumptions of the nature of the relationship.

Neural network has three layers; input layer, hidden layer and output layer. Input layer just takes the data and behaves like an independent variable therefore amount of neuron in input layer depends on the variable. Output layer behaves like a dependent variable and amount of neuron in this layer depends on the dependent variables (forecasting variables).

If the networks output shows with $\hat{Y}$ and actual value with Y, the purpose of network training is to find the networks weight to minimize the network error. If the error of forecasting determined with Sum of Squared Errors (SSE) purpose is to minimize the Equation (2) [10].

$$\mathrm{SSE} = \sum\left(Y_i - \overline{Y}_i\right)^2 \tag{2}$$

Fitting, Neural Network

The Neural Network Fitting Tool helps to select data, create and train a network and evaluate its performance using mean square error and regression analysis.

A two-layer feed-forward network with sigmoid hidden neurons and linear output neurons Neural Network Fitting can fit multi-dimensional mapping problems arbitrarily well, given consistent data and enough neurons in its hidden layer.

The network will be trained with Levenberg-Marquardt backpropagation algorithm, unless there is not enough memory, in which case scaled conjugate gradient backpropagation will be used [11].

To define a fitting problem, arrange a set of Q input vectors as columns in a matrix then, arrange another set of Q target vectors (the correct output vectors for each of the input vectors) into a second matrix [10].

The process of finding the best set of weights for the neural network is referred to as training or learning. The approach used by most commercial software to estimate the weights is backpropagation. Each time the network cycles through the training data, it produces a predicted value for the target variable. This value is compared to the actual value for the target variable and an error is computed for each observation. The errors are "fed back" through the network and new weights are computed to reduce the overall error. Despite the neural network terminology, the training process is actually a statistical optimization procedure. Typically, the procedure minimizes the sum of the squared residuals in Equation (3) [12].

$$\mathrm{Min}\left(\sum\left(Y - \hat{Y}\right)^2\right) \tag{3}$$

In Fit Neural Network the data of the research contain a predefined set of input and target vectors. The input vectors define data regarding the insurance premiums revenue for the period 1970 to 2011 and the target values define relative values of the insurance premiums. The input matrix consists of one column vectors of insurance premiums revenue investment for 41 samples and target matrix consist of one column vector of the corresponding 41 relative valuations samples. The 1 × 41 inputs and targets vectors are randomly divided into three sets, 60% of the vectors are used to train the network, and the network is adjusted according to its error. 20% of the vectors are used to validate how well the network generalized and to halt training when generalization stops im proving. Finally, the last 20% of the vectors are used to test the network which has no effect on training and provides an independent measure of network performance during and after training. Figure 2 illustrates fit neural network structure.

The next step is to create a network and train it until it has learned the relationship between the inputs and targets. The fit neural network has 5 neurons in the hidden layer. The numbers of neurons in the output layer are automatically set to one vector for 41 samples and the number of elements in each vector of target. Fit Neural Network can potentially represent any input-output relationship with a finite number of discontinuities.

EXPERIMENTAL RESULT

This section demonstrates the common steps of solving a problem with fit neural network. The first step is to define the problem.

For supervised networks, such as Fit Neural Networks trained with backpropagation, this means a set of input vectors and a set of associated desired output vectors called target vectors, as shown in**Figure 3**.

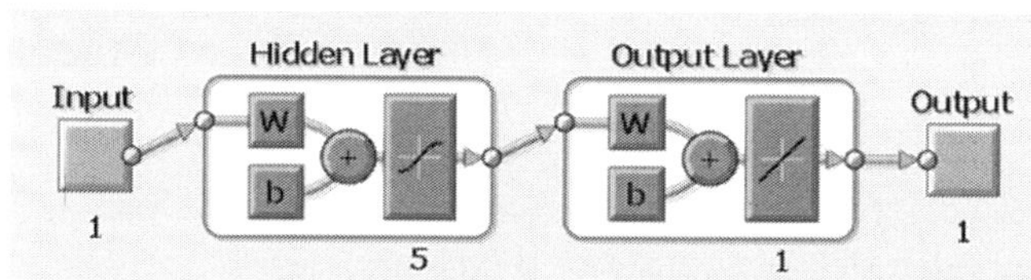

Figure 2: Fit neural network structure.

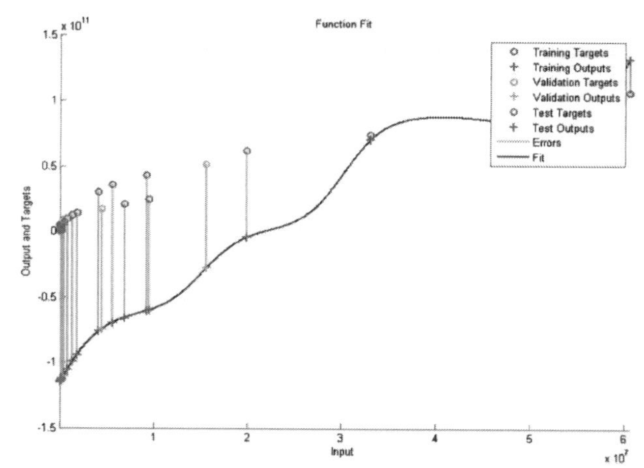

Figure 3: The fitting neural network function.

According to the results

- The network stopped at 1 iteration
- Time was ~0
- The mean squared error was 1.15E + 22
- The gradient (slope) was at 2.76E + 22 when it stopped
- The LM update value was 1.00E + 11 At the one epoch the best validation performance in 0 iteration and training state in one epoch are shown in Figures 4 and 5. The network will be trained with Levenberg-Marquardt back propagation algorithm at epoch1. In fitting problem, a neural network is used to map between a data set of numeric inputs and a set of numeric targets.

The Neural Network Fitting Tool helps to select data, create and train a network and evaluate its performance using mean square error and regression analysis, as shown in **Table 2**.

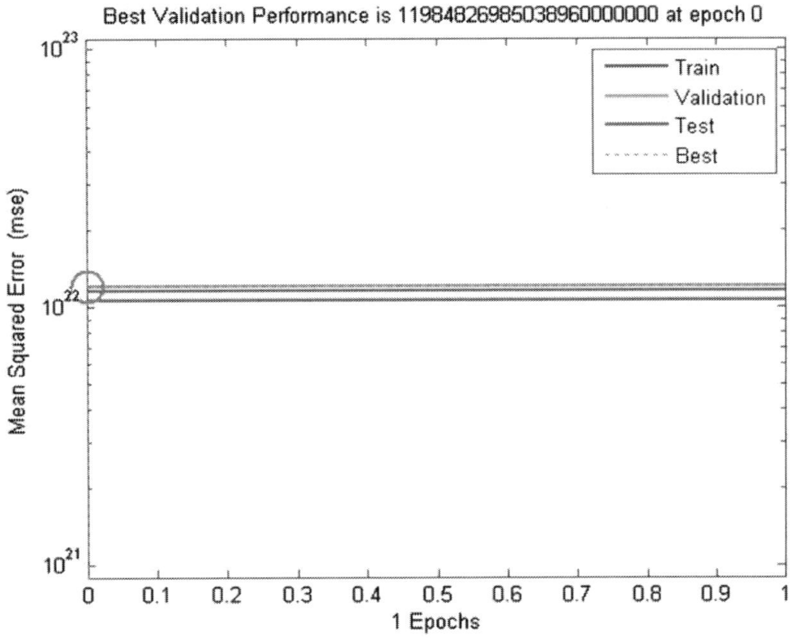

Figure 4: The best validation performance.

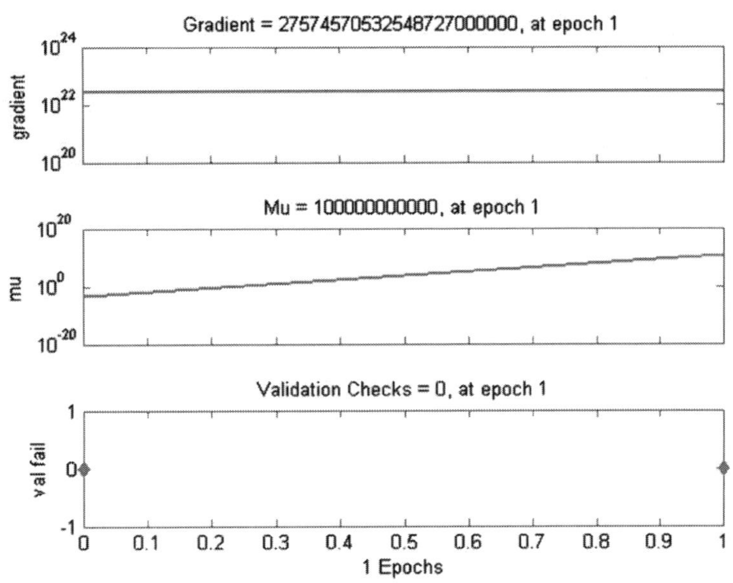

Figure 5: The training state.

Regression R Values measure the correlation between outputs and targets. An R value of≈ 1 means a close relationship and 0 a random relationship, as shown in Figure 6.

Mean Squared Error is the average squared difference between outputs and targets. Lower values are better. Zero means no error. The Mean Squared Error (MSE) is a measure of how close a fitted line is to data points. For every data point, take the distance vertically from the point to the corresponding value on the curve fit (the error), and square the value, MSE is a network performance function. It measures the network's performance according to the mean of squared errors, as shown in Figures 7 and 8.

DISCUSSES THE RESULT

A Fitting Neural Network topology was adopted for the forecast model. During the development of the forecasting model various architectures were developed and evaluated. The input layer of the neural network had one vector, represented 41 samples of insurance premiums revenue of one element (41 × 1). The output from this neuron was linearly de-normalised to produce a value for the fore casted number of epochs to stop training in the range 0 - 1000.

Table 2: The MSE and regression for three sets.

	MSE	Regression
Train	1.15E + 22	0.976193013
Validation	1.20E + 22	0.984037461
Test	1.05E + 22	0.993632741

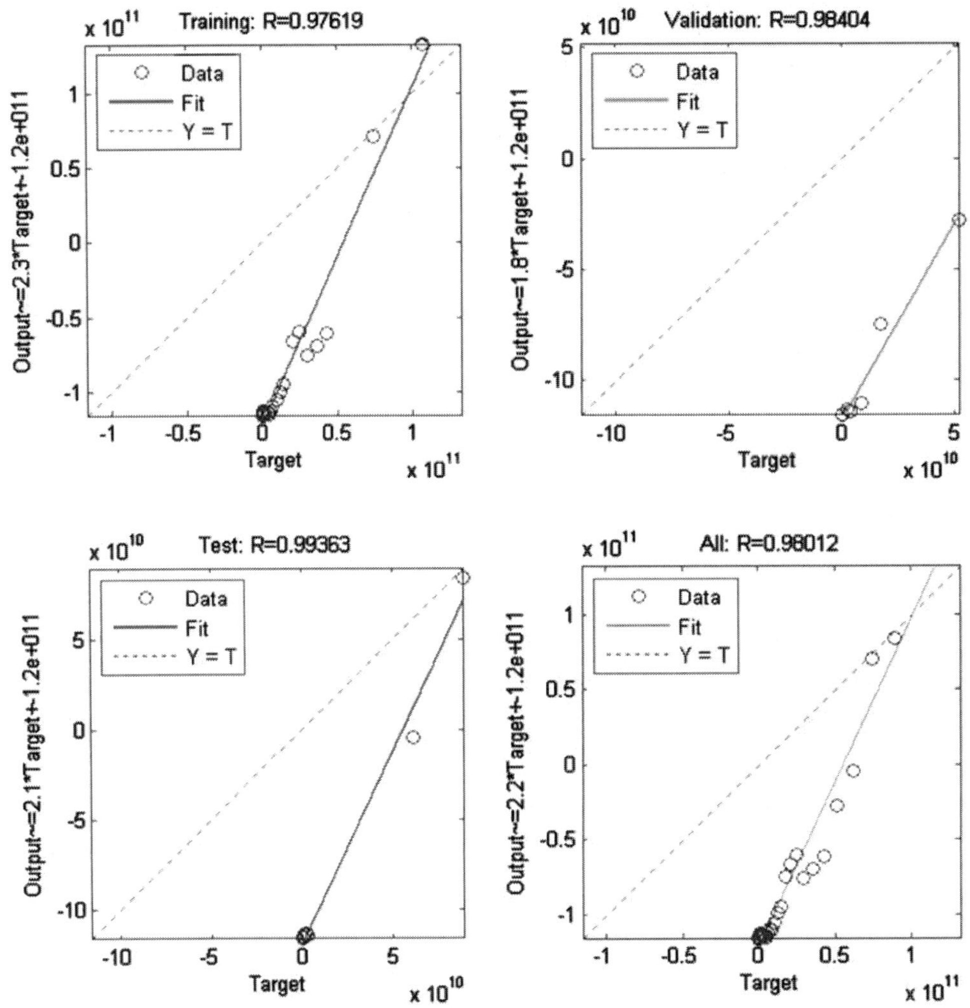

Figure 6: The regression for training, validation, test and all samples.

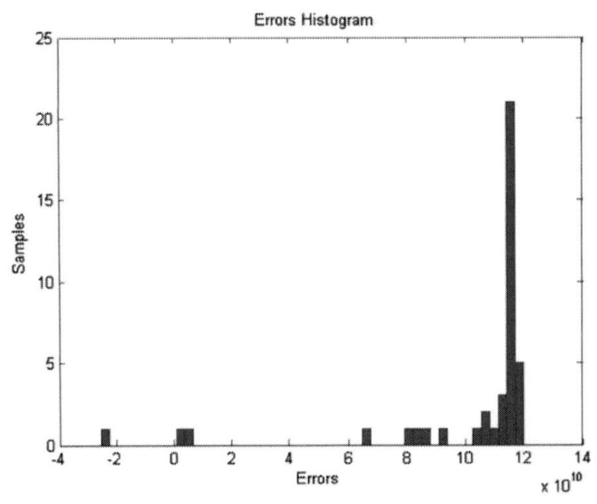

Figure 7: The errors histogram.

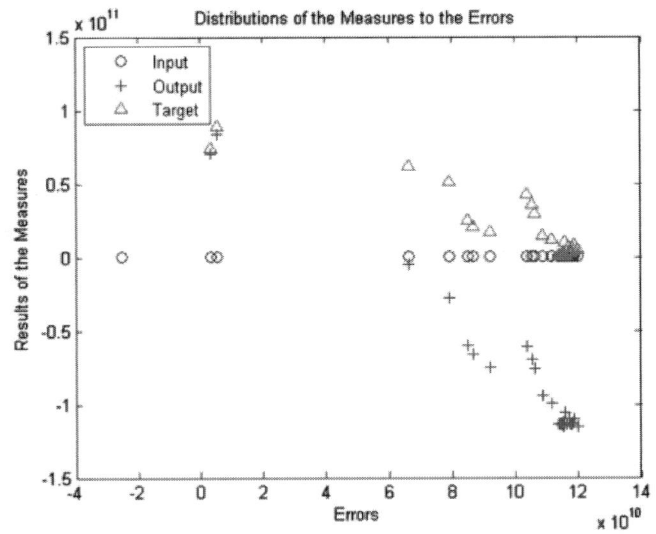

Figure 8. Distribution the errors for input, target and output samples.

The neural network generated for the required forecasting model had a 1-5-1 architecture. The forecast performance of Fitting Neural Network model was satisfactory (MSE (train) = 1.15E + 22, MSE (validation) = 1.20E + 22, MSE (test) = 1.05E + 22).

The simulated value was almost the same with actual value. Take a look at the regression plot of all state **Figure 6**. Each of the Figures corresponds to a specific target from the output array. As all the R parameters are very close to 1, this means that the correlation between the outputs and the targets is very high, as illustrated in **Table 2**. The fit neural network based on the training data and the results shows an increment in the insurance premiums revenue for approximately 120% in the future for the period from 2012 to 2053.

CONCLUSIONS

Artificial Neural Network is a well known approach for estimation and forecasting of various economic and accounting variables. The aim of this research is to forecast the insurance premiums revenue of the National Insurance Company in Iraq using Artificial Neural Network for the annual data of the years between 1970 and 2011. This approach is established with investment income of the National Insurance Company as independent (Input) variable.

The results showed that forecasting the insurance premiums revenue with Artificial Neural Network is possible and provides strong results of forecasting. Best architecture for fitting neural network as one input vector, five hidden layer and the output is one vector (1-5-1), the ratio of increasing the insurance premiums revenue is approximately 120% for the period between 2012 and 2053 as a forecast for the future.

REFERENCES

1. National Insurance Company Site. http://www.nic.gov.iq/index_files/Page419.htm
2. M. Safdari and M. Shamsoddini, "Using Artificial Neural Networks and Monte Carlo Simulation in Terms of Uncertainty for Prediction of Budget Deficit in Iran," Interdisciplinary Journal of Contemporary Research in Business, Vol. 4, No. 2, 2012, p. 132.
3. M. Sarchami and M. Eftekhari, "Using Artificial Neural Networks for Forecasting per Share Earnings," African Journal of Business Management, Vol. 6, No. 11, 2012, pp. 4288-4294.
4. G. Tkacz and S. Hu, "Department of Monetary and Financial Analysis Bank of Canada Ottawa, Ontario, Canada K1A 0G9, Forecasting GDP Growth Using Artificial," Neural Networks, Bank of Canada Working Paper 99-3, 1999.
5. A. Vahedi, "The Predicting Stock Price Using Artificial Neural Network," Journal of Basic and Applied Scientific Research, Vol. 2, No. 3, 2012, pp. 2325-2328.
6. P.-C. Chang, C.-H. Liu, J.-L. Lin, C.-Y. Fan and C. S. P. Ng, "A Neural Network with a Case Based Dynamic Window for Stock Trading Prediction," Expert Systems with Applications, Vol. 36, No. 3, 2009, pp. 6889-6898.
7. R. Law and N. Au, "A Neural Network Model to Forecast Japanese Demand for Travel to Hong Kong," The Hong Kong Polytechnic University, Kowloon, 1999. doi:10.1016/S0261-5177(98)00094-6
8. R. G. Hoptroff, "The Principles and Practice of Time Series Forecasting and Business Modelling Using Neural Nets," Neural Computing and Applications, Vol. 1, No. 1 1993, pp. 59-66. doi:10.1007/BF01411375
9. J. Kamruzzaman and R. A. Sarker, "Artificial Neural Networks: Applications in Finance and Manufacturing," 2006.
10. M. Beale, M. T. Hagan and H. Demuth, "Neural Network Toolbox™ 7 User's Guide," The MathWorks, Inc., Natick.
11. The MathWorks, Inc., "MATLAB® Primer, R2012a" 2012. http://www.eng.umd.edu/~nsw/chbe250/getstart.pdf
12. S. Bridgeland, M. Dorey and J. Palin, "Neural Networks Statistics for Professionals?" 1997.

CHAPTER 8

FINANCIAL TIME SERIES PREDICTION USING ELMAN RECURRENT RANDOM NEURAL NETWORKS

Jie Wang, Jun Wang, Wen Fang, and Hongli Niu

INTRODUCTION

Predicting stock price index is difficult due to uncertainties involved. In the past decades, the stock market prediction has played a vital role for the investment brokers and the individual investors, and the researchers are on the constant look out for a reliable method for predicting stock market trends. In recent years, the artificial neural networks (ANNs) have been applied to many areas of statistics. One of these areas is time series forecasting. References [1–3] reveal different time series forecasting by ANNs methods. ANNs have been also employed independently or as an auxiliary tool to predict time series. ANNs are nonlinear methods which mimic nerve system. They have functions of self-organizing, data-driven, self-study, self-adaptive, and associated memory. ANNs can learn from patterns and capture hidden functional relationships in a given data even if the functional relationships are not known or difficult to identify. A number of researchers have utilized ANNs to predict financial time series including backpropagation neural networks, back radial basis function neural networks, generalized regression neural networks, wavelet neural networks, and dynamic artificial neural network [4–9]. Statistical theories and methods play an important role in financial time series analysis because both financial theory and its empirical time series contain an element of uncertainty. Some statistical properties for the stock market fluctuations are uncovered in the literatures such as power-law of logarithmic returns and volumes, heavy tails distribution of price changes, volatility clustering, and long-range memory of volatility [1, 10–12].

The backpropagation neural network (BPNN) is a neural network training algorithm for financial forecasting, which has powerful problem-solving ability. Multilayer perceptron (MLP) is one of the most prevalent neural networks, which has the capability of complex mapping between inputs and outputs that makes it possible to approximate nonlinear function. Reference [13] employs MLP in trading and hybrid time-varying leverage effects and [14] in forecasting of time series. The two architectures have at least three layers. The first layer is called the input layer (the number of its nodes corresponds to the number of explanatory variables). The last layer is called the output layer (the number of its nodes corresponds to the number of response variables). An intermediary layer of nodes, the hidden layer, separates the input from the output layer. Its number of nodes defines the amount of complexity which the model is capable of fitting. In previous studies, forward networks have frequently been used for financial time series prediction, while, unlike forward networks, recurrent neural network uses feedback connections to model spatial as well as temporal dependencies between input and output series to make the initial states and the past states of the neurons capable of being involved in a series of processing. References [15–17] show the applications in different areas of recurrent neural network. This ability makes them applicable to time series prediction with satisfactory prediction results [18]. As a special recurrent neural network, the Elman recurrent neural network (ERNN) has been used in the present paper for

Citation: Jie Wang, Jun Wang, Wen Fang, and Hongli Niu, "Financial Time Series Prediction Using Elman Recurrent Random Neural Networks," Computational Intelligence and Neuroscience, vol. 2016, Article ID 4742515, 14 pages, 2016. doi:10.1155/2016/4742515

prediction. ERNN is a time-varying predictive control system that was developed with the ability to keep memory of recent events in order to predict future output.

The nonlinear and nonstationary characteristics of the stock market make it difficult and challenging for forecasting stock indices in a reliable manner. Particularly, in the current stock markets, the rapid changes of trading rules and management systems have made it difficult to reflect the markets' development using the early data. However, if only the recent data are selected, a lot of useful information (which the early data hold) will be lost. In this research, a stochastic time effective neural network (STNN) and the corresponding learning algorithm were presented. References [19–22] introduce the corresponding stochastic time effective models and use them to predict financial time series. Particularly, [23] has shown a random data-time effective radial basis function neural network, which is also applied to the prediction of financial price series. The present paper has optimized the ERNN model which is different with the above models; also at first step of the procedures we employ different input variables from [23]. At the last section of this paper, two new error measure methods are first introduced to evaluate the better predicting results of the proposed model than other traditional models. For this improved network model, each of historical data is given a weight depending on the time at which it occurs. The degree of impact of historical data on the market is expressed by a stochastic process, where a drift function and the Brownian motion are introduced in the time strength function in order to make the model have the effect of random movement while maintaining the original trend. In the present work, we combine MLP with ERNN and stochastic time effective function to develop a stock price forecasting model, called ST-ERNN.

In order to display that the ST-ERNN can provide a higher accuracy of the financial time series forecasting, we compare the forecasting performance with the BPNN model, the STNN model, and the ERNN model by employing different global stock indices. Shanghai Stock Exchange (SSE) Composite Index, Taiwan Stock Exchange Capitalization Weighted Stock Index (TWSE), Korean Stock Price Index (KOSPI), and Nikkei 225 Index (Nikkei225) are applied in this work to analyze the forecasting models by comparison.

PROPOSED APPROACH

Elman Recurrent Neural Network (ERNN)

The Elman recurrent neural network, a simple recurrent neural network, was introduced by Elman in 1990 [24]. As is well known, a recurrent network has some advantages, such as having time series and nonlinear prediction capabilities, faster convergence, and more accurate mapping ability. References [25, 26] combine Elman neural network with different areas for their purposes. In this network, the outputs of the hidden layer are allowed to feedback onto themselves through a buffer layer, called the recurrent layer. This feedback allows ERNN to learn, recognize, and generate temporal patterns, as well as spatial patterns. Every hidden neuron is connected to only one recurrent layer neuron through a constant weight of value one. Hence the recurrent layer virtually constitutes a copy of the state of the hidden layer one instant before. The number of recurrent neurons is consequently the same as the number of hidden neurons. To sum up, the ERNN is composed of an input layer, a recurrent layer which provides state information, a hidden layer, and an output layer. Each layer contains one or more neurons which propagate information from one layer to another by computing a nonlinear function of their weighted sum of inputs.

In Figure 1, a multi-input ERNN model is exhibited, where the number of neurons in inputs layer is m and in the hidden layer is n and one output unit. Let x_{it} ($i = 1, 2, \ldots, m$) denote the set of input vector of neurons at time t, y_{t+1} denotes the output of the network at time $t+1$, z_{jt} ($j = 1, 2, \ldots, n$) denote the output of hidden layer neurons at time t, and ujt ($j = 1, 2, \ldots, n$) denote the recurrent layer neurons. wij is the weight that connects the node i in the input layer neurons to the node j in the hidden layer. c_j, V_j are the weights that connect the node j in the hidden layer neurons to the node in the recurrent layer and output, respectively. Hidden layer stage is as follows: the inputs of all neurons in the hidden layer are given by

$$\text{net}_{jt}(k) = \sum_{i=1}^{n} w_{ij} x_{it}(k-1) + \sum_{j=1}^{m} c_j u_{jt}(k),$$
$$u_{jt}(k) = z_{jt}(k-1), \quad i = 1, 2, \ldots, n, \quad j = 1, 2, \ldots, m. \tag{1}$$

The outputs of hidden neurons are given by

$$z_{jt}(k) = f_H\left(\text{net}_{jt}(k)\right) = f_H\left(\sum_{i=1}^{n} w_{ij} x_{it}(k) + \sum_{j=1}^{m} c_j u_{jt}(k)\right), \tag{2}$$

where the sigmoid function in hidden layer is selected as the activation function: $f_H(x) = 1/(1 + e^{-x})$. The output of the hidden layer is given as follows:

$$y_{t+1}(k) = f_T\left(\sum_{j=1}^{m} v_j z_{jt}(k)\right), \tag{3}$$

where $f_T(x)$ is an identity map as the activation function.

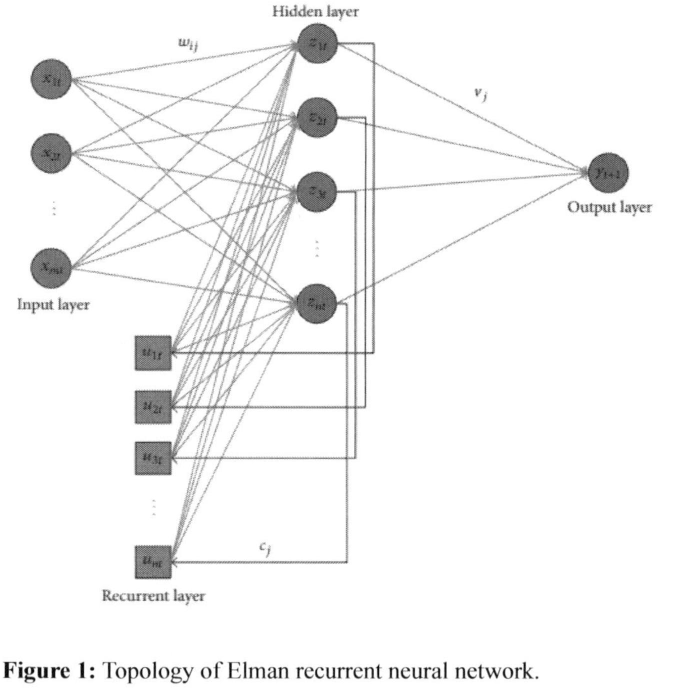

Figure 1: Topology of Elman recurrent neural network.

Algorithm of ERNN with a Stochastic Time Effective Function (ST-ERNN)

The backpropagation algorithm is a supervised learning algorithm which minimizes the global error E by using the gradient descent method [18, 21]. For the STERNN model, we assume that the error of the output is given by $\varepsilon_{t_n} = d_{t_n} - y_{t_n}$ and the error of the sample n is defined as

$$E(t_n) = \frac{1}{2}\varphi(t_n)\left(d_{t_n} - y_{t_n}\right)^2, \tag{4}$$

where tn is the time of the sample n $(n = 1, \ldots, N)$, d_{t_n} is the actual value, y_{t_n} is the output at time t_n, and $\varphi(t_n)$ is the stochastic time effective function which endows each historical data with a weight depending on the time at which it occurs. We define (t_n) as follows:

$$\varphi(t_n) = \frac{1}{\beta}\exp\left\{\int_{t_0}^{t_n}\mu(t)\,dt + \int_{t_0}^{t_n}\sigma(t)\,dB(t)\right\}, \tag{5}$$

where β (> 0) is the time strength coefficient, t_0 is the time of the newest data in the data training set, and t_n is an arbitrary time point in the data training set. (t) is the drift function, (t) is the volatility function, and $B(t)$ is the standard Brownian motion.

Intuitively, the drift function is used to model deterministic trends, the volatility function is often used to model a set of unpredictable events occurring during this motion, and Brownian motion is usually thought as random motion of a particle in liquid (where the future motion of the particle at any given time is not dependent on the past). Brownian motion is a continuous time stochastic process, and it is the limit of or continuous version of random walks. Since Brownian motion's time derivative is everywhere infinite, it is an idealised approximation to actual random physical processes, which always have a finite time scale. We begin with an explicit definition. A Brownian motion is a real-valued, continuous stochastic process$\{Y(t), t \geq 0\}$ on a probability space (Ω, F, $\mathbb{P}$), with independent and stationary increments. In detail, we have the following: (a) continuity: the map $s \mapsto$ (s) is continuousPa.s.; (b) independent increments: if $s \leq t$, $Y_t - Y_s$ is independent of $\mathcal{F} = (Y_u, u \leq s)$; (c) stationary increments: if $s \leq t$, $Y_t - Y_s$ and $Y_{t-s} - Y_0$ have the same probability law. From this definition, if $\{(t), t \geq 0\}$ is a Brownian motion, then$Y_t - Y_0$ is a normal random variable with mean rt and variance σ^2 t, where r and σ are constant real numbers. A Brownian motion is standard (we denote it by (t)) if $(0) = 0$ $\mathbb{P}$ a.s., $\mathbb{E}[B(t)] = 0$, and $\mathbb{E}[B(t)]^2 = t$. In the above random data-time effective function, the impact of the historical data on the stock market is regarded as a time variable function; the efficiency of the historical data depends on its time. Then the corresponding global error of all the data at each network repeated training set in the output layer is defined as

$$\begin{aligned} E &= \frac{1}{N}\sum_{n=1}^{N}E(t_n) = \frac{1}{2N} \\ &\cdot \sum_{n=1}^{N}\frac{1}{\beta}\exp\left\{\int_{t_0}^{t_n}\mu(t)\,dt + \int_{t_0}^{t_n}\sigma(t)\,dB(t)\right\} \\ &\cdot \left(d_{t_n} - y_{t_n}\right)^2. \end{aligned} \tag{6}$$

The main objective of learning algorithm is to minimize the value of cost function E until it reaches the preset minimum value ξ by repeated learning. On each repetition, the output is calculated and the global error E is obtained. The gradient of the cost function is given by $\Delta E = \partial E / \partial W$. For the weight nodes in the input layer, the gradient of the connective weight w_{ij} is given by

$$\Delta w_{ij} = -\eta\frac{\partial E(t_n)}{\partial w_{ij}} = \eta\varepsilon_{t_n}v_j\varphi(t_n)f_H'\left(\text{net}_{jt_n}\right)x_{it_n}, \tag{7}$$

for the weight nodes in the recurrent layer, the gradient of the connective weight c_j is given by

$$\Delta c_j = -\eta\frac{\partial E(t_n)}{\partial c_j} = \eta\varepsilon_{t_n}v_j\varphi(t_n)f_H'\left(\text{net}_{jt_n}\right)u_{jt_n}, \tag{8}$$

and for the weight nodes in the hidden layer, the gradient of the connective weight V_j is given by

$$\Delta v_j = -\eta\frac{\partial E(t_n)}{\partial v_j} = \eta\varepsilon_{t_n}\varphi(t_n)f_H\left(\text{net}_{jt_n}\right), \tag{9}$$

where η is the learning rate and $f_H'(\text{net}_{jt_n})$ is the derivative of the activation function. So the update rules for the weights w_{ij}, c_j, and V_j are given by

$$\begin{aligned} w_{ij}^{k+1} &= w_{ij}^{k} + \Delta w_{ij}^{k} \\ &= w_{ij}^{k} + \eta\varepsilon_{t_n}v_j\varphi(t_n)f_H'\left(\text{net}_{jt_n}\right)x_{it_n}, \\ c_j^{k+1} &= c_j^{k} + \Delta c_j^{k} = c_j^{k} + \eta\varepsilon_{t_n}v_j\varphi(t_n)f_H'\left(\text{net}_{jt_n}\right)u_{jt_n}, \\ v_j^{k+1} &= v_j^{k} + \Delta v_j^{k} = v_j^{k} + \eta\varepsilon_{t_n}\varphi(t_n)f_H\left(\text{net}_{jt_n}\right). \end{aligned} \tag{10}$$

Note that the training aim of the stochastic time effective neural network is to modify the weights so as to minimize the error between the network's prediction and the actual target. In Figure 2, the training algorithm procedures of the stochastic time effective neural network are displayed, which are as follows. Step 1. Perform input data normalization. In ST-ERNN model, we choose four kinds of stock prices as the input values in the input layer: daily opening price, daily highest price, daily lowest price, and daily closing price. The output layer is the closing price of the next trading day. Then determine parameters of the network such as learning rate η which is between 0 and 1, the maximum training iterations number K, and initial connective weights. Also, the topology of the network architecture is the number of neural nodes in the hidden layer in this paper. Step 2. At the beginning of data processing, connective weights w_{ij}, V_j, and c_j follow the uniform distribution on $(-1, 1)$. Step 3. Introduce the stochastic time effective function (t) in the error function E. Choose the drift function (t) and the volatility function (t). Give the transfer function from the input layer to the hidden layer and the transfer function from the hidden layer to the output layer. Step 4. Establish an error acceptable model and set preset minimum error ξ. Based on network training objective $E = (1/N)\sum_{n=1}^{N}E(t_n)$, if E is below preset minimum error, go to Step 6; otherwise go to Step 5. Step 5. Modify the connective weights: calculate the gradient of the connective weights w_{ij}, Δw_{ij}^k, v_j, Δv_j^k, c_j, and Δc_j^k. Then modify the weights from the layer to the previous layer, w_{ij}^{k+1}, v_j^{k+1}, or c_j^{k+1}. Step 6. Output the predictive value $y_{t+1} = f_T(\sum_{j=1}^{m}v_jf_H(\sum_{i=1}^{n}w_{ij}x_{it} + \sum_{j=1}^{m}c_ju_{jt}))$.

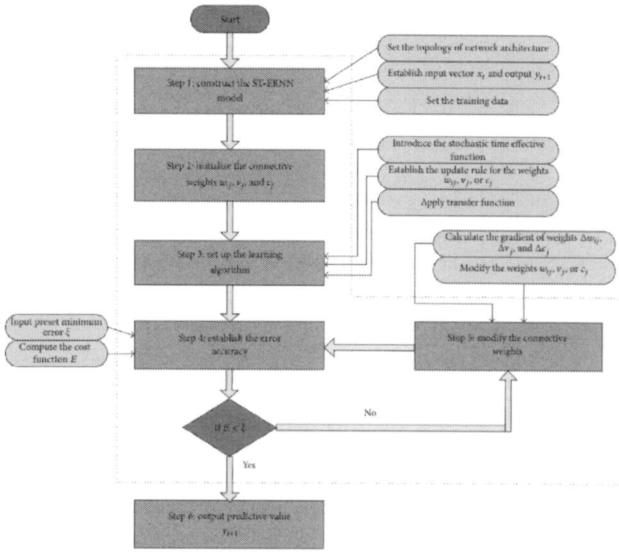

Figure 2: Training algorithm procedures of ST-ERNN.

FORECASTING AND STATISTICAL ANALYSIS OF STOCK PRICE

Selecting and Preprocessing of the Data

To evaluate the performance of the proposed ST-ERNN forecasting model, we select the daily data from Shanghai Stock Exchange (SSE) Composite Index, Taiwan Stock Exchange Capitalization Weighted Stock Index (TWSE), Korean Stock Price Index (KOSPI), and Nikkei 225 Index (Nikkei225) to analyze the forecasting models by comparison. In Table 1 we show that the selected number of each index is 2000.The SSE data cover the time period from 16/03/2006 up to 19/03/2014, the TWSE is from 09/02/2006 up to 19/03/2014, and KOSPI used in this paper is from 20/02/2006 up to 19/03/2014 while Nikkei225 is from 27/01/2006 up to 19/03/2014. Usually, the nontrading time periods are treated as frozen such that we adopt only the time during trading hours. To reduce the impact of noise in the financial market and finally lead to a better prediction, the collected data should be properly adjusted and normalized at the beginning of the modelling. There are different normalization methods that are tested to improve the network training [27, 28], which include "the normalized data in the range of [0, 1]" in the following equation, which is also adopted in this work:

$$S(t)' = \frac{S(t) - \min S(t)}{\max S(t) - \min S(t)}, \tag{11}$$

where the minimum and maximum values are obtained on the training set during the training process. In order to obtain the true value after the forecasting, we can revert the output variables as

$$S(t) = S(t)' (\max S(t) - \min S(t)) + \min S(t). \tag{12}$$

Table 1: Data selection.

Index	Date sets	Total number	Hidden number	Learning rate
SSE	16/03/2006~19/03/2014	2000	9	0.001
TWSE	09/02/2006~19/03/2014	2000	12	0.001
KOSPI	20/02/2006~19/03/2014	2000	10	0.05
Nikkei225	27/01/2006~19/03/2014	2000	10	0.01

Training and Forecasting by ST-ERNN Model

In the STERNN model, after we have done the experiments repeatedly on the different index data, different number of neural nodes in the hidden layer were chose as the optimal; see Table 1. The dataset was divide into two subsets: the training set and the testing set. It is noteworthy that the lengths of the data points we chose for these four time series are the same; the lengths of training data and testing data are also set the same. The training set with 75% of data was used for model building; and the testing set, with the last 25%, was used to test on the out-of-sample set the predictive part of a model. The training set is totally 1500 data, for the SSE is from 16/03/2006 to 22/02/2012 while that for the TWSE is from 09/02/2006 to 08/03/2012, for KOSPI is from 20/02/2006 to 09/03/2012, and for Nikkei is from 27/01/2006 to 09/03/2012. The number of the rest is 500, defined as the testing set. We preset the learning rate and the maximum training cycle by referring to [21, 29, 30]; then we have done the experiment repeatedly on the training set of different index data; different numbers of neural nodes in the hidden layer are chosen as the optimal; see Table 1. The maximum training iterations number K is 300, different dataset has different learning rate η, and, here, after many times experiments of the training data we choose 0.001, 0.001, 0.05, and 0.01 for SSE, TWSE, KOSPI, and Nikkei225, respectively. And the predefined minimum training threshold $\xi = 10^{-5}$. When using the ER-STNN model to predict the daily closing price of stock index, we assume that (t) (the drift function) and (t)(the volatility function) are as follows:

$$\mu(t) = \frac{1}{(c-t)^2},$$

$$\sigma(t) = \left[\frac{1}{N-1}\sum_{i=1}^{N}(x-\overline{x})^2\right]^{1/2}, \tag{13}$$

where c is the parameter which is equal to the number of samples in the datasets and $\overline{x}$ is the mean of the sample data. Then the corresponding cost function can be written by

$$E = \frac{1}{N}\sum_{n=1}^{N} E(t_n) = \frac{1}{2N}\sum_{n=1}^{N}\frac{1}{\beta}\exp\left\{\int_{t_0}^{t_n}\frac{1}{(c-t)^2}dt + \int_{t_0}^{t_n}\left[\frac{1}{N-1}\sum_{i=1}^{N}(x-\overline{x})^2\right]^{1/2} dB(t)\right\}\left(d_{t_n} - y_{t_n}\right)^2. \tag{14}$$

Figure 3 shows the predicting results of training and testing data for SSE, TWSE, KOSPI, and Nikkei225 with the ST-ERNN model correspondingly. The curves of the actual data and the predictive data are intuitively very approximating. It means that with many times experiments the financial time series have been well trained; the forecasting results are desired by ST-ERNN model.

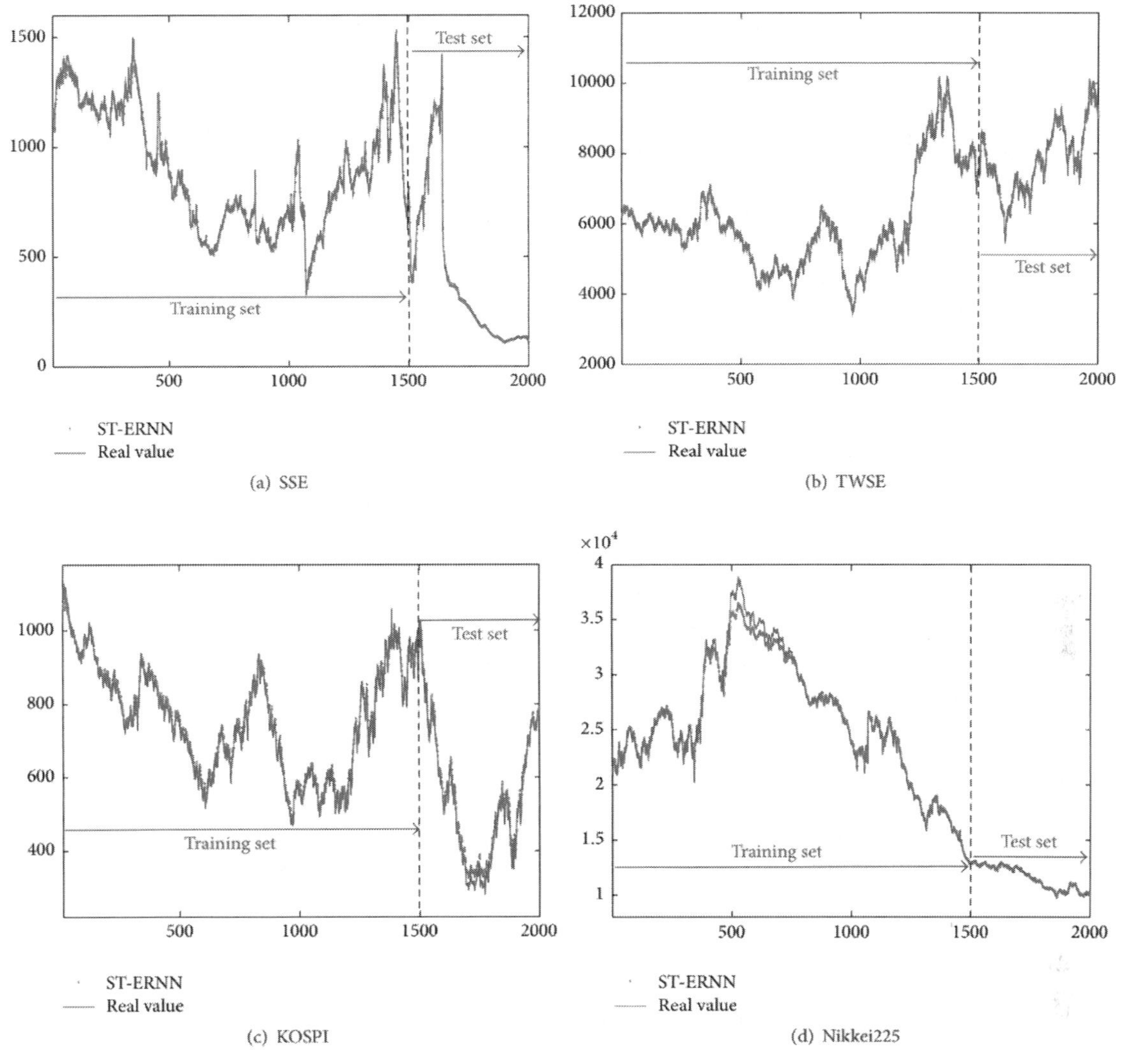

Figure 3: Comparisons of the predictive data and the actual data for the forecasting models.

The plots of the real and the predictive data for these four price series are, respectively, shown in Figure 4. Through the linear regression analysis, we make a comparison of the predictive value of the ST-ERNN model with the real price data. It is known that the linear regression can be used to fit a predictive model to an observed data set of Y and X. The linear equations of SSE, TWSE, KOSPI, and Nikkei225 are exhibited, respectively, in Figures 4(a)–4(d). We can observe that all the slopes of the linear equations for them are drawn near to 1, which implies that the predictive values and the real values are not deviating too much.

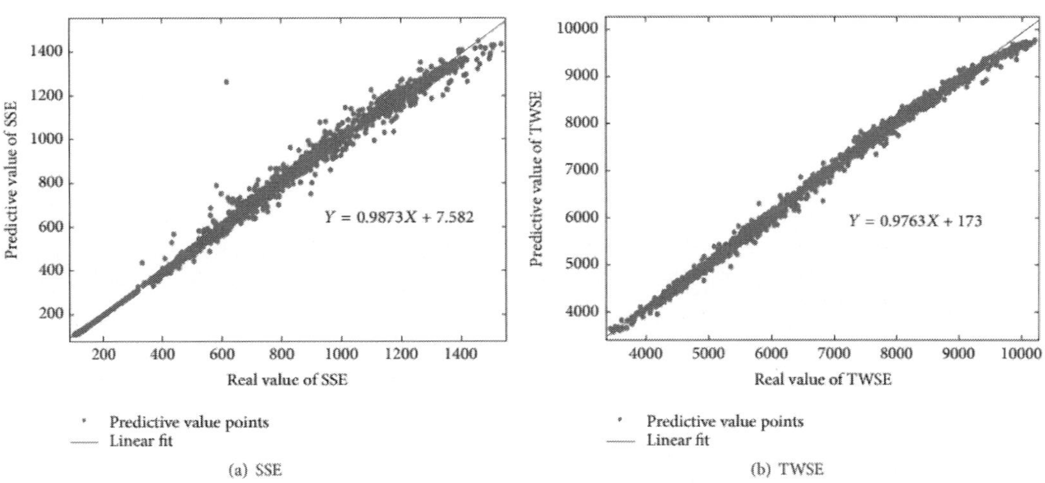

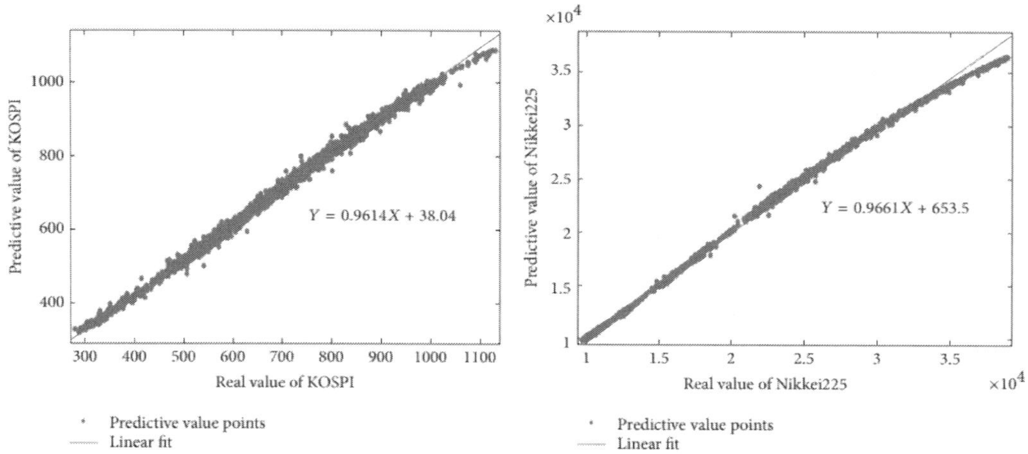

(c) KOSPI (d) Nikkei225

Figure 4: Comparisons and linear regressions of the actual data and the predictive values for SSE, TWSE, KOSPI, and Nikkei225.

A valuable numerical measure of association between two variables is the correlation coefficient R. Table 2 shows the values of a, b, and R for the above indices.$R$is given as follows:

$$R = \frac{\sum_{i=1}^{N}\left(d_t - \bar{d}_t\right)\left(y_t - \bar{y}_t\right)}{\sqrt{\sum_{i=1}^{N}\left(d_t - \bar{d}_t\right)^2 \sum_{i=1}^{N}\left(y_t - \bar{y}_t\right)^2}}, \quad (15)$$

where d_t is the actual value, y_t is the predicting value, $\bar{d}_t$ is the mean of the actual value, $\bar{y}_t$ is the mean of the predicting value, and N is the total number of the data.

Table 2: Linear regression parameters of market indices.

Parameter	SSE	TWSE	KOSPI	Nikkei225
a	0.9873	0.9763	0.9614	0.9661
b	7.582	173	38.04	653.5
R	0.992	0.9952	0.9963	0.9971

Comparisons of Forecasting Results

We compare the proposed and conventional forecasting approaches (BPNN, STNN, and ERNN model) on the four indices mentioned above, where STNN is based on the BPNN and combined with the stochastic effective function [19]. For these four different models, we set the same inputs of the networks, including four kinds of series: daily open price, daily closing price, daily highest price, and daily lowest price. The network output is the closing price of the next trading day. In the stock markets, the practical experience shows us that the above four kinds of data of the last trading day are very important indicators when predicting the closing price of the next trading day. To choose better parameters, we have carried out many experiments on these four different indices. In order to achieve the optimal networks of each forecasting approach, the most appropriate numbers of neural nodes in the hidden layer are different; the learning rates are also varying by training different models; see Table 3. In Table 3, "Hidden" stands for the number of neural nodes in the hidden layer, and "L. r" stands for learning rate. The hidden number is also chosen by referring to [21, 29, 30]. The experiments have been done repeatedly to determine hidden nodes and training cycle in the training process. The details of principles of how to choose the hidden number are as follows: If the number of neural nodes in the input layer is N, the number of neural nodes in the hidden layer is set to be nearly $2N + 1$, and the number of neural nodes in the output layer is 1. Since the ERNN model and the ST-ERNN model have similar topology structures, in Table 3, the number of neural nodes in hidden layer and the learning rate are chosen approximatly in the two models of training process. Also, the BPNN model and the STNN model are similar, so the chosen parameters are basically the same. Figures 5(a)–5(d) show the predicting values of the four indexes on the test set. From these plots, the predicting values of the ST-ERNN model are closer to the actual values than the other models curves. To compare the training and forecasting results more clearly, the performance measures RMSE, MAE, MAPE, and MAPE(100) are uncovered in the next part.

Table 3: Different parameters for different models.

Index data	BPNN		STNN		ERNN		ST-ERNN	
	Hidden	L. r	Hidden	L. r	Hidden	L. r	Hidden	L. r
SSE	8	0.01	8	0.01	10	0.001	9	0.001
TWSE	10	0.01	10	0.01	12	0.001	12	0.001
KOSPI	8	0.02	8	0.02	10	0.03	10	0.05
Nikkei225	10	0.05	10	0.05	10	0.01	10	0.01

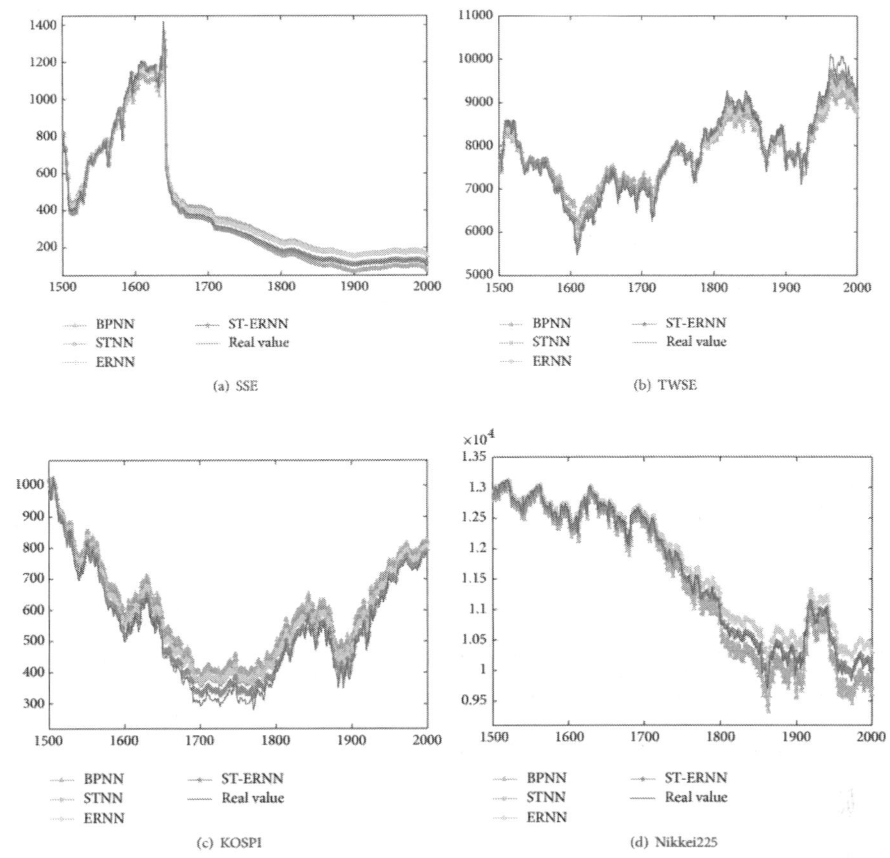

Figure 5: Predictive values on the test set for SSE, TWSE, KOSPI, and Nikkei225.

To analyze the forecasting performance of four considered forecasting models deeply, we use the following error evaluation criteria [31–35]: the mean absolute error (MAE), the root mean square error (RMSE), and the correlation coefficient (MAPE); the corresponding definitions are given as follows:

$$\text{MAE} = \frac{1}{N}\sum_{t=1}^{N} |d_t - y_t|,$$

$$\text{RMSE} = \sqrt{\frac{1}{N}\sum_{t=1}^{N} (d_t - y_t)^2},$$

$$\text{MAPE} = 100 \times \frac{1}{N}\sum_{t=1}^{N} \left|\frac{d_t - y_t}{d_t}\right|, \qquad (16)$$

where d_t and y_t are the real value and the predicting value at time t, respectively. N is the total number of the data. Noting that MAE, RMSE, and MAPE are measures of the deviation between the prediction values and the actual values, the prediction performance is better when the values of these evaluation criteria are smaller. However, if the results are not consistent among these criteria, we choose the MAPE as the benchmark since MAPE is relatively more stable than other criteria [16].

Figures 6(a)–6(d) show the forecasting results of SSE, TWSE, KOSPI, and Nikkei225 for four forecasting models. The empirical research shows that the proposed ST-ERNN model has the best performance; the ERNN and the STNN both outperform the common BPNN model. The stock markets showed large fluctuations which are reflected in Figure 6; we can see that the large fluctuation period forecasting is relatively not accurate from these four models. When the stock market is relatively stable, the forecasting result is nearer to the actual value. Compared with the BPNN, the STNN, and the ERNN models, the forecasting results are also presented in Table 4, where the MAPE(100) stands for the latest 100 days of MAPE in the testing data. Table 4 shows that the evaluation criteria by the ST-ERNN model are almost smaller than those by other models. From Table 4 and Figure 6, we can conclude that the proposed ST-ERNN model is better than the other three models. In Table 4, the evaluation criteria by the STNN model and ERNN model are almost smaller than those by BPNN for four considered indices. It illustrates that the effect of financial time series forecasting of STNN model is superior to that of BPNN model, and the dynamic neural network is effective, robust, and precise than original BPNN for these four indices. Besides, most values of MAPE(100) are smaller than those of MAPE in all stock indexes. Therefore, the short-term prediction outperforms the long-term prediction. Overall training and testing results are consistent with the measured data, which demonstrates that the ST-ERNN predictor has higher forecast accuracy.

Table 4: Comparisons of indices' predictions for different forecasting models.

Index errors	BPNN	STNN	ERNN	ST-ERNN
		SSE		
MAE	45.3701	24.9687	37.262647	12.7390
RMSE	54.4564	40.5437	49.3907	37.0693
MAPE	20.1994	11.8947	18.2110	4.1353
MAPE(100)	5.0644	3.6868	4.3176	2.6809
		TWSE		
MAE	252.7225	140.5971	151.2830	105.6377
RMSE	316.8197	186.8309	205.4236	136.1674
MAPE	3.2017	1.7303	1.8449	1.3468
MAPE(100)	2.2135	1.1494	1.3349	1.2601
		KOSPI		
MAE	74.3073	56.3309	47.9296	18.2421
RMSE	77.1528	58.2944	50.8174	21.0479
MAPE	16.6084	12.4461	10.9608	4.2257
MAPE(100)	7.4379	5.9664	4.9176	2.1788
		Nikkei225		
MAE	203.8034	138.1857	166.2480	68.5458
RMSE	238.5933	169.7061	207.3395	89.0378
MAPE	1.8556	1.2580	1.5398	0.6010
MAPE(100)	0.7674	0.5191	0.4962	0.4261

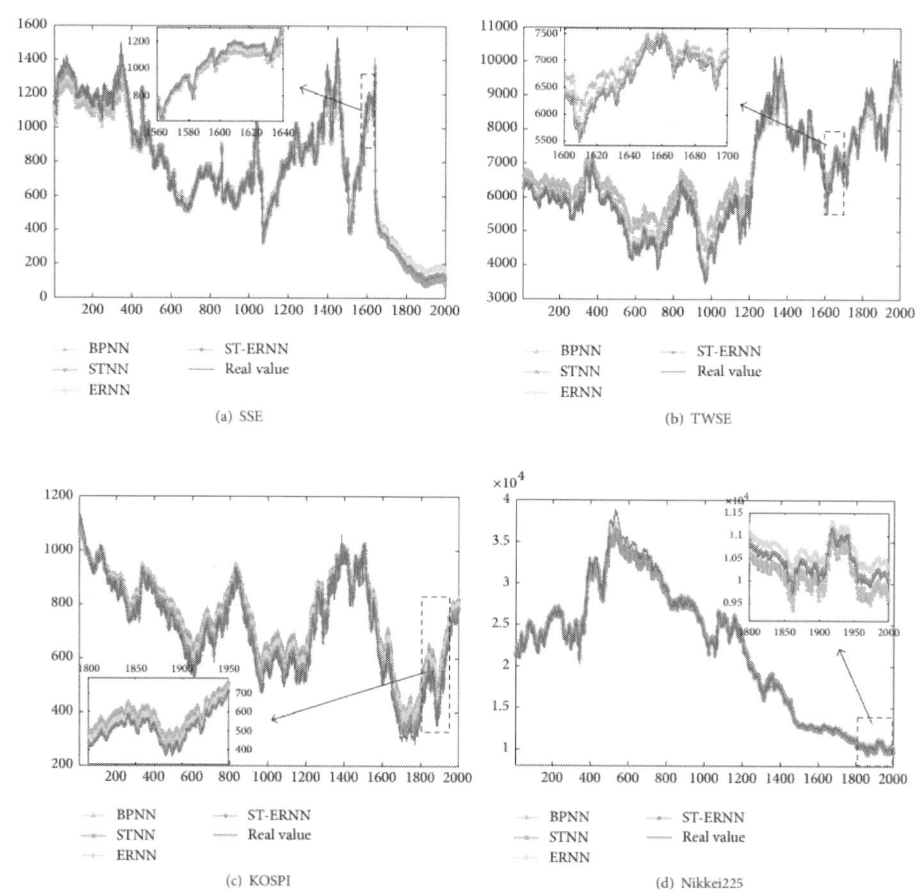

Figure 6: Comparisons of the actual data and the predictive data for SSE, TWSE, KOSPI, and Nikkei225.

In Figures 7(a), 7(b), 7(c), and 7(d) we considered the relative errors of the ST-ERNN forecasting results. Figure 7 depicts that most of the predicting relative errors for these four price series are between −0.1 and 0.1. Moreover, there are some points with large relative errors of forecasting results in four models, especially on the SSE index, which can attribute to the large fluctuation that leads to the large relative errors. The definition of relative error is given as follows:

$$e(t) = \frac{d_t - y_t}{d_t}, \tag{17}$$

where d_t and y_t denote the actual value and the predicting value, respectively, at time t, $t = 1, 2, \ldots$.

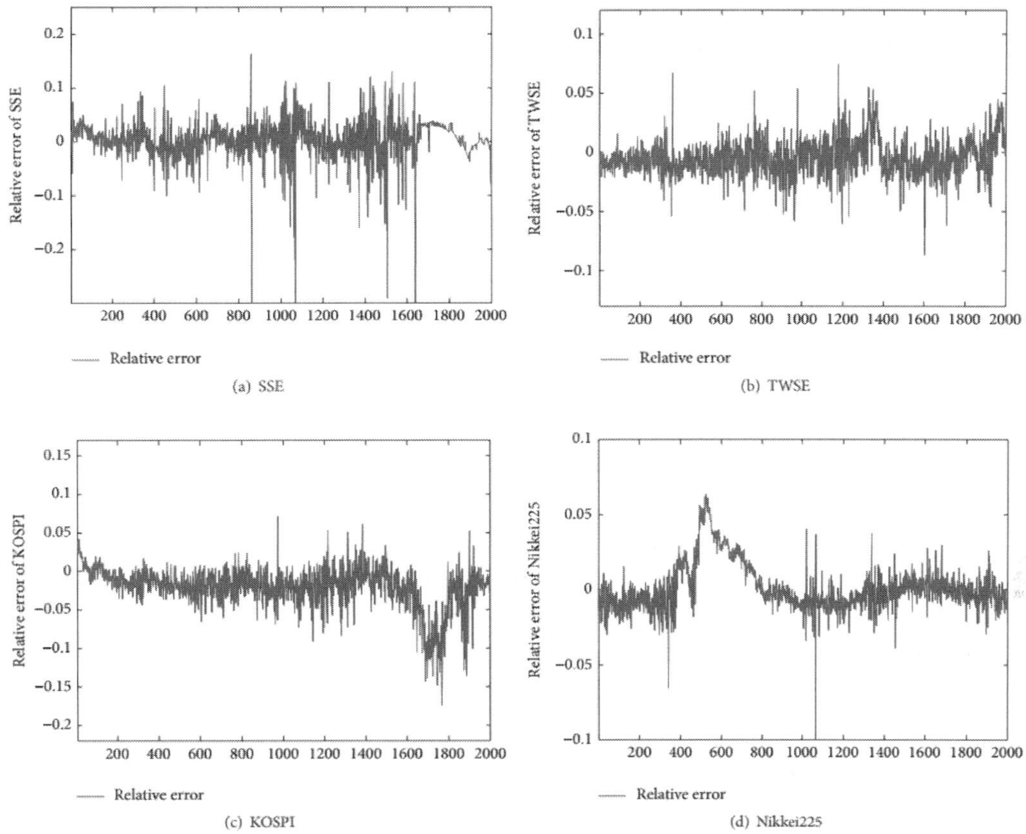

Figure 7: ((a), (b), (c), and (d)) Relative errors of forecasting results from the ST-ERNN model.

CID AND MCID ANALYSIS

The analysis and forecast of time series have long been a focus of economic research for a more clear understanding of mechanism and characteristics of financial markets [36–42]. In this section, we employ an efficient complexity invariant distance (CID) for time series. Reference [43] shows that complexity invariant distance measure can produce improvements in classification and clustering in the vast majority of cases.

Complexity invariance uses information about complexity differences between two time series as a correction factor for existing distance measures. We begin by introducing Euclidean distance and use this as a starting point to bring in the definition of CID. Suppose we have two time series, P and Q, of length n. Consider

$$P = p_1, p_2, \ldots, p_i, \ldots, p_n,$$
$$Q = q_1, q_2, \ldots, q_i, \ldots, q_n. \tag{18}$$

The ubiquitous Euclidean distance is

$$\mathrm{ED}(P, Q) = \sqrt{\sum_{i=1}^{n} (p_i - q_i)^2}. \tag{19}$$

The Euclidean distance, ED(P, Q), between two time series P and Q, can be made complexity invariant by introducing a correction factor

$$\mathrm{CID}(P, Q) = \mathrm{ED}(P, Q) \times \mathrm{CF}(P, Q), \tag{20}$$

where CF is a complexity correction factor defined as

$$\mathrm{CF}(P, Q) = \frac{\max(\mathrm{CE}(P), \mathrm{CE}(Q))}{\min(\mathrm{CE}(P), \mathrm{CE}(Q))} \tag{21}$$

and CE(T) is a complexity estimate of a time series T, which can be computed as follows:

$$\mathrm{CE}(T) = \sqrt{\sum_{i=1}^{n-1} (t_{i+1} - t_i)^2}. \tag{22}$$

It is worth noticing that CF accounts for differences in the complexities of the time series being compared. CF forces time series with very different complexities to be further apart. In the case that all time series have the same complexity, CID simply degenerates to Euclidean distance. The prediction performance is better when the CID distance is smaller; that is to say the curve of the predictive data is closer to the actual data. The actual values can be seen as the series P and the predicting results as the series Q. Table 5 shows CID distance between the real indices values of SSE, TWSE, KOSPI, and Nikkei225 and the corresponding predictions from each network model. It is clear that the CID distance between the real index values and the prediction by ST-ERNN model is the smallest one; moreover the distances by the STNN model and the ERNN model are smaller than those by the BPNN for all the four considered indices.

Table 5: CID distances for four network models

Index	BPNN	STNN	ERNN	ST-ERNN
SSE	3052.1	1764.7	2320.2	1659.9
TWSE	27805	9876.3	10830	6158.1
KOSPI	3350.4	2312.8	2551.0	1006.0
Nikkei225	44541	23726	32895	25421

In general, the complexity of a real system is not constrained to a sole scale. In this part we consider a developed CID analysis, that is, the multiscale CID (MCID). The MCID analysis takes into account the multiple time scales while measuring the predicting results, and it is applied to the stock prices analysis for the actual data and the predicting data in this work. The MCID analysis should comprise two steps. (i) Considering one-dimensional discrete time series $\{x_1, x_2,\ldots,\ldots,x_N\}$, we construct consecutive coarse-grained time series $\{y^{(\tau)}\}$, corresponding to the scale factor τ, according to the following formula:

$$y_j^{(\tau)} = \frac{1}{\tau} \sum_{i=(j-1)\tau+1}^{j\tau} x_i, \quad 1 \leq j \leq \frac{N}{\tau}. \tag{23}$$

For scale one, the time series $\{^{(1)}\}$ is simply the original time series. The length of each coarse-grained time series is equal to the original time series divided by the scale factor τ. (ii) Calculate the CID for each coarse-grained time series and then plot as a function of the scale factor. Figure 8 shows the MCID values between the forecasting results and the real market prices from BPNN, ERNN, STNN, and STERNN models. In Figure 8, it is obvious that the MCID from ST-ERNN with the actual value is the smallest one in any scale; that is, the ST-ERNN (with the stochastic time effective function) for forecasting stock prices is effective.

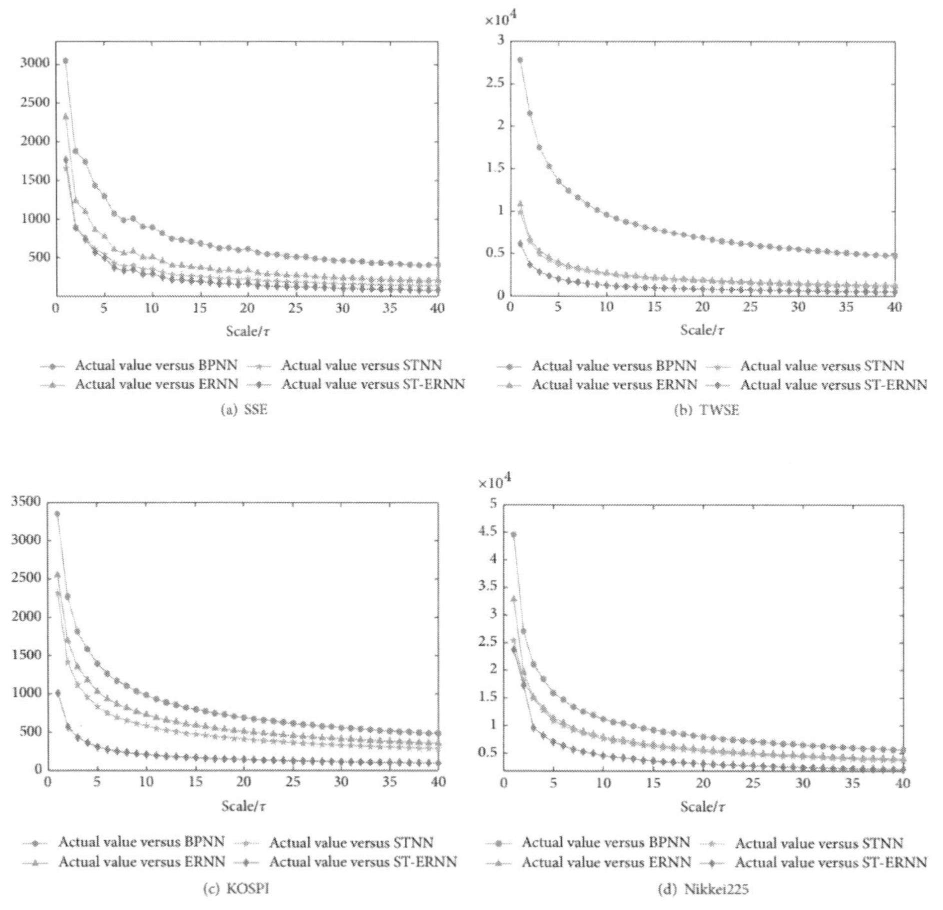

Figure 8: ((a), (b), (c), and (d)) MCID values between the forecasting results and the real market prices from BPNN, ERNN, STNN, and ST-ERNN models.

CONCLUSION

The aim of this research is to develop a predictive model to forecast the financial time series. In this study, we have developed a predictive model by using an Elman recurrent neural network with the stochastic time effective function to forecast the indices of SSE, TWSE, KOSPI, and Nikkei225. Through the linear regression analysis, it implies that the predictive values and the real values are not deviating too much. Then we take the proposed model compared with BPNN, STNN, and ERNN forecasting models. Empirical examinations of predicting precision for the price time series (by the comparisons of predicting measures as MAE, RMSE, MAPE, and MAPE(100)) show that the proposed neural network model has the advantage of improving the precision of forecasting, and the forecasting of this proposed model much approaches to the real financial market movements. Furthermore, from the curve of the relative error, it can make a conclusion that the large fluctuation leads to the large relative errors. In addition, by calculating CID and MCID distance the conclusion was illustrated more clearly. The study and the proposed model contribute significantly to the time series literature on forecasting.

ACKNOWLEDGMENT

The authors were supported in part by National Natural Science Foundation of China under Grant nos. 71271026 and 10971010.

REFERENCES

1. Y. Kajitani, K. W. Hipel, and A. I. McLeod, "Forecasting nonlinear time series with feed-forward neural networks: a case study of Canadian lynx data," Journal of Forecasting, vol. 24, no. 2, pp. 105–117, 2005.
2. T. Takahama, S. Sakai, A. Hara, and N. Iwane, "Predicting stock price using neural networks optimized by differential evolution with degeneration," International Journal of Innovative Computing, Information and Control, vol. 5, no. 12, pp. 5021–5031, 2009.
3. K. Huarng and T. H.-K. Yu, "The application of neural networks to forecast fuzzy time series," Physica A, vol. 363, no. 2, pp. 481–491, 2006.
4. F. Wang and J. Wang, "Statistical analysis and forecasting of return interval for SSE and model by lattice percolation system and neural network," Computers and Industrial Engineering, vol. 62, no. 1, pp. 198–205, 2012.
5. H.-J. Kim and K.-S. Shin, "A hybrid approach based on neural networks and genetic algorithms for detecting temporal patterns in stock markets," Applied Soft Computing, vol. 7, no. 2, pp. 569–576, 2007.
6. M. Ghiassi, H. Saidane, and D. K. Zimbra, "A dynamic artificial neural network model for forecasting time series events," International Journal of Forecasting, vol. 21, no. 2, pp. 341–362, 2005.
7. M. R. Hassan, B. Nath, and M. Kirley, "A fusion model of HMM, ANN and GA for stock market forecasting," Expert Systems with Applications, vol. 33, no. 1, pp. 171–180, 2007.
8. D. Devaraj, B. Yegnanarayana, and K. Ramar, "Radial basis function networks for fast contingency ranking," International Journal of Electrical Power and Energy Systems, vol. 24, no. 5, pp. 387–395, 2002.
9. B. A. Garroa and R. A. Vázquez, "Designing artificial neural networks using particle swarm optimization algorithms," Computational Intelligence and Neuroscience, vol. 2015, Article ID 369298, 20 pages, 2015.
10. Q. Gan, "Exponential synchronization of stochastic Cohen-Grossberg neural networks with mixed time-varying delays and reaction-diffusion via periodically intermittent control," Neural Networks, vol. 31, pp. 12–21, 2012.
11. D. Xiao and J. Wang, "Modeling stock price dynamics by continuum percolation system and relevant complex systems analysis," Physica A: Statistical Mechanics and its Applications, vol. 391, no. 20, pp. 4827–4838, 2012.
12. D. Enke and N. Mehdiyev, "Stock market prediction using a combination of stepwise regression analysis, differential evolution-based fuzzy clustering, and a fuzzy inference Neural Network," Intelligent Automation and Soft Computing, vol. 19, no. 4, pp. 636–648, 2013.
13. G. Sermpinisa, C. Stasinakisa, and C. Dunisb, "Stochastic and genetic neural network combinations in trading and hybrid time-varying leverage effects," Journal of International Financial Markets, Institutions & Money, vol. 30, pp. 21–54, 2014.
14. R. Ebrahimpour, H. Nikoo, S. Masoudnia, M. R. Yousefi, and M. S. Ghaemi, "Mixture of mlp-experts for trend forecasting of time series: a case study of the tehran stock exchange," International Journal of Forecasting, vol. 27, no. 3, pp. 804–816, 2011.
15. A. Bahrammirzaee, "A comparative survey of artificial intelligence applications in finance: artificial neural networks, expert system and hybrid intelligent systems," Neural Computing and Applications, vol. 19, no. 8, pp. 1165–1195, 2010.
16. A. Graves, M. Liwicki, S. Fernández, R. Bertolami, H. Bunke, and J. Schmidhuber, "A novel connectionist system for unconstrained handwriting recognition," IEEE Transactions on Pattern Analysis and Machine Intelligence, vol. 31, no. 5, pp. 855–868, 2009.
17. M. Ardalani-Farsa and S. Zolfaghari, "Chaotic time series prediction with residual analysis method using hybrid Elman-NARX neural networks," Neurocomputing, vol. 73, no. 13–15, pp. 2540–2553, 2010.
18. M. Paliwal and U. A. Kumar, "Neural networks and statistical techniques: a review of applications,"Expert Systems with Applications, vol. 36, no. 1, pp. 2–17, 2009.
19. Z. Liao and J. Wang, "Forecasting model of global stock index by stochastic time effective neural network," Expert Systems with Applications, vol. 37, no. 1, pp. 834–841, 2010.
20. L. Pan and J. Cao, "Robust stability for uncertain stochastic neural network with delay and impulses,"Neurocomputing, vol. 94, pp. 102–110, 2012.

21. H. F. Liu and J. Wang, "Integrating independent component analysis and principal component analysis with neural network to predict Chinese stock market," Mathematical Problems in Engineering, vol. 2011, Article ID 382659, 15 pages, 2011.

22. Z. Q. Guo, H. Q. Wang, and Q. Liu, "Financial time series forecasting using LPP and SVM optimized by PSO," Soft Computing, vol. 17, no. 5, pp. 805–818, 2013.

23. H. L. Niu and J. Wang, "Financial time series prediction by a random data-time effective RBF neural network," Soft Computing, vol. 18, no. 3, pp. 497–508, 2014.

24. J. L. Elman, "Finding structure in time," Cognitive Science, vol. 14, no. 2, pp. 179–211, 1990.

25. M. Cacciola, G. Megali, D. Pellicanó, and F. C. Morabito, "Elman neural networks for characterizing voids in welded strips: a study," Neural Computing and Applications, vol. 21, no. 5, pp. 869–875, 2012.

26. R. Chandra and M. Zhang, "Cooperative coevolution of Elman recurrent neural networks for chaotic time series prediction," Neurocomputing, vol. 86, pp. 116–123, 2012.

27. D. K. Chaturvedi, P. S. Satsangi, and P. K. Kalra, "Effect of different mappings and normalization of neural network models," in Proceedings of the National Power Systems Conference, vol. 9, pp. 377–386, Indian Institute of Technology, Kanpur, India, 1996.

28. S. Makridakis, "Accuracy measures: theoretical and practical concerns," International Journal of Forecasting, vol. 9, no. 4, pp. 527–529, 1993.

29. L. Q. Han, Design and Application of Artificial Neural Network, Chemical Industry Press, 2002.

30. M. Zounemat-Kermani, "Principal component analysis (PCA) for estimating chlorophyll concentration using forward and generalized regression neural networks," Applied Artificial Intelligence, vol. 28, no. 1, pp. 16–29, 2014.

31. D. Olson and C. Mossman, "Neural network forecasts of Canadian stock returns using accounting ratios," International Journal of Forecasting, vol. 19, no. 3, pp. 453–465, 2003.

32. H. Demuth and M. Beale, Network Toolbox: For Use with MATLAB, The Math Works, Natick, Mass, USA, 5th edition, 1998.

33. A. P. Plumb, R. C. Rowe, P. York, and M. Brown, "Optimisation of the predictive ability of artificial neural network (ANN) models: a comparison of three ANN programs and four classes of training algorithm,"European Journal of Pharmaceutical Sciences, vol. 25, no. 4-5, pp. 395–405, 2005.

34. D. Ö. Faruk, "A hybrid neural network and ARIMA model for water quality time series prediction,"Engineering Applications of Artificial Intelligence, vol. 23, no. 4, pp. 586–594, 2010.

35. M. Tripathy, "Power transformer differential protection using neural network principal component analysis and radial basis function neural network," Simulation Modelling Practice and Theory, vol. 18, no. 5, pp. 600–611, 2010.

36. C. E. Martin and J. A. Reggia, "Fusing swarm intelligence and self-assembly for optimizing echo state networks," Computational Intelligence and Neuroscience, vol. 2015, Article ID 642429, 15 pages, 2015.

37. R. S. Tsay, Analysis of Financial Time Series, John Wiley & Sons, Hoboken, NJ, USA, 2005.

38. P.-C. Chang, D.-D. Wang, and C.-L. Zhou, "A novel model by evolving partially connected neural network for stock price trend forecasting," Expert Systems with Applications, vol. 39, no. 1, pp. 611–620, 2012.

39. P. Roy, G. S. Mahapatra, P. Rani, S. K. Pandey, and K. N. Dey, "Robust feed forward and recurrent neural network based dynamic weighted combination models for software reliability prediction," Applied Soft Computing, vol. 22, pp. 629–637, 2014.

40. X. Gabaix, P. Gopikrishnan, V. Plerou, and H. E. Stanley, "A theory of power-law distributions in financial market fluctuations," Nature, vol. 423, no. 6937, pp. 267–270, 2003.

41. R. N. Mantegna and H. E. Stanley, An Introduction to Econophysics: Correlations and Complexity in Finance, Cambridge University Press, Cambridge, UK, 2000.

42. T. H. Roh, "Forecasting the volatility of stock price index," Expert Systems with Applications, vol. 33, no. 4, pp. 916–922, 2007.

43. G. E. Batista, E. J. Keogh, O. M. Tataw, and V. M. de Souza, "CID: an efficient complexity-invariant distance for time series," Data Mining and Knowledge Discovery, vol. 28, no. 3, pp. 634–669, 2014.

CHAPTER 9 FUZZIFIED DATA BASED NEURAL NETWORK MODELING

Deepti Moyi Sahoo and S. Chakraverty

INTRODUCTION

System identification methods in structural dynamics, in general, solve inverse vibration problems to identify properties of a structure from measured data. The rapid progress in the field of computer science and computational mathematics during recent decades has led to an increasing use of process computers and models to analyze, supervise, and control technical processes. The use of computers and efficient mathematical tools allows identification of the process dynamics by evaluating the input and output signals of the system. The result of such a process identification is usually a mathematical model by which the dynamic behaviour can be estimated or predicted. The system identification problem has been nicely explained in a recent paper [1]. The same statements from [1] are reproduced below for the benefit of the readers.

The study of structures dynamic behaviour may be categorized into two distinct activities: analytical and/or numerical modelling (e.g., finite element models) and vibration tests (e.g., experimental modal models). Due to different limitations and assumptions, each approach has its advantages and shortcomings. Therefore, in order to determine the dynamic properties of the structure, reconciliation processes including model correlation and/or model updating should be performed. Model updating can be defined as the adjustment of an existing analytical/numerical model in the light of measured vibration test. After adjustment, the updated model is expected to represent the dynamic behaviour of the structure more accurately as proposed by Friswell et al. [2]. With the recent advances in computing technology for data acquisition, signal processing, and analysis, the parameters of structural models may be updated from the measured responses under excitation of the structure. This procedure is achieved using system identification techniques as an inverse problem. The inverse problem may be defined as determination of the internal structure of a physical system from the system's measured behaviour, or estimation of an unknown input that gives rise to a measured output signal according to Tanaka and Bui [3].

Comprehensive literature surveys have been provided on the subject of model updating of the structural systems by Alvin et al. [4], and Time series methods for fault detection and identification in vibrating structures were presented by Fassois and Sakellariou [5]. Shear buildings are among the most widely studied structural systems. Previous works on model updating of shear buildings rely mostly on using modal parameter identification and physical or structural parameter identification to drive the corresponding update procedures. As regards the publications, Marsi et al. [6] gave various methodologies for different types of problems in system identification. Various techniques for improving structural dynamic models were reviewed in a review paper by Ibanez [7], and studies made by Datta et al. [8] related to system identification of buildings done until that date were also surveyed. Some of the related publications may be mentioned as those of Loh and Tou [9] and Yuan et al. [10].

It is known that, the systems which may be modeled as linear, the identification problem often turns in to a non-linear optimization problem. This requires an intelligent iterative scheme to have the required solution. There exists various online and offline methods, namely, the Gauss-Newton, Kalman filtering and probabilistic methods such as maximum likelihood estimation, and so forth. However, the identification

Citation: Deepti Moyi Sahoo and S. Chakraverty, "Fuzzified Data Based Neural Network Modeling," Advances in Artificial Neural Systems, vol. 2013, Article ID 962734, 12 pages, 2013. doi:10.1155/2013/962734.

problem for a large number of parameters, following two basic difficulties are faced often:

(i) objective function surface may have multiple maxima and minima, and the convergence to the correct parameters is possible only if the initial guess is considered as close to the parameters to be identified;

(ii) inverse problem in general gives nonunique parameter estimates.

To overcome these difficulties, researchers have developed various identification methodologies for the said problem by using powerful technique of Artificial Neural Network (ANN). Chen [11] presented a neural network based method for determining the modal parameters of structures from field measurement. Using the observed dynamic responses, he trained the neural network based on back-propagation technique. He then directly identified the modal parameters of the structure using the weight matrices of the neural network. In particular, Huang et al. [12] presented a novel procedure for identifying the dynamic characteristics of a building using a back-propagation neural network technique. Another novel neural network based approach has been presented by Kao and Hung [13] for detecting structural damage. A decentralized stiffness identification method with neural networks for a multidegree of freedom structure has been developed by Wu et al. [14]. Localized damage detection and parametric identification method with direct use of earthquake responses for large-scale infrastructures has also been proposed by Xu et al. [15]. A neural network based strategy by Xu et al. [16] was developed for direct identification of structural parameters from the time domain dynamic responses of an object structure without anyeigen value analysis.

System identification on the other hand tries to identify structural matrices of mass, damping and stiffness directly. Among various methodologies in this regard Chakraverty [17], Perry et al. [18], Wang [19], Yoshitomi and Takewaki [20], and Lu and Tu [21] developed different techniques to handle the system identification problems. Yuan et al. [10] developed a methodology that identifies the mass and stiffness matrices of a shear building from the first two orders of structural mode measurement. Koh et al. [22] proposed several Ga-based substructural identification methods, which work by solving parts of the structure at a time to improve the convergence of mass and stiffness estimates particularly for large systems. Chakraverty [17] proposed procedures to refine the methods of Yuan et al. [10] to identify the structural mass and stiffness matrices of shear buildings from the modal test data. The refinement was obtained using Holzer criteria. Tang et al. [23] utilized a differential evolution (DE) strategy for parameter estimation of the structural systems with limited output data, noise polluted signals, and no prior knowledge of mass, damping, or stiffness matrices. Recent works on model updating of multistory shear buildings for simultaneous identification of mass, stiffness, and damping matrices using two different soft-computing methods have been developed by Khanmirza et al. [1]. It may be seen from above that Artificial Neural Networks (ANNs) provide a fundamentally different approach to system identification. They have been successfully applied for identification and control of dynamics systems in various fields of engineering because of excellent learning capacity and high tolerance to partially inaccurate data.

It is revealed from the above literature review that various authors developed different identification methodologies using ANN. They supposed that the data obtained are in exact or crisp form. But in actual practice the experimental data obtained from equipments are with errors that may be due to human or equipment error, thereby giving uncertain form of the data. Although one may also use probabilistic methods to handle such problems. Then, the probabilistic method requires huge quantity of data which may not be easy or feasible. Thus in this paper, a minimum number of data are taken in fuzzified form to have the essence of the uncertainty. Accordingly, in this paper, identification methodologies for multistorey shear buildings have been proposed using the powerful technique of Artificial Neural Network (ANN) models which can handle fuzzified data. It is already mentioned that identification with crisp data is known and also neural network method has already been used by various researchers for this case. Here, the input and output data may be in fuzzified form. This is because in general we may not get the corresponding input and output values exactly (in crisp form), but we have only the uncertain information of the data. This uncertain data has been assumed to be in terms of fuzzy numbers.

In this paper, the initial design parameters, namely, stiffness and mass and so the frequency of the said problem is known. But after a large span of time, the structure may be subjected to various manmade and natural calamities. Then, the engineers want to know the present health of the structure by system identification methods. It is assumed that only the stiffness is changed and the mass remains the same. As such equipments are available to get the present values of the frequencies and using these one may get the present parameter values by ANN. But while doing the experiment, one may not get the exact values of the parameters. But we may get those values as uncertain, namely, in fuzzy form. So if sensors are placed to capture the frequency of the floors in fuzzy (uncertain) form, then those may be fed into the proposed new ANN model to get the present stiffness parameters in fuzzified form. In order to train the new ANN model, set of data are generated numerically beforehand. As such, converged ANN model gives the present stiffness parameter values in interval form for each floor. Thus, one may predict the health of the uncertain structure. Corresponding example problems have been solved, and related results are reported to show the reliability and powerfulness of the model.

ANALYSIS AND MODELLING

System identification refers to the branch of numerical analysis which uses the experimental input and output data to develop mathematical models of systems which finally identify the parameters. The floor masses for this methodology are assumed to be $[\underline{m_1}, m_1c, \overline{m_1}]$ $[\underline{m_2}, m_2c, \overline{m_2}], \ldots, [\underline{m_n}, m_nc, \overline{m_n}]$, , and the stiffness $[\underline{k_1}, k_1c, \overline{k_1}], [\underline{k_2}, k_2c, \overline{k_2}], \ldots, [\underline{k_n}, k_nc, \overline{k_n}]$, are the structural parameters which are to be identified. It may be seen that all the mass and stiffness parameters are taken in fuzzy form. As such here for each mass m_i, we have $\underline{m_i}$ as the left value, m_ic as the centre value, and $\overline{m_i}$ as the right value. Similarly for the stiffness parameter for each mass k_i, we have $\underline{k_i}$ as the left value, k_ic as the centre value, and $\overline{k_i}$ as the right value. The n-storey shear structure is shown in Figure

1. Corresponding dynamic equation of motion for n-storey (supposed as n degrees of freedom) shear structure without damping may be written as

$$\{\widetilde{M}\}\{\ddot{\widetilde{X}}\} + \{\widetilde{K}\}\{\widetilde{X}\} = \{\widetilde{0}\}, \tag{1}$$

where $\{\ddot{\widetilde{x}}\} = \{\ddot{\underline{x}}, \ddot{x}c, \ddot{\overline{x}}\}$, $\{\widetilde{x}\} = [\underline{x}, xc, \overline{x}]$.

$\{\widetilde{M}\} = [\underline{M}, Mc, \overline{M}]$ is $n \times n$ mass matrix of the structure and is given by

$$\{\widetilde{M}\} = \begin{bmatrix} [\underline{m_1}, m_1c, \overline{m_1}] & 0 & \cdots & \cdots & 0 \\ 0 & [\underline{m_2}, m_2c, \overline{m_2}] & 0 & \cdots & 0 \\ \cdots & \cdots & \cdots & \cdots & \cdots \\ \cdots & \cdots & 0 & [\underline{m_{n-1}}, m_{n-1}c, \overline{m_{n-1}}] & [\underline{m_n}, m_nc, \overline{m_n}] \\ 0 & \cdots & \cdots & 0 & 0 \end{bmatrix}. \tag{2}$$

$\{\widetilde{K}\} = [\underline{K}, Kc, \overline{K}]$ is $n \times n$ stiffness matrix of the structure and may be written as

$$\{\widetilde{K}\} = \begin{bmatrix} \widetilde{k}_1 + \widetilde{k}_2 & \widetilde{k}_2 & 0 & \cdots & 0 \\ -\widetilde{k}_2 & \widetilde{k}_2 + \widetilde{k}_3 & -\widetilde{k}_3 & \cdots & 0 \\ \cdots & \cdots & & & \cdots \\ 0 & \cdots & -\widetilde{k}_{n-1} & \widetilde{k}_{n-1} + \widetilde{k}_n & \widetilde{k}_n \\ 0 & & \cdots & -\widetilde{k}_n & \widetilde{k}_n \end{bmatrix}, \tag{3}$$

and $\{\widetilde{X}\} = \{\widetilde{x}_1, \widetilde{x}_2, \ldots, \widetilde{x}_n\}^T$ are the vectors of displacement.

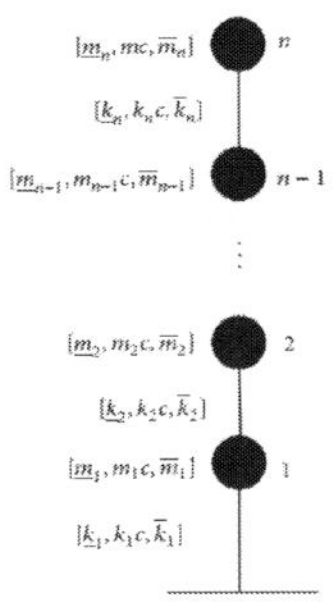

Figure 1: Multistorey shear structure with n-levels having fuzzy structural parameters.

We will first solve the above free vibration equation for vibration characteristics, namely, for frequency and mode shapes of the said structural system in order to get the stiffness parameters in fuzzified form. Accordingly putting $\{\widetilde{X}\} = \{\widetilde{\phi}\}e^{i(\widetilde{\omega})t}$ in free vibration equation (1), we get

$$\left(\{\widetilde{K}\} - \{\widetilde{M}\}[\widetilde{\omega}]^2\right)\{\widetilde{\phi}\} = \{\widetilde{0}\}, \tag{4}$$

where $\{\widetilde{\omega}\}^2 = [\underline{\omega}, \omega c, \overline{\omega}]^2 = [\underline{\lambda}, \lambda c, \overline{\lambda}]$ are eigenvalues or the natural frequency and $\{\widetilde{\phi}\}$ are mode shapes of the structure, respectively.

BASIC CONCEPT OF FUZZY SET THEORY

Definition 1: Let X be a universal set. Then, the fuzzy subset A of X is defined by its membership function

$$\mu_A : X \longrightarrow [0, 1], \tag{5}$$

which assigns a real number $\mu_A(x)$ in the interval [0, 1], to each element $x \in X$, where the value of $\mu_A(x)$ at x shows the grade of membership of x in A.

Definition 2: Given a fuzzy set A in X and any real number $\alpha \in [0, 1]$, then, the α-cut or α-level or cut worthy set of A, denoted by A_α, is the crisp set

$$A_\alpha = \{x \in X \mid \mu_A(x) \geq \alpha\}. \tag{6}$$

The strong α-cut, denoted by $A_{\alpha+}$, is the crisp set

$$A_{\alpha+} = \{x \in X \mid \mu_A(x) \geq \alpha\}. \tag{7}$$

Definition 3: A fuzzy number is a convex normalized fuzzy set of the real line R whose membership function is piecewise continuous.

Definition 4: A triangular fuzzy number A can be defined as a triplet $[a_1, a_2, a_3]$. Its membership function is defined as

$$\mu_A(x) = \begin{cases} 0, & x < a_1 \\ \dfrac{x - a_1}{a_2 - a_1}, & a_1 \leq x \leq a_2 \\ \dfrac{a_3 - x}{a_3 - a_2}, & a_2 \leq x \leq a_3 \\ 0, & x > a_3. \end{cases} \tag{8}$$

Above TFN may be transformed to an interval form A_α by α-cut as

$$A_\alpha = \left[a_1^{(\alpha)}, a_3^{(\alpha)}\right] = \left[(a_2 - a_1)\alpha + a_1, -(a_3 - a_2)\alpha + a_3\right]. \tag{9}$$

OPERATION OF FUZZY NUMBER

In this section, we consider arithmetic operation on fuzzy numbers and the result is expressed in membership function:

$$\forall x, y, z \in R. \tag{10}$$

(1) Addition: $A(+)B$

$$\mu_{A(+)B}(z) = \bigvee_{z=x+y} (\mu_A(x) \wedge \mu_B(y)). \tag{11}$$

(2) Subtraction: $A(-)B$

$$\mu_{A(-)B}(z) = \bigvee_{z=x-y} (\mu_A(x) \wedge \mu_B(y)). \tag{12}$$

(3) Multiplication: $A(\cdot)B$

$$\mu_{A(\cdot)B}(z) = \bigvee_{z=x \cdot y} (\mu_A(x) \wedge \mu_B(y)). \tag{13}$$

(4) Division: $A(/)B$

$$\mu_{A(/)B}(z) = \bigvee_{z=x/y} (\mu_A(x) \wedge \mu_B(y)). \tag{14}$$

(5) Minimum: $A(\wedge)B$

$$\mu_{A(\wedge)B}(z) = \bigvee_{z=x \wedge y} (\mu_A(x) \wedge \mu_B(y)). \tag{15}$$

(6) Maximum: $A(\vee)B$

$$\mu_{A(\vee)B}(z) = \bigvee_{z=x \vee y} (\mu_A(x) \wedge \mu_B(y)). \tag{16}$$

ARTIFICIAL NEURAL NETWORK (ANN) AND ERROR-BACK PROPAGATION TRAINING ALGORITHM (EBPTA) FOR FUZZIFIED DATA

Traditional ANN and EBPTA are well known, but here for the sake of completeness, those are developed for fuzzy case. In ANN, the first layer is considered to be input layer and the last layer is the output layer. Between the input and output layers, there may be more than one hidden layer. Each layer will contain number of neurons or nodes (processing elements) depending upon the problem. These processing elements operate in parallel and are arranged in patterns similar to the patterns found in biological neural nets. The processing elements are connected to each other by adjustable weights. The input/output behavior of the network changes if the weights are changed. So, the weights of the net may be chosen in such a way so as to achieve a desired output. To satisfy this goal, systematic ways of adjusting the weights have to be developed to handle the fuzzified data which are known as training or learning algorithm. Neural network basically depends upon the type of processing elements or nodes, the network topology, and the learning algorithm. Here, error back-propagation training algorithm and feedforward recall have been used but to handle the uncertain system. The typical network is given in Figure 2.

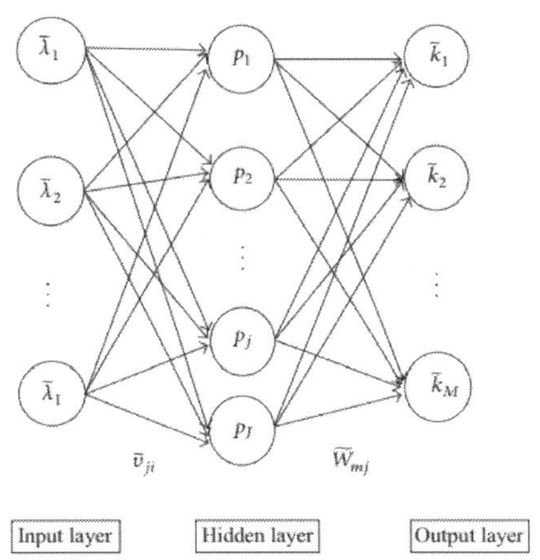

Figure 2: Layered feed-forward fuzzy neural network.

In this Figure, Z_i, P_j, and O_m are input, hidden, and output layers, respectively. The weights between input and hidden layers are denoted by V_{ji}, and the weights between hidden and output layers are denoted by W_{kj}. Here, $\tilde{Z}_i = [\underline{\lambda_i}\ \ \lambda_i c\ \ \overline{\lambda_i}]$ and $\tilde{O}_k = [\underline{k_m}\ \ k_m c\ \ \overline{k_m}]$.

Given R training pairs $\{\tilde{Z}_1, \tilde{d}_1; \tilde{Z}_2, \tilde{d}_2; \ldots, \tilde{Z}_R, \tilde{d}_R\}$ where $\tilde{Z}_i(I \times 1)$ are input and $\tilde{d}_i(M \times 1)$ are desired values for the given inputs, the error value is computed as

$$\tilde{E} = \frac{1}{2}\left(\tilde{d}_m - \tilde{O}_m\right)^2, \quad m = 1, 2, \ldots M, \tag{17}$$

for the present neural network as shown in Figure 2.The error signal terms of the output $(\tilde{\delta}_{Om})$ and hidden layers $(\tilde{\delta}_{Pj})$ are written, respectively, as

$$\tilde{\delta}_{Om} = 0.5 * \left(\tilde{d}_m - \tilde{O}_m\right)\left(1 - \tilde{O}_m^{\,2}\right), \quad m = 1, 2, \ldots M,$$

$$\tilde{\delta}_{Pj} = 0.5 * \left(1 - \tilde{P}_j^2\right) \sum_{m=1}^{M} \tilde{\delta}_{Om} \tilde{W}_{Pj}, \quad j = 1, 2, \ldots J. \tag{18}$$

Consequently, output layer weights $(\tilde{W}_{mj})$ and hidden layer weights $(\tilde{v}_{ji})$ are adjusted as

$$\tilde{W}_{mj}^{(\text{New})} = \tilde{W}_{mj}^{(\text{Old})} + \eta \tilde{\delta}_{Om} P_j, \quad m = 1, 2, \ldots M, \ j = 1, 2, \ldots J,$$

$$\tilde{v}_{ji}^{(\text{New})} = \tilde{v}_{ji}^{(\text{Old})} + \eta \tilde{\delta}_{Pj} Z_i, \quad j = 1, 2, \ldots J, \ i = 1, 2, \ldots I, \tag{19}$$

RESULTS AND DISCUSSION

To investigate the present method here, examples of oneand two-storey shear structures are considered. So, for example, the floor masses for two-storey shear structure are $[\underline{m_1}, m_1 c, \overline{m_1}]$, $[\underline{m_2}, m_2 c, \overline{m_2}]$ and the stiffnesses $[\underline{k_1}, k_1 c, \overline{k_1}]$, $[\underline{k_2}, k_2 c, \overline{k_2}]$ are the structural parameters. Here, masses are assumed to be constant (as mentioned earlier). So, we will identify the stiffness parameter in fuzzy form using the fuzzy form of the frequency where frequency may be obtained from some experiments. In the following paragraphs, we have used the proposed method to identify the stiffness parameter for one-, two-, five-, and ten-storey frame structures. Here, we have considered the cases with crisp data for five- and ten-storeys and then fuzzified data for one- and two-storeys. The training data are also considered with the influence of noise, namely, in terms of triangular fuzzy number data. Accordingly we have considered the following four cases:

Case(i): Five-storey shear structure with crisp data,

Case(ii): Ten-storey shear structure with crisp data,

Case(iii): Single-storey shear structure with fuzzified data,

Case(iv): Double-storey shear structure with fuzzified data.

Computer programs have been written and tested for variety of experiments for the above cases. For the first two cases, namely, Case(i) and Case(ii), the inputs are taken as the crisp frequency values and the outputs are the stiffness parameters which are also in crisp form. On the other hand, for Cases(iii) and (iv), the inputs are taken as the fuzzified frequency values and the outputs are the stiffness parameters again in fuzzified form in the developed Fuzzy Neural Network (FNN) algorithm.

For the first case, an example of a storey shear structure is taken where the masses are $m_1 = m_2 = m_3 = m_4 = m_5 = 36000$ and the stiffness parameters are within the range $k_1 =$ [100000 200000], $k_2 =$ [50000 100000], $k_3 =$ [40000 60000], $k_4 =$ [30000 50000], and $k_5 =$ [20000 30000]. A comparison between the desired and ANN values has been presented in Table 1. This table has been plotted in Figure 3.

Table 1: Comparison between the desired and the ANN values of k_1, k_2, k_3, k_4, and k_5 for a five-storey shear structure

Data number	k_1 (Ann)	k_1 (Des)	k_2 (Ann)	k_2 (Des)	k_3 (Ann)	k_3 (Des)	k_4 (Ann)	k_4 (Des)	k_5 (Ann)	k_5 (Des)
1	181277.7318	181472.3686	57722.68	57880.6541	53111.561	53114.814	44531.8138	44120.9218	24304.5301	24387.4436
2	195883.7223	190579.1937	98497.3362	98529.6391	40890.7789	40714.2336	30510.5884	30636.6569	24013.4116	23815.5846
3	110889.324	112698.6816	97540.2878	97858.3474	56939.1333	56982.5861	35467.0709	35538.4597	27905.0723	27655.1679
4	191334.6369	191337.5856	74367.0906	74268.7824	58151.3678	58679.865	30921.7444	30923.4278	27758.983	27951.999
5	162671.148	163235.9246	90080.9291	90014.0234	53507.0758	53574.7031	31851.263	31942.6356	21775.0509	21868.726
6	109757.8778	109754.0405	57034.3391	57094.3169	55073.904	55154.8026	46360.9403	46469.1566	24899.5619	24897.644
7	127671.411	127849.8219	71003.1282	71088.0641	54999.758	54862.6494	43688.9611	43896.5725	24554.2598	24455.862
8	154429.3614	154688.1519	98500.0073	95786.7763	48031.3148	47844.5404	36250.0047	36341.9896	27719.1389	26463.1301
9	196399.16	195750.6835	89751.9025	89610.3665	53100.0372	53109.5578	48498.0106	49004.441	27950.5364	27093.6483
10	193722.4668	196488.8535	98520.881	97974.6213	43228.929	43423.7338	30822.0268	30688.9216	26813.9637	27546.8668

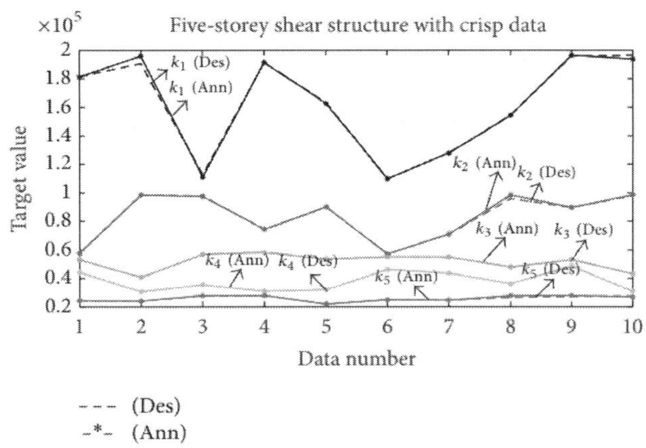

Figure 3: Comparison between the desired and the ANN values of $\widetilde{K}$ for a single-storey shear structure.

In Case(ii), an example for a ten-storey shear structure has been considered with constant masses similar to Case(i) and the stiffness parameters are in the range k_1 = [100000 200000], $k_2 = k_3 = k_4 = k_5 = k_6 = k_7 = k_8 = k_9 = k_{10}$ = [20000 30000]. The desired and ANN values for k_1 to k_5 and k_6 to k_{10} are compared in Tables 2(a) and 2(b), respectively.

Table 2: (a) Comparison between the desired and the ANN values of k_1, k_2, k_3, k_4, and k_5 for a ten-storey shear structure. (b) Comparison between the desired and the ANN values of k_6, k_7, k_8, k_9, and k_{10} for a ten-storey shear structure

(a)

Data number	k_1 (Ann)	k_1 (Des)	k_2 (Ann)	k_2 (Des)	k_3 (Ann)	k_3 (Des)	k_4 (Ann)	k_4 (Des)	k_5 (Ann)	k_5 (Des)
1	116900.6563	114999.7254	23626.293	23947.0748	25255.905	24299.2141	29078.6982	29493.0391	27766.1413	28842.8102
2	137413.4659	135922.821	22400.1311	21970.538	22076.7651	22160.1892	28671.6078	29898.7215	23928.6799	23185.2425
3	174166.5579	171165.6706	26751.8243	27587.6627	28439.4836	28089.9027	28056.19	27636.7332	28909.5075	29349.7909
4	185745.6345	187147.6518	28203.5977	29952.1598	23288.5994	23565.0893	25414.2964	25588.2055	24175.8385	24794.8455
5	131376.8088	132868.9612	22531.4396	21865.7144	20887.9013	20732.4343	22490.5032	21838.4294	21747.4496	22317.9161
6	174687.251	165011.8025	25813.5863	27811.4527	25015.1015	25909.9146	25615.7328	24979.4882	24612.1573	23962.9025
7	185115.3655	197483.6148	24841.291	21957.9798	27352.9705	29101.8783	25184.1779	25178.456	27414.6225	27050.7748
8	107439.5782	107596.7361	28408.1614	29923.5897	22079.0745	21937.6594	29361.5732	29942.4301	25283.6014	25585.5903
9	164872.2954	158701.9167	25498.9862	28022.6157	26269.1879	24323.6779	28505.5766	28548.5168	27421.7863	27566.307
10	134496.3197	136428.6869	23984.6699	23091.3643	26528.5422	27288.6387	20735.4877	20391.8449	26590.0291	26789.4101

(b)

Data number	k_6 (Ann)	k_6 (Des)	k_7 (Ann)	k_7 (Des)	k_8 (Ann)	k_8 (Des)	k_9 (Ann)	k_9 (Des)	k_{10} (Ann)	k_{10} (Des)
1	21170.0974	20899.5068	25777.6655	25605.5953	28204.3487	29899.5021	27503.4171	25859.8704	27163.5463	25814.4649
2	22417.1364	20549.7415	27621.6492	28654.3859	27612.505	28451.7819	28303.9996	29823.0322	22093.3505	22094.0508
3	29672.9685	29638.7013	25998.8211	27124.1481	22438.2305	21982.2179	26315.5549	26153.251	27684.8546	29019.9081
4	19962.2582	19656.5635	21156.2588	20166.7471	22269.5196	21950.7153	23818.7821	23766.1108	27240.5745	27020.6645
5	20161.805	20514.4829	25387.6098	28009.2088	23922.4631	23268.3965	27519.8427	28771.8175	23219.6412	23774.551
6	22307.0935	23043.4895	21527.1166	21425.0932	27311.6444	28803.3786	27670.7454	27848.5243	27234.7985	27349.5593
7	27804.4452	25801.9183	24442.8169	24784.7447	25319.1653	24711.0187	25870.6554	24649.5428	27640.8021	29541.0279
8	25509.2344	25309.6445	22738.1369	22568.3535	23936.8813	24039.6937	28924.1116	28139.7693	25172.6749	25428.1311
9	28341.8519	29012.0809	25380.1928	23690.9169	23071.1828	21792.3148	28034.5751	28984.4414	26519.4395	25401.0583
10	27911.2912	29624.314	26475.8553	24319.8061	21306.3632	21696.0881	25327.5363	24074.5574	24485.2563	23343.2942

For Case(iii), the first example is that of a single-storey shear structure with masses $\widetilde{M} = 36000$ and the stiffness parameters lie within the range $\underline{K} = [100000\ 200000]$, $Kc = [100010\ 200010]$, and $\overline{K} = [100020\ 200020]$. A comparison between desired and the ANN values has been incorporated in Table 3. This table has been plotted in Figure 4. In the second example, a single-storey shear structure is considered with masses $\widetilde{M} = 36000$ and the stiffness parameter varying within the range $\underline{K} = [50000\ 100000]$, $Kc = [50010\ 100010]$, and $\overline{K} = [50020\ 100020]$. Comparison between the desired and the ANN values is tabulated in Table 4 and is plotted in Figure 5.

Table 3: Comparison between the desired and the ANN values of $\widetilde{K}$ for a single-storey shear structure.

Data number	$\underline{K}$ (Ann)	$\underline{K}$ (Des)	Kc (Ann)	Kc (Des)	$\overline{K}$ (Ann)	$\overline{K}$ (Des)
1	124932.9319	124189.1286	135932.8213	135095.2381	191905.7285	190281.611
2	135763.4956	140411.2146	152464.2896	151324.954	191726.9669	194488.719
3	110291.5736	109665.4525	141591.1084	140180.8034	148514.9196	149096.4092
4	107394.0584	107596.6692	115134.7117	113217.3293	149119.797	148935.2638
5	124430.5911	123991.6154	134455.7107	133781.941	192947.0787	194225.0591
6	112574.5401	112331.8935	188853.0283	190015.3846	194542.4439	195633.454
7	120988.7913	118390.7788	138166.8698	136934.6781	157619.3944	157540.8595
8	108960.7756	105997.9543	113526.3083	111130.2755	126504.2017	123995.2526
9	124700.9011	123497.9913	143556.5197	141726.7069	179985.5092	178035.2068
10	105227.009	104965.443	135988.057	135335.8571	140612.991	138983.8837

Table 4: Comparison between the desired and the ANN values of $\widetilde{K}$ for a single-storey shear structure.

Data number	$\underline{k}$ (Ann)	$\underline{k}$ (Des)	kc (Ann)	kc (Des)	$\overline{k}$ (Ann)	$\overline{k}$ (Des)
1	62365.0341	62104.5643	67644.4378	67547.619	95458.8463	95145.8055
2	67613.8959	70215.6073	75826.931	75662.477	95893.1612	97249.3595
3	55005.0087	54842.7263	70556.3936	70090.4017	74368.7997	74553.2046
4	53128.7186	53798.3346	56947.542	56618.6646	74261.1768	74472.6319
5	62246.1626	61995.8077	66881.2194	66895.9705	96278.4523	97122.5295
6	55957.2602	56165.9467	94391.1219	95012.6923	97271.6645	97826.727
7	60056.7259	59195.3894	68223.7328	68472.3391	78385.7211	78780.4298
8	53587.3374	53008.9771	55747.5298	55570.1378	61968.3882	61997.6263
9	62126.6388	61758.9957	71196.546	70863.3535	89991.9346	89022.6034
10	52238.7913	52482.7215	67702.5259	67677.9286	69679.1387	69496.9418

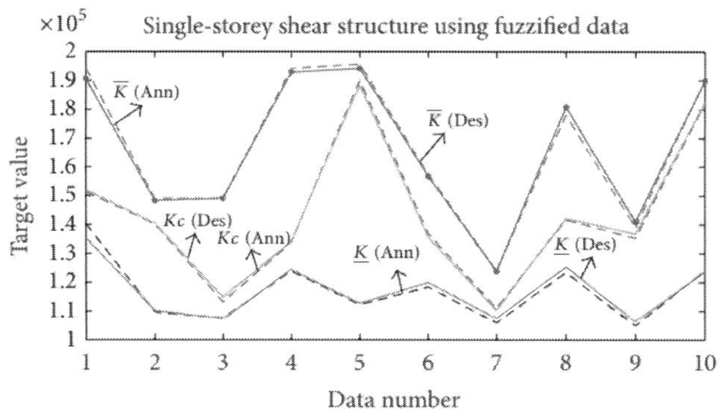

Figure 4: Comparison between the desired and the ANN values of $\widetilde{K}$ for a single-storey shear structure.

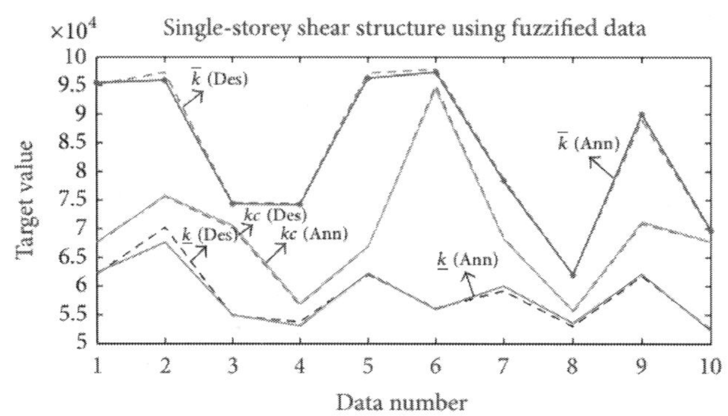

Figure 5: Comparison between the desired and the ANN values of $\widetilde{K}$ for a single-storey shear.

In Case(iv), the first example of a double-storey shear structure is considered where the masses are $\widetilde{m}_1 = \widetilde{m}_2 = 36000$ and the stiffness parameters varying within the range $\underline{k_1}$ = [100000 200000], k_1c = [100010 200010], $\overline{k_1}$ = [100020 200020] and $\underline{k_2}$ = [20000 30000], k_2c = [20010 30010] , and $\overline{k_2}$ = [20020 30020]. The desired and ANN values have been compared in Tables 5(a) and 5(b). This table has also been shown in Figures 6(a) and 6(b). In the second example, a double-storey shear structure is implemented with masses $\widetilde{m}_1 = \widetilde{m}_2 = 36000$ and the stiffness parameters having the range $\underline{k_1}$ = [50000 100000], k_1c = [50010 100010], $\overline{k_1}$ = [50020 100020] and $\underline{k_2}$ = [20000 30000], k_2c = [20010 30010], and $\overline{k_2}$ = [20020 30020]. Comparison between the desired and ANN values are again incorporated in Tables 6(a) and 6(b). This table is plotted in Figures 7(a) and 7(b).

Table 5: (a) Comparison between the desired and the ANN values of $\widetilde{K}_1$ for a double-storey shear structure. (b) Comparison between the desired and the ANN values of $\widetilde{K}_2$ for a double-storey shear structure.

(a)

Data number	$\underline{k_1}$ (Ann)	$\underline{k_1}$ (Des)	k_1c (Ann)	k_1c (Des)	$\overline{k_1}$ (Ann)	$\overline{k_1}$ (Des)
1	113258.5422	113317.1008	133858.2555	133969.3413	162741.2326	162807.3359
2	116526.66	117338.8613	128622.4646	129208.408	193447.2534	195183.0465
3	139119.0131	139093.7802	143501.0894	143175.117	191801.5675	192053.204
4	101316.7594	101558.7126	106512.8803	105287.6998	183040.5812	183137.9743
5	173554.7972	173805.8096	180269.037	180336.4392	198199.4731	198416.3724
6	105985.8857	106047.1179	117592.2043	116726.841	127688.8972	126931.9426
7	110472.1362	110631.6345	140132.9188	139925.7771	142461.6007	142303.5615
8	137120.3743	137250.974	152856.9037	152687.5831	155005.6994	154807.0901
9	119783.849	119821.8403	142480.6438	141679.9468	195824.6624	194293.6984
10	141708.5217	141794.4104	148654.6797	148978.7638	165370.4902	165685.9891

(b)

Data number	$\underline{k_2}$ (Ann)	$\underline{k_2}$ (Des)	k_2c (Ann)	k_2c (Des)	$\overline{k_2}$ (Ann)	$\overline{k_2}$ (Des)
1	58488.0205	58566.0533	91472.5908	92796.1403	99954.016	99152.6233
2	51977.6459	51640.041	65679.199	65072.7474	85856.2114	82258.2268
3	69213.7504	68833.6105	77764.8854	78069.9896	85939.2478	85054.9378
4	60124.2902	59566.1848	83319.0924	83316.9426	93794.9834	94103.325
5	71317.3378	71432.6496	76748.5343	76956.3233	83930.3883	83468.7652
6	59384.591	59531.6634	73687.8221	74121.1031	85087.5853	84905.276
7	56031.7629	56050.5807	68215.603	68455.8273	83728.3652	83326.3957
8	58849.1438	58906.6227	72741.8224	73046.2969	79796.3231	79495.3742
9	57077.8681	56400.72	61035.9761	61329.384	95110.8992	99091.8975
10	57858.7023	57830.2476	69404.8867	69250.9562	99433.354	99954.0197

Table 6: (a) Comparison between the desired and the ANN values of $\widetilde{K}_1$ for a double-storey shear structure. (b) Comparison between the desired and the ANN values of $\widetilde{K}_2$ for a double-storey shear structure.

(a)

Data number	$\underline{k_1}$ (Ann)	$\underline{k_1}$ (Des)	k_1c (Ann)	k_1c (Des)	$\overline{k_1}$ (Ann)	$\overline{k_1}$ (Des)
1	62193.4503	62149.2679	65871.2249	66562.894	69219.2648	69672.8181
2	71578.6175	71235.4748	71816.4848	72130.1157	83311.5254	83571.557
3	63514.5116	63533.5212	84447.6191	84399.8043	86708.0123	87062.8972
4	59459.7849	59872.6899	67907.0231	67971.4105	75148.6421	76002.6234
5	67809.323	67385.6336	85655.9802	86827.0037	91460.6917	91106.0592
6	57879.7498	57499.8627	69206.8111	69745.3738	71387.5577	71516.0705
7	77679.4222	79304.6034	83870.4195	84180.7933	93380.175	94408.5477
8	63484.2106	63107.2659	69028.8134	69579.1498	85313.0398	85212.3715
9	52329.6174	52222.7046	72316.9085	72125.2707	88399.7894	88475.7194
10	50895.5951	50988.8812	69532.938	69859.5759	87547.575	87746.6634

(b)

Data number	$\underline{k_2}$ (Ann)	$\underline{k_2}$ (Des)	k_2c (Ann)	k_2c (Des)	$\overline{k_2}$ (Ann)	$\overline{k_2}$ (Des)
1	27396.6322	27507.0572	27776.8241	27698.5425	28078.4211	28085.141
2	21439.7109	21682.5355	27548.5904	27550.771	29081.9724	28275.8382
3	23717.5546	23773.9554	27948.7301	27919.6303	28617.4807	28629.8048
4	22090.0439	22160.1892	23180.7111	23205.2425	28962.7934	29908.7215
5	25086.5697	25154.2346	25465.6455	25360.6413	27961.1253	27904.0722
6	20724.6386	20919.5068	28645.592	28852.8102	29353.9707	29493.0391
7	20706.4881	21137.0574	23381.0249	23275.6543	25716.8788	25890.2606
8	21056.3736	21382.9255	21574.7879	21557.5235	26851.9289	26712.6437
9	22075.9397	22008.6282	24479.3131	24386.4498	27062.0237	26806.523
10	24070.1411	24079.5484	25009.5776	24971.7702	28009.5803	28335.006

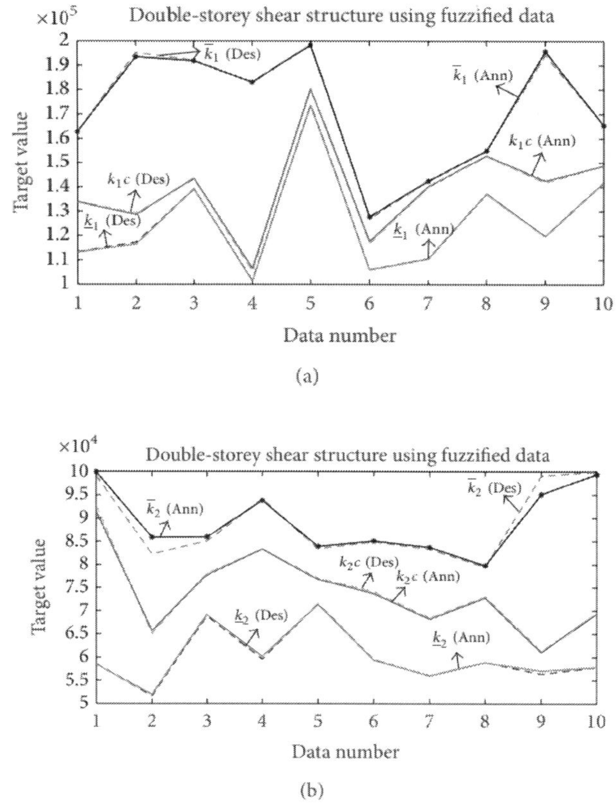

Figure 6: (a) Comparison between the desired and the ANN values of $\bar{k}_1$ for a double-storey shear structure. (b) Comparison between the desired and the ANN values of $\bar{k}_2$ for a double-storey shear structure.

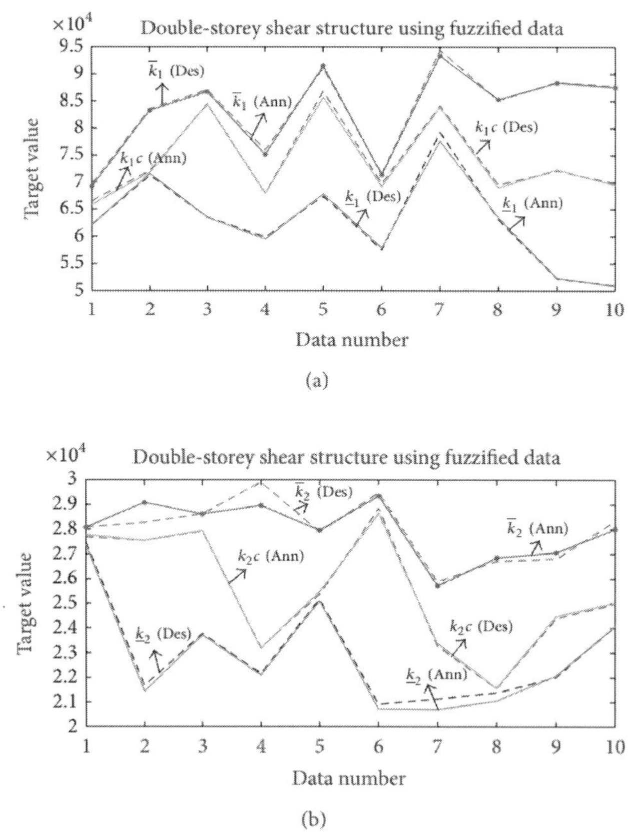

Figure 7: (a) Comparison between the desired and the ANN values of $\bar{k}_1$ for a double-storey shear structure. (b) Comparison between the desired and the ANN values of $\bar{k}_2$ for a double-storey shear structure.

The training data with the influence of noise for two-storey shear structure in TFN form for five sets of data have been presented here. Accordingly, Figures 8(a) and 8(b) refer the fuzzy plot of frequency. Moreover, the Triangular Fuzzy Number (TFN) plots of identified stiffness are cited in Figures 9(a) and 9(b). Also for different alpha values such as $\alpha = 0.3$, $\alpha = 0.5$, and $\alpha = 0.8$, the comparison between the desired and ANN values with another five sets of data has been given in Tables 7(a), and 7(b), and 7(c).

Table 7: (a) Comparison between the desired and the ANN values of $\underline{k_1}$, $\overline{k_1}$ and $\underline{k_2}$, $\overline{k_2}$ for a double-storey shear structure for $\alpha = 0.3$. (b) Comparison between the desired and the ANN values of $\underline{k_1}$, $\overline{k_1}$ and $\underline{k_2}$, $\overline{k_2}$ for a double-storey shear structure for $\alpha = 0.5$. (c) Comparison between the desired and the ANN values of $\underline{k_1}$, $\overline{k_1}$ and $\underline{k_2}$, $\overline{k_2}$ for a double-storey shear structure for $\alpha = 0.8$.

(a)

Data number	$\underline{k_1}$ (Ann)	$\underline{k_1}$ (Des)	$\overline{k_1}$ (Ann)	$\overline{k_1}$ (Des)	$\underline{k_2}$ (Ann)	$\underline{k_1}$ (Des)	$\overline{k_2}$ (Ann)	$\overline{k_2}$ (Des)
1	109470	109250	124660	123870	63676	63908	81668	81670
2	119370	119420	141760	141590	59687	59772	79075	78865
3	141840	141880	154360	154170	63017	63149	77680	77561
4	126590	126380	179820	178510	58265	57879	84888	87763
5	143790	143950	160360	160670	61323	61256	90425	90743

(b)

Data number	$\underline{k_1}$ (Ann)	$\underline{k_1}$ (Des)	$\overline{k_1}$ (Ann)	$\overline{k_1}$ (Des)	$\underline{k_2}$ (Ann)	$\underline{k_1}$ (Des)	$\overline{k_2}$ (Ann)	$\overline{k_2}$ (Des)
1	111790	111390	122640	121830	66536	66826	79388	79513
2	125300	125280	141300	141110	62124	62253	75972	75891
3	144990	144970	153930	153750	65795	65976	76269	76271
4	131130	130750	169150	167990	59057	58865	78073	80211
5	145180	145390	157010	157330	63632	63541	84419	84602

(c)

Data number	$\underline{k_1}$ (Ann)	$\underline{k_1}$ (Des)	$\overline{k_1}$ (Ann)	$\overline{k_1}$ (Des)	$\underline{k_2}$ (Ann)	$\underline{k_1}$ (Des)	$\overline{k_2}$ (Ann)	$\overline{k_2}$ (Des)
1	115270	114590	119610	118770	70827	71203	75968	76278
2	134200	134070	140600	140400	65779	65975	71318	71430
3	149710	149600	153290	153110	69963	70218	74153	74336
4	137940	137310	153150	152200	60244	60344	67851	68882
5	147270	147540	152000	152320	67096	66967	75411	75392

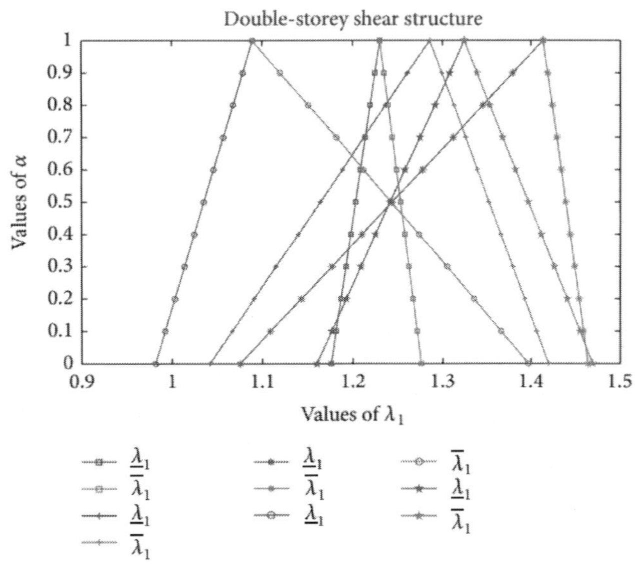

(a)

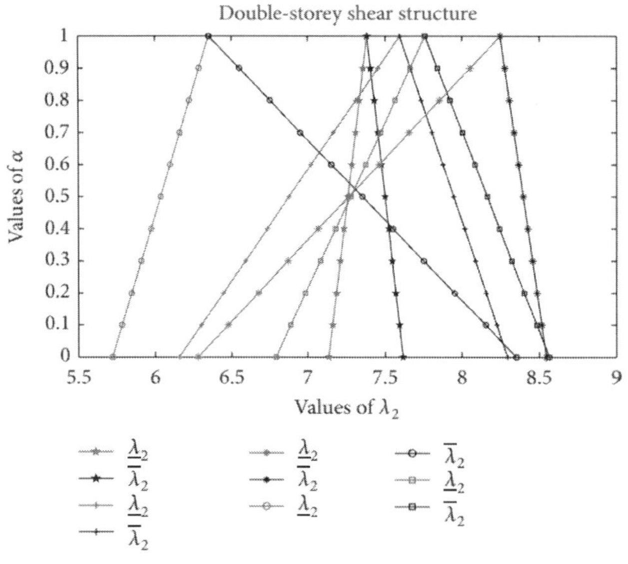

(b)

Figure 8: (a) Comparison of $\underline{\lambda_1}$ and $\underline{\lambda_1}$ with respect to α. (b) Comparison of $\underline{\lambda_2}$ and $\underline{\lambda_2}$ with respect to α.

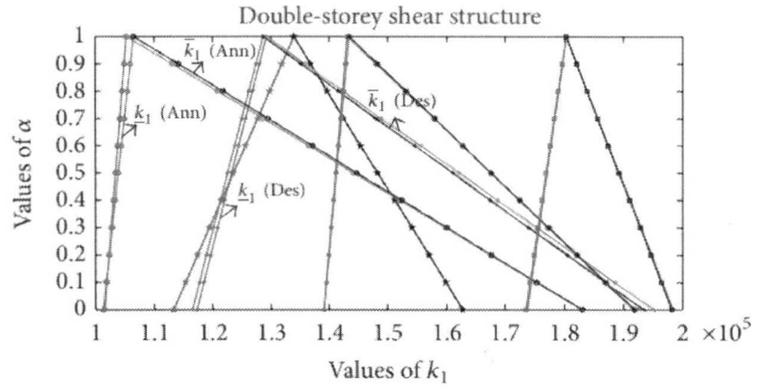

(a)

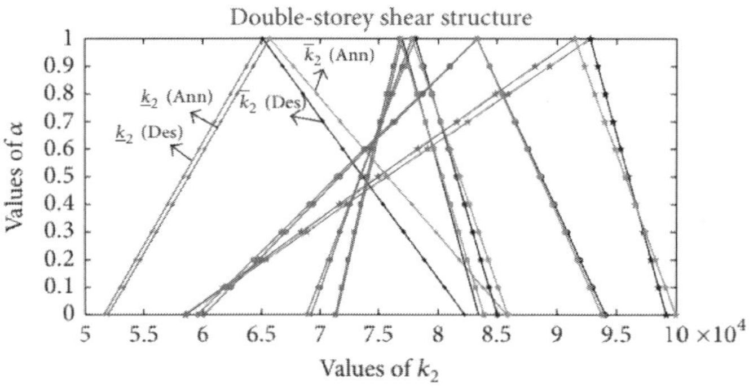

(b)

Figure 9: (a) Comparison of $\underline{k_1}$ and $\overline{k_1}$ with respect to α. (b) Comparison of $\underline{k_2}$ and $\overline{k_2}$ with respect to α.

CONCLUSION

Here, the procedure is demonstrated to identify stiffness parameters for multistorey shear structure using fuzzified data in ANN. The present study considers example problems of one-, two-, five-, and ten-storey shear structures. Identification study for five- and ten-storey shear structures has been done with crisp data. Then, fuzzified data has been considered for one- and two-storey shear structures for the present identification procedure. Initial design parameters, namely, stiffness and mass and so the frequency of the said problem is known in term of fuzzy numbers. The engineers want to know the present health of the structure by system identification methods. It is assumed that only the stiffness is changed and the mass remains the same. The present values of the frequencies may be obtained by available equipments, and using these, one may get the present parameter values by ANN. So, if sensors are placed to capture the frequency of the floors in fuzzy (uncertain) form, then, those may be fed into the proposed new ANN model to get the present stiffness parameters. The methods of one- and two-storey shear structures with fuzzified data may very well be extended for higher storey structures following the present procedure. As regards the influence of noise, it may be seen that the input and output data for two-storey shear structure are actually in terms of Triangular Fuzzy Number (TFN) which themselves dictate the noise in both monotonic increasing and decreasing senses. In order to train the new ANN model, set of data are generated numerically beforehand. As such, converged ANN model gives the present stiffness parameter values in fuzzified form for each floor. Thus, one may predict the health of the structure. Corresponding example problems (as mentioned) have been solved, and related results are reported to show the reliability and powerfulness of the model.

ACKNOWLEDGMENTS

The authors would like to acknowledge funding from the Ministry of Earth Sciences, New Delhi, India. They are also thankful to the anonymous reviewers for their valuable suggestion to improve the paper.

REFERENCES

1. E. Khanmirza, N. Khaji, and V. J. Majd, "Model updating of multistory shear buildings for simultaneous identification of mass, stiffness and damping matrices using two different soft-computing methods,"Expert Systems with Applications, vol. 38, no. 5, pp. 5320–5329, 2011.
2. M. I. Friswell, D. J. Inman, and D. F. Pilkey, "The direct updating of damping and stiffness matrices,"AIAA Journal, vol. 36, no. 3, pp. 491–493, 1998.
3. M. Tanaka and H. D. Bui, Inverse Problems in Engineering Mechanics, Balkema, Rotterdam, The Netherlands, 1994.
4. K. F. Alvin, A. N. Robertson, G. W. Reich, and K. C. Park, "Structural system identification: from reality to models," Computers and Structures, vol. 81, no. 12, pp. 1149–1176, 2003.
5. S. D. Fassois and J. S. Sakellariou, "Time-series methods for fault detection and identification in vibrating structures," Philosophical Transactions of the Royal Society A, vol. 365, no. 1851, pp. 411–448, 2007.
6. S. F. Marsi, G. A. Bekey, H. Sassi, and T. K. Caughey, "Non-parametric identification of a class of non-linear multidegree dynamic systems," Earthquake Engineering & Structural Dynamics, vol. 10, no. 1, pp. 1–30, 1982.
7. P. Ibanez, "Review of analytical and experimental techniques for improving structural dynamic models,"Welding Research Council Bulletin, no. 249, 1979.
8. A. K. Datta, M. Shrikhande, and D. K. Paul, "System identification of buildings: a review," in Proceedings of 11th Symposium on Earthquake Engineering, University of Roorkee, Roorkee, India.
9. C.-H Loh and I.-C Tou, "A system identification approach to the detection of changes in both linear and non-linear structural parameters," Earthquake Engineering & Structural Dynamics, vol. 24, no. 1, pp. 85–97, 1995.
10. P. Yuan, Z. Wu, and X. Ma, "Estimated mass and stiffness matrices of shear building from modal test data," Earthquake Engineering and Structural Dynamics, vol. 27, no. 5, pp. 415–421, 1998.
11. C. H. Chen, "Structural identification from field measurement data using a neural network," Smart Materials and Structures, vol. 14, no. 3, pp. S104–S115, 2005.
12. C. S. Huang, S. L. Hung, C. M. Wen, and T. T. Tu, "A neural network approach for structural identification and diagnosis of a building from seismic response data," Earthquake Engineering and Structural Dynamics, vol. 32, no. 2, pp. 187–206, 2003.
13. C. Y. Kao and S. L. Hung, "Detection of structural damage via free vibration responses generated by approximating artificial neural networks," Computers and Structures, vol. 81, no. 28-29, pp. 2631–2644, 2003.
14. Z. Wu, B. Xu, and K. Yokoyama, "Decentralized parametric damage detection based on neural networks,"Computer-Aided Civil and Infrastructure Engineering, vol. 17, no. 3, pp. 175–184, 2002.
15. B. Xu, Z. Wu, G. Chen, and K. Yokoyama, "A localized identification method with neural networks and its application to structural health monitoring," Journal of Structural Engineering A, vol. 48, pp. 419–427, 2002.
16. B. Xu, Z. Wu, G. Chen, and K. Yokoyama, "Direct identification of structural parameters from dynamic responses with neural networks," Engineering Applications of Artificial Intelligence, vol. 17, no. 8, pp. 931–943, 2004.
17. S. Chakraverty, "Identification of structural parameters of multistorey shear buildings from modal data,"Earthquake Engineering and Structural Dynamics, vol. 34, no. 6, pp. 543–554, 2005.
18. M. J. Perry, C. G. Koh, and Y. S. Choo, "Modified genetic algorithm strategy for structural identification,"Computers and Structures, vol. 84, no. 8-9, pp. 529–540, 2006.
19. G. S. Wang, "Application of hybrid genetic algorithm to system identification," Structural Control and Health Monitoring, vol. 16, no. 2, pp. 125–153, 2009.
20. S. Yoshitomi and I. Takewaki, "Noise-bias compensation in physical-parameter system identification under microtremor input," Engineering Structures, vol. 31, no. 2, pp. 580–590, 2009.
21. Y. Lu and Z. Tu, "A two-level neural network approach for dynamic FE model updating including damping," Journal of Sound and Vibration, vol. 275, no. 3–5, pp. 931–952, 2004.
22. C. G. Koh, Y. F. Chen, and C. Y. Liaw, "A hybrid computational strategy for identification of structural parameters," Computers and Structures, vol. 81, no. 2, pp. 107–117, 2003.
23. H. Tang, S. Xue, and C. Fan, "Differential evolution strategy for structural system identification,"Computers and Structures, vol. 86, no. 21-22, pp. 2004–2012, 2008.

SECTION III: LEARNING AND RECOGNITION APPLICATIONS

CHAPTER 10

HUMAN DETECTION BY ROBOTIC URBAN SEARCH AND RESCUE USING IMAGE PROCESSING AND NEURAL NETWORKS

Fahed Awad and Rufaida Shamroukh

Keywords: Urban Search and Rescue, Human-Robot Interaction, Autonomous Systems, Intelligent Interface, Neural Networks

INTRODUCTION

In light of recent catastrophes, which are either natural such as earthquake, hurricane, flood, and fire, or manmade such as wars, bombing, and terrorist attacks, the need for creating new ways to rescue the survivors who get trapped under rubble, in the fastest way possible, is a must. According to the field of Urban Search and Rescue (USAR), the probability of saving a victim is high within the first 48 hours of the rescue operation, after that, the probability becomes nearly zero [1] .

During the rescue operation, several human factors are deployed such as fire fighters, policemen, and medical assistants. All of them are exposed to very dangerous situations which are caused by the destructed environment they work in, such as collapsed buildings, landslides, and crater. Hence, the rescuer may become a victim who needs to be rescued. Therefore, the rescue operation imposes a substantial risk on the rescue personnel themselves. From this point of view, looking for alternatives to human rescuers has been of a great demand.

Trained dogs have also been used in this field because of their high sensitivity to any slight motion or human presence. However, in such situations, it is hard to depend totally on them because even if they can detect the presence of a living victim, they still cannot judge the situation or relay the information quickly and systematically. For that reason, dogs cannot work independently but rather side by side as assistants to human rescuer. Therefore, the need is for a totally or partially independent alternative to the human factor.

Meanwhile, robots were achieving relatively good progress in other fields such as education, industry, military, and medicine and have proven their robustness and efficiency in most of what they are designed for. Therefore, robots are expected to play an important role in replacing the human factor in many of these fields.

Even though the USAR field seems to be very challenging for robots, robots have already invaded this field like many other fields. The first real attempt to use USAR robots was during the rescue of the World Trade Center (WTC) disaster in New York in 2001. Since then, a worldwide interest in using robots in rescue operations has been rapidly increasing.

During the WTC rescue operation, six remotely-controlled robots were used to assist human rescuers in finding and locating trapped victims [1] . These robots were remotely-controlled by operators. Each robot was equipped with a camera and a wireless communications link and was supposed to transmit images of the scenes they traverse. However, the attempt faced several critical problems due to the remotely-controlled nature of the robots:

1. More than 25% of the communications between the wireless robot and the control unit was extremely noisy and therefore was useless. This eventually led to a loss of communication between the robots and the operators. As a result, the robots stopped working totally and got lost in the rubble because they do not have any autonomous intelligence to continue on their own.

Citation: Awad, F. and Shamroukh, R. (2014) Human Detection by Robotic Urban Search and Rescue Using Image Processing and Neural Networks. International Journal of Intelligence Science, 4, 39-53. doi:10.4236/ijis.2014.42006.

2. A very high communication cost was incurred due to the large number of transmitted images to the operator, especially when the communication line is very error-prone.
3. A very high processing cost is also incurred by the capturing, storing, and transmitting a large number of images.
4. There was a continuous need for illumination due to the dark nature of these environments. Therefore, a continuous light source would be needed in order to be able to acquire and send images. This requires a relatively large power supply, which is not feasible in such situations.

As a result, the attempt of using robots at the WTC failed to accomplish even a small part of its mission [1] .

This research is an attempt to tackle the problems faced the USAR robots during the WTC rescue operation via equipping the robot with some autonomous intelligence towards the ultimate goal of designing a fully autonomous robot.

In this research, a new approach for detecting surviving humans in destructed environments using an autonomous USAR robot is proposed. The proposed system uses a passive infrared sensor (PIR) to detect the existence of living humans and a low-cost camera to acquire snapshots of the scene as needed. Having detected a sign of a living human, the PIR sensor triggers a camera to acquire an image of the scene. The image is fed into a feed-forward neural network (NN), trained to detect the existence of a human body or part of it in the image for different positions within an obstructed environment. This approach requires a relatively small number of images to be acquired and processed during the rescue operation. In this way, the real-time cost of image processing and data transmission is considerably reduced. The transmitted information may include any relevant phenomena that the robot is prepared to sense such as the location, the temperature, the level of certain types of gases, etc. The information may also include the image itself in order for the rescue team to have a better evaluation of the situation.

The robot is assumed to have the capability to determine its current location in real-time, to wirelessly communicate with the rescue team, and to locally store the status and location information about the trapped victims in case the wireless communications link is temporarily disconnected.

The environment is assumed to have obstacles around the surviving victims such as debris, dust, and collapsed walls such that the human body is partially or mostly covered.

In order to prove the concept and the functionality of the system, the autonomous robot was emulated by attaching a laptop PC (representing the brain of the robot) to a large toy car (representing the navigation mechanism of the robot). The car was fully controlled by the laptop PC via an external interface electronic circuit that was designed and built for such purpose. The laptop PC was equipped with a low-cost, medium-resolution web camera and a PIR sensor, and was running the MATLAB software.

1. By adding such capabilities to the robot, the problems that faced the USAR robots during the WTC rescue operation are tackled as follows:
2. Even if the robot loses communication with the operator temporarily, it still can continue with its mission of looking for survivors until the communication is resumed. The critical collected information is saved in an internal memory and is transmitted as soon as the communication is resumed. The robot may also have the capability to maintain and dynamically update internal coverage map of the wireless communications quality.
3. The communication cost is significantly reduced by mostly sending small-size encoded information to the rescue team about the location, and perhaps the status, of the victim rather than transmitting heavy streams of images. In the worst case, a single image of the scene is transmitted for better evaluation of the situation.
4. The image processing cost is reduced by acquiring only a single image of a scene as needed rather than a stream of images.
5. As a result, the power consumption is considerably reduced easing the requirements on the power source specifications. In the worst case, the light source (e.g. a flash light) is used only for taking the snapshots when the illumination at the scene is insufficient.

A large number of experiments were conducted in order to evaluate the performance of the system. The results of the experiments demonstrated that the system has the potential to achieve high performance in detecting living humans in obstructed environments relatively quickly and cost-effectively. The detection accuracy of the system ranged between 79% and 91% depending on a number of factors such as the body position, the light intensity of the scene, and the relative color matching between the body and the surrounding environment.

The rest of the paper is organized as follows: Section 2 discusses the related work; Section 3 presents the implementation of the proposed system; Section 4 explains the image processing and neural network strategies used; Section 5 presents the experimentation methodology and the test results; and Section 6 provides the conclusion.

RELATED WORK

Image processing, neural networks (NN), and passive infrared sensing were used in detecting the presence or shape of the human body for several applications such as surveillance and emergency rescue services. However, to the best of our knowledge, a combined use of all of them in the way proposed here has not been cited.

In this section, a brief discussion of some of the previously proposed techniques in the literature is presented.

Moradi presented a method that uses the infrared radiation emitted by the human body using an infrared camera that acquires thermal images of the surrounding environment [2] . This system includes six main parts: Image Acquisition, Initial Processing, Feature Extraction, Acquisition Storage, Knowledge Base, and Recognition. The features within the images are then classified using the Dystall NN. The number of nodes and layers in this system depends on the desired accuracy. The difference between the training stage and the testing stage of the NN is compared with a pre-defined threshold. If the difference is more than that threshold, then a human is detected.

This method has a number of advantages that distinguish it from other similar methods such as: real-time processing speed, high efficiency, and fast learning. However, there are several factors that complicate the process of the detection and recognition such as: the absorbency of thermal energy by the environment and the victim's clothes, the existence of identical thermal sources such as fire or another living creature (e.g. an animal), and that the images taken by the IR camera usually have relatively low resolution. In addition to that, the cost of the thermal camera is relatively very high.

Burion presented a project that aimed to provide a sensor suite for human detection for the USAR robots [3] . This study evaluated several types of sensors for detecting humans such as pyroelectric sensor, USB camera, microphone, and IR camera. The pyroelectric sensor was used to detect the human body radiation, but its limitation was its binary output. The USB camera was used for motion detection, but its limitation was its sensitivity to changes in light intensity. The microphone was used for long duration and high amplitude sound detection, but it was severely affected by noise. Lastly, the IR camera was used to detect humans by their heat image, but it was affected by other nearby hot objects. The algorithm was based on collecting data from all these sensors as an attempt to improve the robustness of the final results. The main idea was to detect a change in the image scene by checking the values of the pixels. Several images for the scene were acquired and subtracted from each other to discover if a motion has occurred. The used technique was fairly efficient in detecting the victims. However, the robot was not fully autonomous and was dependent on the operator. No neural network was used in the control program, and no detection of the human shape was used.

Nakajimaa et al. proposed a system that learns from examples in order to recognize the person's body in the images taken indoors [4] . The images were represented by color-based and shape-based features. The recognition process is carried out by using the linear Support Vector Machine (SVM) classifiers. This system works in real-time and it can achieve high recognition rate on normalized color histograms of people's clothes. However, the main limitation of this system is that it demonstrated high performance rates only when both the training and test images were recorded during the same day. When the test set contained images of a day that is not represented in the training set, the performance of the system drops down to about 53% due to the change of clothing the person might have every day.

Mohan et al. presented a hierarchical technique for developing a system that locates people in images [5] . In this Adaptive Combination of Classifiers (ACC) technique, the learning occurs in multiple stages. The system is first trained to find the four components of the human body: the head, legs, left arm, and right arm separately from each other. After ensuring that these parts are present in a proper geometric configuration, the system combines the results in order to classify a pattern as either a "person" or a "non-person". The obtained results demonstrated that this system performed significantly better than a similar full-body person detector [4] . Moreover, the system handles the variations in lighting and noise in an image better than a full-body detector.

Engle and Whalen presented a simulation study for a multiple robots foraging in a simulated environment [6] . The robots were supposed to gather two different sets of resources from a walled environment containing obstacles. Each set of resources must be returned to a specific goal. The robots were equipped with laser range finder for long range obstacle detection, a thermal sensor which detects heat around resources, and a color sensor to discriminate between different types of resources. The robots were supposed to search for humans by their body heat, and distinguish humans from non-human objects by using the color sensor. The final simulation was done using just one robot due to time constraints and implementation complexity and the used navigation algorithm could not cover the whole environment. In addition, the financial cost was of the robot was relatively high.

Cavalcanti and Gomes presented an approach for determining the presence of people in still images [7] . It starts with the segmentation of the skin areas in the image using YCbCr skin filter using a color space with a set of experimental thresholds. Then, the detected skin areas are grouped together to form body regions. This technique was been applied on a database of still images and achieved 77.2% correct classification. The advantage of this approach is its simplicity and relative low processing cost. However, higher-level analysis would be needed in order to achieve higher detection performance.

Several research papers [8] -[12] were published regarding the performance of the National Institute of Standard and Technology (NIST) Standards. The papers list the criteria for designing standard arenas and victim models and their characteristics. The arenas are supposed to simulate the destruction caused by the real catastrophes. In addition, they are supposed to provide tangible, realistic, and challenging environments for mobile robot researchers interested in urban search and rescue applications. The arenas were modeled for buildings in various stages of collapse, where the robots were allowed to traverse and were tested for obstacle avoidance and victim detection by repeatedly testing their sensory, navigation, mapping, and planning capabilities. These arenas differ in their level of complexity. They are divided into three levels, the Yellow arena, the Orange arena, and Red arena. The Yellow arena, which is the simplest one, simulates a home after an earthquake or a similar disaster. The floor of this arena is easy to navigate so that most robots can handle it. There is no loose paper, no ramps, etc. The Orange arena is harder than the Yellow arena. The major distinguishing feature of the Orange arena is a ramp with a chicken-wire. In addition, the floor is covered with paper, which is much harder to traverse by small wheeled robots. The Red arena is much harder than the other two. There are rubble and obstacles all over the place. There is also enough metal to cause serious problems to wireless communication. Moreover, simulated victims with various signs of life can be found throughout the three arenas. Some of these signs are human form, motion, audio, thermal, and chemical signatures that represent victims of various states. The robots are awarded points for accurate mapping and victim detection according to the predefined performance metrics.

Trierscheid et al. proposed a new technique for detecting presence of a victim [13] . The technique depends on the spectral imaging that analyzes an invisible light radiation of the human body, which is a near infrared (NIR) light that has shorter wavelengths. This light has been used too to solve the problem of dust coverings in rescue environments. The advantage of this technique is that it does not depend on temperature, unlike thermal imaging, such that cold bodies (i.e. dead persons) can also be detected. The algorithm was responsible for locating victims and marking them in a given image.

Zhao et al. presented a technique for detecting the breathing and heartbeat signals of a living human [14] . This system can detect passive victims who are either completely trapped or too weak to respond to the existing traditional detection systems. The system depends on sending a low-intensity microwave beam to penetrate through the rubble. If a living human exists, his/her small amplitude body-vibrations due to the breathing and heartbeat will modulate the back scattered microwave signal. After that, the reflected wave from the body is demodulated and the breathing and heartbeat signals can be extracted in-order to locate the buried human. This system was able to detect buried humans under rubbles of nearly 90cm of thickness.

SYSTEM IMPLEMENTATION

In order to emulate the proposed search and rescue robotic system and evaluate its performance, a laptop PC, which represents the main processing and control unit (MPCU) of the system, was attached to a navigation mechanism (e.g. a large toy car) via a navigation control unit (NCU).

The NCU consists of electronic circuitry that interfaces the sensors (as system inputs) and the navigation mechanism (as a system output) to the main processing and control unit. The system was equipped with three types of sensors:

- A PIR sensor to detect the presence of a living human based on body radiation.
- An Infra-Red (IR) range sensor to detect the obstacles in the way of the robot.
- An image sensor, which is a traditional web camera to acquire still images according to orders from the control program when a need arises.

The MPCU consists of the following components (see Figure 1):

- The navigation algorithm, which is responsible for steering the robot throughout the search area and around obstacles, based on the readings of the PIR and the IR sensors while searching for survivors.
- The location tracking algorithm, which is responsible for calculating the real-time coordinates of the robot in order to report the locations of the survivors to the rescue personnel. The real implementation of a search and rescue robot is assumed to be equipped with a Global Positioning System (GPS) or a GPS-like system for location identification.

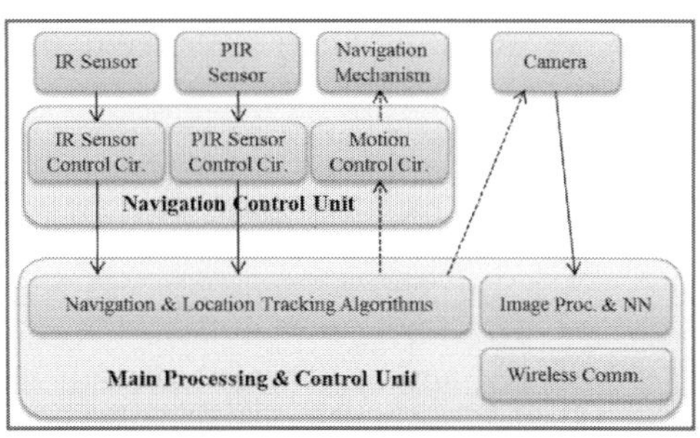

Figure 1: Block diagram of the system.

- The image processing and neural networks unit (IPNNU), which is responsible for detecting a human being in a picture received from the camera. This unit is the core of this research and will be discussed in details in the following sections.
- The wireless communication unit is responsible for providing reliable communication link with the rescue personnel in order to provide the locations of the survivors in addition to any other information the system may be designed to provide such as a snapshot of the scene so that the rescue personnel may be able to assess the situation of the survivor and prioritize their rescue tasks. In our system, the laptop PC was equipped with a wireless local area networking adapter, which was used for communications.

It should be noted that the design of the navigation and location tracking algorithms is beyond the scope of this research. Therefore, simple obstacle avoidance navigation algorithm and simple step counting location identification were used in the system.

The work flow of the system is as follows:

- The MPCU continuously reads the IR range sensor via the NCU. When the IR sensor is triggered (i.e.; an obstacle is detected), the MPCU signals the NCU to change the direction of the movement based on the navigation algorithm and keeps track of the current location and the status of the communication link.
- The MPCU periodically reads the PIR sensor. If the PIR sensor is triggered, the MPCU signals the NCU to stop the robot and the camera to acquire an image.
- The image (i.e.; a still frame) is passed to the IPNNU, where it is preprocessed by the image processing algorithm (e.g.; converting to gray scale, resizing, and canceling some background effects) and is then fed to the pre-trained NN.
- The NN determines whether a human shape or a body part exists in the image and returns the result back to the MPCU by categorizing the image based on the training sets used.
- If a human is detected, the MPCU reports the location to the rescue center. If the communication link is not available, the MPCU may decide to buffer the information and continue its normal operation until the communication is resumed. It may choose to move back to a nearby location where the communication link is known to be usable before it continues. The MPCU might also decide to send the image as well if a need arises. However, the cost of transmitting an image is relatively high in terms of delay, processing, and communication. Therefore, sending an image must be well justified. Otherwise, the battery lifetime of the robot will be reduced significantly. The MPCU may also have the capability to compress the image before sending it, which may reduce the cost significantly, depending on the resources available at the MPCU.

Figure 2 shows the simplified flowchart of the system operation.

Before the experiments were conducted, the detection ranges and coverage angles of the PIR sensor and the camera had to be well-tested and unified in order to make sure that the camera is capable of "seeing" the survivor that has triggered the PIR sensor with enough quality for processing and detecting. The test results were as follows:

- The maximum detection range of the PIR sensor was found to be 5 m at 180°.
- The maximum distance between the camera and the object, D_{max}, of which the image is to be acquired with an acceptable image quality, was found to be 2 m.
- The radius, R, of the image taken at 2 m by the camera was found to be about 1.15 m (seeFigure 3(a)).
- Based on the detection range measurements of the camera, the coverage angle, θ, was calculated as follows:

$$\theta = 2\times\tan^{-1}\left(\frac{R}{D_{max}}\right) = 60^\circ \quad (1)$$

Due to the incompatibility in the detection range and the coverage angle between the PIR sensor and the camera, the following procedure was performed in order to obtain a unified coverage of both:

- In order to reduce the coverage angle of the PIR sensor, an aluminum cap was used. The length of the cap, L, was determined as related to the diameter of the PIR sensor lens, d, which was 9.5 mm, as follows (see Figure 3(b)):

$$\tan\left(\frac{\theta}{2}\right) = \frac{d}{L} \quad (2)$$

$$L = \frac{9.5\text{ mm}}{\tan(30^\circ)} = 16.5\text{ mm} \quad (3)$$

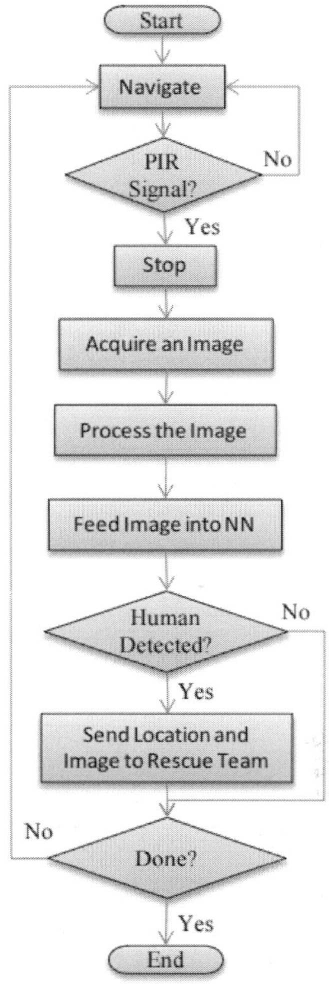

Figure 2: The simplified system operation flowchart.

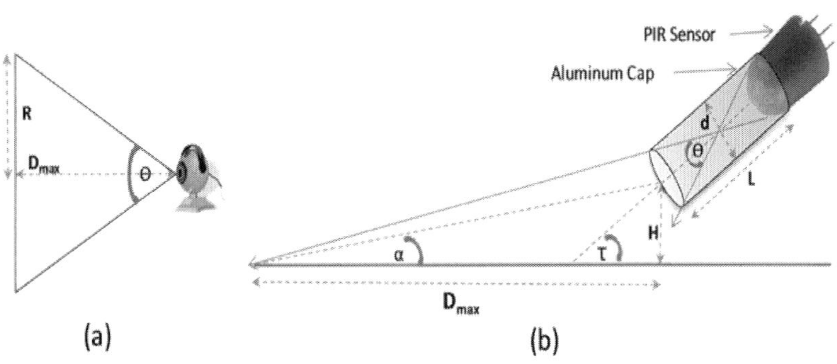

Figure 3: The cover angle of the camera.

- In order to decrease the effective detection range of the PIR sensor from 5 m to 2 m, the PIR sensor was tilted down towards the ground by a calculated degree. Assuming that the PIR sensor is positioned on the robot such that the far edge of the cap is at a certain height, H, from the ground, the tilting angle, τ, of the sensor is calculated as follows assuming that H = 0.5 m:

$$\propto = \tan^{-1}\left(\frac{H}{D_{max}}\right) \quad (4)$$

$$\tau \approx \frac{\theta}{2} + \propto \left(\text{since } d \ll D_{max}\right) \quad (5)$$

$$\propto = \tan^{-1}\left(\frac{0.5\text{ m}}{2\text{ m}}\right) = 14^\circ \quad (6)$$

$$\tau = \frac{60^\circ}{2} + 14^\circ = 44^\circ \quad (7)$$

THE IMAGE PROCESSING AND NEURAL NETWORKS UNIT

As stated previously, when the PIR sensor is triggered, the MPCU signals the camera to acquire an image of the scene, which is passed to the IPNNU for processing and detection. In this section, the IPNNU is discussed.

The Main Features

The type of NN used for the IPNNU is the feed-forward with a supervised learning method [15] [16] .

The process started by training the neural network on a large number of images for human hands, feet, and bodies of different sizes and positions as follows:

- The set of training images, Tr, contained 500 RGB images of 172 × 140 pixels each.
- At each training cycle (or epoch), six images were fed as input to the training stage, of which two are for hands, two for feet, and two for bodies.
- Before feeding an image into the NN, some simple enhancements were first applied in order to reduce the NN processing cost as much as possible [17] . These enhancements were performed as follows:
- The image was converted into gray-scale.
- The resolution was adjusted by down sampling and deleting some unwanted background effects.
- The brightness was adjusted by increasing the contrast.
- The image was converted from a 172 × 140 matrix into a 24,080 × 1 vector in order to feed it as an input to the NN.

The NN used had three layers (see Figure 4):

- The input layer consists of 256 nodes with each representing one of the 8-bit gray scales. The pixels of each image were fed to this layer represented as a vector.
- The hidden layer consists of 256 nodes with each also representing a gray degree.
- The output layer consists of three nodes that represent the desired values. Each node fires only if its desired input is given (i.e.; foot, hand, or body) as input to the first stage.

Neural Network Training and Testing

Before being used in the system, the NN had to go through an iterative training and testing phase. The training set, T_r, was divided into 10 groups of 50 images each. The testing set, T_e, consists of 50 images that the NN was never been trained on. The training and testing procedure was as follows:

- Train the NN on a new set of 50 images from Tr.
- Test the NN using T_e by feeding the images of T_e as inputs to the NN and recording the result for each.
- Calculate the detection accuracy of the NN, which represents the percentage of successful detections.

Repeat the process until all training sets are used.

Figure 5 depicts the detection accuracy, A(n), obtained as a function of the number of training images, n. It is noticed that the detection accuracy monotonically increases with the n. However, it slows downs and starts to saturate for n > 350 to about 84% accuracy at 500 images, which indicates a logarithmic behavior. Therefore, experimental regression analysis was performed on the training results and the trend of A(n) was estimated as:

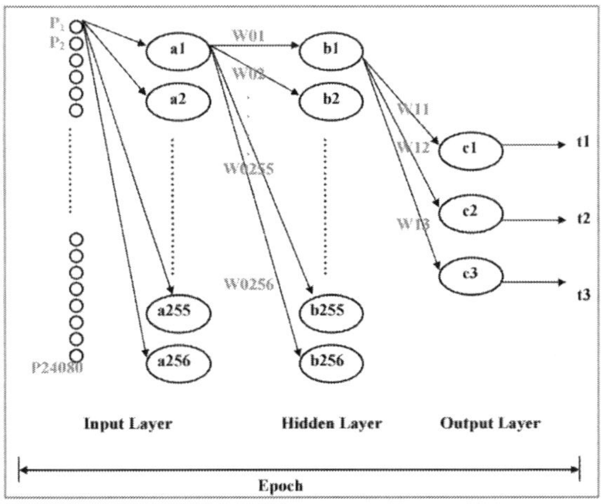

Figure 4: The architecture of the Neural Network used.

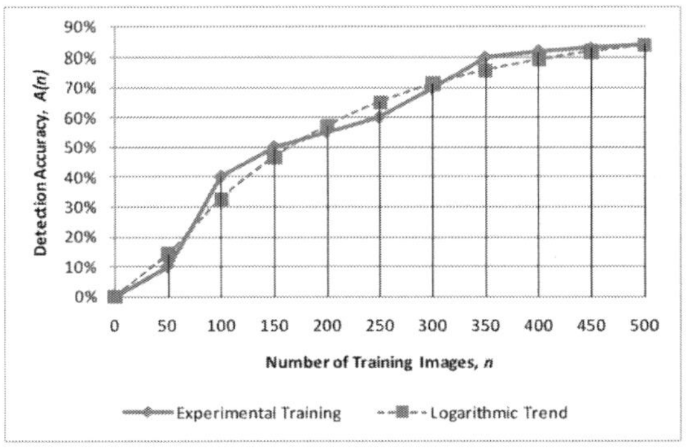

Figure 5: Neural Network detection performance curve.

$$A(n) = 1 - e^{-\left(\frac{n}{180}\right)} \quad (8)$$

EXPERIMENTS AND TEST RESULTS

In order to evaluate the performance of the system, the rescue scenarios were performed by a number of designed experiments. Each experiment consisted of a combination of the following characteristics:

- The human body position such as: the body or part of it is laid down in the middle of the picture or to the side of it, facing forward, facing backward, etc. The different body positions used are listed in Table 1 and Figure 6 shows a sample of the body positions used during the experiments. It should be noted that for Cases 5 and 6, the PIR sensor is triggered, but the IPNNU is not expected to detect a human in the picture because it either almost totally covered (only allowing the body radiation to be sensed) or is in a position, where none of the human body features is clearly visible. Therefore, the detection of a human in these cases is considered as a false positive type of decision.

Figure 6: Sample body positions used for experiments.

- The environmental characteristics around the body such as the lighting level and whether there are features or objects around it. The features and objects were emulated by pieces of furniture for indoor experiments and rocks and trees for outdoor experiments. The different types of environments used and their characteristics are listed in Table 2. This combination of features was used in order to test the robustness of the system in detecting the human body when it is either surrounded or partially covered with debris or rocks or when it is laid in a dark area, etc.

Table 1: The cases of body position.

Scenario	Position Description
Case 1	A full body was laid down facing the camera with no hidden parts
Case 2	A full body was laid on the side of the detection area with no hidden parts
Case 3	Only the hand of a human body is visible
Case 4	Only the foot of a human body is visible
Case 5	A human body was totally covered so that the shape is invisible but the body radiation is allowed to be sensed
Case 6	Human head was placed against the camera such that most other parts are invisible

Table 2: The environments and their characteristics.

Env. Name	Environment Description
ENV1	Very dark environment without any features or objects
ENV2	Very bright environment without any features or objects
ENV3	Fairly lit environment without any features or objects
ENV4	Fairly lit environment with features and objects

- The color levels of clothes dressed by the human being rescued; ranging from very dark to very bright. The reason this factor was added is to test the robustness of the system in recognizing the features of the human body under different combinations of color contrast levels between the body itself and the surrounding environment. The color contrast levels used are listed in Table 3.

Analysis of the Results

All combinations of body positions, environments, and color contrast levels were tested with 5 trials per experiment for a total of 120 experiments and 600 trials.

The detection accuracy test results of all experiments are listed in Table 4. For each experiment, the IPNNU takes a decision as either T, when a human is detected, or F, when no human is detected. For each Case/Environment combination, the total number of T and F decisions is listed.

- The summary of the results for each Case/Environment combination is listed in Table 5 and depicted in Figure 7. The results of this part provide the following observations:
- For Cases 5 and 6, where the system is expected to make only F decisions, as discussed above, the system made a relatively small number of false-positive decisions with an error rate of 7% to 8%.
- Cases 1 and 2 produced a relatively high level of detection accuracy with 11% to 13% error rate since most of the body features were clearly visible.
- For Cases 3 and 4, even though only the hand or the foot of the body was visible, the system performed relatively well in detecting them with 21% to 25% error rate.
- Environments 3 and 4 provided very good conditions for accurate detection with about 9% error rate, while environments 1 and 2 provided moderate conditions for accurate detection with 17% to 21% error rate. The reason is that in Environments 3 and 4, the light intensity was moderate providing enough light to grasp the body features, while in environments 1 and 2, the lack of enough light and the excess of it seem to have blurred the body features and made them less visible.
- It is worth noting that the impact of the features and objects surrounding the body was fairly minimal as there is a negligible difference in performance between Environments 3 and 4.

The summary of the results for each Case/Clothes Color combination is listed in Table 6 and depicted in Figure 8. The results indicate that the very bright and very dark clothes color contrast seem to provide the worst conditions for detection accuracy with 22.5% to 24% error rate, while the medium to dark clothes color contrast provide the best conditions for detection accuracy is all cases and environment conditions with only 6% to 11% error rate.

Table 3: The contrast levels of clothes colors

Symbol	Color Contrast Level
VD	Very dark
D	Dark
M	Moderate
B	Bright
VB	Very Bright

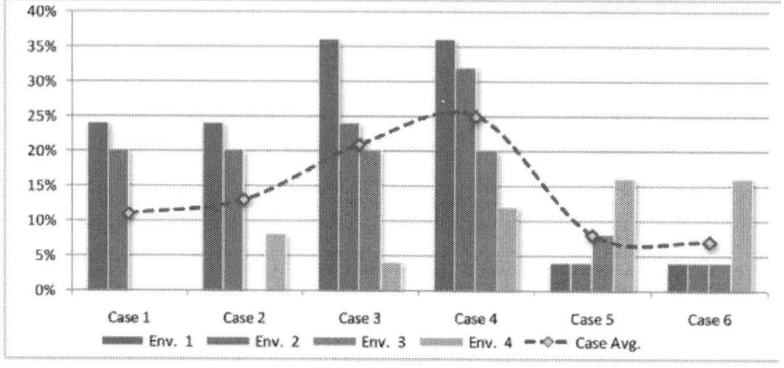

Figure 7: Overall detection error rate statistics per environment type.

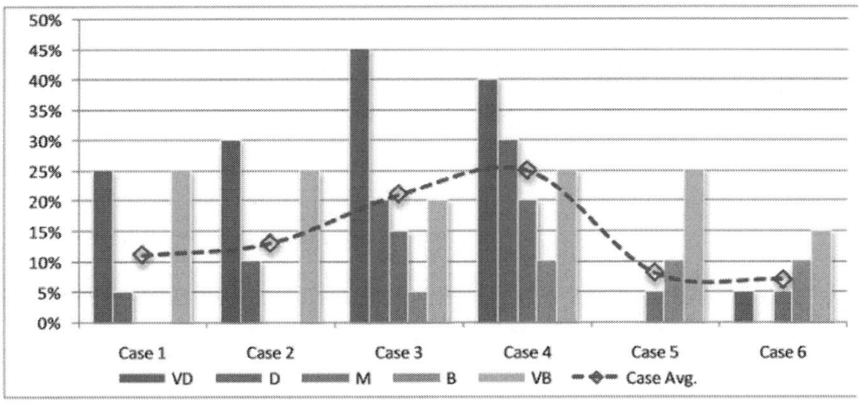

Figure 8: Overall detection error rate statistics per clothes color level.

Table 4: Experimental detection accuracy results.

Env.		ENV1		ENV2		ENV3		ENV4	
Decision		T	F	T	F	T	F	T	F
Case 1									
Clothes Color	VD	0	5	5	0	5	0	5	0
	D	4	1	5	0	5	0	5	0
	M	5	0	5	0	5	0	5	0
	B	5	0	5	0	5	0	5	0
	VB	5	0	0	5	5	0	5	0
SUM		19	6	20	5	25	0	25	0
Case 2									
Clothes Color	VD	0	5	5	0	5	0	4	1
	D	4	1	5	0	5	0	4	1
	M	5	0	5	0	5	0	5	0
	B	5	0	5	0	5	0	5	0
	VB	5	0	0	5	5	0	5	0
SUM		19	6	20	5	25	0	23	2
Case 3									
Clothes Color	VD	0	5	5	0	2	3	4	1
	D	2	3	5	0	4	1	5	0
	M	4	1	4	1	4	1	5	0
	B	5	0	4	1	5	0	5	0
	VB	5	0	1	4	5	0	5	0
SUM		16	9	19	6	20	5	24	1
Case 4									
Clothes Color	VD	0	5	5	0	3	2	4	1
	D	2	3	4	1	4	1	4	1
	M	4	1	4	1	4	1	4	1
	B	5	0	4	1	4	1	5	0
	VB	5	0	0	5	5	0	5	0
SUM		16	9	17	8	20	5	22	3
Case 5									
Clothes Color	VD	0	5	0	5	0	5	0	5
	D	0	5	0	5	0	5	0	5
	M	0	5	0	5	0	5	1	4
	B	0	5	0	5	1	4	1	4
	VB	1	4	1	4	1	4	2	3
SUM		1	24	1	24	2	23	4	21
Case 6									
Clothes Color	VD	0	5	1	4	0	5	0	5
	D	0	5	0	5	0	5	0	5
	M	0	5	0	5	0	5	1	4
	B	0	5	0	5	1	4	1	4
	VB	1	4	0	5	0	5	2	3
SUM		1	24	1	24	1	24	4	21

Table 5: Summary of the experimental detection error rates per environment type.

	C1	C 2	C 3	C 4	C 5	C 6	Avg.
E 1	24%	24%	36%	36%	4%	4%	**21%**
E 2	20%	20%	24%	32%	4%	4%	**17%**
E 3	0%	0%	20%	20%	8%	4%	**9%**
E 4	0%	8%	4%	12%	16%	16%	**9%**
Avg.	**11%**	**13%**	**21%**	**25%**	**8%**	**7%**	**14%**

Table 6: Summary of the experimental detection error rates per clothes color level.

Color	C 1	C 2	C 3	C 4	C 5	C 6	Avg.
VD	25%	30%	45%	40%	0%	5%	**24%**
D	5%	10%	20%	30%	0%	0%	**11%**
M	0%	0%	15%	20%	5%	5%	**8%**
B	0%	0%	5%	10%	10%	10%	**6%**
VB	25%	25%	20%	25%	25%	15%	**23%**
Avg.	**11%**	**13%**	**21%**	**25%**	**8%**	**7%**	**14%**

CONCLUSIONS

In this paper, a new system and methodology for detecting surviving humans in destructed environments using an emulated autonomous robot is proposed. The proposed system applies existing image processing and neural networks techniques for detecting human body or body parts within the camera's range of view. The performance of the system was validated and evaluated via experimentation.

A number of experiments were designed and conducted and a large number of scenarios were tested. For each scenario, the tests were conducted within a number of designed environments that differ in their illumination degree and existing surrounding features. In each environment, different positions of the human body were tested.

The experiments demonstrated that the proposed system can achieve a relatively high detection accuracy of up to 91% in certain conditions and an overall average detection accuracy of 86% for all experiments and environments tested.

This research demonstrates that using relatively simple image processing and neural networks techniques in critical applications such as the urban search and rescue is conceptually efficient and has the potential for playing a significant role in more sophisticated urban search and rescue systems.

REFERENCES

1. Shah, B. and Choset, H. (2004) Survey on Urban Search and Rescue Robotics. Journal of the Robotics Society of Japan, 22, 582-586. http://dx.doi.org/10.7210/jrsj.22.582
2. Moradi, S. (2002) Victim Detection with Infrared Camera in a Rescue Robot. IEEE International Conference on Artificial Intelligence Systems.http://ce.sharif.ac.ir/~rescuerobot/downloads/victim_detection.pdf
3. Burion, S. (2004) Human Detection for Robotic Urban Search and Rescue. Infoscience Database of the Publications and Research Reports, Technical Report.
4. Nakajimaa, C., Pontilb, M., Heiselec, B. and Poggioc, T. (2003) Full-Body Person Recognition System. The Journal of the Pattern Recognition Society, 36, 1997-2006.http://dx.doi.org/10.1016/s0031-3203(03)00061-x
5. Mohan, A., Papageorgiou, C. and Poggio, T. (2001) Example-Based Object Detection in Images by Components. IEEE Transactions on Pattern Analysis and Machine Intelligence, 23, 349-361. http://dx.doi.org/10.1109/34.917571
6. Engle, S. and Whalen, S. (2003) Autonomous Multi-Robot Foraging in a Simulated Environment. UC Davis Report.
7. Cavalcanti, C. and Gomes, H. (2005) People Detection in Still Images Based on a Skin Filter and Body Part Evidence. The Brazilian Symposium on Computer Graphics and Image Processing,
8. National Institute of Standards and Technology (NIST) (2011) Performance Metrics and Test Arenas for Autonomous Mobile Robots. http://www.isd.mel.nist.gov/projects/USAR/
9. Jacoff, A., Messina, E., Weiss, B., Tadokoro, S. and Nakagawa, Y. (2003) Test Arenas and Performance Metrics for Urban Search and Rescue Robots. Proceedings of the 2003 IEEE/RSJ International Conference on Intelligent Robots and Systems, 27-31 October 2003, 3396-3403. http://dx.doi.org/10.1109/IROS.2003.1249681
10. Jacoff, A., Messina, E., and Evans, J. (2002) Performance Evaluation of Autonomous Mobile Robots. Industrial Robot—An International Journal, 29, 259-267.
11. Jacoff, A., Messina, E. and Evans, J. (2001) Experiences in Deploying Test Arenas for Autonomous Mobile Robots. Proceedings of the 2001 Performance Metrics for Intelligent Systems, Mexico, 4 September 2001, 1-8.
12. Jacoff, A., Weiss, B. and Messina, E. (2003) Evolution of a Performance Metric for Urban Search and Rescue Robots. Proceedings of the 2003 Performance Metrics

for Intelligent Systems, Gaithersburg, 16-18 August 2003, 1-11.

13. Trierscheid, M., Pellenz, J., Paulus, D. and Balthasar, D. (2008) Hyperspectral Imaging for Victim Detection with Rescue Robots. Proceedings of the 2008 IEEE International Workshop on Safety, Security and Rescue Robotics, Sendai, 21-24 October 2008, 7-12.http://dx.doi.org/10.1109/SSRR.2008.4745869

14. Zhao, K., Wang, X., Li, Y. and Yu, X. (2006) A Life-Detection System for Special Rescuing Robots. The 9th International Conference on Control, Automation, Robotics and Vision, Singapore, 5-8 December 2006, 1-5.

15. Stergiou, C. and Siganos, D. (2006) Neural Networks. Surveys and Presentations in Information Systems Engineering. SURPRISE 96 Journal.

16. Russell, S. and Norving, P. (2003) Artificial Intelligence—A Modern Approach. 2nd Edition, Prentice Hall, Upper Saddle River.

17. Gonzalez, R. and Woods, R. (2002) Digital image processing. 2nd Edition, Prentice Hall, Upper Saddle River.

CHAPTER 11

MODELING CAMERA IMAGE FORMATION USING A FEEDFORWARD NEURAL NETWORK

Yongtae Do

Keywords: Camera Model, Camera Calibration, Image Formation, Neural Network

INTRODUCTION

A camera can be considered as a device that records objects in three-dimensional (3D) space in the form of their two-dimensional (2D) images. In some technical fields where the use of a camera is required, such as computer vision and image processing, accurate and efficient modeling of the camera's image formation process is a basic problem that must be solved.

For a camera installed in a certain task, the image formation in the camera is characterized with the internal and external parameters of the camera [1]. The internal parameters include focal length, optical image center, and lens distortion coefficients, whereas the external parameters are those for specifying the geometric position and orientation of the camera. The camera model parameter determination process is called camera calibration [2]. Once a camera is calibrated, it is possible to computationally relate objects in 3D world and their projections on the camera's image plane.

Camera modeling and calibration have received great attention in photogrammetry, computer vision, machine vision, and image processing communities particularly since 1980s as cameras and computers became smaller, cheaper, more powerful, and easier to use than before thanks to the rapid technical advances in electronics. The most widely used method is mathematically estimating the parameters of a camera model that best relate control points in 3D world and their corresponding 2D imag points in the model [3-5]. To increase the accuracy of camera calibration, control points must be collected evenly from the space viewed by the camera. However, it is difficult to make accurate position measurements of the 3D points. Methods of automatic calibration [6, 7] and using planar points [7, 8] have been proposed to overcome this difficulty. Existing camera modeling and calibration techniques are well reviewed in [9, 10].

The relationship between the coordinates of a 3D point and the coordinates of its corresponding 2D image point is expressed in terms of a 3×4 matrix when the relationship in a camera is assumed linear. The elements of this transformation matrix can be determined by a regression technique using six or more control points and their image points.

In this paper, we show that the relationship between 3D points and their 2D images can be expressed by a neural network (NN). The model parameter can then be learned by training the NN. The proposed method is quite different from most existing NN-based methods for camera calibration, where NNs are usually used for identifying unknown parts which are not accommodated in a camera model. For example, in [11], an NN is used for learning camera's nonlinearity after linear parameter estimation. The nonlinearity is mostly due to lens distortion [12]. If the linear NN model of this paper is combined with an existing NN for learning nonlinearity, a complete camera model can be constructed with only NNs.

IMAGE FORMATION MODEL

Pin-hole Model

Pin-hole camera model is widely used to relate the image coordinates of an object point visible by a camera and the coordinates of the point in the world coordinate system by distortion-free linear mapping [1, 2]. All rays of sight from 3D

Citation: Y. Do, "Modeling Camera Image Formation Using a Feed-forward Neural Network," Open Journal of Applied Sciences, Vol. 3 No. 1B, 2013, pp. 75-78. doi: 10.4236/ojapps.2013.31B015.

points in a scene are assumed to pass one particular spatial point, pin-hole, in the model. Figure 1 shows the pin-hole camera model, where the following relationships are assumed for a 3D point P $=[x\ y\ z]$ T in the world coordinate system {W}, its corresponding representation $P_C = [x_C\ y_C\ z_C]^T$ in the 3D camera coordinate system {C}, the projected point at $[u, v]^T$ on the 2D image plane, and the optical image center at $[i_O j_O]$ T in the row-column image frame $\{U\}$. A 3D point in {W} can be transformed to the representation in $\{C\}$ by a 3×3 rotation matrix R and a translation vector T.

$$u = i + i_O,\quad v = j + j_O \tag{1}$$

$$P_C = RP + T \tag{2}$$

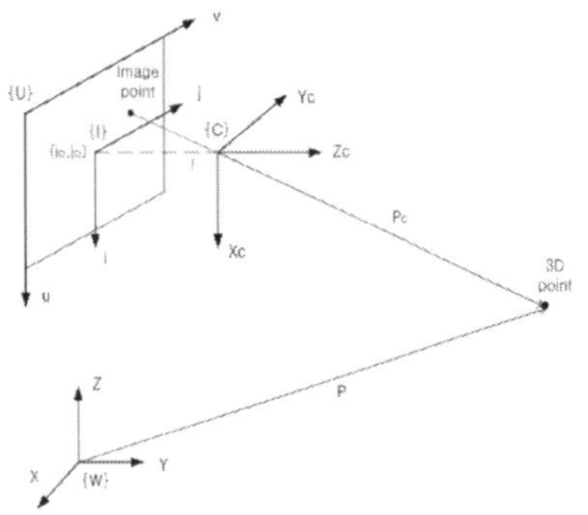

Figure 1: Pin-hole camera model.

The coordinates of an image point are computed in the model from the 3D coordinates in {C} by

$$i = -f\, x_C / z_C,\quad j = -f\, y_C / z_C, \tag{3}$$

where f is the focal length. Combining above equations leads us to the following equation

$$\begin{pmatrix} su \\ sv \\ s \end{pmatrix} = \begin{pmatrix} -f & 0 & i_o \\ 0 & -f & j_o \\ 0 & 0 & 1 \end{pmatrix} \begin{pmatrix} R & T \end{pmatrix} \begin{pmatrix} x \\ y \\ z \\ 1 \end{pmatrix} \tag{4}$$

Neural Network Implementation

A feedforward neural network is capable of computing output values from given input values by propagating weighted values through links between neurons. We want to design an NN as shown in Figure 2 that can represent the image formation process described in Section 2.1. However, it is not possible to build a network in this structure directly from Equation (4) due to the scale factor s, which is the coordinate z_C of a 3D point. Instead, Equation (4) leads us to a structure shown in Figure 3. Figure 4 is a practical network implementation of Figure 3.

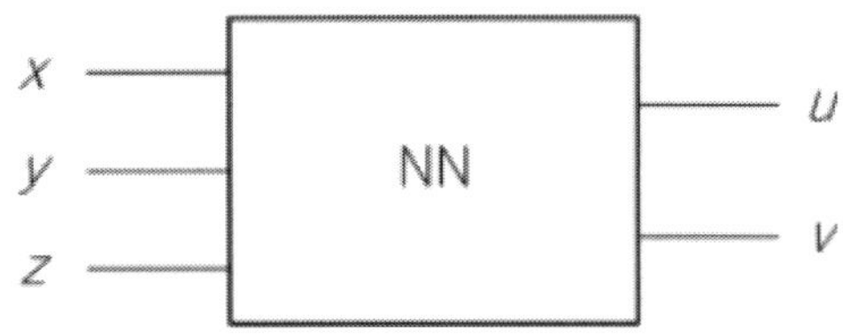

Figure 2: Image formation model by a neural network.

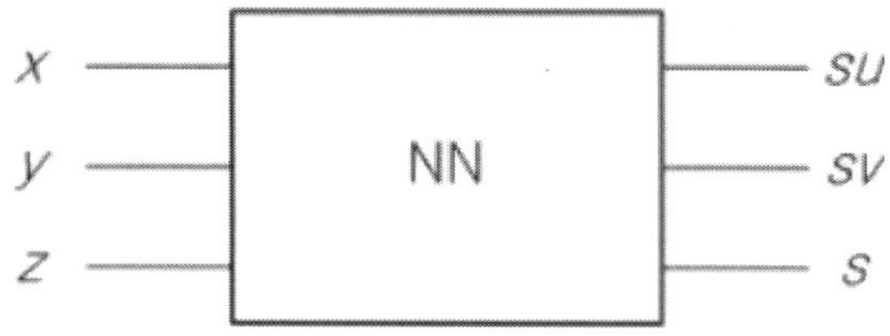

Figure 3: NN built from pinhole camera model.

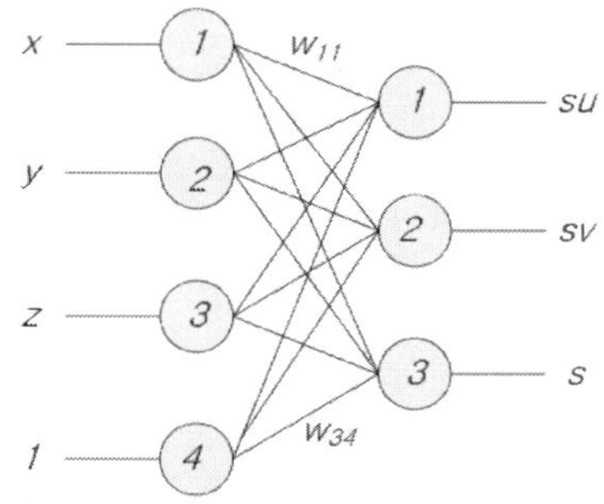

Figure 4: Implementation of the NN of Figure 3

Like most other NNs and their applications, the key issue of the NN implementation presented in Figure 4 is determining the weight of each link between neurons. From Equation (4), the physical meaning of w_{nm}, a link weight from neuron m to neuron n, can be specified as

$$\begin{aligned} &w_{11} = -fr_{11} + i_O r_{31},\quad w_{12} = -fr_{12} + i_O r_{32},\\ &w_{13} = -fr_{13} + i_O r_{33},\quad w_{14} = -ft_1 + i_O t_3,\\ &w_{21} = -fr_{21} + j_O r_{31},\quad w_{22} = -fr_{22} + j_O r_{32},\\ &w_{23} = -fr_{23} + j_O r_{33},\quad w_{24} = -ft_2 + j_O t_3,\\ &w_{31} = r_{31},\quad w_{32} = r_{32},\quad w_{33} = r_{33},\quad w_{34} = t_3, \end{aligned} \tag{5}$$

where r_{pq} are elements of rotation matrix R, and t_p are elements of translation vector T; $1 \le$ p, q ≤ 3.

The network shown in Figure 4 has a quite simple structure. However, it is not simple to train the NN because we do not know the scale factor s for a given 3D point P. We know only the projected image coordinates u and v for a control point P. If the desired output is not available, it is not possible to train the network using a supervised learning algorithm, such as gradient descent optimization [13]. We thus need to develop a method to train the network in the structure of Figure 4.

An error function is defined as

$$E = (e_1^2 + e_2^2 + e_3^2)/2 \tag{6}$$

where

$e_1 = o_1/o_3 - u,\quad e_2 = o_2/o_3 - v,\quad e_3 = ((o_1 o_2)/(uv))^{1/2} - o_3$ for three computed output neuron values, o_1, o_2, and o_3. Note that the error term of the 3rd output neuron, e_3, is derived from

$$o_1 o_2 = (su)(sv) = s^2 uv. \tag{7}$$

Then, the weights are trained by gradient descent. For a weight w_{nm}, n=1 or 2, as shown in Figure 5, a chain rule is applied to the given error E as

$$\frac{\partial E}{\partial w_{nm}} = \frac{\partial E}{\partial e_n}\frac{\partial e_n}{\partial o_n}\frac{\partial o_n}{\partial g_n}\frac{\partial g_n}{\partial w_{nm}} \tag{8}$$

where, assuming a linear activation function for output neurons, $\partial E/\partial e_n = e_n$, $\partial e_n/\partial o_n = 1/o_3$, $\partial o_n/\partial g_n = 1$, $\partial g_n/\partial w_{nm} = o_m$.

For the case of n=3, on the other hand, the following equation can be obtained by gradient descent,

$$\partial E / \partial w_{3m} = -e_3 o_m \tag{9}$$

NUMERICAL EXAMPLE

A camera is assumed to be located at $x=-200$, $y=500$, $z=2000$ and oriented by Z-Y-X Euler angles of $\theta_z=45°$, $\theta_y=-30°$ and $\theta_x=120°$ in the world coordinate system $\{W\}$. It is also assumed that the focal length is $f=25$, the coordinates of the optical image center is (258, 204), and the dimension of a pixel is 0.023×0.023. This camera setup is drawn in Figure 6. An NN can then be built to express the image formation process of the camera as presented in Figure 7.

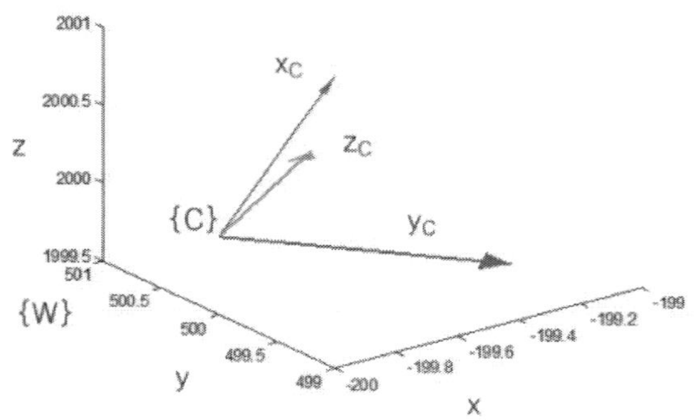

Figure 6: Camera setup assumed as an example.

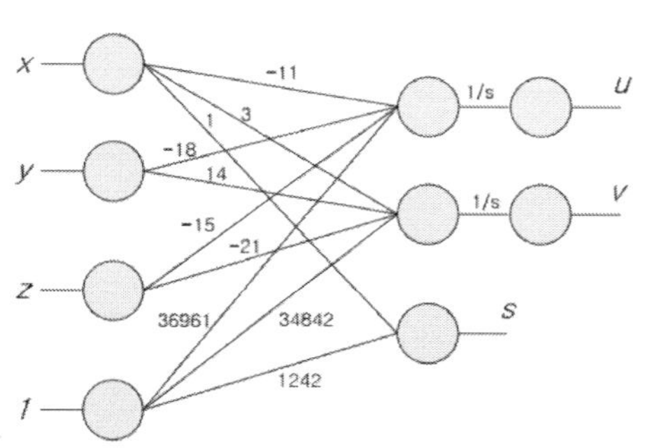

Figure 7: Neural network resulted from the camera setup.

CONCLUDING REMARKS

We have shown that a feedforward neural network can be constructed to express the image formation process of a camera. The network constructed in this paper is in a quite simple structure with four input neurons and three output neurons of linear activation functions. Although most existing applications of NNs to camera modeling have focused on nonlinear lens distortion problem, the network of this paper models the linear perspective transformation. A method to learn the link weights between neurons of the proposed network is also described. The entire image formation of a camera may be modeled accurately if the proposed network is combined with an existing NN-based method developed for correcting lens distortion.

ACKNOWLEDGEMENT

This research was supported by Basic Science Research Program through the National Research Foundation of Korea(NRF) funded by the Ministry of Education, Science and Technology(2012R1A1A4A01010160).

REFERENCES

1. R. Szeliski, "Computer Vision, Algorithms and Applications," Springer-Verlag, London, 2011.
2. R. Y. Tsai, "A Versatile Camera Calibration Technique for High Accuracy 3D Machine Vision Metrology Using Off-the-Shelf TV Cameras and Lenses", IEEE Journal of Robotics and Automation, Vol. 3, No. 4, 1987, pp. 323-344. doi:10.1109/JRA.1987.1087109
3. K. Nakano, M. Oku-tomi and Y. Hasegawa, "Camera Calibration with Precise Extraction of Feature Points Using Projective Transformation," Proceedings of IEEE International Conference on Robotics and Automation, Vol. 3, 2002, pp. 2532-2538. doi:10.1109/ROBOT.2002.1013612
4. J. Weng, P. Cohen, M. Herniou, "Camera Calibration with Distortion Models and Accuracy Evaluation," IEEE Transactions on Pat-tern Analysis and Machine Intelligence, Vol. 14, Issue. 10, pp. 965-980, 1992. doi:10.1109/34.159901
5. K. D. Gremban, C. E. Thorpe, T. Kanade, "Geometric Camera Calibration Using Sys-tems of Linear Equations," Proceedings of IEEE Confe-rence on Robotics and Automation, 1988, pp. 562-567. doi:10.1109/ROBOT.1988.12111
6. R. Hartley and A. Zisserman, "Multiple View Geometry in Computer Vi-sion", Cambridge University Press, 2000.
7. B. Triggs, "Autocalibration from Planar Scenes," Proceedings of European Conference on Computer Vision, 1998, pp. 89-105.
8. Z. Zhang, "A Flexible New Technique for Camera Calibration," IEEE Transactions on Pattern Analysis and Machine Intelligence, Vol. 22, Issue. 11, 2000, pp. 1330-1334. doi:10.1109/34.888718
9. Q. Wang, L. Fu and Z. Liu, "Review on Camera Calibration," Proceedings of Chi-nese Control and Decision Conference, 2010, pp. 3354-3358.
10. J. Salvi, X. Armangué and J. Batlle, "A Comparative Review of Camera Calibrating Methods with Accuracy Evaluation," Pattern Recognition, Vol. 35, Issue 7, 2002, pp. 1617-1635. doi:10.1016/S0031-3203(01)00126-1
11. X. Chen, H. Fang, Y. Yang and S. Qin, "The Research of Camera Distortion Correction Basing on Neural Network," Proceedings of Chinese Control and Decision Conference, 2011, pp. 596-601.

12. J. – P. Tardif, P. Sturm, M. Trudeau and S. Roy, "Calibration of Cameras with Radially Symmetric Distortion," IEEE Transactions on Pattern Analysis and Machine Intelligence, Vol. 31, Issue 9, 2009, pp. 1552-1566. doi:10.1109/TPAMI.2008.202

13. C. M. Christopher, "Pattern Recognition and Machine Learning", Springer Science + Business Media, New York, 2006

CHAPTER 12

MEDICAL IMAGE FUSION BASED ON PULSE COUPLED NEURAL NETWORKS AND MULTI-FEATURE FUZZY CLUSTERING

Xiaoqing Luo and Xiaojun Wu

INTRODUCTION

Image fusion is a kind of information fusion, which refers to the synergistic combination of different sources of sensory image into a single image. The fused image can reflect multiple properties of source images, which makes it more suitable for the purpose of human visual perception and computer processing tasks [1,2]. Recently, multimodal medical image fusion has attracted more attentions due to the increasing demands of clinical applications. Availability of numerous kinds of biomedical sensors makes the medical image fusion a practical topic for researchers and scientists in this field. X-ray, ultrasound, magnetic resonance imaging (MRI) and computed tomography (CT) are a few examples of biomedical sensors. These sensors are used for extracting clinical information, which are generally complementary in nature [1]. Thus, in order to extract more information, medical image fusion combines these contrasting and complimentary features into one fused image. Medical image fusion not only helps in diagnosing diseases, but it also reduces the storage cost by reducing storage to a single fused image instead of multiple-source images [3].

Image fusion can occur at three different levels: pixel level, feature level, and decision level respectively. Generally, pyramid and wavelet transforms are commonly used for multi-resolution image fusion, such as gradient pyramid [4], morphological pyramid [5], DWT pyramid [6], contrast pyramid [7] etc. In the past few years, several researchers have proposed different image fusion methods. Wei proposed a multi-focus image fusion method based on the selection of image blocks from source images by using the energy of image Laplacian [8]. PCNN model derives from the research on cat visual cortex. Its mode of information processing is much closer to the mode of human visual processing. And then PCNN has the flexible structure which can be changed according to different tasks. Additionally, the existing PCNN methods also show PCNN has the higher performance. Su and Wu proposed a image fusion method based on multi-feature fuzzy clustering, which belong to feature level fusion [9]. In this paper, we focus on the image fusion based on the combination of multifeature extraction and PCNN.

The principle of the new image fusion method can be illustrated by Figure 1, where A and B are input medical images, F represents the fused image. One of the source images A is divided into windows. The features of image is defined as $f_{num\times 6}$, where num is the number of windows and 6 is the number of element of feature vector. We use FCM to cluster the feature vectors of image to obtain regions. A and B are decomposed by wavelet transform. l_A and l_B are the low frequency sub-images, y_A and y_B are the high frequency sub-images. The segmentation result is mapped to y_A and y_B. The fusion of l_A and l_B are based on pixel and get by PCNN. The fusion of y_A and y_B are based on region and get by Cauchy similarity of corresponding region. l_F is the low frequency sub-image and y_F is the high frequency sub-image. F can be obtained by inverse wavelet transform.

Citation: Luo, X. and Wu, X. (2012) Medical image fusion based on pulse coupled neural networks and multi-feature fuzzy clustering. Journal of Biomedical Science and Engineering, 5, 878-883. doi: 10.4236/jbise.2012.512A111.

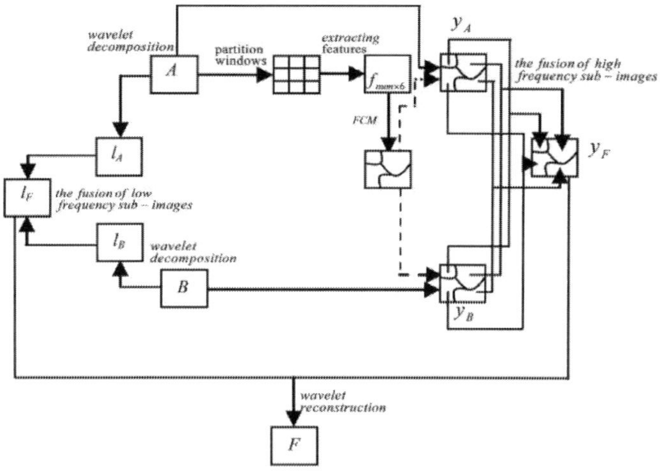

Figure 1: Scheme of the proposed image fusion method.

The proposed method designs more reasonable fusion rules using the global information and multi-feature of image. Compared to weighted average, maximum or region-energy-based rules, the proposed method can obtain better fusion result. The experimental results show that the new algorithm can provide better performance in medical image fusion.

The remainder of the paper is organized as follows: The fusion rule of low frequency sub-images is discussed in Section 2. Section 3 shows the fusion processing of high frequency sub-images. Experimental results and performance evaluations are given in Sections 4. Finally, conclusions are drawn in Section 5.

THE FUSION RULE OF LOW FREQUENCY SUB-IMAGES

The medical images are transformed using wavelet. The fusion of low frequency sub-images is performed using average weighted fusion rule. Let the low frequency subband of two medical images be l_A and l_B respectively, the fusion result of low frequency subband is l_F. i and j are the position of pixels. The fusion rule is given as follows:

$$\begin{aligned} &l_F(i,j) = w_1 l_A(i,j) + w_2 l_B(i,j) \\ &w_1 + w_2 = 1 \end{aligned} \tag{1}$$

It is important that define the weight (w_1 and w_2). In view of the global coupled property and pulse synchronization characteristics of the PCNN [10,11], we use a simplified model and discrete form to determine weights.

In the simplified PCNN model, the PCNN neuron consists of three parts: the dendritic tree, the linking modulation, and the pulse generator [8]. The role of the dendritic tree is to receive the inputs from two kinds of receptive fields. Depending on the type of the receptive field, it is subdivided into two channels (the linking and the feeding). The linking channel receives local stimulus from the output of surrounding neurons, while the feeding channel, besides local stimulus, still receives external stimulus. In the following expressions, the indexes i and j refer to the pixel location in the image, k and l refer to the dislocation in a symmetric neighborhood around one pixel, and n denotes the current iteration(discrete time step). Here n varies from 1 to N (N is the total number of iterations)

$$\begin{cases} F_{ij}(n) = S_{ij}(n) \\ L_{ij}(n) = \exp(-\alpha_L) L_{ij}(n-1) + V_L \sum_{k,l} m_{ij,kl} Y_{ij}(n-1) \\ U_{ij}(n) = F_{ij}(n) \times (1 + \beta L_{ij}(n)) \\ Y_{ij}(n) = \begin{cases} 1 & U_{ij}(n) > T_{ij}(n) \\ 0 & U_{ij}(n) \le T_{ij}(n) \end{cases} \\ T_{ij}(n) = \exp(-\alpha_T) T_{ij}(n-1) + V_T Y_{ij}(n) \end{cases} \tag{2}$$

The dendritic tree is given by $F_{ij}(n)$ and $L_{ij}(n)$. The two main components F and L are called feeding and linking, respectively. $m_{ij,kl}$ are the synaptic weight coefficients and S is the external stimulus. V_L is normalizing constants. α_L is the time constants. The linking modulation is given in the 3rd row of Eq.2, where $U_{ij}(n)$ is the internal state of the neuron. β is the linking parameter and the pulse generator determines the firing events in the model in the 4-th row of Eq.2. $Y_{ij}(n)$ depends on the internal state and threshold. The dynamic threshold of the neuron is the 5-th row of Eq.2, where V_T and α_T are normalized constant and time constant, respectively.

Suppose that the size of each low frequency sub-image is $M \times N$. The corresponding PCNN is then designed for them, and the size of each PCNN is $M \times N$. For each neuron, the feeding input is the intensity of the pixel corresponding to it. The number of neurons in the network is equal to the number of pixels in the input image. There exists a one-to-one correspondence between the image pixels and network neurons. Each pixel is connected to a unique neuron, and each neuron is connected to surrounding neurons.

β is the linking parameter. The pixel with significant feature should give strong response. Therefore, the setting of β should be related to the features of the corresponding pixels of the images. In this paper, local entropy(L_en) and the variance of local entropy of each of pixel (VL_en)are considered as the information of pixel [12]. We define a sliding window, the size of which is $m \times n$. ML_en is defined as the mean of local entropy of each of pixel. ML_en and VL_en are calculated with the sliding window and VL_en is regarded as the distribution feature of local entropy of the center pixel in the sliding window. L_en, ML_en and VL_en can be described as follows:

$$L\_en(i,j) = -\sum_{\omega,x} p_x \ln p_x \tag{3}$$

$$\begin{aligned} &ML\_en(i,j) \\ &= \frac{1}{mn} \sum_{i'=-[m/2]}^{[m/2]} \sum_{j'=-[n/2]}^{[n/2]} L\_en(i+i')(j+j') \end{aligned} \tag{4}$$

$$\begin{aligned} &VL\_en(i,j) \\ &= \frac{1}{mn-1} \sum_{i'=-[m/2]}^{[m/2]} \sum_{j'=-[n/2]}^{[n/2]} (L\_en(i+i')(j+j') \\ &-ML\_en(i,j))^2 \end{aligned} \tag{5}$$

$$\beta(i,j) = L\_en(i,j) \times VL\_en(i,j) \tag{6}$$

L_en can to some extend reflect the amount of information locally. VL_en shows the discrete degree of information distribution in local region, that is , the significant of image feature. Eq.6 defines the linking parameter of each of pixel, which fully reflects the information of pixel. And β is not sensitive to noise because VL_en of noise is small due to the confusion of noise.

The fusion steps of low frequency sub-images using PCNN are described as follows:

1) Let $l_A(i,j)$ and $l_B(i,j)$ separately denote low frequency sub-images of the original medical images A and B. $l_A(i,j)$ and $l_B(i,j)$ are then normalized between 0 and 1, which are denoted as $l'_A(i,j)$ and $l'_B(i,j)$ respectively. $l'_A(i,j)$ and $l'_B(i,j)$ are treated as the feeding input to stimulate a corresponding PCNN.

2) Calculate the L_en and VL_en of $l'_A(i,j)$ and $l'_B(i,j)$ respectively, then, $\beta(i,j)$ can be obtained.

3) If n = N, then iteration stops. $T(i,j)$ is denoted as the total pulse value of the (i,j) neuron of the low frequency sub-image during n iterations. The fused weight can be defined as follows:

$$w_1 = T_A(i,j)/(T_A(i,j)+T_B(i,j)),\ w_2 = 1 - w_1 \tag{7}$$

According to Eq.1, we can get the fusion result of low frequency sub-images.

THE FUSION RULE OF HIGH FREQUENCY SUB-IMAGES

The fusion rule of high frequency sub-images is performed based on multi-feature fuzzy clustering. First, the source images are divided into windows. Multi-feature is extracted from window and the fuzzy C-means (FCM) clustering algorithm [13] is used to segment the image. Second, average weighted fusion method is used to each of region. The weighting factors are constructed based on the local energy and the fuzzy similarity measure defined by Cauchy function [9] .The wavelet coefficients of the fused image are acquired by the weighting factors.

Multi-Feature of Images

To extract texture feature, the input image A is first segmented into wm × wn small windows. Let num be the number of windows in the output image. A feature vector is then extracted from each window, each feature vector,

$f_w(f_w \in R^6, 1 \le w \le num)$, consists of 6 features. Three of them are the texture features, which are denoted by a wavelet transform applied to windows of the image A. The other two features are computed similarly from the LH and HH bands. The fourth feature is the gray value of image denoted by the mean value of window in the spatial domain. The other two are the x-coordinate and ycoordinate on the top left corner of the window, which denotes the spatial location. Finally, we obtain the feature vector f_w, and normalize f_w to $\hat{f}_w$.

Image Segmentation Based on FCM

Image segmentation is an essential step in image fusion. The well known method of fuzzy clustering is FCM Algorithm, which is an unsupervised fuzzy clustering. FCM adopts the iterative algorithm to optimize objective function based by least square algorithm.

FCM algorithm is used to cluster the feature vectors $\hat{f}_w$, we obtain $\mu_{c,w}$ ($1 \le c \le c'$, $1 \le w \le num$), c' is the number of clusters, and $\mu_{c,w} \in [0,1]$ denotes the membership of the feature vector $\hat{f}_w$ in the c-th cluster.

After FCM clustering, the clusters are obtained as follows:

If $\mu_{ci,w} > \mu_{cl,w}$ ($cl = 1,2\cdots,c', ci = 1,2,\cdots,c', cl \ne ci$) then the vector $\hat{f}_w$ belongs to the ci-th cluster. So the set of feature vectors is partitioned into c› groups $\{F_1,\cdots,F_{c'}\}$, and consequently, the image is segmented into c' regions $\{Rg_1,\cdots,Rg_{c'}\}$ with Rg_c being the region corresponding to the feature set F_c. The number of clusters is chosen by cross-validation technique.

Cauchy Fuzzy Similarity

The wavelet coefficients of the c-th region in R level and P band is defined as $y_c^{R,p}$. Let x denote the mean of window and U denote the mean set of windows ($x \in U$). The source image A and B are decomposed by wavelet, the memberships of fuzzy region A and B in a band are given by

$$\mu_{\tilde{A}}(x) = \frac{1}{1+\left(\frac{\|\bar{x}-\bar{\mu}\|^{\alpha}}{d_a}\right)}, \mu_{\tilde{B}}(x) = \frac{1}{1+\left(\frac{\|\bar{x}-\bar{v}\|^{\alpha}}{d_b}\right)} \tag{8}$$

where α determine the kurtosis of Cauchy function, $\bar{\mu}$ and $\bar{v}$ are the regional mean of $y_{c,A}^{R,p}$ and $y_{c,B}^{R,p}$ respectively. d_a and d_b are the mean distance between the centre of clustering. $\bar{y}_{c,A}^{R,p}$ and $\bar{y}_{c,B}^{R,p}$ are the regional mean value.

$$d_a = \frac{2}{c'(c'-1)}\sum_{c=1}^{c'}\sum_{c+1}^{c'}\left\|\bar{y}_{c,A}^{R,p} - \bar{y}_{c+1,A}^{R,p}\right\|$$
$$d_b = \frac{2}{c'(c'-1)}\sum_{c=1}^{c'}\sum_{c+1}^{c'}\left\|\bar{y}_{c,B}^{R,p} - \bar{y}_{c+1,B}^{R,p}\right\| \tag{9}$$

The Cauchy fuzzy similarity is $S(\tilde{A},\tilde{B})$ of fuzzy set A and B, that is, regional matching degree $m_{c,AB}^{R,p}$.

$$S(\tilde{A},\tilde{B}) = \frac{(d_a+d_b)^{\alpha}}{(d_a+d_b)^{\alpha} + \|\bar{\mu}-\bar{v}\|^{\alpha}} \tag{10}$$

Let $E_c^{R,p}$ be the regional information energy. If w_num is the window number of region c, $E_c^{R,p}$ can be defined as follows:

$$E_c^{R,p} = \sum_{wj=1}^{w\_num}\left|\bar{y}_{c,wj}^{R,p}\right|^2 \tag{11}$$

Decision Method

The decision method of image fusion directly affects the quality of fusion result. Let $y_{c,F}^{R}(n/p)$ is the wavelet coefficients of the c-th region of fused image in R level and P band.

$$y_{c,F}^{R}(i,j/p) = \omega_A^{R,p} y_{c,A}^{R}(i,j/p) + \omega_B^{R,p} y_{c,B}^{R}(i,j/p)$$
$$\omega_A^{R,p} + \omega_B^{R,p} = 1 \tag{12}$$

where T is the threshold of $m_{c,AB}^{R,p}$ and $\omega^{R,p}$ is the weighted factor. $\omega_A^{R,p}$ is defined as follows:

$$\omega_A^{R,P} = \begin{cases} 1 & \text{if } m_{c,AB}^{R,P} \le T \text{ and } E_{c,A}^{R,P} > E_{c.B}^{R,P} \\ 0 & \text{if } m_{c,AB}^{R,P} \le T \text{ and } E_{c,A}^{R,P} \le E_{c.B}^{R,P} \\ \frac{1}{2}+\frac{1}{2}\left(\frac{1-m_{c,AB}^{R,P}}{1-T}\right) & \text{if } m_{c,AB}^{R,P} > T \text{ and } E_{c,A}^{R,P} > E_{c.B}^{R,P} \\ \frac{1}{2}-\frac{1}{2}\left(\frac{1-m_{c,AB}^{R,P}}{1-T}\right) & \text{if } m_{c,AB}^{R,P} > T \text{ and } E_{c,A}^{R,P} \le E_{c.B}^{R,P} \end{cases} \quad (13)$$

THE FUSION PROCEDURE AND EXPERIMENTAL RESULTS

The Fusion Procedure

The proposed method can be summarized as follows:

- Select one of medical images to perform multifeature extraction as discussed in Section 3.1.
- We use FCM to segment image based on the results of multi-feature extraction and the segmentation results are mapped into other medical image to be fused.
- Medical images are decomposed by wavelet transform into low frequency and high frequency bands respectively.
- The fusion rule of low frequency sub-images adopts average weighted method based on pixel level. The weighted factor is obtained by PCNN. Then we calculate the L_en and VL_en for each pixel, which is used to define β.
- The fusion rule of high frequency sub-images is the average weighted method based on region. The weighted of region can be got by the regional similarity and region energy.
- The fused image can be got by taking the inverse wavelet transform of the fusion result of low frequency sub-images and high frequency sub-images.

Experimental Results

Medical imaging is taking on an increasingly critical role in healthcare, which has enabled radiologists to quickly acquire images of the human body and its internal structures with effective resolution and realism. These images are often known as multimodality medical images such as computed tomography (CT), ultrasound, positron emission tomography (PET), nuclear magnetic resonance (NMR) etc.. In our experiments, we evaluate the performance of our proposed method by CT and MR images, which come from the web of http://www. imagefusion.org/. The excellent views of bones and other dense structures are given by CT images whereas the excellent views of soft tissues are given perfectly by MR images. In certain situations, both soft and dense tissues are needed to be visualized simultaneously for better diagnosis. Hence, we need medical image fusion of various kinds for better treatment planning.

It is important to perform statistical assessment of the quality of different fusion techniques. Our method is compared to image fusion based on multi-feature fuzzy clustering [13] and image fusion based on DWT [6] and PCA [14]. Several indices are used for fused image quality assessment, including entropy (E), variance (V), mutual information (MI), spatial frequency (SF) and gradient (G) [15].

The size of original CT and MR images is 256 × 256, with 256-level gray scale. When wavelet transform is exploited, three decomposition levels and the wavelet basis "sym4" are used. For the proposed methods, the image block size is 4 × 4 pixels and c› = 50 and T = 0.6 in the experiment. The parameters setting are given as follows:

$$\alpha_L = 1, \alpha_\theta = 0.2, V_L = 1, V_\theta = 20, N = 250$$

$$W = \begin{bmatrix} 0.707 & 1 & 0.707 \\ 1 & 0 & 1 \\ 0.707 & 1 & 0.707 \end{bmatrix}$$

The visual comparison for fused images according to different fusion algorithms are shown in Figures 2 and 3 respectively. From the two figures, it is clear that the proposed algorithm improves better detail information than the existing algorithms. The PCA algorithm gives baseline results because it is not a method based on multi-scale decomposition. Among multi-resolution based algorithms, our method based on multi-feature fuzzy clustering and PCNN has the best visual perception. The fusion method based on DWT lacks the ability that extracts image feature result in the degradation of fusion performance. Statistically, the overall performance and comparison among existing and proposed algorithms using quality metrics are depicted in Tables 1 and 2 respectively. From Table 1, the E, V and MI of PCA are the best and the SF and G of our method are the best. Comparing Figure 2(c) with Figure 2(a), we can find that they are very close that means the main information of Figure 2(c) comes from Figure 2(a). In Table **2**, all metrics except for E are the best for the proposed method. From Table 2, we can easily conclude that the proposed algorithm can preserve high details. The possible reason behind the better performance is the combination of the local entropy and variance of local entropy based PCNN and multi-feature fuzzy clustering, which make more informative detail coefficients are produced when compared to other multi-resolution methods.

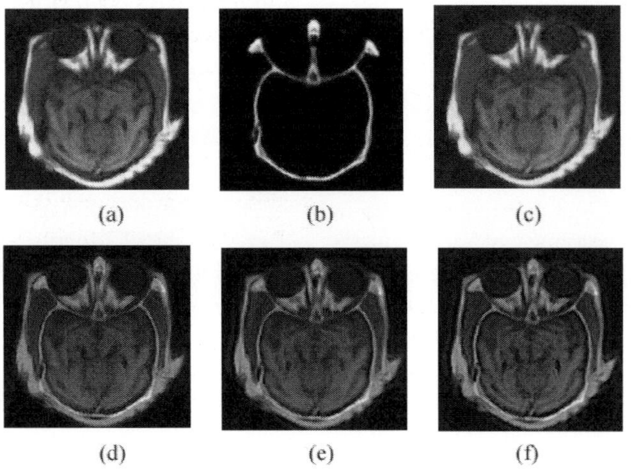

Figure 2: Fusion results for experimental image set 1; (a) heard 1 (MR); (b) heard 2 (CT); (c) fusion with PCA; (d) fusion with DWT; (e) Ref. [13]; (f) proposed method.

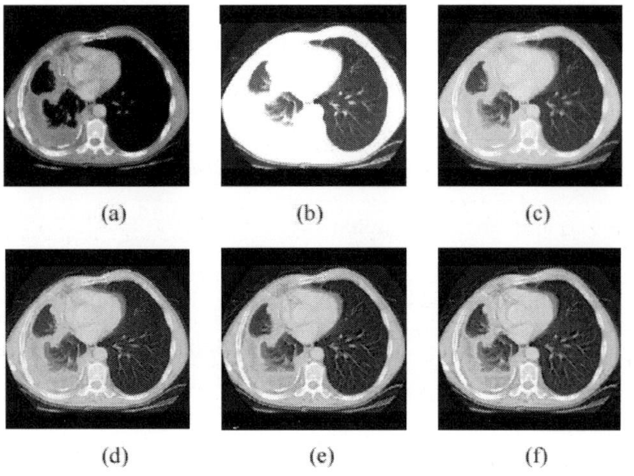

Figure 3: Fusion results for experimental image set 2; (a) head 1 (MR); (b) head 2 (CT); (c) fusion with PCA; (d) fusion with DWT; (e) Ref. [13]; (f) proposed method.

Table 1: The qualities of fusion results for **Figure 2**.

Images	E	V	MI	SF	G
Figure 2(c)	**4.572**	**56.131**	**6.323**	14.291	7.884
Figure 2(d)	4.198	36.823	3.347	14.221	7.677
Figure 2(e)	4.218	37.094	3.331	14.364	7.926
Figure 2(f)	4.244	38.475	2.721	**14.66**	**8.067**

Table 2: The qualities of fusion results for **Figure 3**

Images	E	V	MI	SF	G
Figure 3(c)	4.478	95.538	6.842	25.018	11.657
Figure 3(d)	**4.555**	91.694	4.244	29.705	15.35
Figure 3(e)	4.529	86.608	4.319	31.458	16.056
Figure 3(f)	4.514	**91.939**	**4.335**	**33.355**	**17.072**

CONCLUSION

In this paper, a novel multi-modal medical image fusion algorithm based on PCNN and multi-feature fuzzy clustering is proposed. Considering the human visual system characteristics, two different fusion rules are adopted to fuse the low frequency and high frequency sub-images respectively. For the low frequency sub-images, the fusion weight coefficient based on PCNN. The local entropy and the variance of local entropy of each of pixel reflect the local information, which is used to calculate the linking strength. For the high frequency sub-images, the fusion weight based on region is got by multi-feature fuzzy clustering and Cauchy fuzzy similarity. The proposed algorithm can effectively preserve more information in the fused image with improved quality. The experiments are conducted on CT and MR for image fusion, two groups of CT and MR images are considered. The statistical comparisons demonstrate that the proposed algorithm better preserved the image details and significantly improved the image visual effect than the other fusion methods with very less information distortion. The objective statistical assessment findings agree with the visual perception. Although experiments are conducted only on CT and MR images, we believe that the proposed method can be used for other image fusion applications.

ACKNOWLEDGEMENTS

This research was supported by the grants from Shanghai Commission for Science and Technology (KSCX2-YW-R-112), and Shanghai Leading Academic Discipline Project (J50101).

REFERENCES

1. Bhatnagar, G., Wu, J.Q.M. and Liu, Z. (2012) Human visual system inspired multi-modal medical image fusion framework. Expert Systems with Applications, in press.doi:10.1016/j.eswa.2012.09.011
2. Pajares, G. and Cruz, J. (2004) A wavelet-based image fusion tutorial. Pattern Recognition, 37, 1855-1872. doi:10.1016/j.patcog.2004.03.010
3. Wang, Z.B. and Ma Y.D. (2008) Medical image fusion using m-PCNN. Information Fusion, 9, 176-185. doi:10.1016/j.inffus.2007.04.003
4. Burt, P.J. (1992) A gradient pyramid basis for patternselective image fusion, Society for Information Displays (SID) International Symposium Digest of Technical Papers, 23, 467-470.
5. Toet, A. (1989) A morphological pyramidal image decomposition. Pattern Recognition Letter, 9, 255-261. doi:10.1016/0167-8655(89)90004-4
6. Li, H., Manjunath, B.S. and Mitra, S.K. (1995) Multisensor image fusion using the wavelet transform. Graphical Models and Image Processing, 57, 235-245. doi:10.1006/gmip.1995.1022
7. Toet, A., van Ruyven, L.J. and Valeton, J.M. (1989) Merging thermal and visual images by a contrast pyramid. Optical Engineering, 28, 789-792. doi:10.1117/12.7977034
8. Wang, Z.B., Ma, Y.D. and Gu, J.S. (2010) Multi-focus image fusion using PCNN. Pattern Recognition, 43, 2003-2016. doi:10.1016/j.patcog.2010.01.011
9. Su, D.X. and Wu, X.J. (2006) Image fusion based on multi-feature fuzzy clustering. Journal of CAD and Graphics, 18, 838-843.
10. Eckhorn, R., Reitboeck, H.J., Arndt, M. and Dicke, P.W. (1990) Feature linking via synchronization among distributed assemblies: Simulation of results from cat cortex. Neural Computation, 2, 293-307. doi:10.1162/neco.1990.2.3.293
11. Lindblad, T. and Kinser, J.M. (2005) Image processing using pulse-coupled neural networks. 2nd Edition, Springer, New York
12. Zhang, Y.F. and He, M.Y. (2006) Image fusion algorithm based on local information entropy and its distribution property. Computer Engineering, 32, 22-30.
13. Nikhil, R.P., Kuhu, P. and James, M.K. (2005) A possibilistic fuzzy c means clustering algorithm. IEEE Transactions on Fuzzy Systems, 13, 517-530. doi:10.1109/TFUZZ.2004.840099
14. Zhang, Z. and Blum, R.S. (1999) A categorization of multiscale-decomposition-based image fusion schemes with a performance study for a digital camera application. Proceedings of the IEEE, 87, 1315-1326. doi:10.1109/5.775414
15. Luo, X.Q. and Wu, X.J. (2010) New metric of image fusion based on region similarity. Optical Engineering, 49, 1-13. doi:10.1117/1.3394086

CHAPTER 13

THE USE OF MULTI-OBJECTIVE GENETIC ALGORITHM BASED APPROACH TO CREATE ENSEMBLE OF ANN FOR INTRUSION DETECTION

Gulshan Kumar and Krishan Kumar

Keywords: Ensemble Classifiers, Intrusion Detection System, Intrusion Detection, Multi-Objective Genetic Algorithm

INTRODUCTION

With coming age of Internet and dependence of business applications on it, network security has become key foundation. Information access through Internet provides various ways of attacking the computer system. More and more organizations have become vulnerable to Internet attacks/intrusions. An intrusion or attack can be defined as "any set of actions that attempt to compromise the security objectives". The important security objectives include Availability, Integrity, Confidentiality, Accountability and Assurance [1]. Intrusion detection attempts to detect computer attacks/intrusions by analyzing audit data of the network [2,3]. Intrusion detection system (IDS) is one of the most important components among six anti-intrusion systems namely prevention, preemption, deterrence, deflection, detection, and countermeasures [4]. Detection rate (DR) and False Positive rate (FPR) are two key indicators to evaluate the capability of IDSs. Many efforts have done to improve DR and FPR of IDS [5]. In the beginning, the research focus was on rule based and statistical IDS. But, with large dataset, the results of these IDS become un-satisfactory. Thus, a lot of AI based intrusion detection techniques have been introduced to solve the problem [1,5,7]. Among these techniques, Artificial Neural Networks (ANN) is one of the most widely and robust techniques used to solve complex problems. Many researchers have successfully utilized ANN for IDS [3,8-11] due to its advantages like: 1) High tolerance to noisy data; 2) Ability to classify untrained patterns; 3) Well-suited for continuous-valued inputs and outputs; 4) Successful on a wide array of realworld data; 5) Algorithms are inherently parallel [12]. But, major limitations of ANN based IDSs are: 1) Lower value of DR and high value of FPR, especially for monitory attack classes like U2R and R2L classes; 2) Long training time; 3) Require a number of parameters typically best determined empirically, e.g., the network topology and weights; 4) Poor interpretability: difficult to interpret the symbolic meaning behind the learned weights and of hidden units in the network [12]. The major cause of low results for minority attack classes is that the distribution of different types of attacks is imbalanced [13]. This imbalance results difficulty in learning the features of minority attack classes by ANN. The minority attack classes are also equally important as majority attack classes. The minority attack may cause serious damage if succeeded [9]. For example, if the R2L attacks succeeded, the attacker can get the authority of root user remotely. The attacker can do the whole thing he likes to the targeted computer systems or network device. Although prior research has proposed some approaches for effective intrusion detection systems. But, for improvement of DR and FPR, these approaches still need to be researched to become IDS more effective [5,14]. One limitation with majority of approaches is the lack of control over classification tradeoff the solution they obtains. This issue is identified as general issue while creating classifiers. Striving to create a single best classifier that obtains the highest accuracy may give unfruitful results when used under different scenarios [15].

To solve these problems, we propose an ensemble approach for ANN-based IDS evolved by Multi-objective genetic algorithm (NSGA II) [16], called MANNE (Multiobjective

Citation: G. Kumar and K. Kumar, "The Use of Multi-Objective Genetic Algorithm Based Approach to Create Ensemble of ANN for Intrusion Detection," International Journal of Intelligence Science, Vol. 2 No. 4A, 2012, pp. 115-127. doi: 10.4236/ijis.2012.224016.

genetic algorithm based Artificial Neural Network Ensemble) to improve the DR and FPR of intrusion detection. The procedure for MANNE approach has following phases.

Phase 1: it generates an optimal Pareto front consisting of a set of non-dominated ANN solutions using MOGA, which formulate the base classifiers from training dataset.

Phase 2: it generates another optimal Pareto front consisting of a set of non-dominated ensembles based upon pool of non-dominated ANN solutions as base classifiers (output of phase 1) which exhibit classification tradeoffs.

Phase 3: Prediction aggregation—It gets the final prediction of ensemble from predictions of base classifiers.

In phase 1, we utilized multi objective Genetic algorithm (MOGA) based approach to evolve weights of ANN as base classifiers. It yields an improved Pareto front of solutions. Here, DR of each attack class is treated as separate objective in multi objective approach. Further in phase 2, base classifiers are selected to create ensemble of ANNs to optimize the objective functions. Phase 3 aggregates the predictions of base classifiers to get final prediction of ensemble. To illustrate the applicability and capability of the new approach for intrusion detection, the results of experiments on KDD CUP 1999 dataset [17] are computed. The results demonstrated better performance of MANNE in comparison to widely used intrusion detection approaches. We selected ANN trained using Back Propagation method and most widely used methods for creating ensembles namely Bagging [18], Boosting [19] (ANN as base classifier) to compare MANNE. The results are also compared to other wellknown method such as decision tree, and its ensembles based upon bagging & Boosting in terms of defined performance evaluation metrics.

Article Overview: The rest of the paper is organized as follows. Section 2 presents the literature analysis. Section 3 presents the description of framework and explains the working of MANNE. Section 4 gives the implementation details of MANNE. It highlights the basics of techniques i.e. ANN and MOGA used in the experiments. Section 5 gives details of dataset used to evaluate, evaluation criteria adopted and discuss the results of the experiments. Finally, concluding remarks and future directions are highlighted in Section 6.

LITERATURE ANALYSIS

IDS can be categorized into number of classes based on different criteria [1]. One way to classify IDS is based upon method to process the audit data. Using this criteria, the IDSs can be categorized into two classes namely signature based systems and anomaly based systems [1-3]. Signature based IDS identifies the intrusions by matching the patterns to known attack scenarios/signatures. Whereas, anomaly based IDS works to search for malicious behavior that deviates from established normal patterns.

Another criterion to classify IDS is source of audit data. Based upon this criteria, IDSs can be categorized into two classes namely host based IDS and network based IDS [1]. Host based IDS collects the data from a host to be protected. They collects the data generally from system calls, operating system log files, NT events log file, CPU utilization, application log files, etc. Advantage of Host based IDS is that they are operating system dependent & are very efficient to detect attacks like buffer overflow. These systems become inefficient in case of encrypted data and switched network. Whereas, network based IDS collects the data from network directly in form of packets. These IDSs are operating system independent and easy to deploy to various systems. In this paper, our interest is in network based intrusion detection.

In order to detect the intrusions, various approaches have been developed and proposed over the last decade [1,5,9,20,21]. In the beginning, the research focus was on rule based IDS and statistical IDS. Rule based IDS reported high classification results for known attacks whose signatures are available in database. But, these systems fail to detect novel attacks. The systems require continuous updating of signature database which is very complex and laborious task. Statistical based IDS apply different statistical techniques to design a model to establish threshold values. These IDS requires collection of enough data to build complicated model which is computationally expensive for complicated network traffic [9]. In order to meet deficiency of these methods, a lot of AI based intrusion detection techniques have been introduced [1,6,7,21]. Among these techniques, Artificial Neural Networks (ANN) is one of the most widely and robust techniques used to solve complex problems [9]. Many researchers have successfully utilized ANN for IDS [3,8-11] due to its advantages like: 1) High tolerance to noisy data; 2) Ability to classify untrained patterns; 3) Well-suited for continuous-valued inputs and outputs; 4) Successful on a wide array of real-world data; and 5) Algorithms are inherently parallel [1,12]. ANN can be used in different modes. The modes are: 1) Supervised ANN based IDS; 2) Unsupervised ANN based IDS; and 3) Hybrid ANN based IDS [9]. In supervised ANN based IDS, labeled training data is required to build its model [8,22,23]. Whereas it is not required in case of unsupervised ANN based IDS. In case of hybrid ANN based IDS, there is a combination of supervised ANN and unsupervised ANN, or a combination of ANN with other data mining techniques to detect intrusions [24,25].

Many researchers used ANN as single classifier as well as ensemble classifier for intrusion detection. They reported improvement of detection results by using ensemble of ANN over single ANN. Many researchers utilized ANN in supervised mode for intrusion detection. The main focus was on multi-layer feed-forward (MLFF) neural networks and recurrent neural networks [22,23]. Ryan et al. (1998) used MLFF neural networks for anomaly detection based on user behaviors based upon UNIX commands [8]. The approach was to build a profile for each used based upon the commands executed. The 100 most commonly used commands were selected, thus, giving a 100-dimensional vector of command frequency intervals for each user, which is used as input to the MLP. On average, the system correctly identifies the normal users 93% of the time and 63% of the randomly generated vectors were classified as intrusive. But, practically, the number of training set is very large and distribution is imbalanced leading ANN reaches some local minima and thus lower value of DR.

Ghosh and Schwartzbard (1999) utilized MLP for application based anomaly and misuse detection [26]. Along with MLP, they applied a leaky bucket algorithm to facilitate some form of a memory mechanism since it is necessary to classify sequences of events. One network was trained for each process/program. They used DARPA98 data to evaluate their approach. They reported best results of 77.3% true positives and 3.6% false positives for the anomaly detection. For misuse based detection, the results were nearly 20% false positives at approximately the same true positive rate. They justified the results due to limited amount of intrusive data used for learning.

Han and Cho (2005) proposed an intrusion detection technique based on evolutionary neural networks in order to determine the structure and weights of the call sequences [24]. Chen, Abraham and Yang (2007) proposed hybrid flexible neural-tree-based IDS based on flexible neural tree, evolutionary algorithm and particle swarm optimization (PSO) [27]. Empirical results indicated that the proposed method is efficient.

Engen et al. (2009) presented Multi Objective Evolution of Artificial Neural Network Ensembles (MABLE) to achieve high DR and FPR for minority attack classes [11]. They used multi objective approach to yield Pareto front of ANN solutions. The non-dominated front of solutions is further utilized to create the ensembles of ANN. The approach was evaluated using KDD cup 1999 dataset.

Wang et al. (2010) presented an approach called FCANN, based on ANN and fuzzy clustering [9]. They claimed to achieve higher detection rate, less false positive rate and stronger stability especially for low frequent attacks. The proposed approach generated different training sets by using fuzzy clustering to train different ANN to formulate different base classifiers. The results obtained on KDD cup 1999 dataset [17] were better than decision tree and naïve Bayes methods in terms of precision and stability of detection.

Hansen and Salamon's work shows that the generalization ability of a neural network system can be significantly improved through ensembling a number of neural networks, i.e. training many neural networks and then combining their predictions [28]. For ANN-based intrusion detection, hybrid/ ensemble of ANN has been the trend [9-11,27,29]. But different ways to construct hybrid/ensemble ANN will highly influence the performance of intrusion detection. Different hybrid ANN models should be properly constructed in order to serve different aims.

Empirical results of above cited studies indicated that the ANN based intrusion detection is efficient. Following this stream, we propose an ensemble of ANN, called MANNE, to solve the drawbacks of current ANN-based IDS mentioned in Section 1, i.e. lower DR and high FPR. MANNE approach introduces multi-objective genetic algorithm to evolve ANN as base classifiers. These base classifiers are further used as ensemble members to improve DR and FPR, especially for minority attack classes. The detailed framework of MANNE is described in Section 3. Exploiting a number of views of a same problem with classifier ensembles has been shown to improve the overall accuracy and reliability for a wide range of applications [30]. However, generating an accurate pool of base classifiers and selecting an ensemble among that pool that maximizes prediction accuracy are challenging tasks. One key element in the success of classifier ensembles that has attracted a great deal of interest in recent years is classifier diversity measures. Since diversity is difficult to assess in the input feature space, these measures compute the disagreement between classifiers in the decision space, over several predictions. Through bias-variance error decomposition, it has been shown empirically that considering diversity for ensemble selection improves the generalization capabilities of ensembles [30]. Diversity among the base classifiers mostly lies on "varying" the parameters related to the design and to the training of ANN [31]. In particular, the main methods in the literature can be included in one of the following categories:

Varying the initial random weights: an ensemble of nets can be created by varying the initial random weights, from which each network is trained;

- Varying the network architecture: the nets forming the ensemble exhibit different architectures;
- Varying the network type: different net types (e.g., multilayer perceptrons, radial basis functions neural networks, and probabilistic neural networks) can be used to create the ensemble members;
- Varying the training data: an ensemble of nets can be created by training each network with a different learning set. This can be done in a number of different ways. For example, "sampling" the training data to obtain different learning sets, using learning sets extracted from different data "sources" (e.g., data from different imaging sensors), or by different preprocessing phases (e.g., sets formed by samples characterized by different "features").

Many researchers presented various approaches to design ANN based ensembles. These approaches may be categorized as: 1) direct approach; 2) overproduce and choose approach. The former approach is designed to create an ensemble of diverse ANN directly. For example ASSEMUP, here authors utilized genetic algorithm (GA) to search for an ensemble of diverse ANNs [32].

Whereas later approach (overproduce and choose approach) focuses on creation of an initial large pool of ANNs and the later on choose the subset of the most diverse ANNs to create ensembles. Sharkey and Sharkey also described a design method that follows the "overproduce and choose" strategy [33]. Their choice algorithm is basically guided by a heuristic based on the evaluation of error correlation between pairs of ANNs.

In ensemble classifiers, the predictions of base classifiers can be combined to produce final prediction by using different approaches namely fusion and selection. Fusion approach involves the combination of the predictions obtained by the different classifiers in the ensemble to obtain the final prediction. The important method used for fusion are: 1) Majority voting method; 2) Threshold plurality vote method; 3) Naïve Bayes method; 4) Fuzzy theory method etc. whereas the selection approach, especially its dynamic form, selects one (or more) classifiers from the ensemble according to the prediction performance of these classifiers on similar data from the validation set. The important methods used for selection are: 1) The test and select method; 2) Cascading classifiers method; 3) Dynamic Classifier Selection method; 4) Clustering based selection method etc. Hansen and Salamon (1990) showed that ANN combined by the majority voting method can provide increases in classification accuracy, only if the ANNs make independent errors (diverse in nature) [28].

Therefore, our approach to the design of ANN based ensembles is to create a set of ANN evolved by MOGA exhibiting the highest possible degree of error diversity and ensemble of ANNs thereof using multi-objective approach. The motivation for using multi-objective approach is its advantages over single objective approaches. Single objective approach deals with multiple evaluation functions by transforming them into one objective [16]. Transformation of multiple objectives into single objective often requires prior knowledge about the problem or heuristic that leads the approach to single objective [15]. This means there is requirement of expert in concerned method or approach and specific problem. Even then it is not sure that all the solutions in optimum Pareto front could be found. But multi-objective approaches offer a set of non inferior solutions that reveals different tradeoff between different objectives. This tradeoff is known as Pareto optimum. For example, MOGA may present the Pareto front in single execution without requiring any expert about the method or problem.

FRAMEWORK OF MANNE

This section elaborates our approach, MANNE. The MANNE works in following phases: namely, 1) evolution of pool of ANN as base classifiers; and 2) creation of pool of ensemble of ANNs giving classification tradeoffs; 3) combiner. Phases 1 and 2 are multi-objective. These phases present the user an approximation of the Pareto front of non-dominated solutions of both base classifiers and ensembles. The detection rate of each class is adopted as separate objectives in these phases. Each ANN is evolved by using MOGA to exhibit different classification trade-offs. It helps to maintain diversity among the base classifiers implicitly in MANNE. In phase 2, MANNE optimizes the selection of base classifiers to obtain a Pareto front of ensembles that exhibit different classification trade-offs to the users. Phase 3 combines the predictions of base classifiers to get the final results of ensemble classifier. The details are as follows.

Phase 1: Evolution of pool of diverse ANNs This phase evolves the weights for pool of ANNs to formulate diverse base classifiers using MOGA. The diversity among base classifiers is maintained implicitly by varying initial random weights used for multi objective GA (MOGA) e.g. NSGA II [16]. The detection rate of each class is treated as separate objective. Here, The MOGA is real-coded, uses crossover and mutation operators, an elitist replacement strategy. To enable optimization of multiple objectives, non-dominated sorting is adopted, additionally, an archive function is adopted similar to that of NSGA-II [16] and SPEA [35]. This maintains a set of all non-dominated solutions found from the start of the evolutionary process. This phase of MOGA is able to find optimal Pareto front of nondominated ANN solutions (**Figure 1**). These ANN solutions formulate the base classifiers as candidate solutions for ensemble generation in phase 2.

Phase 2: Evolution of pool of ensembles of ANNs Phase 2 is also multi objective in nature. Phase 2 takes input in form of archive of non-dominated ANN solutions produced by phase 1. The phase evolved ensemble classifiers by combining the Pareto front of nondominated solutions instead of the entire population like other studies [15,36]. The detection rate of each class is treated as separate objective. Here, we are interested in those solutions with non dominated trade off. The predictions of base classifiers are combined using majority voting method. In case of a tie, the winner is randomly chosen. The MOGA method discussed in phase 1 is again applied in phase 2. Here, MOGA is binary coded where 0 represents the non-participation and 1 represents participation of concerned base classifier in creating ensembles. The detection rate of each class is treated as separate objective. The output of phase 2 is an archive of ensemble of ANNs in terms of chromosomes (sequences) of 1's and 0's (**Figure 2**). Here, 1 represents incorporation of corresponding ANN whereas 0 represents absence of corresponding ANN in formation of ensemble. The set of ensembles exhibit the classification trade-off for different objective functions.

Phase 3: Prediction aggregation This phase is responsible for aggregating the predictions of different ANNs base classifiers to get final prediction of ensemble classifier. The phase takes two inputs: 1) archive of non-dominated ANN solutions (output of phase 1); 2) one chromosome (sequence of 1's and 0's) from archive of ensembles (output of phase 2). An ensemble classifier can be selected by using static or dynamic strategy. Here in this work, we selected the ensemble classifier using static strategy based from its performance on the training data in terms of pre-defined performance metric. Based upon the values of chromosome, corresponding ANNs predictions are aggregated to get final prediction of the ensemble. In order to test the proposed approach, the test dataset is directly fed to different ANNs and get the outputs. Final prediction of ensemble is computed by using majority voting method in prediction aggregation module. Here, we used majority voting method to combine the predictions of base classifiers (**Figure 3**).

These three phases of MANNE framework highlights three major issues of current research. The issues are: 1) creation of pool of non-dominated ANN solutions to formulate base classifiers; 2) creation of pool of non-dominated ensemble solutions that exhibit classification trade- off; 3) efficient combination of predictions of base classifiers to get final prediction of ensemble.

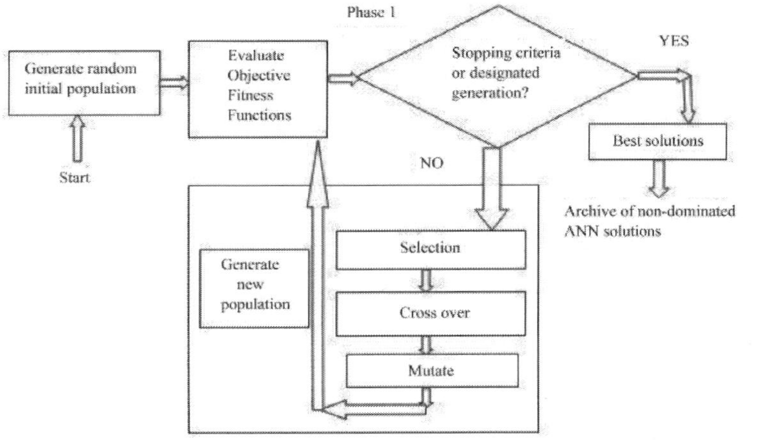

Figure 1: Phase 1 of MANNE approach.

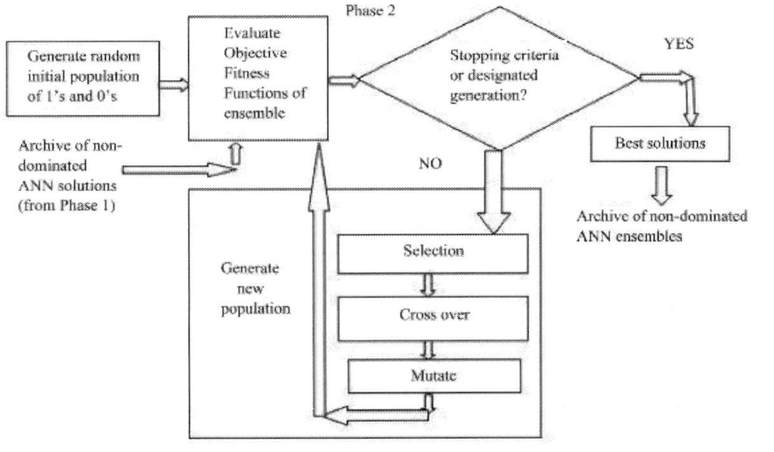

Figure 2: Phase 2 of MANNE approach.

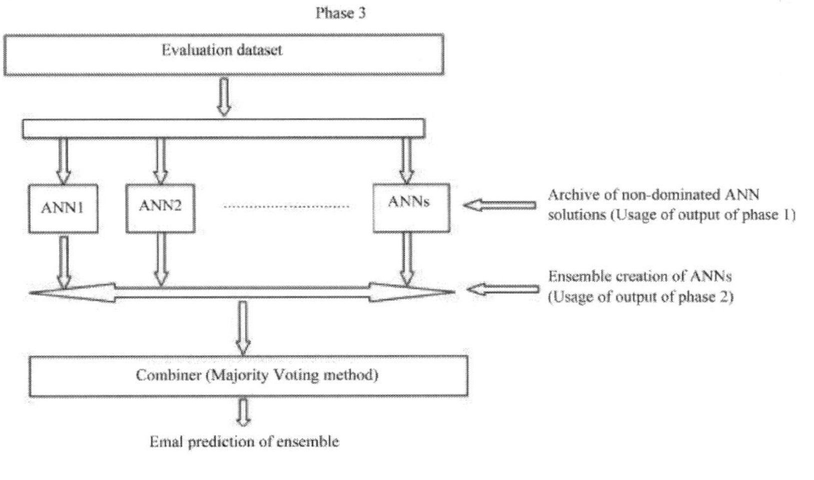

Figure 3: Phase 3 of MANNE approach.

IMPLEMENTATION

To evaluate the performance of MANNE approach, a series of experiments were conducted on KDD CUP 1999 dataset. In these experiments, we implemented and evaluated the proposed methods in VC++ on a Windows PC with Core i3-2330M 2.20 GHz CPU and 2 GB RAM. We used MLPFF ANN as base classifiers. NSGA-II [16], the multi objective genetic algorithm is used to evolve the base classifier and their ensembles. Majority voting method is used as method for combining the predictions of base classifiers. Following sub-sections describe the details of MLPFF ANN and NSGA-II used in this set of experiments.

MLP ANN

An MLP is a network of simple neurons called perceptrons [37]. The perceptron computes a single output from multiple real-valued inputs by forming a linear combination according to its input weights and then possibly putting the output through some non-linear activation function. In other words, MLPs are feed forward ANNs may be trained with the standard back propagation algorithm [37] or by using other alternative techniques as depicted in **Figure 4**. They are supervised networks, so they require a desired response to be trained. They learn how to transform input data into a desired response, so they are widely used for pattern classification. With one or two hidden layers, they can approximate virtually any input-output map. They have been shown to approximate the performance of optimal statistical classifier in difficult problems. The MLPNN used in this study is composed of three neuron layers, namely, the input layer, the output layer and the hidden layer as shown in **Figure 4**. Although the MLPNN can have more than one hidden layer, having more than one hidden layer is rarely beneficial and can lead to gross over-parameterization [38].

For a particular instance i of training/test dataset, the input layer of the MLP ANN used for intrusion detection receives the input vector T from training dataset. The input vector T has general format

$$T_i = \left(t_{i,1}, t_{i,2}, \cdots, t_{i,n}\right) \quad (1)$$

Here, $t_{i,j}$ is the jth feature of ith instance of training/ test dataset. Total number of input neurons in input layer is equal to total features of training/test dataset for intrusion detection. The output layer contains the output neurons. The output neurons are equal to number of classes in dataset.

A hidden layer is a middle layer. This layer adds a degree of flexibility to the performance of the ANN that enables it to deal efficiently with complex nonlinear problems. Each neuron in the single hidden layer receives the same input vector of N elements from the neurons of the input layer, as defined by Equation (1), and produces the output. The input-output transformation in each hidden neuron is achieved by a mathematical non-linear transfer (or activation) function. The general form of activation function is

$$Y_{i,k} = f\left(\sum_{j=1}^{N} w_{j,k} * T_{i,j} + b_k\right) \quad (2)$$

where $Y_{i,k}$ is the output of kth neuron in hidden layer for ith instance of dataset, f( ) is activation function, $w_{j,k}$ is the connection weight assigned to kth hidden neuron and jth neuron in input layer and b_k is the bias of kth hidden neuron. In literature, many activation functions are proposed [38]. The most widely used activation function is the sigmoid function which can be expressed as

$$Y_{i,k} = \left[1 + \exp\left(-\sum_{j=1}^{N} w_{j,k} * T_{i,j} - b_k\right)\right]^{-1} \quad (3)$$

The neurons in output layer produce the final network output. These output neurons receive an input array in form of Equation (4).

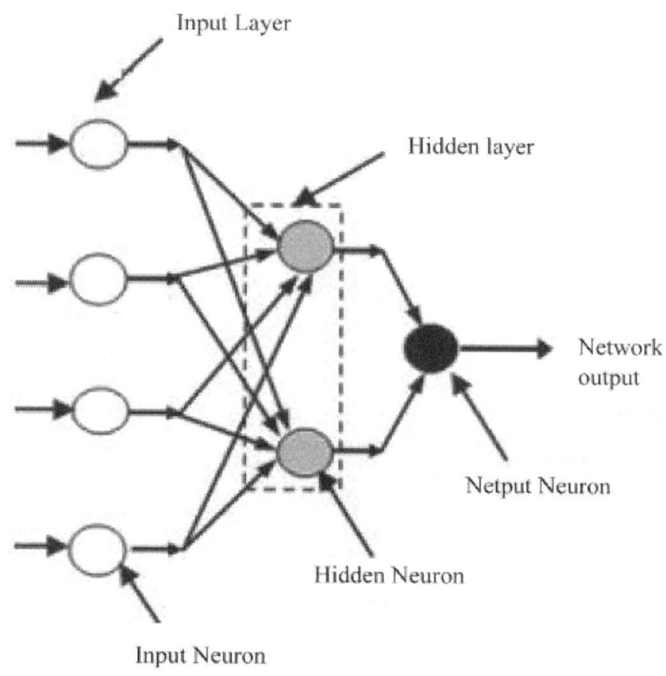

Figure 4: Structure of MLP ANN.

$$Z_i = \left(Y_{i,1}, Y_{i,2}, \cdots, Y_{i,n}\right) \quad (4)$$

The input-output transformation for this output neuron is similar to that of the hidden neurons.

MOGA

For multiple-objective problems like intrusion detection, there exist objectives which generally conflict with each other. For example, the objective may be to minimize cost, maximize detection rate, minimize false positive rates etc. Genetic algorithm (GA) (population based approach) is a popular meta-heuristic that is particularly suited for such class of problems [39]. GA can be applied in two ways to solve multi objective problem. 1) The first way combine the individual objective functions into a single composite function or move all but one objective to the constraint set. Such single objective function can be determined by using methods like utility theory, weighted sum method, etc. But, major limitations are to select the weights of different objectives and proper single objective functions. This approach returns a single solution that lack in examining the trade-offs between objectives [15]; 2) The second way determine a set of entire Pareto optimal solutions which contains solutions that are non-dominated with respect to each other. Pareto optimal solution sets are generally favored to single solution because these solutions can be more useful since the final solution of the decision-maker is always a trade-off between objectives. Thus Multi objective GA may sample the Pareto front in a single run without incorporating any domain knowledge about the problem. These features of MOGA motivated us to apply it to evolve weights of MLPFF ANN.

Many researchers proposed various MOGAs; details can be further explored in [40]. Among many MOGAs proposed in literature, NSGA-II is a fast, elitist and generational algorithm which is widely used for multi-objective optimization problems [16]. The important features of NSGA II are: 1) A full elite preservation strategy and diversity preserving mechanism using crowding distance as distance measure without setting any parameter; 2) Elitism is used to provide the means to keep good solutions among the generations and diversity preserving mechanism is used to allow a better spread among solutions over Pareto front [52]. NSGA-II preserves diversity among non-dominated solutions by use of crowding (instead of sharing). NSGA-II utilizes the concept of dominance to determine the new population after each generation (at which point selection and recombination have taken place to produce an offspring population of the same size as the old population). Before classifying individuals according to the dominance concept, parent and offspring populations of size n are combined to form a global population of size 2n. Non-dominated sorting is then applied to this global population, which identifies sets of non-dominated individuals. A new population of size n is then created from the sets according to their rank. If all individuals of a set cannot fit into the population, niching is used to select individuals in the least crowded region of the set. Consecutive sets, if any, are discarded [15,16,40]. Further details can be found in [16].

Combining MOGA with ANN

Combination of MOGA and ANN remains focus of research community since its first combination in late 80 s. Combination of these autonomous computing methods attempts to solve the problem of ANN. The problem with ANN is that a number of parameters have to be set before any training can begin [41]. However, there are no clear rules how to set these parameters. Yet these parameters determine the success of the training. GA is used to find these parameters. The motivation for this concept of combining MOGA with ANN comes from nature. As in real life, the success of an individual is not only dependent by the knowledge and skills, which he gained through, experience (like ANN training), but it also depends on his genetic heritage (set by MOGA). MOGA combined with ANN proved to be very successful for most of complex problems. In these experiments, we used MLP ANN and NSGA-II with following parameters.

EXPERIMENTS AND RESULTS

In order to evaluate the performance of MANNE approach, we conducted the experiments to evolve ANN using NSGA-II initiated with parameter described in **Table 1** based upon KDD CUP 1999 dataset for intrusion detection.

Table 1: Initialization parameters of MLP ANN and NSGAII

MLP ANN	
Input nodes	41
Hidden layer	1
Hidden nodes	30
Output node	5
Activation function	Sigmoid function
NSGA-II	
No. of generations	500
Population size	100
Cross over rate	0.9
Mutation rate	0.3

Dataset

KDD CUP 1999 dataset [17] for intrusion detection is used to evaluate MANNE approach. The KDD CUP 1999 dataset contains about five million connection records as training data and about two million connection records as test data which are derived from 1998 DARPA intrusion detection evaluation program by MIT Lincoln labs. The connection records have 41 features of continuous, discrete and symbolic features. Each connection record is labeled as either normal or attack type. These attack types can be categorized into four classes namely: 1) Probe; 2) DoS; 3) U2R; and 4) R2L. Although KDD99 data-set might have been criticized for its potential problems [34,42,43], but many researchers give the priority to KDD dataset over other publicly available dataset as benchmark dataset for evaluation of IDS [1, 44]. Tavallaee et al. (2009) proposed a refined form of KDD 99 dataset and called it as NSL KDD dataset [42]. They claimed certain improvement of KDD dataset deficiencies as criticized by McHugh 2000 [43]. Since the number of connection records in NSL KDD dataset is very large, so we randomly selected connection records from training and test dataset to reduce the size of datasets. Total number of instances in reduced training and test dataset are as depicted in **Table 2**. The training and test datasets are further preprocessed to make it compatible with ANN as described in [45].

Evaluation Criteria

In order to evaluate the effectiveness of IDS, we measure its ability to correctly classify events as normal or intrusive along with other performance objectives, such as economy in resource usage, resilience to stress and ability to resist attacks directed at IDS [46]. Measuring this ability of IDS is important to both industry as well as research community. It helps us to tune the IDS in better way as well as compare different IDSs. There exist many metrics that measure different aspects of IDS, but no single metric seems sufficient to objectively measure the capability of intrusion detection systems. Most widely used metrics by intrusion detection research community are True Positive Rate (TPR) and False Positive Rate (FPR). False Negative rate FNR = 1 – TPR and True Negative Rate TNR = 1 – FPR can be used as an alternate. Based upon values of these two metrics only, it is very difficult to determine better IDS among different IDSs. For example, one IDS reporting, TPR = 0.8; FPR = 0.1, while at another IDS, TPR = 0.9; FPR = 0.2. If only the metrics of TPR; FPR are given, it is very difficult to determine the better IDS. To solve this problem, Guofei et al. (2006) proposed a new objective metric called Intrusion Detection Capability (CID) considering base rate, TPR and FPR collectively [46]. CID possesses many important features. For example, 1) it naturally takes into account all the important aspects of detection capability, i.e. FPR, FNR, positive predictive value (PPV [47]), negative predictive value (NPV), and base rate (the probability of intrusions); 2) it objectively provides an essential measure of intrusion detection capability; 3) it is very sensitive to IDS operation parameters such as base rate, FPR and FNR. Detail of CID can be further studied in [46]. Keeping these points in view, we compute TPR, FPR and CID to evaluate the performance of MANNE approach and compare it with other intrusion detection approaches.

Table 2: Summary of training and test dataset used

Dataset	Class	Training instances	Test instances
	Normal	1000	500
	Probe	100	75
Instances	DoS	100	75
	U2R	11	50
	R2L	100	50
Total		1311	750

Results & Discussion

We performed experiments by randomly selecting instances from KDD cup 1999 dataset as described in Subsection 5.1. We compared the results with MLP trained with Back Propagation method (MLP-BP), and other well-known methods such as decision tree (J48). We also compared the results of our approach MANNE with two most widely used ensemble methods i.e. Bagging [18] and Boosting [19]. While creating ensembles using Bagging and Boosting, we used MLP and Decision tree (J48) as base classifiers. These techniques were executed using WEKA Data Mining tool [48]. The results of experiments are shown in Tables 3-8 and Figures 5 and 6.

As described in [46], it is difficult to compare the re- sults of different intrusion detection approaches only by observing the values of TPR and FPR. So, we compare different approaches based upon CID. As shown by above Tables 3-7, we can clearly observe the difference of evaluation criteria (CID) under different attacks types, i.e. Normal, Probe, DoS, U2R and R2L. While MANNE gets comparable results for majority attack classes i.e. Probe and DoS. MANNE reports higher values of CID than Decision tree (J48), MLP and their ensemble approaches for Normal and minority attack classes i.e. U2R and R2L.

Table 3: Performance comparison of various methods (Normal class)

	TPR	FPR	CID
MLP	0.898	0.544	0.1218
Bagged MLP	0.894	0.484	0.1538
Boosted MLP	0.898	0.544	0.1218
J48	0.864	0.516	0.1077
Bagged J48	0.866	0.54	0.0967
Boosted J48	0.892	0.572	0.10099
MANNE	0.848	0.32	0.2195

Table 4: Performance comparison of various methods (Probe class)

	TPR	FPR	CID
MLP	0.627	0.079	0.2424
Bagged MLP	0.827	0.084	0.4036
Boosted MLP	0.627	0.079	0.2424
J48	0.64	0.059	0.2891
Bagged J48	0.64	0.062	0.2830
Boosted J48	0.68	0.056	0.3285
MANNE	0.8	0.08	0.3852

Table 5: Performance comparison of various methods (DoS class)

	TPR	FPR	CID
MLP	0.507	0.028	0.2596
Bagged MLP	0.52	0.025	0.2790
Boosted MLP	0.507	0.028	0.2596
J48	0.493	0.068	0.1682
Bagged J48	0.507	0.061	0.1882
Boosted J48	0.547	0.027	0.2944
MANNE	0.4267	0.0533	0.1490

Table 6: Performance comparison of various methods (U2R class)

	TPR	FPR	CID
MLP	0	0.544	0
Bagged MLP	0	0.484	0
Boosted MLP	0	0.544	0
J48	0	0.516	0
Bagged J48	0	0.54	0
Boosted J48	0	0.572	0
MANNE	0.022857	0.32	0.07628

Table 7: Performance comparison of various methods (R2L class)

	TPR	FPR	CID
MLP	0.02	0.003	0.0047
Bagged MLP	0.06	0.004	0.0238
Boosted MLP	0.02	0.003	0.0047
J48	0.24	0.006	0.1357
Bagged J48	0.18	0.004	0.1027
Boosted J48	0.14	0.003	0.0797
MANNE	0.42	0.027	0.1898

Table 8: Performance comparison of various methods (based on weighted average of TPR & FPR of all classes)

	TPR	FPR	CID
MLP	0.72	0.374	0.0857
Bagged MLP	0.736	0.334	0.1163
Boosted MLP	0.72	0.374	0.0857
J48	0.708	0.357	0.088
Bagged J48	0.705	0.373	0.0787
Boosted J48	0.732	0.39	0.0841
MANNE	0.727	0.23	0.1825

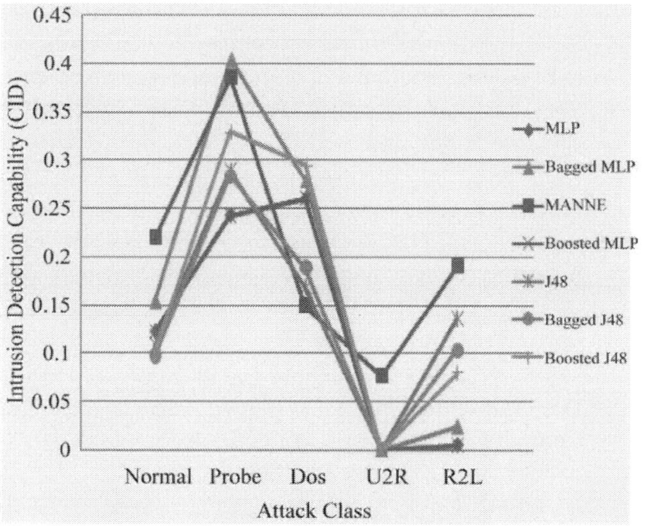

Figure 5: Class-wise comparison of different methods based upon CID.

As depicted in **Figure 5**, all other approaches except Bagged MLP get similar results for Normal, DoS, U2R and R2L classes. For Probe attack class, Bagged MLP shows comparable performance to MANNE. Whereas, for Normal, U2R and R2L classes, MANNE shows better performance than other six intrusion detection approaches used in these experiments. **Table 8** and **Figure 6** present the results of different approaches based upon weighted average of TPR and FPR for all classes. The results clearly indicate that MANNE is better approach for intrusion detection in terms of high TPR, low FPR and more importantly high value of CID. On average results, Bagged MLP shows comparable TPR, high FPR and low CID than MANNE. It may also be observed that bagged MLP has reported improvement over single MLP classifier. However Boosted MLP does not attain significant improvements. This validates the conclusions of prior research that are: 1) performance of bagging and boosting ensemble methods is affected by the training size [49,50]; 2) boosting is the best for large training sample sizes and bagging is useful for critical training sample sizes [50,51]. Due to small size of training dataset adopted in this study, performance of bagged MLP is superior to boosted MLP.

Therefore, we can draw the conclusion that our proposed approach, MANNE can get higher detection TPR, low FPR and high CID especially for Normal and minority classes. But the major limitation of MANNE is the long time to find Pareto front of non-dominated ANN solutions using MOGA. The computation of fitness functions of different ANN consumes is computationally expensive. The limitation can be overcome by computing fitness function of ANNs in parallel.

CONCLUDING REMARKS AND FUTURE DIRECTIONS

In this study, we propose a new intrusion detection approach, called MANNE based upon ensemble of ANN evolved by Multi Objective Genetic Algorithm (MOGA). The MANNE generates Pareto front of non-dominated ANN solutions and their ensembles thereof to exhibit classification trade-offs in different phases. Majority voting method is used to determine the final prediction of ensemble from predictions of base classifiers. The MANNE is validated by using KDD cup 1999 dataset for intrusion detection. The results of experiments conducted validate the usage feasibility of our approach MANNE. The efficiency of MANNE approach over single classifier and their conventional ensembles (Bagging and Boosting) is proved.

Since, calculation of fitness functions in various generations by MOGA is computationally expensive, so MANNE take long time to find Pareto optimal ANN solutions and their ensemble thereof. This is major limita- tion of proposed approach that may be overcome by computing the function values in parallel. Here, we compute the results by limiting the population size and number of generations of MOGA. The results can be further improved by choosing appropriate values of these parameters. We validate our approach using a small subset of KDD CUP 1999 dataset only. The applicability of our approach can be tested for different intrusion detection datasets.

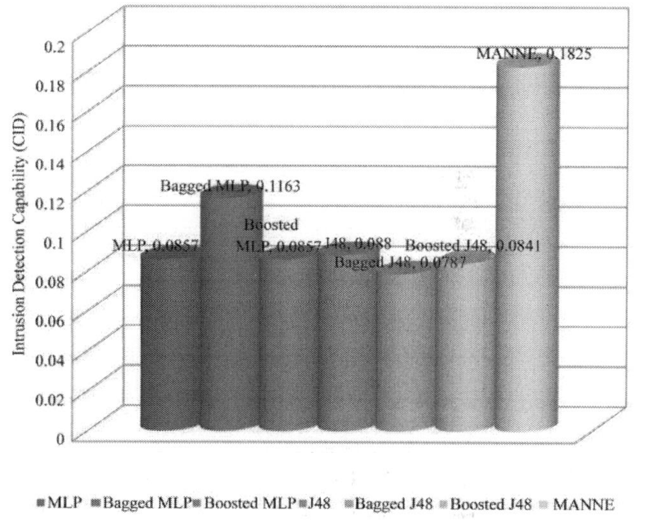

Figure 6: Comparison of different methods based upon CID.

So, our future research will be to carry out more experiments by choosing different values of population size as well as number of generations upon different intrusion detection datasets to improve the classification results. Another direction for research work is to explore different techniques to reduce the training time of ANNs.

REFERENCES

1. G. Kumar, K. Kumar and M. Sachdeva, "The Use of Artificial Intelligence Based Techniques for Intrusion Detection—A Review," Artificial Intelligence Review, Vol. 34, No. 4, 2010, pp. 369-387. doi:10.1007/s10462-010-9179-5
2. J. P. Anderson, "Computer Security Threat Monitoring and Surveillance," Technical Report, James P. Anderson Company, Fort Washington, 1980.
3. C. Endorf, E. Schultz and J. Mellander, "Intrusion Detection and Prevention," McGraw-Hill, New York, 2004.
4. L. R. Halme and R. K. Bauer, "AINT Misbehaving: A Taxonomy of Anti-Intrusion Techniques," Computers and Security, Vol. 14, No. 7, 1995, p. 606. doi:10.1016/0167-4048(96)81669-5

5. A. Patcha and J. M. Park, "An Overview of Anomaly Detection Techniques: Existing Solutions and Latest Technological Trends," Computer Networks, Vol. 51, No. 12, 2007, pp. 3448-3470. doi:10.1016/j.comnet.2007.02.001

6. P. Dokas, L. Ertoz, A. Lazarevic, J. Srivastava and P. N. Tan, "Data Mining for Network Intrusion Detection," Proceedings of NSF Workshop on Next Generation Data Mining, November 2002, pp. 21-30.

7. S. Wu and E. Yen, "Data Mining-Based Intrusion Detectors," Expert Systems with Applications, Vol. 36, No. 3, 2009, pp. 5605-5612. doi:10.1016/j.eswa.2008.06.138

8. J. Ryan, M. Lin and R. Miikkulainen, "Intrusion Detection with Neural Networks," Springer, Cambridge, 2002.

9. G. Wang, J. Hao, J. Ma and L. Huang, "A New Approach to Intrusion Detection Using Artificial Neural Networks and Fuzzy Clustering," Expert Systems with Applications, Vol. 37, No. 9, 2010, pp. 6225-6232. doi:10.1016/j.eswa.2010.02.102

10. M. Govindarajan and R. M. Chandrasekaran, "Intrusion Detection Using Neural Based Hybrid Classification Methods," Computer Networks, Vol. 55, No. 8, 2011, pp. 1662- 1671. doi:10.1016/j.comnet.2010.12.008

11. V. Engen, J. Vincent, A. C. Schierz and K. Phalp, "MultiObjective Evolution of the Pareto Optimal Set of Neural Network Classifier Ensembles," Proceedings of the International Conference on Machine Learning and Cybernetics (ICMLC), Baoding, 2009, pp. 74-79.

12. J. Han, M. Kamber and J. Pei, "Data Mining: Concepts and Techniques," 3rd Edition, Morgan Kaufmann, Burlington, 2011.

13. V. Engen, J. Vincent and K. Phalp, "Exploring Discrepancies in Findings Obtained with the KDD Cup '99 Data Set," Intelligent Data Analysis, Vol. 15, No. 2, 2011, pp. 251-276.

14. D. Joo, T. Hong and I. Han, "The Neural Network Models for IDS Based on the Asymmetric Costs of False Negative Errors and False Positive Errors," Expert Systems with Applications, Vol. 25, No. 1, 2003, pp. 69-75. doi:10.1016/S0957-4174(03)00007-1

15. V. Engen, "Machine Learning for Network Based Intrusion Detection: An Investigation into Discrepancies in Findings with the KDD Cup '99 Data Set and MultiObjective Evolution of Neural Network Classifier Ensembles for Imbalanced Data," Ph.D. Thesis, School of Design, Engineering and Computing, Bournemouth University, Bournemouth, 2010.

16. K. Deb, A. Pratap, S. Agarwal and T. Meyarivan, "A Fast and Elitist Multiobjective Genetic Algorithm: NSGA-II," IEEE Transactions on Evolutionary Computation, Vol. 6, No. 2, 2002, pp. 182-197. doi:10.1109/4235.996017

17. KDD, "KDD Cup 1999 Dataset," 1999. http://archive.ics.uci.edu/ml/datasets/KDD+Cup+1999+ Data

18. L. Breiman, "Bagging predictors," Machine Learning, Vol. 24, No. 2, 1996, pp. 123-140.doi:10.1007/BF00058655

19. Y. Freund and R. E. Shapire, "A Decision-Theoretic Generalization of on Line Learning and an Application to Boosting," Journal of Computer and System Sciences, Vol. 55, No. 1, 1997, pp. 119-139. doi:10.1006/jcss.1997.1504

20. O. Depren, M. Topallar, E. Anarim and M. K. Ciliz, "An Intelligent Intrusion Detection System (IDS) for Anomaly and Misuse Detection in Computer Networks," Expert Systems with Applications, Vol. 29, No. 4, 2005, pp. 713-722. doi:10.1016/j.eswa.2005.05.002

21. P. Garcia-Teodoro, J. Diaz-Verdejo, G. Macia-Fernandez and E. Vazquez, "Anomaly-Based Network Intrusion Detection: Techniques, Systems and Challenges," Computers & Security, Vol. 28, No. 1, 2009, pp. 18-28. doi:10.1016/j.cose.2008.08.003

22. S. Mukkamala, G. Janoski and A. Sung, "Intrusion Detection Using Neural Networks and Support Vector Machines," Proceedings of the IEEE International Joint Conference on Neural Networks, 2002, pp. 1702-1707.

23. R. Cunningham and R. Lippmann, "Improving Intrusion Detection Performance Using Keyword Selection and Neural Networks," Computer Networks, Vol. 34, No. 4, 2000, pp. 597-603. doi:10.1016/S1389-1286(00)00140-7

24. S. J. Han and S. B. Cho, "Evolutionary Neural Networks for Anomaly Detection Based on the Behavior of a Program," IEEE Transactions on Systems, Man and Cybernetics (Part B), Vol. 36, No. 3, 2005, pp. 559-570. doi:10.1109/TSMCB.2005.860136

25. C. Jirapummin, N. Wattanapongsakorn and P. Kanthamanon, "Hybrid Neural Networks for Intrusion Detection System," Proceedings of ITC-CSCC, July 2002, pp. 928-931.

26. A. Ghosh and A. Schwartzbard, "A Study in Using Neural Networks for Anomaly and Misuse Detection," Proceedings of the 8th USENIX Security Symposium, Washington DC, 1999, pp. 141-152.

27. Y. H. Chen, A. Abraham and B. Yang, "Hybrid Flexible Neural-Tree-Based Intrusion Detection Systems," International Journal of Intelligent Systems, Vol. 22, No. 4, 2007, pp. 337-352. doi:10.1002/int.20203

28. L. K. Hansen and P. Salamon, "Neural Network Ensembles," IEEE Transactions Pattern Analysis and Machine Intelligence, Vol. 12, No. 10, 1990, pp. 993-1001.doi:10.1109/34.58871

29. S. Sahin, M. R. Tolun and R. Hassanpour, "Hybrid expert Systems: A Survey of Current Approaches and Applications," Expert Systems with Applications, Vol. 39, No. 4, 2012, pp. 4609-4617. doi:10.1016/j.eswa.2011.08.130

30. J. Francois Connolly, E. Granger and R. Sabourin, "Evolution of Heterogeneous Ensembles through Dynamic Particle Swarm Optimization for Video-Based Face Recognition," Pattern Recognition, Vol. 45, 2012, pp. 2460- 2477. doi:10.1016/j.patcog.2011.12.016

31. G. Giacinto and F. Roli, "Design of Effective Neural Network Ensembles for Image Classification Purposes", Image and Vision Computing, 2001, Vol. 19, No. 9-10, pp. 699-707. doi:10.1016/S0262-8856(01)00045-2

32. D. W. Opitz and J. W. Shavlik, "Actively Searching for an Effective Neural Network Ensemble," Connection Science, Vol. 8, No. 3-4, 1996, pp. 337-353. doi:10.1080/095400996116802

33. A. J. C. Sharkey and N. E. Sharkey, "Combining Neurals Nets," The Knowledge Review, Vol. 12, No. 3, 1997, pp. 231-247. doi:10.1017/S0269888997003123

34. C. Brown, A. Cowperthwaite, A. Hijazi and A. Somayaji, "Analysis of the 1999 DARPA/Lincoln Laboratory IDS Evaluation Data with Netadhict," Proceedings of the 2nd IEEE International Conference on Computational Intelligence for Security and Defense Applications, Piscataway, 2009, pp. 1-7.

35. E. Zitzler and L. Thiele, "Multiobjective Evolutionary Algorithms: A Comparative Case Study and the Strength Pareto Approach," IEEE Transactions on Evolutionary Computation, Vol. 3, No. 4, 1999, pp. 257-271. doi:10.1109/4235.797969

36. H. Ishibuchi and Y. Nojima, "Evolutionary Multiobjective Optimization for the Design of Fuzzy Rulebased Ensemble Classifiers," International Journal of Hybrid Intelligent Systems, Vol. 3, No. 3, 2006, pp. 129-145.

37. C. M. Bishop, "Neural Networks for Pattern Recognition," Oxford University Press, Oxford, 1995.

38. A. Y. Shamseldin, K. M. O. Connor and A. E. Nasr, "A Comparative Study of Three Neural Network Forecast Combination Methods for Simulated River Flows of Different Rainfall—Runoff Models," Hydrological Sciences Journal, Vol. 52, No. 5, 2007, pp. 896-916. doi:10.1623/hysj.52.5.896

39. A. Konak, D. W. Coit and A. E. Smith, "Multi-Objective Optimization Using Genetic Algorithms: A Tutorial," Reliability Engineering and System Safety, Vol. 91, No. 9, 2006, pp. 992-1007. doi:10.1016/j.ress.2005.11.018

40. A. Zhou, B. Y. Qu, H. Li, S. Z. Zhao, P. N. Suganthan and Q. Zhang, "Multiobjective Evolutionary Algorithms: A Survey of the State of the Art," Swarm and Evolutionary Computation, Vol. 1, No. 1, 2011, pp. 32-49. doi:10.1016/j.swevo.2011.03.001

41. P. Koehn, "Combining Genetic Algorithms and Neural Networks: The Encoding Problem," MS Thesis, The University of Tennessee, Knoxville, 1994.

42. M. Tavallaee, E. Bagheri, W. Lu and A. A. Ghorbani, "A Detailed Analysis of the KDD CUP 99 Data Set," Proceedings of IEEE Symposium on Computational Intelligence in Security and Defense Applications (CISDA), 2009. doi:10.1109/CISDA.2009.5356528

43. J. McHugh, "Testing Intrusion Detection Systems: A Critique of the 1998 and 1999 DARPA Intrusion Detection System Evaluations as Performed by Lincoln Laboratory," ACM Transactions on Information and System Security, Vol. 3, No. 4, 2000, pp. 262-294. doi:10.1145/382912.382923

44. C. F. Tsai, Y. F. Hsu, C. Y. Lin and W. Y. Lin, "Intrusion Detection by Machine Learning: A Review," Expert Systems with Applications, Vol. 36, No. 10, 2009, pp. 11994- 12000.doi:10.1016/j.eswa.2009.05.029

45. G. Kumar, K. Kumar and M. Sachdeva, "An Empirical Comparative Analysis of Feature Reduction Methods for Intrusion Detection," International Journal of Information and Telecommunication, Vol. 1, No. 1, 2010, pp. 44- 51.

46. G. Gu, P. Fogla, D. Dagon, W. Lee and B. Skoric, "Measuring Intrusion Detection Capability: An InformationTheoretic Approach," Proceedings of ACM Symposium on InformAction, Computer and Communications Security (ASIACCS'06), March 2006, pp. 90-101.

47. S. Axelsson, "The Base-Rate Fallacy and Its Implications for the Difficulty of Intrusion Detection," ACM Transactions on Information and System Security (TISSEC),Vol. 3, No. 3, 2000, pp. 186-205.

48. I. H. Witten and E. Frank, "Data Mining: Practical Machine Learning Tools and Techniques," 2nd Edition, Morgan Kaufmann, San Francisco, 2005.

49. S. Sun, C. Zhang and D. Zhan, "An Experimental Evaluation of Ensemble Methods for EEG Signal Classification," Pattern Recognition Letters, Vol. 28, No. 15, 2007, pp. 2157-2163.

50. R. Das and A. Sengur, "Evaluation of Ensemble Methods for Diagnosing of Valvular Heart Disease," Expert Systems with Applications, Vol. 37, No. 7, 2010, pp. 5110- 5115.

51. M. Skurichina and R. P. W. Duin, "Bagging, Boosting and the Random Subspace Method for Linear Classifiers," Pattern Analysis and Applications, Vol. 5, No. 2, 2002, pp. 121-135.doi:10.1007/s100440200011

52. E. M. D. Santos, R. Sabouirn and P. Maupin, "Overfitting Cautions Selection of Ensembles with Genetic Algoritms," Information Fusion, Vol. 10, 2009, pp. 150-162.

CHAPTER 14

RECOGNITION OF ARABIC SIGN LANGUAGE (ARSL) USING RECURRENT NEURAL NETWORKS

Manar Maraqa, Farid Al-Zboun, Mufleh Dhyabat, and Raed Abu Zitar

Keywords: Arabic Sign Language, Feedforward Neural Networks, Recurrent Neural Networks, Gesture Recognition

INTRODUCTION

Deaf people use sign language as an alternative to spoken language A sign language provides signs for whole words as well as signs of letters for words that don't have a corresponding sign in that sign language. Hearing people have difficulty to learn sign languages, also it is difficult for deaf people to learn oral languages. Sign language recognition systems can facilitate the communication between those two communities. Also for the hearing people, such systems can help in interacting with machines in a more natural way.

This research aims to reduce the gap of communications between deaf and hearing people by focusing on the recognition of letters, which are the bases of a sign language. Hand gestures recognition systems can be classified into two categories: static and dynamic. A static gesture is a particular hand movements represented by a single image, while a dynamic gesture is a moving gesture represented by a sequence of images. In principle, dynamic gesture recognition is static gesture recognition with frame segmentation functions. These functions decide on the start and end of a single static gesture image frames. This work focuses on the ArSL (Arabic Sign Language) which uses one hand and 28 gestures (see figure 1) to communicate the 28 letters of the Arabic alphabet.

Research on hand gesture usually falls into three categories. The first one is glove-based analysis, which employs sensors attached to the glove. Look-up table software is usually provided with the glove to be used for hand gesture recognition [1].

The second category involves analysis of drawing gestures; this category is merely a character recognition problem. The third category, vision-based analysis, is based on the use of video cameras to capture the movement of the singer' hand that is sometimes aided by making the signer wear a glove that has painted areas indicating the positions of the fingers and the wrist then use those measurements in the recognition process.

As mentioned before, deaf people use their hands in particular movements of palm and fingers to express their thoughts and feelings. Therefore palm orientations of hands' images are estimated to perform gesture recognition. This will be adopted in our work since videobased ArSL recognition methods are still major areas of research and plenty of investigates can be carried in this area. K. Assaleh and M. Al-Rousan [2] proposed the use of polynomial networks as a classification engine for automatic Arabic Sign Language (ArSL) recognition system. They built the system and measured its performance using real ArSL data collected from deaf people. Images were collected from deaf participants performing Arabic sign gestures using a colored glove. Thirty features were extracted from the segmented color regions which represent the fingertips and their relative positions and orientations with respect to the wrist and to each other. They compared the performance of their system with previously published work using ANFIS-based classification on the same data set and the same corresponding feature set. The polynomial-based system has produced superior recognition results to those obtained by the ANFIS-based system for both training and test data. The recognition of the proposed system has shown an excellent performance with a low error rate of 6.59% corresponding to a recognition rate of 93.41%.

Citation: M. Maraqa, F. Al-Zboun, M. Dhyabat and R. Zitar, "Recognition of Arabic Sign Language (ArSL) Using Recurrent Neural Networks," Journal of Intelligent Learning Systems and Applications, Vol. 4 No. 1, 2012, pp. 41-52. doi:10.4236/jilsa.2012.41004.

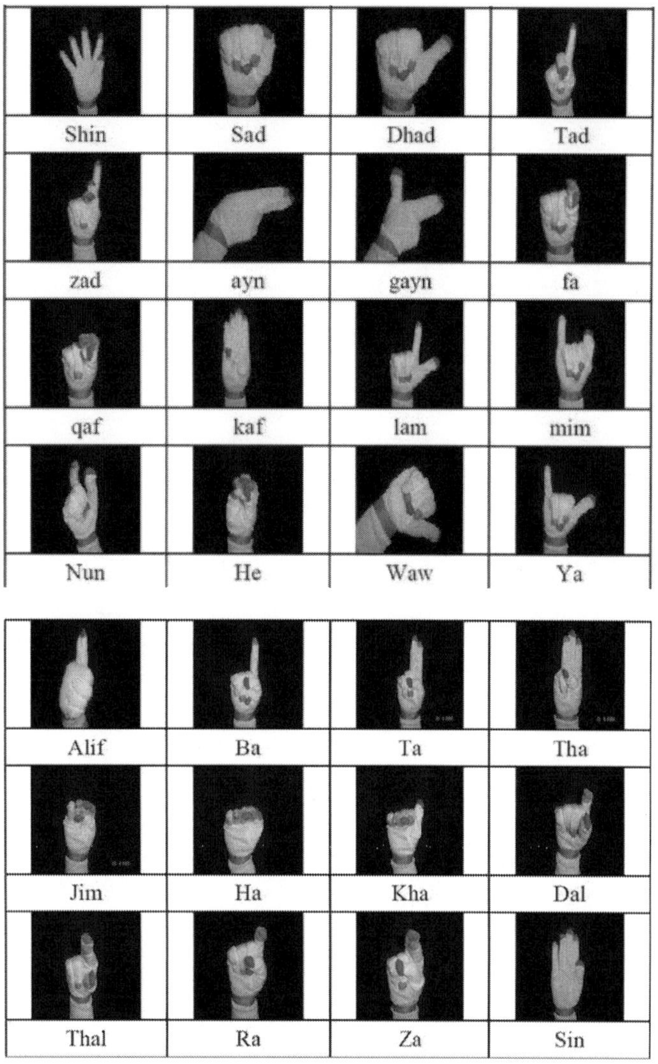

Figure 1: Arabic sign language gestures.

Two cameras with 3-D techniques were used [3] in several applications. It worth mentioning that Gesture recognition was also applied on different languages other than English and Arabic [4]. Techniques such as fuzzy decision trees, transition-movement models, saptio-temporal, or common sense context were applied with remarkable success [5-8].

Y. Yuan, Y. Liu and K. Barner [9] designed a set of command-like gestures for users with limited range and function in their digits and wrist. Trajectory and angle features are extracted from these gestures and passed to a recurrent neural network for recognition. Experiments are performed to test the feasibility of gesture recognition system and determine the effect of network topology on the gesture recognition rate. The proposal approach that they adopted achieved an overall correct rate of approximately 94.5%.

R. Salomon and J. Weissmann [10] this paper is about a data glove as a powerful input device for virtual reality and multi media applications. The data glove system allows the user to present the system with a rich set of intuitive commands. This paper applied algorithms to fine tune pre-learned radial basis function networks. In experiments they held, they used the CyberGlove, which measures the angles of 18 joints of the hand: two for each finger, one each for the angles between neighboring fingers, as well as one each for thumb rotation, palm arch, wrist pitch, and wrist yaw. They choose a set of 20 static hand gestures. The experiments were performed with neural network that has three standard three-layered backpropagation with different structures to exploit a (tentative) correlation between gestures and finger combinations.

F. Florez, J. Garcia, and A. Hernandez [11] in this paper a structure capable of characterizing hand posture and its movement was presented. Topology of a selforganizing neural network determines posture, whereas its adaptation dynamics throughout time determines gesture. To validate this method, they have trained the system with 12 gestures, some of which are very similar, and have obtained high success rates.

M. Mohandes and S. Buraiky [12] introduced a system to recognize isolated signs from the Arabic sign language using the Support Vector Machine algorithm. An instrumented glove was used to get raw measurements sent by the glove in the form of a sequence of frames with values that represent the position of the hand, the roll of the hand, the flexes of the thumb, the index finger, the forefinger and the ring finger. Results obtained in this research were promising.

K. Murakami and H. Taguchi [13] developed a posture recognition system using neural networks which could recognize a finger alphabet of 42 symbols of Japanese sign language. Then developed a gesture recognition system where each gesture specifies a word. To deal with dynamic processes they used a recurrent neural network described a gesture recognition method which can recognize continuous gesture. The recognition rate was found to be 94%.

O. Al-Jarrah, A. Shatnawi, and A.H. Halawani [14] presented two neural network systems for the recognition of the sign language alphabets. The first is based on the feedforward neural network architecture, while the second is based on probabilistic neural networks. The user was not required to wear any electromechanical device or any marker to interact with the system. The system takes images of gestures and converts them to a set of features suitable to be fed to the neural network structure for recognition. The feature extraction involved the orientation and the position of hand within the image. It is shown that an accuracy of 94.4% is achieved using the first system and 91.3% using the second.

C programming language and MATLAB software package were used in this research. MATLAB was used for image processing while the selected neural networks (feedforward and recurrent networks) were designed and implemented using the C programming language.

METHODOLOGY

The methodology of this research includes four stages (see figure 2) which can be summarized as follows: 1) data collection and image acquisition, 2) image processing, 3) feature extraction and finally 4) gesture recognition.

Stage one—image acquisition—is done using a digital camera and a colored glove, hand gestures are performed by participants. The stage of image processing for static and dynamic system is done based on the color system HSI (Hue, Saturation, and Intensity) and then segmentation process will take place to divide the image into six layers representing the five fingertips and wrist.

Next the feature extraction stage comes. This is implemented according to the color layers expanded from the segmented color regions. Thirty features are extracted, same features used by K. Assaleh and M. Al-Rousan [2], and grouped in one vector that represents a single gesture. In dynamic systems, however, same features will be used but with different preprocessing. Our proposed system tries to find the most effective way to decide on the beginning and the end of a gesture. Finally, stage four is concerned with using feedforward Neural Networks with back propagation and Recurrent Neural Networks for the gesture recognition purpose.

IMAGE PROCESSING

This stage includes image acquisition and segmentation.

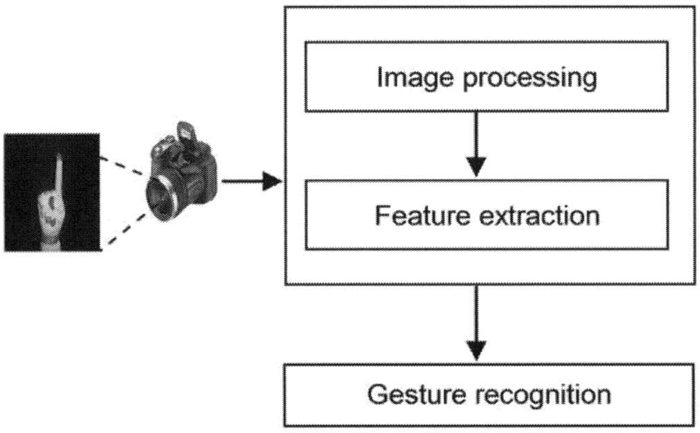

Figure 2: System stages.

Since colored images are being used in this research, the basic fundamentals of images, colors and color models will be introduced.

Image Basics

An image consists of a two-dimensional array of numbers. The color or gray shade displayed for a given picture element (pixel) depends on the number stored in the array for that pixel. The simplest type of image data is black and white. It is a binary image since each pixel is either 0 or 1. The next, more complex type of image data is gray scale; these images are black, white, and shades of gray. Each pixel here takes on a value between zero and the number of gray scales that the scanner can record [15]. The most complex type of image is color images. They have three channels corresponding to the colors red, green, and blue. Thus, each pixel has three values associated with it. Any color processing device uses red, green, and blue filters to produce those values [15].

Color Fundamentals

Color is the brain's reaction to a specific visual stimulus (i.e., an object reflecting light of a certain wavelength) [16]. The ability of the human eye to distinguish colors is based upon the varying sensitivity of different cells in the retina to light of different wavelengths [17].

The human retina has three types of color photoreceptor cells, two of them, rods and cones receive light and transform it into image-forming signals which are transmitted through the optic nerve to the brain [17]. The third and more recently discovered category of photoreceptor cells is probably not involved in image-forming vision.

Rods are photoreceptor cells in the retina of the eye that are effective at extremely low light levels unlike the cone cells that function at bright light. Since rods are more light-sensitive, they are responsible for night vision whereas cones are less sensitive to light than the rod cells but allow the perception of color [17].

The signals from these color sensitive cells (cones), together with those from the rods (sensitive to intensity), combine in the brain to give "sensations" of different colors.

Color Spaces

Since color is subjective, there was a need to attribute numbers to help in the process of describing colors, either between people or between machines or programs. A color space is a method by which we can specify, create and visualize color [18].

There are many different ways of representing color; the most common way in computer graphics is to use a triplet of intensity values. Any unique combination of the

three values yields a distinct color. The three dimensional space which describes the distribution of physical colors is called a color space [18].

Color vectors in each of these spaces differ from one another; this difference means that two colors in one space being separated by one distance value would be separated by a different distance value in another space. A color represented in one space can be changed to another representation by performing some transformation.

The most common color model is the RGB; it is from this space that all other color spaces are derived. However the two color spaces that will be defined and used in this research are both RGB and HSI.

RGB

The RGB color model is commonly used in computer graphics and image processing applications. It is based on the physical (i.e., wavelength) representation of the three primary colors; red, green and blue. An RGB color image can be represented as an $M \times N \times 3$ array of color pixels, where each color pixel is a triplet values corresponding to the red, green and blue component and is usually scaled by 255 for an 8-bit representation [19].

The RGB color space is usually shown graphically as an RGB color cube, as shown in figure 3. The vertices of the cube are the primary (red, green and blue) and secondary (cyan, magenta and yellow) and any RGB color will be defined by its values on the three axes [20]. We can define any color simply by giving its red, green, and blue values, or coordinates, within the color cube [15].

However, it has the drawback that the luminance information is split across all three axes and it doesn't closely model the psychological understanding of color [19].

HSI

HSI color space was developed to be more intuitive in manipulating color and was designed to approximate the way human perceive and interpret color. Humans usually describe a color object by its hue, saturation and brightness. Hue is an attribute that describes a pure color as described by wavelength; saturation gives a measure of the degree to which a pure color is diluted by white light (i.e. the colorfulness of an area relative to its brightness), while intensity describes the color sensation (the overall brightness or the amount of light) [19]. Figure 4 illus- trates a common representation of this space. The cone shape has one central axis representing intensity. Along this axis are all the gray values, with black at the pointed end of the cone and white at its base. The greater the distance along this line from the pointed end, or origin, the brighter or higher the intensity. Since HSI color space decouples the intensity component from the color-carrying information (hue and saturation) in a color image; HSI is considered to be an ideal tool for developing image processing algorithms based on color description and will be adopted in our work [19].

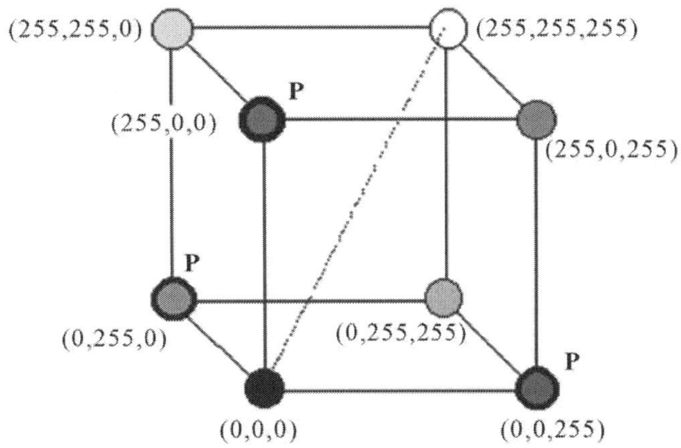

Figure 3: The RGB color space.

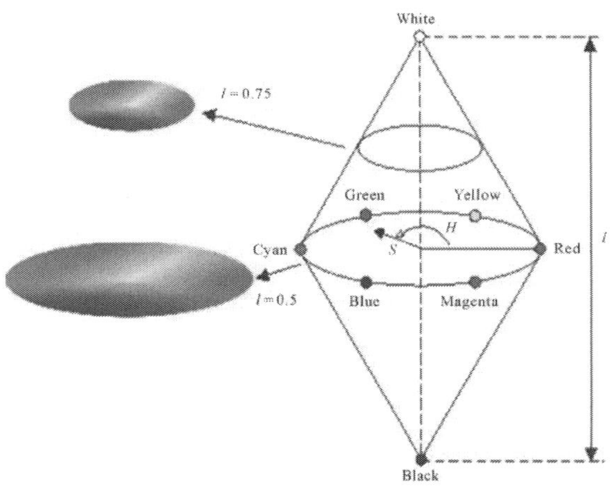

Figure 4: (Gonzalez [19]): The HSI color model based on circular color planes. The circles are perpendicular to the vertical intensity axis.

Converting Colors from RGB to HSI

The transformation required to convert the RGB color system to HSI is as follows:

The H component of each RGB pixel is obtained using the equation:

$$H = \begin{cases} \theta \text{ if } B \le G \\ 360 - \theta \text{ if } B > G \end{cases}, \quad (1)$$

with

$$\theta = \arccos\left[\frac{\frac{1}{2}\left[(R-G)+(R-B)\right]}{\left[(R-G)^2+(R-B)(G-B)\right]^{1/2}}\right]. \quad (2)$$

The saturation component is also obtained by using

$$S = 1 - \frac{3}{R+G+B}\left[\min(R,G,B)\right]. \quad (3)$$

Finally, the intensity component is given by:

$$I = \frac{R+G+B}{3}. \quad (4)$$

The above calculations are performed assuming that the RGB values have been normalized to the range [0,1], and that angle θ is measured with respect to the red axis of the HSI space.

Image Acquisition

Images were captured using a colored digital camera, each one of them was resized to 256 × 256 pixels, and image processing was performed using Matlab 6.5.

The image processing toolbox in Matlab represents color images as RGB (red, green, blue) values directly in an RGB image, which is then transformed to an HSI color space. The color segmentation is performed by grouping the pixels which are similar in some region property such as the H (Hue) value that defines the color. According to this, different color regions are determined by selecting the appropriate H value for each color.

The resulting value is six image layers representing the color areas of the five fingertips and the wrist as shown in figure 5. To determine the best point that represents a color there was a need to use a clustering method which is The Fuzzy c-means.

FEATURES EXTRACTION

Image acquisition was done using a digital camera and a colored glove. 900 colored images have been used to represent the 30 different hand gestures and have been used as a training set; another 900 images have been taken and used as a test set.

Feature extraction stage is then implemented according to the color layers expanded from the segmented color regions, more specifically the colors centers that where determined using the FCM clustering method.

Based on the region centers; thirty features are extracted from each image, the same features which were adopted by K. Assaleh and M. Al-Rousan [2], and grouped in one vector that represents a single gesture.

The thirty features are based on the segmented color regions which are taken from the fingertips and their relative positions and orientations with respect to the wrist and to each other [2]. These features include the vectors from the center of each color region to the center of all other regions, and the angles between each of these vectors and the horizontal axis as shown in figure 6.

To eliminate the effect of the distance separating the camera from the colored glove, the feature vector was normalized by dividing each entry of it by the maximum value of the whole vector [2].

Figure 5: Color segmentation.

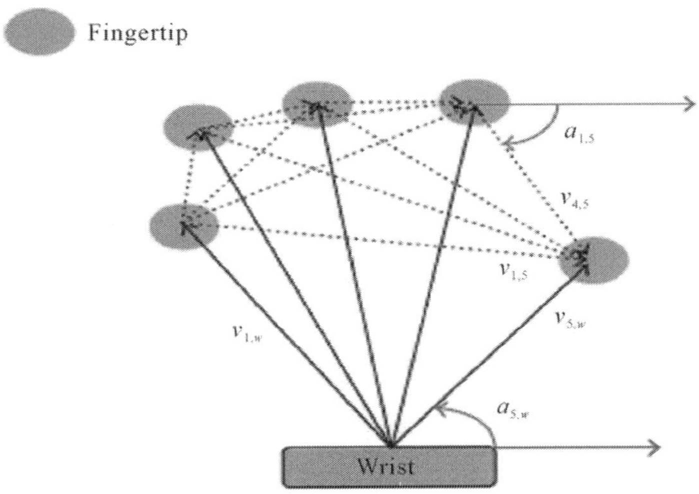

Figure 6: (Assaleh and Al-Rousan [2]): vectors-length and angles.

NEURAL NETWORK ARCHITECTURES

Two main types of neural networks architectures were used; Feedforward networks and recurrent networks.

Feed-Forward Neural Networks

Feedforward neural networks are the most popular and most widely used models in many applications. In this architecture each neuron in one layer has directed connections to the neurons of the subsequent layer; there are no links between neurons in the same layer neither with any of the previous layers [21]. The data flow in a strictly forward behavior. Since single-layer neural network has limited capabilities regarding pattern recognition; a multilayer feedforward neural network will be used.

Multilayer Feedforward Neural Networks

A multilayer feedforward network has a layered structure. The input layer where its neurons serve only as distribution points, one or more hidden layers of computation neurons, and the output layer [22].

Units in each layer receive their input from units from a layer directly below and send their output to units in a layer directly above the unit which means that the values only move from input to hidden to output layers; no values are fed back to earlier layers. Multilayer neural networks have proven their ability to solve many difficult problems such as pattern recognition as well as the ability of to extract more meaningful features from the input patterns through the use of hidden layers [22].

The multilayer network architecture chosen for this research is a three layers neural network, i.e. a network that has one hidden layer. Since each gesture is represented by a vector containing thirty features; the input layer has been chosen to have 30 input units. There is no rule for determining the number of nodes that the hidden layer should have; many simulations lead us to decide on its number; fifteen units. The output layer is 30 units since we have 30 gestures in the Arabic sign language, each output unit will represent one of the gestures.

Each unit in the input layer has been fully connected to every other unit in the second layer—the hidden layer. Also, every unit in the hidden layer is connected to every other neuron in the output layer in a feedforward behavior.

Figure 7 shows a model of the feedforward fully connected multilayer neural network that has been designed and tested for this research.

Recurrent Neural Networks

Recurrent neural networks have been an interesting and important part of neural network research during the 1990's. They are designed to learn sequential or time varying patterns and have been applied to a wide variety of problems that involve many interesting human behaviors [23]. Applications for such networks vary from simple problems (temporal version of XOR) to discovering syntactic/semantic features for words [24].

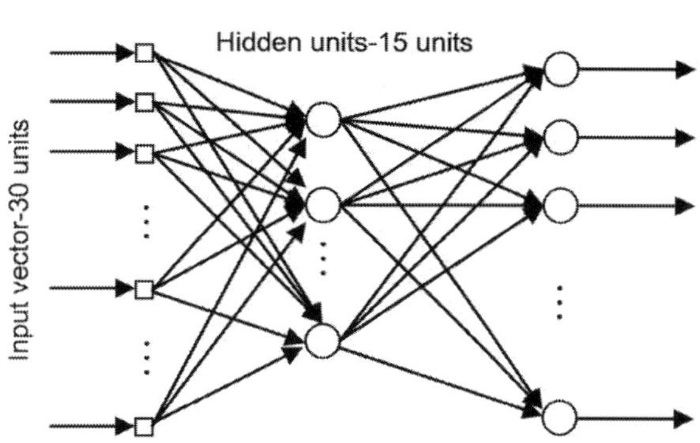

Figure 7: A three layers feedforward network.

Dynamic or recurrent neural networks differ from static neural networks since they are constructed to include feedback, or recurrent connections between the network layers and within the layer itself [25]. This feedback implies that the network has local memory characteristics that is able to store activity patterns and present those patterns to the network more than once, allowing the layer with feedback connections to use its own past activation in its preceding behavior [26].

So at any given time, the network output is calculated by propagating the input pattern forward through the network and the recurrent activations are propagated back to the extra layer—called the context layer—which copies the activation pattern from the output layer on the last instant. Different architectures can be created by adding recurrent connections at different points in the basic feedforward architecture [25]. Two of the most popular recurrent neural networks were introduced by Elman and Jordan are presented next followed by a combination of both; fully recurrent network.

Elman Neural Networks

In 1990, Jeff Elman introduced a recurrent neural network which uses context units. The Elman network is a two-layer network in which the hidden layer is recurrent; each node in the hidden layer is connected through a recurrent link with all the nodes in the hidden layer as well as the typical feedforward connections from each input node [27]. Therefore, at each time step the outputs of the hidden units are calculated, their values are used to compute the output of the network and are all stored as "extra inputs" (called context unit) to be used when the next time the network is operated.

The recurrent contexts provide a weighted sum of the previous values of the hidden units as input to the hidden units and thus provide the network with information about previous activation values [28].

As shown in **Figure 8**, the activations are copied from hidden layer to context layer so that each context node is merely a copy of the previous activation of its corresponding hidden node [29]. This process allows the network to memorize information of its internal state for better patterns detection.

Same number of units as in previous feedforward neural network was used; 30 input units followed by 15 hidden units, and finally 30 output units.

Jordan Neural Networks

Jordan's network is similar to Elman neural network in that the hidden layer is recurrent; each context node (the copied nodes) has recurrent links to all of the other context nodes and it also has a feedback from the output layer to the hidden one, as shown in **Figure 9**. The activity of the output nodes is recurrently copied back into the context nodes, the recurrent connections between the context nodes appear to help the network to stabilize the network's and provide the network with a memory of its previous state [29].

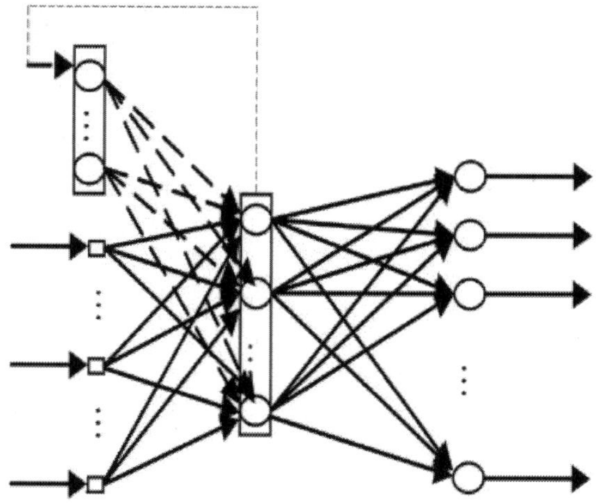

Figure 8: Elman neural network architecture demonstrated using the context layer.

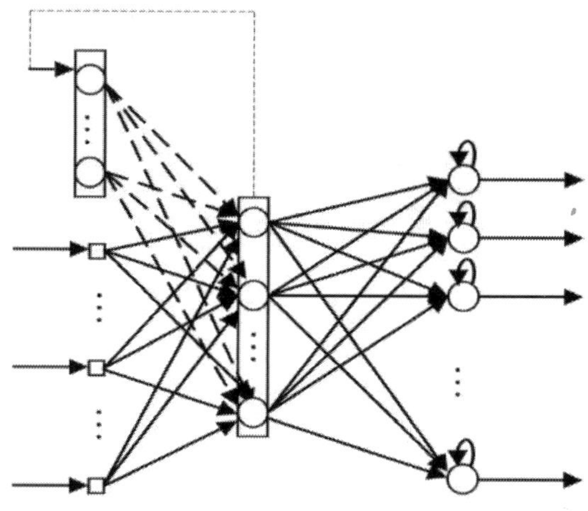

Figure 9: Jordan neural network architecture.

Fully Recurrent Neural Networks

In this type of networks both hidden and output layers are recurrent; moreover, a recurrent link exists to connect the output layer with the input layer (see figure 10).

This architecture is expected to have more complex and time consuming computations since it has more complicated structure; but the existence of those extra recurrent links is supposed to allow the network to reach a better convergence to the optimal weights that leads the network to more accurate gesture recognition.

Training Algorithms

Neural networks learn to perform tasks by being presented with example input patterns and adjusting the weights on the connections between the nodes of the network. Many possible learning algorithms can be used to calculate the necessary weight changes [29].

Standard back-propagation was used to train the feedforward neural networks. Regarding the recurrent neural networks; similar algorithm was used. Simple Recurrent Networks (SRN) was used to train the Elman neural network while Backpropagation through Time (BPTT) was used to train both the Jordan and the fully recurrent network.

SRN method was developed to mimic the backpropagation but with a slight modification, Elman was the first to use it to train his recurrent network [29].

Backpropagation Through Time (BPTT) algorithm is another way to modify backpropagation to be able to work with time sequences on recurrent networks such as Jordan and fully recurrent neural networks. This method is based on converting the network from a feedback system to purely feedforward system by folding the network over time [30]. The network can then be trained if it is one large feedforward network with the modified weights being treated as shared weight [31].

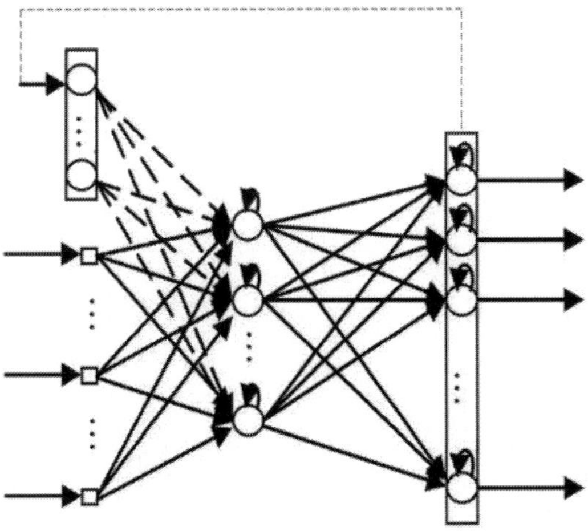

Figure 10: Fully recurrent neural network.

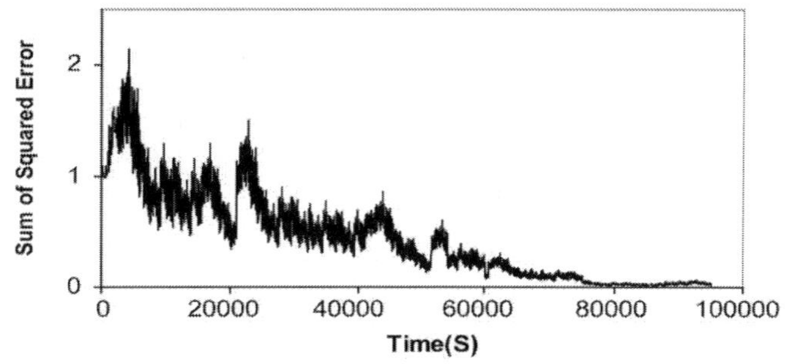

Figure 11: The sum of squared error during the feedforward training process.

Table 1: Recognition results using feedforward neural network

Class	Error rate	Class	Error rate	Class	Error rate
alif	0/30	za	0/30	qaf	0/30
ba	3/30	sin	29/30	kaf	0/30
ta	0/30	shin	3/30	lam	0/30
tha	0/30	sad	28/30	mim	0/30
jim	14/30	dhad	17/30	nun	0/30
ha	0/30	tad	0/30	he	0/30
kha	16/30	zad	0/30	waw	30/30
dal	21/30	ayn	0/30	la	0/30
thal	0/30	gayn	25/30	ya	0/30
ra	0/30	fa	0/30	t	3/30
Total = 186/900 = 20.67%					
Accuracy rate = 79.33%					

Gesture Recognition Using Neural Networks for Static Gesture Recognition

Gesture Recognition Using Feedforward Networks

Figure 11 shows the way in which the sum of squared error declines until it reaches the target value. The training process was slow comparing to the recurrent neural networks. The recognition results where also poor using this type of architecture. One class for instance—Waw class—had zero recognition rate which was totally unacceptable for such a system. **Table 1** shows the recognition rate for each class.

Gesture Recognition Using Elman Neural Networks

A very recognizable improvement has been made when the system was implemented using recurrent neural network; specifically speaking, using Elman architecture. The accuracy rate has risen to 89.66%. But there are still some drawbacks in certain classes and can be noticed by the large error rate for that class and this has to do with the similarities among some hand gestures. **Figure 12** and table 2 both shows the Elman neural network recognition performance.

Gesture Recognition Using Jordan Neural Networks

The results came a bit close to the previous one-Elman neural networkand with nearly the same number of epochs. Figure 13 and table 3 both show the Jordan neural network recognition performance.

Gesture Recognition Using Fully Recurrent Neural Networks

The final architecture of recurrent neural network is the most promising type of the three previous architectures.

That is because of the feedback links that lead the network to stability, convergence and the best accuracy rate among the explored types. **Figure 14**shows the reduction in the sum of squared error values whereas table 4 shows the recognition rate for each class.

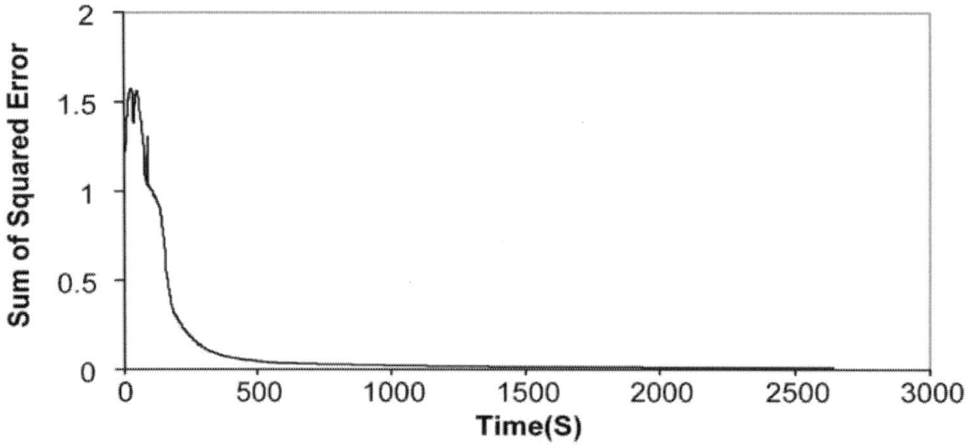

Figure 12: The sum of squared error during the training of Elman neural network.

Table 2: Recognition results using Elman neural network.

Class	Error rate	Class	Error rate	Class	Error rate
alif	0/30	za	0/30	qaf	0/30
ba	28/30	sin	0/30	kaf	0/30
ta	0/30	shin	2/30	lam	0/30
tha	0/30	sad	0/30	mim	0/30
jim	0/30	dhad	15/30	nun	0/30
ha	0/30	tad	19/30	he	0/30
kha	4/30	zad	0/30	waw	3/30
dal	0/30	ayn	0/30	la	0/30
thal	0/30	gayn	17/30	ya	0/30
ra	0/30	fa	0/30	t	5/30

Total = 93/900 = 10.33%

Accuracy rate = 89.66%

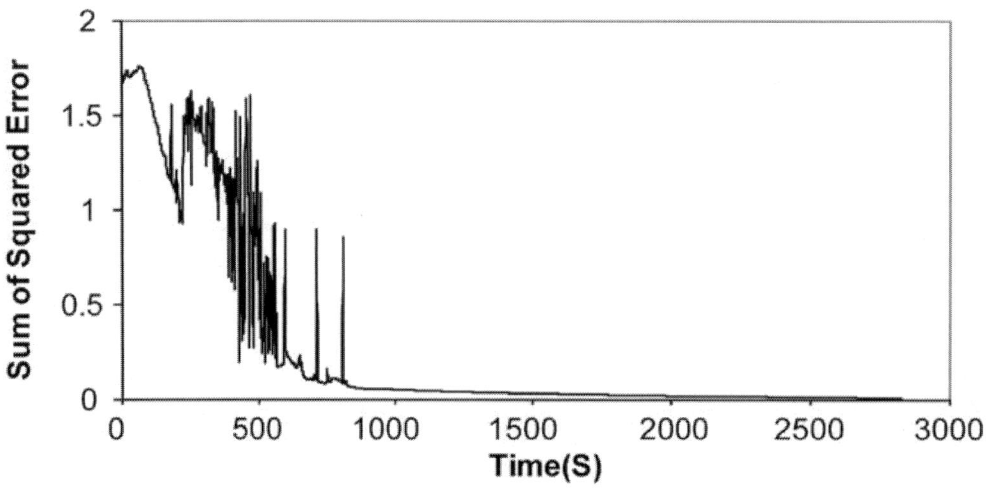

Figure 13: The sum of squared error during the training process of Jordan neural network.

Table 3: Recognition results using Jordan neural network

Class	Error rate	Class	Error rate	Class	Error rate
alif	0/30	za	0/30	qaf	0/30
ba	14/30	sin	6/30	kaf	3/30
ta	4/30	shin	3/30	lam	0/30
tha	6/30	sad	0/30	mim	2/30
jim	0/30	dhad	0/30	nun	0/30
ha	0/30	tad	19/30	he	6/30
kha	22/30	zad	0/30	waw	8/30
dal	25/30	ayn	0/30	la	0/30
thal	0/30	gayn	0/30	ya	0/30
ra	0/30	fa	0/30	t	21/30
Total = 139/900 = 15.44%					

DYNAMIC GESTURE RECOGNITION

The previous results suggest that the best architecture that can help in detecting hand gestures is the fully recurrent neural networks. Based on that, the dynamic process will be implemented using the later architecture. It will be used for recognizing gestures of frames extracted from a video stream of a moving hand performing sign language.

For the research purposes we will introduce a dynamic experiment that was held for video containing three gestures.

Frames were extracted at a rate of 15 frames per second. The idea behind identifying the dynamic gestures is simple; we will train the neural network using the static images as a training set; recall that the training database contains 900 images. Then the extracted images will be presented to the neural network to perform the recognition process, and in order to separate the characters there was a need to use a statistical measurement. It was noticed that the output of each neuron in the output layer of the i-th frame is close in value or related to the output of the same neuron of the (i + 1)-th frame only if they both belong to the same gesture. According to that the correlation value was computed for output values of the neural network for every two successive frames [31]. A correlation coefficient is a number between −1 and 1 which measures the degree to which two data sets are linearly related. Whenever the correlation value gets low comparing to the values around; it means that we have a gesture change. In particular, a correlation value of zero means that there is no correlation at all and hence a change in hand gesture. **Figure 15** shows the correlation values of the extracted frames. Since the number of the extracted frames is large; frame numbers in the image sample in figure 17 do not correspond to their actual order appearance in the original video. Figures that show the correlation values between frames will reflect the actual frames order.

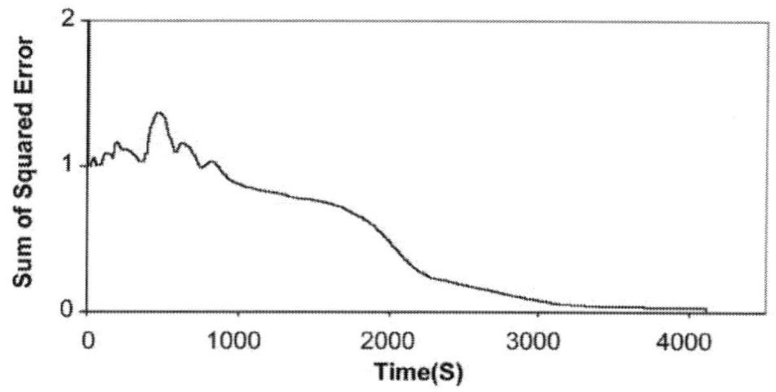

Figure 14: The sum of squared error during the training process of the fully recurrent neural network.

Table 4: Recognition results using fully recurrent neural network

Class	Error rate	Class	Error rate	Class	Error rate
alif	0/30	za	0/30	qaf	0/30
ba	4/30	sin	0/30	kaf	0/30
ta	0/30	shin	3/30	lam	0/30
tha	0/30	sad	0/30	mim	0/30
jim	0/30	dhad	0/30	nun	0/30
ha	0/30	tad	0/30	he	0/30
kha	11/30	zad	0/30	waw	0/30
dal	0/30	ayn	0/30	la	0/30
thal	0/30	gayn	22/30	ya	0/30
ra	0/30	fa	0/30	t	4/30

Choosing a zero threshold value can help in sensing the changes to decide on the beginning of a new character. Figure 15 shows the suggested threshold value.

Words Recognition

To show how this procedure works for complete words; an experiment is conducted for the word Shams (شمس).

Testing Shams (شمس)

The word Shams consists of three gestures; Shin, Mim and Sin (figure 16). A group of 120 frames were extracted from a 8 second length video (figure 17). The correlation test in **Figure 18** was able to detect the two transitions that occur on frames 30 and 74.

CONCLUSIONS AND FUTURE WORK

A static and dynamic hand gesture recognition system was presented in this research using a set of features that take into account the fingertips and the wrist along with orientation between them [32].

Two major network architectures have been presented; feedforward and recurrent neural networks along with a database consisting of 900 images formed by 2 persons performing 30 repetitions of each gesture has been used to train the neural networks.

The images have been captured by a color camera and digitized into 256 × 256 pixel images which have been converted into HSI system. Color segmentation was implemented using Matlab 6.5 and the hand gesture recog- nition system was implemented in C.

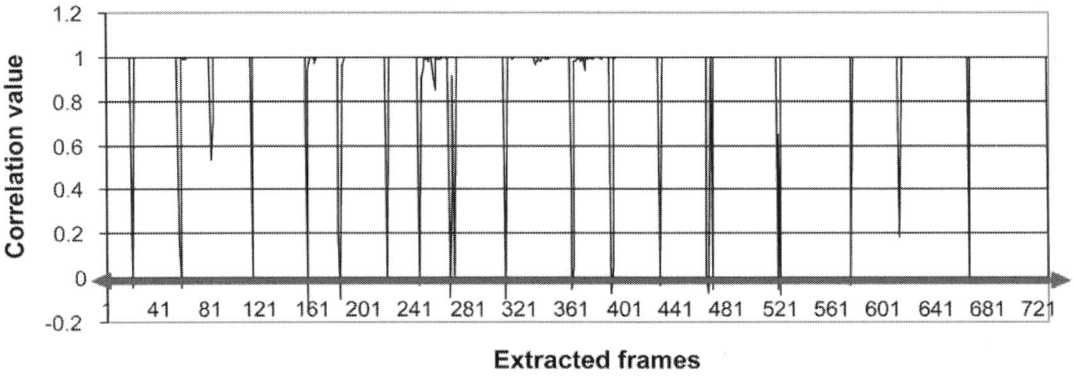

Figure 15: The threshold value that separates one gesture from another.

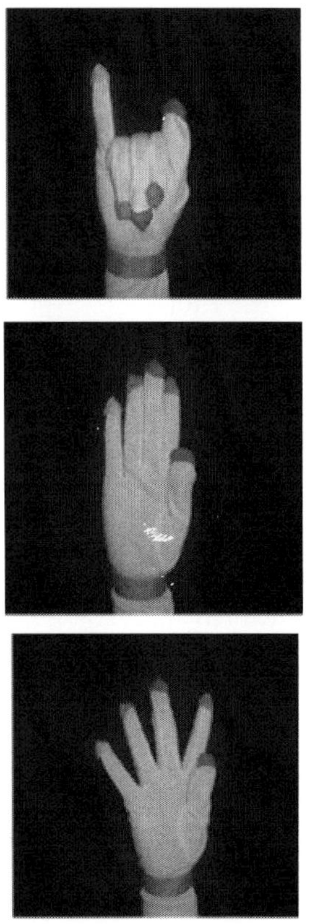

Figure 16: Classes from left: Shin, Sin and Mim.

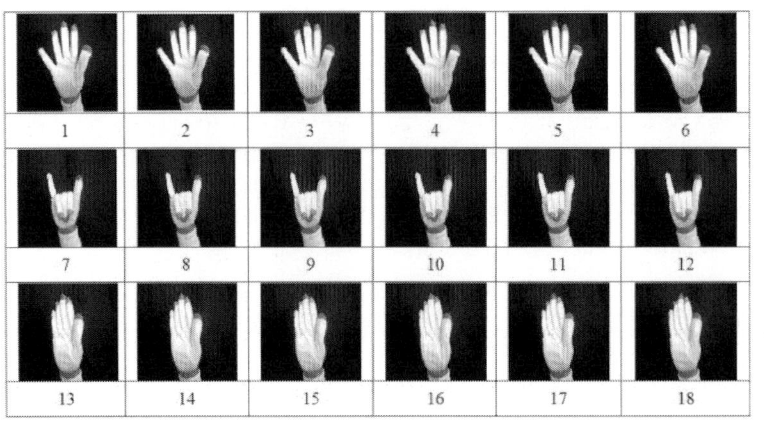

Figure 17: A sample of the extracted frames that contain transitions.

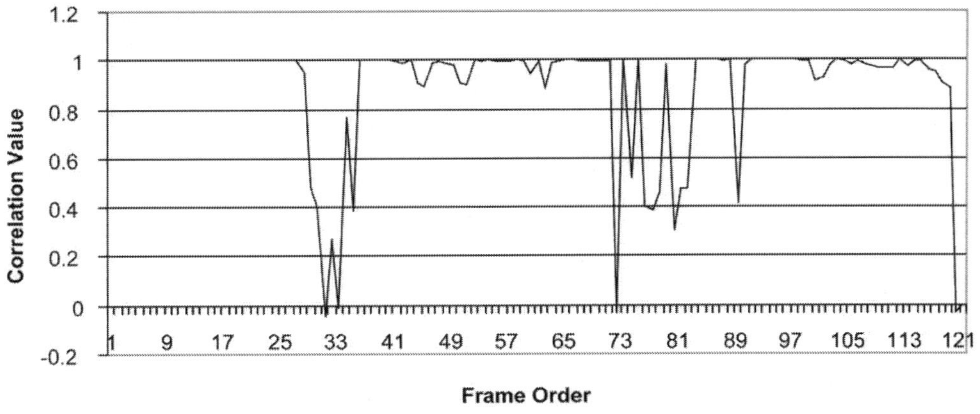

Figure 18: Correlation values which shows that transition has occurred on frames 30 and 74.

The system has been tested using a test set of 900 images; represent all of the 30 gestures. The recognition rate for the static images under the described conditions has showed a significant improvement in the recognition rate that has reached up to 95.11% for the fully recurrent network; it performed better than the Elman's and Jordan's neural networks.

As for the dynamic system, using a simple statistical measure helped in determining the transition between different hand gestures and was useful in recognizing whole words in Arabic Sign Language (ArSL).

Some of the mistakes of the recognition process are due to false feature extraction and others are due to the similarities of some gestures; the results show an improvement in the generalisability of the system when using a fully recurrent network comparing with using other types of neural networks.

One of my major goals was speed and the avoidance of special hardware. This was achieved since the application was written in C. MATLAB is considered to be slower but allowed us to work faster and easier with image processing issues.

This research has also shown that it is feasible to utilize a data glove and neural network classifier to assist in human computer interaction applications. Regarding the future work; research will be devoted to the following topics:

- Using both hands may be a considerable improvement;
- The recognition of gesture sequences imposes the problem of detecting and eliminating unwanted intermediate gestures that might unintentionally be formed during the transition.

REFERENCES

1. J. Eisenstein, S. Ghandeharizadeh, L. Golubchik, C. Shahabi, D. Yan and R. Zimmermann, "Device Independence and Extensibility in Gesture Recognition," Proceedings of IEEE Virtual Reality, Los Angeles, 22-26 March 2003, pp. 207-214.doi:10.1109/VR.2003.1191141
2. K. Assaleh and M. Al-Rousan, "A New Method for Arabic Sign Language Recognition," EURASIP Journal on Applied Signal Processing, Hindawi Publishing Corporation, New York, 2005, pp. 2136-2145.
3. K. Abe, H. Saito and S. Ozawa, "Virtual 3-D Interface System via Hand Motion Recognition from Two Cameras," IEEE Transactions on Systems, Man and Cybernetics, Vol. 32, No. 4, 2002, pp. 536-540. doi:10.1109/TSMCA.2002.804821
4. J.-S. Kim, W. Jang and Z. Bien, "A Dynamic Gesture Recognition System for the Korean Sign Language (KSL)," SMC-B, Vol. 26, No. 2, 1996, pp. 354-359.
5. G. Fang, W. Gao and D. Zhao, "Large Vocabulary Sign Language Recognition Based on Fuzzy Decision Trees," SMC-A, Vol. 34, No. 3, 2004, pp. 305-314.
6. G. Fang, W. Gao and D. Zhao, "Large-Vocabulary Continuous Sign Language Recognition Based on TransitionMovement Models," SMC-A, Vol. 37, No. 1, 2007, pp. 1- 9.
7. T. Shanableh, K. Assaleh and M. Al-Rousan, "SpatioTemporal Feature-Extraction Techniques for Isolated Ges ture Recognition in Arabic Sign Language," SMC-B, Vol. 37, No. 3, 2007, pp. 641-650.
8. I. Infantino, R. Rizzo and S. Gaglio, "A Framework for Sign Language Sentence Recognition by Commonsense Context," SMC-C, Vol. 37, No. 5, 2007, pp. 1034-1039.
9. Y. Yuan, Y. Liu and K. Barner, "Tactile Gesture Recognition for People with Disabilities," IEEE International Conference on Acoustics, Speech, and Signal Processing, Vol. 5, Kyoto, 18-23 March 2005, pp. 461-464.
10. R. Salomon and J. Weissmann, "Evolutionary Tuning of Neural Networks for Gesture Recognition, Evolutionary Computation," Proceedings of the 2000 Congress on Evolutionary Computation, Vol. 2, La Jolla, 16-19 July 2000, pp. 1528-1534.
11. F. Florez, J. Garcia and A. Hernandez, "Hand Gesture Recognition Following the Dynamics of a Topology-Preserving Network," Proceedings of IEEE 5th International Conference on Automatic Face and Gesture Recognition, Washington DC, 19-20 May 2002, pp. 303-308.
12. M. Mohandes and S. Buraiky, "Automation of the Arabic Sign Language Recognition using the PowerGlove," AIML Journal, Vol. 7, No. 1, 2007, pp. 41-46.
13. K. Murakami and H. Taguchi, "Gesture Recognition Using Recurrent Neural Networks," Proceedings of the SIGCHI Conference on Human Factors in Computing Systems, Gaithersburg, 15-17 March 1991, pp. 237-242.

14. O. Al-Jarrah, A. Shatnawi and A. H. Halawani, "Recognition of Gestures in Arabic Sign Language using Neural Networks," Proceeding of Artificial Intelligence and Soft Computing, Palma De Mallorca, 28-30 August 2006.

15. W. K. Pratt, "Digital Image Processing, PIKS Scientific Inside," 4th Edition, A John Wiley & Sons, Inc., Hoboken, 2007.

16. A. Ford and A. Roberts, "Color Space Conversions," 1998. http://www.poynton.com/PDFs/coloureq.pdf

17. A. Balaguer, "Analytical Methods for the Study of Color in Digital Images," 2006. http://www.tesisenxarxa.net/TESIS_UIB/AVAILABLE/TDX-1027106- 4116//tapb1de1.pdf

18. S. Wesolkowski, "Color Image Edge Detection and Segmentation: A Comparison of the Vector Angle and the Euclidean Distance Color Similarity Measures," 1999. http://etd.uwaterloo.ca/etd/swesolko1999.pdf

19. R. Gonzalez, R. Woods and S. Eddins, "Digital Image Processing Using MATLAB," Pearson Prentice Hall, Upper Saddle River, 2004.

20. C. Y. Wen and C. M. Chou, "Color Image Models and Its Applications to Document Examination," Forensic Science Journal, Vol. 3, No. 1, 2004, pp. 23-32.

21. J. Weissmann and R. Salomon, "Gesture Recognition for Virtual Reality Applications Using Data Gloves and Neural Networks," Proceedings of IEEE International Joint Conference on Neural Networks, Washington DC, 10-16 July 1999.

22. S. Hykin, "Neural Networks: A Comprehensive Foundation," 2nd Edition, Prentice Hall, Upper Saddle River, 1998.

23. L. C. Jain, "Recurrent Neural Networks," CRC Press, Boca Raton, 2001.

24. J. L. Elman, "Finding Structure in Time," Cognitive Science, Vol. 14, No. 2, 1990, pp. 179-211. doi:10.1207/s15516709cog1402_1

25. S. Ismail and A. bin Ahmad, "Recurrent Neural Network with Backpropagation through Time Algorithm for Arabic Recognition," Proceeding 18th European Simulation Multiconference, Magdeburg, 13-16 June 2004.

26. N. Sinha, M. Gupta and D. Rao, "Dynamic Neural Networks: An Overview," Proceedings of IEEE International Conference on Industrial Technology, Vol. 1, Goa, 19-22 January 2000, pp. 491-496.

27. S. Zappacosta, G. Baldassarre and S. Nolfi, "Elman Neural Networks and Time Integration for Object Recognition," Technical Report, Istituto di Scienze e Tecnologie della Cognizione, Roma, 2006.

28. T. Chen and V. So, "A Comparative Study of Recurrent Neural Network Architectures on Learning Temporal Sequences," IEEE International Conference on Digital Object Identifier, Vol. 4, 1996, pp. 1945-1950.

29. P. Vamplew, "Recognition of Sign Language Using Neural Networks," PhD Thesis, University of Tasmania, Newnham, 1996.

30. P. Werbos, "Backpropagation through Time: What It Does and How To Do It," Proceedings of the IEEE, Vol. 78, No. 10, 1990, pp. 1550-1560. doi:10.1109/5.58337

31. S. Ismail and A. bin Ahmad, "Recurrent Neural Network with Backpropagation through Time Algorithm for Arabic Recognition," Proceedings 18th European Simulation Multiconference, Magdeburg, 13-16 June 2004.

32. M. Maraqa and R. Abu-Zaiter, "Recognition of Arabic Sign Language (ArSL) Using Recurrent Neural Networks," Proceeding of the First International Conference on Applications of Digital Information and Web Technologies, 2008, pp. 478-481.

CHAPTER 15 HYBRID FUZZY WAVELET NEURAL NETWORK

Jamal Salahaldeen Majeed Alneamy and Rahma Abdulwahid Hameed Alnaish

INTRODUCTION

Heart disease is a term that refers to any disturbance that makes the heart function abnormally [1]. When the coronary arteries are narrowed or blocked, the blood flow to the myocardium is decreased. This represents the main reason for the emergence of heart disease in humans. There are several risk factors for this disease, including diabetes, smoking, obesity, and a family history of heart disease, high cholesterol, and high blood pressure [1–3].

Actually, the incidence rate of heart disease is on the rise. Every year about 720,000 Americans have a heart attack. Among them, 515,000 have their first heart attack and 205,000 people have a second (or third, etc.) heart attack. Heart disease causes the death of about 600,000 people in the United States every year, which makes it responsible for one in every four deaths [4].

Due to the large number of patients with heart disease, it became necessary to have a powerful tool that works accurately and efficiently for diagnosing this disease and helping the physicians make decisions about their patients. This is because the process of diagnosis and decision making is a difficult task and needs a lot of experience and skill.

Recently, a lot of research has been published regarding the field of medical diagnosis of heart disease. In 2008, Kahramanli and Allahverdi designed a hybrid system that represents a combination between fuzzy neural network (FNN) and artificial neural network (ANN), trained by a backpropagation (BP) algorithm. The results have shown that the proposed method is comparable with other methods [5]. Besides, Das et al. in 2009 proposed a system for diagnosing heart disease by using the neural network ensemble model, which combines several individual neural networks that are trained on the same task. However, this method increased the complexity and therefore the execution time [3]. In 2011, Khemphila and Boonjing presented a classification approach to diagnose heart disease using multilayer perceptron (MLP) with a backpropagation learning algorithm, as well as a feature selection algorithm to use 8 features instead of 13. The results have shown that the accuracy rate was enhanced by 1.1% in the training data set and by 0.82% in the testing data set [6]. In 2013, Beheshti et al. applied the centripetal accelerated particle swarm optimization (CAPSO) to evolve the learning of the artificial neural network (ANN), which was used to classify a heart disease data set. The results have shown that the diagnosis rate still needs to be improved [7]. From all previous studies, the classification accuracy did not reach a desirable level. However, the main objective of all previous studies was to make the diagnosis process of heart disease more accurate and efficient.

Moreover, fuzzy neural network (FNN) is the combination of neural network and fuzzy logic in one system that contains both the interpretability property and inference ability of fuzzy logic to handle the uncertainty and the self-learning ability of a neural network to improve the approximation accuracy [8–10]. In spite of the fact that the FNN/NN has many advantages, it still suffers from some drawbacks, such as slow training speed, high approximation error, and poor convergence problems [8].

In recent years, many researchers have emphasized the use of wavelet neural network (WNN), which combines the wavelet function and a neural network. WNN integrates the learning capability of NN with the decomposition capability

Citation: Jamal Salahaldeen Majeed Alneamy and Rahma Abdulwahid Hameed Alnaish, "Hybrid Fuzzy Wavelet Neural Network,"Advances in Artificial Neural Systems, vol. 2014, Article ID 796323, 11 pages, 2014. doi:10.1155/2014/796323

[8, 11], orthogonality [12], and time frequency localization properties [10, 12–14] of the wavelet function. The main advantages of the WNN are better generalization capability [15], faster learning property [8, 15], and smaller approximation errors and size of networks than NN [8]. Therefore, it is able to overcome the obstacles of FNN/NN, especially in highly nonlinear systems [8].

According to the mentioned properties of the WNN and fuzzy system, fuzzy wavelet neural network (FWNN) will be considered in our work. FWNN has been presented in some application areas: function learning [16], chaotic time series identification [14], and the approximation of function, identification of nonlinear dynamic plants, and prediction chaotic time series [17]. FWNN combines the main advantages of a fuzzy system, wavelet function, and neural networks and, therefore, could bring the low level learning and good computational ability of WNN into a fuzzy system and the high humanlike thinking of fuzzy system into the WNN [8].

The training process of FWNN is a crucial task and requires robust optimization techniques to make the performance of this network more accurate and efficient. According to [18–21], which make a comparison study among some naturally inspired optimization algorithms, such as particle swarm optimization (PSO) [22], differential evolution (DE) [23], teaching learning based optimization (TLBO) [24], artificial bee colony (ABC) [25], and firefly algorithm (FA) [26], the TLBO algorithm is accurate, effective, and efficient and shows superior performance in comparison to others. The attractive property of the TLBO algorithm is that it is a simple mathematical model and is one of the most powerful tools to find the optimal solution in a shorter computational time period [18]. In addition, TLBO has balanced exploration and exploitation abilities so it does not get stuck in local minima [27].

In accordance with the above-mentioned advantages of both FWNN and TLBO, in this paper a new method (TLBO-FWNN) is proposed to increase the efficiency of the heart disease diagnosis process.

The rest of this paper is organized as follows: section two represents a background about FWNN; section three explains the TLBO algorithm; in section four, the proposed method of TLBO-FWNN is illustrated; section five describes the heart disease data set; section six demonstrates the *K*-fold cross validation; and finally section seven presents and discusses the experimental results.

THE BACKGROUND OF FUZZY WAVELET NEURAL NETWORK (FWNN)

One of the most commonly used methods for diagnosing of heart disease is artificial neural network (ANN) [6,7]. ANN is considered an effective artificial intelligence method if it has enough training data. The description of an ANN structure is a difficult task [28]. Fuzzy logic [29] has the ability to deal with cognitive uncertainties in a manner like humans [30]. Fuzzy logic is used for improving the ability of the neural network and increasing its learning rate [31]. So, the combination of a neural network and fuzzy logic in one system leads to the creation of another powerful computational tool called fuzzy neural network (FNN), which combines the advantages of both approaches [30, 31].

Most fuzzy neural networks use the sigmoid function as the activation function in the hidden layer, but this type of function leads the training algorithm to converge to the local minima [32] and generally decreases the convergence speed of the network. Therefore, the wavelet function is used as an alternative to the sigmoid function [33, 34]. The wavelet function is a waveform that has limited duration, and the mean value of this duration is zero. This function has two parameters, the dilation parameter and the translation parameter [33].

The combination of the wavelet theory with a fuzzy system and neural network generates the so-called fuzzy wavelet neural network (FWNN) [13]. The structure of the FWNN is described in Figure 1, which contains seven layers [17, 33, 34].

(i) In the first layer, the number of nodes is equal to the number of input variables.

(ii) In the second layer, each node represents one fuzzy set, in which the calculation for the membership value of the input variable to the fuzzy set is carried out.

(iii) In the third layer, each node represents one fuzzy rule. Therefore, the number of nodes is related to the number of fuzzy rules. The output of this layer can be calculated using the following:

$$\mu_i(x) = \prod_{j=1}^{q} A^i_j(x_j), \tag{1}$$

where Π refers to the AND operation and A^i_j represents the membership function used to calculate the membership degrees of the input variables. In this study, a Gaussian membership function is used that can be calculated using

$$A^i_j(x_j) = \exp\left[-\left(\frac{x_j - c^i_j}{\sigma^i_j}\right)^2\right]. \tag{2}$$

In (6), c^i_j and σ^i_j represent the center and the width of the membership function, respectively.

(iv) The fourth layer contains the wavelet functions ψ_{ij} in its neurons, which represents the consequent part of the fuzzy rules. In FWNN, fuzzy rules can be represented by the following equation:

$$R^i: \text{if } x_1 \text{ is } A^i_1,\ x_2 \text{ is } A^i_2, \ldots,\ x_q \text{ is } A^i_q$$
$$\text{then } y_i = w_i \sum_{j=1}^{q} \psi_{ij}(x_j), \tag{3}$$

where R^i refers to the ith rule, and $(1 \le i \le c)$, where c is the number of the rule. x_j refers to the jth input, and $(1 \le j \le q)$, where q is the number of input parameters, while y_i refers to the ith output from the wavelet neural network (WNN).

In the wavelet neural network, which is described in Figure 2, the output can be calculated using

$$y_i = w_i \sum_{j=1}^{q} \psi_{ij}(x_j), \tag{4}$$

where w_i refers to the weight coefficients and ψ_{ij} represents a set of wavelet functions, which is called a wavelet family that can be defined computationally using

$$\psi_{ij}(x_j) = \psi\left(\frac{x_j - b_{ij}}{a_{ij}}\right), \quad a_{ij} \neq 0, \tag{5}$$

where a_{ij} and b_{ij} represent the dilation and translation parameters, respectively, and ψ refers to the mother wavelet that can be calculated using the Mexican hat wavelet function that can be represented in

$$\psi(x) = \frac{1}{\sqrt{|a|}}\left(1 - 2x^2\right)\exp\left(\frac{-x^2}{2}\right). \tag{6}$$

(v) In the fifth layer, multiplication between the outputs of the third layer and the outputs of the fourth layer is done. The output of this layer ($L5$) can be calculated using

$$L_5(i) = \mu_i * y_i, \tag{7}$$

where $1 \leq i \leq c$ and c refers to the number of fuzzy rules and wavelet functions.

(vi) In the sixth layer, the output involves two parts. The first part (L_6^a) aggregates the outputs of the fifth layer, which can be represented using

$$L_6^a = \sum_{i=1}^{c} \mu_i * y_i. \tag{8}$$

The second part (L_6^a) aggregates the outputs of the third layer, which can be represented using

$$L_6^b = \sum_{i=1}^{c} \mu_i. \tag{9}$$

(vii) The seventh layer represents the defuzzification process, which is used to calculate the overall output of FWNN by using

$$u = \frac{\sum_{i=1}^{c} \mu_i y_i}{\sum_{i=1}^{c} \mu_i}. \tag{10}$$

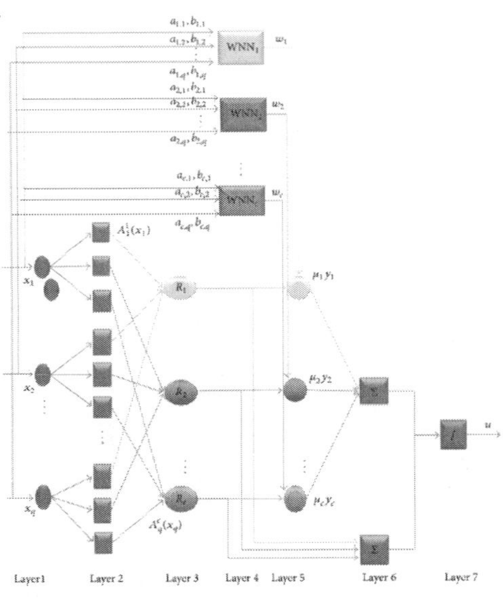

Figure 1: The general structure of the fuzzy wavelet neural network.

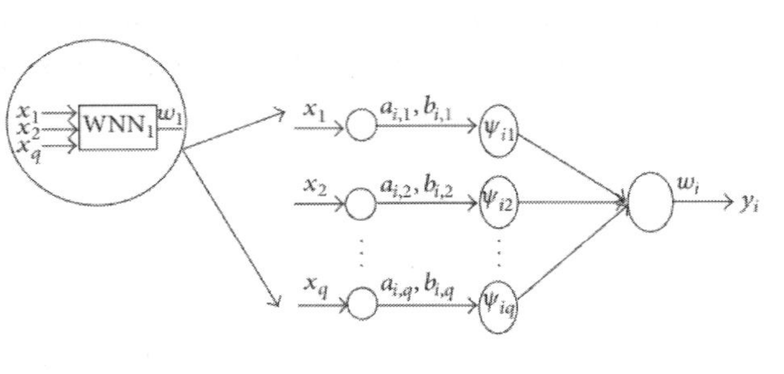

Figure 2: The structure of the wavelet neural network.

REVIEW OF TEACHING LEARNING BASED OPTIMIZATION (TLBO) ALGORITHM

Teaching learning based optimization algorithm (TLBO) is a new optimization algorithm proposed by Rao et al. in 2011 [24]. This algorithm is inspired by learners receiving teaching from the teacher in a class. The teaching process is done either by means of the teacher who is considered to be a highly learned person and has a great influence on the output of students (teacher phase) or through the interaction among learners (learner phase) [20, 21, 24, 35–37].

TLBO is a population-based algorithm in which the population is considered as a class of n learners. Each learner represents a solution and the dimension of each solution that is considered as different subjects offered to the learners actually represents the parameters involved in the objective function of the given optimization problem. The evaluation of each solution (fitness value) of the optimization problem represents the students' grades. The best fitness value is considered to be the teacher [36, 38–40].

The main characteristic of this algorithm is that it does not contain any specific parameters; it includes common parameters only [27, 41]. The implementation of a TLBO algorithm will be explained in the following subsection [24, 38].

(1) Define the optimization problem and initialize the common parameters, which are population size (ps) that represents the number of learners (n) and the dimension of each learner (D), which represents the subjects offered to the learners. In addition, set the value of the maximum number of iterations and the values of the constraints variables (lb, ub), which denote lower and upper boundaries, respectively.

(2) Generate the initial population randomly with (n) rows and (m) columns within [lb, ub] and then calculate the objective function value of each solution using $f(x)$, where x is $1, 2, 3, \ldots, n$. The results were sorted in an ascending order corresponding to ps (ascending order is convenient for finding minimum value; maximum value can be obtained by multiplying by -1 before the objective):

$$\text{Ps} = \begin{bmatrix} A_1^1 & A_2^1 & \cdots & A_{m-1}^1 & A_m^1 \\ A_1^2 & A_2^2 & \cdots & A_{m-1}^2 & A_m^2 \\ \vdots & \vdots & \cdots & \vdots & \vdots \\ A_1^{n-1} & A_1^{n-1} & \cdots & A_{m-1}^{n-1} & A_m^{n-1} \\ A_1^n & A_2^n & \cdots & A_{m-1}^n & A_n^m \end{bmatrix} \begin{matrix} \longrightarrow & f(1) \\ \longrightarrow & f(2) \\ & \vdots \\ \longrightarrow & f(n-1) \\ \longrightarrow & f(n), \end{matrix} \tag{11}$$

where $f(1) < f(2) \cdots < f(n-1) < f(n)$. Therefore, the first learner $A^1 = (A_1^1 \; A_2^1 \; \cdots \; A_m^1)$ is considered to be the best solution (teacher).

(3) In the teacher phase, calculate the mean of the population column wise where

$$A^{mean} = \left\{ \text{mean}\left(\sum_{i=1}^{n} A_1^i\right) \text{mean}\left(\sum_{i=1}^{n} A_2^i\right) \cdots \text{mean}\left(\sum_{i=1}^{n} A_m^i\right) \right\}. \quad (12)$$

(4) The teacher tries to improve the grade average of the students using

$$A^{new,i} = A^i + r_i\left(A^1 - T_F A^{mean}\right) \quad (i = 1, 2, 3, \ldots, n), \quad (13)$$

where $A^{new,}$ represents the improved learners, A^i represents the current learners, r^i is a random number in the interval [0, 1], A^1 is the desired mean, A^{mean} is the current mean [42], and T_F is a teaching factor that is not a parameter of the TLBO algorithm: it is calculated randomly using (14), which decides the value of the mean to be changed [43]:

$$T_F = \text{round}\left[1 + \text{rand}(1)\right]. \quad (14)$$

In $A^{new,}$, if the value of any variable is less than lb or bigger than ub, it is equal to lb or ub, respectively [35]:

$$\text{If } f\left(A^{new,i}\right) < f(A)^i, \text{ then } A^i = A^{new,i} \text{ else } A^i = A^i. \quad (15)$$

(5) In the learner phase, a learner interacts randomly with other learners to enhance his or her knowledge.

(6) Randomly select two learners and A_i and A_j where $i \neq j$:

$$A^{new,i} = A^i + r_i\left(A^i - A^j\right) \text{ if } f\left(A^i\right) < f\left(A^j\right)$$
$$A^{new,i} = A^i + r_i\left(A^j - A^i\right) \text{ if } f\left(A^j\right) < f\left(A^i\right). \quad (16)$$

In $A^{new,}$, if the value of any variable is less than lb or bigger than ub, it is equal to lb or ub, respectively:

$$\text{If } f\left(A^{new,i}\right) < f(A)^i, \text{ then } A^i = A^{new,i} \text{ else } A^i = A^i. \quad (17)$$

(7) The duplicate solutions are modified in order to avoid trapping in the local optima by using mutation process on randomly selected dimensions of the duplicate solutions before executing the next iteration.

(8) Sort the results in an ascending order corresponding to ps.

(9) Repeat processes (3) to (5) until the termination condition is satisfied.

THE PROPOSED METHOD OF TLBO-FWNN

To increase the accuracy of the diagnosis process of heart disease using FWNN, one of the robust optimization algorithms should be used for FWNN training. Thus, the methodology of this study includes two important procedures. The first one is constructing the structure of FWNN for the heart dataset that will be used in both the training and testing phases. The second procedure represents the training process for the constructed FWNN by utilizing the TLBO algorithm. For conducting the training process, a sample of data related to heart disease, which is called training data, is used as the input variables to the FWNN. Then, the mean square error (MSE) is calculated, which represents the difference between the actual output and the desired output of the FWNN. MSE is computed using

$$E_P = \frac{1}{L}\sum_{l=1}^{L}\left(u_l^d - u_l\right)^2, \quad (18)$$

where $1 \leq l \leq L$ represents the number of input patterns, $1 \leq p \leq P$ refers to the iteration number, u_l^d represents desired output, and u_l represents the actual output of the FWNN

The MSE represents the objective function of the TLBO algorithm, which is used to calculate the objective function value of each individual in the population. The population in this algorithm is represented by a set of solutions; each solution refers to one learner and that solution has a number of values that indicate the number of parameters (subjects) to be updated in the FWNN. In this study, the parameters are linkage weights in the FWNN and the wavelet parameters (dilation and translation). The value of these parameters is initialized randomly. Then, these values are updated using the TLBO algorithm to obtain optimal values with the minimum error rate and the highest classification accuracy.

In the testing phase, the optimal values obtained from the training phase with the testing data will be used as the input variables to test the FWNN trained by the TLBO algorithm. The output of the FWNN is calculated and compared with the desired output to investigate the learning ability of the FWNN to classify the heart dataset.

The main steps of training the FWNN using the TLBO algorithm are as follows.

(1) Initialize randomly the values of each learner (i.e., weights, dilation parameters, and translation parameters) within the interval [−1, 1], which represents the lower and upper boundaries, respectively. Then, initialize the common parameters of the TLBO algorithm, which are population size, maximum iteration number, and the dimension.

(2) Put Cycle = 1.

(3) Evaluate each learner by calculating its objective function value based on the FWNN, which gives the error rate of each learner.

(4) Update the weight, dilation, and translation parameters using the TLBO algorithm.

(5) Keep the best learner, which represents the teacher (the best values of weights, dilation, and translation parameters).

(6) Put Cycle = Cycle + 1.

(7) Repeat steps (3) to (6) until the maximum iteration number is reached. Figure 3 represents the flowchart of the TLBO-FWNN method.

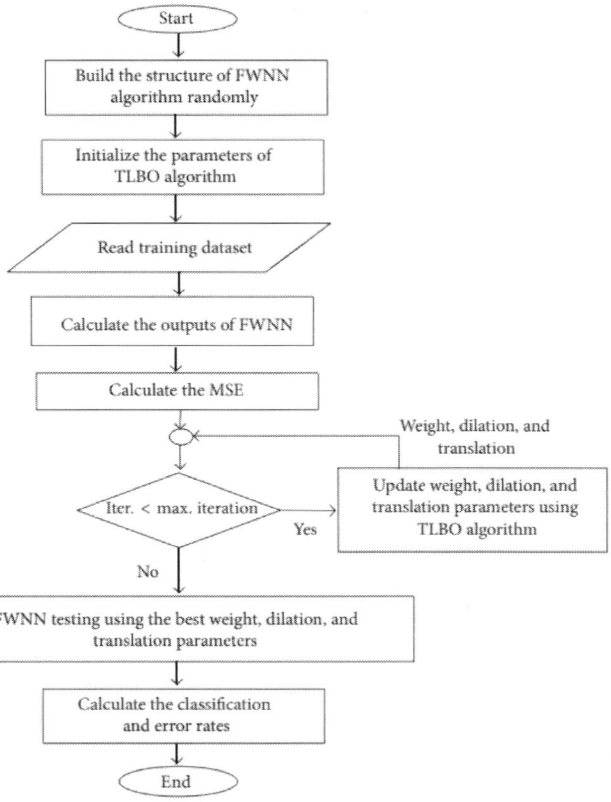

Figure 3: The flowchart of the TLBO-FWNN method.

THE HEART DISEASE DATASET

The Cleveland heart disease dataset was obtained from the Cleveland Clinic Foundation, collected by Robert Detrano. This data was used to predict the presence or the absence of heart disease. It includes 303 instances, but only 297 instances of them were used in this study because 6 instances were missing some of their attributes. The heart dataset contains 160 normal instances and 137 abnormal instances. Each instance has 76 attributes but all published experiments prefer to use 14 of them. Tables 1 and 2 briefly illustrate the properties of these attributes [44].

Table 1: Properties of the input heart dataset's attributes

No.	The name of input variables	Range of the value
1	Age	29–77 (years)
2	Sex	1 (male), 0 (female)
3	Chest pain type (cp)	1, 2, 3, or 4
4	Resting blood pressure (trestbps)	94–200 (mm Hg)
5	Serum cholesterol (chol)	126–564 (mg/dl)
6	Fasting blood sugar >120 mg/dl (fbs)	1 (true), 0 (false)
7	Resting electrocardiographic results (restecg)	0: normal 1: having ST-T wave abnormality 2: showing probable or definite left ventricular hypertrophy
8	Maximum heart rate achieved (thalach)	71–202
9	Exercise induced angina (exang)	1 (yes), 0 (no)
10	ST depression induced by exercise relative to rest (Oldpeak)	0–6.2
11	The slope of the peak exercise ST segment	1: upsloping 2: flat 3: downsloping
12	Number of major vessels (0–3) colored by fluoroscopy	0, 1, 2, or 3
13	Thal	3: normal 6: fixed defect 7: reversible defect

Table 2: Properties of the output heart dataset's attributes.

The type of the output (diagnosis of heart disease)	The value of the output
Abnormal (Probability of diameter narrowing >50%)	1
Normal (Probability of diameter narrowing <50%)	0

K-FOLD CROSS VALIDATION

During the training process of a neural network, the use of *K*-fold cross validation makes the results of the testing process more reliable [45] because it guarantees that all data is used for training and testing. In *K*-fold cross validation, the data is randomly divided into *k* parts called folds, where each fold is equal to another. Among the *K* folds, one fold will be selected for testing and the $K-1$ folds will be used for training. This process is repeated *K* times. Finally, all testing results are averaged to produce a single estimation result [45, 46]. In this study, fivefold cross validation is used.

EXPERIMENTAL RESULTS AND DISCUSSION

In this study, the performance of the proposed system for diagnosing the presence (1) or the absence (0) of heart disease is investigated using a common heart dataset (Cleveland heart disease dataset). We measured error rate, classification rate, and the time taken. The heart dataset is divided into 5 folds: one fold is used for testing and the other 4 folds are used for training. Each fold has 60 instances and each instance has 13 attributes, as shown in Table 1. This process is repeated 5 times. As mentioned previously, the TLBO algorithm has common parameters, which are population size (ps) and the dimension of each solution (*D*). In this research, the value of the *D* parameter is equal to 81, which represents the weight, dilation, and translation parameters. However, the value of the ps parameter is varied because the user of this algorithm does not have adequate knowledge about the appropriate value of this parameter. In this study, the training process is repeated in three separate experiments with three various ps, which are 50, 100, or 150. The maximum iteration number represents the stopping condition, set to 500. In FWNN, the classification of the heart dataset is based on the number of fuzzy sets, fuzzy rules, and wavelet functions, which are equal to three, in addition to the value of each attribute.

In terms of the error rate, which represents the percentage of incorrect classifications for training the FWNN using the TLBO algorithm for the Cleveland heart disease dataset, it is illustrated in Table 3. In this table, the results have shown that the TLBO-FWNN reached the minimum error rate (0.0585) when the population size was equal to 150.

Table 3: Error rate of training the FWNN using TLBO on the heart dataset

Population size	1st time	2nd time	3rd time	4th time	5th time	Mean
50	0.06101	0.0652	0.0632	0.0680	0.0633	0.0641
100	0.0569	0.0628	0.0547	0.0584	0.0623	0.0590
150	0.0567	0.0613	0.0558	0.0577	0.0611	0.0585

Moreover, we noticed from Table 4, which represents the correct classification percentage, that the best classification accuracy is obtained when the population size is equal to 150 (94.1422). Increasing the population size leads to an increase in the training duration, as shown in Table 5, where the average time of training is 138.31 minutes when the population was equal to 150; the average time is 45.39 when the population size was equal to 50. Also, the classification accuracy and the error rate are very close to each other for both population sizes (100 and 150), as shown in Tables 3 and 4.

Table 4: Classification rate of training the FWNN using the TLBO on the heart dataset

Population size	1st time	2nd time	3rd time	4th time	5th time	Mean
50	93.8987	93.4777	93.6709	93.1956	93.6664	93.5818
100	94.3064	93.7180	94.5262	94.1528	93.7668	94.0940
150	94.3238	93.8600	94.4169	94.2263	93.8843	94.1422

Table 5: Time taken for training the FWNN using the TLBO on the heart dataset

Population size	1st time	2nd time	3rd time	4th time	5th time	Mean
50	47	43.75	45.95	47.82	42.43	45.39
100	99	87.96	87	91.41	85.30	90.13
150	131.84	140.77	152.34	134.54	132.09	138.31

Tables 6 and 7 illustrate the MSE and the classification accuracy of testing the FWNN for unseen heart data by using the optimal parameter values obtained from the TLBO algorithm, respectively. In Table 6, the minimum average error rate of 0.0970 is obtained when the population size is equal to 100. In addition, the highest average classification rate (90.2909) is acquired when the population size is equal to 100.

Table 6: Error rate of testing the FWNN on the heart dataset

Population size	1st time	2nd time	3rd time	4th time	5th time	Mean
50	0.1934	0.0617	0.0848	0.0769	0.0838	0.1004
100	0.184	0.0673	0.0899	0.0787	0.0654	0.0970
150	0.1853	0.0624	0.0778	0.0782	0.0858	0.0979

Table 7: Classification rate of testing the FWNN on the heart dataset

Population size	1st time	2nd time	3rd time	4th time	5th time	Mean
50	80.6578	93.8314	91.5186	92.3071	91.6199	89.9869
100	81.5955	93.2665	91.0059	92.127	93.4597	90.2909
150	81.468	93.7626	92.2201	92.1787	91.4164	90.2091

Moreover, the input variables of the FNN are automatically normalized during the fuzzification process. So, the input variables of the WNN should be normalized too to be more homogenous with the input variables of the FNN. The data normalization process is done by finding the maximum value of each column of input variables and then dividing each value in that column on this maximum value.

The error rate of training the FWNN utilizing the TLBO algorithm for the normalized heart disease dataset is illustrated in Table 8. In this table, the results have shown that the TLBO-FWNN reached the minimum error rate when the population size was equal to 100, which is 0.0489 in all experiments.

Table 8: Error rate of training the FWNN using the TLBO on the normalized heart dataset

Population size	1st time	2nd time	3rd time	4th time	5th time	Mean
50	0.0484	0.0522	0.0561	0.0485	0.0543	0.0519
100	0.0476	0.0519	0.0510	0.0481	0.0463	0.0489
150	0.0440	0.0526	0.0522	0.049	0.0513	0.0498

In addition, as shown in Table 9, which represents the correct classification percentage, the highest average classification accuracy (95.0964) is obtained when the population size equals 100.

Table 9: Classification rate of training the FWNN using the TLBO on the normalized heart dataset

Population size	1st time	2nd time	3rd time	4th time	5th time	Mean
50	95.1504	94.7733	94.3811	95.1457	94.5624	94.8025
100	95.2379	94.8006	94.8931	95.1891	95.3613	95.0964
150	95.5908	94.7341	94.7724	95.0860	94.8696	95.0105

The average time taken was equal to 88.498 minutes only when the population size was equal to 100, as shown in Table 10.

Table 10: Duration time for training the FWNN using the TLBO on the normalized heart dataset

Population size	1st time	2nd time	3rd time	4th time	5th time	Mean
50	43.36	48.21	45.03	44.29	43.72	44.922
100	92.17	87.16	88.27	87.65	87.24	88.498
150	144.40	148.67	140.18	132.80	130.37	139.284

Thus, Tables 11 and 12 explain the MSE and classification accuracy when testing the FWNN for normalized unseen heart data, respectively. In Table 11, the lower average error testing rate (0.0997) is obtained when the population size is equal to 50. In Table 12, the highest average classification rate (90.0213) is acquired when the population size was equal to 50.

Table 11: Error rate of testing the FWNN on the normalized heart dataset

Population size	1st time	2nd time	3rd time	4th time	5th time	Mean
50	0.2101	0.0593	0.084	0.0677	0.0778	0.0997
100	0.1898	0.0656	0.0857	0.0764	0.0876	0.1010
150	0.208	0.068	0.071	0.0947	0.0778	0.1039

Table 12: Classification rate of testing the FWNN on the normalized heart dataset

Population size	1st time	2nd time	3rd time	4th time	5th time	Mean
50	78.9873	94.0694	91.5996	93.2322	92.2183	90.0213
100	81.0236	93.4444	91.434	92.3587	91.2441	89.9009
150	79.195	93.2005	92.8955	90.5341	92.2201	89.6090

In conclusion, in comparing the maximum classification rate acquired during the testing of the FWNN on normalized and nonnormalized data, the results have shown that the classification accuracy on nonnormalized data (90.2909) is better than the classification accuracy on normalized data (90.0213).

Also, to investigate the performance of the proposed TLBO-FWNN method, a comparison with eight recently proposed methods from the literature was carried out on the same dataset.

As shown in Table 13 and Figure 4, the results show that the proposed method, TLBO-FWNN, has the best performance for diagnosing heart disease in terms of classification accuracy (90.2909) compared to the results obtained by other methods. The GSA+MLP method was the worst of the others.

Table 13: A comparison of the proposed and existing methods based on classification accuracy

Method	Classification accuracy	Reference	Year
Proposed method (TLBO + FWNN)	**90.2909**	—	—
neural networks ensembles	89.01	Das et al. [3]	2009
CAPSO + MLP	87.04	Beheshti et al. [7]	2013
ANN + FNN + BP	86.8	Kahramanli and Allahverdi [5]	2008
MLP + BP + GA	80.99	Khemphila and Boonjing [6]	2011
MLP + BP	80.17	Khemphila and Boonjing [6]	2011
PSO + MLP	74.07	Beheshti et al. [7]	2013
ICA + MLP	68.52	Beheshti et al. [7]	2013
GSA + MLP	61.11	Beheshti et al. [7]	2013

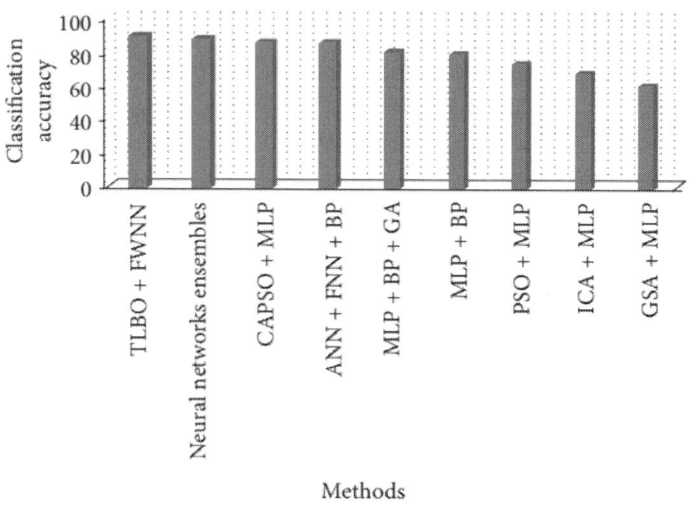

Figure 4: The classification accuracy for the proposed and existing methods.

CONCLUSION AND FUTURE WORK

In this paper, a hybrid fuzzy wavelet neural network and teaching learning based optimization algorithm were used to classify the presence or the absence of heart disease. The teaching learning based optimization (TLBO) algorithm has been proposed for training fuzzy wavelet neural networks (FWNN). The simulation results have shown that when population is of a medium size (100), TLBO-FWNN gives good results in a somewhat short amount of time. In addition, these results demonstrate that the TLBO-FWNN method has superior performance compared to other published methods, giving the highest classification accuracy.

In addition, there are some suggestions that can be applied to enhance the performance of the TLBO-FWNN method in the future, such as using a TLBO algorithm to evolve the structure of the FWNN or utilizing another optimization algorithm to enhance the learning of the FWNN.

REFERENCES

1. K. Polat, S. Güneş, and S. Tosun, "Diagnosis of heart disease using artificial immune recognition system and fuzzy weighted pre-processing," Pattern Recognition, vol. 39, no. 11, pp. 2186–2193, 2006.
2. P. Gayathri and N. Jaisankar, "Comprehensive study of heart disease diagnosis using data mining and soft computing techniques," International Journal of Engineering & Technology, vol. 5, no. 3, pp. 2947–2958, 2013.
3. R. Das, I. Turkoglu, and A. Sengur, "Effective diagnosis of heart disease through neural networks ensembles," Expert Systems with Applications, vol. 36, no. 4, pp. 7675–7680, 2009.
4. centers of disease control and prevention, 2014, http://www.cdc.gov/heartdisease/facts.htm.
5. H. Kahramanli and N. Allahverdi, "Design of a hybrid system for the diabetes and heart diseases," Expert Systems with Applications, vol. 35, no. 1-2, pp. 82–89, 2008.

6. A. Khemphila and V. Boonjing, "Heart disease classification using neural network and feature selection," in Proceedings of the 21st International Conference on Systems Engineering (ICSEng '11), pp. 406–409, IEEE Computer Society, Las Vegas, Nev, USA, August 2011.
7. Z. Beheshti, S. M. H. Shamsuddin, E. Beheshti, and S. S. Yuhaniz, "Enhancement of artificial neural network learning using centripetal accelerated particle swarm optimization for medical diseases diagnosis," Soft Computing, pp. 1–18, 2013.
8. Y. Wang, T. Mai, and J. Mao, "Adaptive motion/force control strategy for non-holonomic mobile manipulator robot using recurrent fuzzy wavelet neural networks," Engineering Applications of Artificial Intelligence, vol. 34, pp. 137–153, 2014.
9. E. Lughofer, "On-line assurance of interpretability criteria in evolving fuzzy systems—achievements, new concepts and open issues," Information Sciences, vol. 251, pp. 22–46, 2013.
10. S. Tzeng, "Design of fuzzy wavelet neural networks using the GA approach for function approximation and system identification," Fuzzy Sets and Systems, vol. 161, no. 19, pp. 2585–2596, 2010.
11. E. Karatepe and T. Hiyama, "Fuzzy wavelet network identification of optimum operating point of non-crystalline silicon solar cells," Computers and Mathematics with Applications, vol. 63, no. 1, pp. 68–82, 2012.
12. V. S. Kodogiannis, M. Amina, and I. Petrounias, "A clustering-based fuzzy wavelet neural network model for short-term load forecasting," International Journal of Neural Systems, vol. 23, no. 5, Article ID 1350024, 2013.
13. M. Shahriari Kahkeshi, F. Sheikholeslam, and M. Zekri, "Design of adaptive fuzzy wavelet neural sliding mode controller for uncertain nonlinear systems," ISA Transactions, vol. 52, no. 3, pp. 342–350, 2013.
14. Y. Bodyanskiy and O. Vynokurova, "Hybrid adaptive wavelet-neuro-fuzzy system for chaotic time series identification," Information Sciences, vol. 220, pp. 170–179, 2013.
15. C. M. Lin, A. B. Ting, C. F. Hsu, and C. M. Chung, "Adaptive control for mimo uncertain nonlinear systems using recurrent wavelet neural network," International Journal of Neural Systems, vol. 22, no. 1, pp. 37–50, 2012.
16. D. W. C. Ho, P.-A. Zhang, and J. Xu, "Fuzzy wavelet networks for function learning," IEEE Transactions on Fuzzy Systems, vol. 9, no. 1, pp. 200–211, 2001.
17. M. Davanipoor, M. Zekri, and F. Sheikholeslam, "Fuzzy wavelet neural network with an accelerated hybrid learning algorithm," IEEE Transactions on Fuzzy Systems, vol. 20, no. 3, pp. 463–470, 2012.
18. S. C. Satapathy, A. Naik, and K. Parvathi, "Teaching learning based optimization for neural networks learning enhancement," in Swarm, Evolutionary, and Memetic Computing, pp. 761–769, Springer, New York, NY, USA, 2012.
19. J. Salah Aldeen and R. A. Wahid, "A comparative study among some natural-inspired optimization algorithms," Journal of Education and Science. In press.
20. R. Rao and G. Waghmare, "Solving composite test functions using teaching-learning-based optimization algorithm," in Proceedings of the International Conference on Frontiers of Intelligent Computing: Theory and Applications (FICTA '13), vol. 199, pp. 395–403, Springer, 2013.
21. R. V. Rao, V. J. Savsani, and D. P. Vakharia, "Teaching-learning-based optimization: an optimization method for continuous non-linear large scale problems," Information Sciences, vol. 183, pp. 1–15, 2012.
22. J. Kennedy and R. Eberhart, "Particle swarm optimization," in Proceedings of the IEEE International Conference on Neural Networks, pp. 1942–1948, Western Australia, Australia, December 1995.
23. R. Storn and K. Price, "Differential evolution—a simple and efficient heuristic for global optimization over continuous spaces," Journal of Global Optimization, vol. 11, no. 4, pp. 341–359, 1997.
24. R. V. Rao, V. J. Savsani, and D. P. Vakharia, "Teaching-learning-based optimization: a novel method for constrained mechanical design optimization problems," Computer Aided Design, vol. 43, no. 3, pp. 303–315, 2011.
25. D. Karaboga, "An idea based on honey bee swarm for numerical optimization," Tech. Rep., Computer Engineering Department, Engineering Faculty, Erciyes University, Kayseri, Turkey, 2005.
26. X.-S. Yang, "Firefly algorithms for multimodal optimization," in Stochastic Algorithms: Foundations and Applications, pp. 169–178, Springer, New York, NY, USA, 2009.
27. E. Uzlu, M. Kanka, A. Akpinar, T. Dede, and A. Akpınar, "Estimates of energy consumption in Turkey using neural networks with the teachinglearning-based optimization algorithm," Energy, 2014.
28. H. Malek, M. M. Ebadzadeh, and M. Rahmati, "Three new fuzzy neural networks learning algorithms based on clustering, training error and genetic algorithm," Applied Intelligence, vol. 37, no. 2, pp. 280–289, 2012.
29. L. A. Zadeh, "Fuzzy sets," Information and Computation, vol. 8, pp. 338–353, 1965.
30. M. M. Gupta and D. H. Rao, "On the principles of fuzzy neural networks," Fuzzy Sets and Systems, vol. 61, no. 1, pp. 1–18, 1994.
31. T. Hassanzadeh, K. Faez, and G. Seyfi, "A speech recognition system based on Structure Equivalent Fuzzy Neural Network trained by Firefly algorithm," in Proceedings of the International Conference on Biomedical Engineering (ICoBE '12), pp. 63–67, IEEE, Penang, Malaysia, February 2012.
32. A. K. Alexandridis and A. D. Zapranis, "Wavelet neural networks: a practical guide," Neural Networks, vol. 42, pp. 1–27, 2013.
33. R. H. Abiyev and O. Kaynak, "Fuzzy wavelet neural networks for identification and control of dynamic

plants—a novel structure and a comparative study," IEEE Transactions on Industrial Electronics, vol. 55, no. 8, pp. 3133–3140, 2008.

34. R. H. Abiyev and O. Kaynak, "Identification and control of dynamic plants using fuzzy wavelet neural networks," in Proceedings of the IEEE International Symposium on Intelligent Control (ISIC '08), pp. 1295–1301, September 2008.

35. V. Toĝan, "Design of planar steel frames using teaching-learning based optimization," Engineering Structures, vol. 34, pp. 225–232, 2012.

36. A. Baykasoğlu, A. Hamzadayi, and S. Y. Köse, "Testing the performance of teaching-learning based optimization (TLBO) algorithm on combinatorial problems: flow shop and job shop scheduling cases,"Information Sciences. An International Journal, vol. 276, pp. 204–218, 2014.

37. R. V. Rao and G. Waghmare, "A comparative study of a teachinglearning-based optimization algorithm on multi-objective unconstrained and constrained functions," Journal of King Saud University—Computer and Information Sciences, 2013.

38. W. Cheng, F. Liu, and L. Li, "Size and geometry optimization of Trusses using teaching-learning-based optimization," International Journal of Optimization in Civil Engineering, vol. 3, no. 3, pp. 431–444, 2013.

39. R. V. Rao, V. J. Savsani, and J. Balic, "Teaching-learning-based optimization algorithm for unconstrained and constrained real-parameter optimization problems," Engineering Optimization, vol. 44, no. 12, pp. 1447–1462, 2012.

40. R. V. Rao, V. D. Kalyankar, and G. Waghmare, "Parameters optimization of selected casting processes using teaching-learning-based optimization algorithm," Applied Mathematical Modelling, 2014.

41. G. Waghmare, "Comments on "a note on teaching-learning-based optimization algorithm"," Information Sciences, vol. 229, pp. 159–169, 2013.

42. P. V. Babu, S. C. Satapathy, M. K. Samantula, P. K. Patra, and B. N. Biswal, "Teaching learning based optimized mathematical model for data classification problems," in Proceedings of the International Conference on Frontiers of Intelligent Computing: Theory and Applications (FICTA '13), pp. 487–496, Springer, 2013.

43. R. Venkata Rao and V. D. Kalyankar, "Parameter optimization of modern machining processes using teaching-learning-based optimization algorithm," Engineering Applications of Artificial Intelligence, vol. 26, no. 1, pp. 524–531, 2013.

44. D. Robert, "V.A. Medical Center, Long Beach and Cleveland Clinic Foundation: Robert Detrano, M.D., Ph.DDonor: David W. Aha," vol. 714, pp. 856-879, 1988.

45. N. A. Baykan and N. Yilmaz, "A mineral classification system with multiple artificial neural network using k-fold cross validation," Mathematical and Computational Applications, vol. 16, no. 1, pp. 22–30, 2011.

46. S. T. Ishikawa and V. C. Gulick, "An automated mineral classifier using Raman spectra," Computers and Geosciences, vol. 54, pp. 259–268, 2013.

CHAPTER 16 HYBRID NEURAL NETWORK ARCHITECTURE FOR ON-LINE LEARNING

Yuhua Chen, Subhash Kak, and Lei Wang

Keywords: Neural Networks, Instantaneously Trained Networks, Back-Propagation, On-Line Learning

INTRODUCTION

On-line learning requires the learning of the mode or context, out of a set of many, within which the timevarying system is evolving. A few examples of timevarying systems are: Aircraft during flight since the configurations of control surfaces as well as flight conditions and the weight of the aircraft are continually changing; the human vocal tract, as the shape of the vocal organs gets modified in the production of different vocalizations; electric or computer networks which may have different modes of behavior depending on the time of the day; and the financial system which changes according to the investor sentiment. In this paper, we consider such non-standard pattern recognition and discovery problems where statistical techniques and conventional neural networks are not convenient to use because of their slow speed.

Pattern discovery may be based on statistical methods [1,2] or on neural networks. The currently researched techniques include various kinds of neural networks [3], principal-component analysis [4], principal-component regression [4], partial least-squares regression [5], and combinatorial methods [6]. The Vapnik-Chervonenkis dimension [1] quantifies the ease of learning categories from small data sets, and if the dimension is finite, machine learning of a certain kind can be efficiently done. The time-varying nature of the data sets that we wish to consider here precludes this approach. Machine intelligence that is based on brain models has stressed the use of neural networks [7] that learn from a training set and then generalize on new input data. However, it has been argued [8,9] that such models miss on the short-term learning component of biological systems which is a very important component in adaptation to changing environment.

Biological systems operate in time-changing environments, and they are especially good at learning in such conditions. Biological learning appears to be at the basis of the capacity of biological systems to adapt to timevarying environments [10,11]. The learning components of biological systems may be divided into three types: sensory, short-term and long-term [12]. The sensory component provides immediate simple reactions to certain changes in the environment. One example of the sensory component is human reflex, which is almost instant in response to stimulus. The long-term learning component is based on experiences gained over periods of time. The short-term learning stands in between the sensory and long-term learning components, and is capable of performing more complex learning tasks than the sensory component while being able to adapt to the changing environment quickly.

The interplay among these biological learning components appears to provide to the organism the capacity to operate in uncertain environments. In addition, two cognitive processes that help in preventing overloading are sensory gating (by which the brain adjusts its response to stimuli) and selective attention (which allows the brain to concentrate on one aspect to the exclusion of others). This is seen, for example, in the driving of a car, where the driver may not be paying total attention to the road in ordinary circumstances. But when the driving conditions are difficult, a different center takes over the driving completely. The first of the two cases may be ascribed to long-term learning and the second to short-term learning.

Citation: Y. Chen, S. Kak and L. Wang, "Hybrid Neural Network Architecture for On-Line Learning," Intelligent Information Management, Vol. 2 No. 4, 2010, pp. 253-261. doi: 10.4236/iim.2010.23030.

In this paper, we propose a hybrid architecture for on-line learning of a time-varying system that is inspired by biological learning. The proposed hybrid architecture employs a surface learning component which can adapt to quick changes in system conditions, as well as a deep learning component which is highly accurate to minimize errors within the same regime of operation. A high level cognitive agent monitors the outputs from the surface learning and deep learning components, and automatically generates desirable system outputs.

We show that the proposed approach provides much better performance compared to traditional approaches. The proposed model provides a framework which may lead to flexible intelligence that is able to adapt to changing environment quickly. It will be helpful for processing of information associated with complex "intelligent" tasks in the real world with dynamic and intentional phenomena in the presence of uncertainty about the environment. Specifically, we will be able to explore novel and hybrid methods that extend the breadth of reasoning to include uncertain and dynamic environments, and also consider the performance with interacting agents.

The rest of the paper is organized as follows. Section 2 describes the proposed hybrid system architecture. Section 3 discusses some candidate components in building the hybrid system. Section 4 evaluates the performance of the proposed hybrid system. We conclude our work in Section 5.

HYBRID SYSTEM ARCHITECTURE FOR ON-LINE LEARNING

The proposed hybrid system can be applied to a broad range of applications such as function approximation, time series prediction, and pattern classification. Each of these areas naturally covers many specific applications. For example, time series prediction may be applied to financial or signal data, and pattern recognition includes application to engineering, military, or medical systems. In this section, we describe the general framework of the proposed hybrid system architecture that enables fast and accurate on-line learning of a time-varying system.

Figure 1 shows the proposed hybrid system architecture, which consists of a surface learning agent, a deep learning agent, and a cognitive agent. In the hybrid system architecture, the surface learning agent and the deep learning agent work in parallel in responding to the changes of the environment. In particular, the surface learning agent picks up the short-term structure of the information signal, and performs quick analysis to respond to the stimulus. The deep learning agent seeks out long-term structure of the information, and abstracts longer correlations present within the system. The high level cognitive agent monitors the environment, as well as the decisions made by the surface and deep learning agents, and automatically generates the most desirable system output based on the situation. The switching between the deep and the surface learning agents may be associated with hysteresis to introduce smoothness in the transition.

Consider the system shown in Figure 2 where the input $X(t)$ is generated by a random switching between several random processes $\{X_i(t), i = 1,\ldots,N\}$; S is a dynamic system; and $Y(t)$ is the output random process. The objective is to predict the realization $Y(t)$ of the output process from its past values.

The motivation for solving this problem is the consideration of real world processes where the input is time varying in such a manner that it is best represented as a series of different random processes. For an agent that wishes to predict $Y(t)$ based on its past, it is essential to learn which of the N X_is is at the input, where it is assumed that the statistical characteristics of the X_is are known so that its prediction can be made relatively easily. The problem arises from the fact that the input signal switches between different processes and therefore no single statistical technique will work at the output all the time.

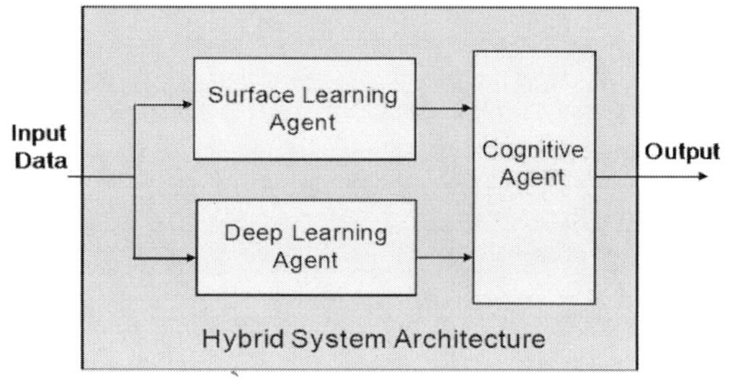

Figure 1: Hybrid system architecture.

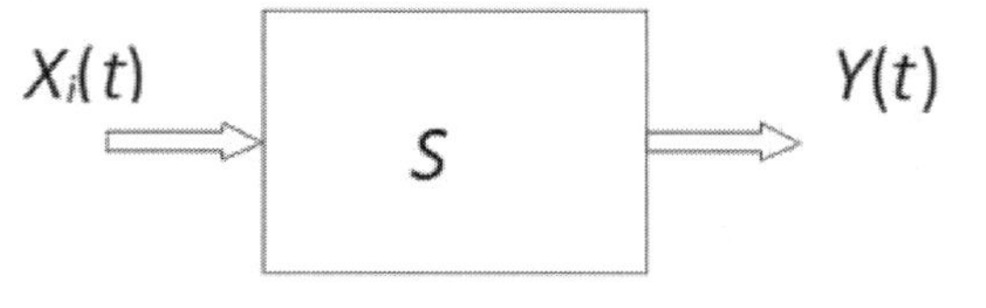

Figure 2: System under consideration.

We divide the problem of prediction into two components: deep learning and surface learning. Deep learning operates within the regime of a specific index i of X_i and provides the best performance with respect to some criterion (such as minimization of RMS errors). One would expect that it would take the deep learning agent some amount of time to adapt to the statistical characteristics of the signal at the input and, therefore, it would be assumed that the switching between the modes takes place slower than this characteristic time. Surface learning operates best during the transition regime between, let us say, the indices i and j.

The dichotomy of the surface and deep learning agents in the proposed hybrid system can find its success in linguistics [13]. For example, in speech or text understanding, without knowing the context, a narrative may appear meaningless. The syntax is provided by the surface structure, whereas the semantics come from the deep structure. Clearly, the surface learning and deep learning agents in the proposed hybrid system is not quite identical to that of syntax and semantics, but it does constitute a step in this direction.

The role of the cognitive agent can be as simple as making a binary decision of selecting the system output from either the surface learning agent or the deep learning agent, or as complex as synthesizing the outputs of the two learning agents into a high level of intelligence. For example, the cognitive agent in the hybrid architecture monitors the errors produced by the surface learning agent and the deep learning agent, and automatically switches the system output according to system conditions. When the system function changes suddenly, the surface learning agent is able to catch up with the changes quickly while the deep learning agent requires more time to produce results with acceptable outputs. In this case, the cognitive agent will use the outputs produced by the surface learning agent. When the system stabilizes in a certain operational region, the deep learning agent will eventually catch up and produces outputs with more accuracy. When this happens, the cognitive agent will select the outputs from the deep learning agent instead. As a result, the hybrid architecture can respond to the changing system quickly and accurately.

BUILDING BLOCKS OF HYBRID ARCHITECTURE

The deep learning agent in the hybrid system must have the property of disregarding quick changes or transients in the input. In other words, it must learn such exemplars that are typical of an established mode. The deep learning agent is, therefore, not very good at determining the transition between modes and this is the reason why it takes more time than an agent that is focused on learning quick changes in the signal. In the biological domain, the deep learning agent is the collection of long-term learning mechanisms.

Several neural networks listed in the section on historical notes of [14] could serve as the deep learning agent. In this paper, we use the multi-layer perceptron with back-propagation as the deep learning agent because it is able to learn the long-term characteristics of the patterns most efficiently [15]. For the rest of the section, we focus on the choices of surface learning agent, which is the most challenging component in designing in the hybrid system.

The surface learning agent needs to be able to learn the changed system function instantaneously or nearinstantaneously. The performance of the surface learning agent directly affects the performance of the hybrid system. We describe two candidates for the surface learning agent in detail as follows.

Corner Classification (CC) Networks

The corner classification (CC) network is based on the idea of phonological loop and the visio-spatial sketchpad. It was proposed by Kak in three variations [8,9]. These and its more advanced variants are also known as the class of Kak neural networks. There are four versions of the CC technique, represented by CC1 through CC4. The concept of radius of generalization was introduced in CC3 and thus this neural network overcame the generalization problem that plagued the earlier CC2 network. Each node in the network acts as a filter for the training sample. The filter is realized by making it act as a hyper plane to separate the corner of the n-dimensional cube represented by the training vector and hence the name corner-classification technique. The CC4 is shown to be better than the other networks in the CC category [16], and is described in detail as follows.

CC4 uses a feedforward network architecture consisting of three layers of neurons as shown inFigure 3. The number of input neurons is equal to the length of input patterns or vectors plus one, the additional neuron being the bias neuron, which has a constant input of 1. The number of hidden neurons is equal to the number of training samples, with each hidden neuron corresponding to one training example. The last node of the input layer is set to one to act as a bias to the hidden layer. The binary step function is used as the activation function for both the hidden and output neurons. The output of the activation function is 1 if summation is positive and zero otherwise.

Input and output weights are determined as follows. For each training vector presented to the network, if an input neuron receives a 1, its weight to the hidden neuron corresponding to this training vector is set to 1. Otherwise, it is set to –1. The bias neuron is treated differently.

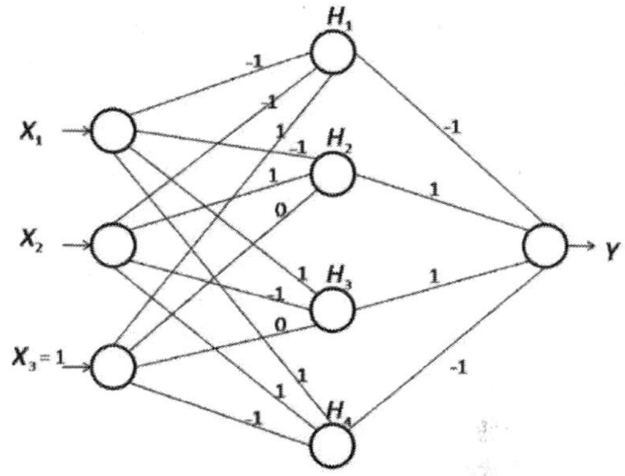

Figure 3: CC4 network architecture for learning the XOR function.

If s is the number of l's in the training vector, excluding the bias input, and the desired radius of generalization is r, then the weight between the bias neuron and the hidden neuron corresponding to this training vector is r –s + 1. Thus, for any training vector x_i of length n including the bias, the input layer weights are assigned according to the following equation:

$$w_i[j] = \begin{cases} 1 & \text{if } x_i[j]=1 \\ -1 & \text{if } x_i[j]=0 \\ r-s+1 & \text{if } j=n. \end{cases}$$

The weights in the output layer are equal to 1 if the output value is 1, and –1 if the output value is 0. This amounts to learning both the input class and its complement and thus instantaneous. The radius of generalization, r can be seen by considering the all-zero input vectors for which $w_{n+1} = r + 1$. The choice of r will depend on the nature of generalization sought. Figure 3 presents a network for the implementation of the XOR example using CC4. Since the weights are 1, –1, or 0, it is clear that actual computations are minimal. In the general case, the only weight that can be greater in magnitude than 1 is the one associated with the bias neuron.

Fast Classification (FC) Network

Here we present another candidate for the surface learning agent, the fast classification (FC) network [17,18], which is a generalization of the CC networks. Whereas the CC networks perform nearest-neighbor generalization of data as binary vectors, the FC network does the same by considering analog-valued vectors. The FC network uses some appropriate metric to compare the stored vectors of the data to the input data. It depends on the concept of "nearest neighbor" for generalization and consists of three layers—an input layer, a hidden layer and an output layer.

The input data is normalized and presented as input vector x. The hidden neuron is represented by the weight vector w_i and its elements are represented by $w_{i,j}$, i = 1,2,…,S and j = 1,2,…,R, where R is the number of components of the input vector and S is the number of hidden neurons (the number of training samples). The output is the dot product of the vectors μ and u, where μ is the vector at the output of the rule base and u is the vector of weights in the output layer as shown inFigure 4. This network can be trained with just two passes of the samples, the first pass assigns the synaptic weights and the second pass determines the radius of generalization for each training sample by fuzzification of the location of the each training sample and by assigning fuzzy membership functions of output classes to new input vectors.

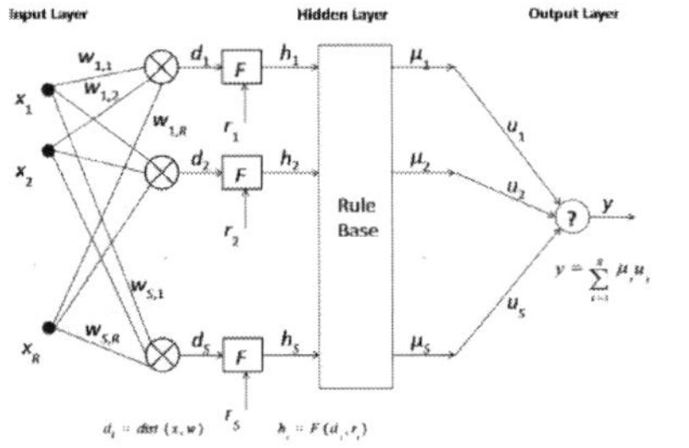

Figure 4: FC network architecture.

The network behaves as a 1NN classifier and a kNN classifier (1- or knearest neighbor classifier) according to whether the input vector falls within the radius of generalization of a training vector or not. The radius of generalization acts as a switch between the 1NN classifier and the kNN classifier. The FC network meets the specifications set by traditional function approximation that every data point is covered in the given training sample and also Cover's theorem on separability of patterns [19]. In a practical case, the k values are determined by the sample size and can be a fraction of the sample size. If k = S then the FC network operating as a kNN classifier can be viewed as a RBF network [14] provided that the membership function is chosen to be Gaussian distributed. On the other hand, if the weighting function is chosen to be the membership function, the FC classifier can be considered as kernel regression [18]. As in the CC networks, this network requires as many hidden neurons as the number of training samples (although the number of hidden neurons could be trimmed to a certain extent).

As mentioned before, the CC networks work on binary data, which requires quantization of input values. If that is a constraint one wishes to avoid for certain reasons, one can use FC networks, which are a generalization of CC networks and they work on continuous valued data. FC networks require a comparison with stored information in one pass, and, therefore, they are not quite instantaneous, but the calculation can be done in time that could be smaller than the time instant at which the next data comes in.

PERFORMANCE EVALUATION

In this section, we evaluate the performance of the hybrid system using several benchmarks.

Mackey-Glass Time Series Prediction

Time series prediction is widely used in financial data for prediction of stocks, currency, interest rates and engineering such as electric load demand. The network is trained by historical data set with time index and the network predicts the future values based on past values. Mackey-Glass (MG) time series is a chaotic time series based on Mackey-Class differential equation,

$$\frac{dx(t)}{dt} = -B \times x(t) + a \times \frac{x(t-D)}{1 + x(t-D)^{c}}$$

where the choice of D has important influence on its chaotic behavior. In most research work, D is set to be 17 or 30 because of the interesting quasi-periodic behaviors these two values present.

We investigate the system response of the hybrid system when the MG series migrates from parameter set 1 to parameter set 2. More specifically, the hybrid system is first trained to predict MG series with parameter set 1 (P1 = {A = 0.8, B=0.1, C=10, D=30}), and then the MG series with parameter set 2 (P2 = {A=0.8, B=0.1, C=10, D=17}). The sliding window is of size 6, and thus inputs consist of 6 consecutive points that are use to predict the very next point ahead:

$$x(k+1) = f(x(k), x(k-1), \ldots, x(k-5)) .$$

We obtained the raw data from the Working Group on Data Modeling Benchmarks (under IEEE Neural Networks Council Standards Committee). The first 3500 points in the initialization stage are not used for either training or testing. The next 1000 points are used for training and validation. Another 500 points are used for testing.

The performance of CC and FC are compared as the potential candidates for the surface learning agent. The multi-layer perceptron with back-propagation (BP) is used for the deep learning agent. We are interested in studying how CC, FC and BP will respond to the change of parameters in the MG series. We use the RMS error as the performance measure of the system response to the relearning process. In Figure 5, we observe that as the candidates for the surface learning agent, CC and FC has reduced RMS error almost instantaneously. On the other hand, it takes some time for the deep learning agent BP to converge to new parameters. However, in a long run, the RMS errors produced by the deep learning agent BP are smaller than the surface learning agent CC or FC. The vertical line marks the stopping point (at 1886-th adaptation cycle) which is determined by the RMS error validation set so as to avoid system over-fitting.

Since FC produces smaller RMS errors than CC, we use FC and BP as the surface learning agent and the deep learning agent in the hybrid system, respectively. The cognitive agent automatically selects the output from the surface learning agent FC once it detects that the system function changes, and switches to the deep learning agent BP after it catches up. The RMS error of the hybrid system is shown in Figure 6. It is clear that the hybrid system has enhanced performance, taking advantage of the surface learning agent and the deep learning agent.

CATS Benchmark Test

The CATS benchmark arises from the well-known Time Series Prediction Competition held in 2004, in which participants were invited to predict 100 missing points from a 5000-point artificial time series. This 100 data points were divided into 5 groups, each located in the position range 981-1000, 1981-2000, 2981-3000, 3981-4000 and 4981-5000, respectively. Participants proposed several prediction methods, linear as well as nonlinear and the winner suggests that good division of the problem into short-term prediction and long-term prediction lead to good result. Since we are interested in the system response of the hybrid system, we skip the input selection stage and only the use short-term prediction. The short-term prediction is known as $\hat{x}(t+1) = f(x(t), x(t-1), \ldots, x(t-W+1))$, where W indicates the window size.

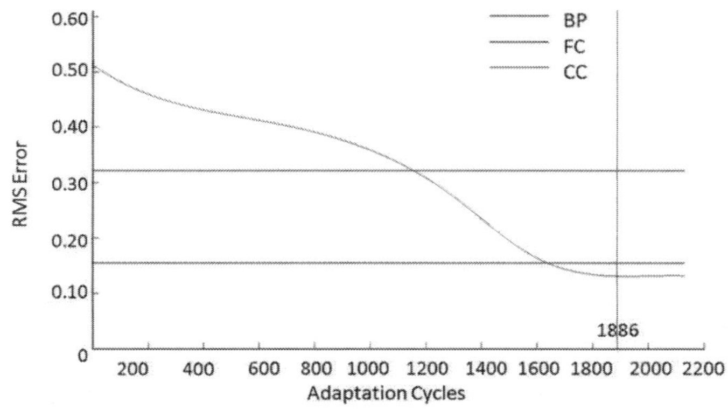

Figure 5: RMS errors vs. adaptation cycles.

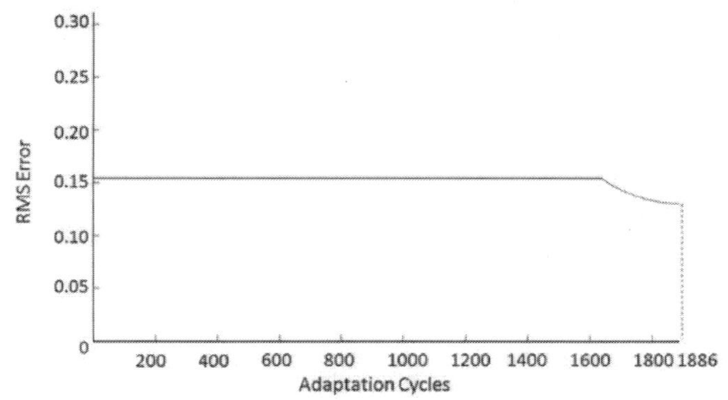

Figure 6: RMS error of the hybrid system.

Each time after a prediction is made, the oldest point in the window will be dropped and the newly predicted point is appended on the other side, becoming the current value to predict the next point. We use validation sets of 10 points (from the known points) to find the best window size, with which we train the final network. We first train the networks to learn points 1-980 and 1001-1980 to predict points 981-1000. Thereafter, based on the trained network, relearning is launched to learn another two segments 3001-3980 and 4001-4980. The system response during the relearning process is thus evaluated. In both cases, 10-point validation sets are utilized, and they are selected to be points 971-980 and 3971-3980, which are adjacent to the to-be-predicted points 981-1000 and 3981-4000, respectively. CC precision is fixed at 256 and window size is selected to be 30 based on the results of validation sets.

Figure 7 plots the E1 errors for points 3981-4000 produced by BP, CC and FC during the relearning process. The BP result is obtained by averaging the results of 10 different trials. Note that the average stopping point for BP is at the 502ed adaptation cycle determined by the validation set. As expected, FC produces good results almost instantly. BP converges slowly but achieves better results eventually. The large error produced by CC is due to the precision. Since FC is consistently better than CC, we use FC as the surface learning agent and BP as the deep learning agent for the hybrid system. The hybrid system switches automatically between the surface learning agent FC and the deep learning agent BP in the relearning process based on whose error is lower for the previously predicted values. The E_1 error of the hybrid system is shown in Figure 8.

$$\frac{\sum_{t=3981}^{4000} (y_t - \hat{y}_t)^2}{100}$$

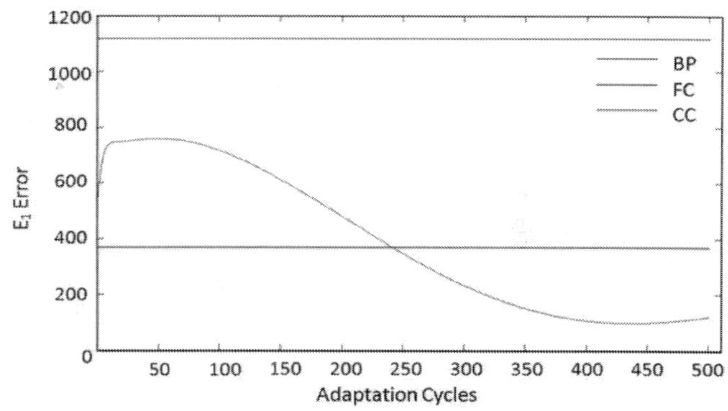

Figure 7: E_1 errors during the relearning process.

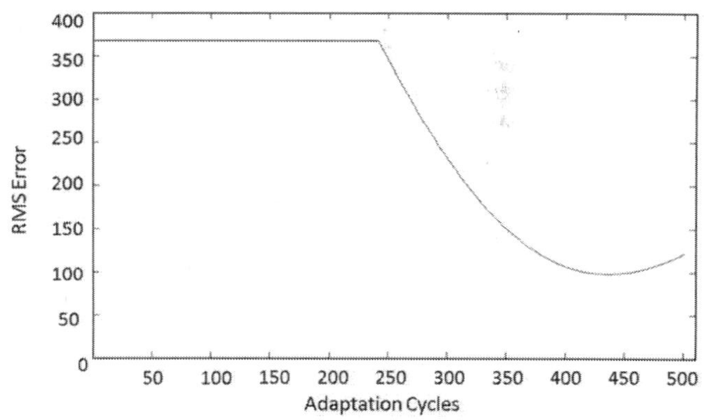

Figure 8: E1 error produced by the hybrid system.

This further demonstrates the advantages of the hybrid system.

Smooth Function Approximation

The problem in smooth function approximation is to implement a function, F(x), which approximates an unknown smooth function, f(x), with a priori as the input-output pairs in a Euclidian sense for all inputs.

Again we use the CC and FC as the potential candidates for the surface learning agent, and BP as the deep learning agent. The hybrid system is first trained to approximate a smooth function with parameter set P1, and then relearns the function as the parameter set changes to P2. The objective smooth function is selected to be the probability density function (pdf) of the Multivariate Normal Distribution,

$$f_X(x_1,x_2)=\frac{1}{2\pi|\Sigma|^{1/2}}\exp(-\frac{1}{2}(x-\mu)^T\Sigma^{-1}(x-\mu))$$

The configurations of the two parameter sets are shown in Table 1. The training set is constructed by uniformly sampling 900 points in the 2-D input space, and another 1600 points make up the testing set.

To understand how the deep learning agent and the surface learning agent in the hybrid system respond to the changed function, we plot a series of transitional plots as follows. The actual functions with parameter set P1 and P2 are plotted in Figures 9 and 10, respectively. Figures 11-13 capture the relearning processes for the deep learning agent BP. It can be observed that the deep learning agent BP adapts from parameter set P1 to P2 gradually. Figure 14 and Figure 15 show the approximation of the surface learning agent candidates CC and FC after instantaneous training, respectively.

The RMS errors produced by the BP, CC and FC during the relearning processes are plotted in Figure 16. As we can see from the figure, it takes a considerable number of adaptation cycles for the deep learning agent BP to catch up with the surface learning agent CC or FC. Since FC produces smaller RMS errors, we choose FC as the surface learning agent for smooth function approximation. The RMS errors of the hybrid system are plotted in Figure 17.

Table 1: Smooth function parameter configuration

P1	*P2*
μ={0,0}	μ={−0.2,0.7}
Σ={0.8 0.2;0.2 0.1}	Σ={0.25 0.3;0.3 1}

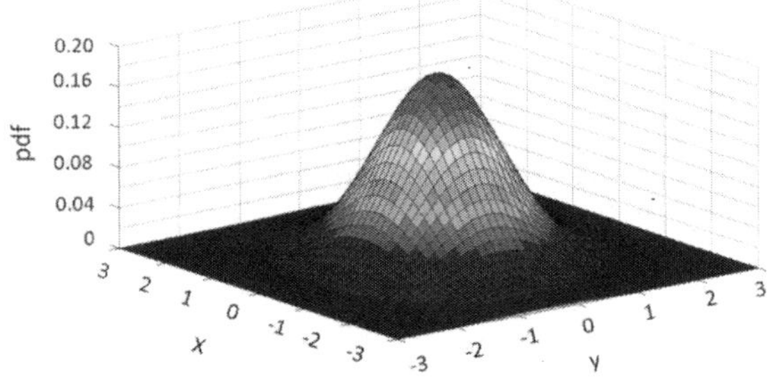

Figure 9: Actual smooth function with parameter P1.

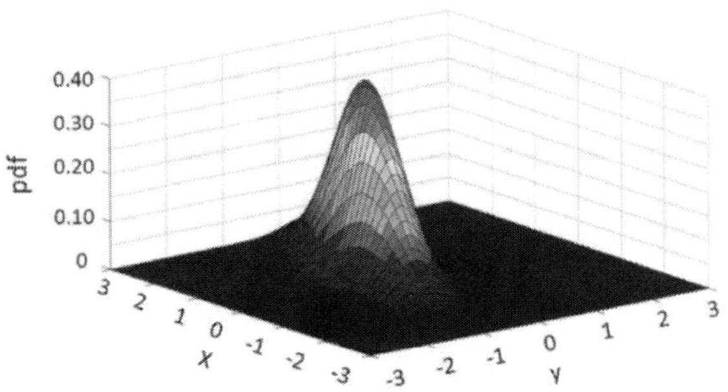

Figure 10: Actual smooth function with parameter P2.

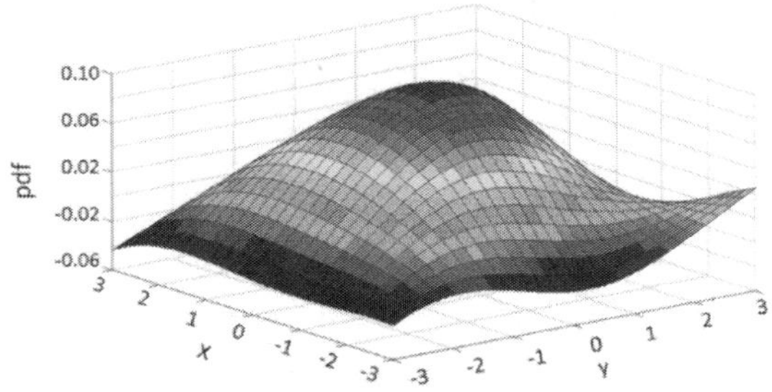

Figure 11: BP shape after 1 adaptation cycles.

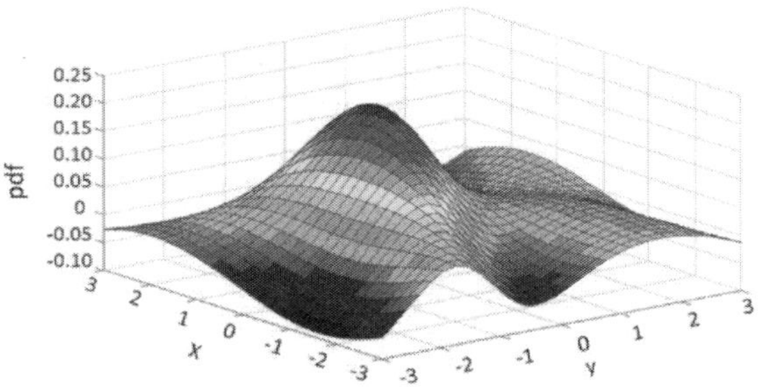

Figure 12: BP shape after 5001 relearning adaptation cycles.

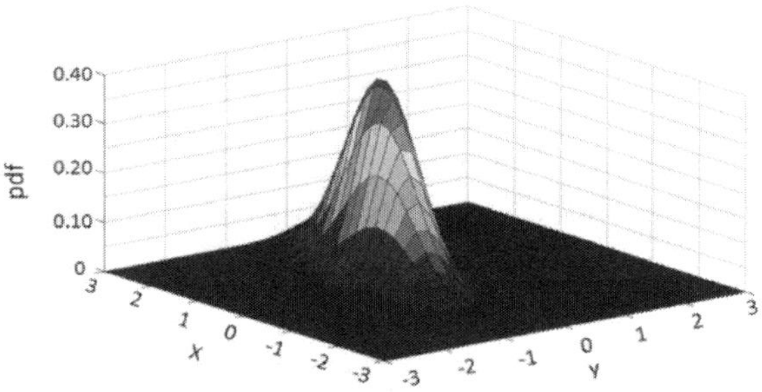

Figure 13: BP shape after 300003 relearning adaptation cycles.

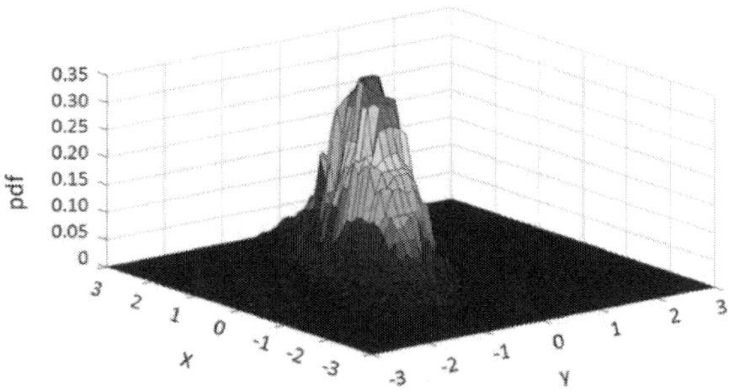

Figure 14: CC approximation of P2 after instantaneous training.

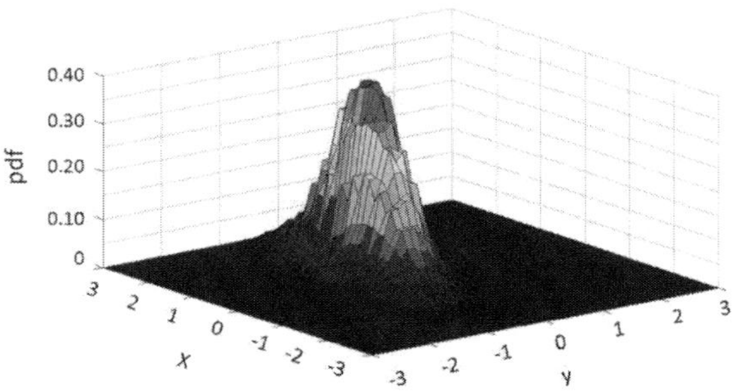

Figure 15: FC approximation of P2 after instantaneous training.

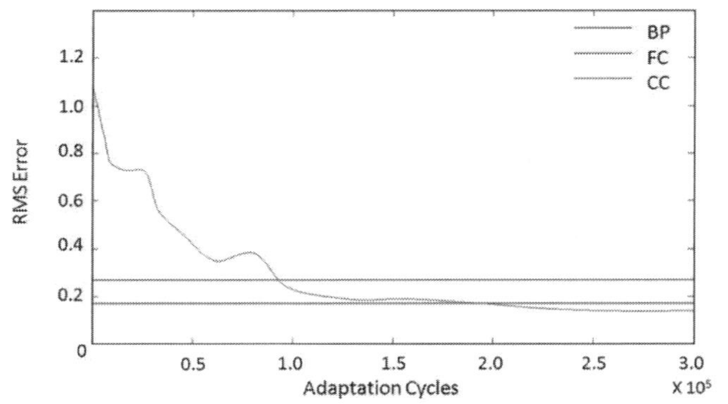

Figure 16: RMS errors vs. adaptation cycles.

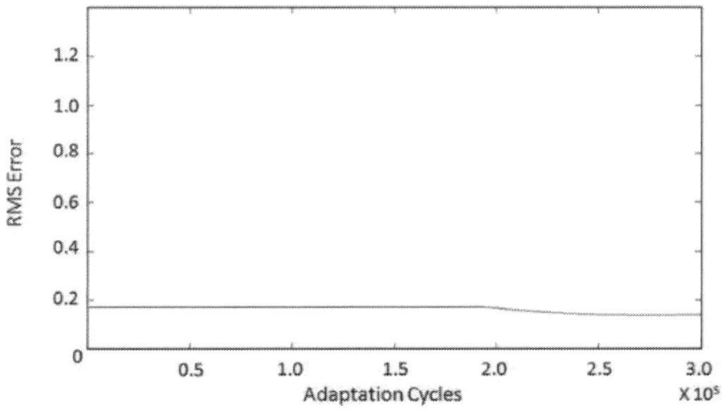

Figure 17: RMS of the hybrid architecture.

CONCLUSIONS

This paper has proposed a hybrid neural network architecture that uses two kinds of neural networks simultaneously: 1) a surface learning network that can quickly adapt to new modes of operation; and, 2) a deep learning, accurate network for use within a specific regime of operation. This may be viewed as the development of a bicameral learning scheme that is inspired by the dual nature of biological memory, in which one agent learns quickly and the other more slowly, corresponding to short-term and long-term memory. It makes it meaningful to look at other aspects of these two aspects of biological memory that may be of relevance to machine intelligence.

The two networks of the hybrid architecture platform should not be seen as arbitrary submodules and, therefore, our method represents an approach that has a pre-defined structure to it. Such a hybrid architecture can be based on different classes of learning systems although in this paper we have considered CC and FC fast learning networks on the one hand and back-propagation networks on the other.

The performance of the hybrid architecture has been compared with that of multi-layer perceptron with back-propagation and the CC and FC networks for chaotic time-series prediction, the CATS benchmark test, and smooth function approximation. It has been shown that the hybrid architecture provides a superior performance based on a RMS error criterion.

We expect the applications of our hybrid neural network architecture to problems in finance, control, timeseries prediction, and economic forecasting.

REFERENCES

1. V. N. Vapnik, "The Nature of Statistical Learning Theory," Springer-Verlag, Berlin, 1995.
2. M. J. Kearns and U. V. Vazirani, "An Introduction to Computational Learning Theory," MIT Press, Cambridge, 1994.
3. C. G. Looney, "Pattern Recognition Using Neural Networks," Oxford University Press, New York, 1997.
4. I. T. Joliffe, "Principal Component Analysis," SpringerVerlag, Berlin, 2002.
5. I. Frank and J. Friedman, "A Statistical View of Some Chemometrics Regression Tools," Technometrics, Vol. 35, No. 2, 1993, pp. 109-148.
6. C. H. Papadimitrou and K. Steiglitz, "Combinatorial Optimization," Dover Publications, New York, 1998.
7. C. M. Bishop, "Neural Networks for Pattern Recognitio," Oxford University Press, Oxford, 1996.
8. S. Kak, "Three Languages of the Brain: Quantum, Reorganizational, and Associative," In K. Pribram and J. King, Eds., Learning and Self-Organization, Mahwah, Lawrence Erlbaum Associates, 1996, pp. 185-219.
9. S. Kak, "Faster Web Search and Prediction Using Instantaneously Trained Neural Networks," IEEE Intelligent Systems, Vol. 14, No. 6, 1999, pp. 79-82.
10. S. Kak, "Stream Computing," arXiv: 0801.1336, 2008.
11. S. Kak, "Artificial and Biological Intelligence," ACM Ubiquity, Vol. 6, No. 42, 2005, pp. 1-20.
12. E. R. Kandel, "In Search of Memory: The Emergence of A New Science of Mind," W. W. Norton, New York, 2007.
13. N. Chomsky, "Syntactic Structures," Mouton, 1957.
14. S. Haykin, "Neural Networks," Prentice-Hall, Upper Saddle River, 1999.
15. A. R. Barron, "Universal Approximation Bounds for Superpositions of A Sigmoidal Function," IEEE Transactions on Information Theory, Vol. 39, No. 3, 1993, pp. 930-945.
16. K. W. Tang and S. Kak, "A New Corner Classification Approach to Neural Network Training," Circuits, Systems, Signal Processing, Vol. 17, No. 4, 1998, pp. 459-469.
17. S. Kak, "A Class of Instantaneously Trained Neural Networks," Information Sciences, Vol. 148, 2002, pp. 97-102.
18. K. W. Tang and S. Kak, "Fast Classification Networks for Signal Processing," Circuits, Systems, Signal Processing, Vol. 21, No. 2, 2002, pp. 207-224.
19. T. M. Cover, "Geometrical and Statistical Properties of Systems of Linear Inequalities with Applications in Pattern Recognition," IEEE Transactions on Electronic Computers, Vol. 14, No. 3, 1965, pp. 326-334.

SECTION IV: MODELING AND CONTROL ALGORITHMS

CHAPTER 17

COURSE CONTROL OF UNDERACTUATED SHIP BASED ON NONLINEAR ROBUST NEURAL NETWORK BACKSTEPPING METHOD

Junjia Yuan, Hao Meng, Qidan Zhu, and Jiajia Zhou

INTRODUCTION

Tracking control performance for surface vessel along the predefined route has been an essential control problem for marine autopilot system design, and it has received considerable attractions from control community. In 1922, proportional-integral-derivative (PID) autopilot for ship steering was presented by Nicholas Minosky [1]. PID controller greatly improved the performance of autopilots. Until the 1980s almost all makes of autopilots were based on these controllers. One challenge for tracking control of surface vessel based on above method is that the systems are often underactuated by the sway motion due to weight, complexity, and efficiency considerations and exhibit nonholonomic constraints, which meets Brocket's theorem that there is no continuous or even smooth time-invariant state feedback law that can stabilize the system to the origin [2]. Another challenge is that the vessel model itself exhibits severe nonlinear characteristic and model uncertainties induced by the ocean environment [3, 4].

For the ship with nonlinear maneuvering characteristics and without uncertainties, a state feedback linearization control law was designed [5], while feedback linearization with saturation and slew rate limiting actuators was discussed [6]. Later, combined with a genetic algorithm, the backstepping method was employed to develop a nonlinear ship course controller by Witkowska and Smierzchalski [7], where the ship course parameters were automatically tuned to the optimal values with the aid of a genetic algorithm. Even considering the ship steering model with both constant parametric uncertainties and input disturbance with unknown bound, a robust adaptive nonlinear control law was presented based on projection approach and Lyapunov stability theory [8]. Recently many papers have tackled these problems based on Lyapunov theory [9–12]. In [13–15] a global tracking controller for underactuated ship is addressed with nonzero off-diagonal terms, the reference trajectory is generated by using a virtual target guidance algorithm, and the controller designed is facilitated by an introduction of changing the ship outputs, several coordinate transformations, and backstepping method. And the controller design is heavily depending on accurate dynamic model; the robustness against disturbance has not been addressed. A method using backstepping adaptive dynamical sliding mode control is presented for path following control of USV in [16], the control system takes account of the modeling errors and disturbances, and simplified tracking error dynamics are obtained by assuming that the sway velocity is small which can be neglected in the controller design and only for straight line path tracking can be achieved. The LOS based guidance law is also used in the controller design which causes the complexity of computing high-order derivative of virtual control. In [17], a transformation of vessel kinematics to the Serret-Frenet frame is introduced by exploring an extra degree of freedom by controlling explicitly the progression rate of the virtual target along the path and overcomes the major singular problem; approach angle is introduced for controller design via backstepping method. Neural networks are introduced to enhance system stability and transient performance, which can handle the known dynamics and uncertainties of systems well [18–20]. Particularly in [12] a single hidden layer neural network (SHLNN) is adopted to obtain the adaptive signal

Citation: Junjia Yuan, Hao Meng, Qidan Zhu, and Jiajia Zhou, "Course Control of Underactuated Ship Based on Nonlinear Robust Neural Network Backstepping Method," Computational Intelligence and Neuroscience, vol. 2016, Article ID 3013280, 11 pages, 2016. doi:10.1155/2016/3013280

online, but the choice of the single hidden layer neural network is limited by the number of hidden layer node selections that will affect the online learning speed and accuracy and cannot produce a better estimation effect on the fast changing disturbances.

Therefore, a solution to the course control of underactuated surface vessel is addressed in this paper. In view of the characteristics of the underactuated performance, the backstepping control method is used to deal with above problem. The direct adaptive neural network is adopted to design control law by using the RBF neural network to overcome the problem that the ideal virtual control cannot be used directly in practice. The weights of the neural network are updated by adaptive technique to guarantee the stability of the closed-loop system through Lyapunov stability theory. Simulation results are illustrated to verify the performance of the proposed adaptive neural network controller with good precision.

ADAPTIVE ROBUST NEURAL NETWORK CONTROLLER DESIGN

Problem Description

Consider the following nonlinear systems:

$$\begin{aligned} \dot{x}_i &= f_i(\bar{x}_i) + g_i(\bar{x}_i)x_{i+1} + d_i, \quad 1 \le i \le n-1, \\ \dot{x}_n &= f_n(\bar{x}_n) + g_n(\dot{x}_n)u + d_n, \quad n \ge 2, \\ y &= x_1, \end{aligned} \tag{1}$$

where $\bar{x}_i = [x_1, x_2,...,x_i]$ is system state, u is control input, and y is system output. The control objective is to design an adaptive neural network controller and make y track yd. yd meets the smooth bounded reference model as follows:

$$\begin{aligned} \dot{x}_{di} &= f_{di}(x_d), \quad 1 \le i \le m \\ y_d &= x_{d1}, \quad m \ge n, \end{aligned} \tag{2}$$

where $x_d = [x_{d1}, x_{d2}, \ldots, x_{dm}]^T \in R^m$ is state constant, $y_d \in R$ represents system output, and $f_{di}(\cdot)$, $i = 1, 2, \ldots, m$, denote nonlinear function, assuming that the reference model for each state is bounded as $x_d \in \Omega_d$, $\forall t \ge 0$.

Assumption 1. There is an unknown constant p_i^* to meet, $\forall(\bar{x}_n, t) \in R^n \times R^+$, $|d_i(\bar{x}_n, t)| \le p_i^* \rho_i(\bar{x}_i)$, and $\rho_i(\bar{x}_i)$, and $\rho_i(\bar{x}_i)$ is a known positive smooth function.

Direct Adaptive Neural Network Controller Design

In view of the problems and solutions described in the last section, the direct adaptive neural network controller for nonlinear systems with RBF neural network is chosen. Detailed design steps will be described in the following

Step 1. Let $z_1 = x_1 - x_{d1}$, $z_2 = x_2 - \alpha_1$, and then

$$\dot{z}_1 = f_1(x_1) + g_1(x_1)x_2 + d_1 - \dot{x}_{d1}. \tag{3}$$

Consider the following Lyapunov function:

$$V_1 = \frac{1}{2g_1(x_1)}z_1^2 + \frac{1}{2}\widetilde{W}_1^T\Gamma_1^{-1}\widetilde{W}_1, \tag{4}$$

where $\widetilde{W}_1 = \widehat{W}_1 - W_1^*$, W_1^* represents the ideal weight vector of neural network, $\widehat{W}_1$ represents the estimated value of the neural network weight vector, $\widetilde{W}_1$ represents the estimation error of weight vector, $\Gamma_1 = \Gamma_1^T > 0$ is the adaptive gain matrix, and the derivation of V_1 can be computed as

$$\begin{aligned} \dot{V}_1 &= \frac{z_1\dot{z}_1}{g_1(x_1)} + \frac{\dot{g}_1(x_1)z_1^2}{2g_1^2(x_1)} + \widetilde{W}_1^T\Gamma_1^{-1}\dot{\widehat{W}}_1 \\ &= \frac{z_1}{g_1(x_1)}\left(f_1(x_1) + g_1(x_1)x_2 + d_1 - \dot{x}_{d1}\right) \\ &\quad + \frac{\dot{g}_1(x_1)z_1^2}{2g_1^2(x_1)} + \widetilde{W}_1^T\Gamma_1^{-1}\dot{\widehat{W}}_1 \\ &= z_1\left(z_2 + \alpha_1 + \frac{f_1(x_1) - \dot{x}_{d1}}{g_1(x_1)}\right) + \frac{z_1 d_1}{g_1(x_1)} \\ &\quad + \frac{\dot{g}_1(x_1)z_1^2}{2g_1^2(x_1)} + \widetilde{W}_1^T\Gamma_1^{-1}\dot{\widehat{W}}_1. \end{aligned} \tag{5}$$

According to Assumption 1, we can get

$$\begin{aligned} \dot{V}_1 &\le z_1\left(z_2 + \alpha_1 + \frac{f_1(x_1) - \dot{x}_{d1}}{g_1(x_1)}\right) + \frac{z_1^2\rho_1^2}{2g_1^2(x_1)} + \frac{P_1^{*2}}{2} \\ &\quad + \frac{\dot{g}_1(x_1)z_1^2}{2g_1^2(x_1)} + \widetilde{W}_1^T\Gamma_1^{-1}\dot{\widehat{W}}_1 \\ &= z_1\left(z_2 + \alpha_1 + \frac{f_1(x_1) - \dot{x}_{d1}}{g_1(x_1)} + \frac{z_1\rho_1^2}{2g_1^2(x_1)}\right) + \frac{P_1^{*2}}{2} \\ &\quad + \frac{\dot{g}_1(x_1)z_1^2}{2g_1^2(x_1)} + \widetilde{W}_1^T\Gamma_1^{-1}\dot{\widehat{W}}_1. \end{aligned} \tag{6}$$

There is an ideal virtual feedback control law:

$$\alpha_1^* = -c_1z_1 - \left[\frac{f_1(x_1) - \dot{x}_{d1}}{g_1(x_1)} + \frac{z_1\rho_1^2}{2g_1^2(x_1)}\right], \tag{7}$$

where $_{c1} > 0$ is designed controller parameter

Because of the unknown smooth functions $f_1(x_1)$ and $g_1(x_1)$, we cannot actually get the ideal feedback control law α_1^*; from (7) we can see that the unknown part $(f_1(x_1) - \dot{x}_{d1})/g_1(x_1)$ is smooth function of x_1 and $\dot{x}_{d1}$, so that

$$\begin{aligned} h_1(Z_1) &\triangleq \frac{f_1(x_1) - \dot{x}_{d1}}{g_1(x_1)} + \frac{z_1\rho_1^2}{2g_1^2(x_1)}, \\ Z_1 &\triangleq [x_1, \dot{x}_{d1}]^T \subset R^2. \end{aligned} \tag{8}$$

RBF neural network $W_1^T S_1(Z_1)$ is used to approximate the unknown function $h_1(Z_1)$, and α_1^* can be expressed as

$$\alpha_1^* = -c_1z_1 - W_1^{*T}S_1(Z_1) - e_1, \tag{9}$$

where $|e_1| \le e_1^*$ is estimated error and meets $e_1^* > 0$.

Because W_1^* is unknown, the virtual control law is selected as follows:

$$\alpha_1 = -c_1z_1 - \widehat{W}_1^T S_1(Z_1) \tag{10}$$

and then

$$\begin{aligned} \dot{V}_1 &\le z_1z_2 - c_1z_1^2 + \frac{\dot{g}_1(x_1)z_1^2}{2g_1^2(x_1)} + z_1e_1 + \frac{P_1^{*2}}{2} \\ &\quad - \widetilde{W}_1^T S_1 z_1 + \widetilde{W}_1^T\Gamma_1^{-1}\dot{\widehat{W}}_1. \end{aligned} \tag{11}$$

Adaptive law can be chosen as follows:

$$\dot{\widehat{W}}_1 = \dot{\widetilde{W}}_1 = \Gamma_1 \left[S_1(Z_1) z_1 - \sigma_1 \widehat{W}_1 \right], \tag{12}$$

where $\sigma_1 > 0$ and then

$$\dot{V}_1 \leq z_1 z_2 - c_1 z_1^2 + \frac{\dot{g}_1(x_1) z_1^2}{2 g_1^2(x_1)} + z_1 e_1 + \frac{P_1^{*2}}{2} - \sigma_1 \widetilde{W}_1^T \widehat{W}_1. \tag{13}$$

Let $c_1 = c_{10} + c_{11}$, where $c_{10} > 0$ and $c_{11} > 0$, and then the upper equation becomes

$$\dot{V}_1 \leq z_1 z_2 - \left(c_{10} + \frac{\dot{g}_1}{2 g_1^2} \right) z_1^2 - c_{11} z_1^2 + z_1 e_1 + \frac{P_1^{*2}}{2} - \sigma_1 \widetilde{W}_1^T \widehat{W}_1. \tag{14}$$

According to the complete square formula,

$$\begin{aligned} -\sigma_1 \widetilde{W}_1^T \widehat{W}_1 &= -\sigma_1 \widetilde{W}_1^T \left(\widetilde{W}_1 + W_1^* \right) \\ &\leq -\sigma_1 \left\| \widetilde{W}_1 \right\|^2 + \sigma_1 \left\| \widetilde{W}_1 \right\| \left\| W_1^* \right\| \\ &\leq -\frac{\sigma_1 \left\| \widetilde{W}_1 \right\|^2}{2} + \frac{\sigma_1 \left\| W_1^* \right\|^2}{2}, \end{aligned}$$

$$-c_{11} z_1^2 + z_1 e_1 \leq -c_{11} z_1^2 + z_1 \left| e_1 \right| \leq \frac{e_1^2}{4 c_{11}} \leq \frac{e_1^{*2}}{4 c_{11}}. \tag{15}$$

Because $-(c_{10} + (\dot{g}_1/2g_1^2))z_1^2 \leq -(c_{10} - (g_{1d}/2g_{1m}^2))z_1^2$, we can make $(c_{10}^* \triangleq c_{10} - (g_{1d}/2g_{1m}^2)) > 0$ by choosing the appropriate c_{10} and obtain the following inequality:

$$\dot{V}_1 \leq z_1 z_2 - c_{10}^* z_1^2 - \frac{\sigma_1 \left\| \widetilde{W}_1 \right\|^2}{2} + \frac{\sigma_1 \left\| W_1^* \right\|^2}{2} + \frac{e_1^{*2}}{4 c_{11}} + \frac{P_1^{*2}}{2}. \tag{16}$$

The cross coupling $z_1 z_2$ in (16) will be eliminated in the next step.

Step 2. Let $z_2 = x_2 - \alpha_1$; then

$$\dot{z}_2 = f_2(\overline{x}_2) + g_2(\overline{x}_2) x_3 + d_2 - \dot{\alpha}_1. \tag{17}$$

From (10) we can see that α_1 is a function of x_1, x_d, and $\widehat{W}_1$, and $\dot{\alpha}_1$ can be written as

$$\begin{aligned} \dot{\alpha}_1 &= \frac{\partial \alpha_1}{\partial x_1} \dot{x}_1 + \frac{\partial \alpha_1}{\partial x_d} \dot{x}_d + \frac{\partial \alpha_1}{\partial \widehat{W}_1} \dot{\widehat{W}}_1 \\ &= \frac{\partial \alpha_1}{\partial x_1} \left(g_1(x_1) x_2 + f_1(x_1) \right) + \varphi_1, \end{aligned} \tag{18}$$

where $\phi_1 = (\partial\alpha_1/\partial x_d)\dot{x}_d + (\partial\alpha_1/\partial \widehat{W}_1)[\Gamma_1(S_1(Z_1)z_1 - \sigma_1 \widehat{W}_1)]$ can be calculated.

Consider the following Lyapunov function:

$$V_2 = V_1 + \frac{1}{2 g_2(\overline{x}_2)} z_2^2 + \frac{1}{2} \widetilde{W}_2^T \Gamma_2^{-1} \widetilde{W}_2, \tag{19}$$

where $\Gamma_2 = \Gamma_2^T > 0$ is an adaptive gain matrix.

Then the derivation of V_2 can be calculated as

$$\begin{aligned} \dot{V}_2 &= \dot{V}_1 + \frac{z_2 \dot{z}_2}{g_2(\overline{x}_2)} + \frac{\dot{g}_2(\overline{x}_2) z_2^2}{2 g_2^2(\overline{x}_2)} + \widetilde{W}_2^T \Gamma_2^{-1} \dot{\widehat{W}}_2 \\ &= \dot{V}_1 + \frac{z_2}{g_2(\overline{x}_2)} \left(f_2(\overline{x}_2) + g_2(\overline{x}_2) x_3 + d_2 - \dot{\alpha}_1 \right) \\ &\quad + \frac{\dot{g}_2(\overline{x}_2) z_2^2}{2 g_2^2(\overline{x}_2)} + \widetilde{W}_2^T \Gamma_2^{-1} \dot{\widehat{W}}_2 \\ &= \dot{V}_1 + z_2 \left(z_3 + \alpha_2 + \frac{f_2(\overline{x}_2) - \dot{\alpha}_1}{g_2(\overline{x}_2)} \right) + \frac{z_2 d_2}{g_2(\overline{x}_2)} \\ &\quad + \frac{\dot{g}_2(\overline{x}_2) z_2^2}{2 g_2^2(\overline{x}_2)} + \widetilde{W}_2^T \Gamma_2^{-1} \dot{\widehat{W}}_2. \end{aligned} \tag{20}$$

According to Assumption 1 we can get

$$\begin{aligned} \dot{V}_2 &\leq \dot{V}_1 + z_2 \left(z_3 + \alpha_2 + \frac{f_2(\overline{x}_2) - \dot{\alpha}_1}{g_2(\overline{x}_2)} \right) + \frac{z_2^2 \rho_2^2}{2 g_2^2(\overline{x}_2)} \\ &\quad + \frac{P_2^{*2}}{2} + \frac{\dot{g}_2(\overline{x}_2) z_2^2}{2 g_2^2(\overline{x}_2)} + \widetilde{W}_2^T \Gamma_2^{-1} \dot{\widehat{W}}_2 \\ &= \dot{V}_1 + z_2 \left(z_3 + \alpha_2 + \frac{f_2(\overline{x}_2) - \dot{\alpha}_1}{g_2(\overline{x}_2)} + \frac{z_2 \rho_2^2}{2 g_2^2(\overline{x}_2)} \right) \\ &\quad + \frac{P_2^{*2}}{2} + \frac{\dot{g}_2(\overline{x}_2) z_2^2}{2 g_2^2(\overline{x}_2)} + \widetilde{W}_2^T \Gamma_2^{-1} \dot{\widehat{W}}_2. \end{aligned} \tag{21}$$

There is an ideal feedback control law:

$$\alpha_2^* = -z_1 - c_2 z_2 - \left[\frac{f_2(\overline{x}_2) - \dot{\alpha}_1}{g_2(\overline{x}_2)} + \frac{z_2 \rho_2^2}{2 g_2^2(\overline{x}_2)} \right], \tag{22}$$

where $c_2 > 0$ is a designed controller parameter.

Because of the unknown smooth functions $f_2(\overline{x}_2)$ and $g_2(\overline{x}_2)$, we cannot actually get the ideal feedback control law α_2^*; from (22) we can see that the unknown part is a smooth function of $\overline{x}_2$ and $\dot{\alpha}_1$; let

$$h_2(Z_2) \triangleq \frac{f_2(\overline{x}_2) - \dot{\alpha}_1}{g_2(\overline{x}_2)} + \frac{z_2 \rho_2^2}{2 g_2^2(\overline{x}_2)}, \tag{23}$$

where $Z_2 \triangleq [\overline{x}_2^T, (\partial\alpha_1/\partial x_1), \phi_1]^T \subset R^4$. RBF neural network $W_2^T S_2(Z_2)$ is used to approximate the unknown function $h_2(Z_2)$, and α_2^* can be expressed as

$$\alpha_2^* = -z_1 - c_2 z_2 - W_2^{*T} S_2(Z_2) - e_2, \tag{24}$$

where W_2^* is expressed as the ideal constant weight vector and $|e_2| \leq e_2^*$ is the estimated error and meets $e_2^* > 0$.

Because W_2^* is unknown, select the following virtual control law:

$$\alpha_2 = -z_1 - c_2 z_2 - \widehat{W}_2^T S_2(Z_2), \tag{25}$$

where $\widehat{W}_2$ is the estimated value of W_2^* then

$$\begin{aligned} \dot{V}_2 &\leq \dot{V}_1 - z_1 z_2 + z_2 z_3 - c_2 z_2^2 + \frac{\dot{g}_2(\overline{x}_2) z_2^2}{2 g_2^2(\overline{x}_2)} + z_2 e_2 \\ &\quad + \frac{P_2^{*2}}{2} - \widetilde{W}_2^T S_2 z_2 + \widetilde{W}_2^T \Gamma_2^{-1} \dot{\widehat{W}}_2, \end{aligned} \tag{26}$$

where $\widetilde{W}_2 = \widehat{W}_2 - W_2^*$.

Adaptive law can be chosen as

$$\dot{\widehat{W}}_2 = \dot{\widetilde{W}}_2 = \Gamma_2 \left[S_2 (Z_2) z_2 - \sigma_2 \widehat{W}_2 \right], \tag{27}$$

where $\sigma_2 > 0$; then

$$\dot{V}_2 \le \dot{V}_1 - z_1 z_2 + z_2 z_3 - c_2 z_2^2 + \frac{\dot{g}_2 (\overline{x}_2) z_2^2}{2 g_2^2 (\overline{x}_2)} + z_2 e_2 + \frac{P_2^{*2}}{2} - \sigma_2 \widetilde{W}_2^T \widehat{W}_2. \tag{28}$$

Let $c_2 = c_{20} + c_{21}$, c_{20}, $c_{21} > 0$; then the upper equation becomes

$$\dot{V}_2 \le \dot{V}_1 - z_1 z_2 + z_2 z_3 - \left(c_{20} + \frac{\dot{g}_2 (\overline{x}_2)}{2 g_2^2 (\overline{x}_2)} \right) z_2^2 - c_{21} z_2^2 + z_2 e_2 + \frac{P_2^{*2}}{2} - \sigma_2 \widetilde{W}_2^T \widehat{W}_2. \tag{29}$$

According to the complete square formula,

$$\begin{aligned} -\sigma_2 \widetilde{W}_2^T \widehat{W}_2 &= -\sigma_2 \widetilde{W}_2^T \left(\widetilde{W}_2 + W_2^* \right) \\ &\le -\sigma_2 \left\| \widetilde{W}_2 \right\|^2 + \sigma_2 \left\| \widetilde{W}_2 \right\| \left\| W_2^* \right\| \\ &\le -\frac{\sigma_2 \left\| \widetilde{W}_2 \right\|^2}{2} + \frac{\sigma_2 \left\| W_2^* \right\|^2}{2}, \end{aligned}$$

$$-c_{21} z_2^2 + z_2 e_2 \le -c_{21} z_2^2 + z_2 |e_2| \le \frac{e_2^2}{4 c_{21}} \le \frac{e_2^{*2}}{4 c_{21}}. \tag{30}$$

Because $-(c_{20} + (\dot{g}_2 / 2 g_2^2)) z_2^2 \le -(c_{20} - (g_{2d} / 2 g_{2m}^2)) z_2^2$, then we can make $(c_{20}^* \triangleq c_{20} - (g_{2d} / 2 g_{2m}^2)) > 0$ by selecting the proper c_{20}; then

$$\begin{aligned} \dot{V}_2 &\le \dot{V}_1 - z_1 z_2 + z_2 z_3 - c_{20}^* z_2^2 - \frac{\sigma_2 \left\| \widetilde{W}_2 \right\|^2}{2} + \frac{\sigma_2 \left\| W_2^* \right\|^2}{2} + \frac{e_2^{*2}}{4 c_{21}} + \frac{P_2^{*2}}{2} \\ &\le z_2 z_3 - \sum_{k=1}^{2} c_{k0}^* z_k^2 - \sum_{k=1}^{2} \frac{\sigma_k \left\| \widetilde{W}_k \right\|^2}{2} + \sum_{k=1}^{2} \frac{\sigma_k \left\| W_k^* \right\|^2}{2} + \sum_{k=1}^{2} \frac{e_k^{*2}}{4 c_{k1}}. \end{aligned} \tag{31}$$

The cross coupling $z_2 z_3$ in (31) will be eliminated in the next step.

Step i ($3 \le i \le n - 1$). The derivative of $z_i = x_i - \alpha_{i-1}$ can be calculated as

$$\dot{z}_i = f_i (\overline{x}_i) + g_i (\overline{x}_i) x_{i+1} - \dot{\alpha}_{i-1}, \tag{32}$$

where

$$\begin{aligned} \dot{\alpha}_{i-1} &= \sum_{k=1}^{i-1} \frac{\partial \alpha_{i-1}}{\partial x_k} \left(g_k (\overline{x}_k) x_{k+1} + f_k (\overline{x}_k) \right) + \varphi_{i-1}, \\ \phi_{i-1} &= \sum_{k=1}^{i-1} \left(\frac{\partial \alpha_{i-1}}{\partial x_d} \right) \dot{x}_d + \sum_{k=1}^{i-1} \left(\frac{\partial \alpha_{i-1}}{\partial \widehat{W}_k} \right) \left[\Gamma_k \left(S_k (Z_k) z_k - \sigma_k \widehat{W}_k \right) \right]. \end{aligned} \tag{33}$$

Consider the following Lyapunov function:

$$V_i = V_{i-1} + \frac{1}{2 g_i (\overline{x}_i)} z_i^2 + \frac{1}{2} \widetilde{W}_i^T \Gamma_i^{-1} \widetilde{W}_i, \tag{34}$$

where $\Gamma_i = \Gamma_i^T > 0$ is an adaptive gain matrix.

Then the derivation of V_i can be calculated as

$$\begin{aligned} \dot{V}_i &= \dot{V}_{i-1} + \frac{z_i \dot{z}_i}{g_i (\overline{x}_i)} + \frac{\dot{g}_i (\overline{x}_i) z_i^2}{2 g_i^2 (\overline{x}_i)} + \widetilde{W}_i^T \Gamma_i^{-1} \dot{\widehat{W}}_i \\ &= \dot{V}_{i-1} + \frac{z_i}{g_i (\overline{x}_i)} \left(f_i (\overline{x}_i) + g_i (\overline{x}_i) x_{i+1} + d_i - \dot{\alpha}_{i-1} \right) + \frac{\dot{g}_i (\overline{x}_i) z_i^2}{2 g_i^2 (\overline{x}_i)} + \widetilde{W}_i^T \Gamma_i^{-1} \dot{\widehat{W}}_i \\ &= \dot{V}_{i-1} + z_i \left(z_{i+1} + \alpha_i + \frac{f_i (\overline{x}_i) - \dot{\alpha}_{i-1}}{g_i (\overline{x}_i)} \right) + \frac{z_i d_i}{g_i (\overline{x}_i)} + \frac{\dot{g}_i (\overline{x}_i) z_i^2}{2 g_i^2 (\overline{x}_i)} + \widetilde{W}_i^T \Gamma_i^{-1} \dot{\widehat{W}}_i. \end{aligned} \tag{35}$$

According to Assumption 1 we can get

$$\begin{aligned} \dot{V}_i &\le \dot{V}_{i-1} + z_i \left(z_{i+1} + \alpha_i + \frac{f_i (\overline{x}_i) - \dot{\alpha}_{i-1}}{g_i (\overline{x}_i)} \right) + \frac{z_i^2 \rho_i^2}{2 g_i^2 (\overline{x}_i)} + \frac{P_i^{*2}}{2} + \frac{\dot{g}_i (\overline{x}_i) z_i^2}{2 g_i^2 (\overline{x}_i)} + \widetilde{W}_i^T \Gamma_i^{-1} \dot{\widehat{W}}_i \\ &= \dot{V}_{i-1} + z_i \left(z_{i+1} + \alpha_i + \frac{f_i (\overline{x}_i) - \dot{\alpha}_{i-1}}{g_i (\overline{x}_i)} + \frac{z_i^2 \rho_i^2}{2 g_i^2 (\overline{x}_i)} \right) + \frac{P_i^{*2}}{2} + \frac{\dot{g}_i (\overline{x}_i) z_i^2}{2 g_i^2 (\overline{x}_i)} + \widetilde{W}_i^T \Gamma_i^{-1} \dot{\widehat{W}}_i. \end{aligned} \tag{36}$$

There is an ideal feedback control law as

$$\alpha_i^* = -z_{i-1} - c_i z_i - \left[\frac{f_i (\overline{x}_i) - \dot{\alpha}_{i-1}}{g_i (\overline{x}_i)} + \frac{z_i \rho_i^2}{2 g_i^2 (\overline{x}_i)} \right], \tag{37}$$

where $c_i > 0$ is designed controller parameter.

Because of the unknown smooth functions $f_i(\overline{x}_i)$ and $g_i(\overline{x}_i)$, we cannot actually get the ideal feedback control law α_i^*; from (37) we can see that the unknown part is a smooth function of $\overline{x}_i$ and $\dot{\alpha}_{i-1}$, and let

$$h_i (Z_i) \triangleq \frac{f_i (\overline{x}_i) - \dot{\alpha}_{i-1}}{g_i (\overline{x}_i)} + \frac{z_i \rho_i^2}{2 g_i^2 (\overline{x}_i)}, \tag{38}$$

where

$$Z_i \triangleq \left[\overline{x}_i^T, \frac{\partial \alpha_{i-1}}{\partial x_1}, \ldots, \frac{\partial \alpha_{i-1}}{\partial x_{i-1}}, \varphi_{i-1} \right]^T \subset R^{2i}. \tag{39}$$

By introducing the direct variable $(\partial \alpha_{i-1} / \partial x_1), \ldots, (\partial \alpha_{i-1} / \partial x_{i-1})$, φ_{i-1}, we can make the number of neural networks minimized. RBF neural network $W_i^T S_i(Z_i)$ is used to approximate the unknown function $h(Z_i)$, and α_i^* can be expressed as

$$\alpha_i^* = -z_{i-1} - c_i z_i - W_i^{*T} S_i (Z_i) - e_i, \tag{40}$$

where $|e_i| \le e_i^*$ is estimated error and meets $e_i^* > 0$.

Because W_i^* is unknown, select the following virtual control law:

$$\alpha_i = -z_{i-1} - c_i z_i - \widehat{W}_i^T S_i (Z_i), \tag{41}$$

where W_i^* is the estimated value of $\widehat{W}_i$; then

$$\dot{V}_i \le \dot{V}_{i-1} - z_{i-1} z_i + z_i z_{i+1} - c_i z_i^2 + \frac{\dot{g}_i (\overline{x}_i) z_i^2}{2 g_i^2 (\overline{x}_i)} + z_i e_i + \frac{P_i^{*2}}{2} - \widetilde{W}_i^T S_i z_i + \widetilde{W}_i^T \Gamma_i^{-1} \dot{\widehat{W}}_i, \tag{42}$$

where $\widetilde{W}_i = \widehat{W}_i - W_i^*$.

The following adaptive law can be selected as

$$\dot{\widehat{W}}_i = \dot{\widetilde{W}}_i = \Gamma_i \left[S_i(Z_i) z_i - \sigma_i \widehat{W}_i\right], \tag{43}$$

where $\sigma_i > 0$; then

$$\dot{V}_i \le \dot{V}_{i-1} - z_{i-1}z_i + z_i z_{i+1} - c_i z_i^2 + \frac{\dot{g}_i(\bar{x}_i) z_i^2}{2g_i^2(\bar{x}_i)} + z_i e_i + \frac{P_i^{*2}}{2} - \sigma_i \widetilde{W}_i^T \widehat{W}_i. \tag{44}$$

Let $c_i = c_{i0} + c_{i1}$, c_{i0}, $c_{i1} > 0$; then (44) can be rewritten as

$$\dot{V}_i \le \dot{V}_{i-1} - z_{i-1}z_i + z_i z_{i+1} - \left(c_{i0} + \frac{\dot{g}_i(\bar{x}_i)}{2g_i^2(\bar{x}_i)}\right) z_i^2 - c_{i1} z_i^2 + z_i e_i + \frac{P_i^{*2}}{2} - \sigma_i \widetilde{W}_i^T \widehat{W}_i. \tag{45}$$

According to the complete square formula,

$$\begin{aligned} -\sigma_i \widetilde{W}_i^T \widehat{W}_i &= -\sigma_i \widetilde{W}_i^T \left(\widetilde{W}_i + W_i^*\right) \\ &\le -\sigma_i \left\|\widetilde{W}_i\right\|^2 + \sigma_i \left\|\widetilde{W}_i\right\| \left\|W_i^*\right\| \\ &\le -\frac{\sigma_i \left\|\widetilde{W}_i\right\|^2}{2} + \frac{\sigma_i \left\|W_i^*\right\|^2}{2}, \end{aligned}$$

$$-c_{i1} z_i^2 + z_i e_i \le -c_{i1} z_i^2 + z_i \left|e_i\right| \le \frac{e_i^2}{4c_{i1}} \le \frac{e_i^{*2}}{4c_{i1}}. \tag{46}$$

Because $-(c_{i0} + (\dot{g}_i/2g_i^2))z_i^2 \le -(c_{i0} - (g_{id}/2g_{im}^2))z_i^2$, then we can make $(c_{i0}^* \triangleq c_{i0} - (g_{id}/2g_{im}^2)) > 0$ by selecting the proper c_{i0}; then

$$\begin{aligned} \dot{V}_i &\le \dot{V}_{i-1} - z_{i-1}z_i + z_i z_{i+1} - c_{i0}^* z_i^2 - \frac{\sigma_i \left\|\widetilde{W}_i\right\|^2}{2} + \frac{\sigma_i \left\|W_i^*\right\|^2}{2} + \frac{e_i^{*2}}{4c_{i1}} + \frac{P_i^{*2}}{2} \\ &\le z_i z_{i+1} - \sum_{k=1}^{i} c_{k0}^* z_k^2 - \sum_{k=1}^{i} \frac{\sigma_k \left\|\widetilde{W}_k\right\|^2}{2} + \sum_{k=1}^{i} \frac{\sigma_k \left\|W_k^*\right\|^2}{2} + \sum_{k=1}^{i} \frac{e_k^{*2}}{4c_{k1}} + \sum_{k=1}^{i} \frac{P_k^{*2}}{2}. \end{aligned} \tag{47}$$

The cross coupling $z_i z_{i+1}$ in (47) will be eliminated in the next step.

Step n. The derivative of $z_n = x_n - \alpha_{n-1}$ can be calculated as

$$\dot{z}_n = f_n(\bar{x}_n) + g_n(\bar{x}_{n-1}) u - \dot{\alpha}_{n-1}, \tag{48}$$

where

$$\dot{\alpha}_{n-1} = \sum_{k=1}^{n-1} \frac{\partial \alpha_{n-1}}{\partial x_k} \left(g_k(\bar{x}_k) x_{k+1} + f_k(\bar{x}_k)\right) + \phi_{n-1}, \tag{49}$$

where

$$\phi_{n-1} = \sum_{k=1}^{n-1} \left(\frac{\partial \alpha_{n-1}}{\partial x_d}\right) \dot{x}_d + \sum_{k=1}^{n-1} \left(\frac{\partial \alpha_{n-1}}{\partial \widehat{W}_k}\right) \left[\Gamma_k \left(S_k(Z_k) z_k - \sigma_k \widehat{W}_k\right)\right]. \tag{50}$$

Consider the following Lyapunov function:

$$V_n = V_{n-1} + \frac{1}{2g_n(\bar{x}_n)} z_n^2 + \frac{1}{2} \widetilde{W}_n^T \Gamma_n^{-1} \widetilde{W}_n, \tag{51}$$

where $\Gamma_n = \Gamma_n^T > 0$ is an adaptive gain matrix. Then the derivation of V_n can be calculated as

$$\begin{aligned} \dot{V}_n &= \dot{V}_{n-1} + \frac{z_n \dot{z}_n}{g_i(\bar{x}_i)} + \frac{\dot{g}_n(\bar{x}_n) z_n^2}{2g_n^2(\bar{x}_n)} + \widetilde{W}_n^T \Gamma_n^{-1} \dot{\widehat{W}}_n \\ &= \dot{V}_{n-1} + \frac{z_n}{g_n(\bar{x}_n)} \left(f_n(\bar{x}_n) + g_n(\bar{x}_n) u + d_n - \dot{\alpha}_{n-1}\right) + \frac{\dot{g}_n(\bar{x}_n) z_n^2}{2g_n^2(\bar{x}_n)} + \widetilde{W}_n^T \Gamma_n^{-1} \dot{\widehat{W}}_n \\ &= \dot{V}_{n-1} + z_n \left(z_{n+1} + u + \frac{f_n(\bar{x}_n) - \dot{\alpha}_{n-1}}{g_n(\bar{x}_n)}\right) + \frac{z_n d_n}{g_n(\bar{x}_n)} + \frac{\dot{g}_n(\bar{x}_n) z_n^2}{2g_n^2(\bar{x}_n)} + \widetilde{W}_n^T \Gamma_n^{-1} \dot{\widehat{W}}_n. \end{aligned} \tag{52}$$

According to Assumption 1 we can get

$$\begin{aligned} \dot{V}_n &\le \dot{V}_{n-1} + z_n \left(z_{n+1} + u + \frac{f_i(\bar{x}_i) - \dot{\alpha}_{n-1}}{g_i(\bar{x}_i)}\right) + \frac{z_n^2 \rho_n^2}{2g_n^2(\bar{x}_n)} + \frac{P_n^{*2}}{2} + \frac{\dot{g}_n(\bar{x}_n) z_n^2}{2g_n^2(\bar{x}_n)} + \widetilde{W}_n^T \Gamma_n^{-1} \dot{\widehat{W}}_n \\ &= \dot{V}_{n-1} + z_n \left(z_{n+1} + u + \frac{f_n(\bar{x}_n) - \dot{\alpha}_{n-1}}{g_n(\bar{x}_n)} + \frac{z_n^2 \rho_n^2}{2g_n^2(\bar{x}_n)}\right) + \frac{P_n^{*2}}{2} + \frac{\dot{g}_n(\bar{x}_n) z_n^2}{2g_n^2(\bar{x}_n)} + \widetilde{W}_n^T \Gamma_n^{-1} \dot{\widehat{W}}_n. \end{aligned} \tag{53}$$

There is an ideal feedback control law as

$$u^* = -z_{i-1} - c_i z_i - \left[\frac{f_i(\bar{x}_i) - \dot{\alpha}_{i-1}}{g_i(\bar{x}_i)} + \frac{z_i \rho_i^2}{2g_i^2(\bar{x}_i)}\right], \tag{54}$$

where $c_n > 0$ is designed controller parameter.

Because of the unknown smooth functions $f_n(\bar{x}_n)$ and $g_i(\bar{x}_i)$, we cannot actually get the ideal feedback control law u^*; from (54) we can see the unknown part is a smooth function of $\bar{x}_n$ and $\dot{\alpha}_{n-1}$, and let

$$h_n(Z_i) \triangleq \frac{f_n(\bar{x}_n) - \dot{\alpha}_{n-1}}{g_n(\bar{x}_n)} + \frac{z_n \rho_n^2}{2g_n^2(\bar{x}_n)}, \tag{55}$$

where $Z_n \triangleq [\bar{x}_n^T, \partial\alpha_{n-1}/\partial x_1, \ldots, \partial\alpha_{n-1}/\partial x_{n-1}, \phi_{n-1}]^T \subset R^{2n}$.

RBF neural network $W_n^T S_n(Z_n)$ is used to approximate the unknown function $h(Z_n)$, and u^* can be expressed as

$$u^* = -z_{n-1} - c_n z_n - W_n^{*T} S_n(Z_n) - e_n, \tag{56}$$

where $|e_n| \le e_n^*$ is estimated error and meets $e_n^* > 0$.

Because W_n^* is unknown, select the following virtual control law:

$$u = -z_{n-1} - c_n z_n - \widehat{W}_n^T S_n(Z_n), \tag{57}$$

where $\widehat{W}_i$ is the estimated value of W_i^*; then

$$\dot{V}_n \le \dot{V}_{n-1} - z_{n-1} z_n + z_n z_{n+1} - c_n z_n^2 + \frac{\dot{g}_n(\bar{x}_n) z_n^2}{2g_n^2(\bar{x}_n)} + z_n e_n + \frac{P_n^{*2}}{2} - \widetilde{W}_n^T S_n z_n + \widetilde{W}_n^T \Gamma_n^{-1} \dot{\widehat{W}}_n, \tag{58}$$

where $\widetilde{W}_n = \widehat{W}_n - W_n^*$.

The following adaptive law can be selected as

$$\dot{\widehat{W}}_n = \dot{\widetilde{W}}_n = \Gamma_n\left[S_n(Z_n)z_n - \sigma_n\widehat{W}_n\right], \quad (59)$$

where $\sigma_n > 0$; then

$$\dot{V}_n \le \dot{V}_{n-1} - z_{n-1}z_n + z_nz_{n+1} - c_nz_n^2 + \frac{\dot{g}_n(\bar{x}_n)z_n^2}{2g_n^2(\bar{x}_n)} + z_ne_n + \frac{P_n^{*2}}{2} - \sigma_n\widetilde{W}_n^T\widehat{W}_n. \quad (60)$$

Let $c_n = c_{n0} + c_{n1}$, c_{n0}, $c_{n1} > 0$; (60) can be rewritten as

$$\dot{V}_n \le \dot{V}_{n-1} - z_{n-1}z_n + z_nz_{n+1} - \left(c_{n0} + \frac{\dot{g}_n(\bar{x}_n)}{2g_n^2(\bar{x}_n)}\right)z_n^2 - c_{n1}z_n^2 + z_ne_n + \frac{P_n^{*2}}{2} - \sigma_n\widetilde{W}_n^T\widehat{W}_n. \quad (61)$$

According to the complete square formula,

$$\begin{aligned} -\sigma_n\widetilde{W}_n^T\widehat{W}_n &= -\sigma_n\widetilde{W}_n^T\left(\widetilde{W}_n + W_n^*\right) \\ &\le -\sigma_n\left\|\widetilde{W}_n\right\|^2 + \sigma_n\left\|\widetilde{W}_n\right\|\left\|W_n^*\right\| \\ &\le -\frac{\sigma_n\left\|\widetilde{W}_n\right\|^2}{2} + \frac{\sigma_n\left\|W_n^*\right\|^2}{2}, \end{aligned}$$

$$-c_{n1}z_n^2 + z_ne_n \le -c_{n1}z_n^2 + z_n\left|e_n\right| \le \frac{e_n^2}{4c_{n1}} \le \frac{e_n^{*2}}{4c_{n1}}. \quad (62)$$

Because $-(c_{n0}+(\dot{g}_n/2g_n^2))z_n^2 \le -(c_{n0}-(g_{nd}/2g_{nm}^2))z_n^2$, then we can make $(c_{n0}^* \triangleq c_{n0} - (g_{nd}/2g_{nm}^2)) > 0$ by selecting the proper c_{n0}; then

$$\dot{V}_n \le -\sum_{k=1}^{n}c_{k0}^*z_k^2 - \sum_{k=1}^{n}\frac{\sigma_k\left\|\widetilde{W}_k\right\|^2}{2} + \sum_{k=1}^{n}\frac{\sigma_k\left\|W_k^*\right\|^2}{2} + \sum_{k=1}^{n}\frac{e_k^{*2}}{4c_{k1}} + \sum_{k=1}^{n}\frac{P_k^{*2}}{2}. \quad (63)$$

Let $\delta \triangleq \sum_{k=1}^{n}(\sigma_k\|W_k^*\|^2/2) + \sum_{k=1}^{n}(e_k^{*2}/4c_{k1}) + \sum_{k=1}^{n}(P_k^{*2}/2)$, $c_{k0}^* \ge (\gamma/2g_{km})$, $c_{k0} > (\gamma/2g_{km}) + (g_{kd}/2g_{km}^2)$, $k = 1, 2, \ldots, n$, where $\gamma > 0$, $\sigma_k \ge \gamma\lambda_{\max}\{\Gamma_k^{-1}\}$, $k = 1, 2, \ldots, n$; then

$$\begin{aligned} \dot{V}_n &\le -\sum_{k=1}^{n}c_{k0}^*z_k^2 - \sum_{k=1}^{n}\frac{\sigma_k\left\|\widetilde{W}_k\right\|^2}{2} + \delta \\ &\le -\sum_{k=1}^{n}\frac{\gamma}{2g_{km}}z_k^2 - \sum_{k=1}^{n}\frac{\gamma\widetilde{W}_k^T\Gamma_k^{-1}\widetilde{W}_k}{2g_{km}} + \delta \\ &\le -\gamma\left[\sum_{k=1}^{n}\frac{1}{2g_k}z_k^2 + \sum_{k=1}^{n}\frac{\widetilde{W}_k^T\Gamma_k^{-1}\widetilde{W}_k}{2}\right] + \delta \\ &\le -\gamma V_n + \delta. \end{aligned} \quad (64)$$

The stability and control performance of the closed-loop adaptive system are demonstrated by the following theorem.

Theorem 2. In the initial conditions, by formula (1), reference model (2), control law (57), and neural network weight update rate in (12), (27), (43), and (59), supposing that there is a large enough set of closed sets $\Omega^i \in R^{2i}$, $i = 1, 2, \ldots, n$, for any given moment $t \ge 0$, making $Z_i \in \Omega_i$, the following conclusions can be obtained as follows:

(1) The signal of the whole closed-loop system is bounded, and the state variable $\bar{x}_n$ and the neural network estimation errors $\widetilde{W}_1^T, \ldots, \widetilde{W}_n^T$ will eventually converge to the closed set as follows:

$$\Omega_{s1} \triangleq \left\{\bar{x}_n, \widetilde{W}_1, \ldots, \widetilde{W}_n \mid V < \frac{\delta}{\gamma},\ x_d \in \Omega_d\right\}. \quad (65)$$

(2) By choosing the proper control parameters, the output tracking error $(t) - y_{d1}(t)$ is close to a small neighborhood of zero [21].

ADAPTIVE ROBUST NEURAL NETWORK CONTROL FOR SHIP COURSE

Problem Formulation

This section introduces a simplified dynamic model of an underactuated surface vehicle with only one control input δ for heading control. A surface ship usually has three degrees of freedom for path following control in horizontal plane. Assuming that the vessel has three planes of symmetry, for most underactuated vessels have port/starboard symmetry, it can be neglected to simplify the vessel model for controller design. The detailed model which considers the environment disturbances can be set as follows:

$$\begin{aligned} \dot{y} &= U\sin\psi, \\ \dot{\psi} &= r, \\ \dot{r} &= -\frac{1}{T}r - \frac{\alpha}{T}r^3 + \frac{K}{T}\delta + \Delta, \\ y_1 &= y, \\ y_2 &= \psi, \end{aligned} \quad (66)$$

where y denotes transverse displacement in the earth inertial coordinates; $U = \sqrt{u^2 + V^2}$ is resultant velocity of ship; ψ is course angle; r is yawing angular velocity; K, T represent performance index for ship steering; α is coefficient of nonlinear term; δ is control rudder angle; y_1, y_2 represent system output.

The control objective is to design the controller δ to make the control output y, ψ achieve the setting value (y_d, ψ_d). Because the dimension of the system control input is less than the degree of freedom of the system, it is an underactuated system.

Dynamic Controller Design

Selection of coordinate transformation is as follows:

$$w_e = \psi + \arcsin\left(\frac{ky}{\sqrt{1+(ky)^2}}\right). \quad (67)$$

The original system can be transformed into a single input single output system:

$$\begin{aligned} \dot{x}_1 &= \frac{k\dot{y}}{1+(ky)^2} + x_2, \\ \dot{x}_2 &= -a_1x_2 - a_2x_2^3 + bu + \Delta, \end{aligned} \quad (68)$$

where $a_1 = 1/T$, $a_2 = \alpha/T$, $b = K/T$, $x_1 = w_e$, $x_2 = r$, $u = \delta$, and the output of whole system is x_1.

For system model (67) and (68), the controller design is carried out by using backstepping method.

Step 1. Let $z_1 = x_1$, $x_{d1} = 0$; then

$$\dot{z}_1 = \frac{k\dot{y}}{1+(ky)^2} + x_2. \tag{69}$$

For the subsystem z_1, $\alpha_1^* \triangleq x_2$ is chosen as virtual control input. Select the Lyapunov function $V_{z1} = (1/2)z_1^2$, and there is

$$\dot{V}_{z1} = z_1\dot{z}_1 = \left(\frac{k\dot{y}}{1+(ky)^2} + x_2\right)z_1. \tag{70}$$

Let $z_2 = x_2 - \alpha_1$; then $x_2 = z_2 + \alpha_1$,

$$\dot{V}_{z1} = \left(\frac{k\dot{y}}{1+(ky)^2} + z_2 + \alpha_1\right)z_1. \tag{71}$$

Select the following virtual control law:

$$\alpha_1^* = -c_1 z_1 - \frac{k\dot{y}}{1+(ky)^2}. \tag{72}$$

$\dot{V}_{z1} = z_1 z_2 - c_1 z_1^2$, because $k\dot{y}/(1+(ky)^2)$ is unknown function, $h_1(Z_1) = k\dot{y}/(1+(ky)^2)$, and we will adopt RBF NN to estimate $h_1(Z_1)$ and get $h_1(Z_1) = W_1^{*T}S_1(Z_1) + \varepsilon_1$. But the actual use of the NN for the system is $h_1(Z_1) = \widehat{W}_1^T S_1(Z_1)$.

Actual virtual control input is $\alpha_1 = -c_1 z_1 - \widehat{W}_1^T S_1(Z_1)$; then

$$\begin{aligned}\dot{z}_1 &= \frac{k\dot{y}}{1+(ky)^2} + z_2 + \alpha_1\\ &= \left(z_2 - c_1 z_1 - \widetilde{W}_1 S_1(Z_1) + \varepsilon_1\right),\end{aligned} \tag{73}$$

where $\widetilde{W}_1 = \widehat{W}_1 - W_1^*$.

Select Lyapunov function as

$$V_1 = V_{z1} + \frac{1}{2}\widetilde{W}_1^T \Gamma^{-1}\widetilde{W}_1; \tag{74}$$

then

$$\begin{aligned}\dot{V}_1 &= \dot{V}_{z1} + \widetilde{W}_1\Gamma^{-1}\dot{\widehat{W}}_1 \le z_1\left(z_2 + \alpha_1 + h_1(Z_1)\right)\\ &= z_1\left[z_2 - c_1 z_1 - \widehat{W}_1 S_1(Z_1) + W_1^* S_1(Z_1) + \varepsilon_1\right]\\ &\quad + \widetilde{W}_1\Gamma^{-1}\dot{\widehat{W}}_1\\ &= z_1\left[z_2 - c_1 z_1 - \widetilde{W}_1 S_1(Z_1) + \varepsilon_1\right] + \widetilde{W}_1\Gamma^{-1}\dot{\widehat{W}}_1.\end{aligned} \tag{75}$$

The adaptive law of neural network can be designed as

$$\dot{\widehat{W}}_1 = \dot{\widetilde{W}}_1 = \Gamma_1\left[S_1(Z_1)z_1 - \sigma_1\widehat{W}_1\right], \tag{76}$$

where $\sigma_1 > 0$. Let $c_1 = c_{10} + c_{11}$, where $c_{10}, c_{11} > 0$.

Furthermore,

$$\dot{V}_1 = z_1 z_2 - c_{10}z_1^2 - c_{11}z_1^2 + z_1\varepsilon_1 - \sigma_1\widetilde{W}_1^T\widehat{W}_1; \tag{77}$$

then

$$\begin{aligned}-\sigma_1\widetilde{W}_1^T\widehat{W}_1 &= -\sigma_1\widetilde{W}_1^T\left(\widetilde{W}_1 + W_1^*\right)\\ &\le -\sigma_1\left\|\widetilde{W}_1\right\|^2 + \sigma_1\left\|\widetilde{W}_1\right\|\left\|W_1^*\right\|\\ &\le -\frac{\sigma_1\left\|\widetilde{W}_1\right\|^2}{2} + \frac{\sigma_1\left\|W_1^*\right\|^2}{2}\end{aligned} \tag{78}$$

because

$$-c_{11}z_1^2 + z_1\varepsilon_1 \le -c_{11}z_1^2 + z_1\left|\varepsilon_1\right| \le \frac{\varepsilon_1^2}{4c_{11}} \le \frac{\varepsilon_1^{*2}}{4c_{11}}. \tag{79}$$

Finally we can get

$$\dot{V}_1 < z_1 z_2 - c_{10}^* z_1^2 - \frac{\sigma_1\left\|\widetilde{W}_1\right\|^2}{2} + \frac{\sigma_1\left\|W_1^*\right\|^2}{2} + \frac{\varepsilon_1^{*2}}{4c_{11}}. \tag{80}$$

Step 2. Let $z_2 = x_2 - \alpha_1$; derivation of z_2 can be calculated as

$$\begin{aligned}\dot{z}_2 &= f_2(\overline{x}_2) + g_2(\overline{x}_2)u + \Delta - \dot{\alpha}_1\\ &= -a_1 x_2 - a_2 x_2^{\ 3} + bu + \Delta - \dot{\alpha}_1.\end{aligned} \tag{81}$$

Because $V_{z2} = (1/2b)z_2^2$, then

$$\begin{aligned}\dot{V}_{z2} &= \frac{1}{b}z_2\dot{z}_2 = \frac{1}{b}z_2\left(-a_1x_2 - a_2x_2^{\ 3} + bu + \Delta - \dot{\alpha}_1\right)\\ &= z_2\left[u + \frac{1}{b}\left(-a_1x_2 - a_2x_2^{\ 3} - \dot{\alpha}_1\right)\right] + \frac{\Delta}{b}z_2\\ &\le z_2\left[u + \frac{1}{b}\left(-a_1x_2 - a_2x_2^{\ 3} - \dot{\alpha}_1 + \frac{\rho^2 z_2}{2b}\right)\right]\\ &\quad + \frac{p^2}{2},\end{aligned} \tag{82}$$

where $\Delta \le p \cdot \rho(x)$, p is unknown parameter, $\rho(x)$ is known nonlinear function, and then

$$u^* = -z_1 - c_2 z_2 - \frac{1}{b}\left(-a_1x_2 - a_2x_2^{\ 3} - \dot{\alpha}_1 + \frac{\rho^2 z_2}{2b}\right). \tag{83}$$

Let

$$h_2(Z_2) = \frac{1}{b}\left(-a_1x_2 - a_2x_2^{\ 3} - \dot{\alpha}_1 + \frac{\rho^2 z_2}{2b}\right). \tag{84}$$

Equation (83) can be rewritten as

$$u^* = -z_1 - c_2 z_2 - h_2(Z_2). \tag{85}$$

In the same way we use RBF NN estimate $h_2(Z_2)$:

$$h_2(Z_2) = W_2^{*T}S_2(Z_2) + \varepsilon_2. \tag{86}$$

The actual use of the NN for the system and controller can be expressed as

$$\begin{aligned}&h_2(Z_2) = \widehat{W}_2^T S_2(Z_2),\\ &\quad u = z_1 - c_2 z_2 - \widehat{W}_2^T S_2(Z_2).\end{aligned} \tag{87}$$

Select Lyapunov function as

$$V_2 = V_1 + V_{z2} + \frac{1}{2}\widetilde{W}_2^T\Gamma^{-1}\widetilde{W}_2. \tag{88}$$

The derivation of V_2 can be calculated as

$$\begin{aligned}\dot{V}_2 &= \dot{V}_1 + \dot{V}_{z2} + \widetilde{W}_1\Gamma^{-1}\dot{\widehat{W}}_1\\ &\le z_1 z_2 - c_{10}^* z_1^2 - \frac{\sigma_1\left\|\widetilde{W}_1\right\|^2}{2} + \frac{\sigma_1\left\|W_1^*\right\|^2}{2} + \frac{\varepsilon_1^{*2}}{4c_{11}}\\ &\quad + z_2\left[-z_1 - c_2 z_2 - \widehat{W}_2 S_2(Z_2) + W_2^* S_2(Z_2) + \varepsilon_2\right]\\ &\quad + \frac{p^2}{2} + \widetilde{W}_1\Gamma^{-1}\dot{\widehat{W}}_1\end{aligned}$$

$$= -\sum_{i=1}^{2} c_{i0}^{*} z_i^2 - \sum_{i=1}^{2} \frac{\sigma_i \|\widetilde{W}_i\|^2}{2} + \sum_{i=1}^{2} \frac{\sigma_i \|W_i^{*}\|^2}{2} + \sum_{i=1}^{2} \frac{\varepsilon_i^{*2}}{4c_{11}}$$
$$+ \frac{p^2}{2}. \tag{89}$$

Therefore, all signals in the close loop of course tracking system are stable, and the tracking errors can be made arbitrarily small by selecting appropriate controller parameters. So the final control law can be designed as

$$u = z_1 - c_2 z_2 - \widehat{W}_2^T S_2 (Z_2). \tag{90}$$

NUMERICAL SIMULATIONS AND ANALYSIS

The simulation experiment can be operated based on an experimental ship. The nonlinear mathematical model for the ship has been presented in [22], which captures the fundamental characteristics of dynamics and offers good maneuverability in the open-loop test. To illustrate the effectiveness of the theoretical results, the proposed control scheme is implemented and simulated with the above nonlinear model with tracking task.

The characteristic parameters of the ship used in the simulation are given as $K = 0.478$, $T = 216$, and $\alpha = 30$. Neural network contains 25 neurons; that is, $l_1 = 25$; the center vector μ_l $(l = 1, 2, \ldots, l_1)$ is uniformly distributed in the width $[-2, 2]\times[-2, 2]\times[-2, 2]$. Neural network $\widehat{W}_2^T S_2(Z_2)$ contains 135 neurons; that is, $l_2 = 125$; the center vector μ_l $(l = 1, 2, \ldots, l_2)$ is uniformly distributed in the width $[-4, 4] \times [-4, 4] \times [-4, 4] \times [-4, 4] \times [-4, 4] \times [-4, 4] \times [-4, 0] \times [-6, 6]$. The controller design parameters are given as follows which satisfy the condition mentioned in design procedure: $k = 0.1394$, $c_1 = 4$, $c_2 = 120$, $\Gamma_1 = \mathrm{diag}\{3\}$, $\Gamma_2 = \mathrm{diag}\{4\}$, and $\sigma_1 = 4$, $\sigma_2 = 2$. The initial linear and angular velocity of ship used in the simulation are given as $[u, V, r] = [0.1, 0, 0]^T$, $[x, y, \psi]^T = [10, 30, -\pi/4]^T$ is the initial position and orientation vector of ship, and the desired velocity of ship is given as $u_d = 1$ (m/s). We choose the reference trajectory as $10 \cos \omega t$.

In order to further verify the validity of the proposed control method, the algorithm of this paper is compared with the simulation results in [12]. So the robustness of trajectory tracking controller against the disturbance and model uncertainties can be evaluated. All the simulation results are depicted in Figures 1–4. Figure 1 shows the trajectory tracking of ship with the given path, and the ship can track and converge to the reference path with more accuracy in [12]. Figure 2 plots the position tracking errors; the along-track and cross-track errors asymptotically converge to zero faster. Figure 3 gives the control inputs response. Surge, sway, yaw velocities, and orientation of ship during the trajectory tracking control process are plotted in Figure 4, which gives a clear insight into the model response involved in nonlinear dynamics.

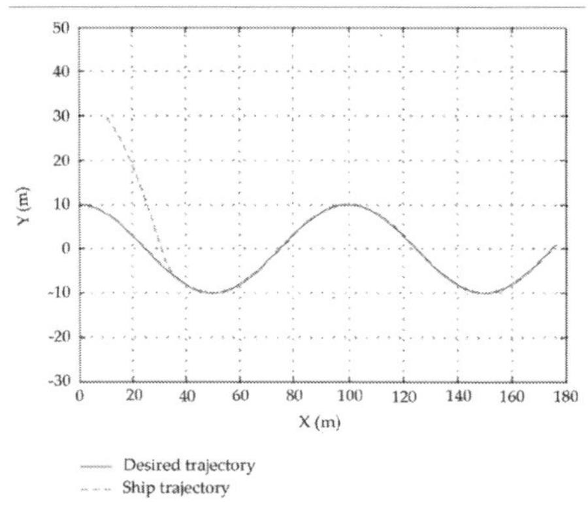

Figure 1: Ship tracking performance of proposed control method.

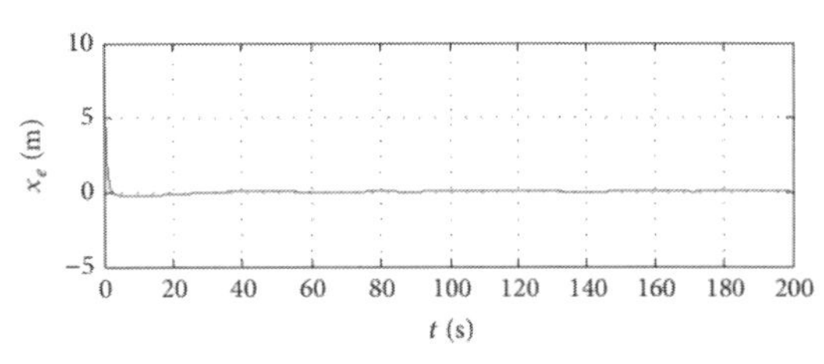

Figure 2: Tracking errors of surge and sway.

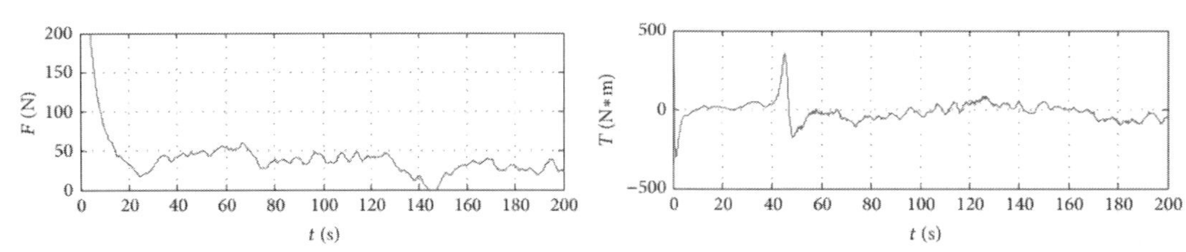

Figure 3: Control force and torque of ship.

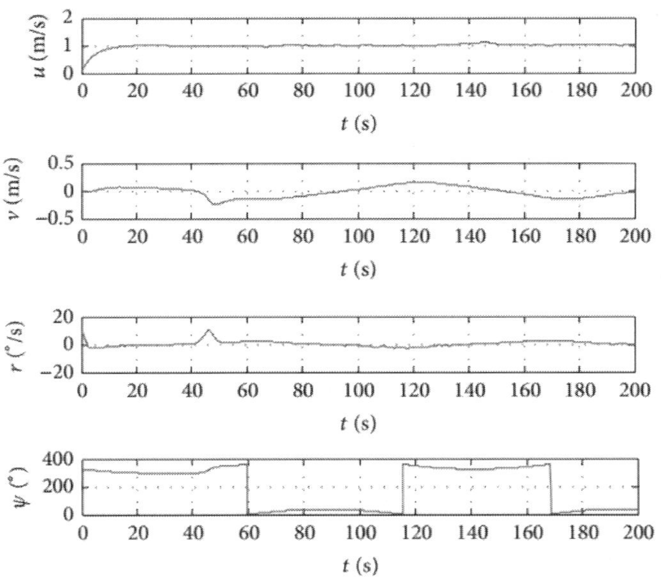

Figure 4: State changing curves of ship.

CONCLUSIONS

In this paper, we proposed a solution to the course control of underactuated surface vessel. Firstly, the direct adaptive neural network control and its application are introduced. Then the backstepping controller with robust neural network is designed to deal with the uncertain and underactuated characteristics for the ship. Neural networks are adopted to determine the parameters of the unknown part of the ideal virtual control and the ideal control; even the weights of neural network are updated by using adaptive technique. Finally uniform stability for the convergence of tracking errors has been proven through Lyapunov stability theory. The simulation results illustrate the performance of the proposed course tracking controller with good precision.

ACKNOWLEDGMENT

This work was supported by the National Natural Science Foundation of China, under Grant 51309067/E091002.

REFERENCES

1. T. I. Fossen, "A survey on nonlinear ship control: from the oryto practice," in Proceedings of the 5th IFAC Conference on Manoeuvring and Control of Marine Craft, pp. 1–16, Aalborg, Denmark, 2000.
2. L. Lapierre and D. Soetanto, "Nonlinear path-following control of an AUV," Ocean Engineering, vol. 34, no. 11-12, pp. 1734–1744, 2007.
3. J. He-ming, S. Wen-long, and C. Zi-yin, "Bottom following control of underactuated AUV based on nonlinear backstepping method," Advances in Information Sciences and Service Sciences, vol. 4, no. 12, pp. 362–369, 2012.
4. B. Sun, D. Zhu, and S. X. Yang, "A bio-inspired cascaded approach for three-dimensional tracking control of unmanned underwater vehicles," International Journal of Robotics and Automation, vol. 29, no. 4, 2014.
5. T. I. Fossen, "High performance ship autopilot with wave filter," in Proceedings of the 10th International Ship Control Systems Symposium (SCSS '93), pp. 2271–2285, Ottawa, Canada, 1993.
6. C. Y. Tzeng, G. C. Goodwin, and S. Crisafulli, "Feedback linearization design of a ship steering autopilot with saturating and slew rate limiting actuator," International Journal of Adaptive Control and Signal Processing, vol. 13, no. 1, pp. 23–30, 1999.
7. A. Witkowska and R. Smierzchalski, "Nonlinear backstepping ship course controller," International Journal of Automation and Computing, vol. 6, no. 3, pp. 277–284, 2009.
8. Y. S. Yang, "Robust adaptive control algorithm applied to ship steering autopilot with uncertain nonlinear system," Shipbuilding of China, vol. 41, no. 1, pp. 21–25, 2000 (Chinese).
9. J. He-Ming, S. Wen-Long, and C. Zi-Yin, "Nonlinear backstepping control of underactuated AUV in diving plane," Advances in Information Sciences and Service Sciences, vol. 4, no. 9, pp. 214–221, 2012.
10. J.-H. Li, P.-M. Lee, B.-H. Jun, and Y.-K. Lim, "Point-to-point navigation of underactuated ships,"Automatica, vol. 44, no. 12, pp. 3201–3205, 2008.
11. M. Bao-li, "Global K-exponential asymptotic stabilization of underactuated surface vessels," Systems & Control Letters, vol. 58, no. 3, pp. 194–201, 2009.
12. L.-J. Zhang, H.-M. Jia, and X. Qi, "NNFFC-adaptive output feedback trajectory tracking control for a surface ship at high speed," Ocean Engineering, vol. 38, no. 13, pp. 1430–1438, 2011.
13. K. D. Do, Z. P. Jiang, and J. Pan, "Robust adaptive path following of underactuated ships," Automatica, vol. 40, no. 6, pp. 929–944, 2004.
14. K. D. Do and J. Pan, "State- and output-feedback robust path-following controllers for underactuated ships using Serret-Frenet frame," Ocean Engineering, vol. 31, no. 5-6, pp. 587–613, 2004.
15. K. D. Do, "Practical control of underactuated ships," Ocean Engineering, vol. 37, no. 13, pp. 1111–1119, 2010.
16. Y.-L. Liao, L. Wan, and J.-Y. Zhuang, "Backstepping dynamical sliding mode control method for the path following of the underactuated surface vessel," Procedia Engineering, vol. 15, pp. 256–263, 2011.
17. K. D. Do and J. Pan, "Global robust adaptive path following of underactuated ships," Automatica, vol. 42, no. 10, pp. 1713–1722, 2006.
18. V. Sakhre, S. Jain, V. S. Sapkal, and D. P. Agarwal, "Fuzzy counter propagation neural network control for a class of nonlinear dynamical systems," Computational Intelligence and Neuroscience, vol. 2015, Article ID 719620, 12 pages, 2015.
19. C.-Z. Pan, S. X. Yang, X.-Z. Lai, and L. Zhou, "An efficient neural network based tracking controller for autonomous underwater vehicles subject to unknown dynamics," in Proceedings of the 26th Chinese Control

and Decision Conference (CCDC '14), pp. 3300–3305, IEEE, Changsha, China, June 2014.

20. L. A. Wulandhari, A. Wibowo, and M. I. Desa, "Improvement of adaptive GAs and back propagation ANNs performance in condition diagnosis of multiple bearing system using grey relational analysis,"Computational Intelligence and Neuroscience, vol. 2014, Article ID 419743, 11 pages, 2014.

21. M. M. Polycarpou, "Stable adaptive neural control scheme for nonlinear systems," IEEE Transactions on Automatic Control, vol. 41, no. 3, pp. 447–451, 1996.

22. L. Moreira, T. I. Fossen, and C. Guedes Soares, "Path following control system for a tanker ship model,"Ocean Engineering, vol. 34, no. 14-15, pp. 2074–2085, 2007.

CHAPTER 18

WATER QUALITY MODELING IN RESERVOIRS USING MULTIVARIATE LINEAR REGRESSION AND TWO NEURAL NETWORK MODELS

Wei-Bo Chen and Wen-Cheng Liu

INTRODUCTION

Water is an important resource for the survival and health of humans and ecosystems. The quality of water is also crucial. The wording, water quality, can be used to address the condition in water column which included the characteristics of physical, chemical, and biological characteristics. Assessing the water quality variables is needed to develop best planning and management for water resources [1, 2].

The definition of eutrophication is the nutrient enrichment which means the excessive phosphorus and nitrogen loads in lakes and reservoirs, resulting in a serious problem. The natural or artificial enrichment of inland water bodies can cause eutrophication with algal blooms to deteriorate the water quality for human use and the decrease of dissolved oxygen levels, resulting in adverse effects on fisheries. The application of some modeling techniques to predict the behavior of enriched water bodies allows for combating adverse effects [3–5].

Due to the advanced computing capabilities, two-dimensional/three-dimensional reservoir hydrodynamic and water quality models have been developed and widely applied to resolve water quality problems [6–9]. Although deterministic models have been adopted for modeling water quality, these models require input data, model parameters, and extensive information to obtain results [10]. Because a large number of factors affecting the water quality have complicated nonlinear relationships with the variables, traditional deterministic models are not easy to handle.

Because of the existing difficulties and challenges in the simulating of water quality conditions using the hydrodynamic and water quality model, relatively novel computational approaches, artificial neural networks (ANNs), which have found wide acceptance in many disciplines, provide an alternative method for understanding and managing the water quality in reservoirs. ANNs are well-suited for this application because of their informative processing characteristics, such as nonlinearity, parallelism, noise tolerance, and learning and generalization capabilities [11, 12].

One of the successful applications of artificial intelligence techniques including knowledge-based systems, genetic algorithms, artificial neural networks, and fuzzy inference systems has been simulating complex nonlinear systems [13]. In particular, artificial neural networks have been successfully used as tools to simulate and predict water quality in water bodies [14–18]. The ANN model which is a black-box model does not require knowledge of any of the parameters [19]. ANNs have several advantages including learning ability, dealing with complex nonlinear data, and parallel processing ability. Prediction with ANN can be performed by the network learning experimentally generated data or using validated models [20].

Recently, Ranković et al. [21] developed a feed-forward neural network model to simulate the dissolved oxygen in the Gruza Reservoir in Serbia. Soltani et al. [22] combined a water quality simulation model and a hybrid genetic algorithm to determine the optimal operating polices for different reservoir outlets. The water quality simulation model is based on an adaptive neural fuzzy inference system that was trained using

Citation: Wei-Bo Chen and Wen-Cheng Liu, "Water Quality Modeling in Reservoirs Using Multivariate Linear Regression and Two Neural Network Models," Advances in Artificial Neural Systems, vol. 2015, Article ID 521721, 12 pages, 2015. doi:10.1155/2015/521721

the results of a numerical water quality simulation model. Again, Ranković et al. [15] used an adaptive network-based fuzzy inference system model to simulate the dissolved oxygen in the Gruza Reservoir in Serbia. However, evaluating the efficiency of multivariate linear regression and artificial neural network models to predict the water quality parameters in reservoirs has not been reported.

The main objective of this study is to establish a multivariate linear regression (MLR) model and two artificial neural network models, including a radial basis function neural network (RBFN) and an adaptive neurofuzzy inference system (ANFIS), to simulate the dissolved oxygen (DO), the total phosphorus (TP), the chlorophyll a(Chl a) content, and the Secchi disk depth (SD), which are commonly used as indicators of the eutrophication of reservoirs. A further aim is to demonstrate the application of these models to identify complex nonlinear relationships between the inputs and outputs in the Mingder Reservoir, Taiwan. The simulated and measured DO, TP, Chl a, and SD values were compared using the MLR, RBFN, and ANFIS models.

MATERIALS AND METHODS

Description of Study Area and Data Collection

The Mingder Reservoir (Figure 1) is located in central Taiwan. The reservoir, completed in 1970, has a total watershed area of 61 km^2 and an effective storage volume of 1.65×10^8 m^3 and was built as a water supply source to Miaoli County for industrial supply, irrigation, and flood control. The dam site of the Mingder Reservoir is located at the tributary of the Houlong River and is approximately 7 km from Miaoli City.

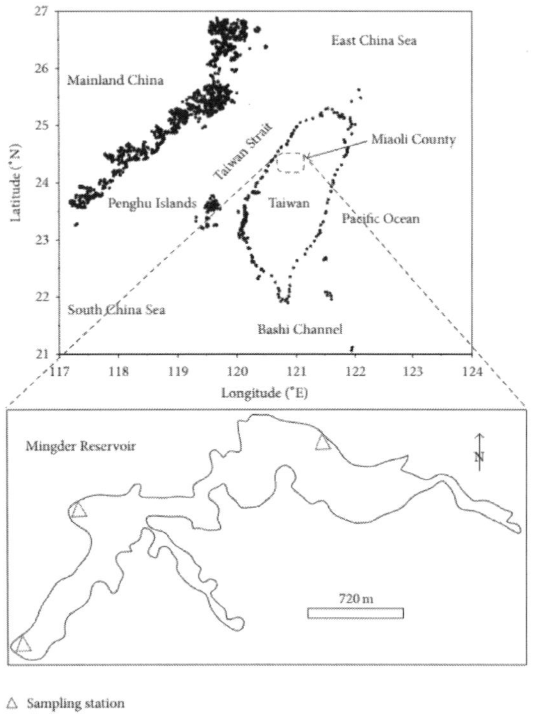

Figure 1: The Mingder Reservoir and water quality sampling stations.

The Mingder Reservoir is an in-channel reservoir that was formed by the construction of an earth dam and has a surface area of 1.62 km^2. Its water quality has been routinely monitored over the past two decades, once per season since 1993. There are three water quality sampling stations in the reservoir.

Carlson [23] proposed a trophic state index (CTSI) related to the diverse aspects of the trophic state found in multiparameter indices. The CTSI has the simplicity of a single parameter index for the water quality assessment of impounded water bodies. The CTSI has been adopted by the Taiwan Environmental Protection Administration (TEPA) to determine eutrophication status. It is calculated with three variables: the Secchi disk depth (SD), the total phosphorus (TP), and the chlorophyll a concentration (Chl-a). For this reason, these three water quality variables were predicted using three approaches presented in this study.

Figure 2 shows the CTSI values of the Mingder Reservoir from 1993 to 2013. A CTSI value above 50 indicates that the water body is eutrophic, as shown in Figure 2 for the Mingder Reservoir. This figure shows that the reservoir is in a status between mesotrophic and eutrophic. Agricultural activities are the major sources of nutrients and provide excessive nutrient loads to the reservoir.

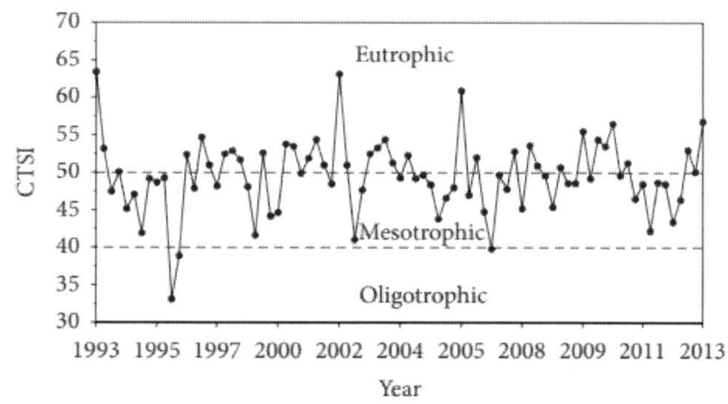

Figure 2: Carlson trophic state index (CTSI) for the Mingder Reservoir.

The historical water quality data, including the water temperature, pH, electrical conductivity, turbidity, suspended solids, total hardness, total alkalinity, Secchi disk depth, dissolved oxygen, chlorophyll aconcentration, total phosphorus, nitrate nitrogen, and biochemical oxygen demand from 1993 to 2013, were collected from the TEPA and analyzed. A statistical summary of the water quality variables is shown in Table 1.

Table 1: The statistic summary of the water quality variables in the Mingder Reservoir

Variables	Minimum	Maximum	Mean	St. Dev.	C. V
Water temperature (°C)	13.70	33.60	23.46	5.18	0.22
pH	5.28	9.50	8.11	0.67	0.08
Electrical conductivity (μmho/cm 25°C)	78.00	447.00	234.74	52.33	0.22
Turbidity (NTU)	0.87	750.00	13.64	58.63	4.30
Suspended solids (mg/L)	1.48	438.00	10.49	33.31	3.18
Total hardness (mg/L)	1.20	190.00	96.67	22.70	0.23
Total alkalinity (mg/L)	29.40	174.00	90.80	22.40	0.25
Secchi disk depth (m)	0.15	3.40	1.50	0.52	0.35
Dissolved oxygen (mg/L)	0.00	14.80	7.68	3.15	0.41
Chlorophyll *a* (μg/L)	0.10	52.80	7.96	6.84	0.86
Total phosphorus (μg/L)	3.00	191.00	22.01	16.97	0.77
Nitrate nitrogen (mg/L)	0.01	1.90	0.12	0.21	1.69
Biochemical oxygen demand (mg/L)	0.69	50.98	8.67	5.78	0.67

St. Dev.: standard deviation.
C. V.: coefficient of variation (St. Dev./Mean).

Adaptive Neurofuzzy Inference System (ANFIS)

The ANFIS is a fuzzy Sugeno model with multilayer feed-forward network which potentially captures the benefits of artificial neural networks and fuzzy logic approaches in a single framework. ANFIS provides easy learning and adaptation since it is a framework of adaptive systems. The Sugeno system is the most commonly adapted fuzzy model for ANFIS framework to deal with the complicated nonlinear problems because of less computational time [24].

To easily understand the architecture of ANFIS, we assume that the fuzzy inference system has two inputs, x_1 and x_2, and only one output, y. Therefore two fuzzy if-then rules based on a first-order Sugeno fuzzy model is provide as below [25]:

Rule 1: if x_1 is A_1 and x_2 is B_1, then $y_1 = p_1x_1+q_1x_2+r_1$,

Rule 2: if x_1 is A_2 and x_2 is B_2, then $y_2 = p_2x_1+q_2x_2+r_2$,

where A_i and B_i are the fuzzy sets and p_i, q_i, and r_i are the parameters that will be determined during the training and testing processes. The architecture of ANFIS with two rules is shown in Figure 3, in which circles represent fixed nodes and squares indicate adaptive nodes. A brief introduction of the ANFIS model follows.

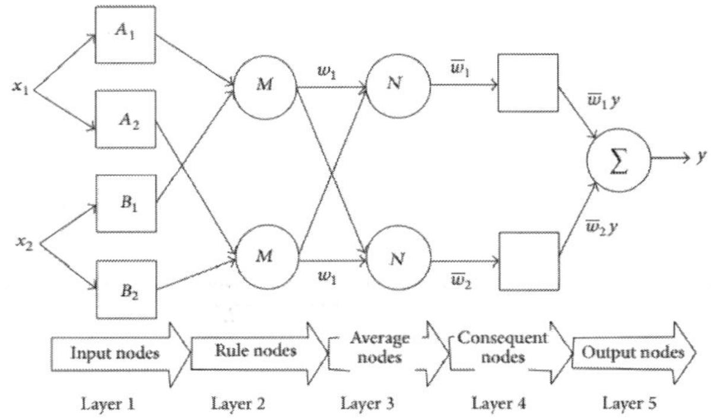

Figure 3: Architecture of the adaptive network-based fuzzy interface system (ANFIS).

Layer 1. Each node i in this fuzzy layer is an adaptive node with a node function

$$O_{1,i} = \mu_{A_i}(x_1), \quad i = 1,2,$$

$$O_{1,i} = \mu_{B_{i-2}}(x_2), \quad i = 3,4, \tag{1}$$

where x_1 and x_2 are the inputs to node i; A_i and B_i are the linguistic labels; and $\mu_{A_i}$and $\mu_{B_{i-2}}$ are the membership functions for the A_i and B_i linguistic labels, respectively. Although many membership functions such as the trapezoidal membership function, the Gaussian membership function, the Gaussian combination membership function, the splinebased membership function, and the sigmoidal membership function can be used. Chau [26] investigated the effect of different membership functions on the performance of ANFIS model and found that the differences are insignificant. In this study, we adopted the generalized bell-shaped membership function which is a commonly used function [26]:

$$\mu_{A_i} = \frac{1}{1+\left|(x_1-c_i)/a_i\right|^{2b_i}},$$

$$\mu_{B_{i-2}} = \frac{1}{1+\left|(x_2-c_i)/a_i\right|^{2b_i}}, \tag{2}$$

where a_i, b_i, and c_i are the parameter sets. The parameters in this layer are the premise parameters.

Layer 2. Each node in this layer is a fixed node which is marked with circle and labeled with M in Figure 3. The outputs of this layer, which are called the firing strengths ($O_{2,i}$), are the products of the corresponding degrees obtained from Layer 1 (the input layer):

$$O_{2,i} = w_i = \mu_{A_i}(x_1) \times \mu_{B_i}(x_1), \quad i = 1,2. \tag{3}$$

Layer 3. Every node in this layer is a circle node labeled *N* (Figure 3). The third layer contains fixed nodes that calculate the ratio of the firing strengths of the *i*th rule to the sum of all rules' firing strength:

$$O_{3,i} = \overline{w}_i = \frac{w_i}{w_1+w_2}, \quad i = 1,2. \tag{4}$$

Layer 4. The nodes in this layer are adaptive and adjustable. The output of each node is the product of normalized firing strength, $\overline{w}_i$, from the third layer:

$$O_{4,i} = \overline{w}_i y_i = \overline{w}_i (p_i x + q_i y + r_i), \quad i = 1,2, \tag{5}$$

where p_i, q_i, and r_i in this layer are consequent parameters.

Layer 5. The single node computes the overall output by summing all of the incoming signals:

$$O_{5,1} = \sum_{i=1}^{2} \overline{w}_i y_i = \frac{\sum_{i=1}^{2} w_i y}{w_1+w_2}. \tag{6}$$

The details and mathematical background for these algorithms can be found in Jang [24].

Radial Basis Function Neural Network (RBFN)

A radial basis function neural network (RBFN) contains a feedforward structure including one input layer, a single hidden layer, and one output layer, as shown in Figure 4. The concept of the RBFN is to establish a radial basis function (ϕ) and to determine the relationship between the input and the output using curve-fitting approaches [27, 28]. A single output RBFN with m hidden layer neurons can be described as

$$y = \sum_{i=1}^{m} \omega_i \phi_i(x), \tag{7}$$

where x is the input vector; ω_i is the connecting weights between the hidden layer and the output layer; and $\phi_i(x)$ is the output value of the neuron in the hidden layer after transfer by the radial basis function. Many radial basis functions can be used in RBFN model. The most common radial function is the Gaussian function [29] which is adopted in the present study:

$$\phi_i(x) = \exp\left(-\frac{\|x-c_i\|}{2\sigma^2}\right), \tag{8}$$

where c_i is center vector of the *i*th neuron in the hidden layer; σ is defined as $\sigma = d_{max}/\sqrt{nc}$, d_{max} is the maximum distance among c_i and nc is the number of the center vectors; and $\|x-c_i\|$ denotes the Euclidean distance between x and c_i. The approach used to determine nc is the orthogonal least squares (OLS) approach developed originally by Chen et al. [30] and improved by Ham and Kostanic [31] and Kecman [32]. The simplest way to select RBFN centers is random method [33]. However, the OLS algorithm provides an optimum number of centers (nc) in RBFN model from the training patterns [34].

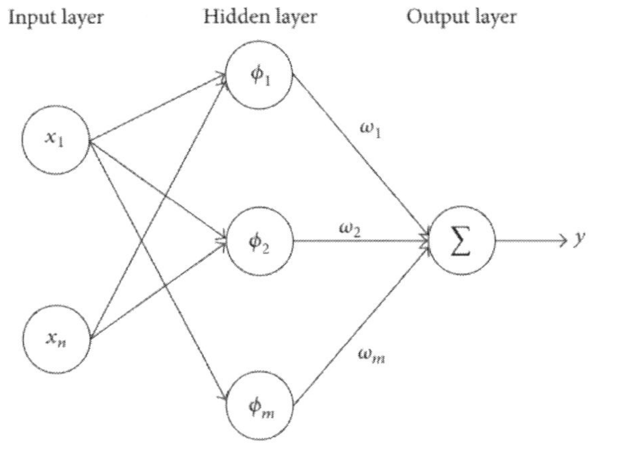

Figure 4: Architecture of the radial basis function neural network (RBFN).

Multilinear Regression

Multilinear regression (MLR) is used to model the linear relationship between a dependent variable and one or more independent variables. MLR is based on least squares: the model is fit such that the sum of the squares of the differences between the observed and simulated values is minimized [35]. The model expresses the value of a predicted variable as a linear function of one or more predictor variables:

$$y = b_0 + b_1 x_1 + b_2 x_2 + \cdots + b_i x_i, \tag{9}$$

where x_i is the value of the ith predictor, b_0 is the regression constant, and b_i is the coefficient of the ith predictor.

Indices of Simulation Performance

Many statistical indexes can be used to evaluate the performance of models. The most common indexes for evaluating the performance of ANN models are the root mean square error (RMSE) and the correlation coefficient (R). To strictly evaluate the performance of MLR, RBFN model, and ANFIS model, three criteria, mean absolute error (MAE), RMSE, and R, are employed in this study. These criteria can be defined by the following equations:

$$\text{MAE} = \frac{1}{N}\sum_N \left|(C_p)_N - (C_m)_N\right|,$$

$$\text{RMSE} = \sqrt{\frac{1}{N}\sum_N \left[(C_p)_N - (C_m)_N\right]^2},$$

$$R = \frac{\sum_N \left[(C_p)_N - \overline{C_p}\right]\left[(C_m)_N - \overline{C_m}\right]}{\sqrt{\sum_N \left[(C_p)_N - \overline{C_p}\right]^2 \sum_N \left[(C_m)_N - \overline{C_m}\right]^2}}, \tag{10}$$

where N is the total number of data points, C_p is a simulated water quality variable, C_m is a measured water quality variable, and $\overline{C_p}$ and $\overline{C_m}$ denote the average simulated and measured water quality variables, respectively.

RESULTS AND DISCUSSION

Selecting the Input Variables

The selection of an appropriate set of input variables for the MLR, RBFN, and ANFIS models is important for predicting the water quality variables in reservoirs [36]. It is difficult to determine how many input variables and which input variables should be adopted in the MLR, RBFN, and ANFIS models. The straight and useful way is to find the correlation coefficient between the individual dependent variables and water quality (DO, TP, Chl a, and SD). A total of 389 data sets collected from 1993 to 2013 were used for the analyses. Table 2 shows the correlation coefficient (R) between the individual dependent variables and DO, TP, Chl a, and SD, respectively. A correlation coefficient greater than 0.1 was set as the threshold for selecting the input variables. It indicates that the most effective inputs to affect DO are the pH value, chlorophyll a concentration, water temperature, total phosphorus, nitrate nitrogen, and biochemical oxygen demand. The most important water quality variables that affect the TP are the turbidity, suspended solids, pH value, dissolved oxygen, electrical conductivity, and nitrate nitrogen. It also illustrates that the most important input variables that affect Chl a and SD are, respectively, the six variables of the pH value, dissolved oxygen, water temperature, biochemical oxygen demand, nitrate nitrogen, and total hardness, and the six variables of the suspended solids, electrical conductivity, turbidity, total hardness, total alkalinity, and total phosphorus.

Table 2: The correlation coefficient () between individual dependent variable and DO, TP, Chl a, and SD.

Variables	R value between dependent variable and DO	R value between dependent variable and TP	R value between dependent variable and Chl a	R value between dependent variable and SD
Water temperature (WT)	0.2025	0.0861	0.3642	0.0571
pH	0.6339	0.2401	0.4090	0.0765
Electrical conductivity (EC)	0.0890	0.1769	0.0938	0.2164
Turbidity (TB)	0.0715	0.3505	0.0003	0.2140
Suspended solids (SS)	0.0812	0.3505	0.0094	0.2394
Total hardness (TH)	0.0289	0.0145	0.1051	0.1989
Total alkalinity (TA)	0.0250	0.0239	0.0488	0.1707
Secchi disk depth (SD)	0.0062	0.0982	0.0916	—
Dissolved oxygen (DO)	—	0.1917	0.3963	0.0062
Chlorophyll a (Chl a)	0.3963	0.0453	—	0.0916
Total phosphorus (TP)	0.1917	—	0.0453	0.1080
Nitrate nitrogen (NO_3)	0.1763	0.1740	0.1410	0.0978
Biochemical oxygen demand (BOD)	0.1199	0.0507	0.1777	0.0528

Water Quality Prediction Using the Multilinear Regression Model

The multilinear regression models were used to predict DO, TP, Chl a, and SD. The multilinear regression models in (11) to (14) were obtained from the input water quality variables:

$$DO = 2.8083 \times pH + 0.0887 \times Chl\ a - 0.074 \times WT - 0.0045 \times TP - 0.4928 \times NO_3 - 0.0055 \times BOD - 13.851, \quad (11)$$

$$TP = 0.039 \times TB + 0.07 \times SS - 4.4717 \times pH - 0.2463 \times DO - 0.0553 \times EC + 70.2402, \quad (12)$$

$$Chl\ a = 1.1423 \times pH + 0.5528 \times DO + 0.3228 \times WT + 0.1079 \times BOD - 1.7734 \times NO_3 - 0.0103 \times TH - 12.8466, \quad (13)$$

$$SD = -0.0119 \times SS - 0.0025 \times EC + 0.0042 \times TB - 0.0016 \times TH - 0.0010 \times TA - 0.0017 \times TP + 2.4449, \quad (14)$$

where BOD is the biochemical oxygen demand (mg/L); EC is the electrical conductivity (μmho/cm 25∘ C); NO3 is the nitrate nitrogen (mg/L); pH is the pH value; SS is the suspended solids (mg/L); TA is the total alkalinity (mg/L); TB is the turbidity (NTU); TH is the total hardness (mg/L); and WT is the water temperature (∘ C).

Equation (11) was used to predict the DO concentration for the training and testing phases. 272 and 117 data sets were used for training and testing the MLR model, respectively. Table 3 shows the performance evaluation using the MLR model for DO, TP, Chl a, and SD. The MAE, RMSE, and *R* values for the DO training phase were 1.81 mg/L, 2.33 mg/L, and 0.67, and these values for the DO testing phase were 1.81 mg/L, 2.41 mg/L, and 0.64, respectively.The MAE, RMSE, and *R* values for the TP training phase were 9.82 μg/L, 15.29 μg/L, and 0.55, and these values for the TP testing phase were 9.99 μg/L, 14.70 μg/L, and 0.31, respectively. The MAE, RMSE, and *R* values for the Chl a training phase were 3.96 μg/L, 5.85 μg/L, and 0.50, and these values for the Chl *a* testing phase were 4.18 μg/L, 5.92 μg/L, and 0.55, respectively. The MAE, RMSE, and *R* values for the SD training phase were 0.34 m, 0.45 m, and 0.43, and these values for the SD testing phase were 0.37 m, 0.53 m, and 0.35, respectively

Table 3: Performance evaluation during the training and testing phases for multilinear regression model

Water quality variable	Training phase			Testing phase		
	MAE	RMSE	*R*	MAE	RMSE	*R*
DO	1.81 mg/L	2.33 mg/L	0.67	1.81 mg/L	2.41 mg/L	0.64
TP	9.82 μg/L	15.29 μg/L	0.55	9.99 μg/L	14.70 μg/L	0.31
Chlorophyll *a*	3.96 μg/L	5.85 μg/L	0.50	4.18 μg/L	5.92 μg/L	0.55
SD	0.34 m	0.45 m	0.43	0.37 m	0.53 m	0.36

Water Quality Prediction Using the RBFN Model

Due to the poor performance using the multilinear regression model, the RBFN model was applied to predict the DO, TP, Chl a, and SD in the reservoir. The same data sets adopted in the multilinear regression model were used for training and testing the RBFN model.

Table 4 shows the performance evaluation for the DO, TP, Chl a, and SD during the training and testing phases. The MAE, RMSE, and *R* values for the DO during the training phase were 1.49 mg/L, 1.97 mg/L, and 0.77, and these values during the testing phase were 1.45 mg/L, 1.96 mg/L, and 0.79, respectively. The MAE, RMSE, and *R* values for the TP during the training phase were 8.89 μg/L, 11.77 μg/L, and 0.75, and these values during the testing phase were 7.95 μg/L, 9.91 μg/L, and 0.73, respectively. The MAE, RMSE, and *R* values for Chl a during the training phase were 3.09 μg/L, 4.39 μg/L, and 0.79, and these values during the testing phase were 2.86 μg/L, 4.08 μg/L, and 0.75, respectively. The MAE, RMSE, and *R* values for SD during the training phase were 0.29 m, 0.39 m, and 0.68, and these values during the testing phase were 0.23 m, 0.31 m, and 0.76, respectively. The performances for the DO, TP, Chl a, and SD using the RBFN model were better than using the MLR model during the training and testing phases.

Table 4: Performance evaluation during the training and testing phases for RBFN model

Water quality variable	Training phase			Testing phase		
	MAE	RMSE	*R*	MAE	RMSE	*R*
DO	1.49 mg/L	1.97 mg/L	0.77	1.45 mg/L	1.96 mg/L	0.79
TP	8.89 μg/L	11.77 μg/L	0.75	7.95 μg/L	9.91 μg/L	0.73
Chl *a*	3.09 μg/L	4.39 μg/L	0.79	2.86 μg/L	4.08 μg/L	0.75
SD	0.29 m	0.39 m	0.68	0.23 m	0.31 m	0.76

Some specific parameters may cause significant changes in ANN model [37]. In order to avoid overfitting or underfitting, we repeated ANN model until the minimum of errors occurred. Through the reiterative runs, the sum of error reduction ratio in RBFN model is set to 0.85 for providing the best performances. However, the statistical errors for the *R* value were still lower than 0.8 using the RBFN model, which means that the RBFN model is not good enough for predicting the water quality variables.

Water Quality Prediction Using the ANFIS Model

An alternative approach, the ANFIS model, was used to predict the water quality variables. The network was trained using the training data set (i.e., 272 data sets), and then it was tested with the testing data set (i.e., 117 data sets). Figures 5 and 6 show the comparison of the model-predicted DO and model-measured DO for the training and testing phases and scatter plots, respectively. The error values, representing the predicted DO minus the measured DO, are also shown in Figure 5. The MAE, RMSE, and R values for the training phase were 1.30 mg/L, 1.74 mg/L, and 0.85, while these values for the testing phase were 0.92 mg/L, 1.32 mg/L, and 0.88, respectively, as shown in Table 5. Figures 7 and 8 compare the model-predicted and model-measured TP concentrations for the training and testing phases and scatter plots, respectively. The MAE, RMSE, and R values for the training phase were 6.45 μg/L, 9.22 μg/L, and 0.86, while these values for the testing phase were 5.44 μg/L, 7.42 μg/L, and 0.86, respectively. Number of membership functions of ANFIS model is specified as 2 to obtain the best performances.

Table 5: Performance evaluation during the training and testing phases for ANFIS model

Water quality variable	Training phase			Testing phase		
	MAE	RMSE	R	MAE	RMSE	R
DO	1.30 mg/L	1.74 mg/L	0.85	0.92 mg/L	1.32 mg/L	0.88
TP	6.45 μg/L	9.92 μg/L	0.86	5.44 μg/L	7.42 μg/L	0.86
Chl *a*	3.19 μg/L	4.67 μg/L	0.77	2.25 μg/L	3.05 μg/L	0.83
SD	0.21 m	0.31 m	0.80	0.15 m	0.24 m	0.89

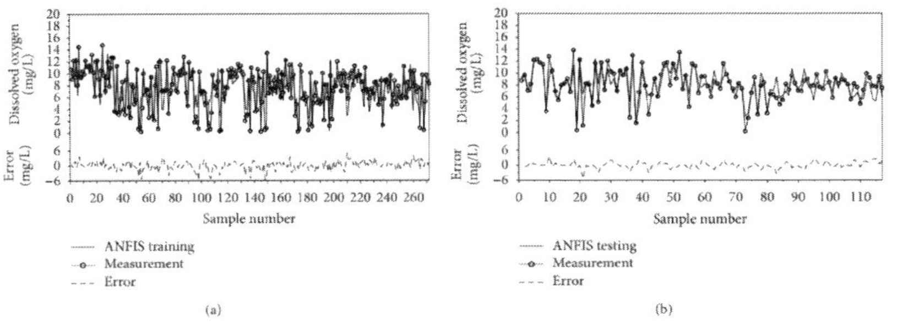

Figure 5: Comparison of predicted and measured dissolved oxygen using ANFIS model for the (a) training phase and (b) testing phase.

Figure 6: Scatter plots of predicted and measured dissolved oxygen using ANFIS model for the (a) training phase and (b) testing phase.

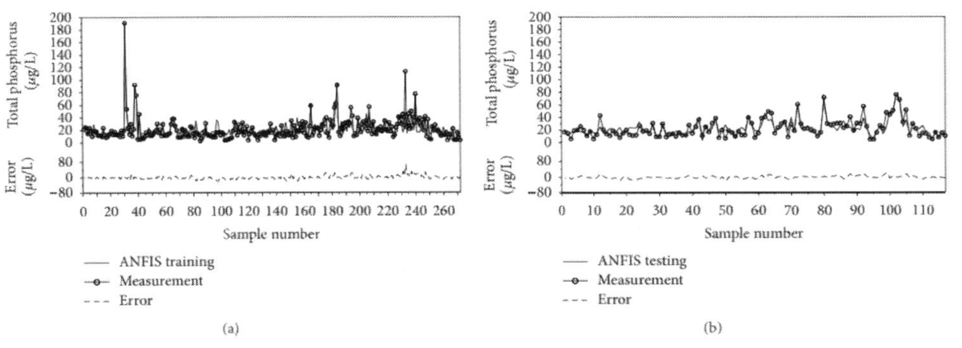

Figure 7: Comparison of predicted and measured total phosphorus using ANFIS model for the (a) training phase and (b) testing phase.

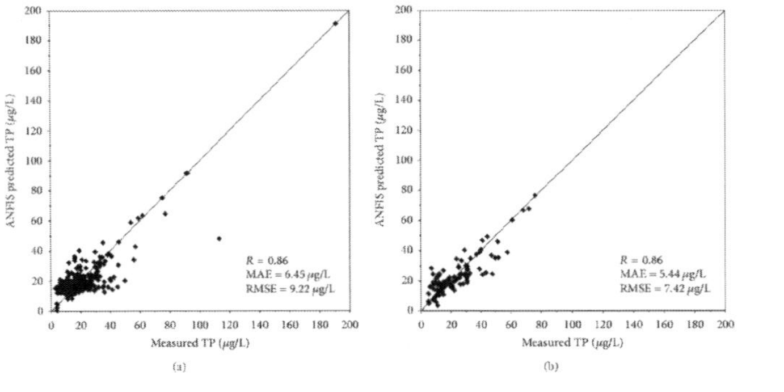

Figure 8: Scatter plots of predicted and measured total phosphorus using ANFIS model for the (a) training phase and (b) testing phase.

Figures 9 and 10 compare the model-predicted and model-measured chlorophyll a concentrations for the training and testing phases and scatter plots, respectively. The MAE, RMSE, and R values for the training phase were 3.19 μg/L, 4.67 μg/L, and 0.77, and these values for the testing phase were 3.25 μg/L, 3.05 μg/L, and 0.83, respectively. The performance evaluation for predicting the Chl a concentration using the ANFIS model during the training phase is slightly inferior to that using RBFN model, but the performance evaluation for predicting the Chl a concentration using the ANFIS model during testing phase is superior to that using RBFN model (Table 4). This result may be the reason that the predicted Chl a concentration using the ANFIS model underestimated the high Chl a concentration in the observational data during the training phase.

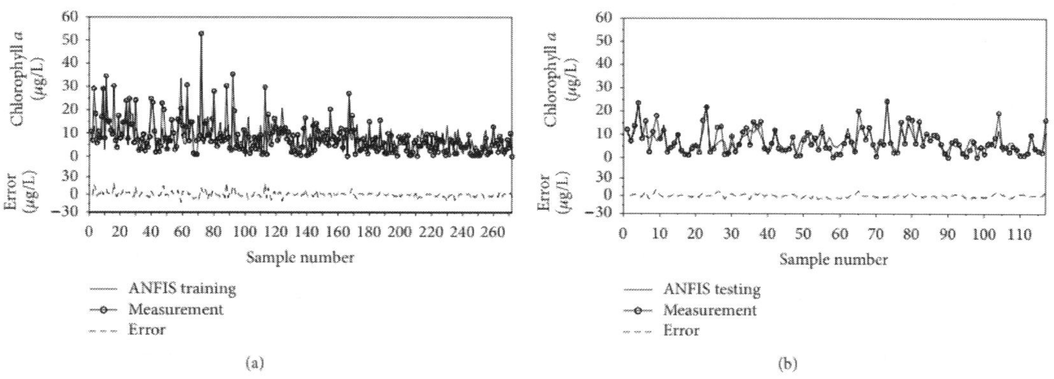

Figure 9: Comparison of predicted and measured chlorophyll a using ANFIS model for the (a) training phase and (b) testing phase.

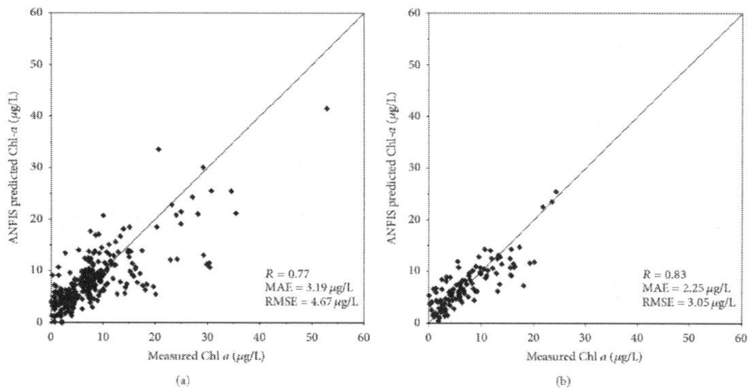

Figure 10: Scatter plots of predicted and measured chlorophyll a using ANFIS model for the (a) training phase and (b) testing phase.

Figures 11 and 12 illustrate the comparison of the modelpredicted and model-measured Secchi disk depth for the training and testing phases and scatter plots, respectively. The MAE, RMSE, and R values for the training phase were 0.21 m, 0.31 m, and 0.80, while these values for the testing phase were 0.15 m, 0.24 m, and 0.89, respectively. Overall, the performances of the DO, TP, Chl a, and SD with the ANFIS model are better than those with the multilinear regression model and the RBFN model. The performance evaluations with ANFIS during the testing phase are superior to those during the training phase. A similar result is also found in Rankovic et al. [′ 15].

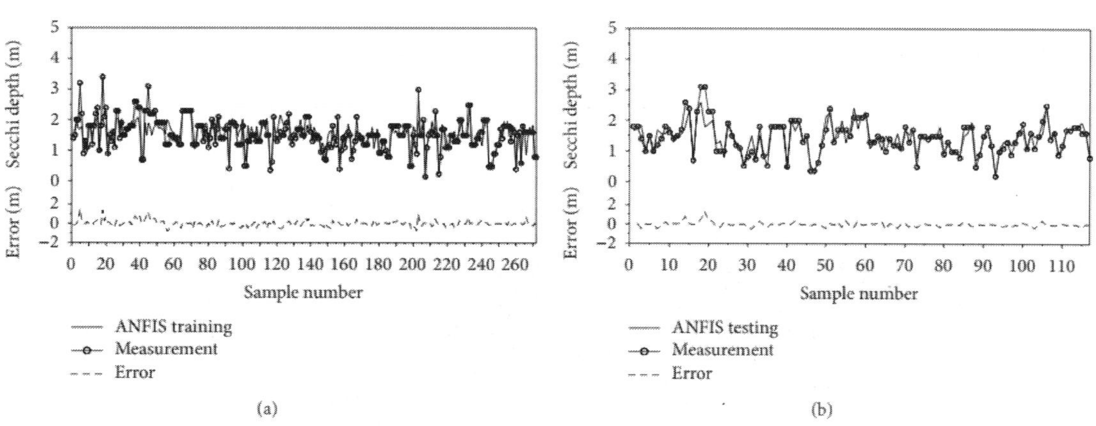

Figure 11: Comparison of predicted and measured Secchi disk depth using ANFIS model for the (a) training phase and (b) testing phase.

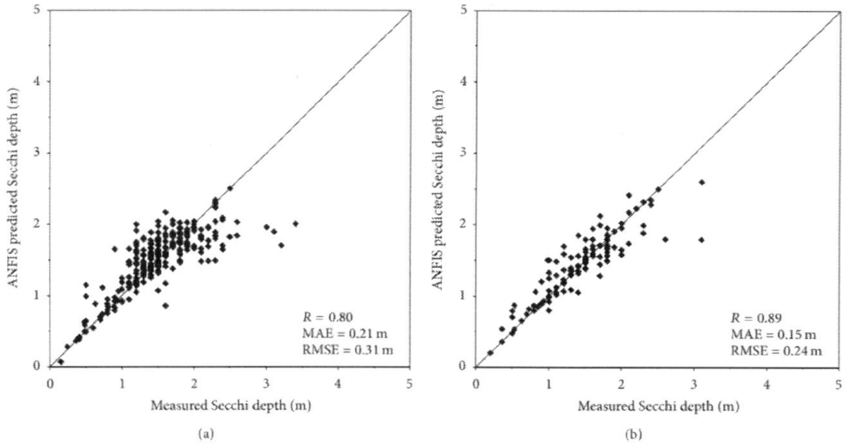

Figure 12: Scatter plots of predicted and measured Secchi disk depth using ANFIS model for the (a) training phase and (b) testing phase.

Akkoyunlu et al. [14] applied two ANN models and an MLR model to estimate the DO concentration in Lake Iznik, Turkey. They found that the MLR model performed less accurately to predict the DO. In the current study, the MLR model not only is less accurate for predicting the DO concentration but also does not simulate the TP, Chl a, or SD well.

DISCUSSION

In general, the neural network models provide better performance than the MLR model in this study. The MLR model is still a useful tool for simple and fast predicting water quality, although the predicted results by MLR model are of insufficient accuracy. For instance, Chenini and Khemiri [38] adopted MLR approach to evaluate the ground water quality in Maknassy Basin, central Tunisia. Thoe and Lee [39] used MLR to forecast the daily water quality of Hong Kong Beach.

Chau [26] performed a benchmarking comparison for predicting the river flow discharge using ANN and ANFIS models. His study indicated that the ANFIS model exhibited better performance than ANN model, but the performance of these two models were very close. Our study showed that the predictions of water quality using RBFN and ANFIS models had significant differences. It may be the reason that the characteristics of input data are different. Chau [26] used antecedent flow data (i.e., Q_t, Q_{t-1}, and Q_{t-2}) as input vector, while input data with different independent variables is adopted in the present study.

CONCLUSIONS

ANN models (i.e., RBFN and ANFIS models) and an MLR model were developed to predict the DO, TP, Chl a, and SD in the reservoir. The performances of the RBFN, ANFIS, and MLR models were evaluated using the mean absolute error, the root mean square error, and the correlation coefficient. The linear regression between the water quality variables (DO, TP, Chl a, and SD) and the individual dependent variables was used to select the major input variables for the RBFN, ANFIS, and MLR models.

These models were then constructed to predict the DO, TP, Chl a, and SD in the Mingder Reservoir of central Taiwan. The water quality variables predicted using the MLR model did not yield good results. The correlation coefficient between the predicted water quality variables and the measured data was less than 0.8 using the RBFN model. In general, the ANFIS model better predicts the water quality variables than the RBFN model does. The ANN model, including the RBFN and ANFIS model, can preserve the nonlinear characteristics between the input and output variables, which are superior to conventional statistical approaches (i.e., the MLR model). In the real world, temporal and spatial distributions in observational data do not exhibit simple regularities; therefore, they are difficult to accurately predict. It is necessary to use nonlinear models, such as the ANN model, which are suitable for complex nonlinear systems. The proposed approach using the ANFIS model has yielded valuable information that can be used by decision-makers for aiding reservoir water quality management.

In the present study, we focus on the prediction of water quality instead of forecast. In a future study, different lead-time forecasts in the water quality can be developed to assist the local authorities for water quality management. The soft computing techniques, such as the combining fuzzy optimal model with genetic programming [40, 41], support vector machine [42, 43], and particle swarm optimization training algorithm for a neural network [44], can also be develop to improve the prediction of water quality in the reservoirs.

ACKNOWLEDGMENTS

The project under which this study was conducted is supported by the National Science Council (NSC), Taiwan, under Grant no. NSC100-2625-M-239-001. The authors would like to express their appreciation to the Environmental Protection Administration, Taiwan, for providing the measured data.

REFERENCES

1. W.-C. Liu, W.-B. Chen, and N. Kimura, "Impact of phosphorus load reduction on water quality in a stratified reservoir-eutrophication modeling study," Environmental Monitoring and Assessment, vol. 159, no. 1–4, pp. 393–406, 2009.
2. A. Najah, A. El-Shafie, O. A. Karim, and A. H. El-Shafie, "Performance of ANFIS versus MLP-NN dissolved oxygen prediction models in water quality

monitoring," Environmental Science and Pollution Research, vol. 21, no. 3, pp. 1658–1670, 2014.

3. F. Recknagel, A. Talib, and D. van der Molen, "Phytoplankton community dynamics of two adjacent Dutch lakes in response to seasons and eutrophication control unravelled by non-supervised artificial neural networks," Ecological Informatics, vol. 1, no. 3, pp. 277–285, 2006.
4. R. O. Strobl, F. Forte, and L. Pennetta, "Application of artificial neural networks for classifying lake eutrophication status," Lakes & Reservoirs: Research and Management, vol. 12, no. 1, pp. 15–25, 2007.
5. A. Afshar and M. Saadatpour, "Reservoir eutrophication modeling, sensitivity analysis, and assessment: application to karkheh reservoir, Iran," Environmental Engineering Science, vol. 26, no. 7, pp. 1227–1238, 2009.
6. P. Kudu, A. Debsarkar, and S. Mukherjee, "Artificial neural network modeling for biological removal of organic carbon and nitrogen from slaughterhouse wastewater in a sequencing batch reactor," Advances in Artificial Neural Systems, vol. 2013, Article ID 268064, 15 pages, 2013.
7. G. He, H. Fang, S. Bai, X. Liu, M. Chen, and J. Bai, "Application of a three-dimensional eutrophication model for the Beijing Guanting Reservoir, China," Ecological Modelling, vol. 222, no. 8, pp. 1491–1501, 2011.
8. C. Lindim, J. L. Pinho, and J. M. P. Vieira, "Analysis of spatial and temporal patterns in a large reservoir using water quality and hydrodynamic modeling," Ecological Modelling, vol. 222, no. 14, pp. 2485–2494, 2011.
9. C. Zhang, X. Gao, L. Wang, and Y. Chen, "Analysis of agricultural pollution by flood flow impact on water quality in a reservoir using a three-dimensional water quality model," Journal of Hydroinformatics, vol. 15, no. 4, pp. 1061–1072, 2013.
10. J. M. P. Vieira, J. L. S. Pinho, N. Dias, D. Schwanenberg, and H. F. P. van den Boogaard, "Parameter estimation for eutrophication models in reservoirs," Water Science and Technology, vol. 68, no. 2, pp. 319–327, 2013.
11. C. T. Cheng, K. W. Chau, Y. G. Sun, and J. Y. Lin, "Long-term prediction of discharges in Manwan Reservoir using artificial neural network models," in Advances in Neural Networks—ISNN 2005, vol. 3498 of Lecture Notes in Computer Science, pp. 1040–1045, Springer, Berlin, Germany, 2005.
12. W. C. Liu and C. E. Chung, "Enhancing the predicting accuracy of the water stage using a physical-based model and an artificial neural network-genetic algorithm in a river system," Water, vol. 6, no. 6, pp. 1642–1661, 2014.
13. K.-W. Chau, "A review on integration of artificial intelligence into water quality modelling," Marine Pollution Bulletin, vol. 52, no. 7, pp. 726–733, 2006.
14. A. Akkoyunlu, H. Altun, and H. K. Cigizoglu, "Depth-integrated estimation of dissolved oxygen in a lake," Journal of Environmental Engineering, vol. 137, no. 10, pp. 961–967, 2011.
15. V. Ranković, J. Radulović, I. Radojević, A. Ostojić, and L. Čomić, "Prediction of dissolved oxygen in reservoirs using adaptive network-based fuzzy inference system," Journal of Hydroinformatics, vol. 14, no. 1, pp. 167–179, 2012.
16. H. B. Chu, W. X. Lu, and L. Zhang, "Application of artificial neural network in environmental water quality assessment," Journal of Agricultural Science and Technology, vol. 15, no. 2, pp. 343–356, 2013.
17. O. Kisi, N. Akbari, M. Sanatipour, A. Hashemi, K. Teimourzadeh, and J. Shiri, "Modeling of dissolved oxygen in river water using artificial intelligence techniques," Journal of Environmental Informatics, vol. 22, no. 2, pp. 92–101, 2013.
18. M. Ay and O. Kisi, "Modelling of chemical oxygen demand by using ANNs, ANFIS and k-means clustering techniques," Journal of Hydrology, vol. 511, pp. 279–289, 2014.
19. K. P. Singh, A. Basant, A. Malik, and G. Jain, "Artificial neural network modeling of the river water quality-A case study," Ecological Modelling, vol. 220, no. 6, pp. 888–895, 2009.
20. E. Dogan, B. Sengorur, and R. Koklu, "Modeling biological oxygen demand of the Melen River in Turkey using an artificial neural network technique," Journal of Environmental Management, vol. 90, no. 2, pp. 1229–1235, 2009.
21. V. Ranković, J. Radulović, I. Radojević, A. Ostojić, and L. Čomić, "Neural network modeling of dissolved oxygen in the Gruža reservoir, Serbia," Ecological Modelling, vol. 221, no. 8, pp. 1239–1244, 2010.
22. F. Soltani, R. Kerachian, and E. Shirangi, "Developing operating rules for reservoirs considering the water quality issues: application of ANFIS-based surrogate models," Expert Systems with Applications, vol. 37, no. 9, pp. 6639–6645, 2010.
23. R. E. Carlson, "A trophic state index for lakes," Limnology and Oceanography, vol. 22, no. 2, pp. 361–369, 1977.
24. J. S. R. Jang, "ANFIS: adaptive-network-based fuzzy inference system," IEEE Transactions on Systems, Man and Cybernetics, vol. 23, no. 3, pp. 665–685, 1993.
25. T. Takagi and M. Sugeno, "Fuzzy identification of systems and its applications to modeling and control,"IEEE Transactions on Systems, Man and Cybernetics, vol. 15, no. 1, pp. 116–132, 1985.
26. K. W. Chau, Modelling for Coastal Hydraulics and Engineering, Spon Press, 2010.
27. J. C. Mason, R. K. Price, and A. Tem›me, "A neural network model of rainfall-runoff using radial basis functions," Journal of Hydraulic Research, vol. 34, no. 4, pp. 537–548, 1996.
28. Y. B. Dibike, D. P. Solomatine, and M. B. Abbott, "On the encapsulation of numerical-hydraulic models in artificial neural network," Journal of Hydraulic Research, vol. 37, no. 2, pp. 147–161, 1999.
29. M. Verleysen and K. Hlavackova, "Learning in RBF networks," in Proceedings of the International Conference on Neural Network (ICNN ‹96), pp. 199–204, Washington, DC, USA, June 1996.

30. S. Chen, C. F. N. Cowan, and P. M. Grant, "Orthogonal least squares learning algorithm for radial basis function networks," IEEE Transactions on Neural Networks, vol. 2, no. 2, pp. 302–309, 1991.

31. F. M. Ham and I. Kostanic, Principles of Neurocomputing for Science and Engineering, McGraw-Hill, New York, NY, USA, 2001.

32. V. Kecman, Learning and Soft Computing: Support Vector Machine, Neural Networks, and Fuzzy Logic Models, MIT Press, Cambridge, Mass, USA, 2001.

33. S. Haykin, Neural Networks: A Comprehensive Foundation, Prentice Hall, Upper Saddle River, NJ, USA, 2nd edition, 1999.

34. M. M. Zirkohi, M. M. Fateh, and A. Akbarzade, "Design of radial basis function network using adaptive particle swarm optimization and orthogonal least squares," Journal of Software Engineering and Applications, vol. 3, no. 7, pp. 704–708, 2010.

35. S. Weisberg, Applied Linear Regression, John Wiley & Sons, New York, NY, USA, 2nd edition, 1985.

36. S. Soyupak, F. Karaer, H. Gürbüz, E. Kivrak, E. Sentürk, and A. Yazici, "A neural network-based approach for calculating dissolved oxygen profiles in reservoirs," Neural Computing & Applications, vol. 12, no. 3-4, pp. 166–172, 2003.

37. I. V. Tetko, D. J. Livingstone, and A. I. Luik, "Neural network Studies. 1. Comparison of overfitting and overtraining," Journal of Chemical Information and Computer Sciences, vol. 35, no. 5, pp. 826–833, 1995.

38. I. Chenini and S. Khemiri, "Evaluation of ground water quality using multiple linear regression and structural equation modeling," International Journal of Environmental Science and Technology, vol. 6, no. 3, pp. 509–519, 2009.

39. W. Thoe and J. H. W. Lee, "Daily forecasting of Hong Kong beach water quality by multiple linear regression models," Journal of Environmental Engineering, vol. 140, no. 2, Article ID 04013007, 2014.

40. O. Kisi and T. M. Cengiz, "Fuzzy genetic approach for estimating reference evapotranspiration of Turkey: Mediterranean region," Water Resources Management, vol. 27, no. 10, pp. 3541–3553, 2013.

41. C. T. Cheng, C. P. Ou, and K. W. Chau, "Combining a fuzzy optimal model with a genetic algorithm to solve multi-objective rainfall-runoff model calibration," Journal of Hydrology, vol. 268, no. 1–4, pp. 72–86, 2002.

42. J.-Y. Lin, C.-T. Cheng, and K.-W. Chau, "Using support vector machines for long-term discharge prediction," Hydrological Sciences Journal, vol. 51, no. 4, pp. 599–612, 2006.

43. H. Tabari, O. Kisi, A. Ezani, and P. Hosseinzadeh Talaee, "SVM, ANFIS, regression and climate based models for reference evapotranspiration modeling using limited climatic data in a semi-arid highland environment," Journal of Hydrology, vol. 444-445, pp. 78–89, 2012.

44. K. W. Chau, "Particle swarm optimization training algorithm for ANNs in stage prediction of Shing Mun River," Journal of Hydrology, vol. 329, no. 3-4, pp. 363–367, 2006.

CHAPTER 19

TIME SERIES MODELING OF RIVER FLOW USING WAVELET NEURAL NETWORKS

B. Krishna, Y. R. Satyaji Rao, and P. C. Nayak

Keywords: Time Series, River Flow, Wavelets, Neural Networks

INTRODUCTION

Water resources planning and management requires, output from hydrological studies. These are mainly in the form of estimation or forecasting of the magnitude of hydrological variables like precipitation, stream flow and groundwater levels using historical data. Forecasting of hydrological variables especially stream flow is utmost important to provide a warning of the extreme flood or drought conditions and helps to develop operation systems of multipurpose reservoirs. Similarly, groundwater level modeling is useful for consumptive use studies for better watershed management.

Time series modeling for either data generation or forecasting of hydrological variables is an important step in the planning and management of water resources. Most of the time series modeling procedures fall within the framework of multivariate Auto Regressive Moving Average (ARMA) model [1]. Traditionally, ARMA models have been widely used for modeling water resources time-series modeling [2]. The time series models are used to describe the stochastic structure of the time sequence of a hydrological variable measured over time. Time-series models are more practical than conceptual models because it is not essential to understand the internal structure of the physical processes that are taking place in the system being modeled. Time series analysis requires mapping complex relationships between input(s) and output(s), since the forecasted values are mapped as a function of observed patterns in the past. On the other hand, classical non-linear techniques typically require large amounts of exogenous data, which are not always available [3]; some non-linear approaches outperform the linear techniques, as periodic gamma autoregressive processes (PGAR) for instance [4], but they can only be applied to a single site, i.e., they are limited to be univariate models. Owing to the difficulties associated with non-linear model structure identification and parameter estimation, very few truly non-linear system theoretic hydrologic models have been reported [5-7]. It seems necessary that nonlinear models such as neural networks, which are suited to complex nonlinear problems, be used for the time series modeling of river flow.

Artificial Neural Networks (ANN) has been used successfully to overcome many difficulties in time series modeling of river flow. Time series modeling using ANN has been a particular focus of interest and better performing models have been reported in a diverse set of fields that include rainfall-runoff modeling [8-12] and groundwater level prediction [13-16]. It is also reported that ANN models are not very satisfied in precision for forecasting because it considered only few aspects of time series property [17]. In order to raise the forecasted precision and lengthen the forecasted time, an alternative model should be envisaged. In this paper, a new hybrid model called wavelet neural network model (WNN), which is the combination of wavelet analysis and ANN, has been proposed. The advantage of the wavelet technique is that it provides a mathematical process for decomposing a signal into multi-levels of details and analysis of these details can be done. Wavelet analysis can effectively diagnose signals of main frequency component and abstract local information of the time series. In the past decade, wavelet theory has been introduced to signal processing analysis. In recent years, the

Citation: B. Krishna, Y. Rao and P. Nayak, "Time Series Modeling of River Flow Using Wavelet Neural Networks,"Journal of Water Resource and Protection, Vol. 3 No. 1, 2011, pp. 50-59. doi: 10.4236/jwarp.2011.31006.

wavelet transforms has been successfully applied to wave data analysis and other ocean engineering applications [18,19].

In recent years, wavelet theory has been introduced in the field of hydrology [17,20-22]. Wavelet analysis has recently been identified as a useful tool for describing both rainfall and runoff time-series [21,23-26]. By coupling the wavelet method with the traditional AR model, the Wavelet-Autoregressive model (WARM) is developed for annual rainfall prediction [27]. Coulibaly [28] used the wavelet analysis to identify and describe variability in annual Canadian stream flows and to gain insights into the dynamical link between the stream flows and the dominant modes of climate variability in the Northern Hemisphere. Due to the similarity between wavelet decomposition and one hidden layer neural network, the idea of combining both wavelet and neural network has resulted recently in formulation of wavelet neural network, which has been used in various fields [29]. Results show that, the training and adaptation efficiency of the wavelet neural network is better than other networks. Dongjie [30] used a combination of neural networks and wavelet methods to predict ground water levels. Aussem [31] used a Dynamical Recurrent Neural Network (DRNN) on each resolution scale of the sunspot time series resulting from the wavelet decomposed series with the Temporal Recurrent Back propagation (TRBP) algorithm. Partal [32] used a conjunction model (wavelet-neurofuzzy) to forecast the Turkey daily precipitation. The observed daily precipitations are decomposed to some sub series by using Discrete Wavelet Transform (DWT) and then appropriate sub series are used as inputs to neurofuzzy models for forecasting of daily precipitations.

In this paper, an attempt has been made to forecast the time series of Daily River flow by developing wavelet neural network (WNN) models. Time series of river flow was decomposed into wavelet sub-series by discrete wavelet transform. Then, neural network model is constructed with wavelet sub-series as input, and the original time series as output. Finally, the forecasting performance of WNN model was compared with the ANN and AR models.

METHODS OF ANALYSIS

Wavelet Analysis

The wavelet analysis is an advance tool in signal processing that has attracted much attention since its theoretical development [33]. Its use has increased rapidly in communications, image processing and optical engineering applications as an alternative to the Fourier transform in preserving local, non-periodic and multiscaled phenomena. The difference between wavelets and Fourier transforms is that wavelets can provide the exact locality of any changes in the dynamical patterns of the sequence, whereas the Fourier transforms concentrate mainly on their frequency. Moreover, Fourier transform assume infinite-length signals, whereas wavelet transforms can be applied to any kind and size of time series, even when these sequences are not homogeneously sampled in time [34]. In general, wavelet transforms can be used to explore, denoise and smoothen time series, aid in forecasting and other empirical analysis.

Wavelet analysis is the breaking up of a signal into shifted and scaled versions of the original (or mother) wavelet. In wavelet analysis, the use of a fully scalable modulated window solves the signal-cutting problem. The window is shifted along the signal and for every position the spectrum is calculated. Then this process is repeated many times with a slightly shorter (or longer) window for every new cycle. In the end, the result will be a collection of time-frequency representations of the signal, all with different resolutions. Because of this collection of representations we can speak of a multiresolution analysis. By decomposing a time series into timefrequency space, one is able to determine both the dominant modes of variability and how those modes vary in time. Wavelets have proven to be a powerful tool for the analysis and synthesis of data from long memory processes. Wavelets are strongly connected to such processes in that the same shapes repeat at different orders of magnitude. The ability of the wavelets to simultaneously localize a process in time and scale domain results in representing many dense matrices in a sparse form.

Discrete Wavelet Transform (DWT)

The basic aim of wavelet analysis is both to determine the frequency (or scale) content of a signal and to assess and determine the temporal variation of this frequency content. This property is in complete contrast to the Fourier analysis, which allows for the determination of the frequency content of a signal but fails to determine frequency timedependence. Therefore, the wavelet transform is the tool of choice when signals are characterized by localized high frequency events or when signals are characterized by a large numbers of scale-variable processes. Because of its localization properties in both time and scale, the wavelet transform allows for tracking the time evolution of processes at different scales in the signal.

The wavelet transform of a time series f(t) is defined as

$$f(a,b)=\frac{1}{\sqrt{a}}\int_{-\infty}^{\infty} f(t)\psi\left(\frac{t-b}{a}\right)dt \qquad (1)$$

where $\psi(t)$ is the basic wavelet with effective length (t) that is usually much shorter than the target time series f(t). The variables are a and b, where a is the scale or dilation factor that determines the characteristic frequency so that its variation gives rise to a 'spectrum'; and b is the translation in time so that its variation represents the 'sliding' of the wavelet over f(t). The wavelet spectrum is thus customarily displayed in time-frequency domain. For low scales i.e. when $|a| \ll 1$, the wavelet function is highly concentrated (shrunken compressed) with frequency contents mostly in the higher frequency bands. Inversely, when $|a| \gg 1$, the wavelet is stretched and contains mostly low frequencies. For small scales, we obtain thus a more detailed view of the signal (also known as a "higher resolution") whereas for larger scales we obtain a more general view of the signal structure.

The original signal X(n) passes through two complementary filters (low pass and high pass filters) and emerges as two signals as Approximations (A) and Details (D). The approximations are the high-scale, low frequency components of the signal. The details are the low-scale, high frequency components. Normally, the low frequency content of the signal (approximation, A) is the most important part. It demonstrates the signal identity. The high-frequency component (detail, D) is nuance. The decomposition process can be iterated, with successive approximations being decomposed in turn, so that one signal is broken down into many lower resolution components (Figure 1).

Mother Wavelet

The choice of the mother wavelet depends on the data to be analyzed. The Daubechies and Morlet wavelet transforms are the commonly used "Mother" wavelets. Daubechies wavelets exhibit good trade-off between parsimony and information richness, it produces the identical events across the observed time series and appears in so many different fashions that most prediction models are unable to recognize them well [35]. Morlet wavelets, on the other hand, have a more consistent response to similar events but have the weakness of generating many more inputs than the Daubechies wavelets for the prediction models.

An ANN, can be defined as a system or mathematical model consisting of many nonlinear artificial neurons running in parallel, which can be generated, as one or multiple layered. Although the concept of artificial neurons was first introduced by McCulloch and Pitts [36], the major applications of ANN's have arisen only since the development of the back-propagation method of training by Rumelhart [37]. Following this development, ANN research has resulted in the successful solution of some complicated problems not easily solved by traditional modeling methods when the quality/quantity of data is very limited. ANN models are 'black box' models with particular properties, which are greatly suited to dynamic nonlinear system modeling. The main advantage of this approach over traditional methods is that it does not require the complex nature of the underlying process under consideration to be explicitly described in mathematical form. ANN applications in hydrology vary, from real-time to event based modeling.

The most popular ANN architecture in hydrologic modeling is the multilayer perceptron (MLP) trained with BP algorithm [8,9]. A multilayer perceptron network consists of an input layer, one or more hidden layers of computation nodes, and an output layer. The number of input and output nodes is determined by the nature of the actual input and output variables. The number of hidden nodes, however, depends on the complexity of the mathematical nature of the problem, and is determined by the modeler, often by trial and error. The input signal propagates through the network in a forward direction, layer by layer. Each hidden and output node processes its input by multiplying each of its input values by a weight, summing the product and then passing the sum through a nonlinear transfer function to produce a result. For the training process, where weights are selected, the neural network uses the gradient descent method to modify the randomly selected weights of the nodes in response to the errors between the actual output values and the target values. This process is referred to as training or learning. It stops when the errors are minimized or another stopping criterion is met. The BPNN can be expressed as

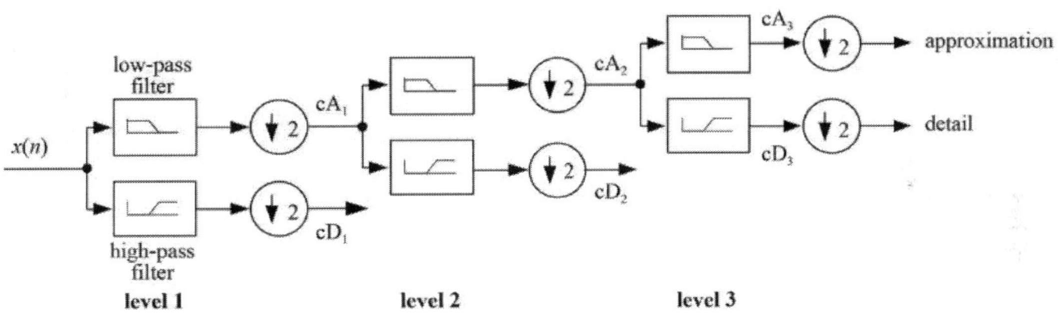

Figure 1: Diagram of multiresolution analysis of signal.

$$Y = f\left(\sum WX - \theta\right) \tag{2}$$

where X = input or hidden node value; Y = output value of the hidden or output node; f (.) = transfer function; W = weights connecting the input to hidden, or hidden to output nodes; and θ = bias (or threshold) for each node.

METHOD OF NETWORK TRAINING

Levenberg-Marquardt method (LM) was used for the training of the given network. Levenberg-Marquardt method (LM) is a modification of the classic Newton algorithm for finding an optimum solution to a minimization problem. In practice, LM is faster and finds better optima for a variety of problems than most other methods [38]. The method also takes advantage of the internal recurrence to dynamically incorporate past experience in the training process [39].

The Levenberg-Marquardt algorithm is given by

$$X_{k+1} = X_k - \left(J^T J + \mu I\right)^{-1} J^T e \tag{3}$$

where, X is the weights of neural network, J is the Jacobian matrix of the performance criteria to be minimized, m is a learning rate that controls the learning process and e is residual error vector.

If scalar m is very large, the above expression approximates gradient descent with a small step size; while if it is very small; the above expression becomes GaussNewton method using the approximate Hessian matrix. The Gauss-Newton method is faster and more accurate near an error minimum. Hence we decrease m after each successful step and increase only when a step increases the error. Levenberg-Marquardt has great computational and memory requirements, and thus it can only be used in small networks. It is faster and less easily trapped in local minima than other optimization algorithms.

Selection of Network Architecture

Increasing the number of training patterns provide more information about the shape of the solution surface, and thus increases the potential level of accuracy that can be achieved by the network. A large training pattern set, however can sometimes overwhelm certain training algorithms, thereby increasing the likelihood of an algorithm becoming stuck in a local error minimum. Consequently, there is no guarantee that adding more training patterns leads to improve solution. Moreover, there is a limit to the amount of information that can be modeled by a network that comprises a fixed number of hidden neurons. The time required to train a network increases with the number of patterns in the training set. The critical aspect is the choice of the number of nodes in the hidden layer and hence the number of connection weights.

Based on the physical knowledge of the problem and statistical analysis, different combinations of antecedent values of the time series were considered as input nodes. The output node is the time series data to be predicted in one step ahead. Time series data was standardized for zero mean and unit variation, and then normalized into 0 to 1. The activation function used for the hidden and output layer was logarithmic sigmoidal and pure linear function respectively. For deciding the optimal hidden neurons, a trial and error procedure started with two hidden neurons initially, and the number of hidden neurons was increased up to 10 with a step size of 1 in each trial. For each set of hidden neurons, the network was trained in batch mode to minimize the mean square error at the output layer. In order to check any over-fitting during training, a cross validation was performed by keeping track of the efficiency of the fitted model. The training was stopped when there was no significant improvement in the efficiency, and the model was then tested for its generalization properties. Figure 2 shows the multilayer perceptron (MLP) neural network architecture when the original signal taken as input of the neural network architecture.

Method of Combining Wavelet Analysis with ANN

The decomposed details (D) and approximation (A) were taken as inputs to neural network structure as shown in Figure 3. In Figure 3, i is the level of decomposition varying from 1 to I and j is the number of antecedent values varying from 0 to J and N is the length of the time series. To obtain the optimal weights (parameters) of the neural network structure, LM back-propagation algorithm has been used to train the network. A standard MLP with a logarithmic sigmoidal transfer function for the hidden layer and linear transfer function for the output layer were used in the analysis. The number of hidden nodes was determined by trial and error procedure. The output node will be the original value at one step ahead.

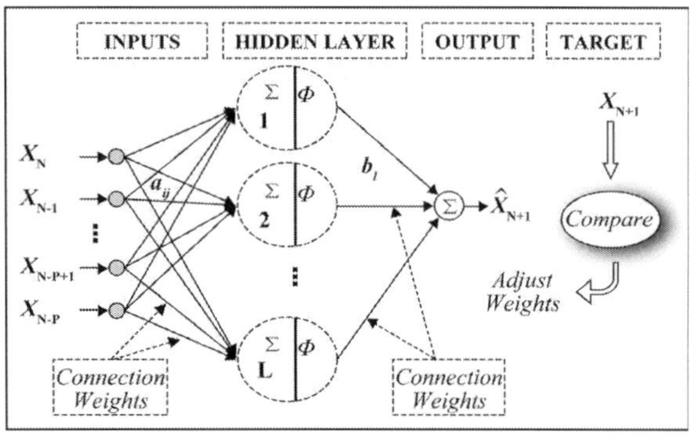

Figure 2: Signal data based multilayer perceptron (MLP) neural network structure.

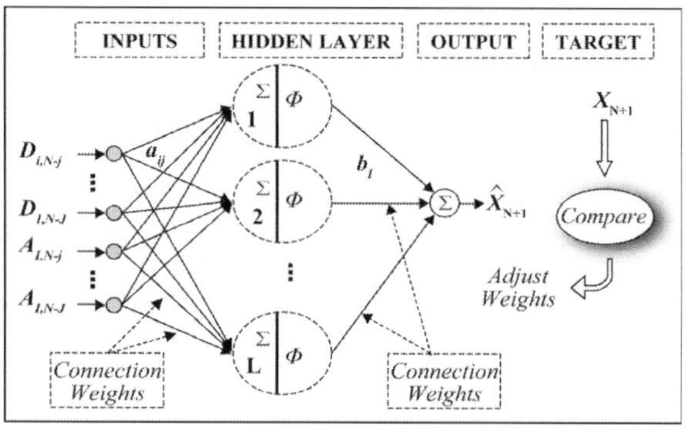

Figure 3: Wavelet based multilayer perceptron (MLP) neural network structure.

Linear Auto-Regressive (AR) Modeling

A common approach for modeling univariate time series is the autoregressive (AR) model:

$$X_t = \delta + \phi_1 X_{t-1} + \phi_2 X_{t-2} + \cdots + \phi_p X_{t-p} + A_t \tag{4}$$

where X_t is the time series, A_t is white noise, and

$$\delta = \left(1 - \sum_{i=1}^{p} \phi_i\right)\mu \tag{5}$$

where μ is the mean of the time series. An autoregressive model is simply a linear regression of the current value of the series against one or more prior values. AR models can be analyzed with linear least squares technique. They also have a straightforward interpretation. The determination of the model order can be estimated by examining the plots of Auto Correlation Function (ACF) and Partial Auto Correlation Function (PACF). The number of non-zero terms (i.e. outside confidence bands) in PACF suggests the order of the AR model. An AR (k) model will be implied by a sample PACF with k non-zero terms, and the terms in the sample ACF will decay slowly towards zero. From ACF and PACF analysis for river flow, the order of the AR model is selected as 1.

1. Performance Criteria The performance of various models during calibration and validation were evaluated by using the statistical indices: the Root Mean Squared Error (RMSE), Correlation Coefficient (R), Coefficient of Efficiency (COE) and Persistence Index (PI).
2. Study Area In this paper, a hybrid model wavelet neural network (WNN) used to forecast the river flow of the Malaprabha River basin (Figure 4) in Karnataka state of India. The river Malaprabha is one of the tributary of river Krishna, originated from Kanakumbi in the Western Ghats at an altitude of 792.48 m in Belgaum district of Karnataka State. The river flows in an easterly direction and joins the River Krishna. The Malaprabha river upto Khanapur gauging station was considered for the present study. It is having a total catchment area of 520 Sq.km. and lies between 15° 30' to 15° 50' N latitude and 74° 12' to 74° 32' E longitude. About 60% of the basin was covered with forests covering upstream area of the basin and northern part of the basin is used for agricultural purpose. Major portion of the catchment is covered with tertiary basaltic rock, whereas, the sedimentary rocks have confined to the southeastern part of the catchment. Most of the rainfall

of the basin experiences from southwest monsoon. The average annual precipitation is 2337 mm from seven rain gauges, which are uniformly distributed throughout the basin (Figure 4). The average daily river flow data of 11 years (1986-1996) used for the current study. The maximum value of the testing data set is fall within the training data set limit. This means that the trained neural network models do not face difficulties in making extrapolation.

DEVELOPMENT OF WAVELET NEURAL NETWORK MODEL

The original time series was decomposed into Details and Approximations a certain number of sub-time series $\{D_1, D_2, \cdots, D_P, A_P\}$ by wavelet transform algorithm.

These play different role in the original time series and the behavior of each sub-time series is distinct [17]. So the contribution to original time series varies from each other. The decomposition process can be iterated, with successive approximations being decomposed in turn, so that one signal is broken down into many lower resolution components, tested using different scales from 1 to 10 with different sliding window amplitudes. In this context, dealing with a very irregular signal shape, an irregular wavelet, the Daubechies wavelet of order 5 (DB5), has been used at level 3. Consequently, D_1, D_2, D_3 were detail time series, and A_3 was the approximation time series.

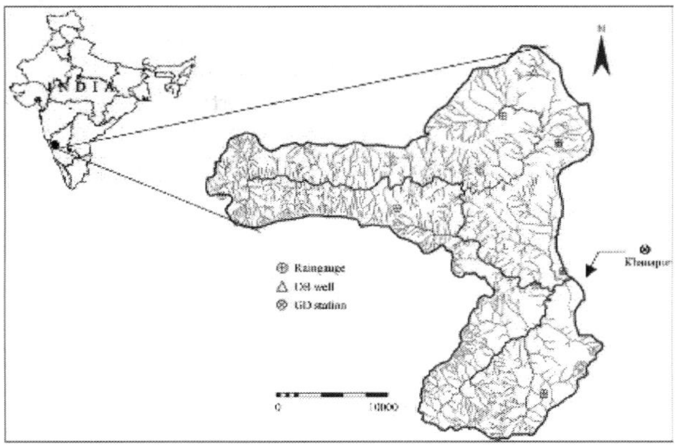

Figure 4: Location of study area.

Table 1: Model inputs.

Model I	X (t) = f (x [t-1])
Model II	X (t) = f (x [t-1], x [t-2])
Model III	X (t) = f (x [t-1], x [t-2], x [t-3])
Model IV	X (t) = f (x [t-1], x [t-2], x [t-3], x [t-4])
Model V	X (t) = f (x [t-1], x [t-2], x [t-3], x [t-4], x [t-5])

An ANN was constructed in which the sub-series $\{D_1, D_2, D_3, A_3\}$ at time t are input of ANN and the original time series at t + T time are output of ANN, where T is the length of time to forecast. The input nodes are the antecedent values of the time series and were presented in Table 1. The Wavelet Neural Network model (WNN) was formed in which the weights are learned with Feed forward neural network with Back Propagation algorithm. The number of hidden neurons for BPNN was determined by trial and error procedure.

RESULTS AND DISCUSSION

To forecast the river flow at Khanapur gauging station of Malaprabha River (Figure 4), the daily stream flow data of 11 years was used. The first seven years (1986-92) data were used for calibration of the model, and the remaining four years (1993-96) data were used for validation. The model inputs (Table 1) were decomposed by wavelets and decomposed sub-series were taken as input to ANN and the original river flow value in one day ahead as output. ANN was trained using backpropagation with LM algorithm. The optimal number of hidden neurons was determined as three by trial and error procedure.

The performance of various models estimated to forecast the river flow was presented in Table 2. From Table 2, it was found that low RMSE values (8.24 to 18.60 m^3/s) for WNN models when compared to ANN and AR (1) models. It was observed that WNN models estimated the peak values of river flow to a reasonable accuracy (peak flow during the study was 774 m^3/s). From Table 2, it was observed that the WNN model having four antecedent values of the time series, estimated minimum RMSE (8.24 m^3/s), high correlation coefficient (0.9870), highest efficiency (> 97%) and a high PI value of 0.881 during the validation period. The model IV of WNN was selected as the best-fit model to forecast the river flow in one-day advance.

Table 2: Goodness of fit statistics of the forecasted river flow for the calibration and validation period.

Model	Calibration				Validation			
	RMSE (cumecs)	R	COE (%)	PI	RMSE (cumecs)	R	COE (%)	PI
WNN								
Model I	17.76	0.952	90.76	0.627	18.60	0.931	86.69	0.395
Model II	8.66	0.989	97.80	0.911	10.46	0.979	95.78	0.809
Model III	9.44	0.986	97.38	0.894	10.33	0.979	95.89	0.814
Model IV	**6.07**	**0.995**	**98.91**	**0.956**	**8.18**	**0.987**	**97.38**	**0.881**
Model V	5.90	0.994	98.97	0.959	10.01	0.980	96.14	0.825
ANN								
Model I	26.09	0.894	80.07	0.195	23.45	0.889	78.86	0.039
Model II	25.39	0.900	81.13	0.238	23.15	0.893	79.40	0.064
Model III	26.07	0.895	80.10	0.196	23.17	0.893	79.36	0.062
Model IV	25.96	0.896	80.27	0.203	23.16	0.898	79.37	0.062
Model V	25.32	0.901	81.23	0.242	23.73	0.887	78.35	0.061
AR 1	28.30	0.876	76.55	0.053	23.26	0.890	79.05	0.046

An analysis to assess the potential of each of the model to preserve the statistical properties of the observed flow series was carried out and reveals that the flow series computed by the WNN model reproduces the first three statistical moments (i.e. mean, standard deviation and skewness) better than that computed by the ANN model. The values of the first three moments for the observed and modeled flow series for the validation period were presented in Table 3 for comparison. In Table 3, AR model performance was not presented because of its low efficiency compared to other models.Table 3 depicts the percentage error in annual peak flow estimates for the validation period for both models. From Table 3 it is found that the WNN model improves the annual peak flow estimates and the error was limited to 18%. However, ANN models tend to underestimate the peak flow up to 55% error in peak estimation.

Figure 5 shows the observed and modeled hydrographs for WNN and ANN models. It was found that values modeled from WNN model correctly matched with the observed values, whereas, ANN model underestimated the observed values. The distribution of error along the magnitude of river flow computed by WNN and ANN models during the validation period has been presented in Figure 6. From Figure 6, it was observed that the estimation of peak flow was very good as the error is minimum when compared with ANN model. Figure 7 shows the scatter plot between the observed and modeled flows by WNN and ANN. It was observed that the flow forecasted by WNN models were very much close to the 45 degrees line. From this analysis, it was worth to mention that the performance of WNN was much better than ANN and AR models in forecasting the river flow in one-day advance.

CONCLUSIONS

This paper reports a hybrid model called wavelet based neural network model for time series modeling of river flow. The proposed model is a combination of wavelet analysis and artificial neural network (WNN). Wavelet decomposes the time series into multi-levels of details and it can adopt multi-resolution analysis and effectively diagnose the main frequency component of the signal and abstract local information of the time series. The proposed WNN model was applied to daily river flow of Malaprabha river basin in Belgaum district of Karnataka State, India. The time series data of river flow was decomposed into sub series by DWT. Each of sub-series plays distinct role in original time series. Appropriate sub-series of the variable used as inputs to the ANN model and original time series of the variable as output. From the current study it is found that the proposed wavelet neural network model is better in forecasting river flow in Malaprabha basin. In the analysis, original signals are represented in different resolution by discrete wavelet transformation, therefore, the WNN forecasts are more accurate than that obtained directly by original signals.

Table 3: Statistical moments of the observed and modeled river flow series during validation period.

Statistical moments	Year	Observed (cumecs)	WNN	ANN
Mean	1993	45.84	46.00	46.06
	1994	64.23	63.78	63.12
	1995	30.92	31.98	31.25
	1996	31.08	31.21	33.02
Standard deviation	1993	65.67	63.83	61.01
	1994	85.32	82.14	77.36
	1995	54.89	56.39	53.76
	1996	40.94	40.38	44.69
Skew ness	1993	2.85	2.79	2.09
	1994	1.98	1.81	1.45
	1995	3.20	3.29	2.84
	1996	2.21	2.27	2.26
			%Error in peak estimation	
Peak value	1993	432.00	−0.49	−28.53
	1994	430.61	−9.23	−35.62
	1995	360.65	−17.36	−30.88
	1996	224.65	2.50	−54.80

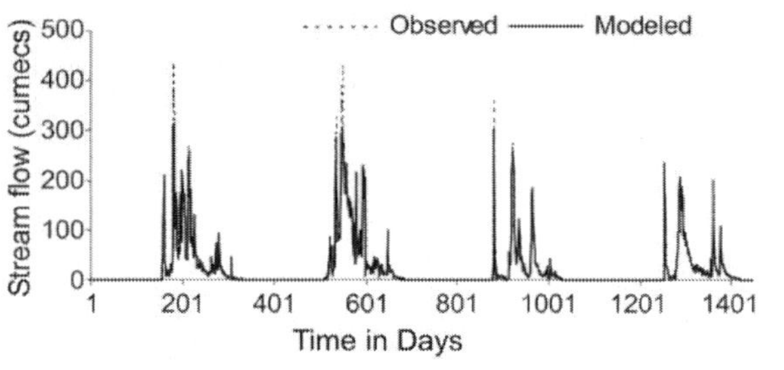

(a)

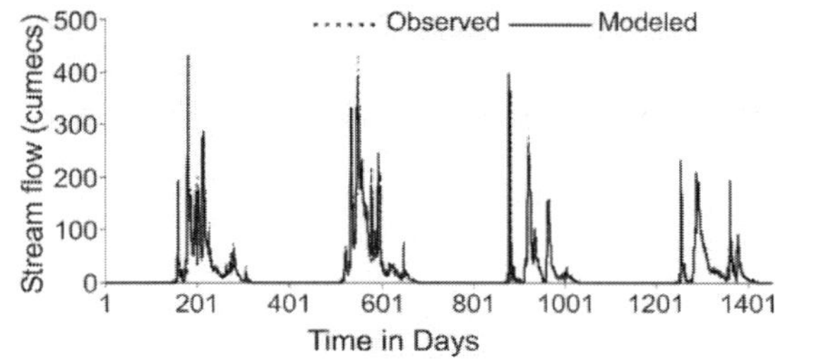

(b)

Figure 5: Plot of observed and modeled hydrographs for (a) WNN and (b) ANN model for the validation period.

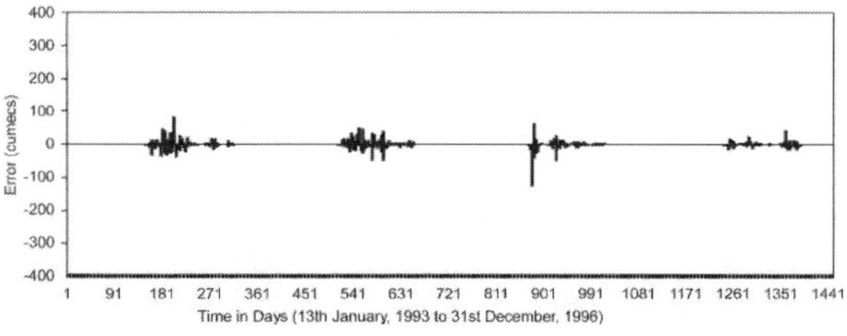

(a)

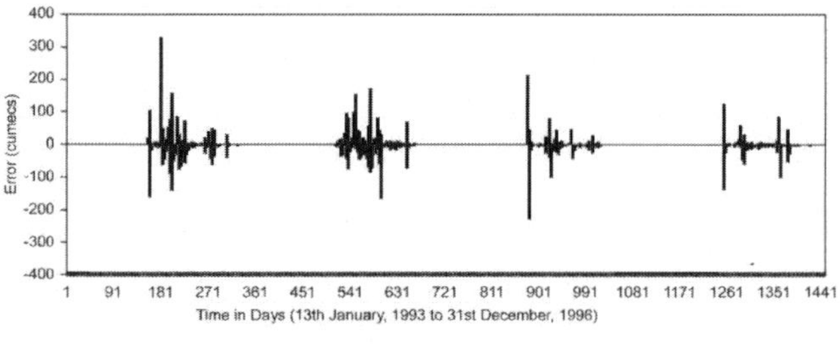

(b)

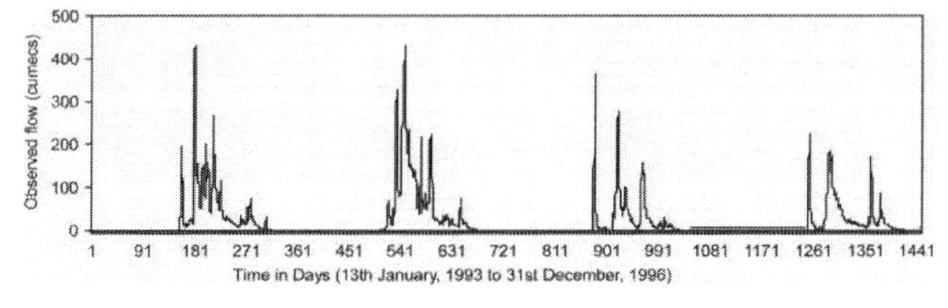

(c)

Figure 6: Distribution of error plots along the magnitude of river flow for (a) WNN model and (b) ANN model during validation period.

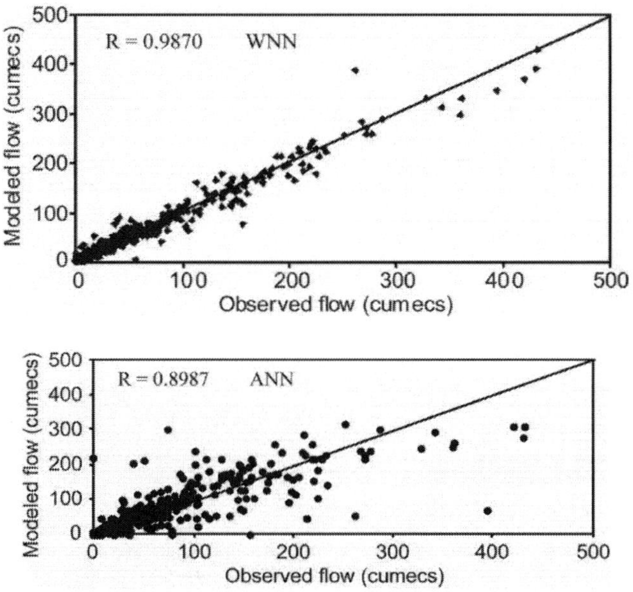

Figure 7: Scatter plot between observed and modeled river flow during validation period.

REFERENCES

1. H. Raman and N. Sunil Kumar, "Multivariate Modeling of Water Resources Time Series Using Artificial Neural Networks," Journal of Hydrological Sciences, Vol. 40, No. 4, 1995, pp. 145-163. doi:10.1080/02626669509491401
2. H. R. Maier and G. C. Dandy, "Determining Inputs for Neural Network Models of Multivariate Time Series," Microcomputers in Civil Engineering, Vol. 12, 1997, pp. 353-368.
3. M. C. Deo and K. Thirumalaiah, "Real Time Forecasting Using Neural Networks: Artificial Neural Networks in Hydrology," In: R. S. Govindaraju and A. Ramachandra Rao, Kluwer Academic Publishers, Dordrecht, 2000, pp. 53-71.
4. B. Fernandez and J. D. Salas, "Periodic Gamma Autoregressive Processes for Operational Hydrology," Water Resources Research, Vol. 22, No. 10, 1986, pp. 1385- 1396.doi:10.1029/WR022i010p01385
5. S. L. S. Jacoby, "A Mathematical Model for Non-Linear Hydrologic Systems," Journal of Geophysics Research, Vol. 71, No. 20, 1966, pp. 4811-4824.
6. J. Amorocho and A. Brandstetter, "A Critique of Current Methods of Hydrologic Systems Investigations," Eos Transactions of AGU, Vol. 45, 1971, pp. 307-321.
7. S. Ikeda, M. Ochiai and Y. Sawaragi, "Sequential GMDH Algorithm and Its Applications to River Flow Prediction," IEEE Transactions of System Management and Cybernetics, Vol. 6, No. 7, 1976, pp. 473-479. doi:10.1109/TSMC.1976.4309532
8. ASCE Task Committee, "Artificial Neural Networks in hydrology-I: Preliminary Concepts," Journal of Hydrologic Engineering, Vol. 5, No. 2, 2000(a), pp. 115-123.
9. ASCE Task Committee, "Artificial Neural Networks in Hydrology-II: Hydrologic Applications," Journal of Hydrologic Engineering, Vol. 5, No. 2, 2000(b), pp. 124-137.
10. D. W. Dawson and R. Wilby, "Hydrological Modeling Using Artificial Neural Networks," Progress in Physical Geograpgy, Vol. 25, No. 1, 2001, pp. 80-108.
11. S. Birikundavy, R. Labib, H. T. Trung and J. Rousselle, "Performance of Neural Networks in Daily Stream Flow Forecasting," Journal of Hydrologic Engineering, Vol. 7, No. 5, 2002, pp. 392-398. doi:10.1061/(ASCE)1084-0699(2002)7:5(392)
12. P. Hettiarachchi, M. J. Hall and A. W. Minns, "The Extrapolation of Artificial Neural Networks for the Modeling of Rainfall-Runoff Relationships," Journal of Hydroinformatics, Vol. 7, No. 4, 2005, pp. 291-296.
13. E. J. Coppola, M. Poulton, E. Charles, J. Dustman and F. Szidarovszky, "Application of Artificial Neural Networks to Complex Groundwater Problems," Journal of Natural Resources Research, Vol. 12, No. 4, 2003(a), pp. 303- 320.
14. E. J. Coppola, F. Szidarovszky, M. Poulton and E. Charles, "Artificial Neural Network Approach for Predicting Transient Water Levels in a Multilayered Groundwater System under Variable State, Pumping and Climate Conditions," Journal of Hydrologic Engineering, Vol. 8, No. 6, 2003(b), pp. 348-359.
15. P. C. Nayak, Y. R. Satyaji Rao and K. P. Sudheer, "Groundwater Level Forecasting in a Shallow Aquifer Using Artificial Neural Network Approach," Water Resources Management, Vol. 20, No. 1, 2006, pp. 77-90. doi:10.1007/s11269-006-4007-z
16. B. Krishna, Y. R. Satyaji Rao and T. Vijaya, "Modeling Groundwater Levels in an Urban Coastal Aquifer Using Artificial Neural Networks," Hydrological Processes, Vol. 22, No. 12, 2008, pp. 1180-1188. doi:10.1002/hyp.6686
17. D. Wang and J. Ding, "Wavelet Network Model and Its Application to the Prediction of Hydrology," Nature and Science, Vol. 1, No. 1, 2003, pp. 67-71.
18. S. R. Massel, "Wavelet Analysis for Processing of Ocean Surface Wave Records," Ocean Engineering, Vol. 28, 2001, pp. 957-987. doi:10.1016/S0029-8018(00)00044-5
19. M. C. Huang, "Wave Parameters and Functions in Wavelet Analysis," Ocean Engineering, Vol. 31, No. 1, 2004, pp. 111-125. doi:10.1016/S0029-8018(03)00047-7

20. L. C. Smith, D. Turcotte and B. L. Isacks, "Stream Flow Characterization and Feature Detection Using a Discrete Wavelet Transform," Hydrological Processes, Vol. 12, No. 2, 1998, pp. 233-249. doi:10.1002/(SICI)1099-1085(199802)12:2<233::AID-HYP573>3.0.CO;2-3

21. D. Labat, R. Ababou and A. Mangin, "Rainfall-Runoff Relations for Karstic Springs: Part II. Continuous Wavelet and Discrete Orthogonal Multiresolution Analyses," Journal of Hydrology, Vol. 238, No. 3-4, 2000, pp. 149-178. doi:10.1016/S0022-1694(00)00322-X

22. P. Saco and P. Kumar, "Coherent Modes in Multiscale Variability of Stream Flow over the United States," Water Resources Research, Vol. 36, No. 4, 2000, pp. 1049- 1067.doi:10.1029/1999WR900345

23. P. Kumar and E. Foufoula-Georgiou, "A Multicomponent Decomposition of Spatial Rainfall Fields: Segregation of Largeand Small-Scale Features Using Wavelet Transforms," Water Resources Research, Vol. 29, No. 8, 1993, pp. 2515-2532. doi:10.1029/93WR00548

24. P. Kumar, "Role of Coherent Structure in the Stochastic Dynamic Variability of Precipitation," Journal of Geophysical Research, Vol. 101, 1996, pp. 393-404. doi:10.1029/96JD01839

25. K. Fraedrich, J. Jiang, F.-W. Gerstengarbe and P. C. Werner, "Multiscale Detection of Abrupt Climate Changes: Application to the River Nile Flood," International Journal of Climatology, Vol. 17, No. 12, 1997, pp. 1301- 1315.doi:10.1002/(SICI)1097-0088(199710)17:12<1301::AID-JOC196>3.0.CO;2-W

26. R. H. Compagnucci, S. A. Blanco, M. A. Filiola and P. M. Jacovkis, "Variability in Subtropical Andean Argentinian Atuel River: A Wavelet Approach," Environmetrics, Vol. 11, No. 3, 2000, pp. 251-269. doi:10.1002/(SICI)1099-095X(200005/06)11:3<251::AID-ENV405>3.0.CO;2-0

27. S. Tantanee, S. Patamatammakul, T. Oki, V. Sriboonlue and T. Prempree, "Coupled Wavelet-Autoregressive Model for Annual Rainfall Prediction," Journal of Environmental Hydrology, Vol. 13, No. 18, 2005, pp. 1-8.

28. P. Coulibaly, "Wavelet Analysis of Variability in Annual Canadian Stream Flows," Water Resources Research, Vol. 40, 2004.

29. F. Xiao, X. Gao, C. Cao and J. Zhang, "Short-Term Prediction on Parameter-Varying Systems by Multiwavelets Neural Network," Lecture Notes in Computer Science, Springer-Verlag, Vol. 3630, No. 3611, 2005, pp. 139- 146.

30. D. J. Wu, J. Wang and Y. Teng, "Prediction of Underground Water Levels Using Wavelet Decompositions and Transforms," Journal of Hydro-Engineering, Vol. 5, 2004, pp. 34-39.

31. A. Aussem and F. Murtagh, "Combining Neural Network Forecasts on Wavelet Transformed Series," Connection Science, Vol. 9, No. 1, 1997, pp. 113-121. doi:10.1080/095400997116766

32. T. Partal and O. Kisi, "Wavelet and Neuro-Fuzzy Conjunction Model for Precipitation Forecasting," Journal of Hydrology, Vol. 342, No. 1-2, 2007, pp. 199-212.doi:10.1016/j.jhydrol.2007.05.026

33. A. Grossmann and J. Morlet, "Decomposition of Hardy Functions into Square Integrable Wavelets of Constant shape," SIAM Journal on Mathematical Analysis, Vol. 15, No. 4, 1984, pp. 723-736. doi:10.1137/0515056

34. A. Antonios and E. V. Constantine, "Wavelet Exploratory Analysis of the FTSE ALL SHARE Index," Preprint submitted to Economics Letters University of Durham, Durham, 2003.

35. D. Benaouda, F. Murtagh, J. L. Starck and O. Renaud, "Wavelet-Based Nonlinear Multiscale Decomposition Model for Electricity Load Forecasting," Neurocomputing, Vol. 70, No. 1-3, 2006, pp. 139-154. doi:10.1016/j.neucom.2006.04.005

36. W. McCulloch and W. Pitts, "A Logical Calculus of the Ideas Immanent in Nervous Activity," Bulletin of Mathematical Biophysics, Vol. 5, 1943, pp. 115-133. doi:10.1007/BF02478259

37. D. E. Rumelhart, G. E. Hinton and R. J. Williams, "Learning Representations by Back-Propagating Errors," Nature, Vol. 323, No. 9, 1986, pp. 533-536. doi:10.1038/323533a0

38. M. T. Hagan and M. B. Menhaj, "Training Feed forward Networks with Marquardt Algorithm," IEEE Transactions on Neural Networks, Vol. 5, No. 6, 1994, pp. 989- 993.doi:10.1109/72.329697

39. P. Coulibaly, F. Anctil, P. Rasmussen and B. Bobee, "A Recurrent Neural Networks Approach Using Indices of Low-Frequency Climatic Variability to Forecast Regional Annual Runoff," Hydrological Processes, Vol. 14, No. 15, 2000, pp. 2755-2777.doi:10.1002/1099-1085(20001030)14:15<2755::AID-HYP90>3.0.CO;2-9

CHAPTER 20

SELF-CONSTRUCTING NEURAL NETWORK MODELING AND CONTROL OF AN AGV

Jafar Keighobadi, Khadijeh Alioghli Fazeli, and Mohammad Sadeghi Shahidi

Keywords: Wavelet, Neural Networks, Self-Constructing Dynamical Modeling, Trajectory Tracking

INTRODUCTION

Nowadays, wide range applications of AGVs in industry, transportation, inspection and other fields have increased the importance of the trajectory tracking control of nonholonomic AGVs [1-4]. As the base of path-following controllers, kinematic models of nonholonomic systems have been preferred by most researchers in recent literatures [5]. However, dynamical models though increasing the complexity of control systems are essential due to comprising the vehicle inertial effects as long as its Coriolis, centripetal and linear accelerations in the inputs torques. Furthermore, merely using the dynamical models the input torques to the AGV's driving wheels could be considered as direct control commands.

In this paper, following kinematic modeling of the generalized AGV whose center of mass is placed out of the center of rotation between two independent driving wheels, the dynamical models of AGV are developed in both Cartesian and polar coordinate systems. Owing to the nonholonomic constraints on AGV's kinematics, the so-called global dynamical model of AGV includes a coupled constraint equation with two dynamical equations corresponding to 2 DOF of the system. However, the represented dynamical models of AGV by local posture variables don't include the non-integrable constraints. These kind of dynamical models are more appropriate to design sliding surfaces associate with robust switching controllers [4]. However, as model based controllers require the complete knowledge of the AGV parameters including the inertial matrix, the global dynamical models are superior in the estimation of unknown parameters (see [6,7]).

Furthermore, due to the physical meaning of initial off tracks with respect to global coordinate frames, the control systems based on global dynamical models should be selected when the vehicle is out of the desired path.

Inaccuracies in physical models of AGVs usually degrade the performance of trajectory tracking controllers, therefore, different strategies of solution have been proposed in recent two decades. A nonlinear adaptive controller has been designed based on a dynamical model updated by the online estimation of the plant inertial parameters [1]. Furthermore, robust sliding mode control techniques could be used to accomplish perfect path tracking when there are considerable uncertainties in the mathematical model of systems like an AGV [4,8]. Besides the complicated structure of sliding mode controllers integrated with the plant dynamics, this method is suffered by the chattering phenomenon [9].

Considering the lack of the physical models, the artificial neural networks (ANN) method as a universal function approximation generates a well posed mathematical model with adaptive learning capability. Using a multilayer feed-forward ANN, a combined controller of feedback velocity control and torque control techniques could be developed. However, due to the complicated structures of both the controller and the neural networklearning algorithm, the control system is computationally expensive. Jun has proposed a combined neural network with PID control to take advantage of the simplicity of PID controllers and the powerful capability of learning, adaptability and tackling nonlinearity of neural

Citation: Keighobadi, J. , Fazeli, K. and Shahidi, M. (2013) Self-Constructing Neural Network Modeling and Control of an AGV. Positioning, 4, 160-168. doi: 10.4236/pos.2013.42016.

networks [5,10]. As an important imperfection over most of the developed controllers in the documented research works, the control system merely uses the kinematic equations and therefore, the control commands are limited to the steering angle and forward velocity of the Vehicle. Through developing dynamic based controller, the inertial effects are considered in the imposed torques on the driving wheels as direct control commands to the AGV. In this paper, a four layers back propagation ANN control system for trajectory tracking control of nonholonomic AGVs is designed. A new learning scheme is derived to train the weights of each layer of the neural network by minimizing a criterion prescribed in a quadratic form of the error between desired and followed trajectories by the AGV. A simple torque combined system consisting of a computed torque controller and a neural network controller with parallel structure is presented for trajectory tracking control of nonholonomic AGVs. In the classic NN system, the main drawbacks are undesirable local minima and slow convergence of back-propagation learning. Moreover, the implementation of multiple feed-forward neural networks suffers from the lack of efficient constructive approaches, both for determining parameters of neurons and for choosing network structures. To overcoming the disadvantages of global approximation ANN, the global activation function is substituted with localized wavelet neural networks in the controller [4]. Due to the local properties of wavelets, arbitrary functions can be approximated by the truncated discrete wavelet transform [7].

A self-constructing four-layer wavelet network including input, wavelet, product, and output layers is used to modeling and trajectory tracking control of the vehicle. Using orthogonal wavelet functions as node functions of the network, both the structure and the parameters of the controller are learned in online. In the structure learning process, the degree measure method is used to find the proper wavelet bases and to minimize the number of wavelet bases generated from input space. In parameter learning scheme, the supervisory gradient descent algorithm is used to adjust the shape of wavelet functions and the connection weights of the network. The computed torque SCWN controller based on feedback error learning strategy results in perfect tracking control performance. The rest of the paper is organized as follows.

In Section 2, kinematic and dynamic modeling of AGV is derived. Section 3 is devoted to wavelet neural network modeling of the AGV. Trajectory tracking controllers are represented in Section 4. Software simulation and concluding remarks are presented in Sections 5 and 6, respectively.

AGV Kinematics

According to the schematic of AGV in Figure 1, it comprises a plate body carried by two independent driving wheels. The other two caster wheels prevent the vehicle from tipping over as it moves on a plane. Owning to very small inertial moments of the casters, their dynamical effects on the AGV's motion could be ignored. Per as Figure 1, a is the distance between the center of mass of the vehicle (shown by C) and the connection center of driving wheels. Furthermore, 2l and R denote the length of driving axel and the radius of driving wheels, respectively. The fixed axes of local coordinates, x-y on the vehicle body are centered on point C.

In the dynamical modeling of AGV, the generalized coordinates vector is considered as:

$$p=[X \quad Y \quad x \quad y \quad \theta \quad \varphi_R \quad \varphi_L]^T \tag{1}$$

where, X and Y show the position of the AGV's center of mass in the global coordinate system with axes X-Y; the heading angle between y and Y axes, θ represents the orientation of the AGV in plane motions; and φ_R, φ_L are the rotation angles of the right and left driving wheels, respectively. To explain the AGV's position in global polar coordinates, the components (ρ, ψ) could also be used.

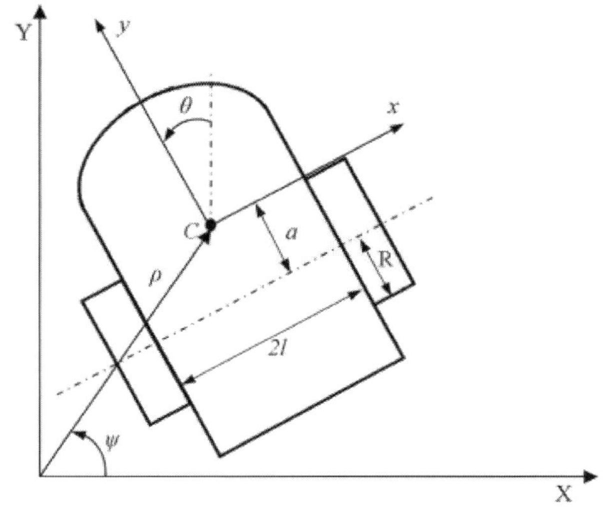

Figure 1: Schematics of AGV.

The assumption of pure rolling and not slipping motion of driving wheels leads to a non-integrable constraint in the kinematical model of the nonholonomic vehicles. Therefore, the AGV's posture could be determined completely using at least three generalized coordinates though its dynamical model comprises only two differential equations.

Considering the AGV kinematics, the following holonomic constraints are valid for movements on non-sliding and smooth surfaces.

$$\dot{x}=-\frac{aR}{2l}(\dot{\varphi}_R-\dot{\varphi}_L) \tag{2}$$

$$\dot{y}=\frac{R}{2}(\dot{\varphi}_R+\dot{\varphi}_L) \tag{3}$$

$$\dot{\theta}=\frac{R}{2l}(\dot{\varphi}_R-\dot{\varphi}_L) \tag{4}$$

Transforming the local velocity components of AGV to the global components results in the nonholonomic constraints as:

$$\begin{bmatrix}\dot{X}\\ \dot{Y}\end{bmatrix}=\begin{bmatrix}\cos\theta & -\sin\theta\\ \sin\theta & \cos\theta\end{bmatrix}\begin{bmatrix}\dot{x}\\ \dot{y}\end{bmatrix} \tag{5}$$

These constraints could be rewritten using (1) through (4) to obtain direct transformation matrix between the global velocity components and the local translationalrotational velocity components as:

$$\begin{bmatrix}\dot{X}\\ \dot{Y}\\ \dot{\theta}\end{bmatrix}=\begin{bmatrix}-\sin\theta & -a\cos\theta\\ \cos\theta & -a\sin\theta\\ 0 & 1\end{bmatrix}\begin{bmatrix}v\\ \omega\end{bmatrix} \tag{6}$$

where, the local velocity components v and ω stand for the linear forward velocity of AGV and its angular velocity around the vertical axis, respectively.

Using the posture variables of polar coordinate system, $\rho = \sqrt{X^2 + Y^2}$ and $\psi = \tan^{-1}(Y/X)$ in (6), the kinematical model of AGV in polar coordinates is obtained as follows.

$$\begin{bmatrix} \dot{\rho} \\ \dot{\psi} \\ \dot{\theta} \end{bmatrix} = \begin{bmatrix} \sin(\psi-\theta) & -a\cos(\psi-\theta) \\ \dfrac{\cos(\psi-\theta)}{\rho} & \dfrac{a\sin(\psi-\theta)}{\rho} \\ 0 & 1 \end{bmatrix} \begin{bmatrix} v \\ \omega \end{bmatrix} \tag{7}$$

The considered distance between the centers of rotation and mass of the AGV, a leads to an enlarged application range of the proposed methods to different kind of industrial, service and entertainment vehicles.

Owing to excluding the inertial effects, the designed controllers based on the kinematical models (2) through (7) may not be very satisfied in real world at least for mechanical engineers. Furthermore, the dynamical models of AGV should be used as the base of control systems to obtain the input torques to AGV as direct control commands.

DYNAMIC MODELLING OF AGV

In the dynamical models, the applied torques to the driving wheels would be obtained as terms of the vehicle accelerations, velocities, and posture variables as well as the inertial parameters. In this paper, the well-known Lagrange's method is used to determine the dynamical equations of motion as:

$$\frac{d}{dt}\left(\frac{\partial L}{\partial \dot{q}}\right) - \frac{\partial L}{\partial q} = T + A^{T}(q)\lambda \tag{8}$$

where, λ is a Lagrange multiplier; $A^{T}(q)$ is given by the nonholonomic constraints; and T is the control torque vector with components, T_R and T_L which are generated by separate actuator motors of the right and left driving wheels, respectively. Now the following Lagrangian could be considered for the AGV dynamic modeling [1].

$$L = \frac{1}{2}m\left(\dot{X}^2 + \dot{Y}^2\right) + \frac{1}{2}I_t\dot{\theta}^2 + \frac{1}{2}I_w\left(\dot{\varphi}_R^2 + \dot{\varphi}_L^2\right) \tag{9}$$

where, m is the total mass of the vehicle; I_t is the AGV's moment of inertia around the normal axis of X-Y plane crossing through the point C; and I_w denotes the inertia moment of driving wheels. Applying (9) in (8) and using the kinematical constraints (2) through (5) gives:

$$M(q)\ddot{q} + G(q,\dot{q}) = B(q)\tau - A^{T}(q)\lambda \tag{10}$$

$$q = [X, Y, \theta]^{T} \tag{11}$$

$$\tau = [T_R, T_L]^{T} \tag{12}$$

$$M(q) = \begin{bmatrix} m + \dfrac{2I_w}{R^2}\sin^2\theta & \dfrac{-I_w}{R^2}\sin 2\theta & 0 \\ \dfrac{-I_w}{R^2}\sin 2\theta & m + \dfrac{2I_w}{R^2}\cos^2\theta & 0 \\ 0 & 0 & I_t + \dfrac{2l^2 I_w}{R^2} \end{bmatrix} \tag{13}$$

$$G(q,\dot{q}) = \begin{bmatrix} \dfrac{2I_w}{R^2}\left(\dot{X}\dot{\theta}\sin 2\theta - \dot{Y}\dot{\theta}\cos 2\theta\right) \\ \dfrac{2I_w}{R^2}\left(-\dot{X}\dot{\theta}\cos 2\theta - \dot{Y}\dot{\theta}\sin 2\theta\right) \\ \dfrac{I_w}{R^2}\left(\dot{Y}^2\sin 2\theta - \dot{X}^2\sin 2\theta + 2\dot{X}\dot{Y}\cos 2\theta\right) \end{bmatrix} \tag{14}$$

$$A(q) = [\cos\theta \quad \sin\theta \quad a] \tag{15}$$

$$B(q) = \begin{bmatrix} \dfrac{-\sin\theta}{R} & \dfrac{-\sin\theta}{R} \\ \dfrac{\cos\theta}{R} & \dfrac{\cos\theta}{R} \\ \dfrac{l}{R} & \dfrac{l}{R} \end{bmatrix} \tag{16}$$

As represented by Hu and Huo [11], many nonholonomic mechanical systems could be described by Equation (10) in which in general form, $q \in R^n$ and $\tau \in R^r$ are the generalized configuration and the control input vectors, respectively; $\lambda \in R^m$ is the constraint force vector; $M(q) \in R^{m \times n}$ is a positive definite matrix; $V(q,\dot{q}) \in R^n$ is the term which includes centripetal and Coriolis forces; $B(q)$ is a $n \times r$ full rank transformation input matrix; $A(q)$ is a $m \times n$ full rank matrix associated with the constraints.

In order to achieve an applicable model for control purposes, the constraint force vector, λ should be eliminated from (10). Depending on using which set of kinematical equations, four different dynamical models are presented in this paper. Using constraints (2) through (5), the following so called local dynamic model is obtained.

$$\begin{bmatrix} T_R \\ T_L \end{bmatrix} = \begin{bmatrix} m_{11} & m_{12} \\ m_{21} & m_{22} \end{bmatrix} \begin{bmatrix} \ddot{\varphi}_R \\ \ddot{\varphi}_L \end{bmatrix} + m\frac{aR^3}{4l^2} \begin{bmatrix} \dot{\varphi}_R\dot{\varphi}_L - \dot{\varphi}_L^2 \\ \dot{\varphi}_R\dot{\varphi}_L - \dot{\varphi}_R^2 \end{bmatrix} \tag{17}$$

$$m_{11} = m_{22} = I_w + m\left(\frac{R^2}{4} + \frac{a^2R^2}{4l^2}\right) + I_t\left(\frac{R}{2l}\right)^2 \tag{18}$$

$$m_{12} = m_{21} = m\left(\frac{R^2}{4} - \frac{aR^2}{4l^2}\right) - I_t\left(\frac{R}{2l}\right)^2 \tag{19}$$

Using (2) and (3) in (17) to replacing φ_R, φ_L by x, y results in another so-called local dynamical model of AGV as:

$$\begin{bmatrix} T_R \\ T_L \end{bmatrix} = \begin{bmatrix} (m_{12} - m_{11})l/aR & (m_{12} + m_{11})/R \\ (m_{22} - m_{21})l/aR & (m_{21} + m_{22})/R \end{bmatrix} \begin{bmatrix} \ddot{x} \\ \ddot{y} \end{bmatrix} + m\frac{R}{2l} \begin{bmatrix} -\dot{x}\dot{y} - \dfrac{l}{a}\dot{x} \\ \dot{x}\dot{y} - \dfrac{l}{a}\dot{x} \end{bmatrix} \tag{20}$$

Using local dynamical models as the base of path following control systems results in uncompensated initial position off tracks though the tracked orientation trajectory by the AGV becomes accurate [4]. To overcome this difficulty, two dynamical models of AGV are developed using global posture variables. Therefore, using constraints (5) to replacing the local velocity and acceleration components in (20) by corresponding global kinds results as:

$$\begin{bmatrix} T_R \\ T_L \end{bmatrix} = \begin{bmatrix} m_{11}^1 & m_{12}^1 \\ m_{21}^1 & m_{22}^1 \end{bmatrix} \begin{bmatrix} \ddot{X} \\ \ddot{Y} \end{bmatrix} + V^1\left(\dot{X}, \dot{Y}, \dot{\theta}, \theta\right) \tag{21}$$

The elements of inertial matrix and nonlinear vector, V^1 associated with the global dynamical model (21) are obtained as:

$$m_{11}^1 = -E_1\cos\theta - E_2\sin\theta \tag{22}$$

$$m_{12}^1 = -E_1\sin\theta + E_2\cos\theta \tag{23}$$

$$m_{21}^1 = E_1\cos\theta - E_2\sin\theta \tag{24}$$

$$m_{22}^1 = E_1 \sin\theta + E_2 \cos\theta \tag{25}$$

$$V_1^1 = E_1\left(\dot{X}\dot{\theta}\sin\theta - \dot{Y}\dot{\theta}\cos\theta\right) + E_2\left(-\dot{X}\dot{\theta}\cos\theta - \dot{Y}\dot{\theta}\sin\theta\right) - \frac{R}{2a}M\left(\dot{X}\cos\theta + \dot{Y}\sin\theta\right)^2$$
$$-\frac{R}{2l}M\left(\dot{X}\cos\theta + \dot{Y}\sin\theta\right)\left(-\dot{X}\sin\theta + \dot{Y}\cos\theta\right) \tag{26}$$

$$V_2^1 = E_1\left(-\dot{X}\dot{\theta}\sin\theta + \dot{Y}\dot{\theta}\cos\theta\right) + E_2\left(-\dot{X}\dot{\theta}\cos\theta - \dot{Y}\dot{\theta}\sin\theta\right) - \frac{R}{2a}M\left(\dot{X}\cos\theta + \dot{Y}\sin\theta\right)^2$$
$$+\frac{R}{2l}M\left(\dot{X}\cos\theta + \dot{Y}\sin\theta\right)\left(-\dot{X}\sin\theta + \dot{Y}\cos\theta\right) \tag{27}$$

where:

$$E_1 = \left(\frac{maR}{2l} + \frac{l}{aR}I_w + \frac{R}{2la}I_t\right) \tag{28}$$

$$E_2 = \left(\frac{1}{R}I_w + m\frac{R}{2}\right) \tag{29}$$

By use of kinematical model (6), $\dot{X}$ and $\dot{Y}$ could be written in terms of v and $\omega = \dot{\theta}$. Hence, (21) is changed to the second dynamical model in global coordinate system as:

$$\begin{bmatrix} T_2 \\ T_3 \end{bmatrix} = \begin{bmatrix} m_{11}^2 & m_{12}^2 \\ m_{21}^2 & m_{22}^2 \end{bmatrix} \begin{bmatrix} \dot{v} \\ \ddot{\theta} \end{bmatrix} + V^2\left(v, \dot{\theta}\right) \tag{30}$$

$$m_{11}^2 = m_{21}^2 = E_2 \tag{31}$$

$$m_{12}^2 = -m_{22}^2 = E_1 d \tag{32}$$

$$V_1^2 = \frac{Rmd}{2}\left(\frac{v\dot{\theta}}{l} - \dot{\theta}^2\right) \tag{33}$$

$$V_2^2 = \frac{Rmd}{2}\left(\frac{v\dot{\theta}}{l} - \dot{\theta}^2\right) \tag{34}$$

Unlike the model (21), the represented model (30) is simple and its inertial matrix doesn't include the posture variables of AGV. Therefore, this new dynamical model (30) is not affected by probable measurement noises of orientation variable, θ.

WAVELET NEURAL NETWORK (WNN)

As the base of a control system, the mathematical models are not preferred due to modeling uncertainties and exogenous inputs affecting real systems. In this section dynamical modeling of the AGV is considered as a self-constructing wavelet neural network (SCWNN) system. As shown in block diagram of Figure 2, the SCWNN receives a vector of desired reference position, velocity and orientation trajectories, q_d that should be tracked by the AGV. Through the learned SCWNN, the input torque vector, T which should be imposed on the driving wheels of the AGV is generated. Therefore, the AGV will track the desired position and orientation posture variables by applying the intelligently produced torque vector, T. The structure of the designed wavelet neural network (WNN) model is shown in Figure 3.

The proposed SCWNN has a four-layer structure comprising of the input layer, wavelet layer, product layer, and output layer. The input data to the first layer of the network is a n-dimensional vector of posture variables as, $q = [q_1, q_2, \cdots, q_n]$ which is normalized into the interval $[0,1]$. The activation functions of wavelet nodes in the second layer are derived from the mother wavelet, $\varphi(q)$ with a dilation, d and a translation t as: $\varphi_{d,t}(q) = 2^{d/2}\varphi\left(2^d q - t\right)$. The mother wavelet is selected in such a way that it constitutes an orthonormal basis in $L^2(R^n)$. The derivation of a differentiable Mexican-hat function is considered as a mother wavelet herein [8],

$$\varphi(q) = \left(1 - \|q\|^2\right)e^{-\|q\|/2} \tag{35}$$

where $\|\ \|$ stands for 2-norm of vector. Consequently, the activation function of the j-th wavelet node connected with the i-th input data is represented as:

where, n is the number of input-dimensions and m is the number of the wavelets. The wavelet functions (35) with various dilations and translations are presented in Figure 4. Then, each wavelet in the product layer is labeled P, i.e., the product of the jth multidimensional wavelet with n input dimensions $q = [q_1, q_2, \cdots, q_n]^T$, can be defined as

$$\psi_j(q) = \prod_{i=1}^{n} \varphi_{d_j t_j}(q_i) \tag{37}$$

According to the theory of multi-resolution analysis (MRA), see [8], any $f \in L^2(R)$ can be regarded as a linear combination of wavelets at different resolution levels. For this reason, the function f is expressed as

$$Y(X) = f(X) \approx \sum_{j=1}^{m} w_j \varphi_j(X) \tag{38}$$

If $\varphi_j = [\varphi_1, \varphi_2, \cdots, \varphi_m]$ is used as a nonlinear transformation function of hidden nodes and weight vectors and $w_j = w_1, w_2, \cdots, w_m$ defines the connection weights, then Equation (38) can be considered the functional expression of the SCWN modeling function Y.

Self-Constructing Learning Algorithm

In this section, the degree measure method and the well-known back propagation (BP) algorithm are used concurrently for constructing and adjusting the SCWN algorithm. The degree measure method is used to determine the number of wavelet bases in the wavelet layer and the product layer. Furthermore, the BP algorithm is used to adjust the parameters of the wavelet bases and connection weights. At the initial time, the SCWN system does not comprise any wavelet bases. Therefore, the first task is to decide when a new wavelet base should be generated. The partition-based clustering techniques are used to perform cluster analysis in a data set. For each incoming pattern q_i, the firing strength of a wavelet base can be regarded as the degree of the incoming pattern belonging to the corresponding wavelet base. An input datum q_i, with a higher firing strength means that its spatial location is nearer to the center of the wavelet base t_j, than those with smaller firing strength. Based on this concept, the firing strength obtained from Equation (37) in the product layer can be used as the degree measure.

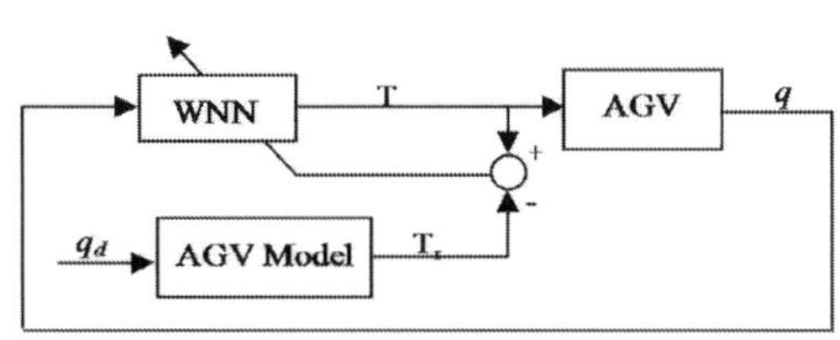

Figure 2: Block diagram of SCWNN modeling system.

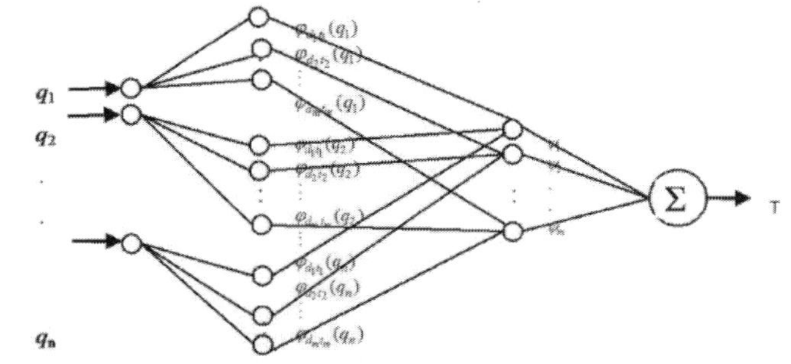

Figure 3: Structure of wavelet neural network.

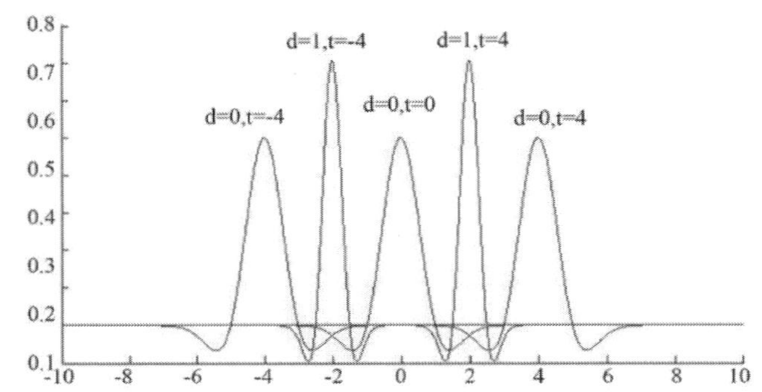

Figure 4: Wavelet functions of (35) with various dilations and translations.

$$F_j = |\varphi_j|, j = 1, \cdots, q \tag{39}$$

where, q is the number of existing wavelet bases and $|\varphi_j|$, is the absolute value of φ_j. According to the degree measure, the criterion of a new wavelet base generated for new incoming data is described in the block diagram of Figure 5.

In Figure 5 $\bar{F}$ is a prespecified threshold that should decay during the learning process, limiting the size of the SCWN model and $t_{q+1}, d_{q+1}, w_{q+1}$ are new wavelet's parameters according as regarded Initially, there are no wavelet bases in the SCWN controller. The first task is to decide when a new wavelet base is generated. We adopt partition-based clustering techniques to perform cluster analysis in a data set. For each incoming pattern q_i, the firing strength of a wavelet base can be regarded as the degree of the incoming pattern belonging to the corresponding wavelet base. An input datum q_i with a higher firing strength means that its spatial location is nearer to the center of the wavelet base t_j than those with smaller firing strength. $\bar{F}$ is defined as, $[0.1^n, 0.5^n]$ where, n is the number of input variables.

After the network structure has been adjusted according to the current training pattern, the network then enters the second learning step to adjust the parameters of the wavelet base and the connection weight (t, d and w) with the same training pattern. The parameterlearning algorithm is based on a set of input/output pairs $\{q, y^d(q)\}$. If the error function is

$$e = y(q) - y^d(q) \tag{40}$$

where $y(q)$ is the model output and $y^d(q)$ is the desired output, then the cost function E can be defined as and can be minimized by all adjustable parameters using an iterative computational scheme. Assuming that W is the adjustable parameter in the wavelet layer and the output layer, the general learning rule used is

$$E = \frac{1}{2}e^2 \tag{41}$$

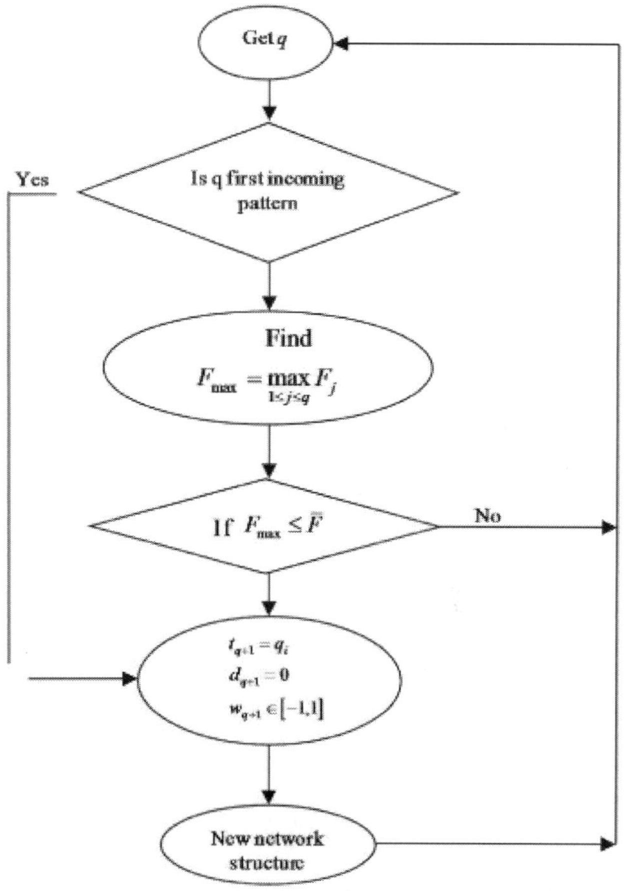

Figure 5: Block diagram for generation of new wavelets in SCWN.

$$W(k+1) = W(k) + \Delta W(k) = W(k) + \eta\left(-\frac{\partial E}{\partial W}\right) \tag{42}$$

where η and k represent the learning rate and the iteration number, respectively. The gradient of the cost function E in Equation (41) with respect to the vector of arbitrarily adjustable parameter W is defined as

$$\frac{\partial E}{\partial W} = -e\frac{\partial y}{\partial W} \tag{43}$$

With the above equation defined, we can infer that the free parameters adjusted in the SCWN are as follows. The connection weight of the output layer is updated by

$$w_j(k+1) = w_j(k) + \Delta w_j$$
$$\Delta w_j = -\eta_w \frac{\partial E}{\partial w_j} = -\eta_w e \tag{44}$$

Similarly, the updated laws of t_{ij} and d_{ij} are shown as follows:

$$t_{ij}(k+1) = t_{ij}(k) + \Delta t_{ij} \tag{45}$$

$$d_{ij}(k+1) = d_{ij}(k) + \Delta d_{ij} \tag{46}$$

where

$$d\Delta t_{ij} = -\eta_t \frac{\partial E}{\partial t_{ij}} = -\eta_t e w_j \psi_j \left\{ \frac{2^{d_{ij}} q_i - t_{ij}}{\left(1-\left(2^{d_{ij}} q_i - t_{ij}\right)^2\right)^2} \left[2 + \left(1 - \left(2^{d_{ij}} q_i - t_{ij}\right)^2\right)\right] \right\} \tag{47}$$

$$\Delta d_{ij} = -\eta_d \frac{\partial E}{\partial d_{ij}} = -\eta_d e w_j \psi_j \left\{ \frac{\ln 2}{2} - 2^{d_{ij}} q_i \ln 2 \left(2^{d_{ij}} q_i - t_{ij}\right) \left[1 + \frac{2}{1-\left(2^{d_{ij}} q_i - t_{ij}\right)^2} \right] \right\} \tag{48}$$

Wavelet Neural Network Control of AGV

Neural networks have known as an attractive method to model the complex non-linear systems due to its inherent ability to approximate arbitrary continuous functions. During the 1980's and the early 1990's, conclusive proofs were given by numerous authors that feed-forward neural networks with one hidden layer are capable of approximating any continuous function on a compact set in a very precise and satisfactory sense [12]. Recently, wavelet decomposition method has been used as a new powerful tool for function approximation in a manner that readily reveals properties of the arbitrary L_2 function (energy-finite and continuous or discontinuous) [13]. Combination of wavelets and neural networks methods results in wavelet neural network models with efficient constructive approach. Besides precise approximation of arbitrary L_2 functions, the wavelet neural networks could result in a convex cost index for which simple iterative solutions such as gradient descent rules are justifiable and are not in danger of being trapped in local minima when choosing the orthogonal wavelets as the activation functions in the nodes [8]. In this paper, the WNN technique is used as the inverse dynamic model of the AGV to generate sufficient robustness against modeling uncertainties and exogenous disturbances. Considering the proposed dynamical model (17), the input variables to the WNN system are supposed as follow.

$$q = [\varphi_2, \varphi_3, \dot{\varphi}_2, \dot{\varphi}_3] \tag{49}$$

Owing to the fact that the nonholonomic AGV is a 2 DOF dynamic system, two separate WNN systems are used to approximate the input torque of every driving wheels of the AGV. In this way, two control actions for trajectory tracking control of the AGV, T_R and T_L are computed by the right and left WNN as shown in Figure 6.

SIMULATION RESULTS

Using simulations, the effects of the proposed wavelet neural network controller on the convergence of AGV to reference trajectories are evaluated. Therefore, the following example trajectories are used to produce the reference position and orientation angle of the AGV.

$$\theta = 3\times10^{-4}t^3 - 7\times10^{-6}t^4 + 5\times10^{-8}t^5 \tag{50}$$

$$\dot{\varphi}_R = 100\psi + 3.9596\dot{\psi} \tag{51}$$

$$\dot{\varphi}_L = 100\psi - 3.9596\dot{\psi} \tag{52}$$

The simulation of the WNN controller results in a perfect trajectory tracking performance of the AGV. The comparison of tracked X, Y and also the complete circular path of the AGV with the reference values are shown in Figures 7-9, respectively. From these figures, the tracking convergence of AGV along both X and Y trajectories is very fast.

CONCLUSION

An intelligent wavelet neural networks modelling and control method of an AGV has been proposed. Owing to the self-constructing nature of the proposed WNNT, the number of nodes in the layers of the WNNT system is adjusted automatically. Therefore, the proposed method does not require the fixed number of nodes and thereby the computation cost is reduced. Unlike kinematic models, the SCWNN dynamic model of the AGV results in considering the inertial, Coriolis and centripetal accelerations in the trajectory tracking control of the vehicle. According to simulation results, the WNNT control system yields a perfect trajectory tracking of the AGV.

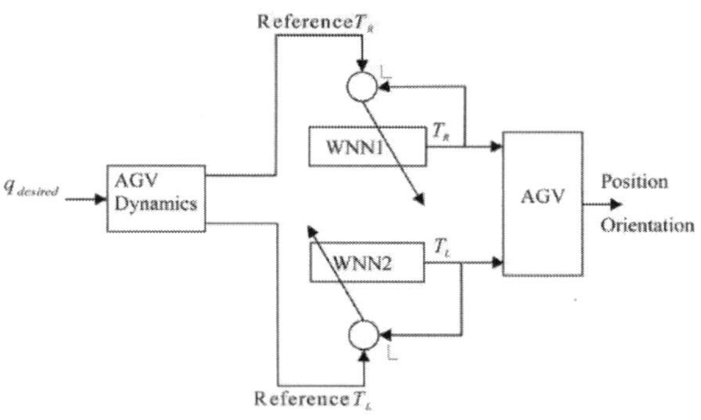

Figure 6: block diagram of AGV control system with inverse dynamic.

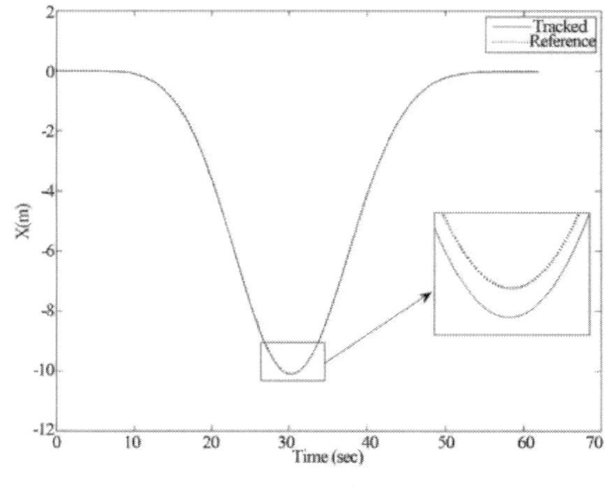

Figure 7. Tracking of AGV along X axes.

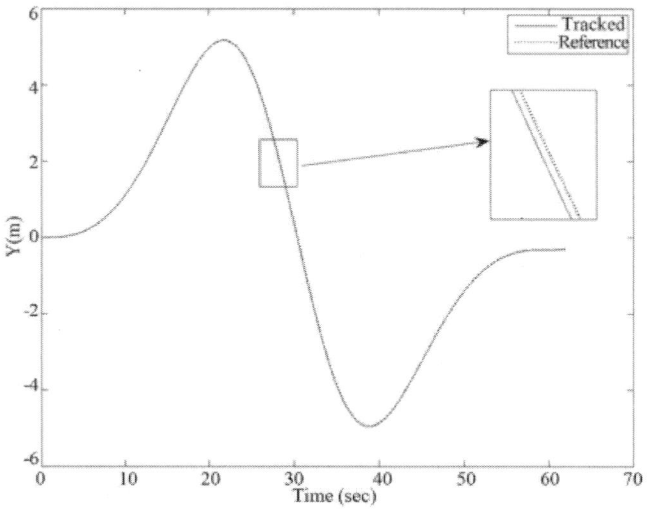

Figure 8: Tracking of AGV along Y axis.

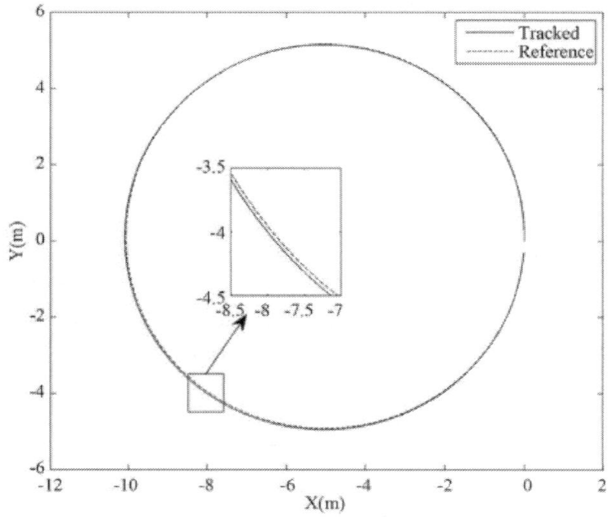

Figure 9: Tracking of AGV on XY plane.

REFERENCES

1. J. Keighobadi, M. B. Menhaj and M. Kabganian, "Feedback Linearization and Fuzzy Controllers for Trajectory Tracking of Wheeled Mobile Robots," Kybernetes, Vol. 39, No. 1, 2010, pp. 83-106. doi:10.1108/03684921011021291
2. J. Keighobadi, "Fuzzy Calibration of a Magnetic Compass for Vehicular Applications," Mechanical Systems and Signal Processing, Vol. 25, No. 6, 2011, pp. 1973-1987.doi:10.1016/j.ymssp.2010.11.005
3. J. Keighobadi, M. J. Yazdanpanah and M. Kabganian, "An Enhanced Fuzzy H∞ Estimator Applied to Low-Cost Attitude-Heading Reference System," Kybernetes, Vol. 40, No. 1, 2011, pp. 300-326. doi:10.1108/03684921111118068
4. J. Keighobadi and M. B. Menhaj, "From Nonlinear to Fuzzy Approaches in Trajectory Tracking Control of Wheeled Mobile Robots," Asian Journal of Control, Vol. 14, No. 4, 2012, pp. 960-973. doi:10.1002/asjc.480
5. Y. Jun, "Adaptive Control of Nonlinear PID-Based Analog Neural Networks for a Nonholonomic Mobile Robot," Neuro-Computing, Vol. 71, No. 7-9, 2008, pp. 1561-1565.doi:10.1016/j.neucom.2007.04.014
6. Q. Zhang, "Using Wavelet Networks in Nonparametric Estimation," IEEE Transactions on Neural Networks, Vol. 8, No. 2, 1998, pp. 227-236. doi:10.1109/72.557660
7. J. Q. Guo, B. Y. Hai and D. X. Ai, "An Online Self-Constructing Wavelet Fuzzy Neural Network for Machine Condition Monitoring," Proceeding of the 4th International Conference on Machine Learning and Cybernetics, Guangzhou, 18-21 August 2005, pp. 18-21.
8. C. J. Lin, "Nonlinear Systems Control Using Self-Constructing Wavelet Networks," Applied Soft Computing, Vol. 9, No. 1, 2009, pp. 71-79. doi:10.1016/j.asoc.2008.03.014
9. J. Keighobadi and Y. Mohamadi, "Fuzzy Robust Trajectory Tracking Control of WMRs," In: S. I. Ao, O. Castillo, and X. Huang, Eds., Intelligent Control and Innovative Computing, Springer, Singapore, 2012, pp. 77-90. doi:10.1007/978-1-4614-1695-1_7
10. L. Gaviphat, "Adaptive Self-Tuning Neuro Wavelet Network Controllers," Ph.D. Thesis, Electrical Engineering Department, Blackburg, 1997.
11. M. Y. Hu and W. Huo, "Robust and Adaptive Control of Nonholonomic Mechanical Systems with Application to Mobile Robots," In: T. P. Leung and H. S. Qin, Eds., Advanced Topics in Nonlinear Control Systems, 2001, pp. 161-192.
12. M. R. Sanner and J. J. E. Slotine, "Structureally Dynamic Wavelet Networks for Adaptive Control of Robotic Systems," International Journal of Control, Vol. 70, No. 3, 1998, pp. 405-421. doi:10.1080/002071798222307
13. F. J. Lin, R. J. Wai and M. P. Chen, "Wavelet Neural Network Control for Linear Ultrasonic Motor Drive via Adaptive Sliding-Mode Technique," IEEE Transactions on Ultrasonics, Ferroelectrics and Frequency Control, Vol. 50, No. 6, 2003, pp. 686-698.doi:10.1109/TUFFC.2003.1209556

INDEX